The Irwin Series in Marketing
Consulting Edito
Gilbert A. Churchill, Jr.
University of Wisconsin, Madison

Readings and Cases in Marketing Management

Edited by

Alvin C. Burns
Department of Marketing
College of Business Administration
University of Central Florida

David W. Cravens
M. J. Neeley School of Business
Texas Christian University

1987

Homewood, Illinois   60430

Preface

Comments to the Course Instructor

Marketing management is an exciting topic to teach to college students. Its concepts and principles are relatively intuitive; its normative guidelines are logical and readily comprehended; and the criticality of marketing decisions to a company's success is universally accepted. In short, marketing is inherently interesting and alive. From our experiences in teaching this course, the typical student becomes increasingly attentive and motivated to learn.

Some excellent marketing textbooks are available today. Each communicates terminology, basic concepts, general principles, and decision-making procedures in a straightforward manner; but all concentrate primarily on content. And much more can be done with marketing management subject matter to make the course come alive and gain relevance—the basic purpose of this book.

More specifically, the objective of this readings and case book is to provide a supplement to your textbook that emphasizes the day-to-day, real-life excitement of marketing management. Perhaps, like you, we have long used case studies and articles from business periodicals as supplements to an already interesting topic. We know that these materials aid in generating class discussion; provide tangible instances of marketing applications; pique curiosity about the rationale for marketing actions; and offer real-world scenarios and problems to be confronted and solved by marketing management students.

The book's contents follow a marketing process orientation beginning with the basics of marketing planning and ending with a section on the societal responsibilities of marketing practitioners. Each section has about six readings that are divided into two categories. The conceptual readings, usually two per section, provide overviews and generalizations of marketing management phenomena. As you would expect, they are written primarily by marketing academicians who have studied several companies or industries. The company articles, written by news reporters or analysts, are stories about specific marketing practices pursued by particular companies. Their purpose is to convey practical information. Our selection of each reading was based on several criteria, such as timeliness, suitability, visibility of the company involved, entertainment value, and demonstration of marketing concepts.

Case studies accompany each section. Some have appeared in other case books; some are new. Here we sought cases that are stimulating, contemporary, of moderate length and difficulty, contain market and financial data, and demonstrate marketing concepts or principles.

We believe the total package will make your teaching enjoyable, just as ours has always been. At the very least, you should find that the readings and cases will truly involve your students in the course.

Comments to the Course Student

This book is a compilation of news stories, magazine and journal articles, and case studies, all related to the area of marketing management. It was conceived with two fundamental objectives: (1) to provide you with contemporary, real-world examples of what marketing managers do and (2) to place you inside the decision problems they confront. It is not a textbook; rather, it is intended as a supplement to your text and regular classroom work on marketing concepts. Thus, the book offers "experiential" learning. In other words, this book contains numerous illustrations and instances of everyday marketing management practice; and the case studies will allow you to vicariously experience the complexities of marketing decision making. Your course instructor will use these readings and cases for class discussion or written assignments to give focus to your learning process.

The book is divided into six major areas, beginning with fundamental concerns in marketing planning and ending with some of the societal impacts of marketing activities. Each readings section has five or six articles. We have broken the readings into two groups to differentiate what we term *conceptual* from *company* articles. The conceptual readings are usually written by marketing professors who have studied marketing phenomena across industries and have thus arrived at guidelines or generalizations. Normally, these articles are written so that they will be instructional for marketing practitioners; many appear in periodicals such as the *Harvard Business Review.* The company readings, on the other hand, are news stories or other descriptions of specific companies' marketing strategies or dilemmas. These articles are usually found in periodicals such as *The Wall Street Journal* or *Fortune* magazine. As you would expect, they are written for their news appeal but do include many marketing principles—if you look for them.

Each section also contains four case studies, with the exception of Section 4, which contains eight. The case studies were all written by respected business case authors, usually professors or graduate students who have studied a company in great depth. Often they interview the executives, inspect the company's financial statements, survey customers and competitors, and may even have served as consultants to the company. Because they believe that significant learning can eventuate from students' wrestling with the company's problems and proposing solutions to them, these case writers have summarized the case facts. Sometimes actual information, perhaps even the name, is disguised to protect the company. At other times, the information is public knowledge, and the case is perfectly faithful to reality. In either instance, be assured that the marketing problems these cases pose are identical to those faced daily by marketing practitioners.

Before any of the readings or cases were selected for this book, they were reviewed by a panel of business students. These students judged each one on several criteria, including readability, timeliness, concepts demonstrated, entertainment value, length, and suitability. All of the final selections were rated "outstanding" or "very good" on these criteria by a majority of the student panel. We certainly hope that you too will find these selections both enjoyable and educational.

Acknowledgments

Many more cases and readings than were ultimately chosen for this book were reviewed. The review process required the dedicated efforts of several graduate students as well as our own time, formalized ratings sheets, and at least three screening stages. In acknowledgment, we wish to thank the following individuals: Project Director Rachel Grenfell; Reviewers Annette Beadle, Kim Sanders, Mark Scyster, Mel Hoskins; and Permissions Expediter Randy Russ. Each of these LSU students played a vital part in bringing this book to completion.

Contents

C₅-16

SECTION 6
Marketing's Broadening Roles   *378*

Readings and Cases in Marketing Management

SECTION 1

Marketing Strategy Planning

*M*arketing strategy planning is the single-most important function of a progressive company in today's volatile business world. Simply stated, it is the process in which a company (1) senses the forces that shape its opportunities and threats; (2) judges the future impacts of these forces; and (3) devises strategies to take advantage of or protect against anticipated changes in the business environment. Stated even more simply, marketing strategy planning means determining where you are, deciding where you want to be, and figuring out how you can best get there. Despite the intuitive nature of this definition, marketing strategy planning is in fact a company's long-term commitment to constant vigilance to changes in its surroundings, coupled with a sensitivity to expected future consequences. Many companies have adopted marketing strategy planning as a central philosophy; to them, it is a logical extension of the marketing concept that has been a driving force in their operations for years.

Why is marketing strategy planning relevant to marketing management? The answer to this question can be found in the open-systems orientation of any company that views itself as a marketing organization. The business environment is characterized by one certainty: it changes. Consequently, the wise company forecasts systematic changes and positions itself to be ready to take advantage of shifts when they occur. Take, for instance, changes in customers. Much has been written about the changes that have occurred among the "baby boomers," who constitute the target market for a vast number of companies. Psychological, income-level, lifestyle, and even physiological changes in these consumers have been well documented, as have their strategic consequences for companies. Virtually all consumer groups undergo subtle mindset alterations over time; competitors too change in form and mentality. AT&T, for instance, now competes aggressively with IBM; television networks are barraged by competition from cable and satellite companies; and even the Coca-Cola Company altered its 100-year-old recipe to respond to Pepsi-Cola's challenges.

Other important areas of change can be found as well: technological advances provide opportunities for more efficient operations; companies encounter supplier problems; public opinion becomes more critical; and legal constraints tighten. Even changes in management philosophies creep into the picture. The list could easily be expanded. But the point is that the astute company embraces the need to constantly monitor and anticipate changes in its environment.

From a marketing strategy planning perspective, there are significant advantages to change. As a general introduction, we will point out three benefits and discuss each one briefly.

■ An understanding of who you are. Perhaps the most important, yet least discussed, benefit of marketing strategy planning is that the board of directors and top management come to grips with an appreciation of what the company stands for. These companies have a firm understanding of their origins and histories. Furthermore, they comprehend their strengths and weaknesses; they know how they are perceived by customers; and they have a grasp of the basic values that motivate the company and its employees. Thus, Sears, Roebuck & Co. acts as a cash-rich consumer goods and services conglomerate while 7-11 Food Stores defines itself as a provider of all types of convenience.

■ A vision of the future. The future can never be known with certainty but it can be articulated via probabilities: companies that embrace marketing strategy planning have entertained the eventualities and debated the consequences. They sense future trends and have forecast the impact points. Because their philosophies are *pro-* rather than *re*active, most have generated scenarios that propose new alternatives for their futures. With these, they have come to realize both the prospective opportunities and/or dangers that lie ahead.

■ A roadmap toward company objectives. Once you know who you are and what seems to lie ahead, the next logical step is to formulate plans and strategies to take full advantage of your future. Again, those companies that have adopted marketing strategy planning as a key tactic have formulated detailed long-range plans with attendant strategies and tactics. Someone once described three types of companies: (1) those who make things happen; (2) those who watch things happen; and (3) those who never saw anything happen. Companies that consistently make things happen are deeply committed to marketing strategy planning.

About the Readings

We have selected six readings for this section. We begin our conceptual overview with an article that stresses the criticality of marketing strategy planning in a rapidly changing business environment. One of the most important keys to success is market knowledge that reveals niches (or segments) and allows a company to position itself against its competitors. The article gives specifics on product planning and the role of distribution, as well as pointing out the importance of a balanced marketing strategy that uses all strategic elements rather than overemphasizing only one. The next article goes one step further in illustrating the growing complexity of marketing strategy planning. Here technological advances are envisioned as equalizing forces that tend to bring consumers' needs and wants closer together, regardless of the nation in which they live. The global marketplace concept means that companies have greatly expanded opportunities and a whole new array of competitors. The third conceptual article addresses the technological interface of marketing strategy planning. In it, the pervasive impact of microcomputers is detailed, especially as it has and will continue to change product complexity, marketing organizational structure, decision making, and the application of the marketing concept.

The four articles dealing with specific companies begin with a panel presentation by a major corporation president. Mr. Fox offers eight guidelines that are fundamental to success in markets such as food products, which have matured to a situation of slow growth and entrenched competitors. Next, we shift to an innovative new product, the Walkman, which was conceived and marketed as a "global" product, thus tapping into consumers' universal need for music while engaged in other activities; the reading provides illuminating insight about the company dynamics during the Walkman's marketing planning. After this reading, we have included an article that describes the intense marketing activities in the home computer industry during the early 1980s. You can see the companies jockeying for position in what has become the hottest new consumer market of the decade. As you read about this stage in the home computer market's evolution, reflect on what has happened to these companies since the product first appeared and how critical flexible marketing planning has been for the winners. The section closes with an article that illustrates how three companies faced with what consultants would characterize as impossible situations successfully found niches in their respective markets and concentrated on planning for profitability rather than market share ∎

Conceptual Readings

Strategic Marketing's New Challenge
David W. Cravens

Business successes and disasters often share one characteristic: strategic planning, or the lack thereof. A&P's poor financial performance and loss of market position in the 1970s, for example, clearly indicate the dangers of faulty corporate and marketing strategies. In contrast, General Mills' management has successfully moved the company into new markets such as restaurants and specialty retailing, using the firm's core business, food processing, to generate capital for pursuing new opportunities. Underlying these moves into new business areas are carefully developed and executed strategic plans. Strategic planning for the enterprise demands perceptive insights about customers' needs and wants, and ways of achieving customer satisfaction through the firm's marketing offer (product, distribution, price, and promotion strategies). Thus, a close working relationship between executives responsible for strategic planning of the enterprise and marketing strategists is essential.

A brief examination of General Mills' Red Lobster restaurant chain operations will illustrate the strong market-centered focus in the firm's strategic planning. When Red Lobster was acquired in 1970, there were five units with total sales of $5 million.[1] In October 1981 the three hundredth unit was opened in Dallas. Sales in 1982 will exceed $600 million, accompanied by equally impressive profit performance. Management, recognizing that stores opened in the early 1970s were in need of a facelift, launched an ambitious remodeling program in 1980. To stay abreast of customer needs and wants, intensive marketing research has been used to select new sites, modify menus, and develop consumer pro-

files. Red Lobster, along with General Mills' other restaurant chains (Casa Gallardo, Darryls, York Steak House, and The Good Earth), is positioned to fit into the broad midprice family dining market segment which is expected to grow faster than the total restaurant market during the next five years. Typically, management has chosen to purchase small chains designed around promising away-from-home eating concepts, and to develop them using General Mills' marketing and operations know-how.

Several key features of marketing strategy are central to strategic planning in any enterprise; I want to identify these and indicate why they form the core of corporate and marketing plans. Interestingly, these features often appear in successful strategic plans, but are absent from those of firms whose performance is marginal or unsatisfactory. Such firms need to diagnose marketing strategies and to spot gaps in strategic marketing plans.[2]

Using Strategic Planning

An overwhelming base of evidence indicates that strategic planning is one of the high priority action areas of U.S. business today. And the reason is clear. The success and survival of the firm are at stake. Compare and contrast, for example, the impressive performance of Delta Airlines to that of Braniff International. Both were strong performers in the late 1970s. By 1982 Braniff was bankrupt, while Delta continued to retain a strong mar-

Reprinted with permission from the March–April 1983 issue of *Business Horizons.* © 1983 *Business Horizons.*

ket position amid turbulent economic conditions and deregulation. Clearly, Delta's management recognized the forces of change and developed strategies to position the airline favorably in a competitive environment.

The glamour and mystery often associated with strategic planning mask what should be viewed as a demanding yet logical process of deciding the mission and objectives of the enterprise and then devising strategies for reaching objectives. Since many corporations have two or more business units, top management must decide the corporate game plan for each unit of the corporation.

The 1970s brought major emphasis on strategic planning of the firm. Several new planning tools were developed, including the Boston Consulting Group's portfolio analysis, General Electric's screening grid, and the Profit Impact of Market Strategy (PIMS) studies of the Strategic Planning Institute. Unfortunately, these tools are often viewed as strategic solutions rather than as the diagnostic aids they were intended to be. Clearly, the emphasis should be upon making sound decisions and then executing them. There is evidence of too much concern about strategic concepts:

> [L]ong-term success does not lie in concepts. It depends on an organization's ability to pool the small incremental improvements and insights of the "antennae" of an organization—its salesmen and engineers and workers—to keep an edge on the competition.[3]

The operations of Delta Airlines offer clear evidence of the success of this hands-on approach to strategy. Every employee in the organization, from pilots to maintenance people to office personnel, seems to know where the firm is going, and why.

While the new planning methods are often useful in highlighting opportunities and problem areas, deciding what to do about them is top management's responsibility. Nucor Corporation is an interesting example of how a

perceptive management has been able to establish a strong position for this small-steel producer amid an industry dominated by giants. Nucor, if analyzed using the popular portfolio grid for market position and market attractiveness in the total steel industry, clearly falls into the "dog" category. Yet, if we define the market as steel joists for industrial construction in the Sun Belt, Nucor suddenly is moved into a much stronger business position and a more attractive market opportunity.

Understanding Markets

Understanding the needs and wants of people and organizations in the markets of interest to the enterprise is critical to business success. Gaining this understanding requires skillful analysis of market size and growth trends, customer characteristics, industry profiles, and key competitor strengths and weaknesses. Analyzing and tracking market trends in the 1980s will demand a close working relationship between corporate and marketing strategists and marketing researchers.

The following analysis of Limited, Inc.'s target market strategy made in 1980 illustrates the importance of understanding markets:

> Consider . . . the impact upon a company such as Limited, Inc., of shifts in the size of the different age groups in the population. In the late 1970s management described the firm's target market as providing medium-priced fashion apparel tailored to the tastes and lifestyles of women 16 to 35 years of age. Census projections of age-group shifts from 1980–90 are (1) the young adults (20-34) segment will grow by only 3 percent, and (2) the teenagers (13-19) segment will actually decline by 17 percent.
>
> The Limited, Inc. is aimed at a no-growth segment of the population. In contrast, the middle-aged segment (35-54) will grow by nearly 30 percent! This information raises some interesting strategic issues. Assuming management wants the

firm to grow, should Limited try to gain greater penetration into the 16-35 segment or should they attempt to appeal to the people who were in this segment in the 1970s, thus shifting their target market to the rapid growth 35-54 segment? The facts are clear; choice of an appropriate strategy is less apparent. Further penetration of a static market will be difficult. Following the original target age-group through its life cycle will require altering the product offering and various other elements of corporate and market strategy.[4]

In late 1981 Limited's target market strategy for the 1980s began to unfold, as described by Leslie H. Wexner, president:

> [W]e are carefully and gradually positioning the business to appeal to fashion conscious women in the 20 to 40 year old age category . . . in other words, the growth market of the 1980s. Among other things, this involved upgrading the quality and taste level of our merchandise and placing more emphasis on those merchandise classifications that appeal to these women. The strategy appears to be working.[5]

Meeting customer needs is what business is all about. Executives who are perceptive about what needs to serve and how to serve them are successful in delivering customer satisfaction while achieving high levels of business performance.

Finding Market Niches

Deciding what people or organizations to serve in the marketplace is one of management's most important and demanding strategic decisions. All operations of the firm revolve around the target market decision. Target market alternatives range from serving all (or most) buyers using a mass strategy, or serving one or more niches (segments) using a different strategy in each niche. Niche strategies are widely used across a broad cross section of industries.

There are clear indications that market niching will become the dominant strategy of many successful firms in the 1980s. Niching is a particularly promising option for those companies which are not market leaders, because high market share is often linked to strong business performance, and because serving a niche or segment of a product market is often the only feasible way for many firms to gain and hold market share. While the niche decision alone will not guarantee high performance, it can be the first step in building a high-performance marketing strategy. For example, the Profit Impact of Market Strategies (PIMS) program continues to signal a key link between market-share position and business success:

> Some of the most dramatic and well-publicized strategic successes of recent years have been based on the principle of segment focus that we advocate. For example, Philip Morris steadily improved its share of the cigarette market throughout the 1970s. Part of the company's success has been due to its heavy support for Merit, a low-tar brand that apparently had special appeal for health-conscious smokers.[6]

Analysis of the target market strategies of firms like Ethan Allen in furniture, Nucor in steel joists, Quaker Chemical in specialty chemicals, and Illinois Tool Works in industrial fasteners, adds further evidence to the benefits of market niching. Recognizing the value of a market niche strategy is only the first step in implementing the strategy. Deciding how to partition the market and selecting the best niche(s) to go after are critical steps in gaining a strong market position.

An illustration will add further insight to the target-market decision. Regional banks are looking for market niches that will enable them to position themselves in the highly competitive financial services area created by deregulation. Some illustrative niche strategies include these:

Hawkeye, Bancorp, Des Moines, Iowa, long a big agricultural lender, has turned to managing farms for absentee owners.

Bank One, Columbus, Ohio, has become a leader in specialized services. It hired out to competition and now processes cash-management accounts for nine brokerage firms, which are prevented from issuing checks.

In Missouri, Mark Twain Bankshares Inc.'s financial consultants sell their expertise in business problems as diverse as cash-flow and strategic planning.[7]

While mass market strategies are used by some firms, many others, like regional banks, have chosen to serve one or more customer groups within the total market.

An important issue in deciding whether to use a niche or total market strategy is estimating the costs and benefits underlying the strategy. Niche analysis may involve costly field research, particularly in consumer markets. And if more than one niche is served by a firm, a different marketing program must be developed for each target. In some situations, new markets for example, niching may not be necessary because of limited competition. In mature markets, however, a niche strategy may be critical to achieving desired market position.

Positioning

Deciding what market targets to go after sets the stage for deciding how to meet the needs and wants of target customers. Meeting these needs is accomplished through the design and implementation of a positioning strategy which consists of an integrated combination of product or service, distribution, price, and promotion strategies. Positioning strategy establishes how a product or brand is intended to be perceived by the target market relative to competitors' offerings. The target-market decision and the positioning decision are like two sides of the same coin. First, decide *what* needs to meet and then determine *how* to meet them.

The marketing strategy used by Loctite Corporation in launching Quick Metal, a new puttylike adhesive for repairing worn machine parts, illustrates the benefits of a carefully designed marketing program positioned to serve the needs of target customers:

> Quick Metal got its start in early 1979, when Mr. Fox [marketing v.p.] and other Loctite marketing executives began looking for ways to revive RC601 [Quick Metal's predecessor]. Instead of depending upon its own chemists and sales experts to design a new product that the market might not want, Loctite asked customers what they were looking for.[8]

Management targeted maintenance workers because a tube of the adhesive can eliminate 800 hours of machine downtime. The positioning strategy included a product designed to repair broken machines, a descriptive name, an aggressive promotional campaign, employee incentives, a high price (85 percent gross margin), and an intensive selling effort. In the first six months sales reached $2.2 million compared to the $300,000 the firm estimated that its traditional marketing approach would have generated.[9]

The Loctite illustration highlights two key issues associated with the design of a positioning strategy. First, blending strategy components into an integrated mix is the key to an effective positioning strategy. Preoccupation with one strategy component, and neglect of others, ignores the interrelationship among product, price, distribution, and promotion. A&P's management paid a huge price to learn this basic fact of marketing programming via the firm's ill-fated discount pricing campaign. In contrast, Loctite designed an integrated strategy, with price determined in conjunction with other supporting strategies. Second, the cost and benefits of alternative positioning strategies should be estimated. Loctite allocated more marketing resources to the Quick Metal program than typically was the case in new product development and introduction programs. Yet the net gain was impressive.

Product or Service Planning

The cutting edge of any marketing program positioning strategy is the product or service offered by the firm. The Loctite example illustrates that new-product planning is far too critical to leave only in the hands of research and development people.

> Product strategy is the core of strategic planning for the enterprise and it plays a pivotal role in shaping marketing strategy. Management's strategic decisions about the products to be offered are among the most important of those affecting the future of a company. No other strategic decision has such widespread impact, cutting across every functional area and affecting all levels of an organization.[10]

Management's strategic decisions about products or services fall into three major categories: (1) deciding what new products to develop or acquire; (2) managing existing products over their life cycles; and (3) eliminating products whose costs exceed their benefits. Since the new product area typically receives much attention from management, the following discussion focuses on existing products, whose strategic aspects may be neglected simply because the products are fully integrated into routine, day-to-day operations.

Often, strategic analysis of existing products will indicate promising opportunities for modifying them and repositioning them with buyers. Let's look at an illustration to see how performance of an existing product can be improved. Procter & Gamble's Crest toothpaste has been the leading brand in the $700 million dentifrice market for two decades.[11] But by

1980 competition was beginning to penetrate P&G's market position. For example, Beecham's Aqua Fresh, by borrowing the best features of Lever and P&G brands, gained a 14 percent market share in less than two years. P&G's management apparently underestimated the market appeal of the gel toothpastes, which now have one third of the market. Using a strategy designed to protect and eventually gain market position, P&G launched an aggressive advertising program for Crest and developed additional products, including Crest gel. Even experienced marketing strategists like P&G must guard against strategic complacency.

While there are dangers in following a totally product oriented strategy, products, nevertheless, are vital to business operations, because without a product or service there is no business. Product decisions are central to shaping both corporate and marketing strategy and should be made within the guidelines of corporate mission and objectives.

Strategic Role of Distribution

Firms which do not sell direct via their own sales forces to the people or organizations that consume their products are aligned into one or more distribution channels. Far too often distribution becomes a passive rather than active instrument of strategy. Yet the selection of a good distribution strategy can establish a strong competitive advantage. One major trend during the last decade has been the design and management of integrated distribution channels comprised of organizations at the different levels in the channel. Examples include Tandy's Radio Shack in electronics, Ethan Allen in furniture, and Entenmanns in bakery products.

Selecting the correct distribution intensity is a critical factor in strategically positioning a firm in the marketplace. North American Philips' Magnavox unit illustrates the importance of adjusting distribution strategy to changing conditions. For decades Magnavox held the premium quality position in the television market, successfully establishing a very selective network of dealers. By the mid-1970s it was clear that more intensive distribution was needed for Magnavox to compete with RCA, Zenith, and the Japanese at the retail level. Interestingly, at this mature stage in the life cycle of color television sets, major differences in quality and performance did not exist. North American Philips acquired Sylvania and Philco in early 1981. The impact of this action on Magnavox's distribution strategy was not apparent by early 1982, although one can speculate that the net effect will be a major expansion of Philips' distribution coverage. How this expansion will be translated into the distribution of the three brands is not clear.

Channel management and distribution intensity decisions are key strategic issues for any business that is part of one or more distribution channels. Both the choice of channel strategy and adjustment of strategy to changing conditions are vital management concerns. Analysis of Ethan Allen's performance during the last decade indicates the pivotal role of distribution strategy in corporate performance. It is noteworthy that Ethan Allen moved toward less intensive distribution using carefully selected dealers, supported by various services and assistance from the manufacturer. In contrast, Magnavox may move toward more intensive distribution. Thus, the distribution intensity decision must be matched to the strategic situation and, when necessary, altered to correspond to changing conditions in the marketplace.

Supporting Strategies

The components of marketing strategy should fit together like the parts of a well-designed system. The target market must be served by an integrated marketing program comprised of product, distribution, price, and promotion strategies. Typically, price and promotion are used to support product and distribution strategies. Overreliance upon any one program component such as price can be dangerous. The parts of the program should function as a team working toward customer satisfaction.

Braniff's struggle in early 1982 to stay in business offers sobering evidence of the risks of trying to gain market position by relying primarily upon price. Management closed sales offices, reduced staff, and announced major price reductions. All price reductions were matched by competing airlines. By March cash-flow problems forced delays in payment of employees' salaries and wages, and eventually the airline failed.

The proper blending of marketing strategy components can have an important effect upon marketing productivity. Too many or too few salespeople, ineffective deployment of advertising dollars, and other incorrect marketing resource allocations will adversely affect performance. Management must continually work toward improving the effectiveness and efficiency of marketing programs. Considering that annual expenditures for advertising and personal selling in the United States are more than $150 billion, it is clear that a huge opportunity for productivity gains exists. And the evidence shows that many firms have not reached an optimal level in the use of marketing resources.

Managing for Results

Financial analysis will become one of the most important responsibilities of the marketing strategist in the 1980s. This is not to suggest that the chief marketing executive should take over financial planning. Rather, managing marketing strategies for results will demand an understanding of financial analysis concepts and tools. Marketing strategies, when implemented, affect financial results in two ways: (1) the strategies, if successful, generate sales; and (2) expenditures upon product, distribution, and promotion consume financial resources. Marketing's new financial responsibility is described below.

> To respond to these pressures positively, marketing managers will need a better understanding of accounting and financial management than that of their predecessors. The characteristic marketing manager's emphasis in analysis and action on sales volume, gross margin, and market share must be replaced by a more general management focus on bottom line profitability and return on investment. Top management will think increasingly in terms of total resource allocation across products and markets, assessing the total product portfolio in terms of complex tradeoffs between business growth opportunities in markets requiring additional investment for future profitability versus cash generation now in markets with limited or negative investment. Heightened awareness of the impact of inflation on measures of corporate financial performance will undoubtedly sharpen management concern for this dilemma. Marketing management must adopt new attitudes, what might be called "a general management orientation," as well as make use of the sophisticated measurements, analytical techniques, and strategic planning approaches that are available to help cope with the new pressures and complexities.[12]

At the heart of managing for results are implementation and control of marketing strategies. Contrast, in the late 1970s, the consistent and high level of services offered by the McDonald's fast-food chain with Kentucky Fried Chicken's rundown facilities and inconsistent services.

> Revenue and profit were falling, along with morale among franchise holders and employees. Many Kentucky Fried Chicken restaurants were sloppy and their food was unappetizing. Even founder Col. Harland Sanders griped publicly that the chain served "the worst fried chicken

I've ever seen" and that the gravy resembled "wallpaper paste."[13]

Clearly, management had allowed KFC's operations to get out of control. In 1977 Heublein, Inc., the parent company, initiated a series of actions to improve the quality and delivery of KFC's services and to position the chain aggressively as a fried chicken specialist. These actions have apparently strengthened the firm's market position and have improved the financial performance of the KFC business unit.

We have examined several aspects of strategic marketing, indicating new challenges and responsibilities facing chief marketing executives in the decade ahead. To a large extent these trends are a continuation of the strategic marketing concerns of the late 1970s. These include a rapidly changing business environment, a critical need for analyzing market behavior, the need for adjusting strategies to changing conditions (for example, The Limited, Inc.), and growth in the importance of distribution strategy. Nevertheless, there is one important difference between the contemporary business environment and that of the 1970s. While a rapidly changing business environment was expected after the oil embargo and other events of the 1970s, the nature and scope of changes have been far beyond those anticipated. For example, consider deregulation in transportation and financial institutions. By early 1983, the future of several firms in these industries was in jeopardy. The pace of change in the next decade will be even faster than we experienced in the last 10 years; new strategies will be needed to cope with the changes.

A major distinction between the last decade and the next decade is marketing's new and rapidly expanding and demanding strategic role. Chief marketing executives will be called upon to participate in strategic planning for businesses. To meet this responsibility, marketing executives must quickly develop their capabilities in strategic analysis and planning, financial analysis, and strategic marketing. The requirements of this new role are much greater than they were in the past. The chief marketing executive will be a major participant in strategic planning for the enterprise. In an increasing number of firms, this executive is directing the strategic planning for the firm because of the strong market-centered focus of strategic planning.

Notes

1. This account is drawn, in part, from General Mills' Quarterly Report to Stockholders, November 29, 1981.
2. See David W. Cravens, *Strategic Marketing* (Homewood, Ill.: Richard D. Irwin, 1982).
3. Richard T. Pascale, "Our Curious Addiction to Corporate Grand Strategy," *Fortune*, January 25, 1982, p. 116.
4. Cravens, *Strategic Marketing*, p. 126.
5. The Limited Inc., First Quarter Report 1982, November 12, 1981.
6. Robert D. Buzzell and Frederik D. Wiersema, "Successful Share-Building Strategies," *Harvard Business Review*, January–February 1981, p. 144.
7. John Helyar, "Regional Banks Search for a Niche in Face of New Rules, Competition," *The Wall Street Journal*, February 4, 1982, p. 25.
8. Bill Abrams, "Consumer-Product Techniques Help Loctite Sell to Industry," *The Wall Street Journal*, April 2, 1981, p. 29.
9. Ibid.
10. Cravens, *Strategic Marketing*, p. 229.
11. This account is drawn, in part, from Bill Abrams, "P&G May Give Crest a New Look After Failing to Brush Off Rivals," *The Wall Street Journal*, January 8, 1981, p. 21.
12. Frederick E. Webster, Jr., James A. Largay III, and Clyde P. Stickney, "The Impact of Inflation Accounting on Marketing Decisions," *Journal of Marketing*, Fall 1980, p. 9.
13. David P. Garino, "At Kentucky Fried Chicken It's Time to Set Itself Apart," *The Wall Street Journal*, March 19, 1981, p. 29.

The Globalization of Markets
Theodore Levitt

A powerful force drives the world toward a converging commonality, and that force is technology. It has proletarianized communication, transport, and travel. It has made isolated places and impoverished peoples eager for modernity's allurements. Almost everyone everywhere wants all the things they have heard about, seen, or experienced via the new technologies.

The result is a new commercial reality—the emergence of global markets for standardized consumer products on a previously unimagined scale of magnitude. Corporations geared to this new reality benefit from enormous economies of scale in production, distribu-

tion, marketing, and management. By translating these benefits into reduced world prices, they can decimate competitors that still live in the disabling grip of old assumptions about how the world works.

Gone are accustomed differences in national or regional preference. Gone are the days when a company could sell last year's models—or lesser versions of advanced products—in the less-developed world. And gone are the days when prices, margins, and profits abroad were generally higher than at home.

The globalization of markets is at hand. With that, the multinational commercial world nears its end, and so does the multinational corporation.

The multinational and the global corporation are not the same thing. The multinational corporation operates in a number of countries, and adjusts its products and practices in each—at high relative costs. The global corporation operates with resolute constancy—at low relative cost—as if the entire world (or major regions of it) were a single entity; it sells the same things in the same way everywhere.

Which strategy is better is not a matter of opinion but of necessity. Worldwide communications carry everywhere the constant drumbeat of modern possibilities to lighten and enhance work, raise living standards, divert, and entertain. The same countries that ask the world to recognize and respect the individuality of their cultures insist on the wholesale transfer to them of modern goods, services, and technologies. Modernity is not just a wish but also a widespread practice among those who cling, with unyielding passion or religious fervor, to ancient attitudes and heritages.

Who can forget the televised scenes during the 1979 Iranian uprisings of young men in fashionable French-cut trousers and silky body shirts thirsting with raised modern weapons for blood in the name of Islamic fundamentalism?

In Brazil, thousands swarm daily from pre-industrial Bahian darkness into exploding coastal cities, there quickly to install television sets in crowded corrugated huts and, next to battered Volkswagens, make sacrificial offerings of fruit and fresh-killed chickens to Macumban spirits by candlelight.

During Biafra's fratricidal war against the Ibos, daily televised reports showed soldiers carrying bloodstained swords and listening to transistor radios while drinking Coca-Cola.

In the isolated Siberian city of Krasnoyarsk, with no paved streets and censored news, occasional Western travelers are stealthily propositioned for cigarettes, digital watches, and even the clothes off their backs.

The organized smuggling of electronic equipment, used automobiles, Western cloth-ing, cosmetics, and pirated movies into primitive places exceeds even the thriving underground trade in modern weapons and their military mercenaries.

A thousand suggestive ways attest to the ubiquity of the desire for the most advanced things that the world makes and sells—goods of the best quality and reliability at the lowest price. The world's needs and desires have been irrevocably homogenized. This makes the multinational corporation obsolete and the global corporation absolute.

Living in the Republic of Technology

Daniel J. Boorstin, author of the monumental trilogy *The Americans,* characterized our age as driven by "the Republic of Technology [whose] supreme law . . . is convergence, the tendency for everything to become more like everything else."

In business, this trend has pushed markets toward global commonality. Corporations sell standardized products in the same way everywhere—autos, steel, chemicals, petroleum, cement, agricultural commodities and equipment, industrial and commercial construction, banking and insurance services, computers, semiconductors, transport, electronic instruments, pharmaceuticals, and telecommunications, to mention some of the obvious.

Nor is the sweeping gale of globalization confined to these raw material or high-tech products, where the universal language of customers and users facilitates standardization. The transforming winds whipped up by the proletarianization of communication and travel enter every crevice of life.

Commercially, nothing confirms this as much as the success of McDonald's from the Champs Elysées to the Ginza, of Coca-Cola in Bahrain and Pepsi-Cola in Moscow, and of rock music, Greek salad, Hollywood movies, Revlon cosmetics, Sony televisions, and Levi jeans everywhere. "High-touch" products are as ubiquitous as high tech.

Starting from opposing sides, the high-tech and the high-touch ends of the commercial spectrum gradually consume the undistributed middle in their cosmopolitan orbit. No one is exempt and nothing can stop the process. Everywhere everything gets more and more like everything else as the world's preference structure is relentlessly homogenized.

Consider the cases of Coca-Cola and Pepsi-Cola, which are globally standardized products sold everywhere and welcomed by everyone. Both successfully cross multitudes of national, regional, and ethnic taste buds trained to a variety of deeply ingrained local preferences of taste, flavor, consistency, effervescence, and aftertaste. Everywhere both sell well. Cigarettes too, especially American-made, make year-to-year global inroads on territories previously held in the firm grip of other, mostly local, blends.

These are not exceptional examples. (Indeed their global reach would be even greater were it not for artificial trade barriers.) They exemplify a general drift toward the homogenization of the world and how companies distribute, finance, and price products.[1] Nothing is exempt. The products and methods of the industrialized world play a single tune for all the world, and all the world eagerly dances to it.

Ancient differences in national tastes or modes of doing business disappear. The commonality of preference leads inescapably to the standardization of products, manufacturing, and the institutions of trade and commerce. Small nation-based markets transmogrify and expand. Success in world competition turns on efficiency in production, distribution, marketing, and management, and inevitably becomes focused on price.

The most effective world competitors incorporate superior quality and reliability into their cost structures. They sell in all national markets the same kind of products sold at home or in their largest export market. They compete on the basis of appropriate value—the best combinations of price, quality, reliability, and delivery for products that are globally identical with respect to design, function, and even fashion.

That, and little else, explains the surging success of Japanese companies dealing worldwide in a vast variety of products—both tangible products like steel, cars, motorcycles, hi-fi equipment, farm machinery, robots, microprocessors, carbon fibers, and now even textiles, and intangibles like banking, shipping, general contracting, and soon computer software. Nor are high-quality and low-cost operations incompatible, as a host of consulting organizations and data engineers argue with vigorous vacuity. The reported data are incomplete, wrongly analyzed, and contradictory. The truth is that low-cost operations are the hallmark of corporate cultures that require and produce quality in all that they do. High quality and low costs are not opposing postures. They are compatible, twin identities of superior practice.[2]

To say that Japan's companies are not global because they export cars with left-side drives to the United States and the European continent, while those in Japan have right-side drives, or because they sell office machines through distributors in the United States but directly at home, or speak Portuguese in Brazil is to mistake a difference for a distinction. The same is true of Safeway and Southland retail chains operating effectively in the Middle East, and to not only native but also imported populations from Korea, the Philippines, Pakistan, India, Thailand, Britain, and the United States. National rules of the road differ, and so do distribution channels and languages. Japan's distinction is its unrelenting push for economy and value enhancement. That translates into a drive for standardization at high-quality levels.

Vindication of the Model T

If a company forces costs and prices down and pushes quality and reliability up—while maintaining reasonable concern for suitability—customers will prefer its world-standardized products. The theory holds, at this stage in the evolution of globalization, no matter what conventional market research and even common sense may suggest about different national and regional tastes, preferences, needs, and institutions. The Japanese have repeatedly vindicated this theory, as did Henry Ford with the Model T. Most important, so have their imitators, including companies from South Korea (television sets and heavy construction), Malaysia (personal calculators and microcomputers), Brazil (auto parts and tools), Colombia (apparel), Singapore (optical equipment), and yes, even from the United States (office copiers, computers, bicycles, castings), Western Europe (automatic washing machines), Rumania (housewares), Hungary (apparel), Yugoslavia (furniture), and Israel (pagination equipment).

Of course, large companies operating in a single nation or even a single city don't standardize everything they make, sell, or do. They have product lines instead of a single-product version, and multiple-distribution channels. There are neighborhood, local, regional, ethnic, and institutional differences, even within metropolitan areas. But although companies customize products for particular market segments, they know that success in a world with homogenized demand requires a search for sales opportunities in similar segments across the globe in order to achieve the economies of scale necessary to compete.

Such a search works because a market segment in one country is seldom unique; it has close cousins everywhere precisely because technology has homogenized the globe. Even small local segments have their global equivalents everywhere and become subject to global competition, especially on price.

The global competitor will seek constantly to standardize his offering everywhere. He will digress from this standardization only after exhausting all possibilities to retain it, and he will push for reinstatement of standardization whenever digression and divergence have occurred. He will never assume that the customer is a king who knows his own wishes.

Trouble increasingly stalks companies that lack clarified global focus and remain inattentive to the economics of simplicity and standardization. The most endangered companies in the rapidly evolving world tend to be those that dominate rather small domestic markets with high value-added products for which there are smaller markets elsewhere. With transportation costs proportionately low, distant competitors will enter the now-sheltered markets of those companies with goods produced more cheaply under scale-efficient conditions. Global competition spells the end of domestic territoriality, no matter how diminutive the territory may be.

When the global producer offers his lower costs internationally, his patronage expands exponentially. He not only reaches into distant markets, but also attracts customers who previously held to local preferences and now capitulate to the attractions of lesser prices. The strategy of standardization not only responds to worldwide homogenized markets but also expands those markets with aggressive low pricing. The new technological juggernaut taps an ancient motivation—to make one's money go as far as possible. This is universal—not simply a motivation but actually a need.

The Hedgehog Knows

The difference between the hedgehog and the fox, wrote Sir Isaiah Berlin in distinguishing between Dostoevski and Tolstoy, is that the fox knows a lot about a great many things, but the hedgehog knows everything about one great thing. The multinational corporation knows a lot about a great many countries and congenially adapts to supposed differences. It willingly accepts vestigial national differences, not questioning the possibility of their transformation, not recognizing how the world is ready and eager for the benefit of modernity, especially when the price is right. The multinational corporation's accommodating mode to visible national differences is medieval.

By contrast, the global corporation knows everything about one great thing. It knows about the absolute need to be competitive on a worldwide basis as well as nationally and seeks constantly to drive down prices by standardizing what it sells and how it operates. It treats the world as composed of few standardized markets rather than many customized markets. It actively seeks and vigorously works toward global convergence. Its mission is modernity and its mode, price competition, even when it sells top-of-the-line, high-end products. It knows about the one great thing all nations and people have in common: scarcity.

Nobody takes scarcity lying down; everyone wants more. This in part explains division of labor and specialization of production. They enable people and nations to optimize their conditions through trade. The median is usually money.

Experience teaches that money has three special qualities: scarcity, difficulty of acquisition, and transience. People understandably treat it with respect. Everyone in the increasingly homogenized world market wants products and features that everybody else wants. If the price is low enough, they will take highly standardized world products, even if these aren't exactly what mother said was suitable, what immemorial custom decreed was right, or what market-research fabulists asserted was preferred.

The implacable truth of all modern production—whether of tangible or intangible goods—is that large-scale production of standardized items is generally cheaper within a wide range of volume than small-scale production. Some argue that CAD/CAM will allow companies to manufacture customized products on a small scale—but cheaply. But the argument misses the point. If a company treats the world as one or two distinctive product markets, it can serve the world more economically than if it treats it as three, four, or five product markets.

Why Remaining Differences?

Different cultural preferences, national tastes and standards, and business institutions are vestiges of the past. Some inheritances die gradually, others prosper and expand into mainstream global preferences. So-called ethnic markets are a good example. Chinese food, pita bread, country and western music, pizza, and jazz are everywhere. They are market segments that exist in worldwide proportions. They don't deny or contradict global homogenization but confirm it.

Many of today's differences among nations as to products and their features actually reflect the respectful accommodation of multinational corporations to what they believe are fixed local preferences. They *believe* preferences are fixed, not because they are but because of rigid habits of thinking about what actually is. Most executives in multinational corporations are thoughtlessly accommodating. They falsely presume that marketing means giving the customer what he says he wants rather than trying to understand exactly what he'd like. So they persist with high-cost, customized multinational products and practices instead of pressing hard and pressing properly for global standardization.

I do not advocate the systematic disregard of local or national differences. But a company's sensitivity to such differences does not require that it ignore the possibilities of doing things differently or better.

There are, for example, enormous differences among Middle Eastern countries. Some are socialist, some monarchies, some republics. Some take their legal heritage from the Napoleonic Code, some from the Ottoman Empire, and some from the British common law; except for Israel, all are influenced by Islam. Doing business means personalizing the business relationship in an obsessively intimate fashion. During the month of Ramadan, business discussions can start only after 10 o'clock at night, when people are tired and full of food after a day of fasting. A company must almost certainly have a local partner; a local lawyer is required (as, say, in New York), and irrevocable letters of credit are essential. Yet, as Coca-Cola's Senior Vice President Sam Ayoub noted, "Arabs are much more capable of making distinctions between cultural and religious purposes on the one hand and economic realities on the other than is generally assumed. Islam is compatible with science and modern times."

Barriers to globalization are not confined to the Middle East. The free transfer of technology and data across the boundaries of the European Common Market countries are hampered by legal and financial impediments. And there is resistance to radio and television interference ("pollution") among neighboring European countries.

But the past is a good guide to the future. With persistence and appropriate means, barriers against superior technologies and economics have always fallen. There is no recorded exception where reasonable effort has been made to overcome them. It is very much a matter of time and effort.

A Failure in Global Imagination

Many companies have tried to standardize world practice by exporting domestic products and processes without accommodation or change—and have failed miserably. Their deficiencies have been seized on as evidence of bovine stupidity in the face of abject impossibility. Advocates of global standardization see them as examples of failures in execution.

In fact, poor execution is often an important cause. More important, however, is failure of nerve—failure of imagination.

Consider the case for the introduction of fully automatic home laundry equipment in Western Europe at a time when few homes had even semiautomatic machines. Hoover, Ltd., whose parent company was headquartered in North Canton, Ohio, had a prominent presence in Britain as a producer of vacuum cleaners and washing machines. Due to insufficient demand in the home market and low exports to the European continent, the large washing machine plant in England operated far below capacity. The company needed to sell more of its semiautomatic or automatic machines.

Because it had a "proper" marketing orientation, Hoover conducted consumer preference studies in Britain and each major continental country. The results showed feature preferences clearly enough among several countries (see Exhibit 1).

The incremental unit variable costs (in pounds sterling) of customizing to meet just a few of the national preferences were:

	£	s.	d.
Stainless steel versus enamel drum	1	0	0
Porthole window		10	0
Spin speed of 800 rpm versus 700 rpm		15	0
Water heater	2	15	0
6 versus 5 kilos capacity	1	10	0
	£6	10 s	0 d

$18.20 at the exchange rate of that time.

Considerable plant investment was needed to meet other preferences.

The lowest retail prices (in pounds sterling) of leading locally produced brands in the various countries were approximately:

U.K.	£110
France	114
West Germany	113
Sweden	134
Italy	57

Product customization in each country would have put Hoover in a poor competitive position on the basis of price, mostly due to the higher manufacturing costs incurred by short production runs for separate features. Because Common Market tariff reduction programs were then incomplete, Hoover also paid tariff duties in each continental country.

How to Make a Creative Analysis

In the Hoover case, an imaginative analysis of automatic washing machine sales in each country would have revealed that:

1. Italian automatics, small in capacity and size, low-powered, without built-in heaters, with porcelain enamel tubs, were priced aggressively low and were gaining large market shares in all countries, including West Germany.

2. The best-selling automatics in West Germany were heavily advertised (three times more than the next most promoted brand), were ideally suited to national tastes, and were also by far the highest priced machines available in that country.

3. Italy, with the lowest penetration of washing machines of any kind (manual, semiautomatic, or automatic) was rapidly going directly to automatics, skipping the pattern of first buying hand-wringer, manually assisted machines and then semiautomatics.

4. Detergent manufacturers were just beginning to promote the technique of cold-water and tepid-water laundering then used in the United States.

The growing success of small, low-powered, low-speed, low-capacity, low-priced Italian machines, even against the preferred but highly priced and highly promoted brand in West Germany, was significant. It contained a powerful message that was lost on managers confidently wedded to a distorted version of the marketing concept according to which you give the customer what he says he wants. In fact the customers *said* they wanted certain features, but their behavior demonstrated they'd take other features provided the price and the promotion were right.

EXHIBIT 1 Consumer Preferences to Automatic Washing Machine Features in the 1960s

Features	Great Britain	Italy	West Germany	France	Sweden
Shell dimensions*	34" and narrow	Low and narrow	34" and wide	34" and narrow	34" and wide
Drum material	Enamel	Enamel	Stainless steel	Enamel	Stainless steel
Loading	Top	Front	Front	Front	Front
Front porthole	Yes/no	Yes	Yes	Yes	Yes
Capacity	5 kilos	4 kilos	6 kilos	5 kilos	6 kilos
Spin speed	700 rpm	400 rpm	850 rpm	600 rpm	800 rpm
Water-heating system	No†	Yes	Yes‡	Yes	No†
Washing action	Agitator	Tumble	Tumble	Agitator	Tumble
Styling features	Inconspicuous appearance	Brightly colored	Indestructible appearance	Elegant appearance	Strong appearance

*34" height was (in the process of being adopted as) a standard work-surface height in Europe.

†Most British and Swedish homes had centrally heated hot water.

‡West Germans preferred to launder at temperatures higher than generally provided centrally.

In this case it was obvious that, under prevailing conditions, people preferred a low-priced automatic over any kind of manual or semiautomatic machine and certainly over higher priced automatics, even though the low-priced automatics failed to fulfill all their expressed preferences. The supposedly meticulous and demanding German consumers violated all expectations by buying the simple, low-priced Italian machines.

It was equally clear that people were profoundly influenced by promotions of automatic washers; in West Germany, the most heavily promoted ideal machine also had the largest market share despite its high price. Two things clearly influenced customers to buy: low price regardless of feature preferences and heavy promotion regardless of price. Both factors helped homemakers get what they most wanted—the superior benefits bestowed by fully automatic machines.

Hoover should have aggressively sold a simple, standardized high-quality machine at a low price (afforded by the 17 percent variable cost reduction that the elimination of £6-10-0 worth of extra features made possible). The suggested retail prices could have been somewhat less than £100. The extra funds "saved" by avoiding unnecessary plant modifications would have supported an extended service network and aggressive media promotions.

Hoover's media message should have been: *this* is the machine that you, the homemaker, *deserve* to have to reduce the repetitive heavy daily household burdens, so that *you* may have more constructive time to spend with your children and your husband. The promotion should also have targeted the husband to give him, preferably in the presence of his wife, a sense of obligation to provide an automatic washer for her even before he bought an automobile for himself. An aggressively low price, combined with heavy promotion of this kind, would have overcome previously expressed preferences for particular features.

The Hoover case illustrates how the perverse practice of the marketing concept and the absence of any kind of marketing imagination let multinational attitudes survive when customers actually want the benefits of global standardization. The whole project got off on the wrong foot. It asked people what features they wanted in a washing machine rather than what they wanted out of life. Selling a line of products individually tailored to each nation is thoughtless. Managers who took pride in practicing the marketing concept to the fullest did not, in fact, practice it at all. Hoover asked the wrong questions, then applied neither thought nor imagination to the answers. Such companies are like the ethnocentricists in the Middle Ages who saw with everyday clarity the sun revolving around the earth and offered it as Truth. With no additional data but a more searching mind, Copernicus, like the hedgehog, interpreted a more compelling and accurate reality. Data do not yield information except with the intervention of the mind. Information does not yield meaning except with the intervention of imagination.

Accepting the Inevitable

The global corporation accepts for better or for worse that technology drives consumers relentlessly toward the same common goals—alleviation of life's burdens and the expansion of discretionary time and spending power. Its role is profoundly different from what it has been for the ordinary corporation during its brief, turbulent, and remarkably protean history. It orchestrates the twin vectors of technology and globalization for the world's benefit. Neither fate, nor nature, nor God but rather the necessity of commerce created this role.

In the United States two industries became global long before they were consciously aware of it. After over a generation of persistent and acrimonious labor shutdowns, the

United Steelworkers of America have not called an industrywide strike since 1959; the United Auto Workers have not shut down General Motors since 1970. Both unions realize that they have become global—shutting down all or most of U.S. manufacturing would not shut out U.S. customers. Overseas suppliers are there to supply the market.

Cracking the Code of Western Markets

Since the theory of the marketing concept emerged a quarter of a century ago, the more managerially advanced corporations have been eager to offer what customers clearly wanted rather than what was merely convenient. They have created marketing departments supported by professional market researchers of awesome and often costly proportions. And they have proliferated extraordinary numbers of operations and product lines—highly tailored products and delivery systems for many different markets, market segments, and nations.

Significantly, Japanese companies operate almost entirely without marketing departments or market research of the kind so prevalent in the West. Yet, in the colorful words of General Electric's chairman John F. Welch, Jr., the Japanese, coming from a small cluster of resource-poor islands, with an entirely alien culture and an almost impenetrably complex language, have cracked the code of Western markets. They have done it not by looking with mechanistic thoroughness at the way markets are different but rather by searching for meaning with a deeper wisdom. They have discovered the one great thing all markets have in common—an overwhelming desire for dependable, world-standard modernity in all things, at aggressively low prices. In response, they deliver irresistible value everywhere, attracting people with products that market-research technocrats described with superficial certainty as being unsuitable and uncompetitive.

The wider a company's global reach, the greater the number of regional and national preferences it will encounter for certain product features, distribution systems, or promotional media. There will always need to be some accommodation to differences. But the widely prevailing and often unthinking belief in the immutability of these differences is generally mistaken. Evidence of business failure because of lack of accommodation is often evidence of other shortcomings.

Take the case of Revlon in Japan. The company unnecessarily alienated retailers and confused customers by selling world-standardized cosmetics only in elite outlets; then it tried to recover with low-priced world-standardized products in broader distribution, followed by a change in the company president and cutbacks in distribution as costs rose faster than sales. The problem was not that Revlon didn't understand the Japanese market; it didn't do the job right, wavered in its programs, and was impatient to boot.

By contrast, the Outboard Marine Corporation, with imagination, push, and persistence, collapsed long-established three-tiered distribution channels in Europe into a more focused and controllable two-step system— and did so despite the vociferous warnings of local trade groups. It also reduced the number and types of retail outlets. The result was greater improvement in credit and product-installation service to customers, major cost reductions, and sales advances.

In its highly successful introduction of Contac 600 (the timed-release decongestant) into Japan, SmithKline Corporation used 35 wholesalers instead of the 1,000-plus that established practice required. Daily contacts with the wholesalers and key retailers, also in violation of established practice, supplemented the plan, and it worked.

Denied access to established distribution institutions in the United States, Komatsu, the Japanese manufacturer of lightweight farm machinery, entered the market through over-the-road construction equipment dealers in rural areas of the Sunbelt, where farms are smaller, the soil sandier and easier to work. Here inexperienced distributors were able to attract customers on the basis of Komatsu's product and price appropriateness.

In cases of successful challenge to prevailing institutions and practices, a combination of product reliability and quality, strong and sustained support systems, aggressively low prices, and sales-compensation packages, as well as audacity and implacability, circumvented, shattered, and transformed very different distribution systems. Instead of resentment there was admiration.

Still, some differences between nations are unyielding, even in a world of microprocessors. In the United States almost all manufacturers of microprocessors check them for reliability through a so-called parallel system of testing. Japan prefers the totally different sequential testing system. So Teradyne Corporation, the world's largest producer of microprocessor test equipment, makes one line for the United States and one for Japan. That's easy.

What's not so easy for Teradyne is to know how best to organize and manage, in this instance, its marketing effort. Companies can organize by product, region, function, or by using some combination of these. A company can have separate marketing organizations for Japan and for the United States, or it can have separate product groups, one working largely in Japan and the other in the United States. A single manufacturing facility or marketing operation might service both markets, or a company might use separate marketing operations for each.

Questions arise if the company organizes by product. In the case of Teradyne, should the group handling the parallel system, whose major market is the United States, sell in Japan and compete with the group focused on the Japanese market? If the company orga-

nizes regionally, how do regional groups divide their efforts between promoting the parallel versus the sequential system? If the company organizes in terms of function, how does it get commitment in marketing, for example, for one line instead of the other?

There is no one reliably right answer—no one formula by which to get it. There isn't even a satisfactory contingent answer.[3] What works well for one company or one place may fail for another in precisely the same place, depending on the capabilities, histories, reputations, resources, and even the cultures of both.

The Earth Is Flat

The differences that persist throughout the world despite its globalization affirm an ancient dictum of economics—that things are driven by what happens at the margin, not at the core. Thus, in ordinary competitive analysis, what's important is not the average price but the marginal price; what happens not in the usual case but at the interface of newly erupting conditions. What counts in commercial affairs is what happens at the cutting edge. What is most striking today is the underlying similarities of what is happening now to national preferences at the margin. These similarities at the cutting edge cumulatively form an overwhelming, predominant commonality everywhere.

To refer to the persistence of economic nationalism (protective and subsidized trade practices, special tax aids, or restrictions for home market producers) as a barrier to the globalization of markets is to make a valid point. Economic nationalism does have a powerful persistence. But, as with the present almost totally smooth internationalization of investment capital, the past alone does not shape or predict the future.

Reality is not a fixed paradigm, dominated by immemorial customs and derived attitudes, heedless of powerful and abundant new forces. The world is becoming increasingly informed about the liberating and enhancing possibilities of modernity. The persistence of the inherited varieties of national preferences rests uneasily on increasing evidence of, and restlessness regarding, their inefficiency, costliness, and confinement. The historic past, and the national differences respecting commerce and industry it spawned and fostered everywhere, is now subject to relatively easy transformation.

Cosmopolitanism is no longer the monopoly of the intellectual and leisure classes; it is becoming the established property and defining characteristic of all sectors everywhere in the world. Gradually and irresistibly it breaks down the walls of economic insularity, nationalism, and chauvinism. What we see today as escalating commercial nationalism is simply the last violent death rattle of an obsolete institution.

Companies that adapt to and capitalize on economic convergence can still make distinctions and adjustments in different markets. Persistent differences in the world are consistent with fundamental underlying commonalities; they often complement rather than oppose each other—in business as they do in physics. There is, in physics, simultaneously matter and antimatter working in symbiotic harmony.

The earth is round, but for most purposes it's sensible to treat it as flat. Space is curved, but not much for everyday life here on earth.

Divergence from established practice happens all the time. But the multinational mind, warped into circumspection and timidity by years of stumbles and transnational troubles, now rarely challenges existing overseas practices. More often it considers any departure from inherited domestic routines as mindless, disrespectful, or impossible. It is the mind of a bygone day.

The successful global corporation does not abjure customization or differentiation for the requirements of markets that differ in product preferences, spending patterns, shopping preferences, and institutional or legal arrangements. But the global corporation accepts and adjusts to these differences only reluctantly, only after relentlessly testing their immutability, after trying in various ways to circumvent and reshape them as we saw in the cases of Outboard Marine in Europe, SmithKline in Japan, and Komatsu in the United States.

There is only one significant respect in which a company's activities around the world are important, and this is in what it produces and how it sells. Everything else derives from, and is subsidiary to, these activities.

The purpose of business is to get and keep a customer. Or, to use Peter Drucker's more refined construction, to *create* and keep a customer. A company must be wedded to the ideal of innovation—offering better or more preferred products in such combinations of ways, means, places, and at such prices that prospects *prefer* doing business with the company rather than with others.

Preferences are constantly shaped and reshaped. Within our global commonality enormous variety constantly asserts itself and thrives, as can be seen within the world's single largest domestic market, the United States. But in the process of world homogenization, modern markets expand to reach cost-reducing global proportions. With better and cheaper communication and transport, even small local market segments hitherto protected from distant competitors now feel the pressure of their presence. Nobody is safe from global reach and the irresistible economies of scale.

Two vectors shape the world—technology and globalization. The first helps determine human preferences; the second, economic realities. Regardless of how much preferences evolve and diverge, they also gradually converge and form markets where economies of scale lead to reduction of costs and prices.

The modern global corporation contrasts powerfully with the aging multinational corporation. Instead of adapting to superficial and even entrenched differences within and between nations, it will seek sensibly to force suitably standardized products and practices on the entire globe. They are exactly what the world will take, if they come also with low prices, high quality, and blessed reliability. The global company will operate, in this regard, precisely as Henry Kissinger wrote in *Years of Upheaval* about the continuing Japanese economic success—"voracious in its collection of information, impervious to pressure, and implacable in execution."

Given what is everywhere the purpose of commerce, the global company will shape the vectors of technology and globalization into its great strategic fecundity. It will systematically push these vectors toward their own convergence, offering everyone simultaneously high-quality, more or less standard-

ized products at optimally low prices, thereby achieving for itself vastly expanded markets and profits. Companies that do not adapt to the new global realities will become victims of those that do.

Notes

1. In a landmark article, Robert D. Buzzell pointed out the rapidity with which barriers to standardization were falling. In all cases they succumbed to more and cheaper advanced ways of doing things. See "Can You Standardize Multinational Marketing?" *Harvard Business Review*, November–December 1968, p. 102.

2. There is powerful new evidence for this, even though the opposite has been urged by analysts of PIMS data for nearly a decade. See Lynn W. Phillips, Dae Chang, and Robert D. Buzzell, "Product Quality: Cost Production and Business Performance—A Test of Some Key Hypotheses," Harvard Business School Working Paper No. 83-13.

3. For a discussion of multinational reorganization, see Christopher A. Bartlett, "MNCs: Get Off the Reorganization Merry-Go-Round," *Harvard Business Review*, March–April 1983, p. 138.

Computer-Aided Marketing
Don E. Schultz and Robert D. Dewar

In Arthur Miller's play *Death of a Salesman*, Willy Loman said the only thing a salesman really needed was "a smile and a shoeshine." But rapidly changing manufacturing technology and increasingly complex products sealed Willy Loman's fate in the play, just as it has spelled the end of thousands of Willy Lomans in sales. They simply couldn't survive in the new, more technical selling arena.

Today, galloping technological change in information gathering and dissemination again threaten what have become traditional marketing approaches during the past 20 to 30 years. Even those industrial companies recently adopting some consumer package goods marketing techniques already find themselves outdated. Others who have yet to comprehend the basic marketing concept find

they are hopelessly behind their more sophisticated foreign competitors.

The challenge to business and industrial marketing management has never been greater. Technology has pushed into obsolescence the sales and management systems which moved companies forward in yesterday's marketplace. Moreover, technology threatens traditional management authority within the organization itself because of the power technology confers on those who know how to use it.

The chief culprit is the computer. Once viewed as a specialized tool for accounting and finance, today the computer is the workday tool for all kinds of marketing activity, becoming as indispensable as the telephone. But beyond just the computer, a host of technologies ranging from satellites to robots to electronic mail create problems for today's marketing managers.

Here's how we believe technology has changed the marketplace in which industrial marketing managers operate, some of the challenges those changes pose, and some suggested solutions. Marketing managers who act now may be able to avoid going the way of Willy Loman.

A Changing Marketplace

Depending on their particular industries, marketing managers either have experienced or will face these effects of technological change:

■ The shift to more complex products will accelerate. Because most of U.S. output is the result of technology, information, and services, the era of the United States as a basic processor of raw materials is over. The increasingly complex and sophisticated products we produce or services we perform will demand new types of marketing from new forms of marketing organizations staffed by a new breed of marketer.

■ Information and transportation technologies have allowed manufacturers' searches for materials and components to shift from the traditional regional or national marketplace to a global one, spurring worldwide competition.

■ Growing purchase decision decentralization has expanded the number of purchase decision influences almost geometrically. Where perhaps only one or two people once were involved in industrial purchasing, the influence exerted by specialists and even workers (such as through quality circles) complicates the selling process. As we move from traditional

mass production to more specialized product processing, this problem will increase.

■ Differing purchase decision criteria make traditional marketing approaches inappropriate. As designers, engineers, and even purchasing agents increasingly use the computer to aid their material and component search and screening, an important step in the decision process has moved to machines and out of the hands of people.

■ More sophisticated, computer-literate purchasers aided by desktop computing are changing the buyer-seller relationship. Today, the purchaser commonly knows as much, or perhaps more, about a product's applicability than does the seller. Where once the seller brought new ideas, new uses, and new concepts to the prospect, today the buyer and the seller are equal in terms of product knowledge and application. That puts the traditional salesperson at a distinct disadvantage.

■ Increasing trade concentration in almost all categories creates fewer customers and fewer prospects for most business-to-business sellers. Larger buyers use their purchasing power to squeeze margins and concessions from sellers. Because trade concentration has quietly crept up in many fields, particularly among those companies who rely on retailers and other distribution middlemen, many sellers encounter a totally new relationship with their customers. It's increasing on a national and global scale.

Organizational Challenge

Those technology-based factors affect almost all industrial marketers. In some industries, the issues are even more complex. But the real question marketing managers face is what those changes mean to them and their organizations.

Most of today's marketing management systems are not geared to deal with the complex marketplace of the future. Yet the systems in place today can't simply be scrapped. They must be adapted.

Problems Now

Sales forces generally haven't changed and have become obsolete. Technology always changes much more rapidly than do people. Thus, many organizations are saddled with a sales force which is unable to work with or relate to new types of buyers and the required new approaches to selling.

Traditional marketing and sales communication systems are outdated. Even though computerized sales reporting, inventory control, and order processing are common, some companies still hand tabulate sales reports, inventories, and even sales leads, causing weeks or even months of unnecessary delay. Important marketing decisions too often are based on inadequate or out-of-date information.

The required technical support systems are not in place. Many organizations haven't adopted the research, data gathering, or strategic planning systems available to provide them with the basic information, the heart of any marketing system.

Problems Tomorrow

While the immediate problems are important, the ones we anticipate marketing management will face in the future are even more critical. The reason is simple. Increasingly complex technology will affect many more individuals as people, not just in the way they accomplish tasks.

Perhaps the most pervasive factor will be the influence of the computer and computer literacy among managers and employees. Some of the problems we see are:

Dealing with Computer Literacy. Managing expertise has never been easy, especially

when it hasn't been fully understood by management. Equally difficult is the opposite problem of managing talent inadequate for the task, such as when marketers must cope with a less skilled sales force to carry out complex tasks.

We see four possible scenarios unfolding as computer literacy increases.

1. If a company's management and sales force both remain computer illiterate, the situation will not continue for long. Competitors will acquire an advantage quickly over such an organization.

2. If management does not acquire computer literacy but subordinates such as on the sales force do, the subordinates will challenge management's authority.

It's a particularly unappealing scenario of organizational chaos. It could occur because computer literacy becomes increasingly easy to obtain, and because it will be increasingly difficult to hire noncomputer-literate personnel.

For example, today's salespeople can easily acquire and use personal computers powerful enough for business needs, often for as little as $4,000. Doing so has distinct advantages for tasks such as tracking accounts, route planning, paperwork processing, etc. Product managers, meanwhile, can use personal computers for product planning, market research, and so on.

Moreover, as computer education spreads through universities, secondary schools, and even the elementary education level, it will be difficult by the late 1980s to hire young marketing talent which is not computer knowledgeable. Many of the better universities already *require* the use of personal computers. And in just two years, we have seen the percentage of student papers typed with a word processor increase from 10 percent to 85 percent.

The challenge is that computer-literate subordinates can simulate their superiors' decisions. Because information, especially the ability to manipulate it and process it, gives organizational power, the computer illiterate manager is likely to feel threatened by obsolescence and subordinates' abilities to make better decisions than he.

Under those conditions, managers may resort to heavy-handed authority. But the subordinates, able to rationally make better decisions, will consider authoritarian management an illegitimate use of power. Resentment and attempts by the computer-literate subordinates to subvert existing controls are the most probable results.

3. If managers are computer literate and subordinates are not, different problems emerge. Overcontrol is a distinct possibility.

Management will have no problem making high-quality decisions, but efforts to implement them likely will encounter suspicion and distrust. Salespeople, for example, may feel management is trying to automate their jobs. They will not understand how decisions are made. They may fear that it is only a matter of time until management replaces them with computer-literate personnel.

Under such conditions, management will be faced with the need to train or replace some of the sales force to assure that it acquires computer literacy.

4. In the most favorable scenario, both marketing management and sales and product subordinates are computer literate. Information will be processed rapidly, telecommunications will be the predominate mode of organizational communication. People will simulate decision making. Information will flow to and from all parts of the organization quicker than it does now, implying work will become much more complex and faster-paced for all.

As a result, primarily collegial management styles will be expected to develop. Decision making will be participative, rules and procedures will carry less weight, and communications will be horizontal instead of vertical.

Decentralizing Decision Making. The diffusion of information engages more people in the organizational learning process. Whether or not managers wish to maintain a bureaucratic and hierarchical management style, it is futile for them to try to arrest the process.

In one large insurance company, for instance, the policy of the data processing vice president is to "control" the personal computer. His department bought only three and kept them under lock and key with access restricted to a few personnel. At first, agents in the field sought help from the data processing department. But not getting satisfaction, they now are buying their own personal computers and automating their own offices.

Never was the biblical saying more appropriate: "He who saves his life will surely lose it." In attempting to monopolize personal computers, the vice president ensured that his data processing department would decline in importance and power. Management that stands in the way of the computer revolution can expect a similar result.

If we assume that, like it or not, most marketing departments will progress to a point at which management and sales and product manager subordinates will be computer literate, what are the implications for management style? Exactly what happens as hierarchical style yields ground to a collegial style?

Computer literacy dramatically increases the speed at which the individual can process complex information. Equipped with a personal computer, even the lowest level person can simulate the effects of alternative decisions. The "mysteries" of market research may become accessible to all. Many will be able to reanalyze market research data and draw their own conclusions.

Such an atmosphere of informational give and take with its cross-fertilization of ideas, jeopardizes the traditional organization pyramid. A concentration of decision making at higher levels, a reliance on order through rules and procedures, a strictly vertical infor-

mation flow and norms of obedience to hierarchy will be seriously undermined because
lower level people will have access to and be
able to process as much information as those
at higher levels.

While that's a nightmare to the bureaucrat,
it has many advantages. The quality of ideas
should improve as they are checked and
cross-checked by a greater number of people.
Any conclusion or decision is likely to be re-
calculated by someone somewhere in the organization. Faults will be exposed quickly.
Higher quality information will make secrets
difficult to keep and power difficult to monopolize.

At first, information will become a great
leveler. But later, power will shift to those
who know the new technology best and can
use it to make the best decisions. Those people won't necessarily move up in a hierarchy
because the pyramid itself will be crumbling.
Instead, the technology-savvy will become
the most important people in networks of information processing. People will seek them
out for advice.

Rules and procedures, job descriptions, titles and positions will change to reflect the
operation of those networks. Groups, task
forces, and committees will assume increased
importance in the organization. Conformity
to organization goals will be more a matter of
consensus and agreed-upon norms, rather
than adherence to rule books.

Finally, vertical information patterns will
be the greatest casualty as computer literacy
encourages the horizontal flow of ideas. The
noncomputer-literate executive will have the
greatest frustration attempting to maintain
control over subordinates who can think faster
and more accurately than he.

Retraining Sales and Marketing Personnel.
Technology will force significant changes in
manpower levels among the components of
marketing. For example, we expect that sales
forces will decline dramatically in importance

as technology takes over much of the customer-vendor relationship.

One large manufacturer of paints has its
computers geared to communicate directly
with its customer's computers, for instance.
The customer's production manager requests,
say, a color change through the computer tied
directly to the seller's production and pricing
departments. Negotiations over pricing and
delivery are concluded within hours and the
new paint delivered within days. Previously,
it took several days for a salesperson to handle the order via telephone or personal visits.

We also expect middle management jobs to
decline because most of them exist to procure
and manipulate information for higher-level
decision making. A desktop computer can accomplish in minutes what a staff department
would take days to produce.

Solutions and Power Shifts

Organizational design and personnel management hold the keys to solving the problems
we've outlined here. We recommend several
steps for management to follow.

Reevaluate the Organization

As we've shown, computer literacy will
change the internal management style of the
marketing department. And it will also affect
the relative power of marketing compared to
other functions in the company. For example,
the computer is a powerful tool for distributors, dealers, wholesalers, and retailers who,
by tracking inventory via product codes,
have reliable information facilitating their
demands on manufacturers to an extent previously unthinkable. Manufacturers are increasingly asked to tailor advertising, to contribute more to discounts and to charge lower
prices because dealers and distributors increasingly perform what were manufacturing

functions. Growing distribution channel concentration has accelerated that effect.

As a result, the power of manufacturing departments will increase relative to that of marketing, especially as success in the marketplace turns on the predictability of quality and delivery. Because of rising concentration, brand and product managers will become less important. Their role will be eclipsed by national, or even international, account managers who will operate suborganizations of their own much as product managers do now. Account managers will orient the company to serving large accounts, rather than promoting brands and individual products.

Market research will be a vital function, providing essential knowledge of markets and customers which dealers and distributors also need. The greater the data manipulation and acquisition skills of the manufacturer's marketing research group, the less likely it is that the manufacturer will be reduced to the status of a captive supplier to his distribution system.

Meanwhile, the group most likely to lose power and decrease in size will be the traditional sales force. We've already pointed to computerized customer-vendor relationships. Another cause is the increased importance of manufacturing and market research.

Those power shifts suggest a considerable need for manpower planning, shifting talented individuals from sales to market research and especially to national account management. The organization will need fewer people with lesser skills.

Additionally, there will be some reprioritization of marketing functions. The heads of sales groups may no longer report to the senior vice president of marketing. Instead they'll report to those running national account management units who most likely will be reporting directly to senior management.

Computer literacy will put pressure on marketing and manufacturing to integrate their activities. For example, customers who access databases for comparison shopping will be less tolerant of extended delivery dates, stock outs, and merchandise which is not custom tailored to their specialized use. In the process of integration, computer-literate managers will have a distinct advantage understanding the technological link between manufacturing and marketing.

In addition to electronic coordination mechanisms, there will still be a need for standard linking mechanisms: liaison roles such as national account managers, product planners, brand and product managers; task forces such as product planning committees; and perhaps even dual reporting arrangements such as in matrix management.

The classic matrix structure and behavior used to integrate four functions (research and development, engineering, marketing, and manufacturing) around the customer's needs can take different forms. For example, one large telecommunications company has a system in which engineering and R&D proposals must be checked by the marketing department which rates their market potential before they can be moved on to their final stage of development. The R&D specialists in that system are accountable to their own department superior, and to the marketing product planning group. Once a product moves to manufacturing, the manufacturing manager becomes partially accountable to the marketing manager.

In a similar vein, 'decision triangles'—the manufacturing manager, his manufacturing superior, and the marketing manager—are expected to balance manufacturing costs, customer specifications, and delivery dates and avoid conflict within the organizational hierarchy.

Restructuring systems is one thing. Staffing them is another. The reorganizations we foresee demand new training systems to develop the required staff talent, especially including computer literacy skills.

One particularly creative approach has been used by the chief executive of a large newspaper publishing company. He installed what he calls a "playroom" complete with personal computers, electronic mail devices, and video games. The point is to encourage staff to experiment with the new technology to reduce resistance to it. The company awards bonuses and prizes for ideas on using the new technology in one's job.

Improve the Marketing Mix

Not all the marketing management problems of the future can be solved simply by redesigning the marketing organization. Some of the answers lie in the actual marketing mix each company develops to cope in the new marketplace.

Generally, we foresee three major trends in that regard:

1. Successful companies will emphasize matching a product to the concept of service. In the broadest sense, a marketing orientation requires seeking out and delivering what customers and prospects need and want. The old concept of "selling what we make" is gone forever. The ability of marketing management to identify potential customer needs and wants will be the key competitive ingredient.

Although industrial marketers have always been more closely attuned to what their customers need and want than have consumer producers, the requirement will be even greater in the future. The marketing organization which succeeds will be the one which can identify markets, move to meet demand early, and abandon outdated products quickly and efficiently.

2. Successful marketers will accelerate use of nonpersonal selling methods. With the increasingly global nature of most businesses, it will be impossible to individually contact each prospect. And as buyers move closer to electronic database product comparisons, they'll increasingly accept nonpersonal sales contact. The development and diffusion of product and service electronic databases will become as common as today's trade publications, facilitating new systems of buying and negotiating among computer-literate businesspeople. One can even visualize computer-linked bid and ask negotiations on commodity type items similar to the way traditional commodity markets presently operate in the United States.

The hardware tools for electronic contact are already available: video discs and tapes, closed circuit television seminars, prerecorded interactive sales presentations, electronic mail and, of course, on-line communication. Using them will require more sophisticated sales presentations based on a much greater understanding of the prospect's needs than ever before, however. With the marketer's ability to match products and services to individual customers, that should be quite possible.

3. Successful marketers will rely on broader and deeper communications methods as purchase influences become more widespread and diffused within customer organizations. Traditionally, vehicles such as publication and direct mail advertising have accomplished that goal to a limited extent, reaching influences which salespeople do not see.

But we expect that in the future communications will be the most important part of the marketing effort. The goal will be to assure that the company's products and services are at least considered in every purchasing situation and that can come only through a widespread, effective, communications effort.

Those marketing managers who now dismiss marketing communications as being less productive than personal selling will find they must change to meet the conditions of the new marketplace. No longer can sellers provide product or sales information at the convenience of their sales forces; the information must be available at the convenience of purchase influences.

So it is not too much a stretch of the imagination to foresee business-to-business marketers approaching their customers just as consumer marketers do today: through broad-scale, brand-oriented, persuasive forms of promotion. Because it will be almost impossible to identify every buying influence, it will become much more practical to cover the entire spectrum of potential influences rather than risk missing some of them.

Certain office automation equipment categories are already moving in that direction.

Technology won't disappear no matter how much tradition-bound marketing managers might wish it would. Nor will technology decline. Rather, it will only increase and force fundamental changes in marketing organization, personnel, and programs.

The solution for marketing management is clear. Adapt and change or disappear. Traditional marketing management methods in the balance of the 1980s and into the 1990s will be as obsolete as Willy Loman's attempts to sell with "a shoeshine and a smile."

========================= ***Company Readings*** =========================

Putting Marketing on a "BU$INE$$" Basis
Robert A. Fox

My thanks to The Conference Board for inviting me to speak on the subject of profitability. I'd like to go on record at the start of my remarks as being in favor of it.

Upon first reading the assigned topic—"Putting Marketing on a 'Business' Basis"—you may have been a bit puzzled. After all, marketing, in one form or another, is an essential part of any profit-making enterprise, so how could it be conducted on anything *but* a "business" basis? But if you'll consider it a moment, I think you'll begin to see what The Conference Board is getting at.

Profitability in the decades ahead may depend importantly on our ability to put marketing on a more businesslike basis, to go beyond traditional or volume oriented marketing practices and achieve a much more selective, profit oriented approach.

That, I believe, is because we have entered a new era.

The first third of this century might best be characterized as "The Age of the Salesman." Markets were young, products were new, and there seemed to be no limit to the number of potential customers. A company's greatest asset was the champion salesman, with the loyalty of Willie Loman and the flair of Professor Harold Hill, traveling the land with a smile and a shoeshine, out-talking the competition.

The middle third of the century might best be characterized as "The Age of the Branded Product." Dozens of brand names became household words from Maine to California; America's evenings were spent with the Chase and Sanborn Hour, the Kraft Music Hall, the Voice of Firestone or the Camel Caravan. Advertising slogans and company logos became as familiar to Americans as the folks next door. Brand marketing had become a nationwide phenomenon.

The '50s and early '60s saw a continuation of prosperity. Population was booming, resources plentiful, and inflation almost nil. Glamorous growth industries were springing up on the nation's technological frontiers, and even maturing products were being pushed to new heights by the developing art of brand management.

For the past fifteen years, however, the marketplace has been changing as our American economy approaches maturity. Well before the current recession, many former growth markets were characterized by flat sales curves, intense competition for a static number of dollars, and eroding profitability. In some of our most basic industries—steel, automobiles, rubber, farm equipment, home appliances—even the blue chip companies were often having to struggle to maintain profitability.

What we have been witnessing, I believe, is the start of a new era. One of "slow" or "no" growth, of even more intense competition; the age, not of the salesman or the brand, but of the total business manager. Good salespeople and good products, while still essential, are not enough. In the future the emphasis must be on total business management—on our ability to take a much more critical approach to products, to costs, to markets, even to volume—than we have in the past.

Today, the traditional product lines of many American companies are firmly positioned in mature markets. Many businessmen tend to

Robert A. Fox, The Conference Board's 1982 Marketing Conference. © 1982 The Conference Board. Reprinted with permission.

think of that as a liability, but I am convinced that, properly managed, these core businesses can be turned into solid assets, earning a very respectable return on the investments they represent.

So my purpose today is to suggest a number of strategies for meeting the profitability challenge with mature products in mature markets. I will focus on the maturity challenge not only because I am very familiar with it, but also because I believe it will be one of the main roads to profitability for most American companies in the next decade.

Even for those of you representing growth companies in growth industries, the day of reckoning is not far off. As the strategies for mature markets are listed on the screen, you might think of them as the handwriting on the wall.

The first step in achieving an acceptable level of profitability with a mature business is to recognize that managing a mature market is not the same as managing a growth market. The difference stems from four basic conditions which characterize the mature market.

First, the rapid growth a mature market may have enjoyed in its formative years is almost certainly over, and efforts to sustain that growth will largely be unproductive.

Second, the fact that mature industries are no longer growing doesn't mean they're no longer changing. Technologies, production methods, packaging, distribution systems, and customer needs will continue to change. In fact, studies show that innovation, especially manufacturing innovation, tends to become more frequent as an industry approaches maturity and companies find themselves facing greater competition.

Third, competition becomes more intense as a market matures. This is because corporate growth objectives often remain long after industry growth has slowed, and participants find themselves fighting for a share of a pie that is growing more slowly, or may even be shrinking.

Fourth, attempts to meet intense competition head-on in traditional ways, such as brand proliferation or heavy promotional activity, are almost always self-defeating. Increased production, inventory, and promotional costs tend to erode profitability, even if they *do* gain additional volume. In a declining market, increased advertising budgets may sometimes be necessary to maintain share of market, but they seldom succeed in reversing a downward trend.

Given those characteristics, there are certain key strategies which a company with a primary position in a mature market can follow to gain a satisfactory level of profitability. In describing those strategies, I will frequently cite my own company, Del Monte Corporation, as an example, not only because I am most familiar with it, but also because it is a classic example of a mature company in a mature industry. For most of Del Monte's 66 years, its primary business has been canning fruits and vegetables, and it has canned more of them than anyone else in the world. The bulk of our assets are tied up in the production of low-margin, long-inventory, commodity products manufactured in plants that operate only a few months out of the year. Its product line was dictated by the demands of production. The basic question was: "What products are we best equipped to produce?" The marketing budget was spent primarily on trade incentives to stimulate volume. Advertising, consumer promotion, and market research were at relatively low levels.

The strategy worked well as long as the market for canned foods was expanding. But as the market matured, it became harder to generate growth in volume or earnings. So for the past several years, we have been forging a new Del Monte.

Today, almost four years after becoming part of R. J. Reynolds Industries, our worldwide product mix embraces a number of brands besides Del Monte, and includes fresh and frozen as well as canned foods. But the core of our business is still canned foods and beverages, and the strategies I'll describe are those we've been pursuing to revitalize the core business.

Strategy Number One. *Establish clear objectives, but do not base them on absolute growth in volume or earnings.* Because in a mature market, rapid growth is almost certainly gone. Marketing managers should not be pressured to pursue high-growth objectives or seek volume for volume's sake. Instead, their performance should be measured by how well they do in improving share of market, profitability, and return on assets or investment.

Companies seeking profitability in mature markets cannot afford to overlook any alternatives—including reduced costs, reduced volume, reduced assets, or increased prices.

For example, in the last four years at Del Monte, we reduced assets; we have divested ourselves of seven businesses which did not fit our plans for improving profitability. In doing so, we had to give up some sales, although with only minor impact on our earnings. Most important, we generated a substantial amount of cash to invest in new products and businesses to improve return on assets.

The reverse side of divestiture is the development, or acquisition, of higher-margin businesses which contribute more significantly to earnings than they add to overall assets. And here Del Monte has made two acquisitions— one into frozen foods and the other into new packaging technology.

The elimination of excess inventory is another way in which returns can be improved. If reduced inventories can be made a permanent characteristic, the improvement can become lasting.

Perhaps the hardest and most frequently avoided method of improving return on assets is simply to increase margins by raising prices. In highly competitive markets, this is never an easy step to take.

In 1980, because of a large oversupply of vegetables, the earnings of Del Monte's Dry Grocery and Beverage Products Group declined sharply, even though the group was posting a volume gain. We decided to bite the bullet and accelerate pricing leadership, increasing margins across the board. We expected to lose some volume and market share, and we did. But in 1981 our Dry Grocery Group's earnings began to climb significantly, and they have kept on climbing since. We traded a small amount of market share for a dramatic increase in profitability—and are now winning back market share in new products which carry significantly higher profit margins.

Strategy Number Two. *Take advantage of existing strengths. A mature company in a mature industry is likely to have been around for some time.* No matter how profitability may have eroded in recent years, the company undoubtedly has strengths which younger competitors cannot match.

One strength can often be found—sometimes unexpectedly—in a company's most mature products. Back in the 1930s, the Richardson Corporation, fearing that an anticipated cure for the common cold would doom sales of its Vicks VapoRub, sought to head off disaster by buying Merrel Drugs and becoming Richardson-Merrel. Last year, almost half a century later, the company shed its consistently disappointing Merrel drug division and renamed itself Richardson-Vicks in honor of the 76-year-old Vicks VapoRub, whose sales were still going strong.

In 1979, General Foods halted a decade-long slide in the sales of Jell-O brand gelatin when it abandoned its customary advertising appeal to cost and versatility, and instead capitalized on nostalgia and its long familiarity to generations of Americans. Today, when family groups enjoy Jell-O, they're not having dessert, they're having fun. And, as far as

Jell-O goes, they're having more of it than ever before.

Another obvious strength is a brand name or corporate logo which has won the respect of generations of consumers. We regard the Del Monte shield as one of our most valuable assets, and we know that it will help us introduce line extensions and new products that would have a much harder time without the Del Monte name behind them.

Strategy Number Three. *Identify and exploit growth segments that exist within every mature market.* Forty years ago most advertising campaigns were aimed at the general public, but today American consumers are segmented into scores of buyers on the basis of image, age, background, geography, and lifestyles. Dayton Hudson's B. Dalton Bookstores today carry over 600 cookbook titles, appealing to everyone from microwave-cooking vegetarians to dieting gourmets. If consumer needs are that specialized in terms of cookbooks, imagine how discriminating consumers are when it comes to buying food, or for that matter almost anything else. The profitable company of the future will be the one that can successfully identify and exploit specialized segments within its overall marketplace.

There are many examples in my own industry.

Increasingly, popular LITE fruits answer a consumer desire for less sugar and fewer calories.

"No Salt Added" vegetables are aimed at a growing consumer concern over the excess use of salt, and the prevalence of hypertension in our society.

The increasingly popular individual serving size addresses the needs of single households, made of young or mature adults, or single parents with children. Such households, which increased by 70 percent in the 1970s, are predicted to grow by an additional 40 percent in the 1980s.

For Del Monte, the preceding products represent extensions of our existing product lines that were produced with very little, if any, capital outlay. But *new* products can also increase profitability if they are aimed at growth segments within their particular markets.

There are many dimensions for identifying such segments.

Customer age is one. A decade ago, Richardson-Vicks bought a little-known product, with annual worldwide sales of $10 million, from two South African entrepreneurs. Today, U.S. sales of Oil of Olay top $100 million, largely because Americans aged 30 to 45 are the fastest growing segment of our population, and those are the years when we begin to worry about looking old.

Ethnic background is another dimension. Hispanics, for example, not only are one of the fastest growing ethnic groups in the United States, but tend to maintain their distinct culture longer. They represent a growing long-term market for specialty foods. Moreover, their foods most likely will continue to gain favor among many Americans, just as pizza, Chinese food, and quiche have done. Our Del Monte line of formulated Mexican foods, which expanded broadly this year, enables us to utilize our existing canning facilities to produce a specialty product for a specific growth segment in a basically static market.

Lifestyle is another dimension for identifying today's growth segments. Several shoe companies have improved their profitability by recognizing this fact, and I'm not referring only to Adidas or Nike. Wolverine Worldwide, makers of the famous Hush Puppies, doubled the sales of boots by recognizing the fact that boots were no longer worn primarily by agricultural and industrial workers, but by hikers, campers, and assorted *urban* cowboys.

Strategy Number Four. *Be prepared to invest heavily in all phases of research and develop-*

ment. Studies show that in mature sectors there is a definite correlation between increased R&D expenditures, product improvement, and return on investment. And this is not necessarily the case in growth markets.

In-depth market and consumer research is needed to identify the growth segments, and to define the products that can take advantage of them. The low success ratio for new products shows that they are not intuitively obvious, even to companies with long experience. Indeed, old-line companies especially should guard against a temptation to stop short of adequate consumer research. This is an area where, to quote Harry Truman, "It's what you learn *after* you know it all that counts."

Technological research is needed to develop innovative, superior, differentiated products to meet specific consumer needs. *Innovative, superior,* and *differentiated* are the key words here. The intense competition that characterizes a mature market is more likely to exhaust a company's resources than increase its profitability, *unless* it can offer its customers a unique, superior product that will be both difficult and expensive for competitors to imitate.

Kodak's new Disc camera, with its lifetime flash, faster film speed, self-focusing lens, automatic advance, and small size and weight, is a superlative example of the importance of technological research. Kodak technicians managed to combine a whole list of features which consumers considered the most appealing, and thus created a best seller in a market where previous surveys said that, by and large, there was no one strong characteristic demanded in a new product.

Let me turn away from retail consumer products for another example. Carpenter Technology Corporation of Cleveland has the capacity to produce only one-tenth of one percent of the millions of tons of steel used in the United States each year, and steel is its only product. Yet it manages to earn a very enviable return on equity in a very depressed industry by concentrating all its efforts on the high-margin, specialty steel market. To illustrate just *how* special, Carpenter expects one of its major growth areas in the years ahead to be steel for human joint replacements. Skyscraper skeletons may require more tonnage, but for Carpenter, human skeletons may be more profitable.

Innovation and differentiation need not be limited to the products themselves. At Del Monte we expect a lot of our growth to come from innovative packaging that will appeal to changing consumer tastes. For example, these large 46-ounce cans, which were a staple of the fruit-based beverage industry, have been declining in volume in the U.S.A. Yet, during that same period aseptic packages have scored a tremendous success internationally; we hope to repeat that success here in the United States, by offering virtually the same amount of beverage in these aseptic, foil-lined paper cartons, known variously as Tetrapaks or Combiblocs.

The point here is that a company seeking to achieve good profitability in a mature market must be willing to risk making its own products, packages, or processes obsolete. This is a fact Procter & Gamble learned long ago. Only by introducing many detergents, each differently branded and competing with one another, has it built and maintained its dominance in that business. P&G knows that if an improvement is possible and they don't exploit it, it's only a matter of time until someone else will.

Strategy Number Five. *Emphasize quality.* Studies have shown that within mature industries there is a high correlation between high-product quality and high return on investment. To gain the essential "competitive edge" in highly competitive mature markets, a manufacturer must offer customers a better product than competitors. This is especially true today in retail packaged goods. According to *Forbes,* the average branded food costs about 15 percent more than the average private label, and about 30 percent more than generics. So when it comes to branded products, says *Forbes,* the key question is: "What's in a name?" And the answer is unequivocal: "It *has* to be quality."

Strategy Number Six. *Get rid of the dead wood.* For an old-line company, this can be one of the hardest decisions to make. For many years, one of Del Monte's proudest claims was that it offered the broadest line of canned fruits and vegetables nationally, and there is satisfaction in the knowledge that we still do. But we have faced up to the fact that today a claim like that costs more than it earns. Therefore, in recent years we have discontinued a number of products which could not achieve our desired level of volume and profitability. They were not clear failures, but neither were they clear winners. All of them—Del Monte figs, spiced peaches, seasoned lima beans, kosher-style dill chips—were profitable, long-established products—but their consumer audience was too limited.

Strategy Number Seven. *Pay increased attention to cost reduction, not just in marketing functions, but in every aspect of the company.* One undervalued advantage of a company with long experience in a mature market is experience itself. A company can tap organizationwide experience to discover ways to cut costs in virtually all areas—materials, production, distribution, and marketing. And even mature businesses should not overlook the value of investments in new, cost-saving methods and machinery.

Consolidations provide further opportunities for meaningful cost savings. Approached on a broad enough scale—closing the least efficient operations to free capital, equipment, and personnel to strengthen the most efficient—this strategy can significantly improve ROA all by itself.

In the past two years, Del Monte closed 12 plants, including eight fruit and vegetable canneries, two distribution centers, and two can manufacturing plants, all with no appreciable loss of capacity. In fact, one of our major consolidations—concentrating all our fresh tomato processing activities in a single facility in California—resulted in a significant gain in productivity and a low-cost producer status. Altogether, these consolidations have substantially reduced our asset base, while at the same time resulting in major savings in operating costs.

We, of course, are not alone in this strategy. Firestone, to cite but one of many examples has discontinued more than a third of its North American tire capacity since 1980. But today, operating at 90 percent of capacity, as opposed to 60 percent just two years ago, it has turned a loss into a profit.

The most outstanding success in cost reduction may be that of Iowa Beef Processors, which, in just two decades came out of nowhere to dominate the U.S. meat-packing industry by moving butchering from retail to factory and by paying meticulous attention to keeping costs below those of competitors. As one IBP executive put it: "We took little bitty fractions all along the line"—in slaughtering, transportation, and marketing costs. They also trimmed waste to the core, finding a market for cattle hides, fat, bone, glands—and even gallstones. That example may be extreme, but it makes the point: profitability in mature, highly competitive markets demands the elimination of all waste and unessential overhead.

Strategy Number Eight. *Finally, seek to insure that the money you do spend is spent as wisely as possible, by developing effective management in every area of the corporation.* This means that a company in a mature industry must nurture and support its managers as carefully as it does its products. It should also position them with as much care, recognizing that different market segments may require different management skills.

A company will have a better chance of revitalizing a mature market if its employees regard the job as a favorable assignment, with as great a potential for advancement as any other. In recent years, we may have tended to equate maturity in the market with dullness and stagnation, and assume that to be successful employees must hitch their wagons to a growth product in a growth industry. It is time that companies reclaim at least some of the managerial stars for positions in their mature businesses, where the possibility of earning worthwhile profits may be just as great, and the challenge of earning them even greater.

Those, ladies and gentlemen, are eight key strategies for making money in mature mar-

kets—mileposts on the road to marketing profitability in today's economy. Traveling that road has never been easy; it has always been uphill, and in the 1980s and '90s, it is likely to be steeper than ever. But it is a road we must take for the same reason George Leigh Mallory climbed Mount Everest: "Because it's there." Our mature markets and mature products are there too and we cannot afford not to capitalize on them.

I am confident that, with proper management, we *can* restore our most basic industries—the industries that once were the marvel of the industrialized world—to very attractive profitability.

I am confident too that we will find one of the old truisms of mountaineering to be equally true in business: the more difficult the climb, the more spectacular the view.

The Selling of the "Walkman"—or, It Almost Got Called "Sound-About"
Shu Ueyama

In the beginning, there were two concepts of listening to sound reproduction. There was high-fidelity audio quality, and there was portability. Any audio fan could tell that the two simply did not mix. Until Walkman came along.

Now you'll see Los Angeles roller skaters boogeying to the high-decibel beat of the Rolling Stones; you'll see London commuters with bowler hats thrumming their briefcase handles in time with Duke Ellington; you'll see skiers on the slopes of St. Moritz in the trendy company of Olivia Newton-John's music. You'll see all these things—but you won't hear any of them. Because Walkman has brought personal stereo directly to the ears of everyone, no matter where they are or what they are doing.

Three million of the epoch-making little machines—in essence, a pocket-size cassette player linked to a pair of featherweight headphones—are already making the day a bit brighter for people around the world. And

sales of the Walkman, introduced first in mid-1979, are still going very strong, with a monthly production of more than 200,000 sets of Walkman II. If we combine all the other Walkman family models, Sony will be marketing more than 3.5 million sets all over the world in 1982 alone.

Birth of the Walkman

As with many other great inventions, the birth of the Walkman was accidental.

In October 1978, there was an organizational change in Sony's audio division. The tape recorder division, which had been producing radio-cassette recorders and tape recorders, was told that it would not be making the former any longer; this product category was transferred to the radio division.

So the tape recorder division was in trouble. It had to generate new business to sustain the same profitability as before. The staff got together and had serious discussions day and night for a week. Then came a brilliant idea: to make a portable stereo recorder.

At that time, Sony had two compact-type recorders. One was a semiprofessional monaural recorder called the "Pressman"; the other was a dictating machine for business usage. Because the latter already had double-track recording and playback facility, it was not too difficult to convert it into a normal four-track stereo recorder.

Sony staff members connected this recorder to a pair of large and heavy headphones. The sound quality was superb. The engineers who made this prototype still recollect the excitement they experienced when they heard the sounds for the first time. This clumsy-looking machine hooked to a pair of clumsy headphones was the beginning of the Walkman. Another accident followed several days later. Masaru Ibuka, honorary chairman and cofounder of Sony, casually dropped in on the tape recorder division and saw this strange-looking prototype. He listened to it and thought it could be an interesting product. But he thought the headphones were too big and heavy. Because he knew that the research laboratory was experimenting with new lightweight headphones at that time, he recommended the two be combined.

Akio Morita, Sony's chairman, heard about this prototype from Mr. Ibuka and asked the engineers to bring the machine to his office. He felt the same excitement he experienced when he first introduced transistor radios.

Mr. Morita borrowed the set during the following weekend. He went to play golf with his friends and took it with him. He and one of his golfing friends listened to the recorder because the machine already had two headphone plug-ins. But they found it rather inconvenient not to be able to converse with each other with their headphones on.

On Monday he proposed to the engineers that a special switch be added to suppress the volume of music momentarily when one wishes to have a conversation. It was later named "the hot-line switch."

The engineers incorporated this idea and several others, and they completed the final design and specifications on March 24, 1979, five months after the tape recorder division lost its radio-cassette business.

The Walkman Team

When Mr. Morita saw a tremendous potential in this new product, he gathered 10 people from different Sony divisions: production, product planning, design, advertising, sales, and export. They became the members of the "Walkman Team," a group set up to decide all the strategies for the Walkman. Mr. Morita appointed himself project manager.

Such a team approach was necessary to launch the Walkman within six months. It usually takes one or two years to make a new product.

At meetings, the team discussed specifications of the new model. The production schedule was drawn, and a decision was made on the quantity to be produced. Cost structure and pricing were also decided. There were heated discussions about what to name the product. Various promotional ideas were formulated. Package designs were presented. Presale consumer tests were conducted. All the conceivable activities surrounding the Walkman business were discussed thoroughly in this group.

Marketing the Walkman

The first prototype was made by converting a set of the Pressman, which retailed at 42,800 yen ($186). Stereo circuitry, a stereo-playback head, and a pair of headphones were added, but the speaker was eliminated. Then, a cost estimate helped establish a price of $217. This was presented at a Walkman Team meeting.

Mr. Morita thought it was too expensive. The customer profile of the Pressman was primarily professional reporters and writers who could afford such a high price. Because he had teenagers in his mind as the target customers for the Walkman, he thought it would be necessary to bring down the price drastically, to around the level of $130.

The price of any mass-produced consumer good goes down as production quantity increases. So, even if a product is showing a deficit in its initial production lot, the production cost lowers when it is produced in the millions.

The cost-reduction curve depends totally on the cumulative production quantity. If the cost of a plastic mold or a die is amortized by millions, then the cost distributed to each unit becomes minimal. But the problem was that nobody was quite sure how many Walkmans could be sold. No one, except possibly Mr. Morita, thought they would eventually become such a sensational best seller all over the world.

Mr. Morita, with a mischievous smile on his face, suggested the selling price of 33,000 yen ($143). He explained the reason to the members of the Walkman Team: "Well, gentlemen, this year we happen to be celebrating the 33rd anniversary of our company."

At this price, the tape recorder division would be losing money in the beginning, however hard it tried to bring down the production cost. But Mr. Morita was convinced the Walkman would eventually make money.

The production started. The factory tried its best to bring down its production costs in each stage. The fact that all the key parts, such as motors, stereo heads, and headphones, were being produced within the Sony operation eliminated unnecessary negotiations for price reduction.

Each division shed a little blood and cooperated with the corporate decision.

Normally, circuitry and mechanical engineers do not get involved in production after they have finished their assignments of designing the product, but in the case of the Walkman, they were deeply involved in its production because of the cost reduction they had to achieve.

Changes in circuitry design were made by incorporating ICs (Integrated Circuitries) instead of normal transistors and resistors, thus bringing down the number of parts and the cost. These efforts and the increase of production gradually brought down the production cost.

Naming the Walkman

There were several ideas for the name of this new product. "Hot Line" was proposed by the design division, but the sales force was not sure this would appeal to the general public in Japan. Then came another idea: "Stereo Walkie."

But it turned out that Toshiba had already registered the name "Walky" for one of its radios, and we could not use Walkie. But this name appealed to team members, nonetheless. They particularly liked the logotype design, which had a pair of legs sticking out from the bottom of the capital letter *A* in *WALK*.

More discussions followed. Then, a suggestion was made to combine *walk* with *man*. Like many other new ideas, it was popular, especially among those who understood the English language. It was a typical Japanese-made English word that would not sound quite right to the ears of an Englishman or an American. However, the team went on to design its logotype with two more legs sticking out from the bottom of the second *A*, making a total of four walking legs.

In the final stages of team discussions, a typical consensus process took place. Members of the team decided on "Walkman," but at the same time they combined the "hot line" as its subcatchword. In this way, the face of the design division, which had proposed "hot line," was not lost. Everyone agreed to this final decision happily.

However, there was not a clear international rule about the naming, and eventually Sony ended up with four different names for the same product: "Walkman" in Japan, Asia, Middle East, and Latin America; "Sound-About" in the United States; "Stowaway" in the United Kingdom; "Freestyle" in Sweden.

Separate logotypes and package designs were made according to these names. Sony's overseas subsidiaries were spending substantial amounts of advertising money to promote different names in different markets.

Mr. Morita thought all these efforts were wasteful and decided to unify these different names into one—"Walkman." Some subsidiaries opposed this idea on the grounds that *walkman* was not a proper English word. The strongest opposition came from the Sony Corp. of America. Mr. Morita flew to Phoenix in April 1980, where Sony America was having a dealer conference, and announced his decision, explaining its marketing significance to our U.S. dealers and Sony America's staff.

After he successfully convinced all of the overseas subsidiaries on the adoption of the worldwide naming of "Walkman," he called another Walkman meeting in Tokyo and started to redesign the package that would be used worldwide. A new logotype was made and a colorful picture was printed on the carton box showing young roller skaters with a set of the Walkman. By making it attractive, we thought all our subsidiaries and their dealers all over the world could save the expense of producing additional point-of-purchase material.

The international warranty system also was introduced; customers in any country could receive aftersales servicing even in other countries. Because the Walkman operates on two dry-cell batteries, customers did not have to worry about differences in voltage, either. All these factors encouraged the casual purchasing of the Walkman from a discount shop in Tokyo or in New York or at an airport shop in Hong Kong.

In this way, Sony started to sell the same Walkman around the world. Although Sony subsidiaries in countries where they had used different names had to make another initial investment to promote the same product under the name "Walkman," it turned out to be the right decision. Because hundreds of publications in the world started to write about the Walkman, its name became almost a generic term rather than a product name. The initial worry of Sony America that it was not a proper English word was forgotten, and the Walkman has become a trendy word.

Advertising

It may sound unbelievable now, but owing to the uncertainty of the sales forecast, we had a very small advertising budget for the Walkman. Therefore, we decided at the beginning to run a commercial only in the Tokyo area.

A very tall American girl and an old Japanese gentleman wore headphones connected to a Walkman and they danced in the street. The film was shot two months before the launching of the Walkman, and they had only one pair of the newly developed lightweight headphones.

So they had to use a pair of big and heavy headphones for the old man. We had worried that the public might think the new lightweight headphones were not as good as the "heavy" ones. So we showed that normal headphones also could be used with the Walkman. For this television campaign, we spent only 6 million yen ($25,000)—a very modest campaign indeed to start the Walkman fever.

As we continued selling, we discovered that the strongest motive to purchase the Walkman was an actual trial of the set. Those who listened for the first time were amazed at the quality of the sound and their eyes would sparkle.

Our second TV commercial featured people with expressions of disbelief and delight on their faces when they tried the Walkman for the first time. We tied up with several Tokyo TV stations. Their reporters went out to local scenic places and let people listen to the Walkman. Because these people were tourists and had not been notified that they would be appearing in a TV commercial, they were totally unprepared when the reporter suddenly appeared in front of them with a Walkman. Therefore, their reactions were very natural, and it made the film all the more effective.

We made our third TV commercial when we introduced the Walkman II. We stressed its small size, comparing it to the case for the cassette tape.

Our most recent TV commercial features a five-year-old boy listening to the Walkman with his dog out in a field. In this spot, instead of showing technological superiority, we wanted to show the wonderful world of the Walkman, even for a little boy and a dog. Since the introduction of the Walkman, we had been emphasizing the technical side, but starting with this particular commercial, we began to appeal to a much broader section of the public.

This change in creative strategy was very much intentional, because of the number of similar products coming into the market. The marketers behind these efforts stressed that their products were now technically superior, that they had a recording capability, they had built-in radios, etc.

In order to identify ourselves in this crowded market and to be above technical aspects of the competition, we decided to use this latest "soft" approach.

However, in contrast, our newspaper ads remained very technical. We showed 204 parts and components of the Walkman on a full-page ad using the two most influential newspapers in Japan.

The copy said, "For the first time in the world, you are watching the inside of the Walkman. We, 204 parts all together, weigh only 280 grams, making the Walkman the smallest and lightest of all in the world."

This kind of differentiation of creative strategy—a soft approach for TV and a hard approach for print—will be our policy for a few years. We carefully study the stage of a product life cycle our product is at or the degree of maturity of the market. Then we adjust our creative strategy accordingly. In the case of the Walkman, we had to educate the public as to what this small gadget could do, how we could reduce the size, how we could reproduce such high-quality sound.

Publicity

Our modest advertising fund was supplemented by unique publicity. It is not too much to say that the worldwide Walkman fever was created through our public relations efforts rather than our advertising.

About a month before the Walkman launching, the advertising division received 100 free sets from the factory to be used for publicity purposes.

Members of the division carefully considered who would be the most influential people to spread the Walkman as a new fashion. They focused on musicians who usually carry tape recorders when they travel and listen to music in their cars, at the airports, or on the plane.

Our people wondered if those heavy tape recorders could be replaced with the Walkman. They gave free samples to leading musicians in Japan, as well as some visiting artists from overseas. They also gave samples to chief editors of leading Japanese magazines.

The Walkman sensation gradually started to spread among the people who were regarded by teenagers as trendy.

We were now ready for the launch. The press announcement was very elaborate. Instead of sending ordinary press release invitation cards to magazines and newspapers, we sent out recorded cassette tapes.

Music and all the necessary information were recorded on the tape, which increased curiosity among the reporters and contributed to maximizing the number attending the actual announcement.

They first gathered at the Sony Building in Tokyo and got on a large sightseeing bus that took them to Yoyogi Park, located in central Tokyo. There, Sony had arranged a group of teenagers roller skating with Walkmans on.

This unusual way of making the announcement was well rewarded by the massive publicity we received in all the newspapers the following day, and in all the magazines during the following few weeks.

All of these public relations activities dovetailed and generated a massive amount of topics for newspapers, magazines, and TV stations to report about. And this small gadget grew into a worldwide phenomenon.

Hawking Hardware—Home Computer Firms Begin to See Marketing as Industry's Salvation
The Wall Street Journal Staff Writers

Home computers—despite all the publicity they get—are as rare as backyard swimming pools. They can be found in only about 5 percent of the nation's 84 million households.

Still, the man who buys microcomputers for Sears, Roebuck & Co. predicts that they will be "the appliance of the '80s," a truly mass-market item. If that happens, it will be as much because of marketing as because of technology.

The home computer business has grown rapidly—sales this year are expected to exceed $2 billion—primarily because manufacturers are turning out low-priced machines. As companies attempt to reach more customers and as major differences among models disappear, success is likely to hinge on competitors' skills in market research, packaging, advertising, and distribution.

All of that is called marketing, and computer-company executives readily admit that they haven't mastered it.

"We don't market," said Steven Ross, the chairman of Warner Communications, Inc., explaining problems the company has had with its Atari home computers. "We've got the best goddamn computer, but we don't market it right. I'm pulling my hair out."

Bad Decisions

Indeed, many of the industry's troubles, such as the huge losses posted recently at Atari and Texas Instruments, Inc., can be traced to faulty marketing decisions. And marketing miscalculations had a lot to do with sudden reverses suffered by Osborne Computer Corp., the portable-computer maker, which late last week laid off nearly 80 percent of its remaining employees.

These problems, which can bedevil any industry, are compounded in the rapidly changing electronics business where, as Texas Instruments learned, a carefully planned new product can be rendered unsalable by a competitor's price cuts.

To avoid repetition of such foul play several leading computer makers have turned for help to executives they have recruited from consumer-products companies. Apple Computer, Inc. hired its president from PepsiCo, Inc., and the new president of Mattel, Inc.'s electronics division used to sell candy and toiletries. Recently, Texas Instruments reached out to Procter & Gamble Co., whose name is practically synonymous with marketing excellence, for the new boss of its consumer business.

Computer makers also are beginning to confront their biggest challenge: telling people why they need computers in their homes. "The entire industry has missed the point," says James Morgan, who recently quit as marketing chief at Philip Morris, Inc.'s domestic cigarette unit to become Atari's chairman.

1983 Home Computer Sales (*Estimated Share of $2 Billion Retail Market*)

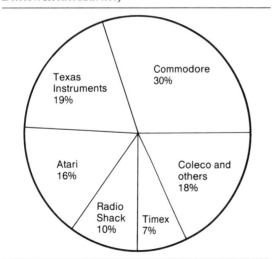

Source: Future Computing Inc.

"All they talk about is RAMs, keyboards, the resolution on the screen. The consumer doesn't know what to do with a computer."

Home computer companies aren't know-nothings about marketing, of course. They have managed to create a large industry and to stir up a lot of interest in their products in a relatively short time.

And some computer manufacturers have done well ignoring marketing precepts. Commodore International, Ltd., whose 30 percent share of the market makes it the industry leader, has cut prices sooner and faster than competitors say is necessary; it plays down the importance of advertising and disdains the formal market research that is sacrosanct at a company like Procter & Gamble. "We believe in putting the product out and letting the consumer tell us what's right and wrong," says Myrrdin Jones, Commodore's marketing vice president.

Home computers have sold well to those consumers who are quick to buy the latest thing. Marketers call such people "early adapters," "innovators," "buffs" and "conspicuous consumers."

"They're the ones who had videocassette recorders seven years ago, bought the Sony Walkman at $150, and have projection TV sets in their living rooms," says James Dragoumis, a vice president of Levine, Huntley, Schmidt & Beaver, an ad agency that once represented Commodore and now works for Acorn Computers, Ltd., a British company trying to crack the U.S. market.

Ironically, the marketing practices of some computer makers may have done as much to undermine their products as to sell them. Because of frequent price cuts and the introduction of ever-more-powerful models, "the consumer constantly is wondering if now is the right time to buy," says David Griesbaum, the home computer buyer for Sears.

Another turnoff: the proliferation of separately purchased printers, disk drives and peripheral hardware, and software programs that must be added to computer consoles to make them truly useful.

Consumer reluctance to invest in computers also may have been fed by the initial success of Timex Corp.'s cheap computer, available for less than $100. Introduced last fall, it was instantly popular; the only drawback was that it didn't do much. Timex buyers "got such a little taste of what computers are all about and such a big taste of what frustration's all about," says Gary Carlston, the chairman of Broderbund Software, Inc., a maker of programs for home computers.

Manufacturers have created problems for themselves by overestimating demand for their products. Early this year Texas Instruments reportedly predicted that industry sales would total 8 million to 10 million units in 1983 and based its production on that estimate. Instead, analysts say, the market will be about half that large.

"The companies knew they had to get a big market to get their costs down," says Robert Conrad, a technology specialist at McKinsey & Co., the management consultants, "so they built up production as if the market was already there." The market for home computers, he adds, "is now saturated for what the products out there are capable of doing."

Manufacturers, especially Atari, have a mixed record of anticipating change. Atari came out with its 5200 "Supergame" video game, which didn't expand to a computer, just as Commodore began promoting its VIC 20 as a game-playing computer and Coleco introduced a video-game player that it promised would eventually be usable with a computer module.

Meanwhile, Atari flopped in its attempts to market a keyboard that would attach to its other video-game units. Last February the company introduced a keyboard under the name My First Computer. It soon was renamed The Graduate and later was abandoned.

Atari "just had lousy strategic decision making" and "didn't turn around fast enough," acknowledges John Cavalier, the company's head of marketing and sales. Atari also failed to match rivals' price cuts, he says, adding: "When you're planning in a market that's moving this quickly, it's tough."

Price War Casualties

Keeping up with frequent price cuts has been Texas Instruments' downfall. Overestimating the persuasiveness of its price reductions, TI flooded dealers with too many machines. When inventory backed up in Texas Instruments warehouses, the company ended up with a $119.2 million second-quarter deficit. Plunging prices also wrecked its plans for a model that would be less expensive than its 99/4A model. When a price war drove the retail price of the 99/4A to $100 from $150, TI abandoned the less-costly version.

Texas Instruments and Atari aren't alone in their marketing mishaps. Timex, bedazzled by the instant popularity of its first computer, failed to consider the novelty factor. And, indeed, after a few months sales fell precipitously.

Mattel has had even more problems. Ever since it introduced its Intellivision video games three years ago, the toy maker has been talking about producing computers. But last week the company said it would sharply reduce marketing of its Aquarius computer, which never made it into national distribution.

All of the fumbling has made some microcomputer manufacturers chary of going after the home computer market. Citing "clear signs of major dissatisfaction with products" in the low-priced end of the market, Apple's president, John Sculley, says he plans to stay out of that sector.

Apple's New Variety

Apple is going after the business market with its $10,000 Lisa computer, gambling that the easy-to-use machine will appeal to big- and medium-sized businesses. Apple is understood to be developing a computer called McIntosh that will incorporate some of the technological advances of the Lisa but at a much lower cost.

To attempt to penetrate the market for computers that can be used at home, Apple plans advertising that will stress the lifestyles of Apple users—"the Apple generation," as Mr. Sculley puts it—rather than the bytes and bits of the machines.

Acorn, the British concern, wanted to enter the home market in the United States but changed its plans after seeing the competitors it would face and the advertising budget—perhaps $50 million a year—it would need. Initially at least, Acorn will pitch its machine to schools.

Others are more optimistic. "Is the home computer boom over?" asks Arnold Greenberg, chairman of Coleco Industries, Inc., which is just entering the market. "It hasn't started yet."

Coleco says the design for its computer, named Adam, was guided in part by what market research turned up about existing products. "We were finding that interest in computers was accelerating," says Mr. Greenberg, "but there was a high frustration factor among consumers."

As a result, Coleco says it tried to make Adam more useful than its predecessors. The company says the machine, which will retail for about $600, will come with built-in word processing software and a printer.

While Coleco figures this marketing strategy will lure buyers, Commodore is sticking with its price oriented approach. Having prospered by cutting prices on its basic console, the company now plans to do likewise with

software. Jack Tramiel, Commodore's chief executive, compares the computer market to the shaving business. "The most important thing is that every home should use a Commodore razor," he says. "Then we should deliver blades to them and make money on the blades."

Despite such different approaches, all the computer makers have recognized that extensive advertising will be necessary for survival. Commodore, for example, says it plans to spend $45 million on ads this year, compared with $10 million in 1982.

Coleco plans to spend $20 million to $25 million advertising Adam in its first year. But perhaps as important as ad budgets will be the messages conveyed. Agencies are scrambling to find what Madison Avenue calls the "hot button"—a sales pitch that works with consumers.

Some advertisers have decided that their hot button will be to dwell on parents' fears that their children will be left behind in life if they don't have computers. Encyclopedias have been sold that way for years, notes one agency executive.

Commodore uses such a ploy for its VIC 20. "Become great at a game machine. Maybe you can score 16 million on Space Invaders," says the announcer in one TV commercial. "Become great at the Commodore VIC 20. Maybe you can score 1600 on the college boards." Atari is believed to have similar ad ideas in the works for commercials featuring actor Alan Alda.

Other attributes also will be plugged. For its higher priced Model 64, Commodore touts its supposedly superiority over the comparable computers of Apple and IBM. Coleco plans to stress the longevity and expansibility of Adam with an ad slogan such as: "We made obsolescence obsolete."

Such messages would help build the market, ad executives say. Manufacturers previously were "yelling at each other in their ads," says an agency chief executive, instead of giving people reasons to buy the product.

Computer makers also have begun to call a cease-fire in their price wars. Mr. Griesbaum of Sears says he expects less discounting this year. Texas Instruments, for example, says it is scrapping certain of its ads featuring comedian Bill Cosby that stress price cuts and rebates.

Elsewhere, there are other signs of marketing's new role. Market research is getting more attention at Atari and Texas Instruments, among others. Companies are working on making their computers better looking. Distributors are being shuffled. Atari, for example, recently dropped 150 of its 190 distributors.

Will the new marketing men and methods work? Certain analysts are skeptical, noting that some of the executives who have been brought from other industries are experienced in slow-growth businesses that have little in common with computers. There's also doubt about the need for many of the software packages being peddled. A bigger boon for home computing, some computer marketers believe, would be the development of widespread networks for home banking and shopping, but they may be several years away.

The Market Share Myth
William Baldwin

Corporate strategy consultants, guided by a mathematical-looking talisman called a "growth/share matrix," define a business with a low share of a stagnant market as a "dog." To succeed, say the experts, a corporation must sell its dog divisions and buy winners.

As you might expect, the matrix helps to sell management consulting services but doesn't always fit the real world. Consider these companies: Unifi, which is in the yarn business; Republic Gypsum, in plaster; and AFG Industries, in glass. Those are commodity industries, where the little guy ought to be doomed. But look.

A decade ago Unifi had a 2 percent market share in its business of texturizing polyester filaments (to give them bulk and stretch). Since then polyester has stagnated, but not Unifi. It earned $10.9 million in fiscal 1982 on $230 million worth of fiber.

Republic Gypsum, a $20 million (fiscal 1982 sales), one-plant wallboard outfit, competes against billion-dollar U.S. Gypsum and Na-

Reprinted by permission of *Forbes* magazine, March 14, 1983. © Forbes Inc., 1983.

tional Gypsum. Last year Republic's operating margin after depreciation was 13.5 percent, triple that of USG and almost quadruple National's.

AFG Industries, a $182 million (1982 sales) glassmaker, boosted its profits last year 18 percent, to $9.4 million, while glass giants PPG Industries and Libbey-Owens-Ford reported operating earnings declines and much smaller profit margins. The dog theory would have dictated the demise of AFG in 1978, when Dee Hubbard, a high school teacher turned glass salesman, created it by consolidating two chronic money losers with a combined 7 percent market share.

Should a corporation dump its dogs? Perhaps, instead, the strategists could learn a lesson from survivors like these three.

Unifi: New Machines, Old Business

G. Allen Mebane, 53, is a throwster—someone who twirls long filaments to make yarn for weaving and knitting. He's a North Carolina country boy who went to the Philadelphia College of Textiles and Science and doesn't know anything about the corporate strategy courses they teach at Harvard. His profession is an old one, except that his raw material is made not by silkworms but by Celanese, Du Pont, Eastman Kodak, and Hoechst.

And behind the whirr of 22,000 spindles at Unifi's plant in Yadkinville, N.C., is a high-tech race for productivity. Since Mebane co-founded Unifi in 1971—40 miles from where a great-great-great-grandfather opened a cotton mill—he has repeatedly installed the newest machines while competitors were still depreciating older ones. "In the last five years I've junked 62 texturizing machines," Mebane brags. He now has 104, mostly German-made; the newest throw yarn onto spindles at 28 miles per hour. Since its founding, Unifi has quintupled output per production worker.

Keeping a year ahead of the industry has not been cheap. Unifi's depreciation rate, as a percentage of original plant and equipment cost, is precisely double that for the average public textile company. The payoff is in Unifi's halving of labor costs per pound of output over the past decade, to six cents. And in performance: an average 27 percent return on equity. Debt, which was once high, is down to 38 percent of capitalization.

Once one of the smallest polyester texturizers, Unifi may now be the largest and lowest cost operator in the world, says analyst Robert Buckman of W.H. Newbold's. But it didn't get to be the lowest cost producer by being the largest. It got to be large by being low cost from the beginning. Competitors are dropping out. Celanese quit the texturizing business last year. Unifi's remaining competition is privately held Macfield and the captive production of large fabric makers.

"Monsanto, Celanese, Hoechst, Phillips, Rohm & Haas, they all stubbed their toes," says Mebane. "It's the chemical company mentality. Monsanto had a plant that made 280 million pounds of fiber and texturized

probably 30 million pounds a year. They had 225 salaried people just on the factory floor." Unifi has 185 all told, plus 826 production workers, moving 220 million pounds a year.

An impatient, energetic man, Mebane quit working for others in 1964 to invest $10,000 in an insolvent company called Throwing Corp. of America. He ran that long enough to make it profitable, sold out to a textile company, and used the proceeds to start a bigger texturizing outfit with several partners. When they needed capital they let Dow Badische, a partnership of the chemical giants, buy in. But when DB wanted to dominate the operation they had DB buy their stock and stomped off to start Unifi. Both the textile company's Throwing Corp. and DB's texturizing operation succumbed in the double-knit collapse of the mid-1970s.

Now Mebane wants Unifi to grow beyond its quarter-billion-dollar size by invading markets traditionally reserved for spun yarns, from bedsheets to sneaker uppers. More than half of today's polyester winds up in spun yarns, in a costly, nature-mimicking process that chops the filament into cottonlike staple, then reassembles it on a spinning wheel. By 1985, say Unifi salesmen, texturized polyester could displace 350 million pounds a year of spun cotton and poly yarn.

The matrix that says Unifi should never have been founded would now define it as a "cash cow." Mebane doesn't. The company does not pay a dividend. Its engineers are tinkering with new twisting mechanisms that could make existing ones obsolete. They recently sank $1 million into automated yarn testers they developed with assistance from MIT. On Mebane's desk are blueprints for $22 million worth of robots.

Robots? The integrated textile and chemical companies Mebane has raced against would probably consider that a bit much. But then, they were only running for their dinner. Unifi was running for its life.

Republic Gypsum: The Backhaulers

"We're not big enough to affect the price," says O. Max Montgomery, 47, chief executive of Republic Gypsum in Dallas. What an understatement. His company, with 2 percent of the U.S. plasterboard market, tags along behind U.S. Gypsum, with 37 percent, and National, with 27 percent. Periodically a recession will send the majors into an I'll-do-it-for-nothing-I-need-the-work price war that decimates everyone's profits. Still, Republic keeps its plant busy in the crossfire, and keeps it efficient. Capacity is 315 million square feet a year, double what it was when the plant started up in 1964, with no increase in manpower.

The Republic plant, sitting on a gypsum deposit in the southwest corner of Oklahoma, can serve Dallas and Oklahoma City very profitably. When construction thins out, it stretches its selling radius to cities like Houston and San Antonio, meeting the local price and absorbing the freight. A big player can't do that, since it would merely cannibalize the territory of another of its own plants. Republic ran at 94 percent capacity last year, versus 70 percent for the industry.

But freight can be the most important cost in this business, far more so than the gypsum itself. Gypsum is only slightly less plentiful than dirt; quarried and crushed, it's worth all of $3 a ton. Getting the wallboard from Oklahoma to Houston, though, costs $34 a ton. Republic's answer is to run its own trucking fleet, plus a wholesale building supplies outfit in Dallas. The trucks load up with asphalt shingles and steel in Houston, so they're filled for most of the backhaul north to Oklahoma. The wholesaling just breaks even, but it eats some of that all-important freight bill. And the fact that companies such as U.S. Gypsum use contract carriers is a selling point for Republic, says Montgomery, a soft-spoken former salesman who joined the company its first day. "They lose control of it once it's on

the truck." A late delivery, of course, might tie up a project's $170-an-hour crane.

If Republic belies the rule that profits go only with big market shares, it illustrates another maxim in spades: stick to what you know. In its 19-year existence, Republic has made forays into mobile home construction, sawmill operation, asphalt shingle manufacturing—all discontinued—plus oil and gas exploration, in each case with sorry results. For now, Montgomery is keeping diversification on the back burner and waiting patiently for economic recovery—earnings were only $778,000 for the first half ended last December—to improve his wallboard prices. That should be good news for stockholders, who saw earnings of $3.79 million, or $1.96 a share, as recently as 1979, and might do much better in the next boom.

AFG Industries: The Wrenching Process

Six years ago the families that owned Fourco Glass Co. in West Virginia had a mess on its hands. "They were losing $1 million a month," recalls R. Dee Hubbard, who was brought in to clean up. "They had 28 different bank accounts. Sales would enter an order, manufacturing would decide not to run it, and never tell sales." Three of Fourco's four plants used a 50-year-old sheet process that was rendered obsolete by the 1959 invention of float glass, which hardens over a puddle of molten tin.

Hubbard, 47, a Butler County (Kansas) Community College graduate who has spent most of his career making and selling windshields, was then head of Lear Siegler's Wichita-based auto-glass division. For two years, as a security blanket, he kept his old job and commuted to the East. As part of the deal Lear Siegler got an option to buy Fourco for $1.2 million.

Clean up Hubbard did. He shut down the sheet plants, laying off 600 workers, and made up the output by running the float line faster. He fired two thirds of the salesmen and half the administrative staff. He hired Wayne Basler, a glass engineer who had once helped Ford Motor reinvent the float process when Ford was initially denied a license by the owner of the technology. Hubbard got Fourco to break even in six months. Then, smartest move of all, he was unpersuasive in urging Lear to exercise that option. Hubbard and some partners bought the company instead.

The new managers pulled in $6.8 million in profits within 10 months and used them to buy a majority interest in ASG Industries of Tennessee. ASG—originally the U.S. arm of the French glass giant St. Gobain—had lost money in 13 of the preceding 20 years. At ASG, Hubbard and Basler worked their usual magic: closing a sheet plant, firing salaried workers, improving yields from a float furnace. They merged the companies in December 1978 as AFG Industries, based in Kingsport, Tennessee. Two years ago they added a third float line by buying Combustion Engineering's glassworks in New Jersey for $32 million. That makes AFG fifth largest in the U.S. flat-glass market, with 435 million square feet a year.

Number five and doing well? Must be in a niche, you might think. Not quite. Hubbard dumped Fourco's two largest customers precisely because they had too many special orders. When other glassmakers were crowding into metallic-coated glass, a specialty, high-margin item, Hubbard got out. He went after home window glass, a commodity item costing a tenth as much. Lots of factories turn out that item, but few do it well, since the float process is more naturally suited to thicker commercial grades. That's where Basler was indispensable.

For his efforts, Basler wound up with AFG stock now worth $22 million. "I'm a strong believer in incentives," Hubbard says. The surviving salesmen make twice as much as before and drive Mercedes-Benzes. Last fall AFG hired Basler's former boss, Edward Sczesny, to head up a consulting business selling float technology to Third World countries. At the time Sczesny was running a similar sideline for Guardian Industries that was yielding $5 million to $30 million a year in fees. His pay at AFG: half the take. For his part Hubbard, a breezy, blustering entrepreneur who wears gold jewelry and likes to talk about his 100 racehorses, is sitting on $42 million worth of AFG stock. "It was a lot of fun," he says.

Not for everybody. Hubbard exacted large concessions from creditors before he walked in Fourco's door. Two thirds of the original ASG and Fourco employees were axed. Last month 263 hourly workers at the former Combustion Engineering plant were locked out when they rejected a contract that would give managers a much freer hand in assigning jobs.

Says Hubbard: "Even the people we laid off told me they didn't like it but they knew it had to be done." If it hadn't been, quite possibly all of the plants would have closed. While 6 of the 31 float furnaces in the United States are cold, none of Hubbard's 3 are. Indeed, he's spending $35 million building a fourth out of the remnants of an obsolete ASG factory.

The resuscitation of America's heavy industries is necessarily a wrenching process. If the giants can't bring themselves to do it, then people like Hubbard will do it for them.

Case Studies

Consolidated Supply Company
Leete A. Thompson

In May 1977, Mr. Robert A. Melon, president, general manager, and sole stockholder of Consolidated Supply Company, Inc., scanned the latest customer orders for some sign of an upturn in sales. After 20 years of steady growth, Consolidated Supply, a Portland, Oregon, wholesale distributor of nails, screws, bolts, nuts, washers, rivets, studs, dowels, anchors, cotter pins, and other industrial fasteners, had experienced a puzzling drop in sales and profits, beginning in 1975.

"I don't know why sales are down," Mr. Melon mused. "I blame the economy, but . . ." He continued:

> We attempt to satisfy the majority of a customer's fastener requirements at a profit. We aren't all things to all people, but we have a good line of fasteners, and we take care of our good customers. Of course, we can't supply everyone with their odds and ends. It doesn't pay.

Mr. Melon also was acutely aware of the competition from firms which sold cheaper Japanese fasteners. In his words:

> We have always dealt solely with domestic fasteners, and we don't believe it's good business to deal with unreliable foreign manufacturers. I know domestic fasteners are a little higher but, as in all things, you usually get what you pay for.

This case was prepared by Professor Leete A. Thompson, California State University, Sacramento.

Marketing Management: Cases and Readings Dennis H. Tootelian, Ralph M. Gaedeke, and Leete A. Thompson, Copyright © 1979 by Harcourt Brace Jovanovich, Inc. Reprinted by permission of the publisher.

The Industry

Sale and distribution of fasteners amounted to more than $2 million in 1977, and sales to manufacturers constituted about two thirds of that total. Construction firms and hardware and specialty stores also were large buyers. Few customers, however, bought in particularly large lots, so much of the profit for distributors lay in converting large-lot purchases into smaller packages.

Distributors tended to be either general suppliers or specialty suppliers. General suppliers carried a broad line of fasteners and dealt in larger quantities than specialists. Specialty houses, by stocking all fasteners in a particular line, had been able to limit competition somewhat and, thereby, keep profit margins higher.

Some general suppliers admitted that they carried fasteners strictly as a convenience item. Such firms typically specialized in machinery, transportation, or construction equipment and were the exceptions. Others, like Thruway Fasteners of upstate New York, stocked 12,000 fasteners, turned inventory six to eight times yearly, and averaged 35 percent on sales of about $10 million. The president of that firm maintained that much of his profit came from being "big enough to enjoy volume discounts." His opinions were shared by a general-line distributor in Louisville, Kentucky, who advised: "Get big in fasteners or you'll lose your shirt." He purchased by the truckload to save freight and to get quantity discounts.[1]

Knowing the right supplier also was viewed as a key to success. A Los Angeles dealer advised: "Source is the name of the game." Thruway's president seemed to concur, for he credited much of his success to being "a conduit for all fastener manufacturers, instead of just one." There were, of course, hundreds of machine shops making fasteners, but some large U.S. firms manufactured almost complete lines. For example, Allen Manufacturing Company of Hartford, Conn., had produced a broad line of fasteners and, in addition, maintained centers near Atlanta, Chicago, Los Angeles, and New York, all of which sold all the firm's products to distributors in their respective areas.[2]

Distributors did not always agree as to the most effective selling practices. One Baltimore firm maintained that it had been successful because of its willingness to "carry the so-called dogs as long as customers want them." The president viewed his inventory as "a collection of many customers' inventories." In his opinion, the customers purchased from him because they lacked either the cash or the space to keep a large stock. A Los Angeles distributor recommended knowing the right machine shops for special orders so that the customer would remember you when he placed a conventional order. Still other distributors disdained small sales and concentrated on large buyers. The Fastener House in Cleveland promoted engineering services to designers who could specify a particular fastener for the product they were designing. They emphasized examining "the total fastener cost" in terms of its quality and labor-saving potentials.[3]

Starting about 1974, foreign imports had forced many U.S. general suppliers to cut margins and concentrate on selling in larger lots. In conjunction with manufacturers, they complained bitterly that Japanese fasteners were being priced below cost.[4] General suppliers seemed to agree that the cheaper foreign fasteners were of lower quality than those produced domestically, but they found that their customers were not easy to convince. Moreover, increased imports of automobiles, appliances, and other manufactured products reduced domestic demand for fasteners.

Nevertheless, 1977 predictions were that general-line fastener sales would increase by 11 percent nationally, and 9 percent in Consolidated's territory, while specialty-line sales were expected to rise by 14 percent.[5] Opportunities were believed to exist in supplying fasteners for metric conversion and OSHA-inspired specification changes in various products. Increased demand also was anticipated because of activities in energy generation, mining, oil, and construction. Accessories, such as hex keys, screwdrivers, gauges, penetrating oils, and sealants were being added by a few general-line distributors. Others even included adhesives, which threatened to replace several kinds of conventional fasteners.

Consolidated Supply's History

In 1955, Robert A. Melon retired as a colonel in the U.S. Army Corps of Engineers and began to sell tools, hardware, fasteners, and associated products to industrial firms near his Portland, Oregon, home. Sales of $10,000 in 1956 convinced him that his venture had potential, so he leased a building, built up his inventory, and gradually began to concentrate on selling industrial fasteners over a wider territory.

By 1960, Mr. Melon felt confident enough to incorporate, with himself as sole common stockholder. He sold preferred stock to friends and relatives to finance Consolidated Supply's further growth. Thereafter, he gradually built an organization around himself, William Holdbert, purchasing agent, Ronald Coburn, a management consultant in sales and finance, and his brother Joseph Melon, an administrative consultant.

By March 1974, sales had reached nearly $1 million and, in anticipation of further expansion, the firm moved from its cramped $100 per month quarters to a 23,000 square-foot office-warehouse, leased for $3,000 per month. Joseph Melon and Ronald Coburn remained as advisers, nominal officers, and members of the board, but most of the increased management burden had fallen upon President Melon and William Holdbert, the purchasing agent and (in fact) the assistant manager. Over the years, Holdbert had come to exercise great influence in supervising employees and in keeping customers happy. Thus, his resignation to join a competitor, as of December 29, 1974, came as something of a shock. Mr. Melon assumed part of Holdbert's responsibilities and hired a new purchasing agent, Herbert Johnson, to take over the remainder.

Consolidated sales were off slightly in the early months of 1975; yet fiscal 1975 set a record of $1.2 million in sales and nearly $75,000 profits. The economy remained sluggish, so there was no great concern when the March 1976 financial statements showed sales to be down about 6 percent and profits off fractionally. However, Mr. Melon was quite worried by March 1977, when annual statements showed that sales had declined another 12 percent and profits had fallen by nearly two thirds. Only 75 percent of the warehouse space was being used in 1977, and it seemed unlikely that the firm would have need of the 10,000 square-foot vacant space behind the building.

Organization and Management

In mid-1977, 11 of Consolidated Supply's 16 active employees reported directly to President Melon (see Exhibit 1). Mr. Melon was involved in almost every detail of operations.

EXHIBIT 1 Consolidated Supply Co., Inc.: Organization Chart

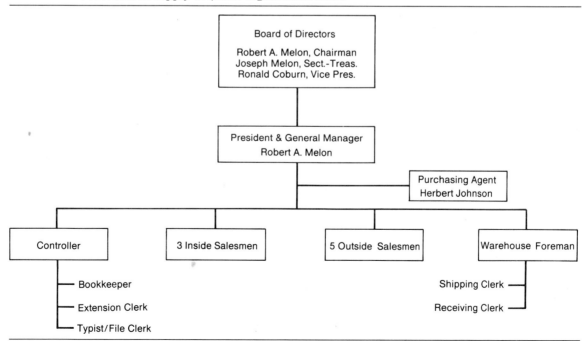

Neither Secretary-Treasurer Joseph Melon nor Vice President Coburn participated in day-to-day decisions, although Coburn did continue to train new salesmen and to provide motivation at the monthly sales meetings.

In general, lateral communications, cross-training, and crossing areas of responsibility were discouraged. Each employee was hired to do a specific job. Anything which required coordination was supposed to move up through organizational channels. Operating policies and procedures all were dated between the years 1965 and 1968. According to President Melon:

I feel that the company is being managed in the most efficient way possible. Over the years we have tried some new things, but in the end we go back to the proven ways.

We don't have any personnel problems. Employees are paid the going wage for a day's work. Salesmen get good commissions. I don't hear any complaints.

There was little doubt, however, that William Holdbert's resignation had affected Consolidated's organizational relationships as well as its management style. Employees observed that Holdbert frequently had bent or broken company policies in order to please customers or placate employees. Indeed, Mr.

EXHIBIT 2 Consolidated Supply Co., Inc.: Income Statement as of March 31 (*in thousands*)

		1977		1976		1975		1974		1973
Sales		$1,028		$1,168		$1,238		$989		$784
Cost of goods sold		595		635		719		572		461
Gross margin		$ 433		$ 533		$ 519		$417		$323
Warehouse expense:										
Wages	$ 37		$ 36		$ 33		$ 24		$ 19	
Labor overhead	7		7		6		5		4	
Other warehouse	3		3		3		2		3	
Total warehouse		47		46		42		31		26
Sales expense:										
Commissions	96		110		117		88		67	
Wages	37		36		29		22		15	
Labor overhead	8		8		7		5		4	
Advertising	5		4		1		1		1	
Freight out	12		13		14		12		7	
Other sales expense	4		4		4		4		4	
Total sales		162		175		172		132		98
Administrative:										
Salary-officer	36		47		49		42		27	
Salaries and wages	52		50		47		40		39	
Labor overhead	8		7		7		6		5	
Bad debts	6		5		8		8		12	
Office expense	21		21		17		19		20	
Lease/rent	36		36		20		7		7	
Phone and utilities	13		13		13		9		8	
Depreciation	5		5		3		3		4	
Other admin. expense	6		22		15		19		14	
Total admin. expense		183		206		179		153		136
Operating profit		$ 41		$ 106		$ 126		$101		$ 63
Other income		5		5		1		—		1
Income taxes		22		40		52		42		24
Net income		$ 24		$ 71		$ 75		$ 59		$ 40

Melon conceded that such practices had been a source of friction between himself and Holdbert, but he had continued to allow Holdbert a considerable amount of freedom in handling personnel, office, warehouse, and purchasing problems because of Holdbert's acknowledged initiative and ability.

Finances

President Melon held a tight rein on Consolidated's finances. Growth in recent years had been financed almost wholly from profits. Mr. Melon even repurchased all outstanding preferred stock in 1974. The firm had borrowed only in emergencies, paid creditors within 30 days, and expected customers to pay their account balances in 30 days. The controller commented:

> We are a cash-producing company which has consistently had a positive cash flow. Collections are good, and our bad debts are still (1977) less than 1 percent of sales . . . I have never had to go to a bank for a loan.
>
> We have a good accounting system. That helps. Accounts receivable, accounts payable, and aging reports all are processed on an IBM minicomputer. The rest is manual, but we are gradually converting to the computer.

Consolidated Supply's financial statements for the five most recent years are shown in Exhibits 2 and 3.

The Market

In 1977, Consolidated Supply's sales territory covered all of Oregon plus southeastern Idaho and parts of southern Washington. No data had been collected on market penetration, although Seattle and Salt Lake City distributors were known to have an impact in fringe areas. Twelve other Portland general suppliers covered some or all of the same territory.

Consolidated's market consisted of anyone in the territory who had need for large quantities of industrial fasteners. Customers were primarily retail hardware stores, auto parts stores, farm equipment suppliers, construction companies, government agencies, and engineering firms, such as heating or air-conditioning contractors. A $10 minimum order size had been strictly enforced since early 1975.

Competition between Consolidated and other general suppliers revolved around price, selling ability, adequate inventories, and rapid delivery of any needed fastener. Firms which handled foreign imports had enjoyed a considerable price advantage, starting about 1974, but Consolidated had been able to offset the price advantage by emphasizing quality and speaking out against foreign imports, according to Mr. Melon.

Planning

Consolidated Supply planned sales and expenditures on an annual basis. In March, each outside salesman was asked to estimate both his volume and his percent of margin for the coming year. These figures were added to expected sales at the warehouse desk to obtain projected annual sales and expected margin. Expenses and budgets for the coming year were based on such sales estimates. Weekly sales and margin reports were checked for variations from target; then appropriate adjustments were made to purchases, sales quotas, personnel, or other operating variables.

Purchasing and Warehousing

Herbert Johnson, the purchasing agent, usually bought fasteners from approximately 100 different U.S. manufacturers during the year.

EXHIBIT 3 Consolidated Supply Co., Inc.: Balance Sheet as of March 31 (*in thousands*)

	1977		1976		1975		1974		1973	
Current assets:										
Cash	$ 96		$ 85		$ 56		$ 48		$ 28	
Accounts receivable	110		121		148		108		101	
Inventory	230		222		192		186		152	
Prepaid expenses	3		3		2		3		4	
Total current assets		$439		$431		$398		$345		$285
Noncurrent assets:										
Motor vehicles	4		4		4		4		4	
Office furniture and equipment	26		25		24		20		20	
Warehouse equipment	20		16		12		12		12	
Less accum. depr. and amortiz.	(38)	12	(33)	12	(28)	12	(25)	11	(23)	13
Deposits and miscellaneous assets		6		6		5		1		1
Total assets		$457		$449		$415		$357		$299
Current liabilities:										
Accounts payable—trade	$ 50		$ 66		$ 90		$ 98		$ 79	
Contracts payable—current	—		—		4		5		5	
Accrued payroll and sales taxes	7		7		12		9		8	
Accrued commissions and payroll	19		22		18		14		—	
Income taxes	10		7		15		26		38	
Total Current Liabilities		$ 86		$102		$139		$152		$130
Noncurrent liabilities— contracts pay		—		—		—		3		15
Total liabilities		$ 86		$102		$139		$155		$145
Capital:										
Preferred stock—7%	—		—		—		—		$ 9	
Common stock—$10 par	$ 20		$ 20		$ 20		$ 20		20	
Retained earnings	351		327		256		182		125	
Total capital		$371		$347		$276		$202		$154
Total liabilities and net worth		$457		$449		$415		$357		$299

A reorder of 90-day stock was placed when the inventory level on a fastener reached a 30-day supply. He explained.

> Our inventory system is kept on a Kardex system (manual), and with over 20,000 different items on hand, it is extremely hard to keep it current and accurate. . . . We have a physical count once a year in February. . . . It takes several months to reconcile and value the inventory afterwards.

Merchandise received was unloaded, opened, and checked on the freight dock before being placed on warehouse shelves. When orders were received, one warehouseman removed the merchandise from shelves, another checked the lot for errors, and the packaged order either awaited customer pickup or was shipped via United Parcel Service or by common carrier freight lines if the orders were larger.

Several new lines of fasteners had been added, and some old lines had been expanded after the firm moved to its present quarters, but demand for most of these had been disappointing. Special orders for fasteners not carried in stock were treated on a case-by-case basis. Mr. Holdbert had accepted as many such orders as possible, even if they involved small orders or foreign imports, but Mr. Melon generally discouraged special orders because of the added costs involved. In 1977, the only special orders freely accepted were large ones which could be drop shipped directly from the manufacturer to the customer. Mr. Johnson explained:

> Special orders are too much trouble. A customer will want some odd size or type of screw, and I'll make a dozen phone calls all over the country trying to locate them for him. If I can't get the fasteners for him, my time has been wasted. If I do get them, the costs eat into profits.

Pricing

Consolidated's pricing was strictly on a markup basis. In general, markups were supposed to insure that an overall margin of 40 percent was earned, though discounts to individual customers varied from 20 percent to about 55 percent on a particular fastener, depending upon the quantity of that fastener the customer normally purchased.

Distribution costs were absorbed, in part, by Consolidated. Company policy dictated that distribution costs not exceed 1 percent of sales; therefore, freight charges were adjusted when it appeared that this limit might be exceeded. By May 1977, all orders over $100 were being shipped freight prepaid. Orders of less than $50 were charged full freight cost, while a 5 cents per pound freight charge was added to orders between $50 and $100.

Marketing

Until 1975, Consolidated had done no advertising other than in the Yellow Pages. Small box listings appeared in the telephone directories of all major population centers throughout the sales territory. President Melon commented:

> I'm not convinced it pays to advertise much. People in the trade know we are here. . . . Recently we've been sending direct mail leaflets to our customers, showing new products or standard items they might use, but it hasn't helped.

Salesmen were compensated entirely by commission, at a rate which varied with the margin achieved on each order. According to one salesman:

> When the economy makes it hard to sell, the front office puts the heat on us, but mainly we are well paid for our sales.

Another salesman observed:

> Our prices are high compared to the competition. We sell by convincing the customer we have what he needs, when he needs it. We stress same-day shipment.

Comments by other salesmen suggested that Consolidated's marketing policies sometimes caused them difficulty, however. For example:

> My job would be easier if we could take back merchandise a little easier. Other houses are more loose in this, and several of them accept returned goods from established customers almost without any question.
> I believe that if we are going to supply fasteners, we should special order all the customers' needs, even if we don't stock the items. If we don't, a customer will just go next door.

Some customers, and former customers, also were critical of Consolidated's marketing policies. A sample of their complaints follows.

Consolidated doesn't want anything to do with the little guy. All they want is big orders.

Consolidated Supply? I can't afford them anymore. They used to give me good service. Their salesman straightened out my shelves and re-stocked them for me automatically. It saved me a lot of work. When their prices were 10 percent or 15 percent high, I figured it was worth it. Now their prices are even higher. I just can't afford them.

I don't always need $10 worth of material. At times I go in there and buy $200 worth. But when I go in to buy a few bolts to get me out of an emergency situation, they won't sell them to me unless I take something else to make up the $10 minimum. Their competitors don't have a minimum at all, so why bother with Consolidated?

Why buy those expensive bolts and nuts when I can get imported ones from Armco Supply at less than half the cost? Customers who come into my hardware store for some bolts don't care whether they were made in Detroit or Tokyo.

Still another retailer in Consolidated's territory commented:

When I select a supply house, I expect them to supply all they can. Consolidated is fine for a run-of-the-mill fastener, but when you ask for something a little different they really hassle you, and if you do get them to special-order it, you pay sky-high prices.

Sometimes we make a mistake in ordering, or our customer makes a mistake. Consolidated won't take anything back unless we agree to a 15 percent to 20 percent restocking charge, and even then we can't get a cash refund. Why deal with a company like that when their competitors do it without a restocking charge? My customers won't pay me a restocking charge.

The Future

President Melon was watching the weekly sales and margin reports carefully in May 1977. He concluded that unless an upturn came soon, he might be forced to consider expanding salesmen's services to customers and/or selling in smaller lots. In either case, he thought, prices would have to rise or other expenses would have to be reduced.

He was reluctant to add a line of Japanese fasteners, although he conceded that they would return an excellent profit margin. He preferred to deal with U.S. manufacturers. Moreover, he was thoroughly convinced that domestic fasteners were superior in quality. A couple of his suppliers had approached him with a plan to lobby and bring political pressure against imports. They were willing to share the costs of modest advertising as well as the costs of hiring a public relations firm to blunt demand for foreign fasteners, but Mr. Melon was still lukewarm to such proposals.

Notes
1. "Profitmakers: Fasteners," *Industrial Distribution,* 3, no. 75, pp. 45–47.
2. Ibid.
3. Ibid.
4. "Japanese Trade Practices under Investigation by Fastener Makers," *Industrial Distribution,* 3, no. 25, pp. 9–11.
5. "31st Annual Survey of Distributor Operations," *Industrial Distribution,* 3, no. 77, pp. 31–45.

ToLee Plantation, Inc.
Richard R. Still and Thomas H. Stevenson

ToLee Plantation in southwest Georgia was one of the Southeast's largest pecan growers; it also grew blueberries, peaches, corn, peanuts, soybeans, and wheat. The owners were considering a change in pecan-marketing strategy. The proposal was to switch from selling to a sheller to shelling and packaging

Richard R. Still and Thomas H. Stevenson, *Cases in Marketing,* pp. 219–24. © 1985; reprinted by permission of Prentice-Hall, Inc., Englewood Cliffs, N.J.

pecans under the ToLee name. The ToLee brand would be sold through mail order and through grocery stores, and bulk sales would be made to commercial buyers. The proposed strategy was attractive because: (1) The National Pecan Marketing Council had plans to educate consumers about pecans and hoped to create a larger demand; (2) Surveys showed consumers preferred pecans over almonds and walnuts; (3) ToLee would be one of the few pecan brands in retail stores; (4) Tolee already had retail distribution of its ToLee Plantation Blueberries.

The owners were convinced that it was important to move quickly. The first brand into the newly expanded market should achieve favored status. If the ToLee brand did not get into the stores first, a competitor might step in and take over the desired position.

The Pecan Industry

Pecans went to market in one of two ways. Some growers sold their crops to shellers for processing and marketing. Other growers handled their own marketing and processing or contracted with shellers for the processing. Some growers kept pecans in cold storage to fill orders year-round rather than just after the harvest. Ninety-four percent of all pecans were marketed shelled for use as a cooking ingredient. Commercial bakers and confectioners bought about 47 percent of the production; retailers, 15 percent; ice cream makers, 5 percent; exporters, 5 percent; gift packers, 5 percent; and other small users, 23 percent.

Three problems confronted pecan growers. First, production varied from year to year, and prices fluctuated with supply. Second, the historically unstable crop size and price created a burden for commercial users, especially makers of pecan candy. If pecans were in short supply, users either could not buy enough or had to pay high prices. Third, pecan growers bore the brunt of highly aggressive marketing techniques used by their major competitors, the walnut and almond growers.

Consumer Perceptions

Marketing research showed consumers preferring pecans over other nuts for baking, but the market share for pecans had dropped steadily. The U.S. Department of Commerce reported annual per capita pecan consumption had fallen in the past 15 years from .44 pounds to .28 pounds, while annual per capita walnut consumption had gone up from .30 pounds to .52 pounds and per capita almond consumption had risen from .27 pounds to .43 pounds. Because of relatively high price and limited availability, pecans generally were used as a holiday item rather than an everyday cooking ingredient.

Also contributing to declining consumption was the fact that pecans were mainly sold commercially while walnuts were mainly retailed. Consumers looked upon pecans as seasonal luxuries, walnuts as everyday necessities. Supermarket managers said that pecans were usually carried only during the holidays because that was when consumers wanted them. Consumers said they bought pecans during the holidays because that was the only time they were on display.

Evidently too a substantial number of consumers believed that pecans were high in cholesterol. Actually, pecans are low in cholesterol, and the meat is nutritious as well as high in energy. Furthermore, nut aficionados say pecans have a richer flavor than most other nuts.

Commercial Users

Commercial users benefited from consumers' beliefs that pecans were for special occasions. People considered candies and other sweets as treats instead of necessities, so treats deserved special ingredients; and because of this pecans were used in sweets more than other nuts. Any nut could supply the crunch, but the pecan offered superior quality and flavor. Some confectioners had found that sales of pecan items did not decline greatly when prices were raised to cover higher nut prices. The commercial user's main concern about pecans was the supply available each year.

The National Pecan Marketing Council

The National Pecan Marketing Council offered membership to all pecan growers and shellers. Its main purpose was to build market demand for pecans. By educating consumers about pecans and their uses, the council hoped to increase the market share of pecans. The council used Atlanta and San Francisco

advertising agencies to develop pecan marketing campaigns. (See Exhibit 1 for a sample advertisement.) Through television, magazine, and trade journal media, the council hoped to refute misconceptions of consumers and commercial users such as: (1) Pecan prices are higher than prices of other nuts; (2) Pecan supplies are unpredictable; (3) Pecans are used only for special dishes; (4) Pecans are not nutritious.

The council believed that once buyers were aware that pecans were always available and versatile in usage, additional demand would develop. With consumers demanding more pecans, retailers would carry them year-round. The council planned too to create a second season for pecans. All varieties of nuts had peak sales during the winter holidays. The council decided to develop an advertising program aimed to develop a summer pecan season, starting the Fourth of July, during which pecans were "excellent for snacking or baking."

EXHIBIT I

Description of Proposed Advertising by National Pecan Marketing Association

Picture: An enlargement of a single pecan nut and one end of a pecan shell. Deep grained wood background. Part of a cracking instrument visible. All in color on top half of the page. Copy against a solid background.

Headline: "Even More Than They're Cracked Up to Be."

Copy: No doubt about it. There is nothing quite like the good old pecan pie. But what a shame to save such a versatile, plentiful nut for pies alone. Especially when the pecan adds so much more to foods than just a decorative touch or crunchy texture. Pecans add flavor. Hearty, robust, full flavor to everything they're baked in, cooked in, tossed with, topped with.

It's no wonder pecans were picked number 1 in a nut preference pool. When asked which nut they preferred in items they buy . . . like cakes, pastries, candy, and dishes of all description . . . people picked the pecan. Over the walnut. Over the almond.

Halved, chopped, or in pieces . . . there's no limit to the number of delicious recipes pecans can be a part of. So if you're looking for new ways to increase sales and please customers, pick the nut they do.

Say the word and we'll send you a whole package of particulars on pecans . . . including aids and ideas designed especially for you and your needs.

PECANS

They make a lot more than just good old pecan pie.

National Pecan Marketing Council
1800 Peachtree Rd. NW/Suite 816/Atlanta, Georgia 30309

ToLee Plantation

At one time ToLee Plantation had its own shelling plant and packaged pecans under the name Mr. Sam's Pecans for sale in bulk to bakeries and through mail order. Later, the shelling plant was sold and ToLee agreed not to buy or build a shelling plant for five years. Since that time ToLee had harvested, cleaned, sized, and graded the pecans, then sold them to shellers. ToLee also stored pecans for future price speculation, and had cold-storage facilities to store one million pounds.[1]

Marketing and Promotion

ToLee had no specialized marketing personnel. The owners contacted buyers for ToLee's crops and negotiated for the best prices. Prices for pecans and the other crops, except peanuts (peanut prices were government regulated), were heavily influenced by market supplies. Often it seemed that pricing was determined by "playing the market" to generate the highest selling prices. The cold storage facilities were useful in this respect, since if ToLee could not get the price desired the crop could be stored in anticipation of higher future prices.[2]

New Strategy

ToLee Plantation's owners felt that the National Pecan Marketing Council was carving out a new market segment. The council's efforts were expected to increase year-round consumer demand for pecans and year-round stocking by the retailers. They wanted ToLee to be the first in designing a retail marketing strategy. Part of the strategy would be to develop packages and displays with strong retailer appeal. Another part was to formulate promotional strategy for ToLee Pecans.

Retailers surveyed by the National Pecan Marketing Council suggested certain changes that might increase pecan sales: (1) Packaging should be improved. The package should be strong and have less writing so the nuts could be seen; (2) Packages should be available in several sizes; (3) Shelf life should be lengthened; (4) Suppliers should provide in-store merchandising aids as well as brand promotion. (Retailers said this improvement was the most important.)

ToLee management planned several packaging moves. The pecans would be packaged in several sizes. Also under consideration was an ultrasmall package to sell as a snack food and a large bag of in-shell nuts. All packages were to have see-through windows, and recipes on the package were under study. Plans too were to design a store display unit to make packages of ToLee pecans a noticeable item in the store.

Promotional strategies were to aim at selling ToLee Pecans during the holidays when demand was high. Additionally, as the Marketing Council created more consumer demand for pecans, promotions would aim to satisfy these new consumer needs.

Starting up a mail-order operation would also require promotion. To reach mail-order buyers, different promotion techniques were under consideration including: (1) cable television advertisements for ToLee Pecans with a toll-free number for placing orders; (2) local television ads; (3) newspaper ads and supplements; (4) magazine ads containing pecan recipes and order forms (this method was being used by almond and walnut growers); (5) direct-mail brochures and order forms.

The owners were optimistic about the chances for marketing success. They had sufficient storage facilities to assure a steady pecan supply for both retailers and mail-order buyers. They had some earlier experience in mail-order operations. They had good relations with major grocery store chains now carrying ToLee Blueberries and this should have favorable impact on the ToLee Pecans. Further, commercial pecan users could still be counted on to buy. Finally, since the five-year moratorium had expired, ToLee was free to buy or build a pecan-shelling plant.

Additional Considerations

Yet details needed working out before going ahead with the project. Most important was the packaging method. Packaging machinery, designed to package different-sized bags with minimum nut breakage, ranged in price from $7,000 to $50,000. Outlays for packaging machinery could be avoided by hiring a contract packager, but this would mean hauling the pecans to Atlanta for packaging, then back to ToLee for distribution; package shelf life would be reduced by the extra transport time.[3] Hand packaging was an alternative requiring very little investment but a heat-sealing machine would be needed.

Competition

There were three different sources of competition. One was from other local pecan growers and sellers. Plantation Pecans and Sunnyland Pecans were two area brands packaged locally and sold through mail order.

A second source of competition was the large nut grocery manufacturers that already were selling packaged pecans in supermarkets. Standard Brands (Planter's Peanuts), Goldkist, and Fisher were three of these manufacturers. If demand for pecans expanded, these manufacturers might decide to market packaged pecans more aggressively. The owners thought that ToLee Pecans could compete with these brands by offering several bag sizes and being first with attractive in-store promotions.

A third source of competition was from other types of nuts—almonds and walnuts, for example. Consumers preferred pecans but if they were not available or too expensive, consumers would substitute walnuts or almonds, both heavily advertised in women's magazines and in some business magazines. The almond growers' cooperative marketing association had recently begun some television advertising, and this might force Tolee to spend more for promotion to make consumers aware of its pecans.

Notes

1. Pecans could be stored for two years.

2. ToLee Blueberries, however, were sold direct to major grocery chains by an employee who contacted the stores and arranged the orders, delivery dates, and selling prices. Deliveries were by a farm van to customers' stores in Georgia, Florida, and Tennessee.

3. Shelf life was an important factor in making retail sales; customers buying rancid pecans likely would not buy them again. And retailers disliked carrying items that spoiled on the shelves.

War Memorial Stadium
Robert D. Hay

Mr. Howard Pearce, general manager of the War Memorial Stadium in Little Rock, Arkansas, sat back in his chair and surveyed the situation facing his stadium commissioners. Sellout crowds were commonplace for the 1977

This case was prepared by Dr. Robert D. Hay of the University of Arkansas, with the assistance of Tom Reed, Nancy Garner, Cindy Kane, and Wendell Fleming, as a basis for class discussion.

University of Arkansas Razorback football team which defeated the Sooners of the University of Oklahoma in the 1978 Orange Bowl game. The Razorbacks had traditionally played four games in Little Rock's War Memorial Stadium (and three games in Fayetteville, home of the Razorbacks) each year. Mr. Pearce wondered if War Memorial Stadium should expand its facilities since sellout crowds occurred in three of the four games played this past 1977 season.

War Memorial Stadium was built 30 years ago at an initial cost of $2 million. Since that time, an additional $2.5 million had been spent in improvements. Rising property values and other factors make the present structure worth approximately $15 million, according to Mr. Pearce.

The stadium, with a present seating capacity of 53,500, is one of approximately only 5 percent of the stadiums in the United States that has no indebtedness. In fact, the stadium's debt on borrowed capital was paid off three years early; Mr. Pearce took great pride in this.

Since the stadium is located in the center of the state, it draws football fans from nearly the whole state, which has a population of two million people. The stadium is somewhat unique in that it was created by an act of the state legislature to serve as a football stadium primarily for the Arkansas Razorbacks, whose home facility is located 200 miles to the northwest, and other state institutions of higher learning.

Mr. Howard Pearce is the present general manager and has held this post for several years, having been appointed to this position by the state legislature. He reports to a commission of eight members, each of whom serves eight years and is appointed by the governor and the legislature. Under Mr. Pearce's leadership, the stadium has been managed as a state business and has shown a profit in its operations.

The fact that the stadium is a profit center is unusual. War Memorial Stadium is run completely on its own and has no tax money used for operations.

The concessions at War Memorial generate yearly gross sales of $175,000. The present facility makes a 39 percent profit on these sales. The national average profit on concessions is around 30 percent. Presently, there are 42 concessions in War Memorial Stadium.

At the present time, approximately 1,750 employees are needed to work the ballgame hours. These employees include parking attendants, police, ushers, concessionaires, gatekeepers, ticket sellers and takers as well as other miscellaneous employees. A source of supply of people has been available in the past years. Cleanup crews are also available since many booster clubs or other organizations work on cleanup as money-making projects.

The stadium is 30 years old. The structure, while solid and architecturally sound, has increasing maintenance and repair problems. Obsolescence is definitely a problem.

Parking area around the stadium is not only very limited, but most of it is owned by the city of Little Rock and state agencies. This is a problem because the stadium has no control over the parking area, which consists of a limited space adjacent to the stadium. Some parking is allowed on the War Memorial Golf Course. The stadium management is responsible for much of the operation of the parking areas, but the city of Little Rock receives most of the revenues. Most stadiums own their own parking areas, and thus have the added revenue.

Access to War Memorial, while not difficult, is not conducive to smooth traffic flow. Traffic tie-ups and congestion are common, before and after a game.

Seating in the present stadium has 26 inches between the rows; new stadiums now have 30 inches between the seats for comfort and ease of crowd flow. Nothing more can be done to make the stadium more comfortable. Capacity crowds are difficult to handle on existing ramps, elevators, and walkways, and little can be done to alleviate the situation.

Maintenance of the present facility is increasing tremendously. A strain on the present facilities is occurring at its present size. An example of increasing maintenance was the $60,000 cost of maintaining rest rooms this year.

The location of the present facility is not in the best neighborhood in Little Rock. Although not in the highest crime area of Little Rock, the area does have problems. The stadium was broken into recently.

Land around the stadium is not available for much expansion. In addition, an estimated three parking spaces for each eight people is needed, and parking space is very limited as previously noted.

Mr. Pearce's philosophy stressed the idea that the University of Arkansas' athletic program and particularly its football team were created for enjoyment by the spectators as well as the participants. The team was produced; it was scheduled to play three or four games regularly in Little Rock; and it was priced reasonably ($8 a ticket) so that as many people as possible could enjoy the benefits of the team. The stadium is indirectly involved in the marketing of the team, and it is a necessary facility for the team to provide the entertainment which fans desire.

The War Memorial Commission believes that to get additional use of the facility, it should try to stage other events in the stadium such as concerts, high school football, professional football events, and other special events.

Mr. Pearce believes that the management of the stadium must be concerned with profitable operations. Although the commission is a nonprofit organization, revenue is used for bond retirement, maintenance, and renovation at times. Excessive profit is not desired, but some kind of profitable operation is necessary.

Further, he believes that the stadium must involve itself in the enforcement and obedience of state, local, and federal laws.

Mr. Pearce wondered about the general economic forecast and its effect on his proposal to expand. He gathered the following information from *Fortune* magazine.

The economic outlook for the United States through 1978 and trends for the years beyond indicate an increasing and expanding economy. The Gross National Product is expected to reach approximately $1,890 billion in 1977, which is an increase of 10.7 percent over 1976, deflating to a real increase of 4.9 percent. In 1978, GNP is expected to have a real increase of 4.5 percent, with further increases through 1980 of 4 percent per year.

Government spending should increase in real terms over the next several years at approximately 5 percent per year. Much of this increase will be in defense, public works, and public jobs. The threat of Soviet superiority will override the desire for a balanced budget, while the increase in public jobs will be a response to the expanded work force. Disposable personal income is expected to rise to a rate of 5.6 percent to 6 percent through 1978, with per capita disposable income reaching $6,500 to $6,750. However, inflation should increase at 7 percent to 8 percent causing a real shrinking of disposable income or at best, break-even.

The unemployment figures for 1977 are expected to be 6.5 percent to 7 percent at the end of the year. But an expanding work force in 1978 and capital expenditures which are mainly replacement will cause unemployment to equal 7 percent to 7.5 percent next year.

In the financial markets, the economy will see further indications of an increasing inflation rate. The prime lending rate after reaching 7.25 percent in late 1977 should move upward to reflect the recent increases. The savings rate for 1978 should climb to a historical average of 6.5 percent. It is currently at 5.3 percent. This rate will provide a stronger base for the construction industry with more funds available at savings institutions to finance increased construction activities.

Overall, the economy is in an upward growth pattern, but at a slower rate than has been experienced in the last few years. Most gains in critical areas will be in gross terms only, as inflation will nullify most gains. In addition, the balance of trade should continue to be a problem with increasing demand for imported sources of energy. However, new construction should provide a bright spot in the economy with an increase of 10 percent a year providing a real benefit to the economy. Industries in Arkansas such as steel, aluminum, wood products, and other construction-related businesses should show positive gains due to the increased construction.

College football attendance figures were kept by Mr. Pearce. They showed the following information:

Year	Collegiate Football Attendance of NCAA Schools	Difference from Year Before
1968	27,025,846	596,207
1969	27,626,160	600,314
1970	29,465,604	1,839,444
1971	30,455,442	989,838
1972	30,828,802	373,360
1973	31,282,540	453,738
1974	31,234,855	(47,685)
1975	31,687,847	452,922
1976	32,012,008	324,161
1977	32,905,178	893,170

Unlike most other large universities, the University of Arkansas is in the unique position of having no direct competition. Although there are several other colleges in the state, most are small AIC Division III teams, with the exception of ASU, a Division I team as directed by NCAA regulations for the 1978

season. The AIC schools draw from a very small area around each school and ASU, although a larger institution, is situated in the northeastern corner of the state and draws little attendance from outside that area. Little Rock is located in the center of the state so that most fans have a relatively short drive from almost any point in the state. Most of the major highways in the state also pass through Little Rock, providing easy access to the city. Razorback football has competition from the other colleges in the state, plus many other sporting events held in Arkansas. However, Arkansas football probably faces its biggest indirect competition from other games that are being televised nationally. Arkansas can even be competition to itself if home games are televised as some fans may prefer staying at home. Other events, meetings, and special activities that are taking place within the state also would provide competition to the games.

Football, like many other sporting events, is a recession-proof commodity. No matter what the economy is doing, football attendance has historically remained relatively strong. Leisure activities have been growing at a rapid pace for the past 20 years, even in economic turndowns, providing a growing market. In addition, football fans' participation itself has also been growing both nationally and in Arkansas. Records of attendance at War Memorial since it was opened in 1948 show a general growth trend with some variations.

War Memorial Stadium, because of its construction, can be used for very few events other than football games. Concerts and special events such as the Billy Graham Crusade are among the few exceptions. This limits the use of the stadium and its revenue drawing power to a very seasonal basis of August through the first of December.

With the exception of the New Mexico State game, all Razorback games played at

War Memorial this year were sold out. In fact, the actual attendance records for the other three games actually exceeded the seating capacity of 53,355. One game in particular, the Oklahoma State game, had an official attendance of 54,280, almost 600 more than the seats available. Because of the number of inquiries for tickets to these games, it was Mr. Pearce's opinion that an additional 8,000 tickets could have been sold easily for these games, probably at higher prices than the $8 now charged.

Arkansas had been particularly fortunate this year to have been televised nationally three times. Mr. Pearce said: "Television coverage has also increased the awareness of football in general, raising it to the number one sport in the United States. It has also served as an educational device, teaching the public the rules of the game and giving them a better understanding of how the game is played. Football has a good image both as a participation activity and as a recreational activity by individuals interested in watching the players. It is looked on as a sport that teaches discipline, self-confidence, and good sportsmanship."

The state's population is increasing with a larger population from which to draw fans. As mentioned earlier, the Razorbacks are somewhat unique as they draw from the whole state. Therefore, any increase in the population of Arkansas gives War Memorial a bigger potential market.

War Memorial is a state-owned operation. Therefore, any funds for expansion must be voted on and approved by the state legislature. This is probably the only way to get the needed financing for any proposed structure.

Construction of the new addition must follow the building codes as set forth by the state and the city of Little Rock. One problem area in the code would be an insufficient amount of bathroom facilities with the extra 8,000 seats. Present facilities include eight bathrooms, each with 16 stalls. With the construction of the upper deck, at least 20 more stalls—one half for each sex—must be constructed.

The new addition, as Mr. Pearce visualized it, would be a cantilever-style deck. This type of deck would have all of the superstructure on the outside of the stadium with the deck itself suspended over the lower level seats by a projected beam. There would be no column supports to obscure vision of the playing field. Ramps to the upper deck would be placed from a hill on the south side of the stadium. This would allow easy access to the upper level without inhibiting the flow of individuals entering or leaving the lower level. It would also not take away any of the present parking facilities on the east side of the stadium.

Mr. Pearce pulled from his desk drawer the following statistics:

War Memorial Stadium Attendance Records

Year	Total Attendance	Number Games	Average per Game	Razorback Win-Loss Record	%
1966	135,000	3	45,017	8-2-0	80
1967	187,634	4	46,908	4-5-1	40
1968	148,221	3	49,407	10-1-0	91
1969	170,717	4	42,679	9-2-0	82
1970	194,000	4	48,500	9-2-0	82
1971	217,244	4	54,311	8-3-1	73
1972	209,102	4	52,227	6-5-0	54
1973	179,542	4	44,885	5-5-1	50
1974	200,309	4	50,077	6-4-1	54
1975	201,575	4	50,393	10-2-0	83
1976	192,463	4	48,115	5-5-1	45
1977	214,991	4	53,747	10-1-0	91

Stadium Attendance Information

1976	Utah State	50,536	1977	New Mexico State	53,167
	Oklahoma State	53,103		Oklahoma State	54,280
	Texas A & M	47,497		Houston	53,924
	Texas Tech	41,327		Baylor	53,620
	(Win-loss at time of game 5–3–1)				

In looking at the figures, Mr. Pearce saw that the average per game attendance had not dropped below 42,000 at any time during the years shown. Of particular interest was the record of attendance in 1976 when the Razorbacks' win-loss record was 5–5–1, one of the worst during Frank Broyles' tenure as head coach. Even at the Texas Tech game, attendance was 41,327 on a wet rainy day in late November. The game-time temperature was 22 degrees and there was a brisk wind blowing. In spite of the adverse weather conditions and the poor record at that point in the season (5–3–1), the attendance still did not drop below 40,000.

Again in 1972, 1973, and 1974 the win-loss record was poor. However, average attendance for those years was 52,227; 44,885; and 50,077. Mr. Pearce believed that only stadium attendance over 40,000 was related to the win-loss record.

A trend-line analysis was made using the average per game attendance for the past five years, as follows:

Year	Expected Attendance
1978	54,172
1979	55,749
1980	57,325
1981	58,901
1982	60,478
1983	62,054

Based on the growth pattern of the past five years, a 61,000-seat stadium would be filled by 1983.

When growth trends for the past 12 years were used, analysis showed that a 61,000-seat stadium would not be filled until 1997. The results were:

Year	Expected Attendance
1978	51,989
1979	52,471
1980	52,953
1981	53,435
1982	53,917
1983	54,399
1984	54,881
1985	55,364
.	.
.	.
1996	60,667
1997	61,149

If additional seats were added, Mr. Pearce asked himself, "What effect will empty seats have on ticket sales until that time when the stadium can be sold out whether it be 1983 or 1997?" Mr. Pearce expressed an opinion that it was better to have a situation where there was a shortage or potential shortage for tickets. As he put it, "People want to want tickets. Psychologically, people seem to want something more if they feel there is going to be a shortage. In the case of football tickets, when people feel there is a shortage, the money for tickets will come in faster and there will be a bigger demand. Not only does the money come in at the first, but more and more people want tickets for later games, giving a bandwagon-type effect. Therefore, there is something to be said for keeping the stadium at its present size."

Mr. Pearce considered the financial costs of adding 8,000 additional seats (this figure is the number that the Stadium Commission would like to consider). Therefore, two construction cost estimates were obtained from two established stadium contractors. One estimate was obtained from a Mr. Baxter, who had taken part in several stadium construction cost estimates and jobs, especially in Memphis. Mr. Baxter had recently estimated that double-decking the Liberty Bowl in Memphis would cost approximately $209 per seat.

Mr. Pearce, however, questioned the $209 per seat estimate. Recently, he has been a member of a committee of the International Association of Auditorium and Stadium Managers which had compiled some cost figures for various stadiums built during the past 15 years (see Exhibit 1). Mr. Pearce estimated

the cost per seat to be approximately $800–$1,000. If he used the $800 estimate, the total construction cost would be approximately $6,400,000 for adding 8,000 seats. This figure would include the cost of additional rest rooms and concession stands on the second level.

The stadium is presently rented to the university for 15 percent of ticket sales (gate receipts) for each game played in the stadium. Another major source of revenue to the stadium is concessions, which amounts to approximately $175,000 gross per year. Addi-

EXHIBIT 1 Costs for Stadiums Completed 1960–1978*

Stadium	Year Completed	Seating Capacity	Total Cost	Per Seat Cost
Stadiums completed since 1970				
King Dome				
Seattle, Wash.	1976	64,275	$62,000,000	$946.61
Pontiac Silver Dome				
Pontiac, Mich.	1975	80,656	51,700,000	640.99
Philadelphia Veterans Stadium				
Philadelphia, Pa.	1971	69,000	48,000,000	695.65
Cincinnati Riverfront Stadium				
Cincinnati, Ohio	1973	58,000	38,000,000	665.77
Average since 1970—$741.60				
Stadiums completed between 1960 and 1969 inclusive				
Las Vegas Stadium				
Las Vegas, Nev.	1968	32,500	3,500,000	107.69
Atlanta Stadium				
Atlanta, Ga.	1965	60,000	18,000,000	300.00
Busch Stadium				
St. Louis, Mo.	1966	51,392	28,000,000	544.83
Anaheim Stadium				
Anaheim, Calif.	1966	56,000	16,000,000	285.71
Busch Memorial Stadium				
St. Louis, Mo.	1964	50,000	20,000,000	400.00
Alameda County Coliseum				
Oakland, Calif.	1964	54,500	13,000,000	238.53
Liberty Bowl				
Memphis, Tenn.	1962	50,180	4,000,000	79.71
			Questionable construction cost	
Falcon Stadium				
Colorado Springs, Co.	1962	40,808	3,500,000	85.72
Mississippi Memorial Stadium				
Jackson, Miss.	1961	46,000	1,800,000	39.13
			Open structure end-zone-type seating	
Average for 1960–69 inclusive: $231.25				

*These figures are based on information obtained from questionnaires completed by stadium managers during the I.A.A.M. convention in January 1978.

tional sources of revenue to the stadium are rental receipts from high school football games, of which there are approximately 30 per year. The stadium receives $1,500 per game or 15 percent of gate receipts, whichever is greater. The average attendance at each high school game is approximately 6,000. The stadium also receives revenue from concession sales at these high school football games. This averages approximately $600 gross per game.

The final source of revenue to the stadium is from parking, which averages less than $10,000 gross per year. The majority of the parking revenue goes to the city, approximately $27,000 net per year. An additional problem is that only a few parking spaces immediately around the stadium are owned by the stadium, the remainder by the city of Little Rock.

Mr. Pearce knew that there were no additional markets which the stadium could tap other than the ones which existed. There were no other professional teams in the area such as soccer, football, and basketball.

The stadium employs 10 people year-round. However, during a University of Arkansas football game there are approximately 1,750 people employed.

Additional income and expense information concerning present financial operations is shown in Exhibit 2.

"The Southeastern Conference is planning to raise ticket prices to $10 per ticket. If this happens as planned, then the Southwestern Conference will most likely follow suit. Therefore, an additional increase in income to the stadium will occur," Mr. Pearce commented.

"Considerable income has been lost each year from tickets being sold at less than full price. The following are examples:

In 1976, we lost $58,975 from selling 10,081 tickets at less than full price to the Utah State game.

In 1976, we lost $48,000 from selling 9,000 tickets at less than full price to the Oklahoma State game.

In 1976, we lost $63,000 from selling 11,000 tickets at less than full price to the Texas A & M game.

"Of course, War Memorial Stadium would have received 15 percent of that income. I feel that the stadium could be filled by selling all tickets at full price," Mr. Pearce continued.

EXHIBIT 2 War Memorial Stadium Commission: Income, Expenditures, Depreciation, and Cash Balances—1969–1977

	June 30, 1969	June 30, 1970	June 30, 1971	June 30, 1972	June 30, 1973	June 30, 1974	June 30, 1975	June 30, 1976	June 30, 1977
Income (Rental revenue, 10% ticket tax, interest earned) net	$143,644	$182,789	$172,070	$199,759	$205,625	$185,725	$220,762	$197,200	$244,665
Expenditures									
Operating	52,548	75,863	79,835	107,903	77,240	98,769	103,150	154,485	188,127
Interest on bonds	4,415	4,276	3,866	3,840	3,296	2,746	2,273	1,791	—
Interest on construction loan and astroturf	—	—	2,477	19,737	16,897	11,504	6,225	—	—
Totals	$ 56,963	$ 80,139	$106,178	$131,444	$ 97,415	$113,019	$111,648	$156,276	$188,127
Depreciation	24,632	27,260	82,375	137,363	138,156	138,337	137,413	137,226	137,128
Cash Balances	273,988	295,655	342,803	386,316	420,927	452,031	473,000	258,673	217,964

"If the new seats were added and were completely sold out for each of the four games in Little Rock, the additional income would be $38,000 per year. This does not take into account concessions, which would be substantial. Also, parking income is not considered.

"I feel that with the addition of 8,000 seats in an upper deck, maintenance would probably not go up for a while as additional people would not have to be hired. In other words, the present employment of a U. of A. game could handle the maintenance work involved at no added costs."

Assuming that additional seating is needed and wanted by the U. of A. Athletic Department it is felt that a combination of the following organizations and individuals could present a strong appeal to the state legislature for financial support: U. of A. board trustees, War Memorial Stadium Commission, Frank Broyles and his staff, and Howard Pearce, stadium manager.

Presently, according to Mr. Pearce, the break-even point per game is approximately 40,000 people. He has not calculated a break-even point if expansion were to take place.

Tickets are distributed through the Fayetteville ticket office (located in the new athletic facility on the University of Arkansas campus). The tickets not sold as season tickets or distributed to students are sent back to Little Rock and sold on a per-game basis. Mr.

Pearce said that the "leftover" tickets are advertised in the newspaper and over the radio.

When asked if any additional promotion efforts would be needed for the proposed addition, Mr. Pearce responded, "No, I would just announce extra tickets were available in a newspaper ad, and then get the hell out of the way to keep from being trampled."

It is possible, according to Mr. Pearce, that a new stadium may be built in the future in the Little Rock area. An unnamed source might give to the state of Arkansas a tract of land that would facilitate a new stadium and adequate parking. While not disclosing the donor, or the exact location of the proposed stadium, Mr. Pearce did say the management was hoping a new stadium would have interstate access, and be located near a large shopping mall so that the mall parking could also serve the stadium on ballgame days. Senator Jim Caldwell, a state senator, felt the attitude of the state legislature would be much more favorable toward a new structure if land acquisition costs were exempted.

Mr. Pearce thought that the state legislature could finance the $6,400,000 cost of expanding War Memorial Stadium with a 5 percent, 30-year maturity bond issue. This would mean yearly payments of approximately $450,000. He was wondering if War Memorial Stadium should be expanded.

Adolph Coors Brewing Company
Thomas V. Greer

One of the largest, oldest, and most interesting brewers in the United States was the Adolph Coors Company. It faced a perplexing set of circumstances, opportunities, and problems as an organization and was part of an industry that showed great structural change and extensive modifications of traditional consumer behavior.

The U.S. Beer Industry

The U.S. brewing industry underwent a massive shake-up and restructuring between 1970 and the early 1980s. Fifty-four brewery com-

Reprinted with permission of Macmillan Publishing Company. From Thomas V. Greer, *Cases in Marketing*, 3rd ed. Copyright © 1983 by Thomas V. Greer.

panies disappeared, some by closing down and some by merging with stronger organizations. Among the 41 remaining companies, a few were in severe difficulty, several faced significant problems, and several others faced problem-laden opportunities.

For a long time fourth in size, behind Anheuser-Busch, Inc., Joseph Schlitz Brewing Company, and Pabst Brewing Company, Coors fell to number five as the seventh-ranked Miller Brewing Company surged into second place in the late 1970s. Formerly independent, Miller had been acquired a few years earlier by Philip Morris, Inc. and had been given needed fixed investment, working capital, and marketing expertise for growth. Coors fell to sixth in 1981 as Heileman Brewing Company expanded.

In late 1981, the number four producer, Heileman Brewing Company, attempted to take over Schlitz, which was in difficulty with declining sales and profits. Schlitz agreed to the proposed takeover. However, the Antitrust Division of the U.S. Justice Department was displeased with the additional ownership concentration that the deal would bring to the brewing industry and with the potential for significantly reduced competition. When the Justice Department announced that it would file suit to block the acquisition, it was canceled. This government action surprised many people, because in a much larger and more important merger about two months earlier, Du Pont acquired Conoco. The reason for the different government posture was that without the Du Pont action Conoco, an important oil, natural gas, and coal producer, would have been taken over by Seagram, a Canadian corporation. In mid-1982 seventh-ranked Stroh Brewing Company took over Schlitz. Thus the rank order became Anheuser-Busch, Miller, Stroh-Schlitz, Heileman, Pabst, Coors.

Heileman, of La Crosse, Wisconsin, was one of the fastest growing companies in the American economy, but Schlitz would have been its first nationally distributed brand. In a unique strategy, Heileman operated a network of regional brewers offering 30 brands. Among its better-known brands were Carling Black Label and National Bohemian along the East Coast, Rainier in the Northwest, and Blatz and Old Style in the Middle West and parts of the East.

There were several other important companies. A fast-growing organization was 12th-ranked Pittsburgh Brewing Company, an independent regional business that made Iron City brand. Its highly regarded president had recently been hired by Schlitz to be its chief executive. Other aggressive and growing regional companies included Olympia, Genessee, and Schmidt.

Many beer drinkers preferred to consume regional beers for various reasons, such as perceived unique taste, desire to enjoy local color, a wish to support local business, or avoidance of beers that were thought to be mass-appeal, mass-produced goods. However, it was well understood in the industry and had been demonstrated experimentally that most beer consumers could not recognize their favorite brands in blindfold tests that compared several brands.

Total demand for beer in the United States was growing, but the rate of growth had declined considerably in recent years. Physical volume (in barrels) was expected to rise about 4 percent per year during the middle and late 1980s. "Light" beers already accounted for 14 percent of beer sold, and the demand for such beers was increasing about twice as rapidly as for beer in general. Among American brewers only Anheuser-Busch had made any serious attempts to market abroad.

Adolph Coors Company was eager to improve its sales, profits, and industry rank. Heileman sales were 16 percent higher than Coors, and Pabst sales only 1 percent higher than Coors. A Coors goal was to take over fourth place and secure a firm hold on it. Schlitz brand was in severe difficulty for several reasons, among them a change in the "recipe" or brewing formula. Pabst was also considered vulnerable. An old established company based in Milwaukee, Pabst had been experiencing high turnover among its managers and sluggish sales and profits for several years. An offer by Pabst to buy Schlitz for a larger sum of money than Heileman proposed was rejected by the Schlitz board of directors. Much of the business public and the industry saw this action as a slap in the face for Pabst and commentary on how Pabst's future was perceived. Nevertheless, Pabst began to consider buying Olympia, which had 3.2 percent of the market.

For Coors to climb to fourth place and lock in that rank without marketing nationwide would be an extraordinary accomplishment, if it could be done at all. Such a feat would require a deep penetration of the existing markets and exceptionally high brand loyalty among consumers. Although fourth place probably could be gained within a reasonable time by cutting prices and using advertising at a saturation level, that would probably not increase profits (and might decrease them), so that was not a feasible policy option.

The Coors Company

Coors was the only brewer in the nation's top six that was not national in scope. This organization, based in Golden, Colorado, a suburb of Denver, distributed its output in 20 states in the West, Southwest, and parts of the South and Midwest. Sales were $801 million in 1981, giving Coors a 7.4 percent share of the market, down from 8 percent in 1977.

This company operated only one brewery, but this facility in Golden was the largest brewing plant in the United States. Golden was reasonably centrally located, considering the present geographical outreach of the

firm's sales. But in terms of the population density of the market currently served, the facility was not centrally located. Coors planned eventually to increase the capacity of this brewery by about two thirds. The company was partially integrated up-channel in that it produced its own bottles and cans. Moreover, it supplied itself with natural gas and coal from its own fields and mines.

Founded in 1873, Adolph Coors Company was now managed by the founder's grandsons, William and Joseph Coors, and Joseph's sons, Jeffrey and Peter Coors. William Coors was chairman of the board, Joseph Coors was president, and Peter and Jeffrey Coors were essentially unspecialized vice presidents. William was 67; Jeffrey, 37; and Peter, 36 years of age. Peter, who held a master's degree in business administration, was the only member of the family who had done graduate study in management. The family owned 86 percent of the corporate stock, and the remaining 14 percent of the shares of stock carried no voting rights. The Coors family was close-knit, inward looking, and conservative. This philosophical stance and personality characteristic had been reinforced by a family tragedy in 1960, when Joseph's other son, Adolph III, was kidnapped and murdered.

The company was rethinking its philosophies of marketing and general management. Some officials, including Peter Coors, described the company as arrogant about itself and its output. Ideas that did not originate within the family were not even considered. The firm was frequently referred to by outsiders and workers as "baronial" and "feudal" and "a nineteenth-century industrial dynasty." A new senior vice president for marketing, Robert A. Rechholtz, age 44, had just come from Schlitz, where he held the same title.

However, allegations of rigid inflexibility were somewhat exaggerated. It was worth noting that Coors was the first brewer to adopt aluminum cans, now widely used in the industry. Management admitted on the other hand, that its improved Press-Tab II, a can that was environmentally appealing to the company's predominantly Western market because it had no pop-top, was a mistake because the average person found it impossible to open.

Management's old-fashioned views and egotism had been temporarily reinforced by a fad occurrence on college campuses during the mid-1970s. Coors beer was the "in" beer among millions of educated young adults. This voguish product was carried long distances outside the normal trade territory by students. An informal distribution network arose among enthusiasts, and few college parties were complete without Coors. The bubble burst by 1977.

Labor relations in recent years had been stormy and harmful to Coors. In 1977, Local 366 of the Brewery Workers Union struck the company's plant and was joined in a boycott by several other groups opposed to the company's policies and practices and to the Coors family's conservative politics. The effect was especially strong in California, the company's largest market. Increased advertising by Miller and Anheuser-Busch simultaneously affected Coors, so it was not known how much effect the unions had on sales. Coors' share of the important California market dropped from 40 percent to 20 percent, recovering to only 24 percent by 1981. To the consternation of the labor movement, about two thirds of Coors employees returned to work soon after the strike began. In December 1977 the workers overwhelmingly rejected Local 366 as their bargaining agent and the federal government accordingly decertified the union. However, infuriated union leaders in other states plus some radical left political groups kept the boycott alive. The Coors fad on college campuses might have lasted longer if it had not been for the boycott call. Students in particular embraced the boycott, even though the Coors workers had overwhelmingly voted out

their union. Many students were also angry about the Coors family's generous donations to right-wing political groups.

Coors had always been production oriented. It concentrated on perfect uniformity and turned out only one beer, a medium-priced product made in an unusual process that avoided pasteurization because the family was convinced that heat caused deterioration. However, in 1978 the company belatedly introduced a second product, Coors Light. Some family members, especially Jeffrey Coors, admitted to being furious that chemists in the organization had been secretly conducting some experimental work leading to the development of a light beer for the company. Management had previously told them not to do so.

The primary competitor was Miller Lite, a successful brand that came out several years earlier in response to consumer consciousness about feelings of fullness and the high calorie count in beers. However, the new Coors Light had 105 calories per 12-ounce serving, versus 96 for Miller Lite. Coors regular beer had 145 calories. Sales figures showed that Coors Light was doing better against Miller Lite than were some other light brands that had been launched in the industry. Miller Light held about 57 percent of the low-calorie market. The second and third largest brands were Michelob Light and Natural Light, both made by Anheuser-Busch. In 1982 Anheuser-Busch also introduced Budweiser Light nationally, after 11 months of test marketing, and supported it with heavy advertising. Natural Light was in danger of being deleted from the product line because of low sales and profits.

In 1980 Coors began a lengthy test market of a superpremium beer tentatively named Herman Joseph's 1868 to honor the year that founder Adolph Coors arrived in the United States as a young stowaway. Following the test market it was planned to roll out the new product, introducing it in several cycles of a few states each until the 20-state market was covered. The new superpremium product was intended to compete with Miller's Lowenbrau, Anheuser-Busch's Michelob, and Heineken. Coors also had in test markets a premium Irish beer labeled George Killian's, under license from a French brewer, Société Brasserie Pelforth. In addition, Coors began discussions with a Belgian brewer concerning the possibility of importing Stella Artois brand.

Imported beers accounted for about 3 percent of the American market, up from .6 percent in 1971. Heineken from Holland was the leading import. It held about 40 percent of this segment of the American market, and 200 other brands accounted for the rest. Americans bought foreign beer for three major reasons: prestige, variety, and the generally heavier, stronger, and more distinctive taste of nearly all imports. Most foreign tourists in the United States and a small percentage of Americans regarded U.S. beers as caramel-colored carbonated water. American commentators and writers on food and beverages generally agreed that American beers were bland by prevailing world standards and were rather similar to each other.

Until recently Coors spent little on advertising. In the early 1970s it budgeted about $3 million annually, but this figure grew to more than $30 million in the early 1980s. Expressed as a ratio to barrels of beer produced, this figure was still about 20 percent per barrel below the advertising outlays for Anheuser-Busch and Miller. Coors had always relied on a conservative in-house advertising department to a greater extent than most other brewers. The company retained a larger national advertising agency under contract for at least media relations but would not delegate much to the agency. For the light beer, Peter Coors was able to switch the advertising to Ted Bates & Company, a major national agency.

Coors took an option to buy a large parcel of rural land near Elkton, Virginia, if it should decide to go nationwide soon. However, the management was philosophically opposed to borrowing money for any purpose. Expansion money had always come from the profits of the organization. If significant expansion, especially nationwide, were to come, there might well have to be capital investments in storage facilities for finished products. The Golden brewery was designed to place output directly in transit toward customers, not to hold any inventory.

SECTION 2

Analyzing the Situation:
Market and Competitor Analyses

*T*he previous section introduced basic concepts in marketing planning. This section delves deeper into two specific areas that account for the majority of attention in a *situation analysis:* (1) target-market analysis and (2) competitive vigilance. These areas have been singled out because they are almost invariably the primary determinants of a company's marketing strategies. There are, of course, several other environmental factors that influence a company's operations; further, on occasion marketing strategy is dictated by legal constraints or other factors. But vast numbers of marketing strategies are predicated on the central tenet of the marketing concept, which advocates satisfying the customer well enough to inspire brand loyalty. Furthermore, most companies explicitly position their marketing strategies against those competitors who have the greatest advantage in the target market.

The marketing concept dictates that a company must consider its market's characteristics of central importance when deciding on strategies and tactics. Inspection of the generic market for any good or service quickly gives rise to the awareness of segments, or pockets, of customers who are uniquely identifiable, and who themselves constitute target markets. Therefore, most companies use specialization by selecting specific segments and competing for market share within them. The factors commonly used to segment markets are similarly valuable as monitors of change within markets. For example, demographic characteristics shift over time and provide tangible barometers of subsequent changes in the preferences of consumers. Lifestyles of consumers evolve, and the wise company will forecast and anticipate when its target moves even a notch along a relevant psychographic dimension. By comparing annual customer surveys to baselines, changes in tastes, shopping preferences, evaluative criteria, benefits sought, or even price, sensitivity can be determined. In short, the successful company constantly monitors and anticipates changes in the vital signs of its target markets.

On the other side of the need for a system that tracks changes in consumers is an equally pressing need for a system that watches competitors. This competitive watchdog system evolves logically from the consumer-monitoring system. It soon becomes evident from marketing research results that consumers tend to limit their choices to a few competing brands, each of which is uniquely positioned in their minds. By identifying those competitors vying for the customer's preferences, a company can begin to learn their strengths and weaknesses and ultimately to exploit competitors' biases and complacencies.

Consumer surveys assist a company in understanding how competitors are perceived by prospective buyers; that is, they profile the images of competing brands. Moreover, a number of other sources of information are available. Annual reports, news articles, industry synopses, test markets, advertising copy, former employees, and even rumors all assist in compiling a file that can be used to profile the predilections of specific competitors. The payoffs of such files are less easily seen than are those for a consumer-monitoring system, but they are just as crucial. Increasingly, corporate competition is compared to a military confrontation: in wartime, an accurate intelligence function almost always determines the outcomes of major battles.

The benefits of good market- and competitor-monitoring systems cannot be overemphasized. First, there is a guarantee that the company will be able to anticipate changes in customers' circumstances and respond to them with optimal timing. Second, the creation and adoption of consumer monitoring assures a company that it will have a strong customer orientation. Third, sensing consumer shifts, along with knowing competitors' strengths and weaknesses, considerably reduces the uncertainties involved in estimating competitors' responses to marketing strategies or tactics. Finally, with a reasonable understanding of how competitors are perceived by customers and knowledge of how aggressive particular competitors tend to be, a company can be forewarned of possible heavy losses before it uses alternative strategies.

About the Readings

The first of our two conceptual readings includes an in-depth analysis of the senior citizen market segment. In this reading, the author explains that demographic shifts have given rise to a large group of consumers whose particular needs for goods and services distinguish it not as an ailing and dependent segment, but rather as an energetic and vital target market for astute companies. Professor Gelb describes the many marketing opportunities that follow from accurate knowledge of this market. In the next article, the product-portfolio method of analyzing a company's product line is expanded to multinational marketing situations. Explicit in this article is the warning about American businesspeople's underestimation of foreign competitors' marketing abilities, as well as our tendency to see everything in American terms.

The first of the four company readings asks if Americans will buy an *Ohio* Honda. This article has an interesting history. Japanese products have evolved from what were first perceived as cheap imitations to goods that evoke an image of frontier technology and high quality. Now, faced with international trade barriers and economic realities, Honda is producing its cars in the United States. Will the stamp "Made in USA" tarnish Japan's foreign-quality image? Immediately following this article on ground transportation is one on air travel. It portrays a marketing success story springing directly from market and competitor analyses. The People Express Airline found a gaping hole in the air-passenger market and targeted the price-sensitive, convenience-insensitive market segment. President Gerald Gitner's marketing commitment permeates this strategy, which thrives on high volume and low price demand, rendering competing airlines' high fixed costs and traditional approaches no contest to People Express. From air travel, our attention shifts to the supermarket industry where Kroger is the recently crowned king. Kroger has embarked on a vertical integration strategy and operates with stringent performance standards for individual stores. The reading emphasizes Kroger's consumer orientation, which stresses surveys and consumer-reaction tests. By valuing innovation and taking an aggressive competitive stance, Kroger dominates its local markets. Finally, we look at a new food product stimulated by market changes. In this reading, surveys are described that identify the demographic characteristics associated with the increased desire for "natural" foods. Affluence and an affinity for ethnic foods mean that soybean-based products, most notably tofu, will be significant products for dieters and other market segments ■

Conceptual Readings

Discovering the 65 + Consumer
Betsy D. Gelb

So far, visible marketing efforts directed at consumers 65 and older are the exception rather than the rule. However, it seems likely that more attention will be paid to this age group and that many industries can benefit from a new perspective concerning the 65 + market segment.

There are two powerful reasons for the expectation of new interest in targeting goods and services to *seniors,* the term now in vogue. One reason is short-term profitability: seniors have dramatically high—and increasing—purchasing power. The second reason stems from societal pressures. Business is now being asked to contribute to a "better image" for older Americans, just as it has been expected to better the image of racial and ethnic minorities and of women.

These two issues are, in fact, mutually supportive. People with money have two kinds of power, direct buying power and indirect political influence. Marketers have always responded to perceived buying power. Now they are beginning to see that a skillful response can be profitable and can also improve attitudes toward business and their particular organization, among society at large and among retirement-age Americans in particular. I should point out that "retirement-age" consumers are being defined here as 65 or older despite the fact that mandatory retirement now is illegal before age 70. Many working people still retire at 65 because full social security benefits become available at that time. Others who retire earlier or later or who never have worked for pay still see 65 as a milestone because medicare benefits and double income tax exemptions begin at that age.

Marketers and Seniors

What precedents exist for targeting a special marketing effort to a particular demographic group? The idea is far from new. Based on societal pressures and on managers' recognition that profitable market segments were being overlooked, the past 20 years have brought visibility to minorities and also to women who are not housewives. Marketing efforts have been designed explicitly to welcome women buyers to product categories previously identified with males (for example, tires) or to welcome male buyers to product categories traditionally associated with females (for example, groceries). The basic principle has been to communicate to a specific category of potential buyers that the advertised goods or services are for "people like you." In the general case, that objective is accomplished by media choice, message (for example, "Attention Ms. Salesperson"), illustration of product users, special pricing or product features for a particular category, or (more likely) some combination of all of these strategies.[1]

When age-group targeting has taken place, however, the category singled out most often has been consumers under 30. A "young image" for goods and services has been seen as desirable for several reasons: the product will be associated with youth by older adults who want to remain young; the product will appeal to younger people who have more years ahead to use it; and the marketing effort will have greater impact among the young because they are not yet set in their brand preferences.[2]

An unintended consequence of such targeting, however, has been to antagonize "pro-age" (their term) activists. Their complaints parallel what business has heard for at least two decades from racial minorities and women. Briefly stated, the argument is as follows:

■ Respect for a group follows from particular kinds of portrayal in the media. Advertising offers an opportunity to portray members of a population group as visible and as sought after by marketers (therefore powerful, at least economically).

■ Self-respect for any group follows from respect by others in society. This self-respect inspires the willingness to take actions (for example, to reenter the job market) that lead to economic power—and therefore lead to further societal respect.

The prediction being offered here is that business will respond to this argument, and that such response will be a significant trend in the 1980s. Business is doing more than just responding to societal pressures, however; as was true of ethnic minorities and women, managers will perceive the profit potential of this new group. There are three major reasons that seniors are becoming an increasingly attractive market:

■ This is a large and fast-growing segment, currently increasing at a rate approximately double that of the general population.[3]

■ They have purchasing power beyond their income. Per-capita assets are highest of any age group, and they are willing to "dis-save."[4]

■ Previous assumptions that older people do not identify with their age segment are being questioned.

I want to examine in greater detail the senior market and also the societal arguments for explicit marketing attention to seniors. The discussion is intended to serve two purposes. First, it can help any manager to appraise both the profitability and social responsibility arguments, to see whether they apply to his or her organization. Second, the discussion can increase the effectiveness of any contemplated targeting effort. For example, to understand what pro-age groups are trying to achieve is an obvious prerequisite to efforts to meet their demands.

Examining the Market

A first step is to describe this market of Americans 65 or older. This age category includes 11 percent of the U.S. population now; it is expected to be 13 percent by the year 2000. Women outnumber men 3 to 2.[5] Fully 95 percent of the individuals in this segment live outside institutions, and only 10 percent of those live with children.[6]

Differences between 65+ Americans and other adults are fewer than often supposed. Health is poorer, but only an estimated 15 percent need special health or social services.[7] More common is sensory deterioration—gradually poorer eyesight, hearing, sense of smell, taste, and touch.[8] Ability to learn does not deteriorate, however, if the older person is allowed to control the pace of learning.[9] Household size is smaller in this age category, but the greatest decrease in household size occurs much earlier, when children leave home. Full-time employment is lower, leading to more seasonal migration (wintering in warm climates) and to earlier bedtimes, yet purchasing power is higher than for younger groups. What distinguishes the later years is the combination of discretionary time and money.

It is erroneous to assume that seniors have low purchasing power. In 1977, per capita income of households headed by persons 65 or older was only 7 percent less than that of the population as a whole. A study by the Congressional Budget Office the same year estimated that the inclusion of government benefits, such as medicare and double tax exemptions, as income equivalents would reduce the number of officially "poor old families" to about 6 percent of the elderly population.[10] The myth of the elderly poor probably persists because marketers see household income data, not per capita income data. Per-household income in this age category does indeed look meager until smaller household size is recognized as a confounding factor.

In this age category, however, income is an overly conservative measure of buying potential. This is the age group with the highest accumulation of assets. Furthermore, there is evidence that, in response to inflation, "retired" will increasingly mean "drawing a pension and working part time at a new job." A nationwide survey research firm reported in 1979 that more than half of all workers wanted to continue working past 65 and nearly half of the retired wished they were still working.[11]

Having been reassured about numbers and purchasing power, managers must next be concerned about the kind of response seniors have to age-group-targeted advertising. A marketer might ask, in effect, whether retirement-age buyers exhibit "gray pride" or "gray shame."

A trend toward the former, toward pride in age identification, has been observed. It is believed to be a product of senior centers, of the women's movement, and of pro-age lobby groups like the Gray Panthers and the American Association of Retired Persons.[12] There is also evidence that, like other groups, 65+ consumers are attracted to marketers who appear to want their business. An attitude study of shoppers 60 or older found 57 percent saying they would visit a hypothetical store with a "Welcome, Seniors" sign in the window, the same proportion who said they would be attracted by ads claiming low prices.[13]

Furthermore, the 65+ group represents the most persuasible age segment, based on their answers to questions in a survey intended to isolate this dimension of self-image.[14] Also, they are, more than other age groups, "conspicuous consumers," who seek approval

from friends and see brands as relevant to that goal.[15] They react negatively to marketing gestures which stereotype the elderly as poor, according to one study. Therefore, the study concluded, a senior citizen discount should be presented as a reward for longtime patronage, not as an implication that older Americans are too poor to pay regular prices.[16]

Marketing to seniors can be as socially useful as it is profitable. Bernice Neugarten, for example, believes that "just the reality of having more old people around" has already improved attitudes toward them.[17] If she is right, having them around in print ads and television commercials may well improve the attitudes even further. There are economic benefits in such attitude changes—for example, the greater likelihood that an employer will see a 65-year-old employee as a candidate for promotion, not just as a time server. Since delaying retirement eases the strain on the social security system, it can be argued convincingly that society benefits when older workers find meaningful challenges in their current jobs or in new ones, and consequently stay in the labor force.

Marketing which is visibly directed to 65+ consumers may also communicate to them and to others that this age segment has substantial resources. If luxury housing developments join arthritis remedies in courting the 65+ consumer, a reminder of the purchasing power of seniors reaches everyone.

Advertising which uses seniors as models and/or spokespersons also has the potential to show their diversity. According to Neugarten:

> The American stereotype of the aged is based on the needy aged; it doesn't resemble the majority of old people, nor are old people a homogeneous group. The stereotype has it that as people age, they become more and more like one another. In truth, they become less and less alike. If you look at people's lives, they're like the spreading of a fan. The longer people live, the greater the differences between them. A group of 18-year-olds is more alike than a group of 60-year-olds. To say

a man is 60 years old tells you nothing about him except that he has lived for 60 years.[18]

Given this degree of diversity among 60 year olds, it is hardly surprising that the difference between someone 65 and someone 85 can be awesome. Thus Neugarten distinguishes between the "young old"—those under 75 or healthy and active beyond that age—and the "old old," whose infirmities create impressions of dependency which are inaccurately projected onto those who are 65 to 75. Since it may be assumed that advertising would more often picture the "young old," if only because there are twice as many of them, a more realistic picture of the vigor of many seniors should emerge.

Beyond the question of image, there are direct benefits to the welfare of older Americans which can flow from directing marketing dollars to them.

■ Astute marketers will use research to learn how older people view and use their products before committing significant budgets to this audience. Better product values, as the 65+ segment perceives value, will result.

■ Products which already would serve the retirement-age segment well, if their benefits were known, will in fact become better known. These range from special condominiums to magazines with large type for the "old old." For the "young old" these products include mopeds, special cosmetics, shared jobs, and travel packages, plus educational opportunities running the gamut from fun courses to colleges for seniors. Both the "young old" and the "old old" would benefit from mental health services, financial services, cable TV instruction, home care and maintenance services, and medium-sized restaurant meals at bargain prices at 5 p.m. Placing a storefront tax assistance, legal, or dental practice next to the social security office building, for instance, is the kind of targeting that can benefit marketers and also their 65+ customers.

■ Marketing aimed at people who have retired may also help to meet some of the seniors' social needs once met by socializing at the workplace. Clearly, social integration has value to the elderly; one study has concluded that the degree of socializing affects their perceptions of unfair tactics in the marketplace and the lack of it prompts action in their own behalf, such as complaining.[19]

■ Media vehicles and programming that could be useful for seniors will prosper. The audience exists, particularly for television programming; in the quintile that watches the most television, the 65+ segment has 172 individuals for every 100 in the adult population as a whole.[20] They read as much in the newspapers as other adult categories, and print media are particularly effective for imparting information to them, for two reasons. First, the pace of stimulus presentation affects learning for seniors, and their continued ability to match the performance of other adults depends upon their ability to control the speed with which information is presented.[21] Furthermore, the preferences of 65+ consumers appear to shift with age, from entertainment to information.[22] Such a shift explains the success of such age-specific magazines as *Prime Time, 50 Plus, Modern Maturity,* and publications of the retired federal employees organization and the National Retired Teachers Association.

The material cited is obviously not all a marketer needs to know. Data are extremely spotty, however, and recommendations on how to apply it are correspondingly limited.

Even if better data were on hand today, however, they would be rapidly out of date as more people, with all the diversity which Neugarten refers to, reach 65. Some 4,000 Americans do so daily, replacing the 3,000 who die. Even if knowledge of this age group of 25 million people were extensive, therefore, it would need to be kept current. Furthermore, a continuing problem is the impossibility in the short term of knowing which findings about 65 + consumers are a function of age and which simply reflect the conditions and values predominating when the current group was growing up. If these cohort-specific factors are more significant, seniors even 5 or 10 years from now may differ from today's seniors in many respects.

A second limitation of this discussion has been the frequent oversimplifications which have ignored the differences between "young old" and "old old." To say, for example, that seniors are disproportionately likely to watch television is to gloss over the cohort-by-cohort differences; all-day viewers of 85 may outweigh occasional viewers of 65 as an average figure is calculated.

Keeping these limitations in mind, however, the overall conclusion remains: marketing to seniors can be expected to increase and can be more effective as managers become more knowledgeable about the 65 + group. In addition, marketing efforts directed to this group can help both business and society—two institutions which are often portrayed as adversaries. In reality, no conflict is necessary—managerial decisions can benefit an organization and the society of which it is a part.

Notes

1. Edward W. J. Faison, *Advertising: A Behavioral Approach for Managers* (New York: John Wiley & Sons, 1980).

2. Fred D. Reynolds and William D. Wells, *Consumer Behavior* (New York: McGraw-Hill, 1977). Chapt. 4.

3. Carole B. Allan, "The Older Consumer: The Time is Now," in *Aging: Agenda for the Eighties*, ed. Julienne Pincau Hubbard (Washington, D.C.: Government Research Corporation, 1979), pp. 35–40.

4. Robert C. Atchley, *The Social Forces in Later Life* (Belmont, Calif.: Wadsworth, 1972), p. 123.

5. Barbara Boyle Terry, "The Demographics of Aging: Implications for Pension Policy," in Hubbard, *Aging: Agenda for the Eighties*, pp. 21–26.

6. Fabian Linden, "Consumer Markets: Midlife and Beyond," *Across the Board*, December 1976, pp. 2–3.

7. Bernice Neugarten, interviewed by Elizabeth Hall, "Acting One's Age: New Rules for the Old," *Psychology Today*, April 1980, pp. 66–80.

8. Leon Pastalan, "How the Elderly Negotiate Their Environment." Paper presented at "Environment for the Aged" (San Juan, P. R.: December 17–20, 1971, University of Michigan Institute of Gerontology).

9. Lynn W. Phillips and Brian Sternthal, "Age Differences in Information Processing: A Perspective on the Aged Consumer," *Journal of Marketing Research*, November 1977, pp. 444–57.

10. Allan, "The Time Is Now," p. 37.

11. "Most Want to Work Past Retirement Age," *Houston Post*, March 1, 1979, p. 4B.

12. James E. Trela, "Some Political Consequences of Senior Center and Other Old Age Group Memberships," *The Gerontologist*, Summer 1971, pp. 118–23.

13. Betsy D. Gelb, "Exploring the Gray Market Segment," *MSU Business Topics*, Spring 1978, pp. 41–46.

14. Simmons Market Research Bureau, Inc., *The 1980 Study of Media and Markets*, Multi-Media Audiences: Adults (New York: SMRB, 1980), p. 0398.

15. J. G. Towle and C. R. Martin, "The Elderly Consumer: One Segment of Many?" in *The Elderly Consumer*, ed. F. E. Waddell (Columbia, Md.: The Human Ecology Center, Antioch College, 1976), pp. 232–42.

16. Gelb, "Gray Market Segment," pp. 41–46.

17. Neugarten, "New Rules for the Old," pp. 66–80.

18. Neugarten, "New Rules for the Old," p. 78.

19. K. Lawther, "Social Integration and the Elderly Consumer: Unfairness Awareness, Complaint Actions and Information Usage," in *AMA Educators Conference Proceedings*, ed. S. C. Jain (Chicago: American Marketing Association, 1978), pp. 341–45.

20. Simmons, *Media and Markets*, p. 0464.

21. Phillips and Sternthal, "Perspective on the Aged Consumer," pp. 444–57.

22. Wilbur Schramm, "Aging and Mass Communications," in *Aging and Society*, ed. M. Riley and J. Riley (New York: Russell Sage Foundation, 1969), pp. 352–75.

Is the International Cash Cow Really a Prize Heifer?
William L. Shanklin and John K. Ryans, Jr.

A growing number of U.S.-based multinational corporations (MNCs) are reporting higher percentage returns on sales in foreign markets than in domestic ones. Further, in absolute dollar terms, more and more of these firms are producing higher foreign than domestic operating income. And many U.S. multinationals now appear to be relying on their foreign operations to bail out their poor domestic performances. Ford Motor Company in recent years has used this approach, but is by no means alone.

A close study of the 1979 annual reports of some 100 major U.S. corporations demonstrated their increasing reliance on overseas markets. Of this group, 65 firms reported that more than one fifth of their net sales took place abroad. Forty-six of the companies had higher percentage returns in overseas than in domestic markets. For 12 of them, foreign operating income actually exceeded that earned in the United States.

At first glance, this seems like good news, coming as it does when the U.S. economy is soft. But unless the successes of international operations are placed in proper perspective, reported results can be misleading and, in fact, can endanger a firm's long-term prospect. Too often a foreign star—a prize heifer— may be treated as a cash cow with the result that hope for its continued growth and improvement is lost. Management's temptation to deplete a promising foreign market or product is especially great in the short run as the firm seeks to overcome current losses in a rapidly deteriorating domestic market.

This article considers traditional product-portfolio analysis and suggests how this valuable strategic planning approach, if specifically adapted to take account of the domestic/ international dichotomy, can help to insure

that the international side of a multinational gets the attention and resources it needs to be a major contributor in the long term. International portfolio analysis can assist corporate policymakers in firms succeeding abroad and faltering at home from forming misleading conclusions about overall company performance. We try to show how multinational management can avoid the mistake of managing an overseas star as a corporate cash cow and transforming it into a problem child.

The Integrated Product Portfolio

Under the original product-portfolio concept developed by the Boston Consulting Group, firms analyze the cash flow potential of their various products. Each product is seen as a star, cash cow, problem child, or dog, based on its individual market share and growth possibilities.

With a simple two-by-two schema, this widely accepted approach to strategic market planning has allowed management to identify a particular product's role in its firm's product mix. The terms used to identify the quadrants of the matrix have become a fundamental addition to business terminology. Still for our purposes here, it is useful to review briefly the basic concepts embodied in the product-portfolio approach.

Both growth and market share are quantifiable. And the products are rated as being either high or low on these measures of potential, as shown in the accompanying figure.

Growth has been referred to as a proxy for the product's stage in the life cycle.[1] Those still in the stage of ascendancy are felt to have high growth opportunity, while those leveling off or showing some decline, that is, mature products, have low growth opportunity. A basic assumption of this analysis is that a high

Reprinted with permission from the March–April 1981 issue of *Business Horizons.* © 1981 *Business Horizons.*

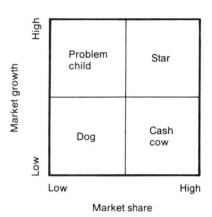

growth product requires significant cash inputs to continue its expansion, while low growth potential suggests excess cash flow which could be used by other products.

Market share has been the easier of the two concepts for most firms to measure and requires a comparison with competitors. Those products that hold a relatively low share of the total market, regardless of market size, are considered low market-share products. Again, there is an underlying cash flow assumption: market share must be bought and high market share requires significant investment. Multinational firms often have more difficulty in analyzing their products than do those firms operating domestically. In particular, it is often harder to make market-share estimates for some of their overseas markets.

While the measures employed are relatively straightforward, it must be recognized that firms may view the same data differently. What may be seen as a low market share for one firm, may in fact be seen as high for another. Recently, one writer suggested that a growth rate of 10 percent or more is high, while parity with the market leader is the "cut-line" for market share.[2] This interpreta-

tion ignores the international arena where a firm may see itself as having a high market share if it has only 7 or 8 percent of all its major Western European markets.

Each of the four cells in the product-portfolio matrix has its own particular definition in terms of cash flow.

■ *Star* has the best of both worlds, a high or dominant market share and continued growth potential. It is assumed to be essential that to achieve stardom, the product's earnings are to be plowed back and not used as a net producer of cash flow.

■ *Cash cow* has probably been a star of the past and has reached its potential. Its cash flow is used to prop up the problem child or to further R&D efforts. The assumption is that the amount of resources needed to maintain the cash cow's market share is less than the revenue it produces and that there is little growth possibility remaining.

■ *Problem child* is often an enigma to the firm's management. Products in this category face a growing market and yet have achieved limited market share themselves. While additional investment may be warranted, the product itself may not be competitive or its market segment correctly identified.

■ *Dog* is appropriately named. This quadrant contains those products that have neither a dominant market share nor a rapidly growing market. Depending upon the product's life-cycle stage and variable product costs, it still may be able to produce a steady, if not spectacular, cash flow. In other instances, the product may be ripe for divestment or abandonment.

Since this product portfolio matrix was introduced, a number of product strategies have become associated with a product's classification. For example, once designated as a cash cow, a product is likely to receive little funding except for necessary modifications and improvements. The strategy recommended for the cash cow is "harvesting" or, as Kotler recently described it, "a strategic management decision to reduce the investment in a business entity in the hope of cutting costs and/or improving cash flow."[3] In other words, a deliberate milking.

While the basis for product analysis seems quite plausible, it now appears that the way the MNC interprets its overseas activities may lead to possible misinterpretation of its products' performances. This is especially true in two instances. First, if a product has peaked domestically but is still in the growth stage abroad, the firm is likely to place it entirely in the cash-cow category. Second, if the product is entirely produced and developed by an overseas subsidiary, the firm may misinterpret a peaking in one market as being representative of its overseas potential.

An even greater concern, however, is the premature sacrificing of overseas opportunities to cover domestic disaster. Regardless of what organizational structure the MNC employs, it is still possible to isolate the contribution of the firm's overseas products and submit them to separate product-portfolio analysis. Where this "harvesting" of overseas operations appears especially evident is in those firms having separate international divisions or geographic structures. Here it seems that it is the international area, which in many firms is continuing to provide profitable operations, that is feeling the brunt of domestic concerns. There are, of course, circumstances under which the apparent long-term sacrifice of potential is justifiable, but it is never justifiable to misread an overseas product's potential.

Early Warning Indicators

There are several incisive, diagnostic questions that top management in a U.S.-based multinational can ask of itself to ascertain whether the company is headed for trouble because it is erroneously handling foreign markets or products as though they were cash cows. These queries all seek to get at how the MNC has been, is now, and ideally should be managing its domestic markets and products vis-à-vis its foreign ones. The questions require top management to make both judgmental and quantitative assessments. Answers that are not in accordance with conventional management practice and theory of portfolio management are probably ominous and valuable early warning indicators that trouble lies ahead if changes of a strategic and philosophic nature are not made.

Management can take a useful first step by asking itself to judge how it views philosophically its domestic and international businesses. Is the international component an integral part of the total enterprise, or is it merely a profitable stepchild? A reliable clue to the answer is the quality of management that the MNC has been sending to its international operations.

Is the international organization mostly a training ground for executives who, once they prove their merit and gain experience, will be returned to a domestic assignment? Or is the international part of the business a dumping ground for executives nearing retirement or for those whom the company wants to relocate out of "more important" areas because of doubts about their managerial ability to function on the "faster track" of the domestic scene? If these kinds of conditions prevail, it is a clue that the domestic side of the business is thought as the major leagues and the foreign counterpart the minor league where unproven, or old, or less competent executives are farmed out. The major/minor league dichotomy is significant because how a component—domestic/international—is thought of by top management is also normally how it is treated when it comes to resource allocation.

Management assuredly would want to look closely at the executive assignments to and from international operations and over a period of, say, the previous five years. Of particular concern is whether the international sector of the multinational had greater managerial turnover than the domestic sector and whether the overall caliber of executives who were assigned internationally was comparable to that of managers assigned domestically.

Quantitative indicators can also be adduced and used critically by top management in determining whether the domestic operations are being unduly emphasized at the expense of the international ones. Management needs to determine whether any of its low or negative growth and profit domestic markets are being artificially propped up by cash flows from more profitable international markets. An affirmative answer to either of the two following questions may very well indicate that a product sold in a foreign market is being milked when, in fact, it is not really a cash cow.

First, is there any rapidly growing international market in which the multinational has had a high share and profits and in which the market is continuing to grow while the MNC's share shrinks? If this is, in fact, the case, it follows that management has an early warning signal coming through loud and clear that a star performer needs attention—and quickly. Only further probing can reveal whether the star is on the decline because of forces beyond the control of management or because the market is undeservedly getting cash cow handling from domestic headquarters.

Second, is any growing international market in which the company presently has a low but promising share of market being cultivated financially and with competent management so that it eventually becomes a high-growth/high-share market for the company? If the answer is no, but there are sound reasons why the market is not being strongly pursued, then it is time for corporate management to think seriously about cutting their losses with

this problem child and withdrawing from the market entirely. But if prospects are bright for making the problem child into a star through additional resource allocations, but management's cash-cow treatment has precluded such a transformation, then a signal for immediate action is unmistakable.

An example of a counterproductive cash-cow treatment of a once growing and profitable international business operation is provided by Ford Motor Company. In 1974, Ford hired then-BMW executive Robert Lutz as chief executive of its West German operations—Ford's largest subsidiary. Lutz was extremely aggressive in acquiring a consumer oriented image for Ford through such notable and innovative measures as West Germany's first one-year auto guarantee. Between 1974, when the highly capable Lutz arrived, and 1976, when he was transferred to Ford's European truck operations, the company's market share in West Germany soared from 10 to 15 percent. By 1980, four years after Lutz's departure, market share had ebbed to just over 9 percent. In an article titled "West Germany, A Ford Cash Cow Has Less For Its Parent," *Business Week* said:

> That slide [in market share] not only means that Ford of Germany will be less of a cash cow for its financially needy Dearborn (Michigan) parent, but it also means that the subsidiary may lose for good the market gains it scored in the mid-1970s. . . . Lutz's successor . . . is not only less colorful but also struggling, Ford insiders say, with demands from Dearborn for cash to help headquarters meet the costly U.S. standards for pollution control and gas mileage. As a result, model innovations for the Taurus and Escort have been delayed by Ford of Germany. By contrast, Volkswagen has introduced more than two dozen new cars and variants on the German domestic market since 1975. Its Passat is also cutting sharply into sales of the Taurus.[4]

In commenting on Ford's domestic problems with its North American automobile operations, *The Wall Street Journal* states:

As recently as last fall [1979], Ford thought it had things under control. Despite red ink in the United States, it believed it could ride out the storm profitably this year [1980] on the strength of overseas sales and other operations. But some major foreign markets it counted on are weakening.[5]

Ford's attempted remedy for these problems includes the naming of Harold Poling as the new executive vice president of the company's North American car operations. Where did this talented executive come from? For several years he was the boss of Ford's then-highly profitable European operations and, during his tenure, earned huge corporate profits abroad for Ford. The transfer of Poling in 1980, and the dependence on European profits to carry North American operations, is reminiscent of the Lutz transfer in 1976 and the resulting atrophy in Ford's West German operations. What is more, both Ford's current CEO and current president—Philip Caldwell and Donald Petersen, respectively—once headed international operations.

International Portfolio Management

The international operations of multinationals are typically structured along the lines of product or geographical areas, and most frequently on combinations of the two dimensions. Whenever the product dimension predominates, each division in the MNC may be responsible for marketing and distributing one class of products worldwide, but more commonly a separate international division is solely responsible for marketing on a worldwide basis most or all products of the multinational's domestic divisions. In contrast, when the organizational setup is geographical, each division in the multinational's international operations is charged with the responsibility for conducting all the company's business within its designated geographical sphere.

The product and geographical approaches can be and are often combined by the major multinationals. General Electric, for instance, formed an organizational structure wherein an international group, headed by a vice president and group executive, was assigned to report directly to top management. This international group—which organizationally was placed on a lateral line with 10 GE product groups—was, in turn, subdivided into 3 area divisions (Europe, the Far East, and Latin America), in addition to the GE Export division. At Dana Corporation, a similar arrangement prevails, whereby an international group consists of 3 major geographical subdivisions.

Regardless of the manner in which a multinational is structured, the potential is always there for top management to give cash-cow treatment undeservedly, and perhaps unwittingly, to some of the firm's internationally marketed products and foreign markets—or worse yet, to the company's entire international operation. Because this threat exists, corporate policymakers are well advised to look at all the company's international markets and products marketed in them, as well as at the international operation as a whole, within the revealing analytical context of the portfolio matrix concept.

No matter how an MNC is organized for doing business abroad, appropriate matrixes can be developed to facilitate classification of the firm's international products and markets. General Electric has used a similar sorting scheme for its products. According to GE Chairman Reginald Jones, all its products have been categorized into one of five groupings:

1. High-growth products deserving the highest investment support.

2. Steady reinvestment products deserving high and steady investment.

3. Support products deserving steady investment support.

4. Selective pruning or rejuvenation products deserving reduced investment.

5. Venture products deserving heavy R&D investment.

This kind of analysis, if tailored to depict a detailed domestic/international breakdown for products and markets, enables top management to determine readily whether an international component of the MNC is being managed correctly. Of particular interest is whether a high-potential product or foreign market is being prevented from realizing its bright future because it is getting cash-cow treatment from MNC headquarters. This stunting effect may not be discernible if domestic and foreign operations are not segregated and compared to one another on relevant performance indicators, such as growth, market-share trends, and profits. Conceivably, a product that legitimately qualifies as a cash cow in the United States could very well be a star in an international market. Yet this important distinction, from a prescriptive managerial point of view, might be blurred by aggregated performance data. Management policy, in terms of resource allocation, naturally needs to be markedly different in the two market situations.

Domestic/international breakdowns of performance information are not hard to come by. For instance, the recent Financial Accounting Standards Board Regulation 14 already requires U.S.-based multinationals to segregate in their annual reports to shareholders specific performance data for the firm's significant foreign geographical operations.

What may be hard to come by, however, is the realization (and appropriate commensurate action) on the part of a multinational's top management that the firm is evolving away from its traditional product/market strengths. Management may be reluctant to admit that the firm's world markets are becoming more important than its domestic market, in terms of actual or potential growth and profits, or

that products other than those upon which the company built its name are the wave of the future. And such reluctance is quite understandable. Management oftentimes becomes attached to products and thus is slow to modify them when necessary to meet prevailing market conditions or, in extreme instances, to give them proper burial. Then, too, there is a natural tendency for management to consider the company to be, say, a "U.S. company since 1894," even though, with the firm's vast network of world markets, this feeling may no longer remotely correspond to reality. Additionally, policymakers in large American-based multinationals work under considerable social, governmental, and political pressure to put U.S. operations first, even when more lucrative foreign markets beckon.

Understandable though it may be, management reluctance to modify radically the company's historical product/market bases can spell trouble ahead. Such reluctance can and often does lead to cash-cow harvesting of growing and promising international products and markets in order to support foundering domestic operations. This sort of robbing-Peter-to-pay-Paul approach is usually thought of as a temporary solution until domestic operations are restored to health. Too often, however, the practice continues on year after year until the short run becomes the long run and the multinational ends up with weakened products and markets, not only at home but also abroad.

Take the case of Singer Company. The firm's future is thought by some, including one of its own executives, to be so bleak that they have suggested that the company self-liquidate. Speaking of Singer's unprofitable U.S. sewing machine operations, which until now management has been reluctant to deemphasize or modify, another of the company's managers says:

What Singer has is a group of high-cost factories, tooled up for a demand that existed perhaps 20 years ago, manned with union people who are not about to let the company off the hook. We're turning out machines there that cost exactly double what machines made in Taiwan cost and we're serving a [U.S.] market that is dropping precipitously.[6]

For some time Singer management has been acquiring nonsewing machine businesses to counter the decline in the sewing machine business in the United States and other industrial nations. (Demand for sewing machines has decreased 50 percent in the last seven years in the United States alone.) Nonetheless, Singer management continued to pursue a recovery program based mainly on the company's traditional core business—sewing machines—which resulted in a $130 million write-off on sewing machine operations in the third quarter of 1979. An earlier write-off on business machines reduced Singer's book value by half.

Now that Singer's management has literally been forced to do something more nontraditional (for Singer), it is greatly restructuring (read, scaling down) its North American and European sewing machine business. It then intends to reallocate $125 million in the next several years to promote its more promising businesses, including defense and the growing and profitable sewing machine markets in less-developed countries.

Returning to Competitive Policies

The focus thus far has been on the perils of management's misreading or misinterpreting the international dimension of product-portfolio analysis. But in some instances, management may knowingly milk the corporate foreign star. Why are many U.S. multinationals doing so?

The answer lies with several provocateurs. It has long been fashionable to use the supposedly devious Japanese, the greedy Arab sheiks, conniving oil executives, and "cheap foreign la-

bor" as straw men who have prevented numerous U.S. businesses from competing effectively in their own domestic markets. Yet while labor cries foul over foreign imports, it disregards its own role in diminished productivity and wage increases that go well beyond those justified by gains in worker output. And management has too often responded like the proverbial ostrich to changing consumer demands. One can hardly fault the hard-pressed American who buys the Honda or Datsun.

But the problem largely is a federal one: simply too much interference in the private sector. And the current climate for business in the United States is the culmination of years of need for redress. While not blameless, neither labor nor management can print money; or confiscatorily tax so-called windfall profits; or use inflation as a means to demotivate wage and salary earners by de facto tax increases brought about by congressional failure to index tax brackets; or impose a staggering regulatory burden upon both business and the public.

Inflation, unemployment, and bail-outs by the U.S. taxpayer of New York City, Chrysler, and Lockheed are but symptoms of an underlying economic malady. The United States has one of the lowest savings rates among the industrialized nations of the Western world, due to federal government-fostered, spend-to-beat-inflation psychology. Understandably, then, capital formation, investment, and industrial modernization have suffered, productivity has fallen, and the competitive edge of many U.S. firms has eroded against foreign competitors.

What is more, by stacking regulation on regulation, the federal government has brought about an environment wherein management and labor can demand assistance whenever they get into trouble. The next step in this inexorable spiral appears to be an expedient like the "big wagon," the Italian government's company which purchases failing private ventures.

Significantly, influential Washington policy-makers of all political stripes are now talking about a reindustrialization of America through what amounts to supply-side economics. When (or if) such talk finds its way into meaningful policy, the pressures in and on U.S. multinationals for deliberate short-run remedies, like milking the foreign star, may subside.

Coming full circle, what will remain is the need for multinational management to make certain that the product potentials in the company's foreign markets are properly analyzed. It may then even be politic to close a failing American operation or to do as Anheuser-Busch intends one day with its domestic beer business—to make current domestic products prime cash cows and then seek new opportunities at home and abroad.

The rewards for management's recognizing that a product with high growth and market share is actually a prize heifer rather than a cash cow are considerable. The long-term performance level of any U.S. multinational may well ride on its management's perceptiveness in making this distinction and resolve to act accordingly.

Notes

1. George S. Day, "Diagnosing the Product Portfolio," *Journal of Marketing*, April 1977, p. 29.

2. Terry Haller, "Strategic Planning: Key to Corporate Power for Marketers," *Marketing Times*, May/June 1980, p. 22.

3. Philip Kotler, "Harvesting Strategy for Weak Products," *Business Horizons*, August 1978, p. 6.

4. "West Germany, A Ford Cash Cow Has Less For Its Parent," *Business Week*, May 12, 1980, p. 42.

5. "Ford's Hot Seat, Harold 'Red' Poling Has Task of Reviving North American Sales," *The Wall Street Journal*, May 7, 1980, p. 1.

6. "Is Singer Headed for Self-Liquidation," *Business Week*, March 31, 1980, p. 116.

Company Readings

Will Americans Buy an "Ohio Honda"?
Jennifer Pendleton

When 34-year-old marketing executive Tim Trainor decided he needed to replace his aging Volkswagen, he considered an array of choices. But his mind kept returning to one alternative, a Japanese car.

The Newport Beach, California, resident had his reasons: "I've always driven a foreign car. They're economical and dependable. And Detroit's cars don't have the same response and styling."

Ask him whether he would ever consider purchasing an American-made car and Mr. Trainor is firm: "Never." And the only reason he'd consider driving one, he adds, is if it were a company car. Mr. Trainor eventually bought a new Honda Civic.

Granted, Mr. Trainor isn't the typical car-buying American—he lives in Southern California, he's single, and he has an above-average income. But he is fairly representative of a large block of the population that eschews American cars. To this group, buying a U.S.-built auto means buying inferior.

That many Americans possess these attitudes is not news to the marketers of Japanese cars in the United States. Having cultivated an image of quality, companies including Toyota, Nissan, and Honda have exploited it, presenting their import cars in advertising as dependable, precision-built vehicles.

The strategy has served them well. More than one in four cars sold in the United States today are imports; in California, imported cars command a whopping 50 percent share of the new car market.

But that may change. The image of quality that Japanese car companies have developed in America is being put to the test. The reason: for the first time some of the most successful Japanese vehicles in America are being made *in* America, and not in the Land of the Rising Sun.

So far, two Japanese auto manufacturers have taken the step of opening U.S. plants, and Nissan Motor Co., Ltd. and Honda Motor Co., Ltd., the second- and third-largest auto importers in the United States respectively.

In 1978, Honda began producing motorcycles at its Marysville, Ohio, plant; the following year, it expanded operations to include a passenger car plant. The first cars made there—Honda Accords—rolled out of the plant last November.

Nissan started building its Smyrna, Tennessee, truck plant in April 1980. On June 16 of this year, the plant's 1,300 employees watched as the president of the new U.S. subsidiary drove the company's first U.S.-manufactured truck off the line. Some think Nissan ultimately will add a car manufacturing facility there.

For Honda and Nissan, the establishment of U.S. operations made sense for practical reasons. The vehicles produced in Marysville and Smyrna aren't subject to the voluntary import restrictions that have limited both companies' growth since they were imposed three years ago. The U.S. government classifies vehicles produced in these plants as domestics; the companies are free to produce as many cars and trucks as they choose. So, for once, these two Japanese auto companies are free to let market forces, not the demands of arbitrary restraints, dictate their growth.

Beyond that, the public relations value of such actions is immense. While the current economic upturn has taken the spotlight away from rising protectionism in this country—news footage of U.S. workers bludgeoning Japanese cars in protest of international trading policies was almost a cliche a few months ago—it is still a concern the Japanese companies must grapple with.

David Cole, director of the University of Michigan's Office for the Study of Automotive Transportation, believes that the Japanese automakers have no choice but to set up U.S. operations. Although the Japanese run the risk of possibly jeopardizing their strong quality image, establishing a U.S. manufacturing base is "essential," Mr. Cole says. "It's a step they must take or face an alternative that's far worse."

Of course, the alternative is that the United States or other important Japanese export markets would take actions against them to severely limit Japan's trading activities. At present, more than 40 percent of all Japan's car exports are shipped to the United States.

While the U.S. economy appears to be picking up, unemployment is still high—9.8 percent, according to the figures released by the Office of Management and Budget in July. And the extent of the recovery is still unknown.

The *Los Angeles Times* conducted a national opinion poll a few months ago to ascertain how Americans view the state of U.S. trade with the Japanese and gauge U.S. attitudes toward Japanese goods. Generally, it found that Americans have a favorable view of Japanese products, but favor protectionist measures aimed at Japan.

When asked if the United States should take steps to restrict foreign imports into this country to protect American industry and jobs, an overwhelming 68 percent favored restrictions. Only 26 percent believed there should be no restrictions; 6 percent weren't sure.

The poll confirmed what most have already acknowledged—"Made in Japan" means quality to a majority of Americans. When asked if Japanese automobiles are usually better value for the dollar than those made here, 40 percent responded they were better, 25 percent said about the same and 22 percent said not as good. Some 12 percent weren't sure and 1 percent refused to answer.

In May, *Newsweek* also carried out a poll on the subject. It reached similar conclusions, that protectionism is strong in the United States and buy-American feelings are rising. Of the poll's 915 adult respondents, 53 percent said they were less inclined to buy imported products, compared with 50 percent in 1982, 42 percent in 1980, 42 percent in 1977 and 34 percent in 1973. A total of 40 percent said they would buy an imported product only if there were no comparable American product available.

When asked to rate U.S. products vis 'a vis others in the field, most American products still came out on top, but with cars the gap was close: forty-eight percent of the respondents said American cars were the best, compared with 45 percent who maintained that vehicles produced overseas were as good or better.

That Japan's automotive marketers have developed a quality image isn't surprising. According to research by J. D. Power & Associates, Westlake Village, California, Japanese cars come out way ahead of domestics in overall quality of workmanship and dependability.

Owners of 1981 model Japanese and domestic cars were asked after a year of ownership if they had had any mechanical problems with their vehicles. Overall, 35 percent of the Japanese cars owners said they had had a problem, compared with 56 percent of the domestic owners.

Quality—or the perception of quality—is an issue that most assuredly has been on Honda's mind since it built the U.S. plant 30 miles northwest of Columbus. "From all the research we have generated, we have been forced to conclude that if a product is made in America, there is a perception of lack of quality," says Gerry Rubin, president of American Honda's U.S. advertising agency, Needham, Harper & Steers, west Los Angeles.

"Honda recognized that as a fact of life," he adds.

So why did they do it? Is this Honda's way of taking the ammunition away from protectionist-minded critics? Not so, according to Mr. Rubin. The decision to start a U.S. operation, he says, was years in the making, long before this country's unemployed took to the streets to stage "buy American" rallies. Rather, Honda's decision was based on a logical desire to make its products more easily accessible to its dealers and a long-held belief that a company should build where it sells, says Mr. Rubin.

It also may have something to do with Honda's need to grow. In Japan, Honda is a relative newcomer in the marketplace, and it lacks existing capacity to meet rising consumer demand. Rather than opting to build new plants in Japan, where land and raw materials are scarce, Honda has sought to put its production where its vehicles are.

And the U.S. market is critical for Honda. During the past fiscal year (ending Feb. 28) Honda sold 33 percent of its total 1.1 million passenger car production in the United States. In North America it sold 414,000 passenger cars, a figure that exceeds the 402,000 units it sold in Japan.

Once the decision to build the plant was made, Honda was determined to produce a vehicle of identical quality to its Japanese counterpart. It invested $250 million to build a plant with state-of-the-art equipment and advanced technology.

Honda has attempted to import its Japanese operating style to the United States. Workers aren't called workers, but "associ-

ates." They are encouraged to make suggestions about changes and improvements in the production process.

The "associates" wear uniforms. They exercise together, eat in the same cafeteria, and are encouraged to form social relationships outside the company. The objective is to make all employes part of the "Honda team," sharing in the goal of producing a high-quality product. The result is, "an *esprit de corps* not often found in U.S. manufacturing plants," says one source.

But some are skeptical that this seemingly harmonious atmosphere will continue indefinitely. American workers are not the same as Japanese workers, and in the end will not adhere to Japanese-style regimentation, they say. "Company songs and uniforms? It goes against the American grain," says one source.

Then there's the threat of unionization. The United Auto Workers has plainly expressed its desire to unionize Honda and Nissan's plants, a drive that at present has received little support from the Marysville and Smyrna workers. But, points out Mr. Cole of the University of Michigan, Honda and Nissan are new in America. "The honeymoon is on" with their new U.S. employes, he says, suggesting that the situation may change as time progresses. (It should be noted that conflict over unionization is one of the main points putting the possible General Motors/Toyota joint venture in Fremont, California, in jeopardy.)

GM and Toyota, Japan's number one automaker, are currently seeking Federal Trade Commission approval on their plan to jointly produce front-wheel drive subcompact cars at GM's idled Fremont assembly plant. If approved, the cars will be sold by GM's Chevrolet dealers in the 1985 model year.

So far, at least, it would seem Honda has successfully transplanted its modus operandi to the United States. By most accounts, the American-built Honda Accords are of equal quality to Honda Accords built in Japan.

Through the first six months of the year, the Ohio plant produced 16,861 Accords.

Motor Trend did a comparative study in which it invited several staff members, Accord owners, and other interested parties to examine both an American-built and a Japanese-built Accord and determine which was which. *Motor Trend* couldn't hide a clue that gave it away to some more sensitive participants (the different brand of tires on the U.S. make), but most were hard-pressed to spot any differences.

The magazine described the early U.S.-built Accord it was reviewing as "most impressive," and concluded its piece with the prediction: "We're betting this Japanese-American partnership will be cranking out 'Honda-quality' vehicles for a long time, right here in the good ol' U.S. of A."

Honda's sales certainly haven't suffered since it began building Accords at Marysville. The car continues to be the top-selling front-wheel-drive sedan in this country.

Yet, most likely because of Honda's reluctance to do anything to jeopardize its position of strength, the company has done little to promote the domestic origin of its four-door Accords. "We wanted the public to know we had done this, but we know there are indeed people who don't want a U.S.-made product," says Honda senior v.p. Cliff Schmillen. "There was very little to be gained by letting the whole world know, and we felt the product should speak for itself."

Last fall, in anticipation of the auto plant opening, Honda started a low-key corporate advertising campaign talking about the plant. "Years ago, we made a commitment that will soon stand" is the headline of one ad featuring a photograph of the Honda auto manufacturing facility under construction. In the copy, it explains that Honda's decision to build in the United States was based on a fundamental Honda principle: "Honda has built its company by building overseas. And

by becoming partners with the markets it serves."

Then it shifts to the quality issue: "We have every confidence that we can manufacture quality products here with American materials and American people. And we're confident those products will match anything Honda makes in Japan."

Other ads in the series make similar points. One explains Honda's philosophy regarding its employes: Rows of uniformclad workers are part of "the Honda Team," says one. "Everyone who joins Honda becomes a member of the team sharing in a common goal—quality." Every once in a while an oriental face pops out of the picture, but there aren't many.

The series of ads ran in the business sections of major newspapers in selected markets, the major newsweeklies and national business publications, including *The Wall Street Journal, Business Week, Automotive News,* and *Forbes.* The target audience: decision makers who may influence trade policies between the United States and Japan. At the same time, Honda hoped the ads might also have a residual effect upon potential Accord buyers, who are, in general, upscale and college educated, likely readers of such media. Honda also ran a network TV spot for a few weeks.

Sources close to Honda admit that at the time the first U.S.-built Accords began appearing in dealer showrooms, some customers were skeptical. "Early on, customers did ask specifically if display cars were Marysville Accords," says one source. "Initially, there was concern that they may not be as good as the Japanese-built cars."

And, surprisingly to some, the question also was asked for the opposite reason. In some instances, says one midwestern Honda dealer, potential buyers have asked about the origin of showroom Accords, because they preferred to buy an American car. "We've had some customers say they want to buy a U.S.-built Accord," says Roy Ellsberry, sales manager of Osmon Honda, Dayton, Ohio.

But mostly, says Mr. Ellsberry, customers have displayed little interest. "I can't remember anyone making a big issue of it," he says. And furthermore, he adds, "a lot of people aren't even aware that the company has set up a U.S. plant."

Of course, if it's true that most people aren't aware of the plant, then Honda's low-key approach to spreading the word must have a lot to do with it. But that's okay, according to Honda. "We purposely decided to keep a low profile," said Honda spokesman Paul Haynie. "We wanted to let things settle down. Make sure the public accepted the cars." And public acceptance, reasons Honda, isn't something it, or anyone else, can buy by taking out an ad.

Nissan apparently shares Honda's attitude. Since the first Smyrna-built Nissan light trucks came off the assembly line, which is near Nashville, this summer, the company hasn't trumpeted the news in paid advertising.

The plant's opening *has* been the object of massive publicity, however. CBS-TV's "60 Minutes" profiled it (favorably), and there have been numerous stories in newspapers, business, and auto industry publications.

But that, according to Nissan, is the result of unprompted media interest in the subject, rather than the result of an orchestrated public relations campaign.

Marvin T. Runyon, the former Ford Motor Co. v.p. heading Nissan's Smyrna plant, says he hired Holder Kennedy & Co., a Nashville public relations agency, to handle the flood of media calls the company was receiving, rather than because of a desire to promote the plant. "We're not out to get publicity," explains Mr. Runyon. "But we're getting it anyway." While Nissan's Smyrna operation is the subject of intense media interest, it's not some-

thing the Japanese car company is particularly comfortable with. Its concerns are much the same as Honda's.

Although on the one hand the company wants to convince the American public it's a good corporate citizen, reinvesting its money into the U.S. economy, creating jobs, it, like Honda, is aware of the stigma that may be attached to the "Made in America" label.

Concern over this issue prompted Nissan to research American attitudes by conducting focus group sessions last fall around the country. The purpose was to find out whether the public harbored strong negative—or positive—feelings over American-made products.

What Nissan found, according to marketing services v.p. Robert Kent, is that the American public is relatively unconcerned. "There were no strong negative, or positive, feelings on the issue," says Mr. Kent, who declines to elaborate on the specifics of Nissan's market research.

But although it may be true that Americans in most parts of the country are indifferent on the issue, there is concern in some parts of the United States, particularly the Midwest, where the domestic auto industry is based, Nissan acknowledges. According to Mr. Kent, Nissan is studying the possibility of using a "Made in America" copy line in some regional advertising for the light trucks.

There are some people who believe Nissan is using the U.S. truck plant as a learning tool, a place to try out its U.S. manufacturing prowess. Its ultimate objective, sources believe, is to set up a passenger car plant on its expansive 782-acre site. "I'd be surprised if that doesn't happen within five years," says Mr. Cole of the University of Michigan.

Mr. Runyon, the head of the Smyrna plant, concedes that it was concern over quality that motivated Nissan to open a truck plant (as opposed to a passenger car assembly line). In addition to costing less—tooling costs associated with trucks are less because trucks have fewer variations and fewer options and accessories—fit and finish are less critical with trucks, Mr. Runyon acknowledges.

Although Honda and Nissan's establishment of U.S. operations is a major undertaking, it's not the first time a successful import car company has taken such a step. The German auto giant Volkswagenwerk AG set up a manufacturing plant in Westmoreland County, Pennsylvania, in 1978 to make Rabbits, the small car that eventually replaced the company's legendary Beetle. It's a story that must give any importer opening a U.S. plant pause.

A few years after Volkswagen successfully launched the Rabbit, the company was confident there was sufficient demand to warrant expansion in the United States.

And at the same time, Volkswagen wanted to do something to keep Rabbit prices down. German currency values relative to the dollar made it difficult, or impossible, for Volkswagen to maintain competitive prices against Japan's small-car models. It was the first time Volkswagen had faced strong competition at the lower price end of the market.

In principle it should have worked. Volkswagen was already very successful building cars in foreign countries, with assembly plants in Latin America and Africa. But it didn't.

First, the company misread the extent of the Japanese challenge. It had had the small-car field virtually to itself, but the market had changed. Japan was selling small cars with su-perior styling and design at a lower price. Many people thought Volkswagen's austere, boxy design came up lacking when compared with what Japan was offering.

Volkswagen apparently believed its reputation alone was enough to secure its future. "The feeling was that Americans would buy German excellence," explains one industry analyst. "It didn't work."

There were also quality problems. As consumer complaints mounted about U.S.-built Rabbits, the car's reputation as a precision-built machine suffered. Rabbit sales took a nose dive. The company canceled ambitious plans to open a second plant. Lately, Volkswagen has improved the quality of the U.S.-built Rabbits, but the company is still trying to recover from the damage its reputation received during this period.

No doubt, Honda and Nissan have studied what happened to Volkswagen. But while Honda and Nissan are grappling with the issue of how to cope with the "Made in America" stigma, there are changes going on in American industry. Detroit's auto companies are making great strides in improving overall quality. Some predict the negative image of U.S.-built cars may be on the way out.

If that happens, then Honda and Nissan's current concerns may seem silly in retrospect. And instead, Honda and Nissan's TV commercials may be revised to say, "The best Japanese cars in the world are Made in America."

A Champ of Cheap Airlines
Peter Nulty

In the last three years airline executives have flown into deregulation, two recessions, the air-traffic controllers' strike, and exhausting price wars. Last year, the worst in airline memory, the U.S. industry had operating losses of around $300 million. There are fears that some airline companies—Braniff and Re-public are frequently mentioned—could go out of business. The turbulence aloft isn't confined to American carriers. Sir Freddie Laker's Skytrain went down on the North Atlantic last month. But in a dingy suite of offices in Newark Airport's old North Terminal, People Express Chairman Donald C. Burr, 40, smiles as though a party is beginning.

One of a half dozen, jet-flying airlines born of deregulation, People Express has executed the fastest takeoff of any. The company started last April with three Boeing 737s traveling from Newark to Buffalo, Columbus, and Norfolk. By year's end it had 13 of the planes flying to 10 cities and was surpassing the older fledglings, Midway and New York Air, in the number of miles it carried paying passengers. People Express flew 95 million revenue passenger miles in December, when New York Air flew 64 million passenger miles and Midway 45 million.

People is the busiest airline at Newark Airport, with 72 departures and landings a day. Although the company lost $9 million on revenues of $38 million last year, it made a profit in December, its eighth month of flying—about $500,000 on revenues of $9 million by *Fortune* estimates. (In January, a slow month for air travel, People slipped back into the red.) Hambrecht & Quist, the venture-capital firm that underwrote People's public offering of three million shares in 1980, predicts the company could make as much as $10 million in 1982 if the air-travel market improves, as Hambrecht & Quist expects it to do later this year.

A Wizard Departs

People's prideful chirps of progress missed a few beats two weeks ago when President Gerald L. Gitner, 36, moved to Pan American as that troubled airline's senior vice president of marketing and planning. Gitner had held a similar position with Texas International before quitting to form People Express in April 1980 with two other Texas International employees, Burr and Melrose K. Dawsey, 33. A wizard of marketing and route selection, Gitner skipped about People's tiny headquar-

ters like a kid in a wading pool, with an infectious spirit of fun and adventure.

Fortunately for People, Burr has a record that suggests he can fly solo. A Harvard Business School graduate, he left the presidency of a New York investment firm that invested solely in airlines to join Texas International in 1973, when it appeared to be going down the tubes. Seven years later, when he left to help found People, he was president and chief operating officer and Texas International had been turned around. Burr is the largest stockholder of People, with 715,000 shares. (Gitner has 330,000 shares. Dawsey, who is People's director of administration, has 41,000 shares, and five other officers have 50,000 shares each.) Burr views air travel with glib good humor as a commodity product like "steel, tennis balls, and dead chickens." He poohpoohs such airline frills as hot meals and free magazines. "To be a winner," he claims, "you have to have the ultimate frill—nice people."

To keep spirits from sagging among People's people, Burr spent the day after Gitner announced his departure in company meetings explaining the move. Says Burr: "Our folks were saying, 'We thought you guys started something new and better. Why should we stay committed if the president is going to leave?' " Burr's answer: "Gerry loves planning and that's already done at People Express." Gitner concurs: "People went from zero to $82 million in assets in a year and a half. It's not a start-up anymore."

The ingredients of People's early success are hardly secret: rock-bottom fares and savvy marketing. People may have had the lowest costs of any airline in the country in 1981. In December People's cost per seat for each mile it flew fell to a phenomenal 5.4 cents, compared with, for example, 9 cents for Piedmont that month. General Manager Larry Martin, 33, says People's cost could fall below 5 cents when the airline adds three more planes to its fleet this month.

The company passes its economies on to passengers, who pay only 9.3 cents a mile for their tickets. According to Goldman Sachs, in the first nine months of 1981 two companies that compete with People on some routes were charging a systemwide average of 16.1 cents a mile (Piedmont) and 18.6 cents (USAir). People's stunningly low fares have forced other airlines to match its prices on competitive routes, even though their costs are higher. In April, for example, Piedmont was charging $82 for a ticket from Newark to Norfolk. When it heard People was going to fly the route, Piedmont slashed fares to meet those of the interloper—to $35 in peak hours and $23 at other times. The fare war is still raging.

The BSA Special

To drive home its price message, People is putting on a mischievous ad campaign poking fun at other airlines and their patchwork quilt of fares. In one TV commercial, a reservation clerk at a fictitious competitor tells a customer:

> You want the BSA Airlines super low-price special. OK? You simply fly one way, and pay the price you pay the other way if you fly two ways. OK? Simply put, each way costs half of either way, both ways, some days. OK?

People probably couldn't survive solely by wresting market share from more established companies. In some cases, its competitors have customer recognition and the financial strength to withstand losses on selected routes indefinitely. When People started flying from Newark to Indianapolis it charged only $79 a ticket in peak hours, $59 off-peak. TWA and USAir, which were charging around $150 between New York and Indianapolis, matched People's prices. People couldn't drum up enough passengers and soon

dropped the route. Says Burr, "We got blasted out of there." TWA and USAir have lifted their fares to $162.

Instead of taking passengers off competing planes, People hopes to lure them from the roads and rails on routes where there is a lot of ground traffic and not much airline service. In effect, People wants to preempt Greyhound's slogan, "Leave the driving to us." People Express ads read: "Flying that costs less than driving." A ticket from Newark to West Palm Beach, for example, costs $89 in peak hours and $69 off-peak. A bus or train ticket is more than $130. The trip by car—figuring 20 cents a mile and not counting food and lodging—costs about $250.

Enticing ground lovers into the skies seems to work. After People started flying to Norfolk, a local newspaper reported that Greyhound sharply cut its service to the city and its environs, citing a decrease in ticket sales. Meanwhile, Norfolk airport traffic increased 18 percent.

Superman Does It

Two kinds of travelers like People's fares: those with little money and those with plenty of money who would like to keep it. Senator Ted Kennedy was a passenger from Baltimore to Florida in December; his niece Caroline flew in February. Christopher Reeve, who played the title role in two *Superman* movies, took People from Newark to Boston. (You would think he could have flown still cheaper on his own.) On the planes, briefcases mix with backpacks, blue jeans and sailors' bell-bottoms with pinstripes. The cabins are clean, the seats close together, and the attendants refreshingly chipper. It's like a McDonald's of the air.

People has federal rule making to thank for its price advantage. For years the Civil Aeronautics Board set fares based on average costs of the industry and prevented new competition from entering the business. Companies competed on service, not price. The high cost of providing the service (and of generous wage contracts) was easily passed along to travelers through regulated rates. After congress changed the rules in 1978, it was a simple matter for newcomers organizing from scratch to move in with efficient operations.

No airline has done more than People Express to pare away extras. The first thing experienced travelers notice when flying People is that a lot of services they used to take for granted are either optional or have been eliminated. There are no hot meals; passengers must buy their snacks and beverages (beer and sandwiches cost $1; coffee is 50 cents). People Express takes reservations by telephone, but it has no ticket desks in the terminals. Nor is People hooked up to the industry's interconnected computerized ticketing systems. All tickets are sold on the plane. Unbundling these services alone knocks at least $18 off a ticket price.

Passengers are encouraged to carry their luggage on board; the planes are designed to take two small suitcases per passenger in the cabin. Bags can be checked before boarding—for a fee of $3 per bag. But checked luggage is not transferred to other airlines, making it necessary for passengers to pick up their own bags if they are connecting with other flights. The chief complaint about the luggage policy has come from the operators of the Columbus airport; all that bag toting by People passengers was wearing out the carpet. The Columbus *Citizen-Journal* responded with a ringing editorial ("Get off People's back"), which advised the airport to "get some carpet that will last."

Lopping off the frills—some would call them necessities—is only the beginning of People's cost-cutting design. The company slashes far greater costs out of basic plant, equipment, and personnel. The founders se-

lected Newark's nearly abandoned North Terminal because there was enough cheap space in the building for their entire headquarters, from reservation switchboards to corporate cubbyholes. Chairman Burr's spartan office, which doubles as a boardroom, rents for $6 per square foot a year; in the Pan Am Building in midtown Manhattan, space goes for about $50 a square foot. Rental fees for People's eight boarding gates are less than half those charged at Newark's ultramodern new terminal a half mile away.

People Express works its sedate-looking tan, brown, and maroon fleet hard. Its 737s were purchased from Lufthansa for $3.7 million each. (A new 737 costs as much as $17 million.) When Lufthansa flew the planes, each had 90 seats and a galley for hot meals. People took out the galleys and the first-class sections and added 28 seats per plane. A People 737 flies between 10 and 11 hours a day, 3 or 4 more than the industry average. The additional seats and flying time more than double a plane's productivity without adding to capital costs. On the average, the planes fly 58 percent full—a good showing.

People gets as much out of people as it does out of planes. The company has about 800 full-time employees, or 57 per aircraft; the industry as a whole has about 149 people per plane. The secret of People's high-labor productivity is not large amounts of overtime, but versatility. Because the company is not unionized, People's employees can be moved around to ease a crunch when one occurs. Each employee is trained—and is willing—to perform many tasks. Pilots fly about 70 hours a month (the industry average is around 45), but they also work as instructors, dispatchers, and schedulers.

Flight attendants are called "customer service managers"; they may spend one week a month looking after passengers aloft and the rest of the time taking reservations or keeping the books. Even executives like Melrose

Dawsey regularly leave their desks to sell tickets and serve coffee. Burr, who occasionally pitches in to take reservations, claims this flexibility reduces the number of people on the payroll by at least 10 percent. Signs taped on corridor walls at headquarters announce: "Reservations needs help at peaks on Thursdays. Sign up, schedules permitting."

In a lot of companies an open-ended call for volunteers would fall on deaf ears. But People employees have an incentive to respond—all, even the newest recruits, are stockholders. People may be the only publicly held company that requires every new employee to purchase 100 shares of stock, at a discount of about 60 percent. About a third of the company's 4.5 million shares are owned by employees. The stock, offered over the counter, has been hovering around $8.50 a share, exactly the price at which it was issued 16 months ago—not bad in this market.

Some Get More

In this People's army, the officer staff totals 15 people. None is a vice president—a remarkable omission in the V.P.-prone airline industry. No one, not even Burr, has a secretary. Burr recalls that when he became president of Texas International in 1976, TI had a corporate staff of 350 and monthly revenues less than People's revenues today.

The company's brass doesn't pay itself excessively. Burr gets $48,000, as did Gitner before his departure. (He won't say what he will be paid at Pan Am.) People pilots earn $30,000 a year to start, compared with an average of $60,000 for members of the Air Line Pilots Association. Other People employees are paid *more* than the going rate for their positions. For example, customer-service managers

start at $17,500 a year, well above entry-level pay for flight attendants at other lines. "This is a very democratic company," says Burr. "We've leveled the compensation scales and we intend to keep it that way. We want people motivated by feelings of ownership and peer pressure."

Being lean and entrepreneurial, People was able to move with remarkable speed at two crucial times in its short history. In January 1980, when the company set up shop in Newark, the headquarters-to-be was little more than a shell infested with rats. Only eight employees were on the payroll. Within four months the founders hired and trained 200 people, and People took to the air on schedule.

The second crucial time came after the air-traffic controllers' strike began in August. Access to most airports was restricted, and People had to abandon plans for flying some routes. The company couldn't afford idle planes, so a new strategy was hammered out during two emergency sessions over Gerry Gitner's dinner table in Morristown, New Jersey. The airline decided to start flying to Florida from smaller cities as well as Newark. Within weeks, People Express was originating Florida flights in Buffalo and Columbus. Business was good, and direct Florida flights largely accounted for the company's profitability in December. Burr says a major airline would have taken months to start flying the new routes.

When he was looking for financial backing a year ago, recalls Burr, investors laughed at his choice of Newark as the principal terminal, "and they thought charging passengers for food and drinks was even funnier. Everybody knows it's coffee, tea, or me—for free. Right?" These days it's Burr who is laughing.

Kroger: The New King of Supermarkets
Bill Saporito

The business Barney Kroger began 100 years ago hawking tea and coffee from a bright red wagon has finally made it to the top. When its shareholders agreed to acquire Dillon Cos. of Hutchinson, Kansas, last week, Kroger seized Safeway's crown as the largest supermarket chain in the United States. In all likelihood, the deal merely accelerated the inevitable. With football field-sized outlets, Kroger has become a paragon of aggressive supermarketing. It tosses out money-losing stores like rotten apples, protects winners like tender tomatoes, and attacks new markets with all the subtlety of a falling watermelon.

Kroger's performance has paid off in profits. Safeway, with 529 stores in four foreign countries, still ranks number one in sales worldwide, but it trailed Kroger-*cum*-Dillon's domestic supermarket revenues of nearly $14 billion by some $700 million last year. Even without Dillon, Kroger's 1982 earnings, estimated at $160 million, will probably top Safeway's, and its stock price has left its rival's in the dust (up 43 percent versus Safeway's 11 percent in five years).

"A few years ago they were not even good," a Dallas grocery executive says of Kroger's management. "Now they have far better stores, their people like the direction they're going in, and they're more formidable competition than they've ever been."

How Kroger attained its present exalted state is a tale in savvy merchandising and hardheaded strategic analysis. It begins in the early 1970s when James P. Herring, then chairman, took a deep look at the business. Like hundreds of other food retailers that embraced self-service in the 1930s, Kroger had fed its expansion on low margins, high volume, and booming population growth. By the late 1960s, however, the company was locked in fierce competition for meager market shares in cities that were stagnating or over-built by rival chains. "In some markets we had a 10 percent share," recalls Lyle Everingham, the current chairman. "In assessing what we had, we developed a priority list of markets to establish our franchise, and we just went down the list."

Kroger was already strong in a core of America's heartland that fell inside a box with corners at Indianapolis, Memphis, Chattanooga, and Columbus. Where the company was weak, the new apostles of market share picked up their onions and blew town. They shuttered 1,237 supermarkets in all, abandoning Chicago, Washington, Milwaukee, Kansas City, Birmingham, Minneapolis, and Cleveland. Kroger now operates 1,199 food stores in 19 states and a 560-unit drugstore chain. It ranks number one or two in 11 of its 13 major food-marketing territories, with a market share of about 50 percent in Ohio.

The rationale for this strategy was straightforward. Whether it has 10 percent or 25 percent of a given market, a chain has to advertise and supply its stores from a warehouse. The higher the share of market, the lower the advertising cost per customer and the faster the warehouse will turn over its inventory. In addition, Kroger has 33 manufacturing plants and a huge fleet of trucks that can deliver goods to retail with tremendous efficiency. The larger its share, the more likely those plants and trucks will be used to capacity.

A sixth of the food scanned through Kroger's computerized checkout system is company-made, high for the industry. Kroger manufactures only fast-moving commodity items such as dairy goods, peanut butter, sugar, and canned goods. "In dairies and bakeries," says Everingham, "we believe we are state-of-the-art." That may not seem much to brag about in an operation the scope of Kroger's, but price wars have been won on the cost of milk and bread.

Trouble has beset other chains that own manufacturing plants. In the mid-1960s A&P built the world's largest processing plant in Horseheads, New York; after running at half capacity or less for years, it was closed in 1982 (but hasn't yet been sold). Kroger wouldn't have waited that long to shoot the wounded. Each line it processes is evaluated continually—and unsentimentally—on a make-or-buy basis. Kroger pulled the plug on a candy-making plant near Cincinnati just before Christmas. "We can make candy as *good* as anyone," says Everingham. "We just can't make it as efficiently."

Being the low-cost supplier gives Kroger the chance to dictate prices. When competitive conditions allow, it charges plenty. Kroger controls half the market in its hometown of Cincinnati, which has, according to the Bureau of Labor Statistics, the fastest rising retail food prices of any city in the nation. Competitors think hard before they'll undercut the market leader. They know Kroger could match them penny for penny—and that they would come out of the battle black and blue.

Once the customers are in the store, the secret of supermarketing is to milk them for all they're worth. That requires creativity where the shoppers meet the spaghetti, imaginative merchandising of a kind Kroger hadn't excelled at for years. After Barney Kroger stepped down in 1928, the company was run by lawyers, financial men, and others who had never been in the supermarket front lines. Everingham was the first up-through-the-ranks retailer to take command since the founder himself. His mother ran a produce department for Kroger in Adrian, Michigan. He met his wife when they both worked at a Kroger store, and his brother manages the company's Houston division. As he rose to the top, he and other merchandisers pressed innovations to differentiate Kroger stores from competitors.

Kroger pulled up its socks in basic areas critical to attracting customers. For instance, it switched from putting produce in uninviting plastic-wrapped packages to using bulk displays, which look better and let shoppers pick one apple instead of a six-pack. It also began expanding stores, adding new classes of merchandise and specialty departments to meet almost every imaginable consumer desire in food and household products. Kroger called the expanded outlets superstores; supermarkets no longer seemed adequately superlative. In the past decade the company added 12 million square feet to existing structures, about equal to 260 new superstores. The average size of a Kroger outlet is now 11 percent bigger than Safeway and 38 percent bigger than A&P.

Kroger surveys 250,000 consumers a year to find out what they want. For the gourmet generation, it has cheese shops and delis. For the "me" generation, health food and cosmetics. For the one-stop shopper, goods from auto parts to ziti and services from banking to pharmaceutical. Kroger is now testing restaurants attached to the stores, beauty salons, fresh pasta sections, and sausage nooks. It broke new ground last year by joining an insurance company to set up in-store financial service centers. It wants to sell mutual funds with the mayonnaise.

The motivation for this is margins. While the gross markup on a can of soup may be 19 percent, flowers can easily fetch 50 percent or more. The drawback is the need for sales help, which adds labor costs usually exceeding $10 an hour in an industry that's productivity crazed. To keep costs down layouts must be arranged so clerks can shift from meat to fish, health foods to flowers—and expend as little of their labor on the customers as possible. "Much, much of what our customers do is self-service even in our delicatessens and bakeries," says Everingham. "While we sell a lot of meat out of the deli counter, we sell beaucoup of the product we put out in front of the case."

Entrenched as it is, Kroger can make life harrowing for any newcomer invading its territory. That's especially true in towns and small cities, often the industry's most profitable markets, where a few superstores can handle all the business. Kroger keeps expanding its stores as necessary, so a newcomer will have trouble winning enough customers to fill an efficient-sized outlet profitably.

None of this means Kroger is invincible. Just last year it shut its Market Basket division in southern California, having struggled for 20 years without winning more than a 5 percent share. "The 65 stores we had there were adequate to compete in the marketplace," Everingham says, "but inadequate for us to implement the kind of strategy that our company knows how to execute." Elsewhere 75 other stores were shed as "underproductive."

Kroger came close to closing shop in Pittsburgh last year when it found itself at a special disadvantage. An ailing regional chain in the recession-stunned city won wage rollbacks from local unions representing clerks and meatcutters. When Kroger demanded comparable concessions, the unions balked— until the company threatened to halt construction of five stores and close seven others.

The unions may have remembered what happened when Kroger made similar demands in western Michigan three years ago. The workers refused and Kroger sold all 21 stores there. In Chattanooga, two newly built stores stood empty until local unions met Kroger's conditions. And when Teamsters in Ohio authorized a strike last August, Kroger accepted 1,000 job applications for replacements before the union, working without a contract, settled in November. The tough labor policy is the product of William G. Kagler, a converted political columnist for the *Cin-*

cinnati Enquirer who as Kroger's president is Everingham's heir apparent. "We are aggressive," he says, "about everything."

In several markets Kroger's chief nemesis is warehouse-store operators. Typically carrying 5,000 to 10,000 different items stacked in packing boxes, warehouse units have lower costs than Kroger: cheaper rents, skimpier wages, and none of the services or amenities of a superstore. In St. Louis warehousers got control of 25 percent of the market and helped mangle Kroger's operation there. When warehousers blitzed Little Rock, Safeway converted two supermarkets to low-cost Food Barn outlets, helping to plunge the market into a price war.

Kroger hasn't let many warehouse operators eat its lunch, though. After shutting its supermarkets in Cleveland, it started four warehouse stores there; it runs them primarily to learn the economics of the business and how best to handle these competitors. When a warehouse threatens a Kroger outlet nowadays, the company advertises, "Warehouse Prices in a Complete Store," and matches the competition price for price. But it is careful to respond in only one or two stores nearest the warehouse, thus avoiding a marketwide price war. The practice is known as zone pricing, but warehousers call it just plain predatory.

They charge that Kroger in particular among the big chains tries to strangle them by selling at a loss in selected stores. In Nashville one of Kroger's 29 outlets has endured a two-year price war with a Waremart no-frills store. Kroger's response has been extremely selective: it runs separate ad circulars for the affected store alone. Claims William D. Long, Waremart's president: "Kroger is just denying me an opportunity to sell low-cost groceries." Price sheets in hand, Long has appealed to the Federal Trade Commission for relief, claiming that Kroger is singling him out for destruction. The FTC investigated but took no action. Long says Kroger's tactic is working: he won't open another store in Nashville.

Everingham has no intention of putting away the long knives. "I don't think anyone can point accusingly and say, 'Kroger started this price war,' " he argues. "But we're gonna defend our market share and our penetration with all the ability we've got."

That means Kroger does unto others before others can do unto it. The company plops down 100 superstores a year from Roanoke to Fort Worth, expanding its share of mature markets and elbowing into new ones. Everingham deems the South and West most promising. Kroger has gained ground in Houston and Dallas, and doubled its Atlanta market share to 24 percent in a six-year burst of store building and price pounding.

Perhaps its quickest, biggest push ever came in San Antonio, which Kroger entered from scratch in 1979. Like a thunderstorm off the Gulf of Mexico, it rolled in with 14 stores and a warehouse in two years. It was betting an estimated $100 million that it could take a big bite of the market—and gain the attendant scale economies—in a single chomp.

To help build traffic, Kroger launched its typical "best prices in town" campaign and waited for customers to pour in. The response, officials admit, was underwhelming. Lo and behold, H. E. Butt Grocery Co., the then and present market leader, knew how to play defense Kroger-style. Butt delayed construction of a new headquarters in order to match Kroger new store for new store, price for price, precipitating a price war the like of which the city had never seen. Two smaller chains went to the bottom.

Despite the escalating costs and slow progress, Kroger is a good bet to eventually get its 20 percent to 25 percent cut of the market. Meanwhile, it is demonstrating yet another talent—ability to bleed profusely and survive.

"We have the good fortune," Everingham says, "not to have many San Antonios."

The surest route around other San Antonios led to the acquisition of Dillon, the 11th-largest U.S. chain, which has a lock on established markets much like Kroger's own. The Dillon Store division has big chunks of Kansas, Missouri, and Arkansas towns: it's the law in Dodge City, for example, with at least a 60 percent share. Out in Colorado, Dillon has two divisions. City Markets, with a grip on the western half of the state, operates on high margins in captive tourist areas and in many one- or two-store towns farther west. King Soopers, based in Denver, commands nearly half the business in the 150-by-50-mile territory along the front range of the Rockies.

At some $600 million in Kroger stock, Dillon was the priciest supermarket acquisition in history. But Everingham figures it was a bargain. Dillon's market-share statistics signal high profits; it earned 24 percent on shareholders' equity last year. Having launched a highly successful generics program, King Soopers now sells 20 percent of its goods from the plain-Jane aisle, which could keep Kroger plants plenty busy. To crack Denver from scratch, as it did San Antonio, Kroger would have had to lay out $500 million, facing price wars and no guarantee of market share.

A saw in the grocery trade holds that volume hides all mistakes. Safeway, A&P, and others have spread themselves thin, vying for scraps of business, no matter how unprofitable, in quest of volume. But by quitting markets where it was competing for survival and limiting itself to those where it could compete for growth, Kroger emerged with the most volume of all. A management capable of casting aside its industry's saws looks like a good bet for the future.

Soyfoods Soar on Demographic Trends
Richard Leviton

Soyfood entrepreneurs like the taste of today's demographics. Like yogurt companies before them, they stand to benefit from Americans' growing interest in natural foods.

What began as an oriental food became a low-budget health food. Now, it is headed up the income ladder. A 1981 survey by FIND/SVP found that 17 percent of tofu eaters, for example, had an income between $10,000 and $16,000, and 14 percent earned less than $10,000—a group likely to be tofu's loyal contingent of alternative-minded vegetarians in their 20s.

But the survey also found that 18 percent earned more than $40,000. In the 25 metropolitan areas surveyed, 39 percent of tofu buyers were aged 25 to 34—the baby-boom generation—more than three fourths were female, and almost half lived out West.

While only 10 percent of the total sample had purchased tofu, and 33 percent were "familiar" with it, fully 85 percent were regular buyers of yogurt, and 25 percent heavy users.

Made from soybeans, soyfoods include tofu, tempeh, miso, and a host of secondary prepared foods. They are high in protein, cholesterol-free, low in fat, and inexpensive.

Since 1975, when tofu made the jump from the Asian market to the mainstream supermarket, about 45 Asian-American companies churned out tofu in various ethnic enclaves in larger U.S. cities. By late 1981, about 180 companies were making 26,000 tons annually, worth over $48 million.

America's tofu entrepreneurs have walked into an infant industry at a time when market conditions and consumer demands are perfect. One study predicts tofu sales will climb by 300 percent by 1985, adding that tofu, promoted as a tasty, versatile food, could capture

© March 1983, *American Demographics.*

a market of at least the size of today's yogurt sales of $504 million.

Tofu marketers know that natural food enthusiasts eat tofu. But they also want to know what types of new consumers can be attracted to tofu. The first is the natural foods shopper.

The Health Food Addict

Simmons Market Research Bureau developed a demographic profile of the "typical health food shopper" in 1980. Health food shoppers are usually women between the ages of 25 and 34, college educated, single, employed part-time in a professional, technical, or clerical occupation. For 48 percent, income exceeds $35,000, while the median is $19,340. They cluster in the Northeast and West and in the 25 largest SMSAs.

The natural foods shopper is more likely (compared to average nonhealth food shoppers) to be diet conscious. About half control blood sugar levels; one third would like to lose weight. This model consumer pursues such sports as hiking, running, cross-country skiing, prefers magazines to television, wine to beer, and is 38 percent more likely than other consumers to buy frozen entrees, 213 percent more likely to be a yogurt user, and 175 percent more likely to use frozen yogurt, the survey reported.

Yogurt users have a similar profile. Only 12 percent of current yogurt users in the FIND/SVP survey purchased tofu. But the yogurt users and natural food shoppers are clearly the market with the most potential for the tofu firms.

Demographic shifts that favor the growth of the soyfoods industry include the increase in single-person households—23 percent of all households in 1981. Dual-income families, on the rise, tend to spend more money on convenience items to save time in food preparation. Today's smaller families—some 63 percent of households are childless—mean that adult tastes are becoming more important in meal selection than children's preferences. These trends also suggest demand for smaller package sizes and more convenience offerings.

Education levels are rising too as at least 35 percent of Americans will have attended college by 1990. This trend means better informed, more discriminating consumers, who seek quality, are willing to pay premium prices, and are more likely to experiment with new brands and products.

Tailored Tofu

Legume, Inc. is a New Jersey tofu-products company that recognizes these demographic shifts and tailors its tofu line accordingly. Gary and Chandri Barat's company distributes nationwide a line of frozen Italian-style tofu entrees (Tofu Lasagna, Ravioli, Pizza, Stuffed Shells) in handsomely decorated boxes. After barely two years, Legume's sales have reached $750,000.

The firm focuses sales efforts primarily in high-volume, high-visibility supermarkets. The line is designed to hold its own against Stouffer's Lean Cuisine and Weight Watcher's entrees, both graphically and calorically. Legume's marketing decision to go with frozen Italian foods made with tofu rested on several key observations.

First, plain, unadorned, and modestly packaged tofu (which is the norm for most of the industry's 180 companies) presupposes that typical shoppers might enjoy experimenting in the kitchen with unfamiliar ethnic foods. Second, prepared convenience offerings not only are in vogue but they are a staple in a society too busy to cook.

Their third observation was that ethnic foods are flourishing. Annual sales are placed

at $3.6 billion in 1982, a figure expected to grow by over 12 percent each year through 1990. A recent Gallup survey of 1,000 consumers revealed that 85 percent had tried Italian dishes while eating out, and 38 percent, the highest percentage, ranked Italian as their favorite ethnic style.

Fourth, the Legume company found that frozen pizza sales have grown by 15 percent yearly since 1976, with 1981 sales of $626 million. This represents nearly 5 percent of the total frozen-foods section sales in supermarkets, while the average consumer purchase totals $10.19 for this category.

The Asian Influence

While the primary marketing emphasis since 1975 has been to take tofu out of its oriental context and place it squarely on middle-American dinner plates, at least one company, New England Soy Dairy in Massachusetts, examined the new demographics on the Asian-American population and decided to emphasize the origins of tofu.

The U.S. Asian population has doubled since 1970 to 3.5 million, or 1.5 percent of the total U.S. population, according to the 1980 census. In the last decade, the Japanese-American population grew by 19 percent, Filipinos were up by 126 percent, Koreans, 413 percent, and Hawaiians, 67 percent, compared to the general population growth of only 11 percent.

The New England Soy Dairy is not trying to sell their brand of tofu to the enlarged ranks of Asian immigrants, however, but to the thousands of consumers influenced by this Asian wave. The company targets consumers who spend their predinner hours leaning over woks, stirring noodles, chopping vegetables, pouring in ginger sauce, and practicing what is now called "nouvelle cuisine"—with tofu.

A 1976 Gallup poll suggested that soy, as a new food, doesn't bubble upmarket as a poor man's staple, but percolates downward as a status food among the affluent. This survey revealed that college-educated, upper-income households were more likely than others to have a positive attitude about using soybeans as food.

The gourmet foods market is strongest in the Northeast and Pacific, and 50 percent of gourmet-food consumers have incomes above $30,000. Their median age is over 40; 50 percent are college educated; 65 percent are women; one- or two-person homes make up 49 percent. Designer foods are in vogue among these urban residents, who enjoy unusual or esoteric foods and prefer adventure in dining.

According to the readership profile for *Bon Appetit,* the gourmet oriented consumer group is 7.5 percent female, has a median age of 41.5, is about 60 percent married, and is likely to have attended college. About half these gourmets live in cities, and nearly 70 percent have incomes over $20,000.

Figures correlating income levels with yogurt and tofu consumption were behind the New England Soy Dairy's decision to part company with the rest of the tofu industry. The practice had been to position tofu as a "quality peasant food" in low-key packaging. Company marketers Madeline Fox and Tom Timmins wanted to go after the other segment with higher incomes and more sophisticated tastes.

In January 1982, New England Soy Dairy launched its ambitious Chinese New Year promotion, distributing 1,200 merchandising kits to New England and mid-Atlantic area supermarkets. The theme was "Happy Chinese New Year with Soy Dairy Cooking." Their "Naturally Gourmet" line (a ginger soy sauce, five-spice powder, egg roll wrappers, wonton skins, and tofu cookbook) debuted to enhance the Chinese image, while expanding uses for tofu. The marketing team conducted dozens of successful one-hour cooking-class demonstrations in department stores, supermarkets, and malls.

"The plan is to make people feel comfortable with oriental dishes," says marketer Madeline Fox, "to make the meals seem exciting, versatile, healthful, and gourmet, but easy to prepare with a distinctively U.S. flavor." The promotion netted an initial 47 percent sales increase followed by a net gain of 20 percent.

New Markets

While astute tofu marketers work to capture the market in affluent professionals demanding quality, convenience, and good nutrition, other population trends suggest tofu markets as yet undeveloped.

The elderly, people over 65, will grow more than 20 percent in the 1980s, to 32 million in 1990. Elderly women living alone will increase by 29 percent, with a total of 50 percent of the elderly living by themselves. Meanwhile, elderly income is projected to increase, after inflation, by less than 1 percent per year. Tofu's potential for this segment is as a low-cost versatile food that meets dietary needs.

The weight conscious of America are another untapped market. This group includes the 70 million Americans on a diet at any given time, with about 30 million of them carrying 20 percent more weight than they prefer.

The "typical" dieter, according to *Weight Watchers* magazine's audience profile, is female and over 35. About three quarters are high school graduates. Almost half have incomes above $20,000. Nearly 70 percent are married and live in cities. This description is more blue-collar and downscale than the typical ethnic- and gourmet-foods patron, and includes primarily the chronically overweight. But it does not reflect the larger number of calorie-aware consumers, people already slim or nearly on target with their weight and planning to stay there with careful food selections.

Tofu is well suited for people concerned about diet. It is even more of a diet food than yogurt because of its low calorie-to-protein ratio. Weight Watchers International, recognizing this attribute, includes a half dozen tofu recipes in its official cookbook. Such soy companies as Legume stress the nutritional and caloric information for their low-salt, low-calorie, nonfattening, tofu raviolis and other products.

Marketing tofu is a matter of matching tofu's virtue for each targeted market, whether it be to "peasant-style" natural food users, trendy oriental-foods buffs, upscale gourmet chic fanciers, calorie-obsessed dieters, or the diet-restricted elderly. Since more Americans are moving into these groups, soyfoods are likely to move along with them.

————————————— *Case Studies* —————————————

The Suburban Centre
Dennis H. Tootelian

Nearing the end of the fiscal year, Mr. Larry Jacobs, manager of the Suburban Centre, was assessing the past performance of the regional shopping center (see Exhibit 1) and trying to develop a plan for the future. Faced with rather poor performance several years ago, and increasing competition at the present time, Mr. Jacobs wanted to prepare a plan to present to the Centre's Board of Trustees. Of particular concern was identifying what types of retail outlets to bring into the mall and a program for attracting them. Mr. Jacobs noted:

> Our best point is our location. If we come up with the right tenant mix, we'll have a good tenant mix AND a good location. This is a sure-fire formula.

Center Profile

The Suburban Centre, a regional shopping center located in a large northwestern city, housed 51 tenants on about 40 acres of land. There were 680,790 square feet of leasable space and 3,500 parking spaces (see Exhibit 2). In 1970, the mall was enclosed, and the conversion allowed customers to enter any store either from the mall entrance or from the individual store's entrance on the parking lot. Mr. Jacobs commented on the enclosed mall conversion and the recent history of Suburban Centre:

> This fact that we're a conversion is a strike against us. The stores can be full, but the mall can be empty, giving the impression that the center is dead. In reality, many stores are doing excellent, have been in overage (paying percentage of sales over minimum rent) for years, and are still growing.
>
> Seven years ago, Suburban Centre was extremely active with a 100 percent occupancy rate. The anchor store was one of the highest volume-per-square-foot producers in the entire country, despite its small size.

This case was prepared by Professor Dennis H. Tootelian, California State University, Sacramento.

Dennis H. Tootelian and Ralph M. Gaedeke. Cases and Classics in Marketing Management. Copyright © 1986 by Harcourt Brace Jovanovich, Inc. Reprinted by permission of the publisher.

EXHIBIT 1 Shopping Center Definitions

For case purposes, a shopping center is a group of retail businesses integrated in such a manner that customers can be provided one-stop shopping for their daily needs of goods and services. Three types of centers are included in this case.

SR—Super Regional Shopping Center	Provides goods and services in full depth and variety, includes three or more full-line department stores as principal tenants, and a total area of 1 million or more square feet with parking for 5,000 or more cars.
R—Regional Shopping Center	Provides goods and services in full depth and variety, includes one or more major department stores as principal tenants and one or more large supermarkets; total area exceeds 300,000 square feet with parking for 1,000 or more cars.
C—Community Shopping Center	Provides a wide variety of goods and services in hard and soft lines, in addition to convenience goods and services. Principal tenants are generally a junior department store or large variety store and a supermarket. Total area usually ranges from 60,000 to 300,000 square feet with parking for 400 or more cars.

EXHIBIT 2 Suburban Centre Mall

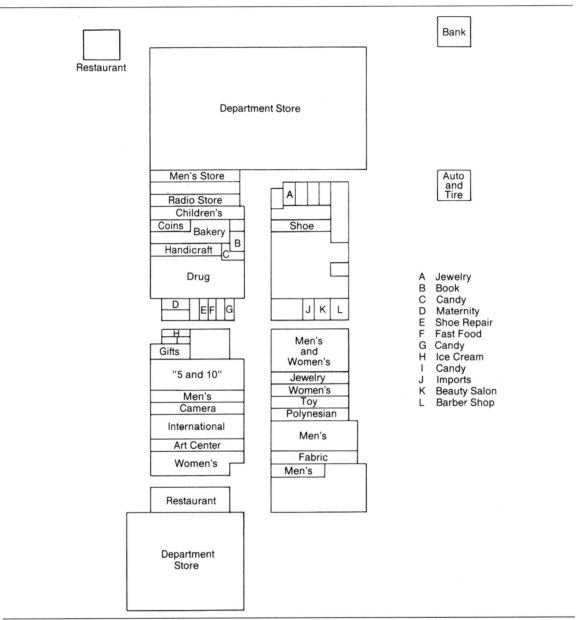

It was at that time that we decided to enclose the mall because of competition. We had been an open mall for about 20 years.

In 1970, we also signed a lease with a big department store. Because of this commitment, we could no longer lease to Apex Supermarket, a 20-year tenant, and they left. At the same time, the anchor store, also a longtime tenant, wanted to expand. We turned them down, too, because we really wanted the big department store. The an-

EXHIBIT 3 Suburban Centre Growth Rate

	1974	1975	1976	1977
Sales	100.0	103.7	106.1	106.4
Total store net profit	100.0	101.1	100.5	99.8
Percent of stores profitable	88.6	89.1	88.9	87.8
Number of stores in centre	41.0	47.0	48.0	51.0

chor store went across the street to what is now Suburban Plaza, which started as a small strip center in 1958, and they built a beautiful 160,000-square-foot store. The plaza became enclosed shortly thereafter.

The deal with the big department store fell through. They just pulled out. That action started the deterioration of the Suburban Centre. Another store left, a discount drugstore did not renew—overnight we had many vacancies. Stores either closed down or went across the street . . . some still even paid rent over here for years, even though they had closed long ago. We've had steady decreases in volume since then. The bottom literally fell out, until two years ago when a big department store signed with us. It opened in March of 1976 and a new discount drugstore just opened.

We've invested over $10,000,000 in the last year and a half, and we've put a lot of thought

EXHIBIT 4 Suburban Centre Projections

Tenant Group	Percent GLA*	Percent Sales	Percent Total Charges
Food	1.31	1.99	3.38
Food services	2.19	2.27	3.9
General merchandise	48.4	47.39	23.92
Clothing and shoes	16.63	24.6	33.35
Dry goods	4.53	5.79	4.37
Furniture	0	0	0
Other retail	12.18	17.39	26.61
Financial	1.65	0	2.45
Offices	0.65	0	0
Services	0.51	0.49	1.21
Other	0.64	0	0.8
Vacant space	11.31	0	0
Total	100.00	100.00	100.00

*GLA = Gross Leasable Area

into our planning. It's sure to pay off. (See Exhibits 3, 4, 5, and 6.)

Management

In 1961, Suburban Centre was purchased by a large investment company located on the East Coast. This firm bought the property

EXHIBIT 5 Financial Data for Enclosed Regional Shopping Centers over 10 Years Old *(Based on GLA*: Suburban Centre 1976)*

Expected Suburban Centre Figures Based on Average Size Store			
Items	*Median*	*Lower Decile*	*Upper Decile*
Sales	$25,569,064	$14,856,294	$33,948,749
Operating receivables	1,184,343	832,060	1,737,931
Operating expenses	352,283	174,464	583,784
Operating balance	852,190	637,465	1,097,111
Net operating income	362,349	23,486	832,060
Funds, after debt service	348,928	110,718	932,712

Expected Figures, Based on Actual GLA National Average			
Items	*Median*	*Lower Decile*	*Upper Decile*
Sales	$51,883,005	$30,145,981	$68,460,666
Operating receivables	2,403,189	1,688,359	3,526,492
Operating expenses	714,830	354,011	1,184,575
Operating balance	1,729,207	1,293,501	2,226,183
Net operating income	735,253	47,655	1,683,354
Funds, after debt service	708,022	255,661	1,892,596

*GLA = Gross Leasable Area

Source: The Urban Land Institute, *Dollars and Cents of Shopping Centers,* 1975 (Washington: The Urban Land Institute; 1975).

EXHIBIT 6 Regional Shopping Center Store Size by Tenant Classification versus Suburban Centre 1976

Average National Regional Shopping Center

Tenant Group	Percent GLA *	Percent Sales	Percent Total Charge†
Food	5.5	7.9	6.0
Food service	2.9	3.6	5.2
General merchandise	53.4	48.5	32.0
Clothing and shoes	16.9	20.4	26.3
Dry goods	1.4	1.5	2.5
Furniture	1.4	1.7	1.8
Other retail	10.1	13.3	16.6
Financial	1.6	0	2.7
Offices	0.4	0	0.6
Services	1.2	1.1	2.7
Other	3.0	2.0	3.6
Vacant space	2.2	0	0
Total	100.00	100.00	100.00

Suburban Centre

Tenant Group	Percent GLA	Percent Sales	Percent Total Charge
Food	0.75	1.17	2.19
Food service	2.19	2.54	4.1
General merchandise	48.4	48.69	25.15
Clothing and shoes	15.48	23.94	32.98
Dry goods	4.53	5.97	4.6
Furniture	0	0	0
Other retail	11.34	17.1	26.29
Financial	1.65	0	2.58
Offices	0.65	0	0
Services	0.51	0.59	1.27
Other	0.84	0	0.84
Vacant space	13.66	0	0
Total	100.00	100.00	100.00

*Gross Leasable Area

†Includes Rent, Overage (if any), Common Area Fees and Misc.

Source: *Dollars and Cents of Shopping Centers,* 1975.

from the original developers and leased it back to them for a period of 11 years. At the end of the lease, the investment company began operating the center through a professional management company which received a management fee plus a commission based on lease volume.

Suburban Centre was governed by a board of trustees, comprised of members of the professional management company and the owners. Policy was largely determined by a sub-

group of the board which met biweekly on the West Coast. Mr. Jacobs had some input, but only of a suggestive nature.

Resident Management

Mr. Jacobs was formerly the shopping center's promotion director for the original developers. When the professional management company took over in 1972, he became the center's manager. Prior to his eight years with the Centre, he was promotion director with three other regional shopping centers on the West Coast and in the Midwest. Concerning his perception of his current responsibilities, Mr. Jacobs commented:

> The basic reason for a resident manager is to make sure that the center stays clean, that mall floors are waxed, and so forth.

Mr. Jacobs was also the spokesman for the Merchants Association, to which all Suburban Centre tenants belonged. This association conducted the advertising in media and mall events, such as sidewalk sales and moonlight sales. Ms. Linda Schmidt was its promotion director.

Tenant Policy

Each lease was different. Negotiations for basic rent and percentage of sales for rent were based on the desirability of the tenant to the center and vice versa. Each tenant paid a certain cost per square foot. The larger the leased space, the lower the cost per foot. In addition, each tenant paid a common area fee for parking lot facilities and mall maintenance. When a predetermined sales volume was reached, a certain percentage of each dollar was paid for additional rent charges (overages). Even though specific rental fee comparisons between shopping centers were difficult to assess, Mr. Jacobs knew that the costs at Suburban Centre were at the higher range. Only Blueridge Mall and Suburban Plaza had higher costs per square foot.

Competition

Although the number of competing shopping centers had not increased appreciably within the last several years, the opening of a super regional about 15 miles from Suburban Centre had hurt the sales of nearly all other malls within the city. Housing 4 major department stores and nearly 100 other specialty stores, Blueridge Mall was especially popular.

One result of the opening of Blueridge was increased competition among the others to attract both customers and desirable retail stores. The major malls competing with Suburban Centre are identified in Exhibit 7. Mr. Jacobs discussed the competition.

> Suburban Plaza, across the street, is not competition. We are partners, more or less. We work together. We promote both sides of the street in what we call Suburban City. It seems like no one realizes that there are two different centers. In order, our competition is Blueridge Mall, Manor Fair, Southwest Center, and maybe the Downtown Mall which is under reconstruction.

Despite Mr. Jacobs's contention that Suburban Plaza was not a competitor, most retailers within the Centre felt differently. Suburban Plaza was second only to Blueridge Mall in terms of retail sales even though it was no bigger than the others. Because of its tenant mix and success in its promotional efforts, the members of the merchant association rated Suburban Plaza its biggest threat. At times, this difference of opinion caused some friction between Mr. Jacobs and the association members.

City Market Survey

In order to make recommendations to the board, Mr. Jacobs gathered data on the metropolitan area and on the buying habits of the various shopping mall customers. A local newspaper recently published the results of a

EXHIBIT 7

Downtown Mall (Open and Enclosed)

Type	Regional
Selling space	127,000 sq. ft. (enclosed)
Parking capacity	None free
Total units	63 occupied
Year opened	1965

Suburban Plaza (Enclosed)

Type	Regional
Selling space	600,000 sq. ft.
Parking capacity	3,500 cars
Total units	48 occupied
Year opened	1960

Suburban Centre (Enclosed)

Type	Regional
Selling space	580,000 sq. ft.
Parking capacity	2,800 cars
Total units	40 occupied
Year opened	1952

Remarks: Addition of 180,000 sq. ft. planned, including a major department store and its auto service center, plus 40,000 sq. ft. of new mall shops.

Manor Fair (Enclosed)

Type	Regional
Selling space	750,000 sq. ft.
Parking capacity	8,000 cars
Total units	69 occupied
Year opened	1959

Remarks: Space currently available, 27,000 sq. ft.

Blueridge Mall (Enclosed)

Type	Super regional
Selling space	1,148,046 sq. ft.
Parking capacity	6,500 cars
Total units	103 occupied
Year opened	1972

Southwest Center (Enclosed)

Type	Regional
Selling space	680,000 sq. ft.
Parking capacity	7,000 cars
Total units	80 occupied
Year opened	1963

Remarks: Space currently available.

shopping center analysis it made, and Ms. Schmidt followed up on some aspects of the report with a study of her own sponsored by the merchants association. Mr. Jacobs hoped that this information would help him to better identify the types of retailers desired to best complete the tenant mix.

Shopper Characteristics

The 16 shopping districts comprising the city contained 918,000 residents (see Exhibits 8, 9, and 10). According to Ms. Schmidt's study, 30 percent of the population within Suburban Centre's district lived within a five-mile radius of the Centre, and accounted for 61 percent of its shoppers. The population within this five-mile radius was predominantly white (87 percent), with a median income of $13,157. Most, furthermore, were white-collar workers (66 percent), and 36 percent of the adult population had at least some college education.

The local newspaper study of Suburban Centre and its major competitors identified two comparative characteristics regarded as highly significant in its findings. First, the Suburban Centre customers were found to be older than those of other shopping centers. Sixty-two percent of the other mall shoppers surveyed by the newspaper were under 35 years of age, whereas only 41 percent of Suburban Centre's customers fell into that age group.

Second, the centre's patrons tended to be more affluent than those of the other shopping malls. Suburban Centre had 27 percent more shoppers from families earning over $25,000 per year, and 20 percent fewer shoppers who came from families making $15,000 or less than the competing centers. Additionally, the Centre's customers ranked first in the number of credit cards possessed. Of nine local and national credit cards identified by the newspaper, the average centre customer held eight.

Although the greater affluence did not bother Mr. Jacobs at all, the age factor did. Catering to an older group, Mr. Jacobs thought, could be problematical. The news-

EXHIBIT 8 Market Profile of the City

	1960	1977	% Increase Since 1960
Population	625,603	918,600	47
Households	187,820	351,300	87
Effective buying Income (in thousands)	$1,565,708	$4,664,122	198
Total retail sales (in thousands)	$ 903,352	$2,876,659	218
Total retail outlets	11,760	21,206	80

EXHIBIT 9 Where They Come From, Where They Shop*

Populations and Households by Districts			
No.	*Population*	*Households*	*% of Households*
1.	59,000	19,800	6.5
2. (Manor Fair)	153,000	51,000	17.5
3. (Suburban Centre, Suburban Plaza)	126,000	39,100	13.4
4.	21,000	6,400	2.2
5.	22,600	7,100	2.4
6.	28,300	9,000	3.1
7. (Downtown Mall)	29,600	16,600	5.7
8.	23,400	10,000	3.4
9. (Blueridge Mall)	69,500	20,500	7.1
10.	87,500	29,000	10.0
11.	102,000	34,500	11.9
12.	13,500	3,900	1.3
13.	14,500	5,100	1.8
14.	61,400	21,000	7.2
15.	31,000	10,500	3.6
16.	25,500	8,500	2.9
Total	867,800	292,100	100.0

*Shoppers at each of the shopping center parking lots were asked to identify where they live by zip code number. Interviewers were trained in this technique. This survey was prepared by the marketing department of the local newspaper.

EXHIBIT 10 Retail Sales and Effective Buying Income *(Comparison Increases: City, State, United States)*

	1973 (in thousands) City	% Increase 4 Years City	% Increase 4 Years State	% Increase 4 Years United States
Effective buying income	$3,664,122	39	37	41
Total retail sales	2,335,659	56	43	48
Food store sales	505,017	47	39	47
Supermarkets (1)	422,103	45	37	56
General merchandise stores	292,894	36	19	21
Department stores (1)	261,805	64	31	38
Apparel store sales	107,001	49	37	47
Furniture and household appliances	120,756	53	43	51
Furniture and home furnishings (1)*	76,968	64	57	67
Automotive dealers**	476,963	57	44	55
Gasoline stations/garages	194,964	54	44	58
Lumber/building/hardware	120,783	111	78	41
Drugstores	99,292	31	22	36
Eating, drinking places	238,169	83	69	72

*3-Year increase.

**Includes dealers selling autos (new or used), motorcycles, house trailers, boats, and bicycles. New or used commercial dealers not included.

(1) Sales included in above category.

Source: Sales Management's Survey of Buying Power, 1974.

paper cited city population estimates showing that the 18 to 35 age group was the fastest growing segment, at least through the early 1980s. The newspaper also noted that the youth population (defined as under 30 years) was moving into the city's suburbs at a rate three times as fast as any other age group.

Shopping Patterns

In terms of shopping patterns, the newspaper characterized the average Suburban Centre shopper as a "hit and run" shopper. It found that the centre had nearly twice as many patrons who spent less than 30 minutes in the mall as any competing shopping center. The centre also tied with Manor Fair for the lowest percentage of customers who shopped for 1 hour or more.

The newspaper study additionally showed that 62 percent of Suburban Centre shoppers rated store selection as good to excellent. This was the lowest rating given by shoppers of all centers. Overall, nearly 85 percent of the shoppers at other malls rated the mall they were in as having a good to excellent selection of stores. Much the same rating was given to

eating facilities. Nearly twice as many patrons at Manor Fair, Southwest Center, and Blueridge Mall evaluated their eating facilities as good to excellent as compared to those at Suburban Centre. One of the few attractions to the centre was found to be the special promotions (art shows, craft exhibits, and the like) it used on occasion. Over 70 percent of the patrons in Suburban Centre said this was an appealing aspect of the mall.

As a follow-up to this particular issue of appeal, Ms. Schmidt's study addressed the question of what could be done to improve the Centre. Her findings are presented in Exhibit 11.

Mr. Jacobs's Recommendation

In light of the stiff competition and of the shoppers' characteristics and buying patterns, Mr. Jacobs was trying to decide on the right mix. Many of the suggestions provided by Ms. Schmidt seemed sound, but he was wondering whether any special effort was necessary. After all, he thought, the rebuilding process took time, and perhaps competition had peaked.

EXHIBIT 11 Suburban Centre *(Shopper's Comments)*

Suggested Improvements for the Centre

Need more stores
More eating facilities
Furniture store
Wine shop
Need a supermarket
Foxy Lady clothing store
Connect plaza and centre with underground walkway
More ladies' specialty shops
More shoe stores
A good all-hours eating place or cafeteria
Public restrooms
Drinking fountains
More parking

Should remain open longer
More varied merchandise
Better selection of young girls' shoes
Stores need clerks who know their merchandise
  and care about customers
More junior shops like Casual Corner
Need a Macy's
More art and craft shows
More parking for moonlight sales
Office supply store
Need 15–20 minute parking for rush buying
  and pickups
More clothing stores

Stores, Services, or Restaurants to Add to the Centre

Large music store
Mr. Steak
More eating places
Furniture store
More department stores
Macy's
Inexpensive shoe store
Wine shop
Quick snack facility
Fabric store
Music center (pianos, organs)
Good clothing store for women
Foxy Lady
Baby shops
Foxmoor
Chess King
Buffet-style restaurant
Drugstore
Specialty shops
Sporting goods store
Discount store
Plant store
Craft store

Fast-food place (ice cream and popcorn)
Dress shops
Frank Moore's
Orange Julius
Pie shop
Expensive restaurant
Sandwich shop
Fashion Conspiracy
Movie theater
Leed's Shoes
Payless drug
Mervyn's
Clothing store for large women
Bookstore
Good cheap coffee shop
Junior apparel shop
Office supply store
Novelty shop
Ladies ready-to-wear
Farrell's
Bible book store
Pet shop
Record and poster shop

Wolverine World Wide, Inc.: Hush Puppies
Kenneth L. Bernhardt

During the spring of 1968, the director of marketing for Hush Puppies at Wolverine World Wide, Inc., was reviewing past marketing strategies as an aid to formulating marketing plans for 1969. Increased competition, rising raw material costs, and a stabilized demand in the past two years made him wonder what changes, if any, might be appropriate in the Hush Puppies marketing program.

Wolverine World Wide, Inc., first started in 1883 as the partnership of Hirth and Krause, a wholesaler of hides, shoes, and leather supplies. Shoemaking and tanning operations

Written by Kenneth L. Bernhardt, Associate Professor, Georgia State University, Atlanta.

S. H. Rewoldt, J. D. Scott, and M. R. Warshaw, 4th ed. *Marketing Management.* © 1981 Richard D. Irwin, Homewood, Ill.

were first begun in 1903. Wolverine, for many years, specialized in the tanning of unusual leathers, enabling the company to occupy a niche for itself in the competitive cowhide field. The firm's main product from the 1920s through the 1950s, when it was called Wolverine Shoe and Tanning Company, was shell horsehide. This was an extraordinarily stiff and strong leather in which the company had a competitive advantage due to the special triple-tanning process which the company had developed. This tannage was highly acid resistant, which was a significant advantage around the farm where there were lactic and other acids. Shell horsehide, a natural leather, dried soft, stayed soft, and was the second toughest leather in the world after kangaroo leather. The company considered itself as selling leather and not just work shoes.

In the late 1930s, the company became concerned about their raw material supply. Horses were becoming more and more scarce (there were 26 million horses in the United States in 1910 and only 4 million in 1950), and the company realized that they could not make shoes out of tractors. Further, the company believed that its success would be linked to the development of other unusual leathers.

It was about this time that a new opportunity presented itself to the company with the introduction, by the meat-packing houses, of prepackaged sliced bacon. Previously, bacon was sold with the skin on it. After hand skinning the bacon, people just threw away the rind. The prepackaging made available large quantities of bacon rind from which the company was able to develop a suede pigskin leather suitable for a line of work gloves. This was the beginning of Wolverine's entry into the pigskin business. The company soon turned its attention from smoked bacon rinds to large-scale processing of "green" (unsmoked) pigskin.

Pigskin possesses certain outstanding qualities. It wears exceptionally well and is highly resistant to deterioration from perspiration. It cannot be damaged by moisture and humidity. Another important characteristic is the fact that pigskins are available in large quantities, as some 70 million pigs are slaughtered each year in the United States alone. Of course, not all this pigskin is acceptable for tanning purposes by shoe manufacturers.

Unfortunately, however, the pig is not easy to skin. With horses and cows, the skin fits loosely, like a coat, and is very easy to remove, much as a banana is peeled. On the other hand, skinning a hog is somewhat like peeling an apple; the hide is bound tightly to the animal by a layer of fat. A highly trained workman requires more than a half hour to "slay" or skin a hog. This is an obvious production bottleneck, when large packinghouses process 600 or more animals each hour.

During World War II, the War Production Board encouraged packers to develop new ways to produce pigskin as a leather source. Wolverine, due to its experience in tanning unusual leathers, was selected to process this pigskin output into work shoes.

Following the war, the pork packers returned to producing bacon. Wolverine, confronted with a diminishing supply of horsehides, bought several units of a wartime mechanical pigskinner and set out to perfect a new pigskinner that satisfied the requirements of both shoemakers and packers. After seven years of research and upward of $2 million in expenditures, the company developed a unique and highly efficient machine for effectively skinning pigs at the packing plant without damaging the skins. Twenty packers were induced to install the perfected skinning machines in their pork-processing operation. Wolverine now had the first and only volume pigskinner.

The company could now produce a skin uniform in size and about two feet square from each side of the animal. The machines, which were owned by Wolverine and cost $15,000 to $18,000 each, could remove pig hides at the rate of about 460 an hour. Another equally expensive unit called a flushing machine removes all excess fat remaining on the skin.

However, the company still had a problem. The only shoes that Wolverine was making at the time were work shoes, and while pigskin made very comfortable footwear, its lightness worked against it in the work-shoe field. In appraising markets, Wolverine decided that the greatest potential lay in easy-to-care-for leisure shoes. Leisure shoes look attractive with a brushed finish, the best finish for pigskin. Brushing pigskin eliminates surface marks and permits distinctive colors. It also leaves the tiny bristle holes in the leather unblocked, giving the shoes natural ventilation.

In 1957, Wolverine had 30,000 pairs of men's shoes made in the new pigskin leather. The soles were cemented to the uppers, not sewn, as was the practice with most shoes. There was one basic pattern in 11 different colors, including scarlet, canary yellow, and kelly green. These shoes were offered to the trade to retail for $7.95, and were distributed nationally through the work-shoe salesmen who generally sold in small rural towns.

A big turning point came in 1958, when Wolverine changed advertising agencies and employed MacManus, John & Adams, Inc. The agency had done no shoe advertising previously, and Wolverine thought that the new agency would therefore be willing to take new approaches and try new ideas in promoting this brand-new product. The first thing the new agency did was to set up a market test. One hundred pairs of shoes were given to consumers, with a follow-up study being done eight weeks later. At the end of the study the researcher told the consumers that the company needed the shoes back, but if they wanted to keep them they could, upon payment of $5. Overwhelmingly, the consumers wanted to keep the shoes. Of course, the company let them keep the shoes without paying the $5.

With strong encouragement from the consumer test, the agency then attacked the problem of what to call the shoes. The only "Hush Puppies" that people had ever heard of at the time was a corn fritter which people in some Southern states threw to their barking dogs with the command, "Hush, puppies." Several of Wolverine's executives liked the name and thought it appropriate to give this name to a comfortable shoe that is kind to the feet and hushes that special kind of "barking dog," one's tired feet.

An outside marketing research firm was commissioned to conduct the name study. Interviews were held with 300 people in Los Angeles and Chicago testing six potential names: Swash Bucks, Lazers, Breathers, Slow Pokes, Ho-Hums, and Hush Puppies. Swash Bucks and Lazers were the best-liked names. The Hush Puppies name had a high association with food and dogs and was the least desirable name. The agency wanted the company to change the name, but the Wolverine sales manager was insistent that Hush Puppies was the name that should be used, and he won out. To go along with the name, a logo was prepared to help create an image for the shoes. A sad-eyed, droopy-eared basset hound was created for this purpose.

The agency and company then set out to reintroduce the new men's leisure-time shoes. Up until this time Wolverine had sold only 30,000 pairs of the Hush Puppies, an extremely small proportion of the total men's shoe market of 200 million pairs per year. This market was, at the time, a relatively stable market, with the men buying an average of only 1.3 pairs of shoes per year and owning an average wardrobe of only 2.5 to 3 pairs of shoes. Research has indicated that men dislike shopping for shoes and feel little need for owning several pairs, which helps explain the lack of growth in the industry.

Initial Marketing Strategy

Wolverine's problem of introducing Hush Puppies was also intensified by the company distribution network in 1958. The company had 57 salesmen who had been selling shell horsehide work shoes and boots, calling on outlets in the small towns and villages of the United States—rarely, if ever, setting foot in the big cities or the growing suburbs. The work shoes and boots were sold primarily to farmers—a main copy point was their stout resistance to "barnyard acid"—whereas the market for Hush Puppies was in the cities and suburbs. A plan to gain new distribution was then worked out.

The company's sales manager was told that the board of directors would approve an advertising budget of 17 percent of anticipated sales, if the sales manager could open 600 new accounts in 35 cities in six weeks. The 35-city plan resulted from an idea to advertise in the 35 cities in which the *This Week* Sunday supplement to newspapers was distributed. This was a large amount of advertising, relative to the industry average of 1.5 percent of sales, and the sales manager accepted the challenge. So in August 1958 all of the company's salesmen were pulled in, literally "transferred" for at least a month, and sent to the 35 cities for a concerted sales drive on Hush Puppies.

It was decided to spend the entire advertising budget in one full-page, four-color advertisement in *This Week* magazine, distributed in 35 leading cities of the country. The extra incentive for the retail stores was that their name would be prominently listed in the Sunday supplement newspaper ad if they ordered the minimum specified assortment of Hush Puppies shoes.

The salesmen were trained by the sales manager on the sales pitch to be used. Each salesman got the highlights of the consumer acceptance study. He carried samples of the

shoes in all 11 colors. He used a demonstration kit showing how the "Breathin' Brushed Pigskin" leather resisted soil, rain, and stains, and he carried a preproof of the color ad showing how the store's name would be handled.

The Wolverine salesmen received orders from 600 major retail accounts—all new—in three weeks, and the ad was run at the end of August. The copy in the ad was unusual compared with normal shoe industry advertising. The shoes were shown on people's feet, and both feet were shown. Previously, most shoe ads had shown just one shoe, so it could be pictured as big as possible, usually against a solid colored velvet or other elegant background.

The ad ran on Sunday, and most retailers sold out their complete stock in a few days. One hundred twenty thousand pairs of Hush Puppies were sold at a retail price of $7.95. Another ad was immediately authorized for the Christmas gift season, again with the dual objectives of (1) selling the concept of leisure shoes, and (2) using dealer listing to gain better distribution in the large markets. It was felt that *This Week* supplement could best satisfy these objectives because of its high impact and penetration into a large number of homes in each city. The Christmas ad was even more successful than the initial ad in August.

Changes in Marketing Strategy, 1959–1963

For 1959, the strategy continued, but expanded into over 50 additional markets covered by *Parade* magazine. The advertising was scheduled for late spring to give the Hush Puppies salesmen time to cover their newly expanded territories, opening up more new retail accounts. Another men's style was added and sales tripled. Promotion effort and sales results both continued to grow. *Family Weekly* Sunday newspaper supplement was later added plus the *Sunday Group* and independent newspapers. By 1961, Hush Puppies was the most heavily promoted brand of shoe in the United States. The advertising budget by this time had leveled off at 7 percent of sales, which was four times the industry average. Demand continued to be greater than capacity, but Wolverine kept on advertising and adding new dealers through the listings. The Sunday supplement promotions were run four times per year: at Easter, at the end of May, in August, and in December. The salesmen would send in a report by telegram on Monday and would file a full report on the promotion's success on Friday of the same week.

The company followed a selective distribution strategy, protecting its dealers so that a proper amount of inventory would be stocked. The price was increased to $9.95, as Wolverine needed a larger margin to support plant expansion and other growth programs, including the largest advertising expenditure for a single brand in the shoe industry. Also, dealers would be more interested in adding the Hush Puppies line if higher margins were offered. All outlets maintained the suggested retail price.

During this period, Wolverine expanded its product line. In 1960, golf shoes were introduced. The total golf shoe market had been about 100,000 pairs per year, but in their first year 94,000 pairs of Hush Puppies golf shoes were sold. In 1961, women's shoes were designed, and by 1963, Hush Puppies were available in styles for the entire family and age spectrum from five years old up.

Until 1963, Wolverine continued to sell Hush Puppies shoes faster than it could ship them, with pairage volume showing great increases (see Exhibit 1). Total company sales increased from a plateau of $11 million to $33 million during this period, with profits in-

EXHIBIT 1 Pairs of Hush Puppies Sold (000)

1957	30
1958	301
1959	1,000
1960	1,500
1961	2,600
1962	4,900

creasing by an even greater percentage. Selected financial statistics are in Exhibit 2.

Up to this point, no one in the company knew the real consumer marketing reasons why sales were increasing this rapidly. The main problems executives had been concerned with centered on how to get more pigskin, more tanning, and more production out of the factories, which were working three shifts a day. There had been no time to think about who was buying Hush Puppies or for what reason. The marketing executives thought that the buyers were from the lower middle class, with emphasis among those people, such as service station attendants, who were on their feet much of the day.

In 1963, the company, in conjunction with its advertising agency, designed a consumer research study to find out more about Hush Puppies' consumers and about what people's experience with Hush Puppies had been. Twenty thousand screening interviews were conducted, followed by 1,000 in-depth interviews. Some of the results are shown in Exhibits 3 and 4. The study showed that 61 percent of the adult population was aware of Hush Puppies, but only 10 percent of the population had bought a pair. The buyers had higher than average income and education, and they generally were professionals or skilled workers. The company, for the first time, really knew who was buying Hush Puppies. When it asked these people why they bought Hush Puppies, comfort kept coming back, followed by light weight and long wear. The company could now plan marketing strategy based on knowledge of both buyers and nonbuyers.

EXHIBIT 2 Wolverine World Wide, Inc.: Selected Financial Information

	Sales ($000)	Profits ($000)	Percent of Profits	Assets ($000)	Shareholders' Equity ($000)	Earnings per Share
1956	$11,313	$ 251	2.2	$ 6,394	$4,750	$0.09
1957	10,925	125	1.1	6,692	4,200	0.05
1958	11,376	341	2.9	6,496	4,387	0.13
1959	15,264	591	3.9	8,025	4,742	0.24
1960	17,929	658	3.7	9,895	6,159	0.22
1961	23,992	1,218	5.1	12,428	7,069	0.40
1962	33,231	1,945	5.9	14,375	8,561	0.64

Source: Wolverine World Wide, Inc., Annual Report, 1968.

EXHIBIT 3 1963 Consumer Research on Hush Puppies' Buyers

	Percent in United States	Percent of Hush Puppies' Buyers
Sex		
Men	48	43*
Women	52	57*
	100	100
Household income		
Under $3,000	20	7
$3,000–$5,000	19	13
$5,000–$7,500	22	31
$7,500–$10,000	21	28
Over $10,000	18	21
	100	100
Occupation (head of household)		
Professional/technical/merchants/ official/proprietor	19	30
Skilled/foreman/craftsman	15	20
Sales-clerical	10	20
Unskilled/operatives	20	11
Farmer	6	1
Service	5	6
Others	25	12
	100	100
Education (head of household)		
Grade school	33	8
High school	46	52
College	21	40
	100	100
Age 18 years and older		
Under 25 years	14	9
25–34 years	20	25
35–44 years	21	34
45–54 years	18	21
55 and over	27	11
	100	100

*Many of these were purchased for others (see Exhibit 4).

EXHIBIT 4 Person for Whom Hush Puppies Were Purchased by Men versus Women

	Percent of Total Buyers	Percent of Men Buyers	Percent of Women Buyers
For self only	46	66	32
For self and others	18	12	22
For others only	36	22	46
	100	100	100

Marketing Strategy, 1963–1966

Armed with information about the consumer, the company was now better able to plan its marketing strategy. To increase the reach and frequency against the new target market, the company began using television in 1964. The "Today" and "Tonight" programs, whose viewers closely matched Hush Puppies' new target market, were tested and subsequently added. This was designed to increase brand awareness and emphasize the comfort theme. It also gave the advertising program some continuity, instead of only the four "waves" per year provided by the Sunday supplement advertisements. Specific advertising objectives were set, and progress was measured. Magazines were added to the media plan to even more effectively reach the newly defined target audience. The following is a list of the magazines which were used: *Good Housekeeping, Parents, Jack and Jill, Esquire, Playboy, True, Mademoiselle, Glamour, Redbook, Seventeen, Ebony, Sports Illustrated, and Family Circle.*

The company continued to use *Family Weekly, This Week, Parade,* and other Sunday supplements at the beginning of each season to introduce the new styles and to provide a promotional peak for retail tie-in advertising.

The consumer study also resulted in a change in Hush Puppies' copy strategy. The 1964 ads stressed the comfort of Hush Puppies, and in 1965 the theme "Hush Puppies make the sidewalks softer" was created and used to illustrate and communicate this comfort.

The company's distribution structure now included 15,000 retail accounts consisting of 60 percent shoe stores and 40 percent department stores (which did 60 percent of the total shoe volume). The company maintained its selective distribution policy, which was somewhat unusual in the shoe industry, where it was common for a company to have several different labels for their shoes, giving each retailer an exclusive franchise for one of the labels. Another unusual aspect of Hush Puppies' distribution strategy was that some of their biggest competitors were also their biggest customers.

Wolverine had maintained the same $9.95 price from 1959 until 1965. At that time, rising costs forced an increase to $11.95. It was not felt that this increase would hurt sales, as the company still had no strong competition in the quality, lower-priced, leisure shoe market.

The company's strategy continued to be successful. Sales grew from $39 million in 1963 to $55.4 million in 1965. Profits nearly doubled. The company had gone from 63d in the industry in 1958 to 6th in the industry at the end of 1965. Eighty-four percent of the adult population was now aware of the brand name, and 22 percent had now purchased at least one pair.

Situation in 1968

By the beginning of 1968, things had changed considerably. Hush Puppies sales were down from the 1966 level, and total company profits were down 40 percent. Selected financial information for this period is included in Exhibit 5. Increased competition and rising raw material costs were known contributors to this financial situation. The management reviewed recent research to find other causes of the leveling off of sales and to find ways to change the marketing strategy to renew the company's growth.

By early 1967, 88 percent of the adult population was aware of the Hush Puppies name and 40 percent had purchased at least one pair (see Exhibit 6). Thus, the percentage of the population which had purchased at least one pair of Hush Puppies had increased sharply in the past few years, and the company management and the advertising agency were concerned with market saturation and what marketing strategy to use to expand sales and profits.

Exhibit 7 revealed another related problem. Fewer former buyers were continuing to buy new pairs. Exhibit 8 showed one possible reason why. Previous buyers who had had their Hush Puppies for over one year were not wearing them for as many or as dressy occasions as new buyers. One of the product's advantages, its resistance to wearing out, was apparently hurting repeat buying. The older pairs were being used for painting, mowing the lawn, etc. The shoes were being downgraded in their usage. However, because the shoes were not worn out, the owners were not buying new pairs.

The executives also reviewed the reasons why people purchased and did not purchase Hush Puppies. This information is in Exhibits 9 and 10. Comfort continued to be the outstanding reason for purchase, but dislike of

EXHIBIT 5 Wolverine World Wide, Inc.: Selected Financial Information

	Sales ($000)	Profits ($000)	Percent of Profits	Assets ($000)	Shareholders' Equity ($000)	Earnings per Share
1963	$39,021	$2,527	6.5	$19,180	$10,424	$0.84
1964	49,083	4,148	8.5	25,080	13,690	1.37
1965	55,357	4,797	8.7	28,266	17,280	1.59
1966	55,813	3,796	6.8	35,393	19,567	1.26
1967	54,839	2,857	5.2	38,295	20,916	0.95

Source: Wolverine World Wide, Inc., Annual Report, 1968.

EXHIBIT 6

	Percent 1967	Percent 1965	Percent 1964	Percent 1963
Awareness of Hush Puppies brand name (total unaided and aided)				
Have heard of Hush Puppies	88	84	67	61
Have not heard of Hush Puppies	12	16	33	39
Base: Total respondents	(1,234)	(17,685)	(70,420)	(68,409)
Prior purchase of Hush Puppies (1967 compared with prior years)				
Have purchased Hush Puppies	40	22	15	10
Have never purchased Hush Puppies	60	78	85	90
Base: Total respondents	(1,234)	(14,855)	(47,181)	(41,729)

EXHIBIT 7 Composition of Total Franchise *(By new, repeat, and former customers)*

	Percent in 1967	Percent in 1965	Percent in 1964
New buyers in past year	21	30	33
Former buyers, bought in past year	16	34	34
Former buyers, prior years but not in past year	63	36	33
	100	100	100
Base: Total buyers	(492)	(3,850)	(10,789)

EXHIBIT 8 Occasions or Purposes for Which Hush Puppies Are Worn *(1967 new buyers in past years versus other buyers in 1967 study, in percent)*

	Men Buyers			Women Buyers		
Occasions	*New in Past Year*	*All Others*	*Difference*	*New in Past Year*	*All Others*	*Difference*
Grocery shopping	90	54	36	85	66	19
In-town shopping	81	48	33	71	44	27
Evening out at friends	78	47	31	51	38	13
A PTA meeting	52	29	23	43	27	16
At regular work	51	33	18	57	41	16
Church	35	19	16	25	12	13
A wedding	13	8	5	6	4	2
Don't know/no answer	4	28	24	1	27	26
Base: Total buyers	(83)	(126)		(79)	(204)	

EXHIBIT 9 Hush Puppies' Product Image—February 1967 *(men only)*

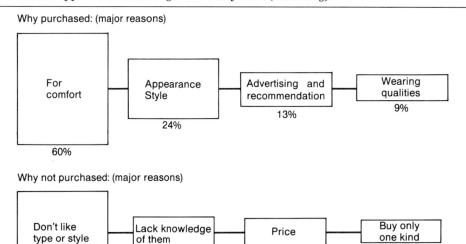

EXHIBIT 10 Hush Puppies' Product Image—February 1967 *(women only)*

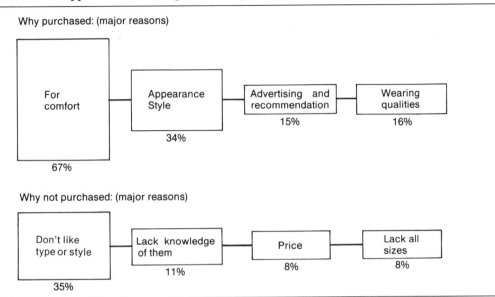

Why purchased: (major reasons)

For comfort — 67%
Appearance Style — 34%
Advertising and recommendation — 15%
Wearing qualities — 16%

Why not purchased: (major reasons)

Don't like type or style — 35%
Lack knowledge of them — 11%
Price — 8%
Lack all sizes — 8%

style was the most important reason for not purchasing Hush Puppies.

After reviewing this information, the executives were trying to find good solutions to the problems they faced. They wondered if they should change the copy approach from the present "comfort" appeal. Should the media strategy be changed, dropping the Sunday supplements, magazines, or both? Should the product itself be changed? In effect, the executives were wondering what changes in their marketing strategy were necessary in light of this new information.

Romano Olive Oil, Inc.
Helene Poist

Founded in the early 1900s in Baltimore, Romano had been importing only the finest quality olive oil from the Mediterranean countries for more than seven decades. Much of the olive oil came directly from groves and processing plants of the parent organization, a growers' cooperative in Spain. Under the policies of the parent organization, the rest of the olive oil had to be purchased through the cooperative. The Spanish cooperative utilized Romano as its marketing organization in the United States. Although the parent wanted to sell as much gallonage as possible through Romano, the American subsidiary's management, almost all U.S. citizens, strongly preferred a healthier "bottom line" (net profit) than what they were achieving. These two goals were somewhat in conflict, apparently because of the price the parent company was charging the American subsidiary for the olive oil. This price was above that that could

Reprinted with permission of Macmillan Publishing Company. Thomas V. Greer, *Cases in Marketing*, 3rd ed. Copyright © 1983 by Thomas V. Greer.

be obtained on the open, free market. Romano accounted for about 10 percent of all olive oil imports into the United States. Since almost all olive oil consumed in the United States was imported, Romano also accounted for about 10 percent of U.S. olive oil sales and was by far the largest marketer of the product.

Olive Oil

In its wild state the olive plant is a low thorny bush, but in its domesticated form it is a tree that can reach 30 feet in height. Native to the Middle East, the olive plant prefers a semidry, mild climate. Because of the fruit and the rich oil obtained from the fruit, the olive became a staple of the diet in the Middle East and spread to all the countries of the Mediterranean Basin in the early years of civilization. Later the olive was brought to California and a few areas of Latin America. Olives and, to a great extent, olive oil became very important exports of Italy, Greece, Spain, and Portugal. California olives were generally sold as canned fruit and were seldom made into oil.

Olive oil was versatile and had been used in various cultures and eras for a variety of purposes besides food preparation. For example, ancient Greeks used olive oil as a body liniment, muscle toner, and relaxant, and for medicinal purposes. The Egyptians mixed it with special herbs and spices to make a perfumed body ointment and cosmetic base. In biblical times olive oil was used in lamps and for religious rituals and blessings. In such times it was used even as a weapon, such as in pouring boiling oil over a fortress wall.

In modern times, however, the primary use of olive oil has been in food preparation. Olive oil has a unique flavor, and it was generally agreed that it surpassed the various vegetable oils in quality. Of particular value was virgin olive oil, which came from the first extraction of the olives. Such a product involved a "cold

press" process, which meant that no hot water or chemical solvents were added to obtain the oil.

Romano's Operations

The oil arrived in drums and tanks in Baltimore harbor, where it was inspected for quality by U.S. Customs, the Food and Drug Administration, and company technicians. At the Romano plant, also in Baltimore, there was continuous quality control by the company laboratory until the product was shipped out to customers. The oil was stored in 32 large, 30,000-gallon, glass-lined, temperature-controlled tanks. The bottling and canning facilities of the plant could process all of the company's retail sizes, that is, 2 ounces, 8 ounces, 16 ounces, and 32 ounces (one quart), as well as the bulk-size institutional and industrial containers. Romano wanted retail distribution of the gallon-size containers but had not been able to convince retailers.

Romano produced a line of olive oil products to suit the various consumer needs. This line consisted of the following: Romano 100 percent Virgin Olive Oil, Romanza 100 percent Olive Oil, Laco Pure Olive Oil, and Avallo 10 and 20 percent Blended Oil. Romanza combined the special flavors of select olive oils and was slightly lower in price than virgin olive oil. Laco had the taste of pure olive oil but was much inferior in quality to virgin and used primarily for the institutional trade. Avallo was a special blend of the less expensive soya cooking oil with a mild taste of pure oil in 10 percent and 20 percent quantities. The Romano brand was the primary line in retail sizes, whereas the other brands were sold primarily to foodservice establishments in the gallon and larger sizes only.

The Spanish parent company sold only the finest grades of olive oil, even though olive oil came in many different grades. At the same time, the average consumer was unable to distinguish among these different grades. Similarly, the prices of the higher grades of olive oil were far above those of the lower grades. Therefore, it was difficult for Romano, Inc., to market a superior product while its competitors marketed an inferior product.

Currently Romano had national distribution, but not in all major supermarket chains and not in all container sizes. The leading seller was the 8-ounce package followed by the 16-ounce and the quart container. Romano had no retail distribution of the gallon size. The main product competition consisted of other imported olive oils, oils that were blended (olive oil and soybean), and the domestic vegetable oils such as Wesson and Mazola. These competitors tended to sell oil in quart and gallon-size containers.

Romano had a network of 19 warehouses throughout the country from which the company served customers in all 50 states. One hundred food brokers represented Romano in their respective marketing areas. Four regional managers and a national sales manager worked closely with these people and the headquarters marketing team to provide the best quality and service possible for all retail and wholesale customers.

Major firms importing olive oil obtained their supplies in several different ways. These included the following:

1. Importing prepackaged oil bearing the exporter's name.

2. Importing prepackaged oil bearing the brand name designed and controlled by the importer.

3. Importing in 128-ounce (one gallon) cans and repacking into retail containers bearing the importer's brand.

4. Importing bulk oil and repacking into retail containers bearing the importer's brand.

Because of the ease of entering the industry, there were a great many regional competitors. They were entrenched in local markets and usually enjoyed lower retail prices than firms that sold nationally. These lower prices were mainly the result of higher freight costs incurred by national competitors to reship the goods. More than 100 different olive oil brands were marketed in the metropolitan New York City market. Romano chose to import in bulk in order to ensure quality and to control shipments to customers. Although this method of importing was the cheapest, freight differentials resulted in the local and regional competitors having lower prices, regardless of the form in which they imported the olive oil.

Because it was both pure and imported, Romano brand olive oil had the disadvantage in the marketplace of selling at a premium price. As indicated previously, Romano competed with several vegetable oils, such as Wesson, which came from much larger companies who had large advertising budgets behind them. Besides being lower in price, such oils made claims of other advantages that might or might not be deterrents to Romano. The first consisted of health related selling points, that is, polyunsaturated fats and low cholesterol. The second was taste appeal, that is, low flavor level.

As to health related selling points, the consumer was presented with data on fat, cholesterol, and saturated and polyunsaturated fat. The corn oil companies heavily advertised and publicized these data in selling the benefits of corn oil. Whereas the cholesterol content of both corn oil and olive oil was zero, olive oil had a higher percentage of the nonsaturated and saturated fats than did corn oil. Corn oil had the advantage of being higher in the polyunsaturated fats. In restricted diets and diets designed to regulate cholesterol, physicians tended to recommend a restriction of the saturated and nonsaturated fats and an increase of the polyunsaturated fats. How much of a factor this had been in terms of influencing the sale of olive oil was not known, but it had to be faced as a possible deterrent to sales. Perhaps because of the heavy use and sales appeal of corn oil and other vegetable oils, many consumers had not acquired a taste for olive oil. In fact, the younger generation had grown up in an era of news, publicity, and advertising of corn oil. It might be possible, however, to counteract this negative factor.

Total olive oil industry sales in the United States had been declining for several years. Two of the reasons were the ethnic connotation of the product and the high and increasing prices of olive oil to the consumer. As Romano's management saw it, the real challenge, in terms of growth, was to expose the nonethnic consumer to the benefits of olive oil.

Romano's strategy of exposing the nonethnic consumer was in line with its current consumer profile. Although its consumers could not be precisely defined in terms of demographics, the majority of them were ethnic. The nonethnic users were primarily (1) women in their early twenties who were inexperienced cooks and followed recipes to the letter, and (2) middle-aged women who were gourmet cooks. Most of Romano's sales were in the smaller containers, whereas many competitors sold primarily the gallon sizes. This led the company to believe that a good many of its consumers were nonethnic users, and that this would ensure Romano an edge in this market if the benefits of olive oil were known by the public.

Olive oil was primarily a commodity, as many people viewed it. Many ethnic consumers bought whatever olive oil was lowest in price, regardless of quality. Also, because of the high price of olive oil, some of these consumers were also moving toward the olive oil and soybean blends. On the other hand, nonethnic consumers tended to buy only the best olive oil and shop for a brand. A company objective was for consumers to buy Romano olive oil and to pay the premium price for it.

Olive oil was almost exclusively a consumer product. Specific data on the end use were currently unavailable. However, trade estimates suggested that upward of 85 percent of all olive oil was sold at retail for home consumption; commercial and institutional users accounted for the remaining 15 percent or less. Trade sources indicated that commercial users consisted only of high-priced hotels and restaurants specializing in European cuisine, which bought olive oil for the sake of authenticity. However, because the price of olive oil was higher than substitute oils, the current use of olive oil was minimal. Generally, olive oil was not used by other sectors of the hotel and restaurant trade. The manufacturing sector did not use olive oil to any appreciable extent because substitute oils were just as good and cost less. The exceptions were small manufacturers of European-style cuisine and gourmet foods. However, the quantity of olive oil used by such firms was insignificant.

Importers believed that the relatively high price of olive oil was the prime reason that consumption was not greater. In their view, this was an almost insoluble problem. The relative price of olive oil was slowly dropping, but the likelihood of the price of olive oil approaching the price of other oils was remote. The price of olive oil was expected to remain at least an order of magnitude greater than that of the vegetable oils. In 1971, the price of olive oil was twice the average price of similar oils, but by 1975 it was three times the price of other oils. The price of olive oil reached a peak of 3.35 times the average of other oils in 1976. After that time the relative price of olive oil declined to about 3.0 and leveled off.

Olive oil was not heavily or widely promoted. The limited promotional monies and activities were aimed at ethnic markets. This was especially true in areas with large numbers of Italians and Puerto Ricans, such as San Francisco, New York City, Miami, Houston, and several New England cities. Actual national expenditures for advertising and sales promotion of olive oil were not available. However, estimates indicated that these figures were insignificant compared to the promotional and advertising expenditures on cooking and salad oils in general.

All importers of olive oil sponsored trade promotions. Various forms were used, but the most common was the conventional "off-invoice." This meant that the retailer received the promotional money off the regular price. In return for $1 or possibly $2 per case (on a $40 per-case value), the retailer provided some or all of the following: in-store displays, reduced retail price, and mention in the retailer's local flier (handbill).

Most of the olive oil industry trade promotions were staged with small retailers in ethnic areas. The major retail chains avoided these trade promotions because the per-case cost was prohibitive. Such a chain's initial outlay was high, but the anticipated sales volume was relatively modest compared to the high turnover items competing for the large retailer's attention. Olive oil trade deals seldom warranted even advertising space in the local newspapers because of the low volume and other items competing for the valuable space.

Research Studies

In order to better understand the consumer, Romano conducted a small but carefully done survey of 250 people in the Baltimore area. The majority of respondents had not used any olive oil within the past year. In rank order the main reasons given by the respondents were the following: (1) cost too much, (2) never thought of it, (3) too greasy, (4) dislike flavor, (5) no reason, (6) not good for health.

Those who used olive oil offered two main reasons for doing so. The first was that recipes called for it and the second was the flavor. The differences between light and heavy users of olive oil appeared to be the following.

EXHIBIT 1 Romano, Inc., Selling Expenses Most Recent Year

	Amount
Salaries and wages	$150,112
Fringe benefits	24,225
Supplies	3,842
Telephone	20,505
Advertising	45,404
Contract services	7,500
Travel and entertainment	90,001
Dues and subscriptions	1,230
Warehouse breakage	4,538
Brokerage commissions	301,446
Unsalable merchandise	6,154
External samples	18,125
Taxes, licenses, and permits	9,545
Insurance	13,494
Depreciation	8,209
Miscellaneous expenses	537
	$704,867

1. Light users used olive oil when recipes called for it. (They tended to buy two- and four ounce packages.)

2. Medium users used olive oil because of flavor and preference as well as the fact that recipes called for it. (They tended to buy 8- and 16-ounce packages.)

3. Heavy users used olive oil because they preferred the taste. They also believed that it was more healthful than other oils. Recipes emerged as only a minor factor for heavy users. (They tended to buy quarts and gallon-size packages.)

Several interesting things had been fairly well established in previous studies in the industry and were rather widely known in the industry. Different ethnic groups bought varying types of olive oil. Preference for olive oil appeared to differ among ethnic groups in the following ways.

1. People of Italian descent preferred a lighter olive oil typical of that supplied by Spanish and Italian exporters.

2. People of Greek and Portuguese descent preferred a heavier oil. In addition, they bought oil to which they were most accus-

tomed. The Greeks bought Greek oil and the Portuguese bought Portuguese oil.

3. First-generation Americans of Mediterranean descent had a latent preference for olive oil. They would prefer to use olive oil whenever they required oil because they preferred its distinct flavor and believed in its health-giving properties. But, because of high prices they restricted their use of olive oil to salads and other purposes where its taste was critical. Where taste was not important they used a cheaper vegetable oil. The implication was that lower prices could induce users to use more olive oil and for all cooking purposes.

4. Upon arrival in the United States most immigrants did not have much discretionary income. As a result, they used cheaper oils. Over time, they became more affluent and switched back to the more costly but preferred oils. The implication was that increasing incomes of new immigrants might result in increased demand for olive oil.

5. High prices and inflation had switched some ethnic users away from olive oil, either partially or completely. Over time, some came to like and prefer these substitute oils. The implication was that some users may have been irrevocably converted to other oils.

Two demographic variables also appeared to influence the use of olive oil. These were the following: (1) the greatest use of olive oil occurred among affluent families. Use declined sharply among families with an annual income of less than $20,000; (2) most of the users of olive oil resided in large metropolitan areas.

In evaluating the nonethnic market, olive oil and salad oils were directly or nearly directly substitutable. That is, one might be substituted for another without significantly affecting the taste, texture, and smell of the oil or any product made from it. However, for some purposes only a specific oil could be used. The degree to which an oil had a uniquely desirable property determined, at least in part, the price that users were prepared to pay for it.

EXHIBIT 2 Romano, Inc., Profit and Loss Statement *(end of most recent year)*

		Amount
Gallons sold		1,207,069
Gross sales		$11,022,150
Less freight	$443,413	
Promotional allowances	381,447	
Discounts allowed	159,130	
Storage and handling	93,242	
Net sales		$ 9,944,918
Cost of sales		7,448,892
Gross contribution		$ 2,496,026
Manufacturing overhead		288,182
Net contribution		$ 2,207,844
Selling expenses	$704,867	
Administrative expenses	325,350	
Net operating income		$ 1,177,627
Other income		42,147
Other deductions		331,168
Net profit before taxes		$ 888,606
Estimated income taxes		455,158
Net profit		$ 433,448

Volkswagen of America
W. Wayne Talarzyk

In January 1974 Volkswagen introduced to the American public a new car model called the Dasher. Positioned as a totally different kind of Volkswagen, the Dasher was promoted as "the perfect car for its time, a car that has all the ingredients needed by the demands of the buying public including contemporary styling, good handling and performance, and economy." However, five months after its introduction, sales were far below projections, and consumer criticisms involving the car's hesitation, squealing brakes, and high price were familiar. It was clear that more knowledge of the Dasher buyer and his or her attitudes and perceptions was needed to evaluate the car's initial position in terms of advertising and merchandising.

Background

The initial Volkswagen concept was developed in the 1920s by a young automobile designer, Ferdinand Porsche. Porsche intended the car to be a completely practical vehicle. At first his plans for an unconventional, small inexpensive automobile were rejected by European automobile manufacturers. The rise of Hitler and his pledge to the German people that every man would own his own car, "The Volkswagen," made Porsche's dream a reality, and manufacture of the Volkswagen got underway. The car's production, however, was disrupted by World War II.

After the war British Occupational Forces controlled the Volkswagen factory until 1949. The factory was then turned over to Heinz Nordoff, who faced the major task of rebuilding the Volkswagen organization. The basic design of the car, however, was not altered, and engineering emphasis was directed toward internal improvements of the automobile. Gradually a global sales and service organization developed. At present, Volkswagen A.G., located in Wolfsburg, is West Germany's largest industrial enterprise with factories located throughout the world.

In its early years, the Beetle, which had become the car's "nickname," had problems gaining acceptance in the American market. To gain initial sales, a foreign-car dealer who had been appointed exclusive importer and agent east of the Mississippi for Volkswagen advocated that dealers who wanted the more popular foreign cars should also purchase a few of the unconventional Beetles. His suggestion was accepted. From this rather humble beginning in the early 1950s, interest in and sales of Volkswagens soon began to increase rapidly.

As can be seen in Exhibit 1, Volkswagen sales peaked in 1970 at 582,500 cars, accounting for almost 7 percent of total sales in the United States. While imports expanded their share of the market as the 1970s continued, Volkswagen began to decline in market share and absolute sales. This decline was partially due to increased foreign-car competition from Japanese firms and the step-up of smaller car production by major U.S. manufacturers. Exhibit 2 displays the shifts in market shares for select automobile makes during the period 1969 to 1973.

The Dasher

As part of the program designed to halt its declining market share, Volkswagen began to restructure its product line with the introduction of the Dasher. The positioning objective

Case prepared by W. Wayne Talarzyk of The Ohio State University.

Roger D. Blackwell, James F. Engel, and W. Wayne Talarzyk, *Contemporary Cases in Consumer Behavior.* Copyright © 1977, The Dryden Press, reprinted by permission of The Dryden Press, CBS College Publishing.

EXHIBIT 1 Volkswagen Share of Total Car Imports into the United States: 1964–1973

Year	Total Imports of Foreign-Made Cars	Total Foreign Imports as Percentage of United States New Car Sales	Total VW Imports	Total VW Imports as Percentage of Total Foreign Car Imports
1964	481,000	6.0	322,900	67.1
1965	569,400	6.1	371,200	65.2
1966	658,100	7.3	427,200	65.0
1967	786,500	9.3	454,800	57.8
1968	985,700	10.4	582,000	59.0
1969	1,061,600	11.2	566,300	53.3
1970	1,230,900	14.6	582,500	47.3
1971	1,487,600	15.1	532,900	35.8
1972	1,529,400	14.6	491,700	32.2
1973	1,719,900	15.1	480,600	27.9

Source: *Ward's Automotive Yearbook, 1973.*

EXHIBIT 2 Percentage Shares of U.S. Automobile Market for Selected Brands: 1969–1973

Brand	1969	1970	1971	1972	1973
Chevrolet	21.8	19.9	22.3	21.9	21.6
Ford	19.9	22.0	19.5	19.7	18.8
Pontiac	8.4	6.5	6.9	6.8	7.1
Buick	7.2	5.9	6.5	6.2	6.1
Plymouth	7.0	8.1	6.7	6.7	6.6
Oldsmobile	6.9	5.5	6.8	7.0	7.1
Dodge	5.7	6.0	5.3	5.3	5.2
Volkswagen	5.7	6.8	5.2	4.6	4.1
Mercury	3.7	3.7	3.3	3.8	3.6
Cadillac	2.6	2.0	2.6	2.5	2.5
American Motors	2.5	3.0	2.5	2.8	3.5
Chrysler	2.2	1.8	1.7	1.8	1.6
Toyota	1.2	2.2	2.8	2.6	2.4
Opel	1.0	1.0	*	*	*
Datsun	*	1.2	1.9	1.8	2.0
Others	4.2	4.4	6.0	6.5	7.8
	100.0	100.0	100.0	100.0	100.0
Industry sales volume	9,446,524	8,388,204	9,830,626	10,409,026	11,350,994

*Less than 1 percent.
Source: R. L. Polk & Co.

for the Dasher involved the approach that it "is a new and remarkable car that does everything a car should do these days."

Characteristics

The Dasher is essentially the same car as the Audi Fox, also manufactured by Volkswagen, with some modifications to the rear body section and the roof by master designer Giorgetto Giugiaro. Offered in three models—two-door sedan, four-door sedan, and five-door wagon—the Dasher was the first Volkswagen model to be sold in the United States without the usual air-cooled engine.

Special design features of the Dasher include:

"Skidbreaker"—this forces the car to brake in a straight line if one side is partially on ice or a front wheel blowout occurs at, say, 50 miles per hour.

Front-wheel drive—the weight of the engine is over the front wheels, which "pulls" the car, allowing far greater control in hazardous driving conditions. It also allows far greater interior space.

Rear window channel—a lip molding around the rear window keeps the glass clear of water for greater visibility.

Safety cell—the engine is designed so that impact forces it down instead of into the passenger compartment.

Safety steering column—a safety element behind the dashboard on the steering column collapses if the driver hits the steering wheel. In addition, the coupling disengages upon impact so that the steering column is forced upward.

In performance tests the Dasher achieved an average of about 25 miles per gallon and was timed 8.5 seconds in accelerating from zero to 50 miles per hour. Introduced at the base sticker price of $3,975, the Dasher included as standard equipment such items as steel-belted radial tires, a rear window defogger, electric clock, vinyl interior, pile carpeting, and rack and pinion steering. Volkswagen also provided a comprehensive warranty plan called the Owner's Security Blanket (Exhibit 3).

Introduction

The Dasher was introduced in January 1974 with a national television and magazine campaign. Regional distributors and local dealers also supported the Dasher's introduction via newspapers and radio as well as spot television. Examples of the introductory advertisements are shown in Exhibits 4, 5, and 6. At the national level about 75 percent of the introduction budget was allocated to television. Among the television shows utilized were "All in the Family," "Sanford and Son," "The Waltons," "Kojak," and "NBA Basketball."

The national print effort included the major weekly and monthly publications and provided a combined circulation of approximately 20 million readers. Special introduction and follow-up spreads were run in *TV Guide* and

---

EXHIBIT 3 Warranty for the Volkswagen Dasher

The New VW Owner's Security Blanket

Once you buy a Dasher we won't leave you out in the cold.

We could begin by listing all the things the new VW Owner's Security Blanket covers. But we think you'd rather see what it doesn't cover during the first 12 months or 20,000 miles, whichever comes first.

List of items not covered by the Security Blanket:

Normal, prescribed maintenance, such as brake, clutch, and valve adjustments.

Filters, fluids, and lubricants.

That wasn't too bad, was it?

Give your car reasonable care, maintain it on schedule, pay for filters and tires when and as they are needed, and we'll handle everything else—parts and labor—free of charge.

All this, plus:

The exclusive VW Computer Analysis—free of charge during the warranty period.

Twenty-four month/24,000 mile (whichever comes first) coverage on major engine and transmission parts.

Free "loaner" service if scheduled warranty repairs keep your car in the shop overnight.

Here and now VW "Express Care" if estimated repair time is half an hour or less.

Six month/6000 mile (whichever comes first) coverage on factory parts and accessories, dealer workmanship included.

And if your warranty coverage has expired, your dealer now offers low-cost Rent-A-Bug to keep you on the road.

The new VW Owner's Security Blanket not only covers your car, it warms your heart.

Check your dealer for complete details.

EXHIBIT 4 Example of Introductory Print Advertisement for the Dasher

Headline: VOLKSWAGEN INTRODUCES THE PERFECT CAR FOR ITS TIME

Text: The perfect car for its time is a new Volkswagen called Dasher, a remarkable car that does *everything* you want a car to do these days.

For example, high power and good gas mileage normally don't go together. But Dasher has an astounding new four-cylinder engine that does a hot 0–50 in 8.5 seconds and *also* gets 25 miles out of the gallon.

If you're like most people you want a roomy car that holds five people comfortably. And you want lots of trunk space. But you also don't want a *big* car. Dasher solves *this* problem too. Technical innovations—some of them will amaze you—have kept Dasher's machinery incredibly compact. So while the car isn't big, the part where the people go is big.

Best of all, wait till you see how Dasher handles.

Dasher's drive wheels are up front, right under the engine. This gives you control you've never felt before in a conventional car. As well as traction on curves and in mud and snow and ice that's nothing less than spectacular.

Dasher also comes with a miraculous little thing called Skidbraker.

Skidbraker *forces* Dasher to move straight ahead as you brake, when one side of the car is riding on ice or snow, a normally ticklish proposition.

Dasher is designed to be reliable (who knows how better than we?) It needs maintenance only at 10,000 mile intervals. It's made easy to repair. It takes computer analysis. And it's covered by the most advanced plan of them all, the VW Owner's Security Blanket.

The Volkswagen Dasher. Once again we've found out how to do it years ahead of anybody else.

Dasher, A New Kind of Volkswagen.

EXHIBIT 5 Storyboard for Introductory Television Commercial

Scene	Visual	Voice Over
1	Body chassis	Volkswagen introduces the perfect car for its time.
2	Dasher coming toward the camera	It's called Dasher. And this is what it does.
3	Body chassis with passengers	It holds five comfortably.
4	Dasher passing camera	It's a powerful car that does zero to fifty in eight and a half seconds,
5	Dasher coming toward the camera	but also gets about 25 miles per gallon.
6	Dasher passing camera	It needs maintenance only once in 10,000 miles.
7	Close-up of front end	It has front wheel drive
8	Close of side front	and rack and pinion steering.
9	Dasher driving away from camera	If you like to hold the road in your own two hands,
10	Dasher cornering	watch this.
11	Dasher cornering	Music
12	Dasher cornering	Music
13	Close-up of engine	Dasher's parts are easy to get at
14	Close-up of engine, parts labeled	and they're covered by the Volkswagen Owner's Security Blanket.

EXHIBIT 5 *(concluded)*

Scene	Visual	Voice Over
15	Close-up of brakes	Then there's Skid Braker.
16	Close-up of brakes	Suppose you have a front wheel blow-out at, say at 50 mph.
17	Blow-out of front tire	Now, watch this.
18	Dasher braking along a no passing line	Skid Braker forces the car to brake in a straight line.
19	Braking Dasher, body chassis with passengers	Dasher, inside and outside, a new kind of Volkswagen.

EXHIBIT 6 Example of Introductory Radio Commercial

Program: Volkswagen Radio
Product: Dasher
Length: 60 "Totally New Car"
Order No. 33-35-36551

Woman:	You bought a new car.
Man:	Not just a new car. A revolutionary new Volkswagen called Dasher that's the perfect car for its time.
Woman:	Why?
Man:	It goes from zero to 50 in only 8.5 seconds.
Woman:	Hmmmmmmm?
Man:	Dasher holds five people comfortably.
Woman:	Uh huh.
Man:	It has front-wheel drive and rack and pinion steering for great handling.
Woman:	Yes . . .
Man:	And Skidbreaker that forces it to brake in a straight line if one side of the car is partly on ice. And . . . oh yeah. It has a security blanket.
Woman:	A Volkswagen Owner's Security Blanket?
Man:	Uh huh.
Woman:	You're right.
Man:	About what?
Woman:	It's perfect.
Announcer:	Volkswagen Dasher. The perfect car for its time.

Reader's Digest. Introduction advertisements also appeared in special-interest magazines with special market readers such as *Road & Track, Car & Driver, Ebony, Black Enterprise, Tennis, Ski,* and *Skiing.*

Initial Sales Responses

Exhibit 7 shows the national registration figures for Dasher and some of the other cars in its classification. Sales reached 3,507 cars in March and then dropped over 500 units in April and again in May. Since these sales levels were not up to those anticipated, special research projects were designed to study the characteristics of Dasher purchasers and their attitudes and perceptions of cars.

Research on Dasher Buyers

A mail survey was sent to 600 Dasher buyers randomly selected from the people who purchased cars in April 1974. From this mailing, 285 respondents returned questionnaires. They form the basis of the selected results shown in Exhibit 8. In another study a group of Dasher owners was compared with owners of four other cars (Fox, Capri, Mustang, and LeMans). These owners were asked to rate their cars on certain features, such as styling, performance, quality, and service warranty. Respondents were also asked to state their purchase criteria and their overall satisfaction with the cars. Results of some of these questions along with the socioeconomic characteristics of the respondents are presented in Exhibit 9. Analysis of the respondent data was expected to clarify the consumer's perception of the Dasher and to help the company reposition the product.

EXHIBIT 7 National Registration Figures for Dasher and Selected Makes in its Classification, January to May 1974

	January		February		March		April		May	
	Units	Percent of Group	Units	Percent of Group	Units	Percent of Group	Units	Percent of Group	Units	Percent of Group
Volkswagen 412	1,503	0.6	1,383	0.5	1,587	0.5	1,530	0.5	1,387	0.4
Volkswagen Dasher	262	0.1	1,795	0.7	3,507	1.2	2,967	0.9	2,410	0.4
Audi Fox	439	0.2	1,130	0.4	2,107	0.7	2,330	0.7	2,420	0.7
Toyota Corona/Mk II	4,900	1.8	5,172	2.0	6,219	2.2	5,555	1.8	4,944	1.5
Datsun 610/710	6,347	2.4	5,587	2.2	5,792	2.0	4,041	1.3	3,421	1.0
Fiat 124 (Ex. Spider and CPE)	679	0.3	974	0.4	1,258	0.4	1,101	0.3	1,008	0.3
Mazda	7,037	2.6	6,039	2.4	5,928	2.1	4,916	1.6	4,874	1.5
Opel 1900 and Manta	5,976	2.2	4,682	1.8	4,217	1.5	3,978	1.3	3,090	0.9
Renault	687	0.3	625	0.2	624	0.2	625	0.2	488	0.1
Omega	3,297	1.2	3,027	1.2	3,318	1.1	3,757	1.2	3,959	1.2
Apollo	3,061	1.1	3,213	1.3	3,473	1.2	3,672	1.2	4,127	1.2
Domestic PC (2)	169,250	63.0	160,989	62.6	183,109	63.5	206,714	65.4	223,778	67.6
Domestic PC (3)	64,825	24.1	62,104	24.2	67,755	23.4	74,392	23.6	75,834	22.8
Others	352	0.1	173	0.1	143	—	86	—	167	0.1
Total	268,615	100.0	256,893	100.0	289,037	100.0	315,664	100.0	331,907	100.0

Source: R. L. Polk & Co.

EXHIBIT 8 Selected Results from April 1974 Survey of Dasher Buyers *(in percentages)*

Primary Reason for Dealership Selection		First Awareness of the Dasher	
Closeness to dealer	40.9	TV commercial	36.7
Previous experience	10.6	Articles (magazines/newspapers)	16.4
Service	8.2	At dealership (showroom/salespeople)	15.7
Dealership personnel	7.8	Advice of friends/relative	6.8
Dealer reputation	7.2	Through Fox/Passat	5.3
Only one	6.2	Newspaper ads	4.7
Trade-in	5.8	Advertising (general)	4.6
Advice of friends	4.0	Magazine ads	4.2
Other	9.3	Other	5.6
Total	100.0	Total	100.0

Salesperson's Sales Points at Time of Purchase*

Gas mileage/economy	28.8
Roominess	17.0
Front-wheel drive	16.2
None (poor salesmanship)	14.8
Handling/ease of driving	14.4
Economy of operation	12.9
Owner's Security Blanket/computer analysis	8.5
No sales points necessary (presold, knew more than salesperson)	8.1
Engine, water-cooled/front-mounted	8.1
Performance	5.9
Design/style	5.5
Features (standard on Dasher but options/accessories on other makes)	5.5
Service	5.5
Quality of workmanship/construction	4.4
Safety	4.4
Engineering	4.4
Other	45.1

Total Purchase		Types of Cars Disposed of in Acquiring a Dasher	
Less than $4000	0.3	Volkswagen	34.8
$4,000–$4,250	10.4	Toyota	1.7
$4,250–$4,500	20.0	Datsun	1.6
$4,500–$4,750	28.0	Other import	5.6
$4,750–$5,000	20.4	Mustang	3.2
$5,000–$5,250	12.5	Other Ford	9.1
$5,250–$5,500	6.3	Vega/Nova	2.9
$5,500–$5,750	1.8	Other Chevrolet	4.9
$5,750 and up	0.3	American Motors Car	4.3
Total	100.0	Other domestic	15.4
		Did not dispose of car	16.5
		Total	100.0

Price of Dasher Compared to Customer's Expectations

Price about what expected	15.9
Price less than expected	—
Little more than expected	47.7**
A lot more than expected	36.4**

Salesperson's Justification for Greater-than-Expected Price of Dasher*

Quality/workmanship	17.7
General inflation	17.1
Didn't (salesperson did not attempt to justify)	12.5
Dollar devaluation	11.8
Features (standard on Dasher, extra on other makes)	9.2

EXHIBIT 8 *(concluded)*

Salesperson's Justification for Greater-than-Expected Price of Dasher*

No reductions from list price	7.8
Unique car (superior/new)	6.5
Couldn't (salesperson tried to justify but, according to customer, failed)	6.5
Increased value of trade-in	5.9
Low operating cost	5.2
Value for the money	3.9
Owner's Security Blanket	3.9
Performance	3.9
Increased production costs	3.9
Gas mileage	3.2

	Dasher Price Was	
	About What	*A Little/Lot*
Satisfaction versus Initial Reaction to Price	*Expected*	*More than Expected*
Completely/very satisfied	70.7	50.7
Fairly well satisfied	19.5	26.9
Somewhat dissatisfied	4.9	19.2
Very dissatisfied	4.9	3.2
	100.0	100.0

*Percentages total up to more than 100 because of multiple mentions.
**About 73 percent discussed price with salesperson.

EXHIBIT 9 Comparisons between Dasher Owner and Owners of Selected Other Cars *(in percentages)*

	Dasher	Fox	Buyers of Capri	Mustang	LeMans
Purchase Criteria Mentioned at Least Once as Reason for Purchase					
Gas mileage	79.7	83.8	81.8	62.7	9.2
Previous experience with make	21.3	1.6	9.0	18.3	42.5
Manufacturer's reputation	28.9	28.4	9.5	9.3	17.9
Resale value	18.0	19.2	17.1	15.8	7.4
Quality of workmanship	22.8	41.6	22.7	4.4	5.3
Interior room	13.0	10.6	2.2	0.5	7.4
Exterior styling	6.5	14.0	29.3	43.9	37.6
Handling ease	13.4	7.8	6.3	5.6	10.6
Value for money	6.6	10.2	16.5	14.9	28.5
Warranty coverage	18.2	1.0	0.4	1.0	4.3
Socioeconomic Characteristics					
Marital status					
Married	74.8	70.0	58.4	60.7	68.7
Single	18.8	27.1	36.3	36.4	22.0
Other	6.4	2.9	5.3	2.9	9.3
	100.0	100.0	100.0	100.0	100.0
Sex					
Male	77.1	68.2	66.0	62.2	65.9
Female	22.9	31.8	34.0	37.8	34.1
	100.0	100.0	100.0	100.0	100.0
Age					
Under 20	0.4	1.0	5.2	6.1	4.0
20–24	8.1	14.8	29.7	30.1	13.7
25–29	24.8	21.3	21.9	19.0	17.9

EXHIBIT 9 *(concluded)*

	Dasher	Fox	Buyers of Capri	Mustang	LeMans
Socioeconomic Characteristics					
30–34	13.0	14.2	10.8	7.8	10.3
35–39	10.8	12.0	6.8	8.2	8.7
40–44	6.6	8.4	6.3	5.5	12.0
45–49	7.2	10.0	7.7	10.7	11.4
50–54	9.1	9.1	6.9	4.7	4.3
55–59	7.8	4.1	2.6	3.6	6.9
60–64	5.4	2.1	1.4	2.3	5.0
65 and over	6.8	3.0	0.7	2.0	5.8
	100.0	100.0	100.0	100.0	100.0
Median age	36.7	34.6	28.4	28.6	37.3
Education					
Grade school only	2.7	1.4	0.3	1.9	3.5
Some high school	5.5	1.8	4.3	6.3	9.0
High school graduate	16.6	9.5	20.2	19.8	33.0
Some college	29.8	19.0	33.8	35.0	30.1
College graduate	18.7	32.1	24.2	21.0	13.6
Some postgraduate	11.5	17.3	6.4	8.9	3.1
Postgraduate degree	15.2	18.9	10.8	7.1	7.7
	100.0	100.0	100.0	100.0	100.0
Occupation					
Professional	40.1	48.0	33.0	28.7	22.2
Managerial	9.6	17.9	16.2	14.4	12.9
Skilled craftsmen	9.6	4.4	10.5	7.2	8.7
Retired	7.8	2.2	1.5	3.1	6.1
Housewife	6.8	5.0	4.8	6.0	13.9
Public service	5.1	3.7	4.9	4.0	4.6
Clerical	4.3	4.6	9.8	12.2	6.5
Sales	4.0	2.5	2.4	4.7	7.5
Military	3.6	2.8	4.9	1.6	1.7
Laborer	2.8	2.2	6.0	5.6	8.9
Student	2.3	4.5	4.4	7.9	2.2
Other	4.0	2.2	1.6	4.6	4.8
	100.0	100.0	100.0	100.0	100.0
Income					
Under $3,000	0.3	0.3	1.1	0.7	0.6
$3,000–$5,000	1.7	1.2	1.1	2.2	2.1
$5,001–$7,500	4.4	3.0	4.1	3.5	5.5
$7,501–$8,500	3.0	3.5	2.5	6.0	4.5
$8,501–$10,000	3.2	4.6	11.7	6.4	12.7
$10,001–$15,000	12.3	9.6	13.9	15.5	12.6
$15,001–$20,000	16.6	19.7	17.6	18.8	22.2
$20,001–$25,000	14.0	11.1	14.9	10.8	11.9
$25,001–$30,000	7.5	8.5	6.1	6.9	4.5
$30,001–$35,000	2.5	6.2	3.0	2.4	2.3
$35,001–$40,000	1.3	5.9	0.4	1.5	1.0
Over $40,000	3.3	11.0	6.2	8.1	3.3
N/A	10.8	5.8	5.7	0.8	0.5
	100.0	100.0	100.0	100.0	100.0
Median income	$16,421	$18,879	$15,303	$14,823	$14,288

Source: Rogers National Research, Inc.

SECTION 3

Marketing Strategy Development

Conceptual Readings

Company Readings

Case Studies

*M*arketing strategy development is the most difficult decision area faced by contemporary businesses. It is difficult because it requires that a manager simultaneously weigh numerous considerations to judge which of several alternative strategies is optimal. After all, the marketing strategy decision largely decides the ultimate success or failure of the company. A good decision may mean millions of dollars in profits, while a mistake may well lead to the company's demise or, at least, a long period of reparative maneuvers to restore the firm to its former position. Fortunately, some general concepts exist that can guide marketing managers through the marketing strategy development phase of business planning.

Before describing these concepts, it is worthwhile to begin with a discussion of the definition and intent of marketing strategy. Marketing strategy is best thought of as the continual process of seeking to hold or gain a long-term differential advantage over competitors. Obviously, market analysis weighs heavily in this process, as does the arsenal of knowledge on specific competitors' strengths and weaknesses. Add to these considerations introspection about your own company's positives and negatives plus a vision of what the future holds, and you have the basic ingredients in marketing strategy development. At this point, there are two general options available to the marketing manager. First, given a current distinct differential advantage over a competitor, you have the opportunity to exploit that advantage. For instance, companies with time-honored images take advantage of their reputational advantages, while new companies keying on new technology rely on their innovativeness as the differentiating factor. Second, the marketing manager can build a long-term differential advantage over time. This option requires that the marketing manager use foresight and planning to coordinate the timing of the advantage's arrival with the opening of an opportunity in the marketplace. With either option, the important point is that marketing strategy ultimately relies on a long-run view of its results.

At least three concepts figure significantly into marketing strategy formulation. The first is the product life cycle (or PLC), which offers insight to the present and prospective competitive and demand circumstances of a product as it moves across its life span. However, since the PLC is a general model, it is necessary for the marketing manager to test it against his or her specific situation. The model was conceived during a period when American industry was undergoing slow and systematic changes. Today, some companies will find themselves in highly volatile industries that skirt the edge of rapid technological change and thus do not fit the model; others will realize that their situations are more consistent with the PLC. A variation of the PLC is the concept of market evolution, where companies in saturated markets engage in product-attribute competition, variously gaining advantages by engineering product characteristics closer to the benefit configurations sought by customers. The soft-drink industry typifies this situation as competitors jockey for position based on less caffeine, no sugar, fewer calories, or taste reformulations.

Finally, there is the portfolio view of a company, another variation that figures into marketing strategy development. Most companies market several product items by dividing them into product lines. In fact, some corporations are best described as holding companies comprised of numerous subsidiaries. If one takes the view that resources such as assets, expertise, or cash can be moved from one profit center to another, the wealth of successful brands can be applied to those products that are less successful but have high potential for future success. With this practice, one part of a company's profits is invested in areas where the future payoffs will be greater than they would if the same profits were reinvested in the original areas. The key here is the company's view of the future. Does it surprise you, for instance, to learn that major newspaper chains have acquired and invested heavily in cable television given the steady decline in newspaper circulation over the last 20 years?

As a final word of introduction to this section, it might be valuable to depict the interplay of market segmentation and investment options. Market segmentation allows a company to identify specific segments of the total market and to analyze their strengths relative to competitors who have targeted the same segments. Each potential target market represents both a different competitive environment and a unique set of requirements for success. If a company can shift marketing resources from one target market to another to gain or exploit a more attractive differential advantage over competitors without negative effects on its total business portfolio, the requirements for marketing strategy development are satisfied.

About the Readings

The first of our conceptual articles describes the marketing evolution of an entrepreneurship: it is especially relevant to contemporary business, where the emphasis is on entrepreneurialism in fast-moving markets that thrive on innovations. The authors point out how a firm progresses from an initial focus on a narrow market opportunity through a series of changes until it becomes a full-fledged, diversified, marketing organization. The second article, in contrast, describes the marketing strategy of "buying in," or locking a buyer into a long-term dependency on the seller. Here, a very different means of achieving loyalty is used. The author notes the strategy's benefits and problems, and even discusses some of the ethical questions inherent in this practice.

The four company related readings begin with an article on IBM (or "Big Blue" as it is known to the computer industry), which describes the marketing philosophies and strategies used by one of the most successful companies of all time. As you read, take note of how IBM's marketing orientation permeates all of its operations, especially the personnel function. You should also be vigilant about how entrepreneurial task forces are used for new-product innovation. IBM provides an excellent example of integrated marketing strategy. The next reading also describes product development, but in this case it is Frito-Lay, which is entering the cookie market with its Grandma brand. The article makes insightful comparisons between Frito-Lay and Nabisco; their marketing styles differ immensely, as do their views about the future of this market. This reading will give you a new appreciation for the marketing weaponry of both these firms.

Next, the scene switches to ulcer treatments where a British pharmaceutical company is entering the U.S. market, which has been dominated by one American firm for seven years. Tagamet, the American product, has exposed weaknesses that can be exploited by Zantac, the British competitor. But Zantac costs more. Who will win is in question, the only certainty being that marketing executives in both companies will end up using their own medicines. The final article is on U.S. Shoe, a company that has been reading demographic trends and quietly pursuing marketing strategies such as specialty retail outlet chains, niching at the high end, and even mail-order lingerie. Pay special attention to how the personality of the president has been instrumental in U.S. Shoe's rapid and profitable ascent in the early 1980s ∎

Conceptual Readings

Growing Ventures Can Anticipate Marketing Stages
Tyzoon T. Tyebjee, Albert V. Bruno, and Shelby H. McIntyre

The theory of evolution suggests that an organism can flourish only if it adapts to environmental changes. No doubt, a business can expect to succeed only if it changes in response to altered external circumstances.

It is through the marketing function that companies must do the bulk of their adjusting to the outside world. Above all, the growing company's marketing apparatus must evolve in an orderly fashion if the company is to avoid a traumatic transition from one growth stage to another. In this article, we identify the important marketing issues for businesses in transition and advise them how to cope with key problems. A premise of our analysis is that top management must not simply react to new situations created by growth but rather that while operating successfully in the present stage, management must take the initiative in planning for the next one. A marketing organization and strategy that are appropriate for one stage can become liabilities as the company passes into its next phase.

Rapidly growing businesses seem to pass through four evolutionary stages, as Exhibit 1 shows. The marketing effort in each stage takes some time to have an impact, and the growth rate during each stage eventually slows as that arrangement becomes constraining.

Stage One: Entrepreneurial Marketing

Fast-growing high-technology companies are often founded by people who have left larger companies to start their own businesses. These entrepreneurs frequently have a wealth of technical expertise and a fund of innovative ideas but little marketing experience.

During the earliest phase of the young ventures' operations, the founders usually rely on a network of personal relationships built up during their previous employment. Early marketing successes are often in the form of sales to friends and acquaintances, and the products specially designed for these customers.

For example, Robert Bozzard, president of the rapidly growing Lexel Corporation (it had $50 million in sales in its sixth year), recalls that:

> During the first few years we built hardware for a few specialized companies. Our first customer, Varian, where we knew several people, wanted a particular type of laser, and we supplied it. I did a lot of engineering on the laser head and the optics, and I also did most of the marketing.

The company in this stage is simply trying to get its foot in the door of the market. It tries to identify customers whose needs are not being met by established competitors—"the elephants." The low production volume at this point cannot support much overhead, so the venture can ill afford a formal marketing organization.

The entrepreneurial marketing approach does furnish the new business with at least one powerful selling point: buyers are assured the undivided attention of top management. Eventually, however, personal atten-

EXHIBIT 1 The Evolution of a Marketing Organization

Problem	Diagnosis	Prescription
Top management suddenly finds itself unable to provide needed attention to marketing.	Stage 1 business is ready for transition to Stage 2.	Hire a sales manager. Continue to hold top management responsible for product planning and pricing and for providing sales support in initial contact with new customers.
There are too many products or markets for top management to coordinate all business functions for each.	Stage 2 company is ready for transition to Stage 3.	Hire product managers and give them support in sales, advertising, and market intelligence. Delegate all marketing responsibility to product managers. Put top management in charge of strategic planning.
Growth opportunities are limited in current product-market scope.	Stage 3 business is ready for transition to Stage 4.	Decentralize marketing activities to divisional level. Establish a corporate marketing group that reviews division marketing plans, furnishes specialized skills in planning and research, manages corporate level marketing communication.

tion becomes a drag on the company's growth.

Thus, entrepreneurial marketing helps to establish the business and generate early growth, but its effectiveness diminishes with the overextension of key people. The customer base is too small, the company's product line is too customized, and the founding managers are spread too thin to meet all their responsibilities effectively.

Stage Two: Opportunistic Marketing

The companies that continue to grow past Stage One do so by changing their operating objective from merely getting a foot in the door to seeking new customers. By the time they reach Stage Two, their credibility and products' technical feasibility have been established. A more standardized product line capable of appealing to a wider set of potential buyers replaces the customized product strategy of Stage One. This expansion means that the business begins to compete directly with established companies. Successful Stage Two businesses usually concentrate on introducing economies of scale and improving their internal reporting systems and financial controls. At the same time, an infant marketing department emerges that is often staffed exclusively by salespeople. Since it is tactical in orientation, product planning and pricing become the responsibility of top management.

The narrow tactical focus tends to create conflicts as new channels of distribution open to serve the broadening customer base. The case of Stoneware, a microcomputer software company, illustrates this point.

In its early days, Stoneware sold its products directly to retail dealers because of the more attractive profit margins available when it bypassed the wholesaler. It grew so rapidly (it had $2 million in sales in its first year) that it began to recruit wholesale distributors. It also continued to sell directly to the dealers with whom it had established relationships. Naturally, the company's new wholesale distributors objected, and since the broad distribution provided by wholesalers was important to Stoneware's growth goals, the company decided to stop selling directly to its original customers and to guarantee its wholesalers exclusive distribution rights. Thus, Stoneware eliminated the last vestige of Stage 1's entrepreneurial hand-holding so as to realize the high volume it needed to achieve economies of scale.

As a company such as Stoneware completes Stage Two, it should be poised for explosive growth. Its narrow customer base and specialized product line have been broadened and standardized, and its manufacturing capability is in place. Many companies at this point, however, fail to organize adequately for the next phase of marketing.

Stage Three: Responsive Marketing

By Stage Three, the company is usually expanding so fast that managers face serious problems of poor organization and division of responsibility. Often they have to make the difficult decision to delegate day-to-day responsibility for key products that have been their pet projects. Relinquishing responsibility is inescapable, but it has a great benefit—it often initiates a process that ends with the creation of a sophisticated marketing department.

Naturally enough, the new product managers emerge as champions for the marketing needs of their wares. Their energetic efforts are rewarded with more people and larger budgets for promotion, customer service, and, ultimately, market research. When the company has integrated such functions, a modern marketing organization emerges.

At this point, effective internal communication is vital to rapidly growing businesses, whose various units risk losing touch with one another and whose customers are becoming so numerous that informal monitoring is unworkable. Successful businesses appear to rely largely on marketing research and their field sales forces for intelligence on customers.

Whereas marketing goals in previous stages are formulated in terms of the needs of the venture, Stage Three marketing goals are driven by customer needs. One company requires key technical personnel to accompany sales personnel periodically on calls to customers. Another company, which sells diagnostic test kits to medical laboratories, has organized an in-house lab to simulate customer use of the products; any new product has to be "sold" to this internal group before it can be put onto the market.

Eventually, market saturation may slow growth, or competitive forces may make additional gains in market share economically infeasible, or the prospect of antitrust action may make further dominance in a single business unattractive. Thus, the Stage Three company must seek other product-market positions to sustain growth.

Stage Four: Diversified Marketing

As a business diversifies, it must reorganize, usually by creating divisions, to cope with increased complexity. As a company progresses into Stage Four, a marketing reorganization also takes place. Depending on the degree of decentralization, each division may operate as a quasi-independent Stage Three unit within a larger portfolio. Each division has a group of product managers with total marketing responsibility for products in the line. Supporting marketing functions such as sales, advertising, and customer research provide the necessary resources to product managers.

The major marketing change in the transition to Stage Four is the emergence of a marketing function at the corporate level. Regardless of the titles on the organizational chart, the marketing function has the responsibility for monitoring the company's divisions and for maintaining a favorable image of the company with customers and the general public. By providing specialized skills in market research and planning, the corporate-level marketing staff acts as an in-house consultant to the division's marketing staff. Marketing also plays a key role in setting the strategic direction for the company, particularly in identifying new growth opportunities.

Building a Marketing Organization

During Stage One, management should carve out identifiable domains of responsibility that it can gradually delegate to the growing staff of specialists. This staff's control over day-to-day operations then expands to incorporate all duties the founding entrepreneurs once performed.

Toward the end of Stage Two, a mature marketing organization is needed to coordinate the product line and monitor the market. Finally, as a company outgrows the narrow focus of product-market coordination and evolves into Stage Four, each division spawns its own product organization. Supporting functions such as advertising and research are decentralized among the divisions into autonomous marketing groups. Exhibit 2 outlines the evolution of a marketing organization.

At the corporate level, a strategic marketing group reviews division plans, manages corporate-level marketing communications, and provides help in marketing research and planning.

What happens after Stage Four? Products and technologies eventually become obsolete, whereas basic market needs generally endure. A slide-rule manufacturer will go out of business when the electronic calculator is invented unless it defines itself as a business to meet calculation needs, not to make slide rules.

The typical Stage Four business has a highly bureaucratized organization that can easily encounter marketing problems. For the Stage Four company, a key issue is whether it can continue to foster a spirit of seeking new venture opportunities, the same spirit that gave birth to the business.

EXHIBIT 2 The Evolution of the Marketing Function

	Stage 1: Entrepreneurial Marketing	Stage 2: Opportunistic Marketing	Stage 3: Responsive Marketing	Stage 4: Diversified Marketing
Marketing strategy	Market niche	Market penetration	Product-market development	New business development
Marketing organization	Informal, flexible	Sales management	Product-market management	Corporate and divisional levels
Marketing goals	Credibility in the marketplace	Sales volume	Customer satisfaction	Product life cycle and portfolio management
Critical success factors	A little help from your friends	Production economies	Functional coordination	Entrepreneurship and innovation

"Buying in" to Market Control
Robert E. Weigand

A Virginia public utility helped pay for underground electric wiring at a large housing development. For all practical purposes, home buyers would have no choice between electricity and gas because the utility and the builder agreed that the homes would be all-electric. The subsidized underground wiring would be paid for—many times over—by the sale of electricity during subsequent years.

■ Both General Motors and Ovitron Corporation submitted bids to build squad radios for the U.S. Army. GM won the bid, but Ovitron challenged the outcome in court, arguing that GM's bid was below cost. The winner, it argued, would be rewarded by charging a higher price on subsequent contracts for the same product. GM's tactic withstood the legal challenge, thus opening the door to future profitable contracts.

■ The city of Oakland built the Oakland-Alameda County Stadium in 1966 so that the Raiders would have a place to play football. The cost was substantial, but the city fathers knew it would be recouped from the rent the team would pay back over the years. However, the stadium could only be paid off if the Raiders remained in Oakland for the long term. When the team wanted to move to Los Angeles recently, the city filed suit. It claimed that the Raiders constitute a public use and necessity. If successful, the city's attorneys will have found a way to link a major capital expenditure made many years ago to a flow of revenue that the city and county have enjoyed over many years.

The above vignettes suggest the general character of a practice that is scarcely acknowledged in business literature but is extremely widespread among many industries. The practice is usually called "buying in," with the subsequent practices and profits referred to as "getting well" or the "follow on."

By buying in I mean linking an initial sale—sometimes made at less than satisfactory profits or even losses—to subsequent more lucrative sales of either the same or related goods or services. The initial buy-in sale itself usually generates volume or margins too small to warrant investment. Follow-on sales, in contrast, allow the seller to get well if the stream of revenue from the follow-on product or service is long enough or if margins are high enough.

The practice of buying in has several important characteristics. First, the seller—not the customer—does the buying in. The seller is buying customer patronage at some future time by offering an attractively priced product or service today.

Second, the process consists of a sequence of sales that are in some way tightly linked. The sequence may be as few as two sales, as when an aircraft manufacturer sells two jet aircraft to a small airline and subsequently sells five more to complete the carrier's needs. Or it may consist of an initial sale followed by a stream of sales for quite some time into the future, such as, from the example cited previously, when GM sold squad radios to the army.

Third, the link between the buy-in and the follow-on sales must be strong if buying in is to succeed. If the first sale does not render follow-on sales a near certainty, the seller has not bought into the future and may simply have spent a lot of money obtaining a low-profit project. Sellers make every effort to solidify the link, while astute customers, rival businesses, and sometimes government agencies attempt to weaken it.

Fourth, the seller must take the view that the profit is to be earned over the life of the products or services. If there is price and profit movement, it will be from low prices and profits during the buy-in to higher prices and profits during the get-well period.

Finally, the customers who are courted and the products or services that are sold during the buy-in may not be the same during the follow-on campaign. For example, the Virginia electric utility mentioned earlier subsidized underground electrical wiring for a major house builder. However, the follow-on sales of electricity were made to those who later bought the houses.

This article focuses on the following: the techniques or methods that managers can use to link a buy-in sale to subsequent get-well sales; the circumstances that should exist and the problems that are created during buy-in situations; and suggestions about how to handle possibly troublesome moral issues that may arise from getting well either too soon or too conspicuously.

Ties that Bind

A seller can use a variety of techniques to encourage a buyer to remain loyal. Strong patents, copyrights, and carefully guarded trade secrets quite obviously act as deterrents to follow-on competition. Polaroid enjoyed a stream of nearly exclusive revenue from instant-picture film sales for more than 30 years, largely because its patents fended off prospective rivals. And anyone who has ever shopped in a large food store knows about encyclopedias. The first volume of a set can be purchased for, say, $1.99. This is the buy-in. But the follow-on volumes, available from the same food store, will cost $4.99 or whatever amount it takes to make the entire pro-

ject profitable. The publisher's copyright, of course, precludes imitators who could break the buy-in.

Less obvious ways are illustrated by the following examples.

■ When Murphy Pacific, a marine salvage company, entered a bid to clear 10 ships from the Suez Canal, it was up against tough bidding from several European companies. The bidding was particularly spirited because the bidders assumed that the winner would be in a unique position to win subsequent dredging and removal contracts—since the company's equipment would already be in place and its engineers would already know the canal's physical characteristics.

■ The Clean Air Act required America's automobile manufacturers to build cars that would be nearly pollution free for their entire life span—defined as 50,000 miles or five years. But factory-installed catalytic converters were expected to last only about 25,000 miles. So each of the four major carmakers told the Environmental Protection Agency that they could assure clean-burning cars only if the replacement converters—installed after about 25,000 miles of driving—were installed by a franchised dealer with genuine factory parts. But independent parts manufacturers and repair shops insisted that this argument was just a ploy to keep them out of the lucrative aftermarket. Since each catalytic converter could cost $100 to $150, access to the follow-on sales was worth arguing about.

The methods for tying the buy-in to follow-on sales fall into five categories.

1. Tying the customer to an operating pattern that encourages continued patronage. For example, Stansaab Elektronik of Sweden successfully beat out such companies as Sperry Rand, IBM, and Raytheon to provide an air-traffic control system for seven Soviet airports. The contract was large—about $72

million—but industry experts say that the follow-on business may be more than 10 times that figure. After all, if the Soviets hope to provide a traffic control system for the entire Soviet Union, its parts must be compatible. Stansaab Elektronik has thus gone a long way toward making follow-on sales.

2. Committing the customer to an inventory of parts and supplies. Airplane manufacturers are among the best illustrations of this approach. Air carriers are anxious to keep the number of engines, tires, light switches, and thousands of other parts to a minimum; they are most likely to do so if they obtain their aircraft fleet from a single manufacturer. Other suppliers of major installations or heavy equipment find making subsequent sales to be much easier than initial ones because customers soon discover how difficult and costly it is to make major changes in inventories of parts and supplies.

3. Committing the customer to the follow-on because a change of suppliers would require retraining employees. Today's managers often view a skilled work force as a fixed asset, much like a piece of equipment. Cost-conscious managers are reluctant to retrain skilled employees unless absolutely necessary. IBM has been accused of preempting commercial markets for computing equipment by seeing to it that employees of prospective customers learned while in college how to operate IBM equipment. IBM accomplished its goal by selling or leasing its equipment to many American colleges and universities at discounts as high as 60 percent off commercial prices. IBM knew that students who learned computing on its machines would not be likely to prefer a rival's equipment once they started working. Rather than retrain their new employees, employers bought IBM equipment. Under legal pressures during the 1970s, IBM sharply curtailed the heaviest discounting. But even today, many computer companies, including IBM, give modest discounts to educational institutions. Each company hopes that it can buy in educationally and get well commercially.

Airbus Industrie, a French company, faced the obstacle of skilled employees trained on the equipment of other companies when it attempted to sell its Airbus jet to Eastern Airlines. All of Eastern's flight and maintenance personnel had been trained on American-made equipment, and management was understandably reluctant to change the practice. So Airbus promised to teach Eastern's captains, first officers, cabin attendants, and maintenance personnel how to work with the A-300 airplane. Industry observers say that the total training costs—paid for by Airbus—could run into several millions of dollars.

But the buy-in worked. Airbus—with its free training, along with a loan of four aircraft for six months for test purposes and a promise of a well-equipped parts and maintenance depot in Miami—cracked the American market. U.S. aircraft makers, government officials, and others charged Airbus Industrie with unscrupulous tactics. But the buy-in now seems to have withstood the test, and Eastern may buy as many as 50 Airbus planes at $50 million each in the current decade.

4. Becoming involved in establishing a product's specifications so that the designer is uniquely suited to meet the specifications. This might best be labeled the "sole savior syndrome." Prospective marketers may argue that they only want to help the prospective customer define his or her needs. This may seem charitable until it turns out that the solution can only be provided by a single supplier—naturally, the one who aided in the design.

For example, few American companies make buses, whether for local or intercity transportation. When the Department of Transportation consults with manufacturers before specifying what sorts of buses it will subsidize for urban mass-transport systems, each manufacturer usually attempts to guide the specifications so that it, and it alone, will be the chosen supplier. Allegations of favoritism—and sometimes lawsuits—often follow contract announcements.

Another example is of a major Western European multinational that invested in a Far Eastern country and that, like a good corporate citizen, earned only a modest profit. It warned highly placed individuals in government ministries about unscrupulous companies that might be inclined to sell poor-quality products to the country. Indeed, the European company even helped government officials write an import policy that would minimize such problems. Not surprisingly, the European company is probably the only one in its industry that can meet the standards it helped establish. It is depending on bureaucratic lethargy to keep the standards in place for a long time. And its critics further believe that its low prices and fair-profit stance will not last long.

5. Withholding information about a buy-in product until the last possible moment before market introduction. Secrecy can act as a significant—although incomplete—barrier to follow-on rivalry. Companies that market safety razors have been known to produce razors that are compatible only with the blades that they market. The specifications of the razors are carefully guarded secrets until the day they are introduced.

Problems of Buying in

Various problems face a company that hopes to buy into a particular market. First, if buying in is to succeed, the tie between the initial and subsequent transactions must be virtually unbreakable. If customers, potential rivals, or government breaks the linkage, both sales volume and gross margins may fall to levels below which it is impossible to recoup the company's initial outlay or bring a satisfactory life-of-the-project return on investment. Each of these three parties has much to gain from making sure that follow-on sales are not monopolized by the original entrant. Some attempts to break the link succeed and some do not, as the following illustrate.

■ Eastman Kodak, easily the dominant company in the photo industry, was accused by Berkey Photo of using its camera trade secrets as a barrier to new competition. By keeping the details of its cameras a secret until introduction day, Kodak had the film sales to itself until prospective rivals could buy the camera and film from the nearest retailer, replicate them, and market them alongside the Kodak brand, which was by then well established. In a lower court, Berkey won the right to compel Kodak to "predisclose" trade secrets about cameras and film far ahead of the introduction date. But Berkey lost its victory in an appeals court, which held that Kodak was entitled to the fruits of its research and was simply "reaping the competitive rewards attributable to its efficient size." Thus the link that Kodak established between its buy-in and its follow-on sales survived Berkey's legal challenge.

■ Public utilities in Pennsylvania, like those in Virginia and nearly everywhere else, often fought hard for new customers, sometimes subsidizing the costs of new household appliances and wiring or piping for housing projects. The utilities knew that they could get well on the subsequent sales of electricity or gas. To stop such practices, the Pennsylvania Public Utility Commission ordered electric and gas utilities in the state to discontinue any practices that would encourage architects, builders, or developers to choose one source of power over another. The consequence of this order is that the initial cost of a home or apartment may be higher by the amount of the utility's previous subsidy, but the buyer may later benefit from lower lighting and heating bills. At the very least, it would seem that those who are not purchasing or renting new homes or apartments will not be obliged to subsidize those who are.

■ Schick began marketing razor blades that would fit both its own Ultrex twin-blade shavers and Gillette's Atra razors. Gillette claimed that Schick had infringed on its patents, so Schick paid Gillette $3 million for the right to market the blades—and not to be sued. But Schick says that once Gillette took the money, it came out with the Atra Invitation, a razor designed to make the original obsolete. Schick sued Gillette in mid-1979, claiming that the changes represented an anticompetitive practice meant to keep Schick out of Gillette's aftermarket sales.

In the automotive industry, the aftermarket for air conditioners, radios, heaters, wire wheels, rustproofing, and a host of other products has traditionally been lucrative. But in recent years, manufacturers have tried to make most of these products standard parts of their automobiles. This means both higher returns to the car manufacturers and smaller shares of aftermarket sales for independent suppliers. In 1979, GM declared that it would factory-install Delco radios—a GM product— on 13 different models, including its new X-body cars. Dealers could no longer order automobiles without a radio. Eleven independent radio distributors brought legal action through their Custom Automotive Sound Association, claiming that the step would foreclose the independents from a huge car-buyer market. Rather than face trial, GM and the association settled out of court. GM agreed not to make radios standard equipment until the end of 1983. It also agreed to give the association four months' notice of any other changes it might make that would affect the competitive position of its members.

The fundamental issue, of course, is whether a radio is an integral part of an automobile or a separate follow-on commodity. GM's legal position quite obviously would be that an automobile surely includes a body, engine, wheels—and a radio. The trade association would claim that radios are optional and that competition for customer allegiance should be open to all.

American law has generally been sympathetic to the protection of industrial property and the right of owners to exploit subsequent business opportunities. However, others have a corresponding right to demonstrate that a greater good is served by opening up those opportunities to outsiders. In short, for others to pick away at the linkage between the buy-in and follow-on sales is perfectly normal—and sometimes successful.

A second condition for successful buying in is possession of the capacity for fulfilling both the buy-in and follow-on sales. For example, much effort is now going into obtaining contracts to provide telecommunications equipment for developing countries. The largest companies—Western Electric, ITT, Siemens, GTE, L.M. Ericsson, Northern Telecom, Nippon Electric, and Philips—are vying to win the initial bids so that they will be in a position to influence and perhaps win subsequent contracts. Small companies that are unable to provide the full gamut of products and services probably need not apply.

If the company that buys in is unable to follow on with the more lucrative downstream sales, it has done no more than prime the market for others. Franchisors who attempted to be sole suppliers to their franchisees learned in a series of court cases that they were restraining trade. The long and steady stream of revenue that should have derived from their monopoly supplier position just did not materialize. Rivals who weren't invited showed up and proved they could supply products that were as good as anyone's. The courts helped both the franchisees and outside suppliers break the buy-in/get-well link. Thus the franchisors primed the market—for someone else.

A third factor is that buying in generally requires more capital for a longer period than single-product marketing. By definition, the buy-in is made at lower-than-normal profits. Follow-on sales may lag by only a few days, in some instances, but in other cases may be months or years in coming. This means at the very least that buying in is not generally attractive to the underfinanced company or to the single-product company with stockholders impatient for dividends. The multiproduct company can afford to wait for its revenue from a buy-in situation simply because it has funds coming in from its other products or services. Thus the cost of a buy-in gets subsidized by the revenue generated by the company's high-profit products or services.

Finally, buying in can create internal company squabbles if the buy-in and get-well products come out of different profit centers—that is, if top management is asking the manager of the profitable get-well division to subsidize the manager of the unprofitable division that helps the company buy in. Which division earns a profit is of little concern to top management but of the utmost importance to the division manager who is up for annual review. Most management groups have had enough experience with similar profit-center problems that they are able to cope reasonably well with the buy-in problem. However, when top management does not acknowledge and deal with the issue, it opens the door to serious personnel difficulties.

Dealing with Ethics and Guilt

A successful buy-in is a mixed blessing. On one hand, it virtually assures future profits during the get-well period. But on the other hand, the practice, if crudely managed, contains the potential for generating an uproar in the marketplace. In its worst form, customers see themselves as exploited and locked into a situation from which there is no exit. They may describe businesses as "monopolist" and see themselves as being "over a barrel" or "with a gun to my head," and so on. And that is often the case. Buying in *is* exploitative under certain circumstances. Managers who are sensitive to increasingly astute and critical customers must face the uncomfortable fact that the intent of buying in is to lock a customer into the selling company.

Perhaps the easiest way to minimize customer antagonism and feelings of entrapment is to maintain, during the get-well period, the quality of product or service that the customer has come to expect. This rule, however, is easy to forget, particularly when management is under pressure to increase profits.

There are other less obvious ways (not all equally defensible) that businesses can use to lessen the potential hostility from customers who are more or less beholden to their suppliers.

The Full-Explanation Solution. During the buy-in period customers should know exactly what their obligations will be and what the seller will deliver during the get-well period. This admonition is easily understood by industrial goods' sellers. Their customers are likely to have engineers who pore over product specifications, attorneys who read the fine print in contracts, accountants who explore every financial option, and so on. Every foreseeable contingency is resolved. In short, when customers put together a buying team that is as astute as the selling team, there are no surprises.

Purchasers of consumer goods, in contrast, are usually less sophisticated. Although they are often shrewd buyers who can carefully weigh the consequences of their decisions, they do not have either the skills or the tools of professional buyers. One example of just how informed (or uninformed) the typical customer can be is provided by the long-standing dispute between Book-of-the-Month Club and the Federal Trade Commission. At issue is whether the company's advertising should make explicit the fact that members must pay handling and shipping charges. The company has argued that a specific statement noting that prices do not include handling and shipping charges is unnecessary because customers expect to pay such charges. However, the FTC has maintained that the fees come as a surprise and that the discount earned by the customer is partly lost when packing and shipping charges are paid. Thus savings are far less than the company's advertising implies, argues the FTC. A forthright explanation of customer rights and obligations in the club's advertising could reduce whatever customer dissatisfaction might exist. But of course it might also make the club's buy-in offer less attractive.

The Multicompany Get-Well Solution. Companies that have succeeded in buying in can reduce antitrust risks and increase customer satisfaction—without necessarily reducing profits—if rival businesses are allowed to participate in the get-well sales. Multiple licensing of get-well patents is one way of allowing rivals in without necessarily damaging profits. Motives are difficult to discern, but I suspect that part of the reason at least a few companies pick up corporate hitchhikers via licensing is that it reduces prospective antitrust attention and customer animosity. Licensing arrangements among rivals generate profits for the licenser but also give customers at least the illusion—and usually the reality—of choice in the marketplace. Licensing is not popular, presumably because many managements believe that profits from licensing are less than profits from monopoly sales. That may help explain why companies such as Kodak, IBM, and Gillette have been so reluctant to allow others to profit from their buy-in situations.

The Sliding-Down-the-Learning-Curve Solution. It is less a matter of business strategy and more a matter of luck to be in an industry where the learning curve is alive and well. Learning-curve theory tells us that cost per unit goes down during a product's life cycle by virtue of the producer's experience with the product. If a product costs, say, one dollar per unit to manufacture in 1980, costs may be only 90 cents by 1983. This decline is brought about by production sophistication rather than economies of scale, which may reduce production costs even more.

One industry in which the learning curve is thriving is the semiconductor industry. Producers are far more efficient now than they were just a few years ago, and this experience is reflected in selling prices that have declined dramatically over the years.

Under such conditions, sellers who have bought into a market can earn generous profits while simultaneously maintaining stable prices or perhaps even gradually reducing them. Of course, costs must go down even faster.

The For-the-Good-of-the-Public Solution. One can argue that businesses which bind customers to purchases that enhance their quality of life are making a positive contribution to consumer welfare. Some psychologists maintain that certain prospective buyers need help in taking the last step toward purchasing products they want. The psychologists contend that many customers are unable to tell a salesperson, "Yes, I'll take it," or cannot bring themselves to sign their name to a mail-order form, even though they know the product will improve their life at least a bit. A tempting buy-in offer made by the seller helps the customer past this mental obstacle.

A formidable problem in persuading hard-to-persuade customers is that they are likely to have substantial postpurchase anxieties about the propriety of their purchases. More than 20 years ago, Leon Festinger pointed out that customers often attempt to provide themselves a comforting rationale for their purchases afterward.[1] They actively seek out and believe information that supports their decision while avoiding or rejecting information that suggests a wrong decision. Festinger's theory explains business strategy that is directed at customers who constitute the follow-on market.

The argument can be made, then, that book clubs use buying in for the public good. Most readers would no doubt accept the argument that a literate public is socially beneficial. So if the psychological theory that people need help overcoming their own purchasing anxieties is right, the clubs that keep sending books unless they are told not to are providing a public service. This presumes, of course, that the money spent on books would otherwise be spent on something of lower social value.

Furthermore, the club managers may have read or even anticipated Festinger's propositions about postdecision dissonance, because their advertising no longer alludes only to the joy of reading. Rather, the advertising also suggests the benefits of owning a collection of fine books. The book clubs learned long ago that while people often buy books to read, they sometimes buy books to leave on their coffee tables and impress their friends. People who buy books but do not read them have their consciences soothed by believing from advertising that ownership of a good book is almost as important as reading it.

The Don't-Get-Well-Too-Quickly Solution. This strategy consists of realizing gross margins during the follow-on sales that are less than what they might be. The approach works best when the seller has the near certainty of a long string of sales into the future and can enjoy the luxury of watching revenue from follow-on sales come drifting in, slowly but surely.

This approach sounds nearly unassailable, but several caveats are worth mentioning. First, it is based on the premise that the link between the buy-in and get-well sales is so strong that the seller will enjoy sales in perpetuity. But the tendency of companies to de-velop "new and improved" products suggests that companies which have bought in would rather not simply let things be. Second, low margins may be unnecessary if placating the consumer market is the only objective, since customers often have little or no idea of what constitutes a fair price. In short, getting well by selling products at high gross margins will generate no ill will in the marketplace if customers do not know that the prices they are paying contribute to high margins. This situation exists with many new consumer products that allow the seller much pricing freedom without risking significant customer criticism.

Sellers who face industrial buyers usually have no such leeway. Industrial customers often can reconstruct prices and have a reasonably accurate idea about the seller's profit margins. They know—better than the household buyer—when the seller is getting well too quickly. For such customers, the slower approach to getting well—meaning a lower selling price and lower margin per unit—may mean higher profits over the life of the project. In addition, rivals may lose interest in breaking the buy-in/get-well link if low prices make the get-well profit potential less attractive.

An ironic danger associated with getting well slowly is that low-margin pricing may smack of a monopolistic approach that appears to foreclose the market to would-be rivals. The irony is that low prices make profit margins too small to encourage market entry by other potential suppliers. Crudely stated, high margins attract rivals, while low margins repel them. Federal antitrust officials have given ample attention in the past to sales of such diverse products as linen and office supplies because entrenched suppliers set prices too low rather than too high. Thus getting well so slowly that it preserves the market for a single well-established supplier can be dangerous legally. Consequently the practice must be handled with great care.

The Muddy-the-Water Solution. This strategy is reserved for those who are morally certain about what they do, though in an open debate the strategy would be hard to defend. One approach consists of separating in the customers' minds the business entity that engages in the buy-in from the one that enjoys the getting well. If enough confusion can be created in the marketing process, customers will not link the two entities and will continue to think well of one unit while any animosity will be directed at the other.

For example, appliance retailers, automobile dealers, and others sell their financing papers via financial institutions. After making a down payment, customers are obligated to a bank or finance company—not to a retailer—for monthly payments. Some retailers have profited rather handsomely by selling get-well financing papers to outside businesses. Some financial institutions, with no reputation to protect, have abused their strong legal position. The retailer in such situations could continue to show much sympathy but give no substantive help to the purchaser. If handled properly, the customer would presumably direct all his or her antagonism toward the financing institution rather than the retailer.

A second and more palatable approach consists of making product design, packaging, or styling changes that hinder comparison with earlier purchases. No seller wants to hear a customer say, "But when I bought this identical product just a year ago it cost me only. . . ." Regular product changes that are announced as improvements are the most common solution, particularly when they are accompanied by style and packaging changes and a phasing out of the older model. Unhappily, business executives may honestly believe that the newer product is a real improvement and that it offers customers more value for their money. But the customers may not notice any real improvement, looking on the changes as purely cosmetic.

In Conclusion

Buying in represents an attempt to monopolize markets. The result, however, is usually far less than a powerful and long-term hold on customer allegiance. Furthermore, most monopolies such as those held in a buy-in/get-well situation are hard to maintain over the years; they tend to deteriorate. This tendency is a tribute to the abilities of customers, government, and rivals to break the link to the get-well stage.

Whatever the effectiveness of buy-in attempts, sensitive executives must not lose sight of the moral issues that buying in may pose. No executive enjoys being in the position of those in the cigarette industry who, until recent years, freely passed out samples of their products on college campuses. Once addicted, the students would pay back the cost of the buy-in many times over. But when the relationship of smoking to health problems became widely known, public criticism forced the companies to stop giving out samples.

Business managers give more attention to buying in than academicians, who would mostly prefer not to acknowledge its importance as a business tool. Even the managers who use the technique often do not use the vocabulary presented here and may not recognize it when they see it in other situations.

Of course, not every product or service is suited to buying in. But the practice occurs often enough, generates serious commercial and legal problems for both seller and buyer, and imposes enough ethical questions that it deserves explicit acknowledgment by both managers and academicians.

Note
1. Leon Festinger, *A Theory of Cognitive Dissonance* (Stanford, Calif.: Stanford University Press, 1957).

===================== *Company Readings* =====================

The Colossus That Works
John Greenwald

IBM. Three of the most famous letters in American business. For years the International Business Machines Corp. towered over the office-equipment industry. Then in the 1970s, besieged by government antitrust charges and challenged by ambitious new rivals, the giant seemed to be staggering, and those three famous letters lost a bit of their luster. Was IBM's dominance in jeopardy?

Not a chance. Under the direction of John Opel, 58, who became chief executive officer in January 1981, the firm has been acting like its brashest competitors—entering new markets, chasing the latest technology, trimming organizational fat, and selling more aggressively than ever. In 1982, IBM had profits of $4.4 billion on sales of $34.4 billion, making it the most profitable U.S. industrial company. Says Stephen McClellan, author of an upcoming book on the computer industry: "In the 1970s, IBM was a battleship in mothballs. Today it is a fleet of killer submarines."

Nowhere was the company's lean new stance more evident than in the way it plunged into the personal computer market in August 1981. Tackling the mass market for computers for the first time, the company broke many of the traditions that had made it so successful in the past. Yet its new machine, the Personal Computer (generally known simply as the PC), has done nothing less than transform the industry. IBM has already captured 21 percent of the $7.5 billion U.S. market for personal computers, a staggering feat in so short a time, and is virtually tied with

pacesetter Apple Computer, which had a four-year head start.

Big Blue, as IBM is nicknamed for the corporate color it puts on many products, is a mighty competitor in a range of products from electric typewriters that sell for $800 to data processing systems that can cost more than $100 million. It commands some 40 percent of the worldwide market for computing equipment and produces some two thirds of all mainframe computers, which are big and medium-size business machines. So great is IBM's preeminence that rivals often seem to be running in a different race. Digital Equipment, the number two computermaker, has less than one fifth of IBM's sales. Says John Imlay, Jr., chairman of MSA, an Atlanta-based software company: "IBM is simply the best-run corporation in American history."

At a time when American business sometimes seems to be slipping, IBM's triumphs have served as a reminder that U.S. industrial prowess and know-how can still be formidable. Struggling U.S. steel and automakers have been severely hurt by Japanese and European imports, but Big Blue's competitiveness is unquestioned. The company is the leading computer firm in virtually every one of the some 130 countries where it does business. "IBM is like your papa," says a Swiss computer-marketing specialist, "because it's so big and it's always there." Even in Japan, which has six major domestic computermakers and restricts access to its markets, IBM is easily the dominant producer of large computers and is fighting Fujitsu for the overall title. Last year IBM sold $1.9 billion worth of equipment in Japan to Fujitsu's $2.1 billion.

For all of its success, IBM has been rethinking some of the ways it does business. In a dramatic departure from its traditional practices, IBM built the PC largely from parts bought from outside suppliers and is selling it through retail outlets like Sears and ComputerLand, as well as its own sales network. The company has begun offering discount prices and introducing new products at an accelerated rate. Last December IBM spent $250 million to acquire 12 percent of Intel, a leading computer-chip maker based in Santa Clara, California. In June IBM paid $228 million for a 15 percent stake in Rolm, also of Santa Clara, a major producer of telecommunications equipment. IBM plans to use Rolm to help create the so-called electronic office. Says Ulric Weil, a top computer analyst for Morgan Stanley & Co.: "We're watching a total transformation of the corporation."

In June IBM Chairman Opel announced that 1983 results were outstripping last year's. That helped push up the price of IBM stock, a leader in the eleven-month-old Wall Street bull rally. After years of hardly moving, IBM shares have nearly doubled in price since the rally started, climbing from 62¼ last August to close last week at 121.

Traditionally, IBM has been so deep in talent that its alumni have gone on to staff laboratories and executive suites throughout the computer industry. "Almost everybody in the business seems to be a former IBMer," observes William Easterbrook, an ex-IBM manager in Copenhagen who now watches the computer industry for Kidder, Peabody, a Wall Street securities firm. Illustrious former employees include Gene Amdahl, founder of Amdahl Corp. (1982 sales, $462 million), which makes large computers; Joe M. Henson, president of Prime Computer (1982 sales, $436 million), a major producer of minicomputers; and David Martin, president of National Advanced Systems, the computer unit of National Semiconductor. Former employees usually speak highly of Big Blue. Says Fla-

vil Van Dyke, president of Genigraphics, a computer-graphics firm: "I still look back fondly at IBM and try to run my company by IBM standards."

Customers of IBM often speak with that same kind of devotion. Some have been known to refuse to see salesmen from rival firms. Says James Marston, vice-president for data processing with American Airlines: "You can take any specific piece of hardware or software and perhaps do better than IBM, but across the board IBM offers an unbeatable system." IBM buyers range from government agencies like the National Aeronautics and Space Administration, which directs space-shuttle missions with Big Blue equipment, to firms as diverse as Bank of America and Coca-Cola.

Longtime industry observers view the loyalty of some customers as a natural outgrowth of the attitudes that IBM drills into its workers from the day they arrive. "IBM creates an environment that is unique because of its strong set of beliefs and principles," says Martin. "It is almost overwhelming how it affects employees and rubs off on customers."

IBM's strong corporate culture is the lengthened shadow of Thomas Watson, Sr., a charismatic executive who joined the Computing-Tabulating-Recording Corp. in 1914, renamed it International Business Machines in 1924, and ran it until a month before his death in 1956. Watson was a visionary who believed above all in his company.

Under Watson, IBM had rules for practically everything. Employees were told what to wear (dark business suits, white shirts, and striped ties) and what to drink (no alcohol, even when off the job), and were urged in signs posted everywhere to THINK. Aspiring executives usually started out in sales and marketing and were transferred so frequently that they took to joking that IBM stood for "I've Been Moved." Observes Gideon Gartner, chairman of the Gartner Group, a computer research firm: "If you understand the marines, you can understand IBM."

Many of the Watson-instilled codes remain in effect today, though in a softened form. All IBMers are subject to a 32-page code of business ethics. Sample warning from the blue-covered rulebook: "If IBM is about to build a new facility, you must not invest in land or business near the new site."

IBM salesmen can now drink at lunch, but if they do they are warned not to make further business calls that day. Male IBMers, who make up 80 percent of the 8,500-member U.S. sales force, must wear suits and ties when meeting prospective customers, although their shirts no longer must be white. Still, a neat and conservative appearance remains the IBM style. "I don't think I've ever seen an IBMer in a pink shirt or an outlandish tie," says Joseph Levy, a vice president for International Data, a Massachusetts-based computer market research firm. The THINK signs have largely vanished, but the old admonition remains the title of the company's employee magazine.

IBM has combined Watson's stern codes with a deep and genuine concern for the welfare of employees, who number 215,000 in the United States, with an additional 150,000 abroad. The company has often fired workers, but it has never laid anyone off to cut costs; instead it retrains and reassigns them. The company's salaries and perks are widely regarded as among the most attractive in the industry. New employees are expected to spend their working lives with the firm, and regularly go through intensive training programs to upgrade their skills. "We hire with a career in mind," says Edward Krieg, director of management development. Although some overseas IBM plants are unionized, the firm has never had a union vote in any U.S. facility.

The generous fringe benefits extend to recreation. The company provides memberships for less than $5 a year in IBM country clubs in Poughkeepsie and Endicott, New York. There, employees can play golf, swim, and participate in numerous other sports.

Watson was especially adept at motivating workers and inspiring loyalty. He personally commissioned a company songbook and led employee gatherings in numbers like *Ever Onward.*[1] The song was belted out with gusto during get-togethers of the IBM 100 percent Club, made up of members who have met 100 percent of their sales goals for the previous year.

Watson was succeeded by his son Thomas Watson, Jr., who served as chief executive officer from 1956 to 1971. A powerful executive in his own right, the younger Watson had helped persuade his father to steer IBM into the computer age. After retirement, Thomas Watson, Jr. was U.S. Ambassador to the Soviet Union under President Carter.

More than anything else, it was IBM's awesome sales skills that enabled the company to capture the computer market. Although it now seems hard to believe, IBM did not introduce the first commercial computer. Remington Rand did that in 1951 with a computer called Univac, which became the name of the firm's computer division. But Big Blue knew far more about winning customers than did Univac. IBM, whose major products at the time included calculators and tabulators, recognized that potential buyers might be frightened by the cost and complexity of computers. When the company entered the market in 1952, it set a high priority on dispelling customer fears. Buyers were promised that IBM service engineers would keep a close watch over the machines and quickly fix any glitches. The salesmen were so knowledgeable and thoroughly trained that their very presence inspired confidence. Univac representatives, by contrast, were seen to dwell on technical details that customers could barely follow.

The race was over by 1956. IBM had won a staggering 85 percent of the U.S. computer market, even though its machines were considered to be technically inferior to Univac's. Years later a Univac executive would lament,

"It doesn't do much good to build a better mousetrap if the other guy selling mousetraps has five times as many salesmen."

The Univac episode helped give rise to the belief that IBM's real strength is in selling while its technical prowess often lags. Says Kenneth Leavitt, president of CGX Corp., a Massachusetts-based maker of high-performance display terminals: "IBM tends to be a step behind in technology but very good at marketing. There are all sorts of new technologies that IBM doesn't have the expertise to get."

Such claims naturally make IBMers bristle. "This is a shibboleth cultivated by certain Wall Streeters," declares Paul Low, manager of the IBM plant in East Fishkill, New York. "Nobody who peeks inside any of our 29 laboratories could fall for that nonsense." Company spokesmen like to point out that IBM spent $3 billion on research, development, and engineering last year, an amount that exceeds the total revenues of many of its rivals. The firm has also taken the offensive in a new advertising campaign that boasts of the more than 11,000 patents IBM inventors have acquired over the past 25 years.

Actually, IBM is skilled at blending both marketing and technical considerations. That goes a long way toward explaining how so huge a company has kept its edge in an industry where key breakthroughs are often made by blue-jeaned engineers working out of their garages.

What IBM seeks, above all, is products that sell. "They have tried to understand what the customer wants," says Stuart Madnick, a professor of management information systems at M.I.T.'s Sloan School. "Often the customer didn't need or want the more advanced technology that others have produced. In many companies the technology has grown faster than the market can absorb."

IBM evaluates buyers' needs in fine detail. "IBM will listen to almost anybody," says Joseph Levy of International Data, which ana-

lyzes computer-market trends. "It is one of our best customers." Big Blue subscribes to virtually every major computer market research service and has a worldwide intelligence-gathering network that includes economists and market analysts.

The company takes equal pains in keeping the skills of its personnel up to date. Last year, for example, IBM invested more than $500 million on employee education and training. Most new IBMers spend much of their first six weeks in company-run classes, and managers are required to take at least 40 hours of additional instruction a year. The classwork often focuses on actual business case studies, in the manner of the Harvard Business School.

The IBM management formula worked so well that the company in the 1960s came to be known as Snow White while its competitors were derisively dubbed the Seven Dwarfs. The dwarfs (Burroughs, Univac, NCR, Control Data, Honeywell, General Electric, and RCA) dwindled to five when GE and RCA quit the computer business in the 1970s, and the others are now collectively referred to by their first initials as the BUNCH.

IBM's very success, however, almost backfired against the company. The Johnson administration on its final working day in office, January 17, 1969, opened a massive antitrust case, accusing the company of monopolistic and anticompetitive practices. The federal suit dragged on endlessly—at a cost to IBM of several hundred million dollars in legal fees—until the Justice Department abruptly dropped it in January 1982, declaring that the case was "without merit." Recalls former IBM Chairman Frank Cary, Opel's predecessor: "The suit was a tremendous cloud that was over the company for 13 years. It couldn't help influencing us in a whole variety of ways. Ending it lifted a huge burden from management's shoulders." Jeffrey Zuckerman, special assistant to Antitrust Division Chief William Baxter, concurs: "We believe

IBM must have been deterred from competing as aggressively as it otherwise would have."

Whatever the reason, IBM's momentum slowed markedly in the 1970s, a period Cary called "a time of planning and consolidation." The company entered the decade with a 60 percent share of the computer market and emerged with a still impressive but slimmed-down 40 percent.

Though IBM was growing at a respectable annual rate of 13 percent, the computer industry was expanding even faster. One challenge came from the Route 128 area around Boston, where Digital Equipment and other firms launched the minicomputer. Such machines were smaller and cheaper than the large ones IBM offered, but still performed a wide range of data processing functions. Revenues of Digital Equipment, the leading maker of minis, have climbed from $265 million to about $4 billion over the past 10 years.

Another challenge came from California's Silicon Valley, where the microprocessor, or computer-on-a-chip, was developed. The tiny devices packed thousands of circuits onto a postage stamp-size silicon chip and gave rise to the microcomputer. Apple recognized the potentially vast appeal of personal computing, and its sales jumped from less than $1 million to $582 million between 1977 and 1982.

By the start of the 1980s, however, IBM had begun to move in new directions, and the dismissal of the lawsuit helped to accelerate the process. The most notable example was in the personal computer field. Although IBM had been monitoring the market for years, it refused to jump in until it began seeing personal computers appear in offices and became convinced that there was enough demand to make their entry pay off. "There's no particular challenge to building a personal computer other than to build one that someone wants," says Cary.

The task of overseeing the creation of the PC fell to a 12-member group in Boca Raton, Florida, led by Philip Estridge, a division vice-president. The team was first assembled in July 1980 and told to develop a competitive and easy-to-use machine within a year. "Twelve-hour days and six- or six and a half-day weeks were commonplace," recalls Estridge. The members made some key moves along the way that help account for the PC's enormous popularity. The planners decided, for example, to build the PC around a 16-bit microprocessor rather than an 8-bit one, which was at that time the industry standard. This move permitted the PC to run faster and handle more complex programs. Says Estridge: "We chose to up the power of the machine so that it could be used without too many changes for the next decade or so."

The group broke with tradition by setting up a so-called open-architecture scheme that makes the PC's technical specifications available to other firms. The idea was to permit outside companies and individuals to write software or build peripheral equipment for the PC and thereby expand its appeal.

The project, however, did not always unfold smoothly and without flaws. Early users discovered that the machine misplaced decimals in certain calculations, but the problem was quickly solved. Also, some owners complained that the keyboard had been poorly designed.

But those problems did not impede sales. "Within just a few months," says Morgan Stanley's Ulric Weil, "the IBM PC was *the* standard for the personal computer market." Orders for the machine, which has a starting price, with standard accessories, of about $3,200, have been pouring in so fast that some buyers have had to wait several months to get one. Last year IBM sold an estimated 200,000 PCs, and this year sales of 800,000 or more are projected. In June, the Travelers Insurance ordered 10,000 PCs, to be delivered over the next two years. New companies with names like Compaq Computer and Eagle Computer have sprung up making machines that are modeled on the PC.

The explosive growth of the IBM entry has set up a confrontation with Apple Computer. Executives of the California-based company, which introduced a fully assembled personal computer in 1977, profess not to be worried. They even greeted the PC the day after it was announced with ads that read "Welcome IBM. Seriously. Welcome to the most exciting and important marketplace since the computer revolution began 35 years ago." Whatever the intent of the message, some IBMers found it condescending.

Apple Chairman Steven Jobs claims that IBM has expanded the personal computer market and that his company's share of it has gone on growing at the expense of weaker rivals like Tandy, which owns Radio Shack. Says he: "Apple has a higher market share than IBM, and we intend to keep it." Indicative of how serious Apple considered the challenge was its decision to hire Pepsi-Cola President John Sculley, a marketing expert, to serve as Apple's president and chief executive. "This is not a bruising fight for market share between Apple and IBM," says Sculley. "It's a sorting out of who the major participants will be."

Some observers are far less confident about Apple's prospects. Gene Amdahl knows IBM from the perspective of a rival and a former 13-year employee. Says he: "IBM waits until some brash young companies develop a market to the point where it's interesting, and then they take it over. In Apple's case the shooting isn't over yet, but I think it's clear how the war will come out."

In fact, IBM's aggressive new posture poses a threat to virtually the entire computer industry. "IBM is creating a dangerous situation for competitors in the marketplace," says computer industry observer Gideon Gartner. Among those most at risk are makers of so-called plug-compatible computers that run IBM software but sell for less. Such firms thrived during the 1970s, when IBM was slow in delivering equipment. Now, however, a

burst of IBM price cuts and new models could badly hurt them.

That has already happened to Magnuson Computer Systems (1982 sales, $18.4 million). The San Jose-based maker of medium-size computers prospered in the late 1970s when IBM failed to ship a rival system on time. But IBM fought back in 1981 by slashing prices and introducing a new model. Then, last October, IBM announced two additional computer models and cut prices again. "There was no question. That was the fatal blow," declares Magnuson President Charles Strauch. The company, which has chopped its work force from more than 640 employees to about 100 over the past 18 months, filed bankruptcy papers in March.

Other firms have also been hit hard. Like Magnuson, Storage Technology enjoyed a big jump in business in 1981 when IBM ran into technical difficulties introducing a new memory device. The Colorado-based company, which makes high-performance memory equipment, gained some 300 customers because of IBM's troubles. However, when Big Blue brought out an improved new line last year, Storage Technology's profits dropped to $64.7 million, from $84.2 million in 1981. Says Jesse Aweida, who cofounded Storage Technology after 13 years with Big Blue: "IBM used to be active in only certain areas of the computer business. Now it wants to be active in the whole business."

One big reason for IBM's clout is the major investments it began making in the late 1970s to upgrade manufacturing facilities. IBM executives point to that drive to cut production costs, launched under Cary, as a foundation of the company's current strength, because it has made the firm extremely cost competitive. IBM has pumped some $10 billion into capital improvements since 1977. The Boca Raton line that turns out the PC is so highly automated that a personal computer can be assembled in 10 minutes of worker time.

The plants use some of IBM's most advanced technology. An engineer in the firm's

La Gaude, France, laboratory can transmit his computerized design information for a new chip via satellite to the IBM facility in East Fishkill, where the chip is actually manufactured. The chip will be floated through tubing on air from one manufacturing station to another and then tested by robotically controlled equipment.

IBM is also the world's largest producer of logic and 64K RAM memory chips, and installs its entire output in its own machines. The company, moreover, can produce at the same plant far denser 256K RAM chips, which Japanese firms are also developing. IBM could start making the chips ahead of the Japanese, perhaps by early next year.

In line with its new aggressiveness, IBM has been cracking down hard on those who would steal its secrets. It cooperated with the FBI last year in a sting operation that nabbed employees of Hitachi and Mitsubishi Electric, two Japanese competitors, for trying to buy confidential IBM information. IBM then brought a separate civil suit against Hitachi, which pleaded guilty to conspiracy charges last February and was fined $10,000. The criminal case against Mitsubishi is still pending.

IBMers claim to be unruffled by Japanese competition. "I think I'll be physically ill if I hear one more time that the Japanese are coming," says Paul Low, manager of the East Fishkill plant. "That's not to say that they're not formidable rivals, because they are, but we're ahead." All six of the major Japanese makers of large computers together have less than 2 percent of the U.S. market for business computers.

Many outsiders believe that IBM is more concerned about the Japanese than it professes. Says Magnuson Computer's Strauch: "I'm sure IBM's basic concern is the Japanese. It is almost certain that what happened to us was a message to the Japanese that if they have any thought of entering the market with a low-to-medium-range mainframe, they had

better be prepared to compete at an extremely low cost." Apple's Jobs believes that IBM's investments in Intel and Rolm are at least partially intended to strengthen IBM's ability to compete with Japan.

The struggle between IBM and its Japanese competitors is most intense in Japan, where IBM lost its number one position to Fujitsu in 1979. IBM Japan, the company's wholly owned subsidiary, is fighting back. "They are becoming surprisingly aggressive," says Yuji Ogino, managing director of IDC Japan, a unit of International Data. IBM Japan, which employs 13,000 Japanese workers, has been slashing prices and launching new marketing drives in a bid to win back its overall lead. Admits a spokesman for a rival Japanese firm: "IBM is an enormous competitor."

At the same time that it has been fighting vigorously for market share, IBM has been forming cooperative agreements with the Japanese. In one, IBM and Matsushita Electric Industrial teamed up to produce a personal computer that converts Japanese phonetic symbols into Chinese characters or Kanji. Typewriters have not been widely used in Japan, partly because, with so many different characters, a typical machine must be packed with about 3,000 Kanji. The new machine, which ranges in price from $4,100 to $12,700 has a keyboard of only 45 phonetic symbols plus the Latin alphabet. More than 15,000 of the machines have been ordered, and there is at least a two-month wait for delivery.

If striking similarities exist between IBM and Japanese companies, the reason is that Big Blue was the model for some Japanese business techniques. For example, IBM developed "quality circles" some 20 years ago. The circles, small teams of workers that get together to discuss ways to improve output and solve production problems, have been widely adopted in Japan and are often cited as a reason for productivity gains there. Both IBM and Japanese executives stress harmonious employee relations, and both place a high priority on becoming the most modern, cost-efficient manufacturer of the products they turn out.

Foreign operations are vital to IBM. Overseas business accounted for 45 percent of IBM's gross income in 1982 and 37 percent of the company's profits. IBM hires mainly local employees at its international locations. There are only 125 Americans among some 1,000 managerial and technical employees in the Paris headquarters of IBM's European, Middle Eastern, and African operations. Says Hans-Olaf Henkel, a vice president in the Paris office: "Europeans like IBM not because it is American, but because it is IBM. It promotes from the inside, and the majority of senior positions are held by nationals of the country."

IBM executives concede that despite its wide-ranging successes, the company has its weaknesses and has made some major mistakes over the years. Despite increased efforts to recruit women and minorities, there are still few of either in management ranks. Only 3,089 of IBM's more than 29,000 managers are women. IBM policies, moreover, can seem high-handed, especially toward women. In December 1981, a California jury awarded $300,000 to an IBM marketing manager who quit after the company objected to her romantic relationship with a former employee who had joined a rival firm. She resigned when her boss, fearing a conflict of interest, tried to transfer her to another division. IBM is appealing the jury verdict.

Some employees find the firm slow to capitalize on opportunities in spite of steps to decentralize decision making. "IBM has more committees than the U.S. Government," complains one insider. To increase its flexibility, IBM has set up 15 small ventures within the company since 1981. These explore new business opportunities in such fields as robotics, specialized medical equipment, and analytical instruments. The new units are independently run, but they can draw on IBM re-

EXHIBIT 1 Big Blue's Market Share *(percent of units installed)*

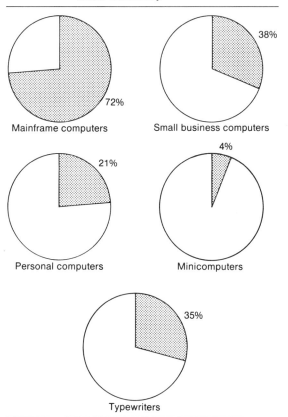

Mainframe computers

Small business computers

Personal computers

Minicomputers

Typewriters

sources. This seems to provide IBM with the benefits of both a large company and a small one. Says Robert Burgelman, an assistant professor of management at Stanford University's Graduate School of Business: "If IBM can integrate these new ventures into its culture, the company is going to be an enormously dangerous competitor in most of the emerging areas of high technology."

IBM stumbled badly when it set out to produce an office copier in the 1970s. Executives first turned down a chance to buy a process that Xerox later used with great success, and then introduced a balky model. Admits Cary: "If you're asking was it a mistake to ship so many copiers before they were really reliable to sell, yes it was a mistake." The company was forced to suspend deliveries until the problems were solved.

IBM, in addition, has not broken into the market for so-called supercomputers, which are used mainly for scientific research. The company launched supercomputer projects in the 1950s and 1960s, but could not produce a design that executives believed would be profitable. IBM has since abandoned the specialized field to Control Data and Cray Research.

Opel is bullish about the future of IBM, and he is very optimistic about the outlook for the whole industry. He notes that while people have limited demands for commodities like shoes and automobiles, they seem to have an insatiable appetite for information. Says he: "I have yet to hear somebody say they could not use more information. Hence the demand for information processing, though perhaps not infinite, is enormous."

What will be coming next out of the IBM laboratories to satisfy that demand? Opel is clearly not ready to sit back and relax despite his company's achievements. Says he: "We've got an enormously successful operation. Therefore you could be complacent; you could play it safe and not change. All the nat-

ural forces in the business pressure you in that direction." But one sign that the pace of the past two years will continue will be the arrival of a home computer, which IBM originally code-named "peanut." This will sell for about $700 and could reach stores in late fall. The machine, fully compatible with the PC, will come with a built-in disc drive and cartridge slot for software. "It will offer the best performance on the market for its price," asserts Clive Smith, a computer watcher with the Yankee Group, a Cambridge, Massachusetts, research firm.

IBM is also developing a raft of exotic technologies. These include Josephson Junction and quiteron switching devices that operate in trillionths of a second at temperatures that approach absolute zero ($-459.67°F$). Says one IBMer: "There's nothing, literally nothing, noteworthy in the field that IBM doesn't have its fingers into."

The biggest future payoff for IBM is likely to come in the field of office automation. The key to the so-called paperless office will be computerized networks that shuttle messages between computer terminals, telephones, and other office equipment. All can then be consolidated into a "workstation" atop a desk. "The world of the future is centered on

EXHIBIT 2 Source of Income

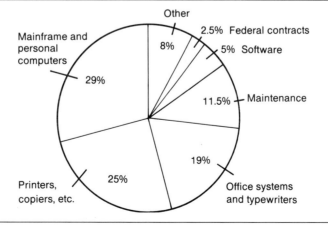

powerful workstations," says Lewis Branscomb, IBM's chief scientist.

Last month IBM showed that it was determined to become a leader in developing the automated office by agreeing to acquire 15 percent of Rolm. That company's advanced PBX system, a type of computerized switchboard, can be used to direct the flow of voice and data traffic between workstations. The investment will enable the two firms to work out ways to link IBM computers with the Rolm PBX.

In fact, IBM has long been deeply involved in telecommunications. In 1975, the company bought a one third interest in Satellite Business Systems, which transmits voice and computer data. IBM is seeking partners for communications ventures in Europe. In March 1982, it won an $18 million contract to upgrade the British telephone system, and it is installing a computer-driven telephone information service in West Germany.

IBM's moves into telecommunications will put it squarely in competition with American Telephone & Telegraph, now the world's biggest company. An extended battle between the two giants seems inevitable in the area where computers and communications overlap to create the Information Age. Once the separation of AT&T from its regulated telephone units goes into effect next January, the company will be able to use its Bell Laboratories and Western Electric facilities to develop products to compete directly with IBM. AT&T through the new American Bell is expected to introduce computers next year, and it already has the capability of offering a wide range of data processing services similar to those IBM provides.

In that upcoming clash of the titans and the continuing fight for the world computer market, IBM will be tough to beat. Its resources—human, technological and financial—are enormous. Its ability to combine salesmanship and service with research and innovation is unmatched in the United States, perhaps anywhere. At a time when the rallying cry "Small is beautiful" can be heard even in business circles and when some critics charge that large corporations are inherently inflexible, IBM has shown how to be a successful colossus.

Note

1. Sample lyric: "Our products are known/ In every zone/ Our reputation sparkles like a gem/ We've fought our way through/ And new fields we're sure to conquer too/ For the ever-onward IBM."

Cookies Are Frito-Lay's New Bag
Ann M. Morrison

Executives in Dallas's 14-story Frito-Lay Tower are no longer content to have millions of people munching bunches of corn and potato chips. Now, after three years of research and testing, the perpetrators of Ruffles, Doritos, and Tostitos are invading an entirely different snack market, the $2.5-billion-a-year retail packaged-cookie business.

In May, Frito-Lay introduced Grandma's cookies in 16 varieties, from sandwich creams to fruit-filled oatmeal, in Kansas City. The first significant new cookie line to elbow its way onto supermarket shelves in a generation, Grandma's will go national soon, though Frito-Laymen won't say when. When it does, it will be taking on Nabisco Brands, the granddaddy of mass-produced cookies.

Meanwhile, at its campus headquarters in the New Jersey suburbs west of Manhattan, Nabisco is plotting a counterinvasion of Frito-Lay's territory, the $6.6-billion-a-year retail market for "salty snacks"—chips, pretzels, cheese puffs, and popcorn. Nabisco aims to be number two to Frito-Lay in salty snacks, a position now held by Borden. Clearly these moves and countermoves could presage an all-out clash of the snack titans, and no one knows it better than D. Wayne Calloway, 46, Frito-Lay's deceptively low-key president and chief executive. "Salty snacks are still a small part of Nabisco Brands' business, like cookies are still a small part of ours," he says in a drawl that comes from somewhere between his native North Carolina and Texas. "We both hope that will change someday, I suspect."

Claude B. Hampton, 57, president of Nabisco's biscuit group, which includes cookies, is blunter: "We aren't going to sit on our high haunches and let 82 years of business go down the drain." So is W. C. (Bill) Korn, 39, a dynamic, idea-a-minute senior vice president at Frito-Lay. In Korn's view, "This has the potential of becoming a Coke-Pepsi thing."

That's no idle comment: Pepsico is the corporate parent of Frito-Lay. Like many companies, Pepsico (1981 sales, $7 billion) shuffles executives around the organization to broaden their experience. Many of the people behind the Grandma's onslaught, including Bill Korn, are veterans of the long-running, no-holds-barred advertising campaign called the Pepsi Challenge. That campaign, which asserts that most consumers prefer Pepsi to Coca-Cola in blind taste tests, has helped Pepsi become the leading soft drink in food stores. Coke is still out in front in total sales, thanks to a commanding lead in restaurants and vending machines.

The struggle for snack supremacy pits two organizations as different as taco chips and chocolate chips. Frito-Lay, believed to have an astonishing 75 percent of the corn chip market, has overwhelmed its rivals in salty snacks, an industry of indulgence whose tonnage increases about 6 percent annually. Nabisco is by far the largest of several nationwide cookie monsters, with 35 percent of the packaged, ready-to-eat business, which hardly grows at all in tonnage. It also has nearly half the slightly zippier cracker market.

A Swashbuckling Style

The two companies' marketing approaches differ enormously. Nabisco marketers pay close attention to demographic trends: fewer kids mean lower cookie consumption; more adults bring in the business for crackers and salty snacks. At Frito-Lay, even the vocabulary is different. Like his colleagues, Korn calls himself a "marketeer," a word with swashbuckling overtones. Says he: "Demographics don't count. Companies forge their own destinies. If you act like you're in a mature market, you certainly will be."

Over the past five years Frito-Lay's sales have more than doubled and earnings have almost tripled, to $270 million in operating profit on $1.9 billion in sales in 1981. These days Pepsico makes more on what is popularly called junk food—somewhat nutritious if you don't mind calories—than on junk drink. Nabisco's biscuit group, which turns out the cookies and crackers, isn't anemic either. Last year it earned about $215 million in operating profit on some $1.4 billion in sales, making it the biggest U.S. unit in $5.8-billion-a-year Nabisco Brands. The brash challengers from Frito-Lay say that theirs is a culture of growth. The calmer heads at Nabisco biscuit, whose sales and earnings have advanced approximately 10 percent annually over the past five years, hold that growth is fine, as long as it doesn't interfere with the bottom line.

In a showdown the two companies would display contrasting strengths and tactics. Frito-Lay has an extremely pervasive yet nimble distribution system geared to the relatively brief shelf life of salty snacks. Nabisco, whose cookie output towers above everyone else's, has a decided cost advantage there—as does Frito-Lay in salty snacks. When it comes to pushing the product, Frito-Lay works mainly on the consumer through heavy advertising and promotion; it claims to spend more on one product, Doritos, than the $12 million or so Nabisco spent last year on its entire cookie line. Nabisco, for its part, prefers to work through the trade with discounts and special offers.

The Dallas marketeers have promised to spend more money advertising and promoting Grandma's by next spring than the entire cookie industry spent last year. The test market may be a sample of the nationwide blitz to come. As one executive in the Frito-Lay Tower says, "World War III has broken out in the cookie aisles in Kansas City." The big cookie manufacturers are firing salvos of coupons, in-store samples, and special trial-size packages, and are bombarding TV and radio with advertising. Cookie sales are up in general, and Grandma's has grabbed the number two spot, at least for now. The Dallasites are already mapping their next test, in Chicago.

Elmer Doolin's $100 Deal

Frito-Lay's success in salty snacks is enough to make any cookie maker quake. Allan Kaplan, a financial analyst for Merrill Lynch, says, "If Frito-Lay were viewed as a separate entity, one would have to conclude that it ranks among the great consumer products companies in the world."

The Frito part of Frito-Lay was started in 1932 in San Antonio by Elmer Doolin, who paid $100 for a corn chip recipe, a potato ricer for making the things, and seven customer accounts. At about the same time, Herman W. Lay, based in Nashville, began distributing potato chips made by an Atlanta manufacturer, which he later bought out. In 1945 he became one of the first franchisees to make and distribute Fritos, and in 1961, two years after Doolin's death, Frito Co. and H. W. Lay & Co.

merged. Four years later Pepsi-Cola acquired Frito-Lay and became Pepsico.

Most of Frito-Lay's sales and earnings come from six products: Lay's and Ruffles potato chips, Doritos and Tostitos tortilla chips, Cheetos cheese puffs, and Fritos corn chips. Each does a crisp business—at least $150 million a year at retail. Doritos, a triangular chip, is the mightiest munchie of them all, bringing in $550 million. Tostitos, a round, light version of Doritos introduced in 1980, hit $140 million in sales during its first year, making it perhaps the most successful new product in the history of packaged goods. Clearly, not all successful chips are made of silicon.

Frito-Lay products, most of which contain no preservatives, have a shelf life of only 45 days. Chips must be speeded from 40 plants through 200 major distribution centers to almost 300,000 retail outlets in less than 2 weeks. An army of some 10,000 route salesmen deliver the products to the stores—not just supermarket chains but also convenience stores, delicatessens, and various mom-and-pop outlets. One half of all Frito-Lay's business comes from smaller customers.

Stacking the Shelves

The route salesmen, who are in a store at least three times a week and as often as eight times, stack the shelves and maintain the Frito displays. In this expensive and hard-to-duplicate "store door" system, the first time store personnel handle a Frito-Lay product is when it's rung up on the cash register. That sale means lots of profit for the retailer, since he has put no money into warehousing, transportation, labeling, or stacking. And the Frito salesman takes back whatever goes stale.

Thomas J. Peters, a management consultant and lecturer at the Stanford Graduate School of Business, says, "No question, 88 percent of the secret of Frito-Lay's magic is its store-door marketing." The company's aggressive growth targets are executed in the Safeways, Krogers, and 7-Elevens around the country by salesmen whose $20,000 to $28,000 annual incomes consist almost entirely of generous 10 percent commissions. "The overriding goal of everyone around here is 'service to sales,'" says Calloway. "It's implanted in everyone's mind, and imprinted on everyone's forehead and shirt and drawers too, I suspect."

Frito-Lay executives have strong notions about market leadership. "A market leader should be growing the category," asserts Calloway. Without referring directly to Nabisco's inability or unwillingness to push cookie volumes higher, Frito-Lay clearly thinks it can do so. "The upside is tremendous and the downside doesn't look too bad," says Calloway. A cookie line would fit beautifully into Frito-Lay's store-door distribution system and benefit from the company's advertising and marketing prowess. On the other hand, Frito-Lay's investment in getting its hand in the cookie jar has amounted to only $70 million, mainly for three plants.

The bold marketeers of Frito-Lay quickly saw indications that the cookie market was far from mature. In-store cookie bakeries have proliferated, and Campbell Soup has scored with its luxury-priced Pepperidge Farm line. The world was ready, the Dallasites figured, for a big-volume packaged cookie that tasted more like homemade. Consumer interviews and tests confirmed that shoppers found run-of-the-shelf cookies hard and dry and not worth the price. Says Vice President John Cranor, 35, "It was Marketing 101."

Frito-Lay's first baking attempts were disasters. Starting with 30 cookies in a regular kitchen oven, then moving up to batches of 1,000 or more, the research and development people found that cookies that tasted great right out of the oven often turned to sawdust or rock after two weeks. Several products judged perfect after a test run could not be duplicated. Truckloads of dough ended up as pig feed.

The Quest for Perfection

Frito-Lay's biggest cookie expenditure was the 1980 acquisition of Grandma's, a privately held bakery in Beaverton, Oregon, skilled in making soft, moist cookies. In the bargain Frito also got a homey trademark, though it quickly restyled Grandma to make her look a bit younger on packages. Grandma's, with sales of $29 million a year, was a strong regional cookie maker with 15 percent of the Northwest market and a full line of products. This included big three-inch cookies sold two to a package—a "single serve" item—which Frito-Lay immediately took national.

Single serves, however, are low-volume impulse items sold at cash registers. Hoping to conquer back in the grocery aisles where the real action is, the Dallas research group continued to look for the perfect cupboard cookie. One objective was a product that consumers would prefer by at least 2 to 1 over the competition in blind taste tests.

Frito-Lay ended up with 16 varieties that, it claims, met its standards, not one an original Grandma's product. They are priced to sell at a 20 percent to 25 percent premium over competing makes. "We can't compete with Nabisco on a cost basis," concedes the Beaverton plant manager. "They have 300-foot ovens, they make their own boxes, mill their own flour." But, he asserts, "we've got quality to sell."

Most of Grandma's cookies do taste fresher than competitive store-bought brands because they are moister—up to 12 percent moisture content rather than about 3 percent. That shortens Grandma's shelf life—two and one half to four months rather than the competition's usual six—but is hardly a problem for a distribution system built to hustle potato chips.

Caches of Grandma's

Security was tight preceding the big Kansas City introduction. Sample products shipped from Oregon were initially stored in sales managers' garages instead of at the regional distribution center. Route trucks were modified to accommodate the new product line before the salesmen were told what it would be. The best guess in Kansas City was that Frito-Lay was bringing out a new line of packaged nut meats.

Three weeks before the launch, senior sales representatives began to call on grocery store executives, seeking space for a product that had never been sold before. Usually parsimonious with shelf space, the trade was undoubtedly eager to accommodate the source of its salty snack profits. "We thought that Frito-Lay's entry would get the whole cookie category off dead center," says an area grocery buyer for Safeway.

According to preliminary readings, it looks as though Grandma's ate up 15 percent to 20 percent of the cookie market in the early days of the Kansas City test. "If you're used to looking at these numbers in consumerland, things like this don't happen often," boasts Korn. "We're way ahead of where we were in Tostitos." These numbers represent only trial purchases, not repeat business over time—the real test of a new product. Still, says Calloway, "it would take an incredible disappointment to make us give up now."

Nabisco has been following the events in Kansas City closely. Hordes of its salesmen were sent there to remind the trade of how long and successful and mutually profitable their relationship has been. Nabisco operatives were glad to advise on how much space Grandma's should get (not as much as Frito wanted) and where that space should come from (definitely not from Nabisco). Nabisco's Hampton has tried Grandma's and finds them "a good product, not an excellent one." Still, a survey shows that Nabisco has lost market share in Kansas City—as have almost all the cookie competitors there. Only American Brands' Sunshine Biscuits—number three

after Nabisco and Keebler nationally—has survived unscathed.

Hampton and his cohorts won't say much about their planned countermove in salty snacks. They are sure to collide with other consumer product giants in the fray for Frito-Lay's business: Borden, the maker of Wise potato chips, which is readying new grain-based snacks; Procter & Gamble, trying again with Pringles, its superprocessed potato chip; and Anheuser-Busch, which has introduced a line of Eagle corn, peanut, and potato snacks, distributed through beer wholesalers.

Of all the potential challengers, Nabisco is the one Frito-Lay fears most. Like Frito-Lay—and unlike most other cookie manufacturers—Nabisco has a store-door network. It's smaller than Frito-Lay's and, because of the longer shelf life of cookies, is a little slower. Nabisco concentrates on large outlets, preferring, as one executive says, "to fish where the fish are." Its 3,000 salesmen make only a 5 percent commission, but because of high base pay, wind up earning about the same amount as the Frito-Lay foot soldiers.

Nabisco has spent 20 years trying to figure out the salty snack market. First, a Nabisco salty snack line packaged in cardboard boxes bombed. Then Nabisco shifted to bags, but snackers didn't like them either. Along the way Nabisco's Mister Salty lost the top position in pretzels to Frito-Lay's Rold Gold. This time Nabisco has vowed to match Frito-Lay corn chip for corn chip. Its products, packaged in special bags to prolong their shelf life to six months, are now in test markets.

To some observers Nabisco has yet to play its best weapon in the snack campaign: the Planters label of peanut fame. Through last year's merger of Nabisco and Standard Brands, Planters and Nabisco are part of the same corporate family, but so far they have kept their operations separate. A product that Planters introduced last year, puffed cheese balls packed in canisters, has been so successful that it has prompted Frito-Lay to reformulate and reposition its somewhat similar Cheetos. The notion of Planters products distributed through Nabisco's network brings out the Alka-Seltzer in Dallas.

A Plant Manager's Lament

The cookie and chip wars ahead are certain to be costly. Each company needs additional consumer testing, plant capacity, and advertising to establish more than a beachhead in the other's territory. The chink in Frito-Lay's armor is inexperience in making cookies. At Beaverton the bakers are still adding a pinch of this and a dollop of that. By now, moans the plant manager, "we thought we'd have a standard recipe, printed on a card."

Unclear too is whether Nabisco's snack products will finally score with consumers. But as these two powers grapple in each other's strongholds, the distinctions between them could begin to blur. Nabisco could become more aggressive. Frito-Lay's competitive spirit could be dampened by profit considerations. In the long run, one could end up looking very much like the other: Coke versus Pepsi.

SmithKline's Ulcer Medicine "Holy War"
Joel Dreyfuss

SmithKline Beckman's patent on Tagamet, the pale green pill that cures ulcers, has been the next best thing to a license to print money. For seven delightfully profitable years, the company enjoyed a virtual monopoly. But competition was bound to rear its head sooner or later. Glaxo Holdings of Britain has brought out a drug, Zantac, that does the same job. A success in Europe, Zantac has just come to market in the United States, and the competitive struggle shaping up will undoubtedly give some SmithKline executives stomach pains.

Since its introduction in 1976, Tagamet has become the largest-selling prescription drug in the world, with sales expected to reach a billion dollars in 1984. SmithKline's sales have climbed from $673 million to $3 billion and earnings per share from $1.21 to $5.51. Tagamet accounts for almost a third of the company's revenues and half its profits. No wonder a SmithKline marketing executive speaks of waging a "holy war" in defense of this lucrative turf.

Cimetidine, the generic name for Tagamet, was a breakthrough in ulcer treatment. It blocks the histamines that trigger the production of stomach acid, and so allows ulcers to heal, often in a matter of weeks. Before Tagamet, the best doctors could do was prescribe substances that coated the stomach and relieved ulcer pains. Often the ulcers lingered on and on, and many intractable cases required surgery.

About four million Americans are treated for ulcers in the course of a year. The odds of being an ulcer patient during one's lifetime are about 1 in 10. It used to be that men got ulcers more often than women in the United States, but it appears that over the past 20 years or so the incidence has declined among men and risen among women. Dr. John H. Kurata, epidemiologist at the Center for Ulcer Research and Education in Los Angeles, reports that these days cases are evenly divided between men and women.

Zantac's compound, ranatidine hydrochloride, is chemically quite different from Tagamet, but it does the same thing for ulcer patients, reducing the secretion of stomach acid. Introduced in Europe in 1981, it has already captured large market shares: 33 percent in Britain, 40 percent in West Germany, and 55 percent in Spain, according to the London investment firm of de Zoete & Bevan.

Glaxo was a big outfit even before it brought out Zantac—the largest pharmaceutical company in Britain. Launched 100 years ago in New Zealand with a dry milk formula and the slogan "Glaxo builds bonnie babies," the company pioneered the large-scale manufacture of penicillin. For years it had a reputation of being strong on science and weak on marketing. But a new management team has moved to shed that image. Worldwide sales have more than doubled since 1976, reaching $1.6 billion last year. This year first half sales were up 24 percent.

In 1978 Glaxo got a foothold in the United States by purchasing Meyer Laboratories, a small company based in Fort Lauderdale, Florida. Two years ago, Joseph J. Ruvane, Jr., 59, an American with 30 years of industry experience, was hired as president of Glaxo, Inc., the U.S. subsidiary. He began planning Zantac's entry into the American market.

A major problem he confronted was too few troops. In an industry where products have to be promoted door to door to tens of thousands of physicians and hospitals, SmithKline's sales force would badly outnumber Glaxo's. It costs $50,000 to $80,000 a year to put a sales representative in the field, so a large force requires a lot of funds. But Glaxo made a bold move to improve its chances. The company worked out an unusual deal with Hoffmann-La Roche, Inc., the Swiss pharmaceutical company, maker of Valium. For a percentage of sales, Hoffmann-La Roche will sell Zantac under the Glaxo name rather than its own, the normal industry practice. Its U.S. sales force of 700, together with Glaxo's—which has grown from 125 to 450— will give Zantac lots of manpower in the struggle for the hearts and minds of physicians. "The equation changed when Glaxo an-

nounced its marketing relationship with Hoffmann-La Roche," observes Ronald M. Nordmann, drug analyst for Oppenheimer & Co. "Hoffmann-La Roche is a very effective, aggressive marketing organization."

Ruvane says his friendship with Hoffmann-La Roche President and CEO Irwin Lerner (they both worked at Organon, Inc., a small New Jersey drug company) opened the door for the joint promotion effort. "Irwin and I are old friends," he adds, "but it's a small industry—everybody sort of knows each other. This was a business deal that worked to the advantage of both." A standard licensing agreement for Zantac was out of the question, Ruvane says. "We wanted to establish our name in this country. It was the absolute primary question." Lerner says he was competing with other companies for a deal with Glaxo. "We had to come up with something different." Ruvane picked Roche because of its size, experience in the market, and—according to one analyst—willingness to provide a lot of up-front money. Roche wanted the deal because its patent on Valium runs out in 1985, and an extra source of revenue could help ease the transition to products still in the R&D pipeline.

In June the Food and Drug Administration gave Glaxo the go-ahead to sell Zantac in the United States. Glaxo's base for the big-money competitive struggle is a new three-story building in North Carolina's Research Triangle Park. A $40-million, 200,000-square-foot manufacturing plant is under construction among the loblolly pines in Zebulon, 23 miles east of the headquarters.

In discussing long-term plans, the deep-voiced, chain-smoking Ruvane says that Zantac's entry into the American market is only a beginning. "We're not coming into this country for just one product. We're in here to stay with a whole range of products. In the next five-year period we want to be in the top 15 companies in the U.S. pharmaceutical industry." Zantac alone could account for a lot of revenue. Irwin Lerner of Hoffmann-La Roche points to estimates by analysts that Zantac will capture between 10 percent and 25 percent of the market within a year. That translates into $50 million to $125 million.

SmithKline, of course, will be putting up a fight, and it has large resources to draw upon. Over the years, it has used its piles of cash from Tagamet to build up the company. Henry Wendt, 50, the president and chief executive who started his career as a SmithKline salesman in 1955, remembers that in the 1950s and 1960s the company failed to do an adequate job of using profits to invest in the future. "We were determined not to make that mistake again," Wendt says, "so we started quickly in the 1970s to strengthen our position internationally."

SmithKline bought companies in Europe and the United States, concentrating in the health care and therapeutics areas it knew best. When Wendt succeeded Chairman Robert F. Dee as chief executive last year, he supervised the integration of Beckman Instruments, a major producer of laboratory instruments, into SmithKline. Wendt concedes that some analysts thought the billion-dollar price paid for Beckman was too high and the timing was wrong because of the recession. "There's no disagreement about timing," he says, "but companies like Beckman aren't available all the time."

The company has also invested heavily in research. Annual expenditures for R&D have leaped from $125 million five years ago to more than $350 million. Two new antibiotics, Cefizox and Monocid, are on the way to market. Awaiting FDA approval is Ridaura, a new treatment for that very common affliction, rheumatoid arthritis.

Still, with all this, SmithKline is largely Tagamet, vulnerable to any large falloff in Tagamet sales. Wendt concedes that the perception of vulnerability is one reason SmithKline's stock is about 10 points below the 12-month high. "I think our share price would be higher if there weren't that concern," he remarks, "but I would say there's more concern from the outside observers than there is inside." The company is confident, he says, that Tagamet "will cross the billion-dollar mark next year regardless of Zantac."

Wendt, who recalls his days in sales with nostalgia, says the struggle with Glaxo excites him. "That's one of the disadvantages of being on the 24th floor. It's not considered good managerial manners to keep daily track, but I certainly talk about it a lot." He plans to go out on a three-day trip to Texas with a sales rep in October "so I can get my hands dirty and really hear doctors talking about the situation."

Knowing that serious competition for Tagamet would come along sooner or later, SmithKline began preparing itself the year after the drug was introduced in the United States. Harry C. Groome III, vice president in charge of pharmaceuticals marketing in the United States, says that as early as 1978, management began holding meetings to assess potential competition. "When we started to profile these compounds," Groome recalls, "we tried to figure out what they would be saying in promotion, how they would be trying to differentiate themselves from Tagamet."

In January 1982, well aware that Zantac was on the way, SmithKline began expanding its sales force from 725 to 850. In August of that year management brought the entire force to Philadelphia for a "national business meeting," dealing with the launch of Zantac as well as new products in SmithKline's development pipeline. Sales representatives got loose-leaf binders on Zantac and lectures on Glaxo's tactics by SmithKline executives from Britain. Sessions covered the technical differences between the two drugs and the arguments Glaxo sales representatives were expected to make. Videotaped role-playing sessions prepared the sales force for questions doctors might ask about the relative merits of the two drugs. By the end of the meeting the sales staff had been worked up to a high pitch of excitement.

The battle for market share will be fought among the 120,000 physicians who prescribe the bulk of ulcer medication. SmithKline has doubled its promotional budget for Tagamet. Both companies are backing up their sales representatives with lavish print material: multiple ad inserts in medical journals and full-color brochures to be dropped off at visits with doctors and hospitals.

The ads for Tagamet and Zantac show radically different tactics in the opening round. SmithKline is taking a laid-back approach. Its ads feature photographs of ordinary people who use Tagamet: a vacationing family, a construction boss, a fireman, a musician. The copy stresses the years of experience, the 30 million people who have used Tagamet, the depth of clinical scrutiny it has undergone, and the low incidence of side effects. "What we basically said is 'Enough science,'" recalls James H. Geddes, product director for Tagamet. "What this drug is really about *now* is people."

The ads for Zantac are strikingly different in style, tone, and message. Computer graphics were used for futuristic illustrations showing molecules floating in space and the pentagonal chemical structure of Zantac. "The graphics have a connotation of newness," explains Alan A. Steigrod, marketing vice president of Glaxo. "We wanted it to look like a scientific piece because it's not a me-too product."

As might be expected from a newcomer challenging an entrenched rival, the Glaxo ads take an aggressive stance: without mentioning the rival by name, they unmistakably try to convey the message that Zantac is safer than Tagamet. In rare cases, patients receiving extraordinarily heavy doses of Tagamet over a period of time have developed unpleasant side effects—gynecomastia (swollen breasts in men), impotence, and mental confusion. Zantac ads show a stylized human fig-

ure, male, being zapped by laserlike beams at critical points, including head and genitals. The accompanying copy tells what side effects Zantac doesn't cause. "No reported mental confusion," for example.

"We're not really comparing Zantac to Tagamet," Steigrod insists. Glaxo, he argues, is saying Zantac doesn't have those side effects. "If the physician perceives that somebody else does, that's his perception."

Steigrod's disclaimer, of course, does little to pacify the folks at SmithKline. "Tagamet's side effects," says Geddes, "are generally low in incidence, well defined, mild in nature, and reversible. Zantac is a new drug in the U.S. and it hasn't been on the market that long. Its clinical profile is still evolving." He suggests that Zantac, which has been used by some two million people, will reveal side effects of its own as use becomes more widespread. SmithKline executives, in mild counterattacks, point to warnings on the Zantac label that the drug can cause headaches, constipation and dizziness.

Outside authorities support SmithKline's contentions that serious side effects from Tagamet are uncommon. According to Dr. Robert T. Jensen, a senior investigator at the National Institutes of Health, the reported cases of swollen breasts and impotence occurred when massive doses were used to treat rare gastric diseases. "It has not been shown that Tagamet causes increased incidence of impotence in regular duodenal ulcer patients receiving conventional doses of the drug," Jensen adds.

The cases of mental confusion, says another expert, may be due to interaction with tranquilizers. Dr. Denis M. McCarthy, a professor of medicine at the University of New Mexico medical school, points out that such reports emerged only after five million people had used Tagamet. McCarthy also observes that side effects from Zantac will probably turn up later on. With some medications, side effects appear only after years of use, he says. "It would be prudent to assume that package inserts will change after the initial marketing." Experts generally agree, however, that both Tagamet and Zantac are safe medications as drugs go.

A major Zantac sales pitch is the convenience of twice-a-day dosage. Tagamet is normally taken four times a day in the United States, and Zantac people argue that twice a day is more convenient. But SmithKline comes armed with a study that shows no difference in compliance among patients, whether they take their prescription twice or four times a day. SmithKline, though, has applied to the FDA for approval of twice-a-day dosage for Tagamet.

One possibly significant difference between the two products is price. For daily doses, Zantac costs about 20 percent more at wholesale than Tagamet. Glaxo argues that Zantac ends up costing less because its prescription information recommends a four-week treatment, while Tagamet is usually prescribed for six to eight weeks. But Dr. Raymond J. Lipicky, an FDA official, says Glaxo's healing rate over four weeks is the same as Tagamet's. "From the data available," he says, "there is no way that Zantac can claim it heals faster than Tagamet." Glaxo just didn't submit data that would support treatment for longer than four weeks, Lipicky explains. Medical experts say most doctors, accustomed to the six-week treatment period for Tagamet, will probably prescribe Zantac in the same way.

So far the FDA has approved Zantac only for duodenal ulcers, which account for 75 percent of cases in the United States, not for gastric (stomach) ulcers. Moreover, the FDA has not yet approved Zantac for long-term maintenance therapy or for use in injectable form. In time, though, Zantac may get FDA approval for all these uses, and it would be imprudent for SmithKline to assume otherwise.

The initial impact of Zantac's entry on SmithKline's sales and profits may be softened by a phenomenon noted in other countries—expansion of the market for ulcer medicine when Zantac arrived on the scene. Apparently the promotion for Zantac prompts some physicians to prescribe ulcer medications for additional patients. Ron Nordmann, the Oppenheimer analyst, points out that in Britain last year, with sales of Zantac growing, unit sales of Tagamet also grew, by 8 percent.

As of now, neither company can substantiate a claim that its ulcer drug is distinctly superior in effectiveness or safety, so the course of the competitive struggle will depend on marketing skill. One rival or the other, or both, may well modify strategy and tactics as sales returns come in. While SmithKline and Glaxo agree that it may take six months before a valid trend emerges, both companies will be watching the weekly numbers intently. At SmithKline the mood is resolute but not ebullient. "We're in the opening round of the battle," says Henry Wendt. "I feel pretty good, so far. But the emphasis should be on the so far."

Any company that gets a large portion of its profits from a competitive advantage in a single product would do well to prepare itself for the day when tough competition comes along. SmithKline did that. It invested profits from Tagamet in building up the company's revenue base, and it rehearsed for the time when Tagamet would have to compete. As a result, SmithKline goes into the battle with arms and armor in good condition. The struggle with Glaxo will be painful, no doubt, but it won't turn SmithKline into an invalid.

What Makes U.S. Shoe Shine
Anne B. Fisher

It used to be a sleepy little shoe company, endangered by cheap imports in a slow-growth business. Not anymore. U.S. Shoe has effloresced into a glamorous $1.3-billion-a-year retailing concern. With a dozen clothing store chains and chichi shoe brands like Pappagallo, Amalfi, and Evan-Picone, profits are soaring.

Behind this transformation is Philip Barach, a chairman who says, "We like to shoot the dice." So far U.S. Shoe has been taking the house for a ride. At the end of August, the company announced second-quarter earnings of $13 million, up 65 percent from the same period last year. Earnings from shoes rose 34 percent, not bad at all in a lackluster market, but the real eye-opener is apparel retailing. Its earnings leapt 198 percent. The company's return on shareholders' equity for 1982 was a more than respectable 18.3 percent.

Investors are betting on more of the same. The company's stock recently sold for $39.50 a share, up from $15.50 a year ago (adjusted for a two-for-one split last June). That's a rise of 155 percent, nearly four times the increase in the New York Stock Exchange index. At a price-earnings multiple of 13, Wall Streeters say the shares are still a bargain. Management seems to agree: in June it persuaded shareholders to pass a stringent "shark-repellent" measure.

U.S. Shoe had been around since 1931, quietly turning out a few popular middle-priced brands of shoes, but it wasn't until Barach became president at age 35, in 1966, that the go-go years began. The company's sales were then only $74 million. Growth in the shoe business was humdrum, and, says Barach, "No matter how hard we swam, it was like swimming against a 30-knot current. Sales just wouldn't rise more than 8 percent or 9 percent a year." Bedeviled by imports and rising costs, shoe companies were going out of business at the rate of 40 or so each year. A few, like Melville Corp., diversified into apparel retailing, putting clothing alongside their shoe stores in suburban shopping centers.

Casting about for new ventures, the young president of U.S. Shoe read a couple of demographic studies that said women in the coming decade would be going out to work in record numbers—and spending record sums on clothes. In hindsight the decision to buy a chain of women's apparel stores doesn't seem very risky, but when Barach presented the idea to the board, he recalls, "They said, 'What do you want to go into the rag business for?' " Admits a longtime board member, "Phil was a brash young kid. It was hard to love him at first." But they let the kid buy, for $5 million, a little group of 20 women's clothing stores called Casual Corner. It's now among the largest such chains in the country, with over 500 stores and annual sales of nearly $400 million.

U.S. Shoe's fast growth in apparel retailing—from $12 million in sales in 1970 to $583 million last year—mirrors the ascendance of so-called specialty retailing. It's a segment of the business that experts say is grabbing market share away from conventional huge department stores, whose forte was serving the mass market. Observes Laurel Cutler, an executive vice president of Leber Katz Partners, a New York advertising agency, "There is no mass market anymore." It has dwindled along with the traditional nuclear family, now only 15 percent of the population. Mom has a job, and she doesn't have time to hunt through seven floors of merchandise. The proliferation of shopping centers in the 1970s also helped speed the age of specialization, as anyone knows who has visited a mall lately and seen a bagel shop across from a doughnut shop next to a croissant shop. It's a trend that shows every sign of strengthening.

The tricky part of specialty retailing is defining the particular narrow market one wants to reach, and that's where U.S. Shoe shines. Barach's knack is for spotting neglected market niches and then betting that he can fill them. As a result, the company has 12 different specialty apparel chains, more than any competitor, and each is intended for a specific kind of customer, from petite sizes to chubby but chic. The latter, Caren Charles stores, are for the woman who, Barach says, "has had two or three kids and she's not a size six anymore, but she's fashion conscious." The Caren Charles chain, which at first drew giggles in the rag trade, has blossomed in three years from 3 stores to 29, with sales per square foot—a standard measure of prosperity in retailing—a robust $200, or about twice the average for department stores.

With a sharp eye for anomalies in a demographic trend, Barach sometimes stacks his chips just as competitors are walking away from the table. In 1981 U.S. Shoe bought Ups 'n Downs, a string of clothing stores for teenage girls. Other retailers, noting that the teen population was declining, were leaving the market in droves. What wasn't much noticed, Barach says, is that most suburban teenagers have part-time jobs and, usually free of the need to pay for food and rent, spend more than half their income on clothes. Ups 'n Downs, with 110 stores, was losing money when Barach bought it from a British company for $10 million. Sales are now over $50 million and climbing. Although U.S. Shoe doesn't disclose divisional profits, Ups 'n Downs has added 37 stores, and sales per square foot have risen to $180, a gain of 40 percent. Part of the secret, Barach says, is to keep the stores small: "Kids don't want to get lost in a sea of polyester."

Sales per square foot in most of U.S. Shoe's stores are enough to make competitors squirm, and nowhere are they higher than in the 600 so-called concept stores the company licenses to independent entrepreneurs. For about $65,000, U.S. Shoe sets up aspiring shopkeepers in cozy boutiques that concentrate on selling one or two brands of the company's shoes in every conceivable size and width. A consumer who likes the look of the Joyce brand, or Red Cross, or Capezio, keeps coming back to the same little store. As with other U.S. Shoe stores, that customer is most often a working woman who doesn't have time to shop around. The result is astonishing sales per square foot—sometimes as high as $800, or about four times the average for shoe stores. Most important, the brand-name boutiques are a captive retail market for U.S. Shoe's footwear, both American-made and imported. The stores, begun in the mid-1970s, are a big reason why shoe earnings have grown at a 20 percent annual rate over the past five years.

Another reason is U.S. Shoe's early plunge into importing. Notes one security analyst, "Barach had a smart attitude: 'If you can't beat 'em, join 'em.' " With cheap shoes pouring in from overseas, Barach decided in 1968 that if U.S. Shoe wanted to stay afloat, it had to grab the upper end of the market—what he calls the "sports cars and convertibles" of shoes. So he started to expand Marx & Newman, a small New York-based import company U.S. Shoe had bought in 1962. By 1980 the division had dibs on a handful of hot-selling "sports cars" that included Bandolino, Amalfi, David Evins, Liz Claiborne, and Evan-Picone. Marx & Newman, which cost U.S. Shoe less than $2 million, had sales last year of over $200 million. It's made U.S. Shoe the biggest importer of high-fashion shoes in the country.

Still, Barach has not given up on domestic shoemaking. A rarity among marketing mavens, he's taken a keen interest in nuts and bolts and is revitalizing U.S. Shoe's manufacturing. The company makes about 60 percent of the shoes it sells, or about $400 million worth a year. While high costs have pushed 300 American shoe manufacturers out of business in the past decade, U.S. Shoe has poured $30 million into its 18 factories to boost productivity. According to Barach, his plant in Wilmington, Ohio, enjoys the highest output per employee of any comparable plant in the world. Each worker turns out 22 pairs of shoes a day, or about 11,000 shoes a year.

The company has controlled costs by taking advantage of some fancy new technology. But the biggest improvements bear the stamp of plain old Yankee ingenuity. U.S. Shoe has hiked production capacity 10 percent by installing more compact conveyor systems to move shoe parts from one place to another in the factories, and by adding balconies to increase the amount of floor space in each plant. Barach figures these moves have given him the equivalent of one new factory without the expense of a new building. The innovations also make workers' tasks faster and easier to do. Despite a 7 percent wage increase last year, U.S. Shoe managed to hold the labor cost increase per pair of shoes to 3½ percent. Its workers, mostly nonunion, average $4.80 an hour in base pay, plus another 22 cents in profit sharing: the total is just under the industry average.

Barach learned Yankee ingenuity from a Russian immigrant—his father, who ran a grocery store in Boston. Barach the younger's first job, at age nine, was to pick out the bruised apples and sell them to customers for applesauce. "I would buttonhole them as they came into the store and say, 'I have a terrific buy for you!' " he says now. "It was good practice at turning a negative into a positive."

After Barach graduated from Harvard Business School in 1955, he planned to go into the fast-food business with a friend. The partners had already picked out the site of their first drive-in restaurant—a vacant lot in Paramus, New Jersey—when the suppliers who had promised financial backing reneged on the

deal. In need of a job, Barach had gone to work for American Hide & Leather Co., a tanning concern that was teetering on the edge of bankruptcy. As a 25-year-old assistant sales manager, Barach got his first taste of acquisitions—his beleaguered employer was buying out smaller companies for their tax losses—and he also met his mentor, Charles Tandy, then American Hide & Leather's largest shareholder. Barach worked for Tandy for a year before joining U.S. Shoe. "Years later, after Radio Shack became such a big thing, Charles used to say to me, 'If you'd stayed with me, you'd be a big man now,' " Barach recalls; "I was president of U.S. Shoe then. I'd say to him, 'Well, I'm making a living, Charles.' "

Barach's current gamble is one that seems at first glance to follow the crowd. Off-price retailing, which offers brand-name and designer clothing at big discounts, has exploded in the past few years. One estimate puts off-price sales at $7 billion a year, with a 35 percent annual growth rate. The field is already chockablock with competition, but U.S. Shoe has waded in with six new ventures, ranging from children's clothing to household linens, whose total sales last year amounted to $80 million. The centerpiece of Barach's off-price strategy is an innovative group of cut-rate emporiums called Front Row. These combine men's, women's, and children's clothing with shoes and housewares all under one 50,000-square-foot roof. Sound like a department store? It isn't. For one thing, Front Row is less than half the size of the average department store. "What we have done," Barach says, "is extract the strongest profit centers most department stores have and put them all on one floor."

It works because Front Row is designed so that a customer walking into one sees every kind of merchandise the store offers in one sweeping glance around the place—no tedious escalator rides from one cavernous floor to another. Barach believes this encourages people to come in because they know they can shop faster. While chatting with customers at a recent Front Row opening in Houston, Barach says he met a young working woman who bought four $150 suits in 25 minutes. That brisk pace pays off: a Front Row that had opened in Houston a few weeks earlier sold $110,000 in merchandise in its first week, despite the hurricane that pounded the city.

Even within off-price, U.S. Shoe has found a niche: the Front Row stores specialize in big-ticket items, like camel's hair coats, that other off-price merchants shun as too far upscale for hard-core bargain-hunters. "Most of the off-price chains have gone after the middle American making $20,000 a year," says Barach. "Our demographics are in much higher incomes." Those customers like bargains too. A Front Row store the company opened in Atlanta last year is chalking up $11.5 million in sales annually. Eight Front Row stores are now operating, and Barach hopes to add two more stores this year. Robert M. Raiff, who follows U.S. Shoe for the securities firm of Cyrus J. Lawrence, predicts that Front Row alone will be a $200-million division by 1986.

Some security analysts have suggested that U.S. Shoe may be trying to do too many things at once. But Barach minimizes risk by starting small. Says he, "If you pay a lot for a business and it flops, it's like a torpedo. But with us, if a division trips up, it's more like a hand grenade to the bow." Barach's venture into direct mail is true to form. Mail order is growing as fast as in-store specialty retailing for the same reason: it saves shoppers time. Two years ago, U.S. Shoe started up a mail-order lingerie business called Intimique. "You can't buy a good mail-order company, they want a leg and an arm," says Barach. "So we developed it ourselves. It's our test-tube baby." Last year, as Intimique's sales reached a modest $2 million, U.S. Shoe bought a tiny, troubled mail-order company specializing in gifts and children's toys. U.S. Shoe gave the owners, a husband and wife, a three-year management contract and assumed their mortgage and other debts. Notes Barach, "We

really paid nothing for it." The move has already added $10 million to mail-order sales. Within five years, Barach expects mail order to bring in $50 million a year even if U.S. Shoe makes no more acquisitions in the business. The reason: the company hopes to expand direct mail by using lines of merchandise it already knows well, like hard-to-find shoe sizes and women's sportswear.

Meantime, Barach plans to spend over $40 million this fiscal year to expand the specialty retailing stores by 27 percent. He wants to double the specialty retailing business, to $1.2 billion, in five years, and he thinks shoes could bring in $1 billion a year by then. That may sound wildly optimistic, but consider: U.S. Shoe is 17 times the size it was when he took over.

If there's a puddle in U.S. Shoe's path, it's the firm's dependence on its chairman. Barach bristles at the view, widely held on Wall Street, that he runs U.S. Shoe almost single-handedly. "How can you run a billion-dollar company as a one-man show?" he protests. But he's the one who threw all the winning dice, and as one director puts it, "He's a family candy store manager at heart. He has his hands in all the jelly bean jars." When he had coronary bypass surgery late last year, a consultant close to the company says, "I feared for the future of U.S. Shoe." Although Barach hints he has already chosen a successor from among the company's four senior vice presidents, U.S. Shoe seems more vulnerable than most companies its size to the loss of its chairman. "If Phil weren't there, I don't think U.S. Shoe would grind to a *complete* halt," says one security analyst. "But almost."

In the fashion industry more than most, risk takers who spot market trends early and exploit them aggressively are needed to make a company soar. But the bigger a company gets, the more vital it is for shareholders, employees, customers, and others that the high fliers, like Phil Barach, also be keenly attentive to what the ground crew is doing.

—————————————————————— *Case Studies* ——————————————————————

Gerber Products Company (A)
Brian Brandt and James Scott

In the spring of 1973, James D. Ryan, vice president of advertising and merchandising, and Frank Sondeen, advertising manager, were discussing what Gerber might do to increase the demand for baby-food products. Trends in birthrates and the feeding habits of mothers had adversely affected the demand for baby food in 1972. Industry sales had dropped 7 percent in the past year.

The possibility of creating a demand for Gerber products in market segments other than babies was being considered. In their discussion Ryan and Sondeen reviewed the product line to determine which items might have an appeal to such prospective buyers. Possibilities mentioned, among others, included fruits, desserts, and juices. It was also recognized that the development of an effective marketing strategy directed at consumers other than babies might well involve changes in packaging, labels, brand names, distribution channels, and pricing, as well as advertising and promotion.

Background

In 1901, the Fremont Canning Corporation was founded in Fremont, Michigan. The founders were experienced in agriculture, but inexperienced in manufacturing and distribution. As a result, the firm eventually got into acute financial difficulty. At this point, Frank Gerber was assigned the task of managing the business on behalf of a local bank, the principal debt carrier. Gerber devoted countless unpaid hours and energy to the task. After several extremely lean years he restored the solvency of the company and turned it into a profitable organization. During this difficult period the founders were offered additional stock as a part of the reorganization, but they preferred cash instead. Accordingly, Frank Gerber emerged with a controlling interest in the company.

Frank Gerber's son, Dan, began the manufacturing of baby food when his wife asked him to strain peas for their baby. Dan Gerber used the factory machinery that was normally used to puree tomatoes for canning. He gave out samples of the new product to mothers in the Fremont community, and enthusiasm grew.

Gerber began advertising in 1928. Advertisements with coupons were placed in *Good Housekeeping, Ladies' Home Journal,* and *Children* (predecessor to *Parents*). At that time, no birth-list compilers were in existence and direct mail to mothers was impossible. In recognition of this lack, for many years Dan Gerber tried to interest advertising agencies in compiling birth lists, but in vain. Throughout the 1930s, he solicited brokers to send in addresses of new mothers. Eventually, in the late 1930s, he pioneered in developing the first national birth lists by establishing a network of county clerks, and hospital and statistical bureau recorders to supply the information. This was accomplished long before standard list-brokers recognized that the utility of such information would justify the cost of gathering it.

After several years of distributing baby foods through food brokers, Gerber started using its own sales force in 1937. The sales-

Written by Brian S. Brandt, research assistant, under the direction of Professor James D. Scott, Graduate School of Business Administration, The University of Michigan, Ann Arbor.

S. H. Rewoldt, J. D. Scott, and M. R. Warshaw, *Marketing Management*, 4th ed. Copyright © 1981, Richard D. Irwin, Homewood, Ill.

men called on doctors, wholesalers, and retailers. By 1942, the year the company name was changed to Gerber, very few food brokers were handling Gerber products. In addition, 1942 marked the time that all adult foods were discontinued and only baby products were produced by the company.

The success of producing baby products only has been evidenced by the need for increased production capacity from plants in California, New York, North Carolina, and Arkansas in addition to the original plant in Fremont, Michigan. Continued success was to be reached by meeting management's marketing objectives, listed in Exhibit 1.

Products

The demand for baby products was unique. Households with babies are a very select market. In 1972, it was estimated that only 1 mother out of 10 was using baby products at any given time. Additionally, Gerber management estimated that Gerber lost customers at a rate of nearly 250,000 per month simply because babies were outgrowing the need for baby food and other baby products (1973 births were 3,141,000). This very select and changing market made the marketing job a tough one.

At that time, the Gerber product line was made up of 160 food items and 95 nonfood items. Boxed baby foods were cereals and cereals with fruit, teething biscuits, animal cookies, and pretzels. Baby food in jars came in two sizes, 7½ ounces and 4½ ounces. The "junior" foods were generally in the 7½-ounce size, while the strained foods for younger babies were in the 4½-ounce size. The products in jars included meat and egg yolks, fruits, vegetables, high-meat dinners, vegetable and meat combinations, wet cereals with fruit, desserts (puddings and cobblers), and toddler meals (beef stew, spaghetti and meatballs, etc.). A variety of fruit juices were sold in single-serving cans.

The nonfood products included baby pants and bibs. These products were sold exclusively in grocery stores, and Gerber was the largest seller of these products *anywhere.* Gerber also sold cotton baby wear and baby-care products such as lotions, powder, and baby oil. Nurser accessories, including bottles and nipples, were also part of the product line. However, the most unusual product was Gerber life insurance. This was an insurance policy on the father's life to provide for the baby's future. It was sold only by mail. Gerber was licensed to sell this insurance in most states.

EXHIBIT 1 Gerber Products Company Marketing Objectives

Long Term

1. To preserve, reinforce, and expand the existing Gerber image and market franchise.
2. To maintain the trustworthy position and reputation of a company dedicated to promoting sound infant nutrition through the manufacture and distribution of premium products.
3. To retain a competitive pricing policy to prevent erosion of sales, distribution, and trade relations.
4. To develop, introduce, and/or acquire new products or services that can contribute to corporate growth and profit.

Short Term

1. To direct a significant proportion of all promotional efforts at the younger, first-time mothers/mothers-to-be to induce product trial and attempt to establish early brand loyalty.
2. To protect the Gerber franchise by providing optimum sustaining promotional support in those sales areas that are now performing at an acceptable level in all product categories.
3. To provide maximum promotional support for the Gerber line or product categories in those sales areas that show evidence of requiring or potentially benefiting from additional support.
4. To coordinate all consumer/trade communications to maximize corporate, product, service, and promotional awareness.

Distribution

Gerber baby foods were sold in most grocery stores nationwide. The company had 33 district sales offices and nearly 1,000 salesmen of its own calling upon retail stores. A separate sales force had been developed to call on doctors.

The Gerber company sold directly to wholesale grocers and national chains. A case (24 4½-ounce jars) of baby food sold to consumers at $3.00 netted Gerber $2.70. Wholesaler's markup was 3.7 percent and retailer's markup was 6.7 percent. Manufacturing costs for a case of baby food were $1.70; Gerber's markup on sales price was 37 percent. Fixed costs were estimated to be $20 million.

All of the baby and food products were generally sold in one spot in the retail store. Since the products were sought by only a small segment of shoppers, this area was usually out of the way or in a less convenient spot than other food items which might be purchased on impulse.

The Gerber sales force was expected to get maximum retail distribution. Shelf space and shelf position were extremely important. It was felt that regular calls on retailers could maintain or improve this situation. The salesmen generally tried to show the retailer that the dollar gross margin per square foot was higher on baby oriented products than on other food items. Salesmen often suggested orders to retailers while giving information and service. Calls on wholesalers were more important when introducing new products. Obviously, a retailer could not get a product that the wholesaler was not handling.

Promotion

Because of the select market for baby food, direct mail was used regularly. New mothers were sent material on Gerber baby foods and Gerber nonfood products. This material often included cents-off coupons to help initiate Gerber purchases. Additionally, Gerber advertised in baby-care magazines. Television advertising was limited since minimal budgets precluded expanding beyond select print vehicles. Service to the mother was the underlying theme behind the consumer promotion. Historically, however, Gerber had led the industry for many years in national network and spot television.

Gerber also used direct mail to doctors in an attempt to get them to endorse Gerber baby foods when counseling new mothers. Gerber also advertised in grocery trade journals to keep grocery buyers and retailers aware of new products and varieties developed through Gerber research.

Competition

Competition was primarily from two other manufacturers, Heinz and Beech-Nut. A large grocery supermarket usually handled Gerber and one of the competitive brands. It was very unusual for any store to carry all three brands. Although competitive products were similar, with Gerber holding the edge on variety, Gerber was able to maintain a price above that of competition.

Gerber had distribution in approximately 90 percent of the retail grocery stores, while both Heinz and Beech-Nut were at or below 50 percent. This wide distribution was supported by the greater share of market held by Gerber.

Brand loyalty was high in the baby-food industry. "Low-priced brands" have not been able to make any significant penetration in the baby-foods category. It may be inferred that mothers will gladly pay a small premium for the self-assurance gained by buying the brand in which they have the most confidence. The consumer distrusts the quality offered by private brands. There is also evidence that quality varies by chain as well as by pack.[1]

Gerber Performance

Sales for the fiscal year ending March 31, 1971, were $261.8 million. Earnings for the same period were $18.5 million. Sales and earnings for the 1972 fiscal year were $282.6 million and $20.3 million, respectively.

Recent Developments

In 1972, total baby-food industry dollar sales dropped 7 percent off the 1971 figure, falling from $383 million to $356 million. This drop was a significant break in the growth trend. The decline was not in any one specific baby-food category. Juices, cereals, strained, and junior foods all experienced a drop in both dollar and unit sales in 1972 (unit sales dropped by 6.8 percent).

An important reason for the drop in sales was the trend in births. Although the number of marriages continued to grow in 1972, the number of births declined for the second straight year, falling from 3.72 million to 3.26 million. Gerber management knew that the birthrate was affected by more family planning and by the desire of more women to work. The questions were, however, would the trend continue, and for how long?

In discussing the impact of this trend, the director of marketing information noted that the declining birthrate had been offset for several years by an increase in consumption per baby, an increase that eventually leveled off. Gerber research had not established the reason for the leveling.

One observer suggested that some mothers might have started preparing their own baby foods as a result of publicity given to comments on commercially prepared baby foods by Ralph Nader, the consumer advocate. Specifically, Nader had claimed in an article appearing in the November 1970 issue of *McCall's* that the nutritional value of certain brands of baby foods was low and that they contained flavoring chemicals that could be harmful to babies.

Gerber challenged such claims in an advertisement entitled "Commercial Baby Foods—Safe, Nutritious, Acceptable, Convenient, Economical." Gerber provided additional facts questioning Nader's claims in a leaflet entitled "Allegations and Facts relative to Recent Statements concerning Baby Foods."

The result of the decline in sales was excess plant capacity. Gerber was working far below capacity in each of its five plants.

Brand Extensibility

To expand the primary demand for its products, Gerber started a "Brand-Extensibility Program." The program's long- and short-term objectives are outlined in Exhibit 2.

Gerber executives felt that they might be able to capitalize on new trends in lifestyles and eating habits. An article in a fall 1971 issue of *Better Homes and Gardens* pointed out that the whole family no longer ate together as it used to. As a result, convenience foods, single-serving foods, snack foods, and fast-food outlets have prospered. People often eat alone and on the run.

Another important trend has been the increasing number of married women in the work force. Working women who are also mothers obviously don't have the time to prepare elaborate meals. In the past decade, the number of women in the work force has grown by 35 percent compared to a 9 percent growth for men. Three out of five working women are married. The average age of working women has been decreasing; in 1971, it was 37.9 years.

EXHIBIT 2 Gerber Brand-Extensibility Marketing Objectives

The long-term objectives were (1) to substantially increase the consumer acceptance and sales of selected Gerber baby foods outside and in addition to the customary area of infant feeding; (2) to acquire an important share of the market category of single-serving, portable snack/dessert foods; and (3) to broaden Gerber's primary image as a producer of high-quality food products for infants to include older children, adults, and consumers with special needs.

The short-term objectives were (1) to specifically identify and match those products and product categories which in combination appeared to have the maximum potential for immediate consumer acceptance and resultant sales; (2) to design and implement a variety of test-marketing programs that would provide appropriate marketing information, such as promotion spending levels, product mix, consumer and trade acceptance, sales levels, advertising spending levels, competitive reaction, etc.; and (3) to expand on a national basis those categories/products which had through test-market experience proved that they could provide acceptable levels of new-product sales.

Some of the categories that were established as targets for future development, which were referred to as "potential usage universes," were as follows.

A. Fruits and desserts concepts.
   1. Carried lunches.
   2. At-home snacks.
   3. High-energy needs.
   4. Institutional desserts.
   5. Vending machine snacks.
B. Ingredient recipe usage, such as cereals, vegetables, juices, fruits, and desserts.
C. Special consumers for all products.

Gerber executives faced certain short-term constraints. The jar and the contents of any product were to be unchanged because of machinery limitations. For example, the existing machines could handle the 7½-ounce jar as a maximum. And the processes for preparing the foods themselves were not easily changed. Management felt that over the long run many changes could be made in the packaging, contents, or any other aspect of the product. Labeling was a simple change that could be made at any time. However, the Gerber management was reluctant to make a financial investment in a "new" product. Sondeen and Ryan knew that children, teenagers, and adults had been eating baby food. However, the percentage of total baby-food usage accounted for by these nonbaby groups had been declining, dropping from 24 percent in 1956 to 11.1 percent in 1971.

One area under consideration by Gerber and its advertising agency, D'Arcy-MacManus-Masius, Inc., was the snack-pack market. A snack pack was a single serving of pudding, fruit, or gelatin in a sealed aluminum cup. The cup could be opened by pulling a tab. The cups were generally five ounces each and sold four to a pack, costing the consumer anywhere from 55 cents to 69 cents for the four cups. Retailer markup was typically around 20 percent of selling price.

Snack packs were introduced nationally by other food companies in the fall of 1969. By the first quarter of 1971 the market for the ready-to-eat puddings had reached $60 million. The snack-pack puddings were considered "plus" sales because dry pudding mixes were not cannibalized. This success of snack packs was due primarily to the large number of schoolchildren and workers who carried their lunch. The snack-pack market was viewed as the 12 billion lunches carried each year. Gerber estimated that the total snack-pack market would reach $100 million by 1974.

Manufacturers in this market were Hunt-Wesson, with 54 percent share of the market; Del Monte, with 23 percent; General Mills, with 8 percent; and General Foods, with 6 percent. The remaining 9 percent of the market share went to small manufacturers, and an increasing share was going to private labels. Since the manufacturers were large and experienced food processors, distribution of the products was extensive.

In addition, each manufacturer spent large amounts for advertising and promotion. For example, when Hunt-Wesson introduced its snack pack in 1970, it spent nearly 75 percent of its total advertising budget of $4.1 million on television advertising. The remainder was spent in newspaper and magazine advertisements, many of which contained coupons. When General Foods introduced its canned-pudding treats in 1971, it spent $1 million on network TV. Couponing in magazines and newspapers and use of television were the popular types of promotion used by snack-pack competitors.

Studies showed that over half of all husbands, housewives, and children 6–12 years old used snack packs. Teenagers and children under six years old used them to a lesser extent. Lunch boxes and evening snacks were the two most popular uses of the snack packs.

Puddings were 71 percent of the market, with fruit at 15 percent.

The snack-pack cups were packed in units of four bound by a cardboard outer wrapper. Gerber had no existing facility for such packaging. Gerber desserts and snack-pack puddings had the same consistency.

Existing Gerber desserts and strained fruits sold for less per ounce than snack packs. Grocers also had a larger markup on snack packs than they did on baby food.

The Research

Shortly after the brand-extensibility objectives were formulated, Gerber received the results of a study of children's, teenagers', and mothers' reactions to older children using Gerber baby foods. The study showed that some baby foods do appeal to nonbaby segments. Among these are puddings and fruits. On the other hand, some products, particularly

EXHIBIT 3 Summary of Research Results

1. Several baby-food categories have considerable appeal to respondents. These foods are perceived as appealing primarily to children and teens rather than adults. Products with appeal are puddings, strained fruits (sauce), pasta products (Chili Mac, Spaghetti and Meatballs, etc.), pretzels, juices, and cookies.
2. Several categories fail to fulfill the expectations of respondents. These include the meats (beef and chicken) and cereals in a jar. These foods vary to an unacceptable extent from the foods they normally eat. Respondents perceive meat as chunky and chewy. The cereals were not thick and creamy like oatmeal.

The strengths and weaknesses of each accepted product category versus respondent recall of competition suggests that fruits (sauce) have great product uniqueness, with puddings and pretzels well liked, and pasta, cookies, and fruit juices having some product disadvantages. Strained fruits are clearly a unique product. Puddings, however, offer no uniqueness versus competition.
4. There are mixed reactions to the baby-food jar and enclosure. The twist-off cap is satisfactory and safer than the snack-pack opening, because there are no sharp edges. However, children have considerable difficulty in opening and closing the jars. Mothers have some fear of the glass jar breaking. Some suggest the use of plastic jars. Eating from the jar is satisfactory. Some would like the opening larger. The size of the jar is perceived as large. Mothers and teenage boys suggest six-pack as well as individual packaging.
5. Respondents have many positive associations toward baby food. However, both mothers and children have fears concerning baby-food consumption by older children. Children/teens fear teasing and/or loss of image. Mothers fear child regression, particularly with younger children (under one). This fear lessens when children reach their teens. Mothers feel that teens are better off to eat baby food than "junk" food. College students need the convenience and easy storage that baby food provides. The jar is a tip-off to children under six that it is baby food. Teenage girls are more likely to eat it than are teenage boys.

Method: A total of three waves of interviewing was conducted among the following categories: (1) children 5–12, six sessions, and three sessions with mothers—a total of nine sessions; (2) teens—six sessions; (3) children 4–5, four sessions, and three sessions with mothers—a total of seven sessions.

Source: "Study of Children's, Teen-agers', and Mothers' Reactions to Gerber Baby Foods for Use by Older Children," prepared by Child Research Service, Inc.

the meats and cereals, fail to meet the expectations of nonbaby respondents. The study also gave the results of research on the baby-food jar and lid, in addition to attitudes and fears about older children eating baby food. Exhibit 3 gives a summary of the results.

In July 1972, the advertising agency of D'Arcy-MacManus-Masius finished a study in which unique and different labels were put on baby-food jars. Coupons offering 10 cents off per jar were mailed to 150,000 households in the Milwaukee area. Also included in the mailing were snack-pack-type labels that could be put over the Gerber label on the jar. It was possible for the consumer to send in to Gerber for more of the paste-over labels. Eighty-four percent of those covered by the research did use the labels. Thirty-six percent said that they would not use the baby food without the different labels.

Another bit of research was completed on April 4, 1973, by D'Arcy-MacManus-Masius. It dealt with single men and women, married men, and elderly men and women.

The results showed some degree of potential acceptance of baby food, especially among single women (including college students) and elderly men and women. The respondents saw convenience and economy as the motivations behind purchasing baby food for snacks and quick meals. They felt that Gerber would be the brand they would try first.

The S&H Green Stamp Promotion

Gerber embarked on a promotion with the Sperry & Hutchinson Company in the fall of 1972 that was to run through June 1, 1973. Leaflets describing topping, sauce, and snack-pack uses of Gerber desserts were distributed at the S&H Green Stamp Redemption Centers. If a consumer sent in 10, 15, or 25 labels from Gerber desserts, she would get 300 bonus S&H Green Stamps in return. In addition blank paste-on labels were sent to the respondent to put over the Gerber label. Illustrations were included to show how messages could be written on the blank labels. For example, "Johnny, you're a peach" could be put on the peach cobbler.

A response of 18,670 was received. This represented 1 percent of the total who received the leaflets. The results showed that 24 percent of the users were nonbabies.

Note
1. *Supermarket News*, August 5, 1974.

Kellogg Rally Cereal
Don E. Schultz and Mark Traxler

In early 1978, A. B. Smith sat in his office in Battle Creek, Michigan, evaluating the nutritional portion of the ready-to-eat cereal market. He was particularly concerned about several trade reports he had seen recently about the success of Quaker Oats Company's LIFE cereal commercial entitled "Mikey." The commercial was being touted as one of the best remembered commercials on the air.

Smith was also concerned about the recent trends in the ready-to-eat (RTE) cereal category such as the success of the bran-type products and the declining interest in the so-called natural cereals. The growth in the nutritional RTE category had been strong. Kellogg's product entries in this category, however, had not shown the same growth as the market leader, LIFE. In addition, LIFE, through the "Mikey" commercial, had

This case was prepared by Professor Don E. Schultz and Mark Traxler of Northwestern University. Reproduced by permission.

strengthened their position as a "nutritional cereal the whole family will like." Kellogg's two nutritional products, Product 19 and Special K, had both been strongly positioned against the adult market.

In the early 1970s, Kellogg had successfully market tested a new product which was directly competitive to LIFE under the name of RALLY. With the growth of the category, the established position of the present Kellogg brands in the nutritional area, and the present consumer concern about sugar content in RTE cereals, Smith was reviewing Kellogg's position in the category prior to making a recommendation to management for 1979. Launching a new brand of RTE cereal was a major undertaking involving several millions of dollars. In addition, Smith was concerned about the potential cannibalization of Kellogg's Special K and Product 19, if another product were introduced.

If LIFE's "all-family" appeal was being communicated through the "Mikey" commercial, was that an area Kellogg was missing? RALLY had been market tested in the early 1970s. Was that test still valid? Could the results of that test be used as a basis for a new product introduction in 1979? All these questions and more were crossing Smith's mind as he pondered the problem.

The Kellogg Company

Kellogg Company had grown out of the Western Health Reform Institute, a nineteenth-century health clinic in Battle Creek, Michigan, affiliated with the Seventh-Day Adventist movement. Dr. John Harvey Kellogg had become head of the institute in 1876. With his younger brother Will, Kellogg became interested in whole-grain cereal products for patients at the clinic. C. W. Post, who had been a patient at the clinic, had the same idea and had developed and promoted some of the foods served at the clinic into successful products. By 1906 Will Kellogg began producing cereal products developed at the clinic under the Battle Creek Toasted Corn Flake Company name. As the company grew and the cereals were widely accepted, the name was changed to Kellogg Company in 1922. Kellogg quickly became the market leader in RTE cereals and presently enjoys an approximate 42 percent share of business, followed by General Mills with 19 percent, General Foods Post Division with 16 percent, and Quaker Oats with 8 percent. Kellogg markets some 15 different brands of RTE cereal, including such famous names as Rice Krispies, Corn Flakes, Sugar Frosted Flakes, Fruit Loops, and Raisin Bran. Kellogg cereal sales totaled $726 million out of total corporate sales of $1.385 billion in 1976. In addition, Kellogg has expanded into other food categories primarily through acquisition of such companies as Salada Foods, Mrs. Smith's Pie Company, Fearn International, and others.

The Breakfast Cereal Market

In 1977, the RTE cereal industry continued its upward climb in total pound and dollar sales. RTE cereals are now the fifth fastest-growing consumer product category, averaging nearly a 5 percent annual increase, according to the U.S. Department of Commerce. Recent sales are shown in Exhibit 1.

Retail sales in 1976 amounted to $1.48 billion, which is approximately 1 percent of all retail food-store sales. Per capita consumption of RTE cereal is increasing also. Between 1972 and 1973, consumption of RTE cereals

EXHIBIT 1 Ready-to-Eat Cereal Sales

Year	Billion Pounds	Percentage Change
1974	1.63	—
1975	1.69	+4
1976	1.81	+7
1977	1.85	+2

EXHIBIT 2 Cold Cereal Consumption by Age

Age (Years)	Pounds/Person/Year
1–2	7.2
3–5	9.4
6–8	12.0
9–11	9.8
12–14	9.8
15–19	5.9
20–54	3.6
55–	5.9

EXHIBIT 4 Cereal Categories by Market Share

Category	Percentage Share
All family	46
Children	24
Highly fortified	9
Bran	7
Granola	4
Variety pack	3
Granola bars	2
Other	5
Total	100

increased from 6 to 8 pounds per person. The Cereal Institute estimates of "cold cereal" consumption by age are given in Exhibit 2.

Since 1974, retail cereal prices have been steadily increasing. Some industry price figures are shown in Exhibit 3.

Consumption of RTE cereals is spread fairly evenly across the country, with nearly 80 percent of all persons using the product. The Target Group Index (TGI) defines "heavy users" as those consuming six or more individual portions of RTE cereal a week. These heavy users comprise nearly 38 percent of all RTE cereal users. There is a slight variance in RTE cereal heavy users geographically. The mid-Atlantic (110) and east central (107) areas index the highest while the southeast (88) and southwest (84) are the lowest (index average equals 100). There is also a slight seasonal sales difference ranging from a high of 110 in July and September to a low of 88 in November (index average equals 100).

Cereals are broken down into seven categories by Selling-Marketing Areas, Inc. (SAMI). These categories and their approximate percentage of the total are given in Exhibit 4. The Target Group Index separates RTE

cereal into three categories: presweetened, natural, and regular. Based on research data, it appears consumers are even less discriminating, preferring to lump RTE cereals into either presweetened or regular. In spite of this generalization, there is consumer recognition of the various types of products available, with a general acceptance of some five to seven "acceptable brands" on most shoppers' lists.

Changes in manufacturer's list prices for RTE cereals are relatively infrequent. The normal retail margin is approximately 18 percent. There are few intermediaries in the RTE cereal channels. Orders flow from the grocery chain buyer or food broker to the manufacturer's sales force to the factory. The goods are shipped to the grocer's warehouse and from there directly to the retail outlet. RTE cereals are fast-moving products with about one box purchased per family per week. Typical RTE promotion to consumers includes cents-off coupons and self-liquidating premiums. The package is used as a breakfast-time entertainment medium by printing interesting information or games on the back and side panels.

While there are certain anticipated trade deals for new products, established brands rely more heavily on consumer advertising and promotion than promotional programs. Because of the large number of brands marketed, there is no one dominant brand. Kellogg Corn Flakes is the largest-selling brand

EXHIBIT 3 Ready-to-Eat Cereal Prices

Year	RTE Average Retail Price per Pound (Dollars)	Percentage Change
1974	0.908	—
1975	0.933	+3
1976	0.951	+2
1977	1.022	+7

with approximately a 7 percent share, followed by Cheerios with approximately 5.6 percent. Others range downward with most in the 1 to 1.5 percent share area.

Nutritional RTE Cereals

The nutritional segment constitutes about 15 percent of the total RTE cereal market when several all-family entries are added to the SAMI "adult highly fortified" category. The adult highly fortified brands are LIFE, Product 19, Special K, Buc Wheats, Golden Grahams, and Total. Other all-family RTE cereals which appear to be directly competitive are Cheerios, Chex (Rice, Corn, Wheat), Wheaties, Shredded Wheat, and Team. Most of the brands in this segment are long established with few recent additions. The range in total RTE brand shares are from a low of approximately 27 percent for Fortified Oat Flakes to approximately 5.6 percent for Cheerios. Kellogg's two entries in this category are Special K with a 2.2 percent share and Product 19 with a 1.2 percent share. The Special K share has been declining slightly over the past two years while Product 19 has remained steady.

The growth of the nutritional segment is much faster than the growth rate for the total RTE cereal market. Exhibit 5 demonstrates some recent growth rates. When new cereals are priced, prices of directly competing products are an important consideration. Typical retail pricing for brands in the nutritional segment are shown in Exhibit 6. Note that Prod-

EXHIBIT 6 Retail Prices for Nutritional Cereals

Brand	Size in Ounces	Price
Buc Wheats	15	$1.11
Cheerios	10	0.83
LIFE	15	0.93
Product 19	12	1.03
Special K	15	1.21
Total	12	1.05

uct 19 and Total, which are in direct competition, are priced accordingly.

Because of the number of brands offered to the consumer, grocery chain buyers frequently reassess which brands to reorder. The decision is based on SAMI and Nielsen data to define the best-selling brands, the grocery's own historical sales data, and, in the case of new products, the national advertising and promotional plans. New products are usually given a six-month trial period by most grocery retailers. However, gaining the necessary two-shelf facings to launch a new brand requires several decisions. It is common for the RTE cereal aisle to be set proportionately to the grocer's sales for each brand. Manufacturer sales forces in the RTE category are highly trained and motivated. Since cereal is an established category, the sales force is usually a key determinant in a successful new product introduction.

Brands in the high nutrition segment invested an average of $6.35 million in measured media in 1977 according to Leading National Advertisers (LNA) annual summary. In 1976, investments in the directly competitive market ranged from less than $1.9 million for Buc Wheats to over $10 million for Cheerios. LIFE expenditures in 1976 were estimated to be approximately $6.4 million compared to the Special K investment of $6.2 million and the Product 19 budget of $2.9 million. With the success of the "Mikey" commercial, LIFE was expected to increase its advertising expenditures in 1978. As a rule of thumb, advertisers in the high-nutrition and all-family cereals invested 60 percent of their funds in

EXHIBIT 5 Growth of the Nutritional Segment of the Ready-to-Eat Cereal Market

Year	Percentage Nutritional Increase	Percentage RTE Increase
1974	+6	N.A.
1975	+13	+4
1976	+14	+7
1977	+16	+2

network television, 33 percent in spot television, and approximately 7 percent in print.

The messages of the major competitors are summarized below.

Special K—An adult cereal with high protein and nutritional campaign stressing weight control and fitness. Copy focuses on the "Special K Breakfast" of less than 240 calories.

Wheaties—Advertising features Bruce Jenner, a current sports celebrity who included Wheaties as part of his winning diet. The brand is known as the "Breakfast of Champions."

Total—Campaign stresses vitamin and nutrition content comparing against other leading cereal brands. Good taste is a secondary message to reassure the consumer.

Cheerios—A long-running family oriented campaign which says, "Get a powerful good feeling with Cheerios."

Product 19—Campaign aimed at adults focusing on good nutrition. The copy asks, "Did you forget your vitamins today?"

LIFE—Uses "Mikey" (described below) as product hero in their long-running campaign.

The essence of the "Mikey" commercial for LIFE is as follows: The commercial shows two skeptical children and a younger child, Mikey, in a kitchen setting. Because they already know that LIFE is supposed to be "good for you," implying that LIFE could not possibly taste good, they use Mikey as a guinea pig to taste LIFE cereal. Mikey innocently eats it while the other two eagerly watch for his reaction. Mikey smiles. Amid shouts of "He likes it!" and "He's eating it!" the two skeptics conclude that LIFE *must* taste good for Mikey to like it.

LIFE cereal has used trial-size sampling to stimulate interest in the product. The packages included three one-ounce servings of LIFE and sold for 10 cents in chain grocery outlets. Sales improved slightly as a result.

The heavy media dollars and promotional efforts that have been described are aimed at the primary purchasers of high protein, high nutrition cereals. They are profiled as women 18 to 49 for products like LIFE, Cheerios, and Wheaties, and slightly older (25 to 54) for Special K, Product 19, Buc Wheats, and Total. They live in Standard Metropolitan Statistical Areas, most have at least a high school education, with an annual household income in excess of $10,000. They are married, with three or more individuals in the household, with children ages 6 to 11 years old, according to Target Group Index data.

The Product

Kellogg's new product development department describes RALLY as a delicately presweetened high-protein cereal for younger adults and children. The actual appearance is a square puffy pillow shape much like Ralston-Purina's Chex cereals. Since RALLY is a rice-based product, it stays crisper in milk than oat or wheat-based cereals. RALLY's delicate presweetening translates into 18 percent sugar by volume as compared to less than 10 percent for nonsweetened brands. Nutritionally, RALLY has 20 percent of the U.S. Recommended Daily Allowance (RDA) of protein with milk and is enriched with eight essential vitamins and iron to 25 percent RDA. Quaker's LIFE is the only other product with such a high protein level and light presweetening with a comparable vitamin and mineral content. RALLY contains 33 percent of the RDA for vitamins B_1, B_2, niacin, and iron, compared with LIFE's 25 percent.

In choosing a package size for RALLY, Kellogg looked at the brand's direct competitor—LIFE cereal. LIFE markets two sizes, the 15- and 20-ounce box. The 15-ounce box retails for 93 cents. To compete with LIFE in the same price range, the largest size Kellogg can offer would be a 13-ounce box at 97 cents because of a difference in cost of raw material. RALLY was tested in a 7-ounce box priced at 75 cents in the 1970 market test.

RALLY's test-market package design showed the red Kellogg logo, a black sticker stating "HIGH PROTEIN" and the name RALLY in big black letters at the top. The bottom portion showed a bowl full of cereal. In the midsection was a set of pennants waving above the bowl as if it were a stadium.

Consumer Test

The 1970 consumer panel preference results for RALLY among women and children were very encouraging (Exhibit 7). The test results indicated that the major advantage of RALLY over LIFE appeared to be based on the comment, "LIFE gets soggy too soon." RALLY was preferred 3 to 1 over LIFE by the panel of children and was rated superior in taste, texture, and sweetness level. Against four leading nutritional brands (LIFE, Total, Product 19, and Special K), women showed a significant preference for RALLY. Consumers also rated RALLY as better than the cereals they were presently using.

Market Test

RALLY was market tested in two eastern cities in the early 1970s. It was positioned as an "all-family nutritional cereal with better taste" directed to children and young adults. RALLY was able to generate and maintain a sales rate equaling a 1 percent share of the total RTE market in these tests.

The introductory sell-in used Kellogg's own sales force to acquaint grocery clients with RALLY and offered a $.75–$1.00 per dozen introductory case allowance to help defray warehousing and stocking expenses. The media plan included network appeals to children and prime-time programming and spot children and daytime programming for the 17-week introductory period.

Summary

In reviewing the RALLY test results, Smith was still undecided about a recommendation to introduce RALLY nationally. On the positive side, consumer response seven years ago was good. RALLY's sugar content would not stir consumer concern as with many presweetened cereals. Every day in the papers consumers read about the importance of good nutrition, and high protein was certainly an important part of nutrition. Finally, RALLY seemed to have overcome the consumer complaints with LIFE that it got soggy in milk too soon.

However, there were problems to be considered, not the least of which was the product name. Should it still be called RALLY? Was Kellogg's target market correct during the test market—young adults and children? As a new product, could RALLY compete with

EXHIBIT 7 1970 Consumer Panel Preferences

	Preferred RALLY	Preferred LIFE	No Preference
General appearance	76%	14%	10%
Shape	54	19	27
Taste	62	20	18
Texture "just right"	83	16	

LIFE in gaining both segments of the target market? After 17 years, LIFE only recently acquired a strong children's following with the "Mikey" commercial. Are the test-market results still valid for a new product introduction in 1979? What about cannibalization of Kellogg's existing brands?

Finally, if the recommendation should be made to introduce RALLY, Smith would have to answer questions such as: What package and pricing changes would be necessary? What improvements in the distribution system would be required? And what sort of advertising strategy and promotion should be used to make RALLY a viable competitor against LIFE and their "Mikey" commercial?

Smithfield-Blume, Ltd.
Jane G. Funk and Thomas F. Funk

In June 1981, the advertising agency of Smithfield-Blume, Ltd. was retained by the Ontario Rutabaga Producers' Marketing Board (ORPMB) to develop a new promotional campaign for Ontario Rutabagas. This was a fairly unusual account for the medium-sized agency which specialized in agribusiness accounts. The average Smithfield-Blume client had a promotional budget of $200,000. The firm's clients included fertilizer, chemical, feed and seed products. They also handled a few other industrial accounts, the largest of which was the $300,000 Warren ("Windows to the World") Window account.

The agency was established in 1952 by Simon J. Smithfield, a former sales representative for Massey Ferguson. Smithfield had started by working with equipment accounts but as the business prospered and the staff expanded, the firm moved into other areas of agribusiness and industrial products. The agency remained fairly conservative in its approach. Smithfield's own specialty was slogans but the real agency emphasis was on "quality" promotion designed to inform customers. Though Smithfield himself had no formal marketing training he was a great believer in hiring account executives with a marketing background because he recognized that ad executives couldn't work in a vacuum.

We have to work on behalf of the client! We have to look at their strategy or help them develop one. Otherwise they may as well toss their money down a rat hole for all the good a flashy ad campaign will do! What's more, we gotta have the guts to tell them their ideas stink! We owe them that honesty!

This philosophy was still at work at Smithfield-Blume though Smithfield had retired. Every junior account man was thoroughly versed in the philosophy and history of S-B.

Though the agency dealt mainly with agribusiness accounts, Smithfield had never been in favor of hiring only those with an agricultural background.

Too narrow-minded! If he grew up on a hog farm in Simcoe then basically he thinks he has the last word on hogs! In this business you need a wide range of experience and a quick, open mind.

Most of S-B's junior ad men came right out of university. One of the latest additions was Ted Banner, a graduate of Western at London, Ontario. Ted had been with S-B for two years. He learned fast and was quite ambitious. To date, his greatest success had been the brochure for Farnum Feed. On the basis of his past performance, S-B executives felt he was ready to take on the ORPMB account.

Ted realized this was his big chance at S-B. The ORPMB account totaled around $150,000 and he planned to make the campaign a real landmark. First, however, he knew he must do his homework, so he carefully studied all the background material he had collected on the ORPMB.

Ontario Rutabaga Producers' Marketing Board

Established in 1979, the ORPMB is made up of a board of directors elected by all the Rutabaga growers in Ontario. The board's objective is "to stimulate and improve the marketing of rutabagas." The board's budget came from licensing fees paid by producers and marketers of rutabagas. In the past the budget had varied greatly and this had seriously affected marketing efforts. The 1980 budget was $82,000; the 1982 budget had risen to $150,000.

The name Rutabaga had become the product's official name in 1967. Prior to this it was known as the Laurentian turnip. Most of the Ontario rutabaga crop was shipped to the United States and was consumed south of the Mason-Dixon Line and east of the Mississippi River. The Board thought that major competition there came from white turnips and turnip greens. Past promotional efforts had been focused mainly in the United States and promoted rutabagas to housewives as a unique and different vegetable. The past campaigns had been rather limited because of small budgets. In 1979, for example, the budget had totaled $30,000.

The 1980 campaign had been more extensive and had used a promotional mix of magazine ads, press releases for radio and newspaper, a television film, and film clips for home economists. All of this was developed around the persona of "June Conway," the fictitious home economist for the board.

Magazine ads appeared in *Woman's Day* and *Family Circle* in November and April. The full-page ads stressed new uses and recipe ideas. Nutrition was mentioned but not stressed and recipe books were available on request.

The media campaign revolved around press releases for radio which were given to the stations and were intended for broadcast at their convenience in late morning or early afternoon women's shows. A $14,000 TV film entitled "Everything You Wanted to Know about Rutabagas but Didn't Know Who to Ask" was distributed upon request to TV cable channels for use at their convenience. The film highlighted the growing of rutabagas and their nutritional value and included attractive recipe ideas. In addition to this a new filmstrip entitled "The Ontario Rutabaga in the Kitchen" was distributed to school home economists. Board member Fred Hunsberger felt very strongly about "Letting those kids know what a good value rutabagas are. If we get them early on we got them for life."

The new board faced a crisis situation at its formation because per capita rutabaga consumption had been declining seriously for the past 20 years and growers were reducing their acreage or leaving the industry altogether. In 1980, board President Clyde Carson presented the board with these depressing statistics and suggested a new "marketing strategy" like that discussed at an agribusiness seminar he had recently attended. As expected, Clyde ran into heavy opposition from other board members who did not understand what a marketing strategy was and who were more interested in increasing their production levels. Fred Hunsberger had been particularly adamant about keeping their current promotional program.

> Clyde, we're already telling 'em about all the vitamins and stuff and offering free recipes. Now what woman won't jump at a free recipe? And that June Conway is a mighty fine woman! The way she talks about those rutabagas just makes my mouth water. And the kids are sure to like the film. I sure would have been pleased to see films when I was in school! That TV cable film is doing the job too. Booked solid all last year. It looks real classy to have our own TV film. Just a fluke that consumption is down. People don't know when they're well off these days. You wait! The old values will come back soon and people will see that turnips—uh—rutabagas are good solid food!

Clyde had persevered and finally got the board to agree to a large-scale study of the North American rutabaga market. The project involved two stages. The first was rutabaga awareness and usage information obtained from 2,000 Canadian and 6,000 U.S. households. More detailed information was obtained in the second stage on usage, attitudes, and preferences from 300 households in Canada and 800 in the United States. Based on the report, Clyde had convinced the board that a drastic overhaul was needed. The first thing they had done was to find a replacement for J. B. Cruikshank, Ltd., the ad agency responsible for "Everything You Always Wanted to Know about. . . ." Fred Hunsberger had insisted that Smithfield-Blume be hired as a replacement because:

> That's a classy outfit! I knew old Sim when he was with Massey and I'll never forget his big "Keep Pace with Case" campaign. That's what we need. A catchy slogan! It will turn the tide in a few weeks. Look at the milk people. My grandkids won't stop singing "Thank you very much milk." Drives me crazy but they say it sells the milk. Why not tur—rutabagas too? Of course, we'll keep June Conway.

Clyde didn't argue with Fred though he privately felt that perhaps Smithfield-Blume was not the best choice and questioned the usefulness of a slogan. Fred, on the other hand, thought that S-B's familiarity with agriculture would be an asset. The two men planned a meeting with S-B's account man.

Research Project Results

Ted Banner sat at his desk in the office of Smithfield-Blume. In front of him were various documents and folders containing background and past promotional programs of the ORPMB. On top of the pile was a report entitled "Consumer Analysis of the North American Rutabaga Market," the report which presented the results of the board's large-scale survey done in 1980. Ted knew that this report had to be the basis of his recommendations for the board. In preparation for his initial meeting with Clyde Carson and Fred Hunsberger, Ted looked through the report and summarized the main points.

Common Product Names

> The report reveals that the product is called by many different names including rutabaga, swede, swede turnip, and turnip. In the United States, 78 percent of the consumers referred to the product as a rutabaga compared to only 20 percent in Canada.

Awareness and Frequency of Use

> Consumers were placed in one of six categories depending on their awareness and frequency of rutabaga use (see Exhibit 1).
> The first category is relatively small and contains people who are not aware of rutabagas. The second category contains people who are aware of rutabagas but never purchased one. This group is relatively small in Canada but large in the United States. The third group contains people who have not purchased a rutabaga in the

EXHIBIT 1 Rutabaga Market Segments, United States and Canada, 1980

	Percent of Population	
Market Segments	Canada	U.S.A.
Nonusers, not aware	11	14
Nonusers, aware	16	40
Lapsed users (not used in past year)	8	14
Light users (less than 4 times a year)	23	19
Medium users (5 to 12 times a year)	25	9
Heavy users (more than 12 times a year)	16	3

last 12 months. These are probably "lapsed users" who have discontinued use of the product. This is a relatively small group.

The last three groups are classified as current rutabaga users and account for 64 percent of Canadian consumers and 31 percent of American consumers. The heavy user segment accounts for 16 percent of Canadian consumers and 3 percent of American consumers.

User and Nonuser Profiles

Analysis of the above groups in terms of demographic characteristics reveals the profiles for both users and nonuser profiles (see Exhibits 2 and 3).

In Canada rutabaga usage tends to be highest among older consumers, consumers who live in rural areas and small communities, French-speaking Canadians, families whose female head is either a homemaker or retired and families whose male and female head have less education. U.S. results are very similar with rutabaga usage being highest among older consumers, lower income families, families whose male and female heads have less education, single-family households, and blacks.

Vegetable Purchase Criteria

Consumers in the study were asked to rank six possible purchase criteria. Highest rank criteria were quality, nutritional value, and taste preference. Price and time needed to prepare the vege-

table were of some but lesser importance. Rutabaga users consistently ranked price higher than taste preference. Nonusers ranked taste preference ahead of price.

Consumer Attitudes

Consumers in both countries responded to a series of statements designed to measure attitudes toward a number of issues related to vegetable and rutabaga usage. The following attitudes emerged:

1. Consumers feel they are eating about the right quantity and variety of vegetables but a sizable group think they should eat more and a greater variety. This is particularly true for the nonuser segment.
2. Rutabagas are not considered expensive in relation to other vegetables but consumers stated that large price increases could cause some reduction in consumption.
3. A large percentage of consumers increased purchases of rutabagas when on special. Most consumers felt that rutabagas were seldom "featured" items at their stores.
4. Most consumers felt that rutabagas are not conveniently located, nor attractively displayed, and frequently not available at their stores.
5. A large percentage of consumers felt that rutabagas are generally too large for the size of their families. They indicated an interest in presliced, ready-to-cook rutabagas, or especially in the United States, ready-to-serve rutabaga casseroles.
6. Most consumers judge product quality by external appearance and many felt that the rough, black and brown spots on the exterior of the rutabaga indicated inferior quality.
7. Many consumers commented on the difficulty of preparing a rutabaga.
8. Most consumers have little information on the nutritional value of rutabagas and would like more.

Reasons for non- and Lapsed Users

Both nonusers and lapsed users listed not liking the taste as the most common reason for nonuse.

EXHIBIT 2 Demographic Profiles of Market Segments, U.S.A., 1980

Demographic Characteristics	Nonusers Not Aware %	Nonusers Aware %	Lapsed Users %	Total Nonusers %	Light Users %	Medium Users %	Heavy Users %	Total Users %
Household income								
Less than $8,000 (21)*	15	31	17	63	23	24	3	37
$8,000–$12,000 (17)	16	38	14	68	18	19	3	32
$12,000–$20,000 (22)	15	48	12	75	17	19	1	25
$20,000–$30,000 (22)	12	44	16	72	18	19	2	28
Over $30,000 (19)	16	43	14	73	16	19	2	27
Age of panel member								
Under 25 (9)	24	51	10	85	9	5	1	15
25 to 34 (22)	18	55	10	83	13	3	1	17
35 to 44 (18)	17	43	14	74	17	17	2	26
45 to 54 (18)	10	40	16	66	21	10	3	34
55 to 64 (16)	9	32	18	59	24	12	5	41
65 and over (18)	11	25	18	54	28	15	3	46
Education of panel member								
Grade school (4)	18	25	14	57	25	14	5	43
High school (47)	16	40	14	70	19	9	2	30
College/university (49)	12	43	15	70	19	9	2	30
Education level of husband								
Grade school (6)	16	32	14	62	24	10	5	38
High school (41)	16	43	12	71	18	8	2	29
College/university (50)	13	47	14	74	16	8	2	26
Employment status of female								
Full time (37)	15	43	14	72	17	7	2	28
Part time (14)	15	42	14	71	18	9	2	29
Not employed (50)	13	39	15	67	21	10	3	33
Household size								
One (14)	11	28	19	58	28	12	3	42
Two (32)	13	37	16	66	20	12	3	34
Three (20)	14	48	13	75	17	5	2	25
Four (20)	17	48	12	77	15	6	2	23
Five or more (14)	17	43	12	72	17	8	3	28
Race								
White (96)	14	41	14	69	19	9	3	31
Black (4)	8	31	20	59	26	12	4	41

*Percent of sample.

EXHIBIT 3 Demographic Profiles of Market Segments, Canada, 1980

Demographic Characteristics	Nonusers Not Aware %	Nonusers Aware %	Lapsed Users %	Total Nonusers %	Light Users %	Medium Users %	Heavy Users %	Total Users %
Age of panel member								
Under 25 (10)*	18	36	9	63	16	15	6	37
25 to 34 (25)	14	21	8	43	21	23	13	57
35 to 44 (17)	12	14	10	36	24	25	14	63
45 to 64 (33)	8	9	7	24	24	30	22	76
65 and over (14)	6	10	9	25	30	27	18	75
Population density								
Rural (21)	12	13	10	35	23	27	16	66
Town (under 30,000) (16)	10	18	6	34	24	21	21	66
City (30,000 to 1 million) (34)	8	15	9	32	22	28	17	67
Metropolitan (over 1 million) (30)	14	18	7	39	24	23	14	61
Language								
English (75)	8	17	9	34	25	25	15	65
French (25)	19	12	7	38	17	25	21	63
Employment status of Female head								
Professional (10)	9	24	8	41	24	24	11	59
White collar (21)	12	16	7	35	22	27	16	65
Blue collar (7)	12	16	9	37	19	24	20	63
Homemaker (50)	12	14	8	34	24	26	16	66
Retired (12)	6	9	10	25	26	24	24	74
Education of female								
Grade school (12)	13	11	6	30	21	29	19	69
High school (57)	11	14	8	33	22	26	19	67
College/university (31)	8	19	9	36	28	25	11	64
Education of male								
Grade school (15)	13	12	6	31	21	29	19	69
High school (49)	12	13	7	32	23	25	20	68
College/university (36)	9	20	8	37	27	24	12	63

*Percent of sample.

use. The second most frequent reply given by nonusers was that they didn't know how to cook or prepare them. Lapsed users listed several secondary reasons: too much trouble to prepare, too hard to cut, poor quality, and prefer more nutritious vegetables.

Purchase and Use

Rutabaga users were asked about their purchase and use of the product. Their responses indicated that (1) approximately one half of all users decide to purchase the product after entering a store; (2) almost all purchases are made in supermarkets; (3) the most popular methods of preparation are boiled and mashed; (4) less than 30 percent of all users serve the vegetable raw; (5) the vegetable's consumers consider close substitutes for rutabagas are carrots and squash; (6) most consumers consider the vegetable as an ordinary everyday dish; (7) over 80 percent of all current users indicated that they were using rutabagas just as often or more often than five years ago; and (8) most consumers obtain recipe ideas from magazines and newspapers.

Ted's Reaction

After thoroughly studying the background information and the research report, Ted knew that the problem he faced was far more complex than he imagined. His telephone conversations with Clyde Carson indicated that Carson was aware of the severity and complexity of the problem but Carson hinted that other board members expected a "magic cure-all" along the lines of the famous "Keep Pace with Case" campaign of a few years earlier. Ted knew he would need to call on all his tact as well as his past marketing background in order to come up with a campaign for the Rutabaga board. He knew the program must take into consideration various promotional tools and their cost (see Exhibit 4). His first task would be to develop a set of recommendations based on the Rutabaga report.

EXHIBIT 4 Selected Advertising Rates

Newspapers	
Toronto Star	One half-page color advertisement run once a month for 9 months, $6,600 per entry
Globe & Mail	One eighth-page color advertisement in Wednesday's food section for nine months; $1,440 per entry
Local paper	One half-page color advertisement; $510 per entry
Magazines	
Chatelaine	One half-page black and one color advertisement run for one edition; $10,130 English edition and/or $3,400 French edition
Radio	
Toronto stations	One 60-second morning announcement; $160 on FM and $170 on AM
Local stations	One 60-second morning announcement; $24 on FM and $31 on AM
Television	
C.T.V.	One 30-second announcement during daytime (noon–7 P.M.) $2,000; during prime time (7 P.M.–11 P.M.) $6,600
C.B.C.	One 30-second announcement during daytime (noon–7 P.M.) $1,000; during prime time (7 P.M.–11 P.M.) $6,500

McDonald's
Thomas V. Greer

McDonald's Corporation was one of the best-known companies in the United States and Canada and constituted a success story seldom equaled. Systemwide sales were about $6.3 billion, and total assets and stockholders' equity were approaching $2.7 billion and $1.2 billion, respectively. Net profits after taxes were very good and, when expressed as net profit per share of common stock, had doubled in the previous four years. No dividends were paid until the 22nd year of the organization's life, all the profits being plowed back into rapid expansion of the system.

Restaurants operated by McDonald's itself furnished about 27 percent of systemwide sales, whereas franchised restaurants accounted for 67 percent of sales. Most franchisers operated 15 to 20 percent of their outlets, but McDonald's operated 26 percent of its outlets. The 353 restaurants operated by several affiliates in foreign countries, chiefly Japan and England, were responsible for about 6 percent of the sales. An affiliate was a company in which McDonald's share of equity was 50 percent or less. The combined sales of foreign affiliates, foreign franchises, and company-owned units abroad amounted to only about 19 percent of company sales, but these sales were rising much faster than domestic sales. There were McDonald's restaurants in 26 countries.

McDonald's held about a 19 percent share of the U.S. market for fast foods and dwarfed the competition. In terms of sales, it was more than twice as large as its nearest rival, Kentucky Fried Chicken. It was 3 times as large as Burger King, more than 4 times as large as Dairy Queen, 5 times as large as Wendy's, 6 times as large as Pizza Hut, 8 times as large as

Hardee's, and 12 times as large as Burger Chef.

McDonald's selected each location and constructed the facilities. A franchisee who operated an establishment paid McDonald's an initial franchising fee of about $250,000, half in cash and half to be paid later, plus an annual franchise fee of 3 percent of sales and an annual building rental of 8.5 percent of sales. The franchise lasted for 20 years and included intensive training at the company's Hamburger University in Elk Grove Village, Illinois; management counseling; assistance with operations, advertising, and public relations; financial advice; materials for employee training; and the financial benefits of volume purchasing. However, McDonald's was not in the business of supplying the franchisees. Instead, it negotiated supply contracts with outside companies.

Growth, Development, and Policies

The company was founded in 1955 by Ray Kroc, a salesman of malted-milk machines. His curiosity was piqued in 1954 when he received an order for eight units from one hamburger restaurant, for that meant that someone had found it necessary to make very large numbers of malts simultaneously. That establishment was McDonald's in San Bernardino, California, an eight-year-old firm owned and operated by Maurice "Mac" and Richard McDonald. The two brothers had developed the concept of the assembly-line hamburger and accompanying french fries. They had pioneered in the use of a standardized beef patty with a standardized sauce, and an infrared lamp to keep the cooked potatoes crisp. In front of the restaurant was a large sign displaying two golden arches. The prices were quite low. Kroc was extremely impressed with what he saw: good value for the money, speedy service, elimination of wastefulness, cleanliness, the absence of anything to be stolen, and standardization. The McDonald brothers had franchised six other establishments in California to use their name and their complete set of procedures, but they were cautious and conservative about expanding further and wanted very much to avoid the traveling that inevitably would go with expanded operations. Kroc talked with them for three days while they assembled hamburgers. Finally they worked out a contract whereby Kroc would have the exclusive right to sell the McDonald's name and complete package of procedures to franchisees and would get a percentage of sales made by franchisees. Six years later, in 1960, Kroc completely bought out the McDonald brothers' interests for $2.7 million.

Ray Kroc believed strongly in the concept of systems. He frequently instructed people, especially franchisees, that there was a science to making and serving a hamburger. He described his operating philosophy with two anagrams, QSC/TLC, which meant "Quality, Service, Cleanliness/Tender Loving Care." He emphasized that the company gave a person a chance to get into business for himself without taking the entire risk alone. But that person had to agree to follow a proven way of conducting the business. Although Kroc saw the extreme importance of systems in creating and running an organization, he believed that systems should be no more complex than necessary. He frequently called attention to a favorite rule of thumb called K.I.S.S. for short, which translated "Keep it simple, stupid."

The system included physical standardization. Kroc believed that the public would react positively to a standardization that featured not only places that turned out the same food but that were extremely clean inside and outside and were staffed by courte-

ous people. Most of the industry of which McDonald's was part had a reputation for slovenly conditions and unconcerned, often surly employees. Another point emphasized to franchisees, managers, and employees was the need to maintain scrupulously clean rest rooms.

McDonald's believed strongly in monitoring the work of franchisees and its own restaurant managers. Standardization and enforcement of policies could not really be accomplished without management audits. Accordingly, twice a year, internal consultants conducted a highly detailed inspection lasting about three days and rendered a written report with grades and comments on management practices. Among the categories critiqued were the food and beverages, cleanliness, speed of service, courtesy, and friendliness.

The company emphasized suburban locations, thus tapping the great population movements of the late 1950s and 1960s. Most existing fast-food firms chose to remain in the cities and ignored the suburbs. In the 1970s McDonald's expanded into the cities and into some small towns.

The Product Line

Although it was realized that the "product" was far more than the food, the heart of McDonald's product was the food itself. The company was devoted to simple, bland foods that would have a rather broad, repetitive appeal and would be easy to make. The hamburger sandwich fitted these criteria, but as food traditions go, it was a relative newcomer. Hamburger meat originated in medieval Eastern Europe as raw beef shredded by a dull knife. Baltic region traders brought it to Hamburg, where it is still eaten both cooked and raw. German immigrants later brought it encased in bread to the United States. It is claimed that the hamburger was introduced by these immigrants in the Cincinnati area and also in St. Louis. There is good documentation that the first large-scale public offering of the hamburger was at the St. Louis World's Fair of 1904. New Haven, Connecticut, however, claims that a restaurant called Louis Lunch was the first to popularize this German dish.

There was always great concern for appropriate product characteristics and an appropriate product mix. Kroc determined that the company's first hamburger patty must measure 1.6 ounces and go in a bun that was 3.5 inches in diameter. He decreed that the bun must contain extra sugar so that it would brown faster and that the sandwich must contain exactly one fourth of an ounce of onion. In 1963 the company introduced its double burger and double cheeseburger. Although it believed passionately in standardization, McDonald's was always interested in new product development and in the improvement of the product line. Despite the fact that it had people engaged in research, McDonald's was quite receptive to product ideas arising from its franchisees. One of the great breakthroughs came from franchisee Lou Groen, who operated a restaurant in a Roman Catholic neighborhood in Cincinnati. On Fridays his sales dropped by about half. In 1961 he began experimenting with a breaded fish filet sandwich and his Friday sales increased. The next year this product became an official part of the McDonald's menu and soon thereafter was named the Filet o' Fish. This was the first expansion beyond burgers, french fries, and beverages. Franchisee Jim Delligatti of Pittsburgh saw that he was losing some trade to a nearby competitor who offered an oversized hamburger. Accordingly, he put two all-beef patties, special sauce, lettuce, cheese, pickles, and onions on a sesame seed bun. The company adopted it in 1968, called it the Big Mac, and it became the best-selling item in the product line.

Something more radical was developed in 1972 by franchisee Herbert Peterson in Santa Barbara, California, who saw that his restaurants might be more profitable if they opened at 7 A.M. rather than 10 A.M. Peterson had always enjoyed eggs Benedict and thought that the masses would like something similar if he could adapt it to the company's price structure and operating system. After six months of experimentation he introduced the Fast-Break Breakfast, a sandwich of Canadian Bacon, cheese, and an egg on an English muffin. Along with earlier openings, this product was introduced in most McDonald's restaurants in the United States in 1976 under the name Egg McMuffin. This product added over 10 percent to sales the first year. Soon thereafter the breakfast menu in the chain was expanded by adding fruit juices, Danish pastries, English muffins, a platter of sausage and hot cakes, and a platter of sausage, scrambled eggs, and hash-brown potatoes. Most units of the chain adopted the 7 A.M. opening except on Sundays, when the opening was usually set at 8 A.M.

The company developed the Quarter Pounder in 1972 to replace the double hamburger. This new product caused McDonald's great public relations difficulties, for an official investigation by the U.S. Department of Agriculture showed that in no instance did the meat used exceed three ounces in weight. A belated advertising campaign by McDonald's emphasized the point that the patty used in the Quarter Pounder weighed a quarter of a pound *before* cooking.

In 1975 the company successfully added McDonaldland cookies, a bland vanilla-flavored product made of flour, sugar, shortening, corn syrup, salt, leavening, lecithin, and artificial flavoring in the shape of fantasy characters from company advertising and sales promotion. It was sold in two-ounce (56 grams) portions packed in pasteboard boxes. Very much like the traditional "animal crackers," these were a hit, especially with children. The cookies were manufactured by the Keebler Company, already well known to children through its famous elves. Hot cherry and apple pies cooked in an individual serving size followed in all locations. Ice cream sundaes were introduced in many locations as a test market. Hot tea was added in most locations in 1977. In 1980 a chopped beefsteak sandwich went into extensive test marketing.

Exhaustive product development research on chicken began in 1971. The cooking of chicken, even merely frying it, offered many options to be evaluated carefully. For example, Kentucky Fried Chicken restaurants in the United States offered a choice of soft or extremely crispy chicken. In 1980 two major chicken products entered test markets. One was the McChicken sandwich, composed of a boneless chicken patty, shredded lettuce, and a dressing that resembled mayonnaise, all on a bun. The other was Chicken McNuggets, bite-size lumps of boneless chicken served with a choice of three sauces or dips. Short-term reception of these items was good enough that they stood a fair chance of being added to the permanent product line, but they would remain in test market for quite a long time.

In markets abroad, McDonald's made a few additions to the standard menu. For example, it added soup in Japan, chicken croquettes and apple sauce in Holland, fried chicken in Australia, wine in France, and beer in West Germany. Market research conducted by various fast-food companies indicated that foreign customers wanted the standard American menus with only a few additions. McDonald's had much more business abroad than any other American restaurant company.

McDonald's had been conservative and cautious in accepting new product ideas. The company used a long lead time and finished off the development process with extensive test marketing. Nevertheless, it had had some failures; the roast beef sandwich, the pineapple burger, and the Tripple Ripple ice cream cone. McDonald's widely test marketed fried

onion cubes in 1979 but decided against them. In the fast-food restaurant industry as a whole, a clear majority of the new products introduced had failed.

The company was anxious to ensure that the cooking process be systematic so as to keep its products consistent. Cybernetic deep fryers continuously adjusted to the moisture in potatoes so that all servings would have the same degree of brownness, and lights on the grills alerted the attendant to flip the patties. Size of potatoes was controlled carefully in purchasing contracts. Because potatoes could not be controlled in advance, special scoops were designed to apportion the cooked potatoes correctly.

Besides preparing the foods according to company policy, McDonald's was vitally interested that the food also be in good condition when served. Therefore, the chain had a policy of throwing away unserved burger patties after 10 minutes, french fries after 7 minutes, and coffee after 30 minutes. Such losses were minimized through careful planning and control, of course. Norms for such losses were built into the budgeting process and franchisees and managers were fully advised about these expectations. The paper and Styrofoam packages around the food and beverages had evoked many complaints from ecologists but served to insulate the products better than those of competitors.

Major competitors of McDonald's were giving increasing attention to their new product development and improvement of their present product lines. Whereas McDonald's was an independent organization, three competitors had been purchased by major conglomerates. Thus, each of these restaurant competitors, although much smaller than McDonald's, now had access to their parent's considerable capital, product development laboratories and expertise, and a tradition of commitment to new-product development. General Foods now owned Burger Chef, Heublein (a large distiller and importer) owned Kentucky Fried Chicken, and Pillsbury owned Burger King. Moreover, through aggressive advertising and on-premises sales promotion, Pillsbury was well on its way toward making the King character as well known and accepted as Ronald McDonald.

Besides the matters already mentioned, there was concern about the image of employment at McDonald's, demographic trends, the taste of the company's food, and criticism of the nutritional characteristics of the company's product line. The first was not as great a problem as the others but was significant. Company employee rolls were dominated by about 165,000 teenagers in the United States. Despite the facts that it was furnishing jobs to an age group that exhibited a relatively high rate of unemployment and that it got along well with nearly all of its employees, McDonald's was attacked by social critics and officials of various labor unions for paying hourly wages that were below average for the nation, although legal. Employee turnover was high compared to business at large but not any higher than the rest of the fast-food industry. The company might have objectively answered these attacks, but could not, for public relations reasons, by pointing out that the employees were, in the words of Theodore Levitt, "totally unskilled machine tenders." This marketing professor and consultant added that "The only choice available to the attendant is to operate it exactly as the designers intended."[1]

Demographic trends were extremely unsettling. It was clear that the company's trade was primarily with children, teenagers, and adults under age 35. Customers 35 years of age or over contributed only about 23 percent of sales, although they constituted about 42 percent of the U.S. population. Children age 15 or under accounted for 20 percent of sales, whereas persons age 16 to 34 accounted for 57 percent. This fact was acceptable as an application of the principle of aiming at a target market. However, the United States birthrate had declined dramatically and the population

was aging. Wendy's, a competitive hamburger chain founded in Ohio in 1969 and not affiliated with any parent or conglomerate, was aiming at the over 25 market and was faring quite well. It featured a stylish decor and its customers were not expected to clear off their tables.

After Ray Kroc went into semiretirement and ownership of McDonald's corporate stock became slightly more diffused, the new board chairman, 46-year-old Fred L. Turner, who had started out as a McDonald's cook, encouraged some physical changes. There were several objectives, one of which was to attract more middle-aged and older adults. McDonald's worked quickly to moderate the garish exterior look of the restaurants, which were often in multi-colored candy stripes. Other factors to be dealt with were the feelings of upper middle-class people who found McDonald's visually jarring at best and unacceptably offensive at worst, occasional ethnic feelings, and occasional zoning regulations. A neat brown-brick exterior of no particular architectural style was the usual result. Moreover, many golden arches signs were greatly reduced in size and some were merely attached to one wall of the building. In addition, the policy that the building had to be freestanding was dropped. Drive-through service bays were added in about 1,000 units in warmer regions of the United States, a throwback to the early years of some competitors. New uniforms for employees were designed and made available in a variety of colors to suit the decor. A few California and Maryland units of the chain experimented with having a hostess, attired at night in an attractive long gown, and substituting candlelight for the usual lighting. In a second cycle of architectural changes, McDonald's authorized 15 new exterior and interior designs: English Tudor, Country French, New England, Western, Spanish, Old English, Dutch Colonial, Tahitian, Caribbean, French Quarter, Alpine, Midwesterner, Williamsburg, Cambridge, and Gaslight.

Although many people were virtually oblivious to the taste of the food they were eating and many were unable or unwilling to give the time it took to savor the taste, there was a modest trend toward increasing American interest in cooking. Gourmet authors and food commentators drew large audiences in person and through the media. Craig Claiborne and Julia Child both found McDonald's french fries good, and James Beard concluded "The whole thing is aimed at the six-year-old palate." Gael Greene noted that the cheese tasted like glue and added "I love the malts—thick, sweet and ice cold. They're better than if they were real."[2]

Social criticism of the nutritional characteristics of food served by McDonald's and other fast-food organizations had been growing for several years.[3] These products were termed "junk food." McDonald's was frequently the focus of criticism, not because it was the worst but because it was the largest. Among the most vocal were black critics who charged that McDonald's expansion into the inner city enticed the poor with low-nutrition food. As a matter of fact, McDonald's had a month-long advertising campaign in the early 1970s on the theme that each person should eat other foods in addition to what the company offered. A detailed research project done by Consumers Union and published in its *Consumer Reports* showed that Big Macs contained more salt per ounce than the burgers served by McDonald's major competitors, but that McDonald's shakes and french fries contained less salt per ounce than the average for the fast-food industry.[4] Nearly all of the company's product line was unquestionably high in fats, sugar, salt, and calories. The real nutritional problem was not just McDonald's food but the severely unbalanced diet of a substantial fraction of the United States population, which included many millions of McDonald's regular customers.

Notes

1. "The Burger That Conquered the Country," *Time*, September 17, 1973, p. 85.

2. Ibid. See also "Love in the Kitchen: The Outcome? Cuisine, Now Chow," *Time*, December 19, 1977, pp. 54–61.

3. The social criticism of McDonald's early years and up to 1976 can be found in the highly opinionated book by Max Boas and Steve Chain, *Big Mac: The Unauthorized Story of McDonald's* (New York: E. P. Dutton, 1976).

4. "Fast Food Chains," *Consumer Reports*, September 1979, pp. 508–13.

SECTION 4

Marketing Program Design

Promotion Decisions Case Studies

Massachusetts State Lottery (A)
Dharmendra T. Verna and Frederick Wiseman

Plas-Tech Corporation (B)
Charles H. Patti

*T*he marketing program for a brand is the articulation of the company's marketing strategy. The essential difference between program and strategy lies in specificity of expression. That is, while the marketing strategy identifies the company's basic philosophies, objectives, and important differential advantages, the marketing program stipulates the precise tactics that have been developed for any one brand. Before moving to specifics, it will be helpful to review some of the options that eventuate from marketing strategy development.

The application of market segmentation yields a number of strategic alternatives ranging from mass marketing to niching. In the first case, the company believes that a sizable chunk of the market is essentially homogeneous and that competitive advantages accrue to economies of scale via mass production, distribution, promotion, and so forth. Here large companies compete for large market shares. On the other end of the continuum are niching companies, those who have targeted their efforts to small segments of the total market; they exist through specialization geared to each target market's characteristics. In these cases, companies are protected by the uniqueness of the segment's marketing requirements and enjoy some insulation because of the segment's small size, which deters larger companies seeking volume sales. Along the midrange of the continuum are companies whose product lines are differentiated to appeal to various segments, but without the uniqueness of the nichers. These companies survive by spreading their presence across several segments, gaining reasonable market shares, and living with full knowledge that competition may injure them in one or more, but probably not *all,* market segments.

209

Regardless of the strategic thrust a company adopts, the result of its marketing program is best described by the concept of positioning. The term *positioning* originates from target-market customers' mental map or perceived image of a brand compared to their map or image of its salient competitors. Most contemporary marketers agree that customers' perceptions of brands determine their preferences and choices; consequently, it is important that the marketing program is orchestrated to have significant beneficial impact on the brand image. There are vivid examples of companies who have managed their images and attained strong positions as a result; for instance, Calvin Klein in the clothes industry, IBM in the computer industry, MTV in the video music arena, Federal Express in the overnight mail industry, or even Disney World in the amusement industry.

In all of these cases, the watchword for marketing program design is *integration*. In some important way the net effect of all marketing program components must be synergistic. In the minds of prospective customers and relative to competition, the marketing program components of product design, pricing, distribution system, and promotion must be complimentary. If they are, a uniquely psychological phenomenon takes place—a brand image—which is used to judge one company's brand against that of others. Admittedly, this process is not completely understood by marketers, but there is general agreement that it operates in the minds of prospective buyers. A useful way to envision synergy is to think about implicit promises represented by marketing program components. For instance, a high relative price implies higher quality and better performance; the use of discount chain outlets signifies mass appeal and average quality; and full-color advertisements in prestigious magazines promise special benefits if that brand is used. Unfortunately, the interactions are usually far more subtle than these examples demonstrate, so the marketing manager must temper intuition with marketing research findings to design a marketing program that has optimal positioning consequences.

About the Readings

The first conceptual article is an in-depth discussion of positioning. Six different positioning methods are described; then a step-by-step process used to position a company's product is offered. Pricing, an often neglected strategic element of the marketing program, is also discussed. Product, advertising, and even distribution-channel examples of positioning abound. In the second conceptual reading, however, the author shows how consumer behavior analysis can be used to price based on the product's value to the customer rather than through the traditional cost-plus-a-margin approach.

The first of our company articles is about advertising campaigns. The advertising theme communicates a brand's position to prospective buyers. In this article, 1982's 25 top advertising campaigns are analyzed from the perspective of why they have been successful in creating lasting impressions and strong brand awareness. After this article, there is a reading on how Coca-Cola's famous "mistake," while seemingly a catastrophe, really must be considered against the many marketing programs orchestrated for the company's several brands. Notice how the intense rivalry between Pepsi-Cola and Coca-Cola drives Coke's marketing programs. The article also illustrates the vital role played by the chief executive officer's personality in shaping both the marketing program's design and its forcefulness.

The final company article explains how the price club concept is revolutionizing the discount-price, high-volume retail business. The article describes Price Club (or Price Co.) on the verge of rapid national expansion to retain its advantage over competitors who are venturing into markets previously dominated by it. While reading this article, notice how Price Club, though somewhat reluctant to take this giant step, is compelled by competitive circumstances and its lack of a strong national image ∎

═══════════════════ *Conceptual Readings* ═══════════════════

Positioning Your Product
David A. Aaker and J. Gary Shansby

How should a new brand be positioned? Can a problem brand be revived by a repositioning strategy? Most marketing managers have addressed these and other positioning questions; however, "positioning" means different things to different people. To some, it means the segmentation decision. To others it is an image question. To still others it means selecting which product features to emphasize. Few managers consider all of these alternatives. Further, the positioning decision is often made ad hoc, and is based upon flashes of insight, even though systematic, research-based approaches to the positioning decision are now available. An understanding of these approaches should lead to more sophisticated analysis in which positioning alternatives are more fully identified and evaluated.

A product or organization has many associations which combine to form a total impression. The positioning decision often means selecting those associations which are to be built upon and emphasized and those associations which are to be removed or deemphasized. The term *position* differs from the older term *image* in that it implies a frame of reference, the reference point usually being the competition. Thus, when the Bank of California positions itself as being small and friendly, it is explicitly, or perhaps implicitly, positioning itself with respect to Bank of America.

The positioning decision is often the crucial strategic decision for a company or brand because the position can be central to customers' perception and choice decisions. Further, since all elements of the marketing program can potentially affect the position, it is usually necessary to use a positioning strategy as a fo-

cus for the development of the marketing program. A clear positioning strategy can ensure that the elements of the marketing program are consistent and supportive.

What alternative positioning strategies are available? How can positioning strategies be identified and selected? Each of these questions will be addressed in turn.

Positioning Strategies

A first step in understanding the scope of positioning alternatives is to consider some of the ways that a positioning strategy can be conceived and implemented. In the following, six approaches to positioning strategy will be illustrated and discussed: positioning by (1) attribute, (2) price quality, (3) use or applications, (4) product user, (5) the product class, and (6) the competitor.

Positioning by Attribute

Probably the most frequently used positioning strategy is associating a product with an attribute, a product feature, or customer benefit. Consider imported automobiles. Datsun and Toyota have emphasized economy and reliability. Volkswagen has used a "value for the money" association. Volvo has stressed durability, showing commercials of "crash tests" and citing statistics on the long average life of their cars. Fiat, in contrast, has made a distinct effort to position itself as a European car with "European craftsmanship." BMW has emphasized handling and engineering efficiency, using the tag line, "the ultimate driving machine" and showing BMWs demonstrating their performance capabilities at a racetrack.

A new product can upon occasion be positioned with respect to an attribute that competitors have ignored. Paper towels had emphasized absorbency until Viva stressed durability, using demonstrations supporting the claim that Viva "keeps on working."

Sometimes a product will attempt to position itself along two or more attributes simultaneously. In the toothpaste market, Crest became a dominant brand by positioning itself as a cavity fighter, a position supported by a medical group endorsement. However, Aim achieved a 10 percent market share by positioning along two attributes, good taste and cavity prevention. More recently, Aqua-fresh has been introduced by Beecham as a gel paste that offers both cavity-fighting and breath-freshening benefits.

It is always tempting to try to position along several attributes. However, positioning strategies that involve too many attributes can be most difficult to implement. The result can often be a fuzzy, confused image.

Positioning by Price/Quality

The price/quality attribute dimension is so useful and pervasive that it is appropriate to consider it separately. In many product categories, some brands offer more in terms of service, features, or performance and a higher price serves to signal this higher quality to the customer. Conversely, other brands emphasize price and value.

In general merchandise stores, for example, the department stores are at the top end of the price/quality scale. Neiman-Marcus, Bloomingdale's, and Saks Fifth Avenue are near the top, followed by Macy's, Robinson's, Bullock's, Rich's, Filene's, Dayton's, Hud-

son's, and so on. Stores such as Sears, Montgomery Ward, and J. C. Penney are positioned below the department stores but above the discount stores like K-Mart. Sears' efforts to create a more upbeat fashion image was thought to have hurt their "value" position and caused some share declines.[1] Sears' recent five-year plan details a firm return to a positioning as a family, middle-class store offering top value. Sears is just one company that has faced the very tricky positioning task of retaining the image of low price and upgrading their quality image. There is always the risk that the quality message will blunt the basic "low-price," "value" position.

Positioning with Respect to Use or Application

Another positioning strategy is associating the product with a use or application. Campbell's Soup for many years was positioned for use at lunch time and advertised extensively over noontime radio. The telephone company more recently has associated long distance calling with communicating with loved ones in their "reach out and touch someone" campaign. Industrial products often rely upon application associations.

Products can, of course, have multiple positioning strategies, although increasing the number involves obvious difficulties and risks. Often a positioning-by-use strategy represents a second or third position designed to expand the market. Thus, Gatorade, introduced as a summer beverage for athletes who need to replace body fluids, has attempted to develop a winter positioning strategy as the beverage to drink when the doctor recommends drinking plenty of fluids. Similarly, Quaker Oats has attempted to position a breakfast food product as a natural whole-grain ingredient for recipes. Arm & Hammer baking soda has successfully positioned their product as an odor-destroying agent in refrigerators.

Positioning by the Product User

Another positioning approach is associating a product with a user or a class of users. Thus, many cosmetic companies have used a model or personality, such as Brut's Joe Namath, to position their product. Revlon's Charlie cosmetic line has been positioned by associating it with a specific lifestyle profile. Johnson & Johnson saw market share move from 3 percent to 14 percent when they repositioned their shampoo from a product used for babies to one used by people who wash their hair frequently and therefore need a mild shampoo.

In 1970, Miller High Life was the "champagne of bottled beers," was purchased by the upper class, and had an image of being a woman's beer. Phillip Morris repositioned it as a beer for the heavy beer-drinking, blue-collar working man. Miller's Lite beer, introduced in 1975, used convincing beer-drinking personalities to position itself as a beer for the heavy beer drinker who dislikes that filled-up feeling. In contrast, earlier efforts to introduce low-calorie beers positioned with respect to the low-calorie attribute were dismal failures. One even claimed its beer had fewer calories than skim milk, and another featured a trim personality. Miller's positioning strategies are in part why its market share has grown from 3.4 percent in 1970 to 24.5 percent in 1979.[2]

Positioning with Respect to a Product Class

Some critical positioning decisions involve product-class associations. For example, Maxim freeze-dried coffee needed to position itself with respect to regular and instant coffee. Some margarines position themselves with respect to butter. Dried milk makers came out with instant breakfast positioned as a breakfast substitute and a virtually identical product positioned as a dietary meal substitute. The hand soap "Caress" by Lever Brothers positioned itself as a bath oil product rather than a soap.

The soft drink 7-Up was for a long time positioned as a beverage with a "fresh clean taste" that was "thirst quenching." However, research discovered that most people regarded 7-Up as a mix rather than a soft drink. The successful "uncola" campaign was then developed to position 7-Up as a soft drink, with a better taste than the "colas."

Positioning with Respect to a Competitor

In most positioning strategies, an explicit or implicit frame of reference is the competition. There are two reasons for making the reference competitor(s) the dominant aspect of the positioning strategy. First, a well-established competitor's image can be exploited to help communicate another image referenced to it. In giving directions to an address, for example, it's easier to say, it is next to the Bank of America building than it is to detail streets, distances, and turns. Second, sometimes it's not important how good customers think you are; it is just important that they believe you are better (or as good as) a given competitor.

Perhaps the most famous positioning strategy of this type was the Avis "We're number two, so we try harder" campaign. The strategy was to position Avis with Hertz as a major car-rental agency and away from National, which at the time was a close third to Avis.

Positioning explicitly with respect to a competitor can be an excellent way to create a position with respect to an attribute, especially the price/quality attribute pair. Thus, products difficult to evaluate, like liquor products, will often be compared with an established competitor to help the positioning task.

For example, Sabroso, a coffee liqueur, positioned itself with the established brand, Kahlua, with respect to quality and also with respect to the type of liqueur.

Positioning with respect to a competitor can be aided by comparative advertising, advertising in which a competitor is explicitly named and compared on one or more attributes. Pontiac has used this approach to position some of their cars as being comparable in gas mileage and price to leading import cars. By comparing Pontiac to a competitor that has a well-defined economy image, like a Volkswagen Rabbit, and using factual information such as EPA gas ratings, the communication task becomes easier.

On Determining the Positioning Strategy

What should be our positioning strategy? The identification and selection of a positioning strategy can draw upon a set of concepts and procedures that have been developed and refined over the last few years. The process of developing a positioning strategy involves six steps.

1. Identify the competitors.
2. Determine how the competitors are perceived and evaluated.
3. Determine the competitors' positions.
4. Analyze the customers.
5. Select the position.
6. Monitor the position.

In each of these steps one can employ marketing research techniques to provide needed information. Sometimes the marketing research approach provides a conceptualization that can be helpful even if the research is not conducted. Each of these steps will be discussed in turn.

Identify the Competitors

This first step is not as simple as it might seem. Tab might define its competitors in a number of ways, including:

a. Other diet cola drinks.
b. All cola drinks.
c. All soft drinks.
d. Nonalcoholic beverages.
e. All beverages.

A Triumph convertible might define its market in several ways:

a. Two-passenger, low-priced, imported, sports-car convertibles.
b. Two-passenger, low-priced, imported sports cars.
c. Two-passenger, low- or medium-priced, imported sports cars.
d. Low- or medium-priced sports cars.
e. Low- or medium-priced imported cars.

In most cases, there will be a primary group of competitors and one or more secondary competitors. Thus, Tab will compete primarily with other diet colas, but other colas and all soft drinks could be important as secondary competitors.

A knowledge of various ways to identify such groupings will be of conceptual as well as practical value. One approach is to determine from product buyers which brands they considered. For example, a sample of Triumph convertible buyers could be asked what other cars they considered and perhaps what other showrooms they actually visited. A Tab buyer could be asked what brand he would have purchased had Tab been out of stock. The resulting analysis will identify the primary and secondary groups of competitive products. Instead of customers, retailers or others knowledgeable about customers could provide the information.

Another approach is the development of associations of products with use situations.[3] Twenty or so respondents might be asked to recall the use contexts for Tab. For each use context, such as an afternoon snack, respondents are then asked to identify all appropriate beverages. For each beverage so identified respondents are then asked to identify appropriate use contexts. This process would continue until a large list of use contexts and beverages resulted. Another respondent group would then be asked to make judgments as to how appropriate each beverage would be for each use situation. Groups of beverages could then be clustered based upon their similarity of appropriate use situations. If Tab was regarded as appropriate with snacks, then it would compete primarily with other beverages regarded as appropriate for snack occasions. The same approach would work with an industrial product such as computers, which might be used in several rather distinct applications.

The concepts of alternatives from which customers choose and appropriateness to a use context can provide a basis for identifying competitors even when market research is not employed. A management team or a group of experts, such as retailers, could employ one or both of these conceptual bases to identify competitive groupings.

Determine How the Competitors are Perceived and Evaluated

The challenge is to identify those product associations used by buyers as they perceive and evaluate competitors. The product associations will include product attributes, product-user groups, and use contexts. Even simple objects such as beer can evoke a host of physical attributes like container, aftertaste, and price, and relevant associations like "appropriate for use while dining at a good restaurant" or "used by working men." The task is to identify a list of product associ-

ations, to remove redundancies from the list, and then to select those that are most useful and relevant in describing brand images.

One research-based approach to product-association list generation is to ask respondents to identify the two most similar brands from a set of three competing brands and to describe why those two brands are similar and different from the third. As a variant, respondents could be asked which of two brands is preferred and why. The result will be a rather long list of product associations, perhaps over a hundred. The next step is to remove redundancy from the list using logic and judgment or factor analysis. The final step is to identify the most relevant product associations by determining which is correlated highest with overall brand attitudes or by asking respondents to indicate which are the most important to them.

Determine the Competitors' Positions

The next step is to determine how competitors (including our own entry) are positioned with respect to the relevant product associations and with respect to each other. Although such judgments can be made subjectively, research-based approaches are available. Such research is termed multidimensional scaling because its goal is to scale objects on several dimensions (or product associations). Multidimensional scaling can be based upon either product associations data or similarities data.

Product-Association-Based Multidimensional Scaling. The most direct approach is simply to ask a sample of the target segment to scale the various objects on the product-association dimensions. For example, the respondent could be asked to express his or her agreement or disagreement on a seven-point scale with statements regarding the Chevette: "With respect to its class I would consider the Chevette to be sporty, roomy, economical, good handling."

Alternatively, perceptions of a brand's users or use contexts could be obtained: "I would expect the typical Chevette owner to be older, wealthy, independent, intelligent." "The Chevette is most appropriate for short neighborhood trips, commuting, cross-country sightseeing."

In generating such measures there are several potential problems and considerations (in addition to generating a relevant product-association list) of which one should be aware:

1. The validity of the task. Can a respondent actually position cars on a "sporty" dimension? There could be several problems. One, a possible unfamiliarity with one or more of the brands, can be handled by asking the respondent to evaluate only familiar brands. Another is the respondent's ability to understand operationally what "sporty" means or how to evaluate a brand on this dimension.

2. Differences among respondents. Subgroups within the population could hold very different perceptions with respect to one or more of the objects. Such diffused images can have important strategic implications. The task of sharpening a diffused image is much different from the task of changing a very tight, established one.

3. Are the differences between objects significant and meaningful? If the differences are not statistically significant, then the sample size may be too small to make any managerial judgments. At the same time, a small difference of no practical consequence may be statistically significant if the sample size is large enough.

4. Which product associations are not only important but also serve to distinguish objects? Thus, airline safety may be an important attribute, but all airlines may be perceived to be equally safe.

Similarities-Based Multidimensional Scaling. Product-association approaches have several conceptual disadvantages. A complete, valid, and relevant product association list is not easy to generate. Further, an object may be perceived or evaluated as a whole that is not really decomposable in terms of product associations. These disadvantages lead us to the use of nonattribute data—namely, similarity data.

Similarity measures simply reflect the perceived similarity of two objects. For example, respondents may be asked to rate the degree of similarity of assorted object pairs without a product-association list which implicitly suggests criteria to be included or excluded. The result, when averaged over all respondents, is a similarity rating for each object pair. A multidimensional scaling program then attempts to locate objects in a two-, three- (or more if necessary) dimensional space termed a perceptual map. The program attempts to construct the perceptual map such that the two objects with the highest similarity are separated by the shortest distance, the object pair with the second highest similarity are separated by the second shortest distance, and so on. A disadvantage of the similarity-based approach is that the interpretation of the dimensions does not have the product associations as a guide.

Analyzing the Customers

A basic understanding of the customer and how the market is segmented will help in selecting a positioning strategy. How is the market segmented? What role does the product class play in the customer's lifestyle? What really motivates the customer? What habits and behavior patterns are relevant?

The segmentation question is, of course, critical. One of the most useful segmentation approaches is benefit segmentation, which focuses upon the benefits or, more generally, the product associations that a segment believes to be important. The identity of important product associations can be done directly by asking customers to rate product associations as to their importance or by asking them to make trade-off judgments between product associations[4] or by asking them to conceptualize and profile "ideal brands." An ideal brand would be a combination of all the customer's preferred product associations. Customers are then grouped into segments defined by product associations considered important by customers. Thus, for toothpaste there could be a decay preventative segment, a fresh breath segment, a price segment, and so on. The segment's relative size and commitment to the product association will be of interest.

It is often useful to go beyond product association lists to get a deeper understanding of consumer perceptions. A good illustration is the development of positioning objectives for Betty Crocker by the Needham, Harper & Steers advertising agency.[5] They conducted research involving more than 3,000 women, and found that Betty Crocker was viewed as a company that is (1) honest and dependable, (2) friendly and concerned about consumers, (3) a specialist in baked goods; but (1) out of date, old, and traditional; a manufacturer of "old standby" products, (2) not particularly contemporary or innovative. The conclusion was that the Betty Crocker image needed to be strengthened and to become more modern and innovative and less old and stodgy.

To improve the Betty Crocker image, it was felt that an understanding was needed of the needs and lifestyle of today's women and how these relate to desserts. Thus, the research study was directed to basic questions about desserts. Why are they served? Who serves them? The answers were illuminating. Dessert users tend to be busy active mothers who are devoted to their families. The primary reasons for serving dessert tend to be psychological and revolve around the family: (1) dessert is a way to show others you care; (2) dessert preparation is viewed as an important duty of a good wife and mother; (3) desserts

are associated with and help to create happy family moments.

Clearly, family bonds, love, and good times are associated with desserts. As a result, the Betty Crocker positioning objective was to associate Betty Crocker uniquely with the positive aspects of today's families and their feelings about dessert. Contemporary, emotionally involving advertising was used to associate Betty Crocker with desserts that contribute to happy family moments.

Making the Positioning Decision

The four steps or exercises just described should be conducted prior to making the actual positioning decision. The exercises can be done subjectively by the involved managers if necessary, although marketing research, if feasible and justifiable, will be more definitive. However, even with that background, it is still not possible to generate a cookbook solution to the positioning questions. However, some guidelines or checkpoints can be offered.

Positioning Usually Implies a Segmentation Commitment. Positioning usually means that an overt decision is being made to concentrate only on certain segments. Such an approach requires commitment and discipline because it's not easy to turn your back on potential buyers. Yet, the effect of generating a distinct, meaningful position is to focus on the target segments and not be constrained by the reaction of other segments.

Sometimes the creation of a "diffuse image," an image that will mean different things to different people, is a way to attract a variety of diverse segments. Such an approach is risky and difficult to implement and usually would be used only by a large brand. The implementation could involve projecting a range of advantages while avoiding being identified with any one. Alternatively, there could be a conscious effort to avoid associations which create positions. Pictures of bottles of Coca-Cola with the words "It's the real thing" superimposed on them, or Budweiser's claim that "Bud is the king of beers," illustrate such a strategy.

An Economic Analysis Should Guide the Decision. The success of any positioning strategy basically depends upon two factors: the potential market size and the penetration probability. Unless both of these factors are favorable, success will be unlikely. One implication of this simple structure is that a positioning strategy should attract a sizable segment. If customers are to be attracted from other brands, those brands should have a worthwhile market share to begin with. If new buyers are to be attracted to the product class, a reasonable assessment should be made of the potential size of that growth area. The penetration probability indicates that there needs to be a competitive weakness to attack or a competitive advantage to exploit to generate a reasonable market penetration probability. Further, the highest payoff will often come from retaining existing customers, so this alternative should also be considered.

If the Advertising is Working, Stick with It. An advertiser will often get tired of a positioning strategy and the advertising used to implement it and will consider making a change. However, the personality or image of a brand, like that of a person, evolves over many years, and the value of consistency through time cannot be overestimated. Some of the very successful, big-budget campaigns have run for 10, 20, or even 30 years.

Don't Try to Be Something You Are Not. It is tempting but naive—and usually fatal—to decide on a positioning strategy that exploits a market need or opportunity but assumes that your product is something it is not. Before positioning a product, it is important to conduct blind taste tests or in-home or in-office use tests to make sure that the product can deliver what it promises and that is compatible with a proposed image.

Consider Hamburger Helper, successfully introduced in 1970 as an add-to-meat product that would generate a good-tasting, economical, skillet dinner.[6] In the mid-1970s, sales suffered when homemakers switched to more exotic, expensive foods. An effort to react by repositioning Hamburger Helper as a base for casseroles failed because the product, at least in the consumers' mind, could not deliver. Consumers perceived it as an economical, reliable, convenience food and further felt that they did not need help in making casseroles. In a personality test, where women were asked to describe the product as if it were a person, the most prevalent characteristic ascribed to the product was "helpful." The result was a revised campaign to position the product as being "helpful."

Monitoring the Position

A positioning objective, like any marketing objective, should be measurable. To evaluate the positioning and to generate diagnostic information about future positioning strategies, it is necessary to monitor the position over time. A variety of techniques can be employed to make this measurement. Hamburger Helper used a "personality test," for example. However, usually one of the more structured techniques of multidimensional scaling is applied.

A variety of positioning strategies is available to the advertiser. An object can be positioned: (1) by attributes—e.g., Crest is a cavity fighter; (2) by price/quality—e.g., Sears is a "value" store; (3) by competitor—e.g., Avis positions itself with Hertz; (4) by application—e.g., Gatorade is for flu attacks; (5) by product user—e.g., Miller is for the blue-collar, heavy beer drinker; (6) by product class—e.g.,—Carnation Instant Breakfast is a breakfast food.

The selection of a positioning strategy involves identifying competitors, relevant attributes, competitor positions, and market segments. Research-based approaches can help in each of these steps by providing conceptualization even if the subjective judgments of managers are used to provide the actual input information to the positioning decision.

Notes

1. "Sears' New 5-year Plan: To Serve Middle America," *Advertising Age*, December 4, 1978.

2. "A–B, Miller Brews Continue to Barrel Ahead," *Advertising Age*, August 4, 1980, p. 4.

3. George S. Day, Alan D. Shocker, and Rajendra K. Srivasta, "Customer-Oriented Approaches to Identify Product Markets," *Journal of Marketing*, Fall 1979, pp. 8–19.

4. Paul E. Green and Yoram Wind, "New Ways to Measure Consumers' Judgments," *Harvard Business Review*, July–August 1975, pp. 107–15.

5. Keth Reinhard, "How We Make Advertising" (presented to the Federal Trade Commission, May 11, 1979), pp. 22–25.

6. Reinhard, "Advertising," p. 29.

Pricing as Creative Marketing
Thomas Nagle

An understanding of buyers increasingly determines what products firms offer, their promotion, and their methods of distribution. This focus, the essence of modern marketing, now widely influences all elements of marketing strategy—except for one. Prices, in many firms otherwise devoted to progressive marketing, are still set not with an eye to the buyer, but with an eye to the seller's production costs, cash flow requirements, or target rate of return.

Why have marketing principles had such little influence in pricing decisions? Probably because, even within the family of marketing, pricing is a somewhat neglected child. In one survey of marketing practitioners, only half rated pricing an important policy decision.[1] In academe, pricing remains the least frequently taught and researched aspect of the marketing mix. Consequently, one is easily left with the impression that the principles of marketing are somehow less relevant to pricing.

In recent years, marketers have begun to dispel that mistaken impression with prescriptions for pricing based on the measurement or calculation of consumer value.[2] These buyer-based pricing procedures are certainly more in the spirit of marketing than the cost-based procedures they are meant to replace. They are, however, but a first step toward the reconciliation of pricing with other aspects of marketing. Pricing still remains a technical problem to be solved by applying a rule or procedure, rather than a creative challenge to be met with the marketer's insight into buyers' motivations.

Yet marketing's detailed attention to buyers—not just the "value" each places on a product but also who they are, why they buy, and how they make their purchase decisions—is no less important for effective pricing than for efficacy in any other aspect of marketing. There are few markets where all buyers place the same value on a product any more than they all want the same product characteristics, appreciate the same promotion, or favor the same distribution channels. The essence of effective marketing is the creative development of segmentation strategies that recognize such buyer diversity. The essence of effective pricing is no different.

Effective pricing can be achieved with neither a rule of thumb nor a mathematical formula. It is, like advertising, a creative process. It requires both insight to identify buyer segments and imagination to design pricing strategies that distinguish among them. Yet creativity comes more naturally when we understand what we are trying to accomplish, and how others have accomplished those goals in similar situations. The aim of this article is to improve our understanding of buyer oriented pricing so that we can better focus our creative efforts.

Understanding Buyers' Motivation

Fortunately, not all companies treat pricing as an afterthought, unrelated to buyers' needs and motivations. We can learn much about pricing from their creative efforts. Ford Motor Company's Mustang automobile provides one example of pricing guided by an awareness of buyer diversity. The Mustang was not designed to be a good sports car, with all the preconceptions of what a sports car "should" be, and then priced to cover costs and a target return. Rather, Ford discovered through extensive study that a market segment existed which valued "sportiness" in a car, but which was unwilling to pay the price for a "sports car." The task Ford successfully completed was to design a car sufficiently sporty to satisfy this segment, but without those elements of a sports car which would drive its costs out of reach.

Ford's strategy was buyer oriented. With buyer oriented pricing, the firm anticipates a price, even before a product's development, by simply evaluating proposed product benefits. Such prices are only tentative and, after each step in the development process, should be reevaluated based on consumer interviews, surveys, and changes in the market. Nevertheless, these tentative prices are an important guide to product development since they can mark potential products as candidates for rejection or redesign. By rec-

ognizing early those products for which tentative prices are too low relative to additional development and production costs, a firm can manage its product development more profitably.

Yet the greatest advantage of buyer oriented pricing is not early determination of the *level* of prices buyers will pay. Much fine tuning is always possible and generally desirable once products are already produced. The most important advantage of buyer oriented pricing is the early detection of *differences* in the way buyers value the same product benefits. That can be important not only for a firm's short-run profitability, but also for its long-run survival.

Many airlines, and certainly many air routes, could not survive if they treated all segments of the air transportation market alike. Were every traveler required to purchase first-class service at a first-class price, airlines would soon go broke for lack of passengers. But were every traveler charged a discount fare, airlines would soon go broke for lack of sufficient revenue per passenger. The planes keep flying because someone had the insight to recognize differences among buyers—in the benefits important to them and in the value they place on those benefits—enabling airlines to offer slightly differentiated products at significantly different prices.

Distinguishing Segments for Pricing

The challenge of buyer oriented pricing is not just to identify different consumer segments. The next step is to design a marketing strategy that effectively distinguishes them for pricing. Airlines successfully distinguish segments simply by requiring a long lead time to reserve a low-price fare. Vacationers are relatively price sensitive and easily able to anticipate their demand for air travel. Business travelers are much less price sensitive but require flexibility. By offering lower fares with inflexible scheduling, airlines can attract enough price-sensitive travelers to support the frequent flights and numerous destinations that the business traveler demands.

Rarely, however, are markets so easily separated. Separation generally requires creative efforts in product design or distribution, which explains why development of a pricing strategy should begin early in the product development process. The market for photocopiers offers a complex but highly informative example.

The most naive product pricer would price a photocopying machine based on production costs, projected sales, and a target return. If he were a bit more sophisticated, he might estimate the market "demand elasticity" for the product so as to estimate a product-maximizing price, but that would still not allow him to identify buyer segments. In contrast, a buyer oriented pricer would first study buyers to determine what product benefits they seek and what value they place on those benefits. In doing so, he would learn that photocopying technology can be used equally well in two ways: for making many copies per original and for making few copies per original.

To the product oriented pricer, that observation would be irrelevant. After all, the technology for making 10 copies from the same original is no different from that for making 10 copies from 10 different originals. In either case, the machine scans the original each time. But it is not differences in technology that call for distinguishing between these two types of copying. It is differences in the buyers.

The buyer oriented pricer would recognize that buyers who make many copies per original have very good alternatives to photocopying. They could use offset presses or duplicators to get high-quality copies at a reasonable cost. But buyers who make few copies per original have no good alternatives. Offsetting

and duplicating are prohibitively costly for a few copies, while carbon paper produces copies of distinctly lower quality. Thus, buyers who make few photocopies per original will value them much more highly than will buyers who make many copies.

To use that information, the buyer oriented pricer would ask what other characteristics distinguish the few-copies-per-original from the many-copies-per-original buyers. Perhaps buyers who make many copies per original also desire collators for sorting those pages into sets, while buyers who make few copies do not value a collator. If so, then the copier firm might find it advantageous to sell collators. Why? Because then the firm could price its copier to reflect its high value to buyers who make few copies per original and so don't need a collator. To avoid losing the more price-sensitive buyers, the firm could offer with each photocopier the right to purchase a collator very cheaply. The firm might even sell the collator "at a loss" in order to sell copiers to price-sensitive buyers, so long as the return over incremental cost on the photocopier exceeded the "loss" on the collator.

Monitoring Use Creatively

Frequently one can also segment buyers of a durable good by the intensity with which they use it. Camera ownership, for example, is certainly valued more by those who make photography a hobby or profession than by those who take pictures only occasionally. Computers and copying machines are likewise valued more highly by those businesses that use them more intensely.

The easiest way to segment such a market for pricing is to require that buyers purchase a consumable good used in conjunction with the durable good. And creative pricers have discovered numerous ways to do so. Kodak, for example, traditionally designed cameras to take only Kodak film. IBM leased its early computing machines requiring that they be used only with IBM cards. Xerox, in the spirit of the duplicator companies that preceded it, also leased its machines so that it could require customers to use only the paper it supplied. The firms in these cases charged a very low explicit price for the durable camera, computer, or copier, usually only the incremental cost of production. The price of supplies, however, carried a substantial margin, resulting in higher prices than those charged by competing sellers. Thus the true price of the durable good was not the low explicit price, but the low explicit price plus the extra cost of supplies. Since intense users of the asset had to buy more supplies, the actual price they paid for the durable good automatically reflected the higher value they placed on it.

Early in American jurisprudence, the courts freely accepted and even supported such tying arrangements as a monitoring device, particularly when the durable good was patented. But after passage of the Clayton Antitrust Act in 1914, the courts began a continuing process of narrowing the acceptability of such arrangements. Photocopier companies can no longer require paper purchase, and IBM can no longer require purchase of its own cards. Even Kodak was ordered not to introduce new cameras without first revealing the technology of the film to its competitors, but that decision was recently overturned on appeal.

Opportunities to segment a market through tying arrangements still exist, however. Certainly maintenance and repair service is so integral to most assets that even when not contractually tied, it can still be used to segment markets for pricing. Moreover, the courts have never ruled against the principle that those who value an asset more highly should pay more than those who value it less. Their concern, rather, has been to maintain competition in the tied good. In the opinion of the Supreme Court, the "illegality in tying arrangements is the wielding of monopolistic leverage; a seller exploits his dominant position in one market to expand his empire into the next." Thus, to be in violation of the law one must be shown to have a monopolistic position in the tying good which excludes substantial competition in the tied good. Consequently, many tying opportunities remain.

In many cases tying arrangements are so common that they are no longer practiced as a conscious strategic decision and their legality remains unquestioned. "Validated" parking, for example, is frequently employed where both a local clientele and drivers patronize a store located where parking normally involves a charge. The free or discount parking, like the discount collator in the example above, reduces the effective price to the relatively price-sensitive buyers, those who place less of a premium on the store's location than do local residents. Likewise, no court has ever considered prohibiting theaters from requiring that popcorn be purchased only from the in-house concession, or considered prohibiting razor manufacturers from creating shaving technologies that tie blades to razors. The law has applied the rule of reason.

The courts have nevertheless severely limited tying arrangements in precisely the cases where they were most dramatically effective. The courts' rulings challenge the buyer oriented pricer to devise a method of monitoring use without restricting competition. Frequently this new creative challenge has been met by monitoring use intensity with simple metering devices.

Xerox Corporation developed monitoring to a science, measuring not only intensity but also type of use. Table 1 shows a pricing schedule for a popular Xerox copier in the early 1970s. The price for the machine includes a usage charge for the number of copies made, in addition to a monthly fixed charge to rent the hardware. Thus consumers who used the machine more intensely paid more to have it. Yet note also that the charge

TABLE 1 Metered Pricing, Typical Xerox Copier, 1974

Basic Monthly Use Charge	Monthly Meter Minimum	Total Monthly Minimum	Meter Rate per Copy from Same Original		
			1–3	4–10	11+
$50.00	$135.00	$185.00	4.6¢	3.0¢	2.0¢

Total cost per month for 10,000 copies, 3 copies per original: $510.00
Total cost per month for 10,000 copies, 50 copies per original: $279.60

differed for the type of copying. The more copies made per original, the lower the per copy charge. The strategic rationale is precisely that for selling collators cheaply with copying machines, to reduce the price to the many-copies-per-original users who value photocopying less highly.

Product Design for Effective Pricing

Notice that all of these pricing tactics called for creative insight based on differences in buyers, not differences in technologies or production costs. Moreover, they required that those differences be identified early in the product development process. Copier firms, for example, needed to recognize at an early stage the need to sell related products, and later the need to include meters of a certain type. Moreover, the decision to use meters might have affected other early design considerations. If a service representative must visit the customer each month to check the meter, more durable parts could be included which require monthly maintenance. In fact, it could even be desirable to include such parts simply to ensure a lessee's cooperation with the meter reading.

Often the product design itself is the mechanism for effective buyer oriented pricing, again requiring formulation of a pricing strategy even before designing the product. Orchestral programming provides an excellent illustration. The most salient benefits that symphony orchestras provide are performances of musical selections. But one need

not talk long with devotees of symphonic music to learn that they are not all alike in their tastes. Many symphonic patrons like hearing "old favorites" and place a much lower value on performances of unusual pieces. A smaller but highly devoted group of patrons prefers hearing pieces which are more avant garde. Both groups would like to attend concerts devoted entirely to their preferred type of music. Yet, invariably, when the programs are scheduled everyone is chagrined to find Ives or Schuller on the same program with Beethoven and Brahms.

Why would program directors so completely ignore consumer preferences in designing programs? In fact, program directors do not ignore consumer preferences but schedule together different types of music precisely because they appeal to different audiences. By bundling features that appeal to different tastes, they are actually segmenting their market for pricing. Thoughtfully combined programs allow symphonies to charge each listener a high price for the music he values most, without driving from the market for that music those patrons with different tastes.

To see how such a program design accomplishes its goal, consider a simple hypothetical example. Traditional music lovers (75 percent of a potential 1,000 patrons) would pay, say, two dollars per composition to hear their old favorites. Thus for a concert of three old favorites they would pay six dollars. But to hear an avant-garde piece they would pay only one dollar. In contrast, those who appreciate the avant garde (the other 25 percent)

TABLE 2 Distribution of Orchestral Patrons and Their Benefit Values for Types of Music

Patron Segment	Value per "Old-Favorite" Piece	Value per "Avant-Garde" Piece
Conservative (75% of patrons)	$2.00	$1.00
Avant garde (25% of patrons)	1.00	3.00

would pay only one dollar to hear an "old favorite," but would pay three dollars to hear a piece by a more contemporary composer. Table 2 summarizes these valuations.

Now how can the program director of an orchestra struggling to pay its bills maximize the income per performance? If a concert consists of three pieces, then four obvious possibilities are:

■ Three old favorites at six dollars per ticket. Only the conservative patrons would attend (since the avant-garde patrons value the concert at only three dollars) filling 750 seats. Resulting income: $4,500.

■ Three old favorites at three dollars per ticket selling all 1,000 seats. Resulting income: $3,000.

■ Three avant garde at nine dollars per ticket. Only avant-garde patrons would attend, filling only 250 seats. Resulting income: $2,250.

■ Three avant garde at three dollars per ticket, selling all 1,000 seats. Resulting income: $3,000.

But the program director can do better, since the following combination generates more income than any of the above:

■ Two old favorites and one avant garde at five dollars per ticket fills 1,000 seats. Resulting income: $5,000.

By scheduling the two styles together in the same concert, the program director earns more revenues because both segments of buyers attend and pay the ticket price. But the excess of the ticket price over three dollars is paid by each segment *for different pieces.* The conservative listeners pay the additional two dollars for the old favorites while the avant-garde listeners pay it for the modern piece. Only with the combination program could either market segment be induced to pay the premium for the style of music it highly valued without pricing the other segment out of the market.

This same practice is used in numerous instances even for pricing other than entertainment and sporting events. Newspaper publishers often sell advertising only as a package for both their morning and evening papers. And radio stations sometimes sell advertising for one program only in combination with another. The practice was first formally analyzed in an article on "block booking" of movies, where movie companies sold films only in blocks of different types.[3] Though the courts found this practice illegal for films, they found it legal for advertising, and it has remained unchallenged in most other uses.

One can also see how this principle of pricing relates to the general problem of product development. Auto manufacturers are constantly developing new product benefits in the form of style, technical improvements, and options. The initial temptation might be to identify buyer groups and combine benefits into car models that most appeal to each group. But that would be exactly like symphonies offering only exclusively "old favorite" or avant-garde concerts. If such cars were priced to reflect the values the most enthusiastic group placed on the benefits, some groups of buyers would be priced out of the market. If prices were set low enough to attract those other buyers, then per-car prices would be insufficient to cover fixed costs. But by deliberately designing benefits that differ-

different buyers find attractive into car models, or into indivisible accessory packages, auto companies can price them to earn more on each model run.

Unfortunately, traditional rules for pricing pay little attention to buyers since they take markets and products as given, along with given levels of demand or cost. Efforts to apply pricing rules suffer without exception from the requirement that the product be already designed, that the markets be already identified and segmented, and that a method of distribution be already in place. With such fundamental decisions assumed invariant, little creative license remains to develop an effective pricing strategy. As the preceding examples illustrate, effective pricing generally requires adjusting other elements of the marketing mix as well as price.

It would nevertheless be shortsighted to label as irrelevant the theoretical models that generate such pricing rules. For example, the economist's theory of "price discrimination," though it offers no operational guide to segment markets, is certainly descriptive of the principles that make some segmentations profitable. Understanding those principles cannot provide management with a prescription for success. Pricing theory cannot be to a pricer what accounting is to a bookkeeper—a surefire set of rules. But it can be what engineering is to an architect—a set of general principles to which a successful idea must conform.

The actual task of pricing falls, however, distinctly and rightly in the domain of marketing because pricing requires more than mere technical expertise. It requires creative judgment and a keen awareness of buyers' motivations. Consequently, the specific strategies of successful pricing are as varied as the imaginations of creative individuals. But what they all have in common is recognition of differences among buyers. Thus, the key to effective pricing is the same one that opens doors to efficacy in other marketing functions: a creative awareness of who buyers are, why they buy, and how they make their purchase decisions. The recognition that buyers differ in these dimensions is as important for effective pricing as it is for effective promotion, distribution, or product development.

Notes

1. Jon G. Udell, "How Important Is Pricing in Competitive Strategy?" *Journal of Marketing,* January 1964, pp. 44–48.

2. See, for example, Benson P. Shapiro and Barbara B. Jackson, "Industrial Pricing to Meet Customer Needs," *Harvard Business Review,* November–December 1978, pp. 119–27; and John L. Forbis and Nitin T. Mehta, "Value-Based Strategies for Industrial Products," *Business Horizons,* May–June 1981, pp. 32–42.

3. George Stigler, "United States v. Loew's Inc.: A Note on Block Booking," in *The Supreme Court Review,* ed., Philip B. Kurland (Chicago: University of Chicago Press, 1963), pp. 152–57.

Company Readings

Making a Lasting Impression
Dave Vadehra

What does it mean to be rated "outstanding" by viewers? First it means they are aware of the campaign and have retained something from it, and second that they have a positive attitude toward the campaign.

Before getting into the specifics of retention, however, it is important to consider the environment in which a commercial reaches its audience. Three things have a significant bearing on this retention. First, clutter. An average viewer is exposed to more than 80 commercials a day. Second, despite all the creativity and research, a commercial occupies only 30 seconds out of an average viewing time of 6½ hours a day. And finally, most viewers indulge in what one in the industry might call rather frivolous activities instead of paying attention to the commercials. Considering this environment, an advertiser is lucky to have his commercial noticed at all. But some of them do manage to break through this indifference and leave a lasting impression.

So what do viewers retain from commercials? Our research shows that, faced with this clutter, viewers generally retain impressions of commercials rather than specific details. In commercials facts are forgotten but feelings remain. The best a commercial can achieve is to impart an impression that is favorable to the product, faithful to the brand but, most important, one retained by the viewers. This retained impression is all that is left of a commercial after it has been processed through human perception and memory.

What do these retained impressions include? We have found a well-defined hierarchy, starting with the brand name. Despite an occasional exception such as Mikey instead of Life cereal or Orson Welles instead of Paul Masson wine, viewers retain the brand name more than any other single element of the commercial. Next to the brand name, the retained impression includes "generics," which are associated both with the brand ("7UP is caffeine-free" or "Federal Express delivers overnight") or the campaign (Levi's commercials are psychedelic or Oscar Mayer has cute kids). Next in order of retention is viewers' attitudinal response. They found the commercial "funny" or "family oriented," "believable," "provocative," or "uplifting." On the negative side these responses often are "talking down," "silly," or "childish."

Next in the decreasing order of retention come commercial specifics. It is the executional elements (the spokesperson, the music, the overall situation and characters) that are most often retained.

The last thing viewers retain is the specific sales message. Over a period of time, however, with repeated exposure and persistence, some sales messages can become product generics and get retained more frequently.

How long and how well do viewers retain these impressions? In today's environment, it is both expensive and difficult to create these impressions. But once created they tend to last for a long time. Unlike campaign specifics, which fade away from viewer's memory within 24 hours, one week or two, the impressions stay much longer—until a purchase decision is made, it is hoped. And how well are these impressions retained? Extremely well. In fact, not only do they last over a long period of time, they also remain current in a viewer's memory. That is, most viewers think they have seen a commercial more recently than they actually have. Over and again we have viewers claiming to have seen the commercial within the past four weeks when, in fact, the commercial has been off the air for months. "Mean Joe Greene" for Coke, "Puppies" for Pepsi and "Plop, plop . . . fizz, fizz" for Alka-Seltzer are all examples of this phenomenon. Perhaps the ultimate compliment was paid by the viewer who claimed to have seen the Marlboro Man, on TV, in the month of November 1982.

How They Made the List

This list of outstanding campaigns (now in its sixth year) is based on more than 22,000 interviews conducted nationwide in 1982. As part of its continuous testing and tracking of TV commercials, Video Storyboard Tests asks TV viewers to name the most outstanding TV commercial they have seen in the past four weeks. They are further asked to list the reasons that makes their chosen commercial "outstanding." The word *outstanding* is intentionally ambiguous, and its meaning is left to individual interpretation. Although the respondents are asked to name one commercial, this list combines all commercials to come up with a roster of campaigns.

The list incorporates two different measures. First, it measures media weight and effectiveness. For a commercial to appear on this list, it must be seen by viewers in the context of their natural TV viewing. This can be accomplished only by media weight of sufficient size to assure adequate exposure.

Second, it is a measure of the creative product of advertising which enables a campaign to break through the clutter and leave a lasting impression with the viewers.

Any confusion in the respondent's mind as to the brand advertised works in favor of the brand thought to be advertised instead of the brand that is actually advertised.

Levels of confusion vary from brand to brand. Overall, less than 5 percent of the respondents named a wrong brand for the commercial they saw. Because of this incorrect perception, their votes were cast for the brands they believed were advertised.

So here are the 25 most retained and best liked TV campaigns of 1982, a distinction awarded not by professionals or experts, but by the group all commercials hope to appeal to: TV viewers.

Lite Beer by Miller (Backer & Spielvogel). "Everything you always wanted in a beer and less" has proved itself everything an advertiser might want in a campaign—and more. For the second consecutive year, as determined by viewers nationwide, Lite beer from Miller Brewing Co. has been voted most outstanding TV campaign.

Lite commercials bear testimony to the durability of a solid theme, engaging personalities, and, as one viewer put it, "light humor, like the beer." In its 10th year, the highlight of the campaign was the 7th annual "reunion" presided over by the never-respected (but ever-remembered) Rodney Dangerfield. "He adds a little something extra every time," a viewer said after observing the comedian's 1982 encounter with the immovable bowling pins.

Six other Lite spots aired in 1982, featuring such Lite beer heavyweights as Big Ben Davidson, Boom Boom Geoffrion, Grits Gresham, Tommy Heinsohn, Lee Meredith, Koichi Numazawa, Carlos Palomino, Boog Powell, Jim Shoulders, Mickey Spillane, and Bob Uecker. And last year's "bowling" reunion brought together 22 alumni. All told, remarked a viewer from Cleveland, "A goofy bunch of guys—just looking at them makes me laugh. They never appeared funny till they started making commercials."

Outstanding TV Campaigns of 1982

1. Miller Lite	14. Velveeta cheese slices
2. Coca-Cola	15. Tab
3. Federal Express	16. Life cereal
4. McDonald's	17. 7UP
5. Pepsi-Cola	18. French's mustard
6. Burger King	19. Toyota
7. Budweiser Light	20. Kibbles 'n Bits
8. Dr Pepper	21. Levi's
9. Atari videogames	22. Kodak
10. AT&T/Long Lines	23. Ford
11. Polaroid	24. MCI
12. Oscar Mayer	25. Wonder bread
13. Shasta	

Reaction to their special brand of humor varies from "humor that is not ridiculous" to "absolutely hilarious" and "outrageously weird." Even those viewers unlikely to be found in beer lines fell for Lite's punchlines. "The way they present it makes me laugh, laugh through the whole thing," said a female teetotaler in Phoenix, adding that the brand of humor is as distinctive as the brand of beer. The humorous unpredictability of each spot, which is calculated to enhance "the regular guy image" of each celebrity, is often described as entertaining, refreshing and "sometimes enlightening."

Coca-Cola (McCann-Erickson). "It's the real thing—Coke and its commercials," said a viewer from Portland, Oregon, about the new Coca-Cola campaign, "Coke Is It." Springing from its introduction on network TV in February 1982, the campaign raced to the top of our top 10 list in the second quarter, settled for second in the third and dropped to fifth in the fourth quarter. Although fifth is Coke's lowest quarterly ranking since the fall of 1978, the advertiser seems hardly concerned. " 'Coke Is It' mirrors the mood of America," said the company. And the mood is more hard sell than "Smile."

"Good singers. Good dancers. Good jingle for a good product," observed a viewer from Detroit. The youthful characters in the Coke commercials (particularly "Song") were rated outstanding and captivating for the tempo of their music and their "snappy energetic style." Besides energy, Coke commercials are full of life, entertaining, refreshing and uplifting to the viewers. "Something is spirited about their commercials. They perk you up and make you happy," said one viewer from the South.

The variety of people used in the campaign—all ages, races, sexes and, in one way or another, all real—left an impression that the commercials had a "personal touch."

Federal Express (Ally & Gargano). With the success registered by its five-year-old "When it absolutely, positively has to be there overnight" campaign, Federal Express had a tough act to follow. But it did so, and did it winningly, with "Federal Express . . . now by 10:30 A.M." The follow-up campaign was not meant to replace "absolutely, positively" so much as it was meant to reinforce the notion that documents received in the morning "can be used or acted upon earlier." Its "Fast-talking man" sequel moved viewers as much as the original (taken off the air after the first quarter), and the two alone placed Federal Express at number three in our annual rankings.

Still, Federal Express did a lot more than just talk fast to viewers last year. The two campaigns consisted of 14 commercials, including such clutterbreakers in their own right as "Paper Blob" and "Presentation." Each spot took a real-life situation, dramatized it to the point of hyperbole, and then proved time and again that people will laugh at the travails of others.

"The exaggerated style is comical and delightful to watch," said a Baltimore businessman. Added another, who took the time to recount his own problems with air carriers, "They make fun of particularly frustrating moments, but they do remind me of work. I can associate . . ." In fact, this association with "reality" scored next to comedy as the campaign's most outstanding element.

To most viewers, the commercials depicted business as usual—almost. "Presentation" was particularly touching in this regard, as one sympathizer noted that while the expressions might have been stretching it, the situation itself was, unfortunately, "very real." "Paper Blob" prompted a viewer to comment: "We are being carried away with office paper—it's a fact of life."

It's also a fact of life that, as good as Federal Express' other characters might have been, none came close to having the recall value of that fast-talking man. "It's the funniest commercial I've ever seen," commented a Californian. Added a midwestern viewer: "His talking draws your attention and makes you listen." A Milwaukee man added what might be considered the highest praise of all: "They get the point across so well that you don't want to fool around with any other carriers."

McDonald's (Leo Burnett USA). McDonald's began the year by airing some of the finest commercials in the "You deserve a break today" campaign and wound up taking the top spot on our first-quarter top 10 list.

From then on, however, some of the fast-food chain's loyal following appeared to be lost by a succession of themes under the "Break" umbrella. "Quality in the bag," "Breakfast," "After four" and "Life style" all came and went—and so did the campaign's rating. The campaign's number seven ranking in the final quarter was the lowest since we began tracking outstanding campaigns.

Children remained true to their beloved Ronald McDonald and his commercials. "He is so appealing," said a female observer. "He makes my baby look up." Ronald also accounts, most likely, for the two year old in Allentown, Pennsylvania, whose mother claims "runs around singing the [McDonald's] tune all day."

There are also signs that McDonald's is beginning to grab adult attention more than before. The campaign's performers, whether children or adult, were consistently rated more "realistic" and less rehearsed than those in other commercials. Aside from making viewers hungry, they made them happy. "Their commercials are full of human interest stories. They focus on aspects of people's lives, things that really happen," said a man in Memphis, Tennessee.

Especially attractive, viewers reported, were last year's "Cup & spoon," "Hop scotch," "Best friends" and "Double Dutch," which was created by Burrell Advertising, Chicago.

Pepsi (BBDO). "Now you see it . . . now you don't" was rated the most outstanding of three Pepsi campaigns last year (Pepsi-Cola, Diet Pepsi and Pepsi Light). It's not as though the campaign for the flagship brand, "Pepsi's got your taste for life," which broke in January 1982, failed to register; viewers did recall this Pepsi generation campaign as warm, lively, and spirited. It's just that it often seemed overshadowed by the companion "Challenge" campaign as well as by Diet Pepsi's "Now you see it" spots. Whatever the reason, "Taste for life" never took hold the way most Pepsi campaigns do.

Diet Pepsi, by comparison, won numerous accolades and even set off a bit of controversy for its interplay of "skinny" women, "muscular" men, and "sticks-in-your-head" music. "They made it seem like I'd enjoy drinking a diet [cola]," a fan said of the three commercials. Others recalled the spots as "really exciting," "light and cheerful" and "graphically outstanding." On the other side, noted a close observer, "Half the bodies are sticking out." And in the Southwest, a mother sniffed: "I'm surprised it was on TV."

As in the past, "Challenge" remained inconclusive. Viewers appeared well aware of the ground rules: "It's done with regular people like you and me," an Oklahoman said. But from those who "agree that Pepsi tastes better" to those who disagree—"I just know it's not true"—many still contested the validity.

Burger King (J. Walter Thompson USA). Burger King broiled more than hamburgers last year. It broiled McDonald's and Wendy's as well with a comparative campaign unrivaled in the fast-food industry for its ability to generate controversy.

The year began innocently enough, with Burger King's new "Aren't you hungry?" campaign checking into our quarterly top 10 list (for the first time) at number seven. Its immediate impact was attributed to a bouncy jingle, some "happy" workers and, most convincingly, the tight focus on food. "The Whopper was mouth-watering and scrumptious," said one viewer. "It does what it sets out to do," said another. "Makes me hungry."

The continuous singing of "Aren't you hungry?"—the best-recalled element of the commercial—with closeups of delicious-tasting food was, at times, cited as "psychological manipulation. By the time you get through it you are always hungry," said a viewer from Orlando, Florida. "I hate Burger King but the commercials make me want to go to it," observed another succumbing to the campaign's nefarious "powers of suggestion."

During the next two quarters, the campaign slipped to the 10th place in our top 10 list as it shifted gears for a comparative platform. This phase of the campaign was occasionally criticized for being "unfair and unbelievable." But a majority cheered for Burger King and "enjoyed the way they cut down McDonald's." Besides flame broiling, size and taste advantages, the impact of these commercials can also be traced to the controversy generated by the legal suits brought on by McDonald's and Wendy's. "Everyone is talking about it," said one viewer from San Antonio.

Finally, the best of Burger King comparative advertising arrived in the form of Sarah Geller in September 1982. Outraged by the 20 percent smaller hamburgers at McDonald's, she moved the campaign to a number two ranking in the fourth quarter. Described by one viewer as "a real gold mine," she generally came across for being as "believable" as "adorable." And Burger King's unusual Christmas message, wishing McDonald's a happy holiday, can hardly be construed as a peace offering.

Budweiser Light (NH&S/USA). Anheuser-Busch brought out its best last year with the introductory campaign for Budweiser Light. The lone Clydesdale galloping on sand (or was it snow) captured for the advertiser "the symbol and spirit of the brand." It also captured the attention of viewers—enough of them, at least, for "Bring out your best" to make our top-10 list even before the campaign went national in the second quarter.

An overwhelming majority considered the Clydesdale introduction "beautiful," with one sentimental observer in Oklahoma going so far as to call it "poetry." The campaign left the masses thirsty for more. "They could lengthen that commercial," said one viewer in Detroit, "and I'd still watch it forever." Another cited the integration of music, mammal, and motion producing the commercial interpretation of "beauty and the beast."

Still, Bud Light had its agency shoot more than horses last year. And it wasn't long before the campaign shifted its focus, quite daringly, from steeds to sports. Bud Light's athletes, if they were to make a mark, had to be used in ways much different than Miller Lite's. And they obviously were, as the sustaining campaign scored well with the viewers for being "fresh," "not pushy" and "not too gimmicky."

The combination of the athletes and the Clydesdale, which serves as a "reminder symbol," resulted in a campaign that tugged on viewers' heartstrings almost as much as it pulled on the advertiser's purse strings. Bud Light spent more than $40 million on TV for 27 spots in 1982, making the brand one of the most lavishly financed introductions of all time. But sales are "extremely encouraging," the company reports, and are running "significantly ahead of expectations." And why shouldn't they be when, as one viewer said of the campaign, "it makes you want to go out and buy beer."

Dr Pepper (Young & Rubicam). The "Be a Pepper" campaign revealed how to become one last year. "All you gotta do is taste," said the soft-drink maker, which continued to use a modest budget with maximum efficiency.

In addition to fortifying its five-year-old campaign with a taste message, Dr Pepper fortified its talent lineup. Celebrities Scott Baio and Ray Bolger stepped in where David Naughton (who owes his fame to Pepperdom) stepped out. The real star, though, was a "revolving room" that allowed Peppers to dance every which way, including upside down. A viewer in Jacksonville said the spot "didn't look like a commercial at all," and certainly not like the many "I walk out on."

Sugar-free Dr Pepper, meanwhile, adopted the "Taste is gonna open your eyes!" theme early in the year to position the brand "as good as regular soft drinks." This campaign's three commercials were targeted at women 25 to 49 and relied heavily on music to present its "Ooh what a surprise" taste message and appearance benefit.

Atari Videogames (Doyle Dane Bernbach). Atari videogames became the first in its category to blip its way onto our list. The Warner Communications unit, which spent nearly $50 million on TV last year, responded early to the videogame controversy by positioning itself as a "family entertainment company."

Since its January 1982, debut, in fact, the "Have you played Atari today?" campaign has conscientiously portrayed "the fun of bringing the family together at home." There was even room for grandpa in the 16 commercials last year, just as there was room for Billy Martin (baseball), "Too Tall" Jones (football) and "E.T." (universal phenomenon).

Music played a major role in the campaign's first six months, with the lyrics varying for each commercial, but settled down in the second half as the pace of offerings stepped up. The tagline was the only musical component of the commercials in the second half of the year.

The commercials themselves were described as humorous, cute, action-packed, eye catching and appealing—the very qualities Atari hopes to package in its game cartridges.

Indeed, one viewer heralded the animated characters marching across the screen as "a totally new concept in advertising. The visual effects are stimulating and the vocal effects are unusual." And it mattered little to him that much of the commercials' content probably came from a game cartridge.

Family togetherness and deep involvement of everyone were often recalled as outstanding elements of several Atari commercials. Most applauded was the Atari Christmas commercial. With "E.T." dressed up as Santa Claus, the commercial "enchanted" its viewers and brought back memories of a clean, wholesome movie.

AT&T/Long Lines (N W Ayer). Anybody not yet moved by AT&T/Long Lines advertising probably can't be reached or touched. The campaign, which completed its fourth year with the "Reach out and touch someone" theme, aired 12 spots in 1982.

"They are so natural, you can feel what people feel," said a viewer in Arizona. In Minneapolis, the commercials' implicit call to action was not at all lost on a consumer used to heavy phone bills. "Made me really want to call my folks," she said and did. "I appreciate them [my folks] more now, because I know how much they mean to me."

"Reach Out" remains one of this list's most touching campaigns, with situations that are realistic, believable, and "portray very sensitive human feelings." These commercials impart a feeling of "closeness" among viewers reminding them of "coming home," "of families caring about each other," "of feeling grateful that my parents are still alive" and also "of calling home."

Basically, "Reach out" commercials reach out to everyone and realistically portray emotions, human feelings and happiness that only a phone call can bring. However, there appears to be a growing feeling in some circles that the campaign is a masterpiece in manipulation, in psychological exploitation, by making viewers lonely. "They try to get right to your guilt center to force you to make that call," proclaimed a Bostonian member of this minority.

Polaroid (Doyle Dane Bernbach). James Garner and Mariette Hartley continued to click with Polaroid last year, although Ms. Hartley held her own alone in the new "Don't pass the moment up, pass it on" campaign for Polaroid films.

Polaroid cameras also received a new campaign last fall (with the Garner/Hartley team intact, of course) that insisted, "If you don't have a Polaroid Sun Camera, something's left out of your life." This campaign, which had four spots on the air by the end of the year, was described by the advertiser as a "translation of rather sophisticated photographic technology concepts into easy-to-understand, consumer-relevant ideas. All this while maintaining a level of entertainment values which makes the commercials enjoyable for consumers to watch."

And watch they did, just as they have for years. "I go running to see a Polaroid commercial with James Garner and Mariette Hartley," said a Sunnyvale, California, viewer.

While Hartley alone garnered her recognition for the film role, Garner collected his share of individual praise. "He is so appealing, with his whimsical manner," said one viewer. And from another: "He is an average kind of guy and represents the reality of everyday situations. He doesn't seem fake."

Still, it was a picture of the pair together that popped up most in viewer's minds. "They complement each other and get your attention through their light-heartedness, sarcasm, low key, and wit," observed a viewer from Tulsa.

Oscar Mayer (J. Walter Thompson USA). No matter what Oscar Mayer's commercials say or sell, viewers always think kids—cute, charming, adorable, "just like mine." "They catch the children in a very natural way," said a longtime fan of the Oscar Mayer commercials. "They don't seem produced."

The cold-cuts campaign, "Ever wonder what Oscar Mayer has in store for you," added three new spots (95 percent fat-free ham, meaty bologna, and convenient variety pack) in 1982 with new lyrics to the familiar jingle— "My bologna has a first name, it's O-S-C-A-R." "We roast the cheese inside," the hot dog campaign, attempted to bring something "new" to the otherwise stagnant category. For all spots, the background jingle was updated from the two-year-old "Let's have a weiner roast."

Not only are they cute, the Oscar Mayer kids are very adept at getting their point across, both to children—"Kid to kid," observed a mother from St. Louis—as well as "young and old, men and women," as a woman from Jacksonville said. And they do sell the product. "They make me feel like going out to buy bologna," said a viewer from Boston.

Shasta (NH&S/USA). Shasta popped up on our list for the first time, thanks to four "up-to-date," "modernistic" spots in the six-month-old campaign, "I wanna pop . . . I wanna Shasta." "We put attractive people on the screen in interesting situations," the advertiser said of its impressive recall, even for soft-drink commercials, "and then we added color and motion and upbeat music."

Hardly a unique formula, but one whose executions, nonetheless, took viewers by surprise. "Whatever you're doing," one observer reported, "it immediately catches your attention and keeps it." Then there was the sex appeal. The bikini-clad women helped, but it was the men in bathing suits (described variously as cute, tan, gorgeous, and muscular) that really moved the (female) masses. "The music is good," said a New England woman. "It gets you to look at the commercial. But it's the guy who keeps you looking." And from a woman in Indianapolis, who had already identified Shasta as her favorite commercial, came the candid reflection, "It creates a spark inside you."

The entire campaign, in fact, created a spark of sorts for its brash and affected integration of acting, dancing, and music. "Don't give me that so-so soda . . . that same old cola," it said.

Velveeta Cheese Slices (J. Walter Thompson USA). "The taste you wouldn't trade for anything," the new campaign for Kraft Inc.'s Velveeta cheese slices, started regionally in January 1982, and moved into other areas to cover the country by October. In the six commercials, its spokesboy, Roger, heralds the availability of Velveeta's great taste in individually wrapped slices. Keeping the brand name in the forefront, the campaign dramatizes Roger's various exploits that generally show him jealousy guarding his cheese and still being taken in by his cronies, sister, and even grandpa.

To the viewers, Roger *was* the Velveeta cheese slices campaign. Fondly recalled were his words, intelligence, naturalness, expressions, and rapport with others. "His facial expressions are precious," said a woman from San Diego.

Tab (McCann-Erickson). "The beautiful drink for beautiful people" successfully completed its sixth year in 1982 by continuing to position Coca-Cola Co.'s Tab as a natural part of an active lifestyle. To go along with the familiar "Girl on the beach" and "Sunday in the park," the campaign added two new spots, "Who gets the Tab?" (vignettes with a beach-and-raft scene) and "Cruise ship" (a combination of Caribbean sunshine and Tab).

The shapely figures of "the girl in the bikini" and "the mother with two kids" were the best-recalled elements of the 1982 campaign. "She is kind of hard to forget," a male viewer from Connecticut said of one or the other. Responses from women, though, suggested wishful thinking of another kind. "It makes you want to buy Tab so you will look like her," observed a woman in Schenectady, New York. "I'd drink Tab forever if I could look like that," promised another. Next to the gorgeous women, viewers applauded the catchy tune "One-calorie Tab."

Life Cereal (BBDO). Life cereal's Mikey is to youngsters what E. F. Hutton is to adults. "They listen to him," a Long Island mother explained. "Mikey gets my kids to try it."

This actor, a teenager by now, has proven staying power. His star vehicle ("Life cereal—nutritious, you know. Delicious, they know") is already in its second decade and is one of the oldest spots on this list. A few additional spots have been added over the years—all based on parent Quaker Oats' strategy for a "nutritious cereal that's so delicious even kids like it"—but none is close to commanding the awareness of that brown-haired, freckled face boy.

Indeed, "Mikey" has been cited in industry circles as the classic commercial in which the performer outshines the product.

But, if so, why have viewers placed the campaign on every one of our annual lists?

Maybe it's because, as one viewer put it, "You can show this commercial to the children . . . [and] it tells them about nutrition." Or maybe it's because the spots combine the brand's taste appeal and kids (recognized by Life as "the pickiest eaters") in a way that's as convincing as it is charming.

"The situation is realistic," confirmed a mother in Tampa, Florida, "and it rings a bell with me."

Whatever the reason, "Mikey" has outperformed all of its companion spots (two in 1982) and will continue its lengthiest of long runs. "No changes planned," the advertiser, who tried unsuccessfully to drop the spot in 1980, responded when asked about 1983.

7UP (N W Ayer). Seven-Up Co. made a bold move last March to switch from mainstream soft-drink positioning to caffeine-free. For the drink that "Never had it, never will" quickly proved that its supporting campaign did, indeed, have *something*—at least in terms of recall. "No caffeine . . . it's just something I'll always remember," said a cola drinker from Atlanta.

For the first few months, the caffeine-free strategy was presented by the "Superstar" campaign with Philadelphia Phillies pitcher Tug McGraw shoving caffeine containing brands right off the screen. In July, 7UP unveiled its new campaign, "Don't you feel good about 7UP," with Geoffrey Holder. Making his first appearance for the brand since it's "uncola" days, Mr. Holder once again mesmerized his viewers with his deep, deep voice and amused them with his laugh. "He catches your attention," said a Holder fan, glad to see him back. Added a viewer in Indianapolis, left with a "light-hearted feeling" by Mr.

Holder's appearance in any one of the three executions, "It cheers me up."

Some viewers were also impressed by the truth and honesty of the strategy because it "shows what we don't need."

Diet 7UP didn't fare badly either, with its three-year-old campaign: "The only thing you give up is calories." Last year's spots brought Arnold Schwarzenegger and Loni Anderson with their "natural dialog" to this calorie-conscious world (Don Rickles was not so readily recalled). It was all in good taste, viewers said of the he-man/she-woman banter, much as the brand itself is supposed to be.

French's Mustard (J. Walter Thompson USA). It again took only $3.4 million—less than any other campaign on this list—for the French's mustard campaign to maintain its place in the top 25.

The little boy, who made his debut in 1981's "Mustard sandwich" spot, continued his winning ways, but he also had help, beginning in May, from a little girl in a companion spot called "Hit dog."

"So young, yet so believable," a woman in North Carolina proclaimed the pair. A young mother in Nashville, obviously taken with the boy's eating a mustard sandwich, was proud to note: "My son would do the same thing."

Both the commercials were rated charming and fun to watch, and many expressed a desire to see more of them. "I'd watch it again. It makes you smile while you're watching," said a viewer from Norfolk, Virginia. "I could watch this commercial for hours," insisted a woman from San Francisco. The ultimate compliment, though, came from a woman in Philadelphia who not only "thoroughly enjoyed" the commercial, but also "added French's to my shopping list" after seeing "Sunshine mustard" in one of its infrequent appearances.

The music, "You Are My Sunshine," no doubt helped to produce the "soft sell" and develop a lingering image that, said one observer, French's was a "brand you can trust." Not bad for a campaign designed to leave its female target audience with such "a good feeling" that should compensate for "the few extra cents" she probably has to plunk down at the counter.

Toyota (Dancer Fitzgerald Sample). After an absence of a year, Toyota once again made the top 25. The campaign, which aired 22 spots in 1982, featured such celebrities as Dan Gurney and Popeye and Olive Oyl. But it was the Toyota jump—a highlight of the "Oh what a feeling!" campaign almost since its inception in 1981—that registered the best with viewers. And, specifically, it was the jump of an Alaskan malamute in an SR5 sports truck spot that made this recall rise the highest.

The "Oh what a feeling" jingle-and-jump combination is designed to communicate owner satisfaction with the car. From a proud owner in Miami came: "I have a Toyota so I relate to their commercials." Added another, "They make you feel good about your Toyota."

While the ending obviously gave the campaign a personality often absent in American auto advertising, the spots also command the viewer's attention in the 20 or so seconds leading to the Toyota jump. This campaign imparted more product benefits to viewers than any other in the list of 25. High gas mileage, bad-weather performance, handling (even on rough roads), and other features were cited by those surveyed. "Oh what a feeling," in other words, campaigned successfully for much more than one feeling.

Kibbles 'n Bits (J. Walter Thompson USA). Of the three pet foods on this list a year ago, only Kibbles 'n Bits remains. And its "Quite a bit better than dry alone" campaign proved itself impressively enough with just one 30-second spot and a TV budget of a mere $5 million.

Quaker Oats Co., when asked to account for its dog-food success, cited the campaign's ability to "generate strong brand-name registration in a low-interest category. The little dogs running home . . . convey a sense of dog excitement/satisfaction with the product."

Of course, one dog's fall into the Kibbles 'n Bits bag at the end of the commercial didn't hurt retention, nor did the use of "canine" voices for a syncopated jingle with a single-minded message ("Kibbles 'n Bits, Kibbles 'n Bits, I'm gonna get me some Kibbles 'n Bits"). This combination struck more than one viewer as "refreshing," and dog owners everywhere were won over by any resemblance of the commercial's canines to their own.

The two dogs in the commercial were considered full of personality, cute, adorable, and well trained. With the brand name repeated 15 times in 30 seconds (nobody even noticed this), "the commercial sticks in your mind. They leave a message and the message is Kibbles 'n Bits, Kibbles 'n Bits," said a dog owner from Tampa. "It keeps going through your head, ringing through your mind. They don't let you forget," added another.

Levi's (Foote, Cone & Belding/Honig). Aside from being "a year too late," no one knows much about Travis—or if they do, they aren't telling. But a lot of people care. So many, in fact, that Levi's followed up the original "Travis" spot for Womenswear 501s, which aired in select markets through August, with a Travis II dubbed "Still making history." In addition, the jeansmaker launched separate campaigns for Youthwear ("Far from Home") and Jeanswear ("The legend goes on").

All three were recalled for their creative and executional excellence. In fact, such Levi's hallmarks as psychedelic visuals, lifelike animation, floating models, and mysterious dialog were never so appreciated. The campaign not only received more compliments for its creativity than any other on our list, but a man from Indianapolis went so far as to declare: "Only Levi's uses imagination in advertising." A woman from Indianapolis basically agreed, except she categorized Levi's commercials as "avant garde, more of an art form" rather than the typical "socko-sell 'em."

This creativity did not come at the expense of strategy. The "look and fit" so important to boys was duly highlighted in the Youthwear campaign, the advertiser said, while the "only original, authentic shrink-to-fit jeans now cut for women" was clearly accentuated in the Womenswear campaign.

Kodak (J. Walter Thompson USA). "Picture a brand new world" launched the disc camera in May 1982. Heralded as the industry's biggest innovation since instant photography, the campaign aired nine spots combining technical imagery and familiar picture-taking situations. Kodak film continued with "America's Storyteller" campaign and aired three spots to demonstrate that Kodak film gives excellent color and sharpness.

Kodak commercials, to the viewers, tell stories of childhood, babies, good times of life, and real people in touching situations. "It's really moving. Gets you in the heart," said a woman from Tulsa. The breathtaking scenery, the colors, the extreme blowups often reflect upon the quality of the product, as well as the viewers trust in it. Michael Landon (Kodak Paper) and James Garner (Polaroid) were the best-recalled elements, along with "Bumble Bee," about realism of Kodak film.

Ford (J. Walter Thompson USA). The new Ford models were introduced last September with "Have you driven a Ford . . . lately?" which rolled out a new generation of fuel-efficient, technically advanced aerodynamic cars. Within this umbrella campaign were individual product commercials—tied together by music, tag line, and Ford logo—and Telly

Savalas' "Believe Best" series. Jackie Stewart was brought in to further emphasize Ford's commitment to quality.

September also saw the landing of the "Ford tough Ranger" campaign. With a series of "Sky dive" commercials, the campaign introduced the Ranger's new 2.2L diesel option and put claims of Ford's traditional toughness up in the sky.

Although some viewers were surprised to see Mr. Savalas in Ford commercials ("I never thought Kojak would do a commercial," moaned one), he was, to most viewers, the best element of the Ford campaign. The visuals in most Ford commercials, meanwhile, were described as colorful, professional, eye-catching and unusual, with the truck's drop from a plane considered a major cinematic accomplishment. Next to the trucks, the Mustang and Escort campaigns were cited most frequently in addition to local dealer spots.

MCI (Ally & Gargano). On the air since 1980, the two campaigns, "The nation's long distance phone company" and "You haven't been talking too much. Just paying too much," have been relentlessly and humorously communicating that MCI rates are 15 percent to 50 percent lower than Bell.

Viewers definitely enjoyed MCI's "sticking it to Ma Bell," "cutting the phone company," and "criticizing" the market leader. But they also applauded the information content of the 1982 campaign's 16 spots—12 for residential use and 4 for commercial use. "It's true," said a viewer in San Diego, referring to the you-pay-too-much message, "not just a lot of joking like other commercials."

Although several MCI commercials were cited as outstanding, its arrival on this list is mostly attributed to a spoof of AT&T's "Joey Called." In the MCI version, the mother was not crying because Joey said, "I love you, Mom"; her tears, rather, were caused by the arrival of the long distance phone bill. Besides noting the obvious spoof, the viewers loved this commercial for its surprise ending and its emotional appeal.

Wonder Bread (Ted Bates Advertising/New York). Wonder bread's "Good nutrition doesn't have to be whole wheat," which first aired in early 1981, appears on this list for the first time. The campaign was designed to convince mothers that Wonder white bread not only has the same important nutrients as whole

wheat bread, but also has the soft fresh taste that children love.

The four spots that aired in 1982 all played on a misconception that whole wheat bread is more nutritious. At the same time, in an effort to maintain its position in the fast-growing whole wheat bread category, Wonder bread launched its first family wheat bread with the campaign "The soft wheat kids love to eat." This campaign's only spot, "Gorgonzola," first aired in June 1982.

Coke's Man on the Spot
Scott Scredon and Marc Frons

Roberto C. Goizueta had never known the taste of failure. Although he fled Cuba immediately after Castro took power, leaving behind a life of prosperity and security, his business career had been marked by one stunning success after another. But ever since the Coca-Cola Co. chief executive scrapped the formula of his company's 99-year-old flagship brand in favor of new Coke in April, he had been under siege: rivals credited him with the marketing blunder of the decade. Longtime Coke drinkers—and even some bottlers—angrily demanded that he bring back the old Coke. On July 11 he did.

It was an odd turn for the man who awakened Coke from its antebellum torpor. In little over four years, Goizueta (pronounced Goy-SWEAT-a) transformed the Atlanta soft-drink maker into a $7.4 billion diversified giant. His moves have always defied Coke tradition: he replaced weak bottlers, bought Columbia Pictures Industries, Inc., and introduced diet Coke. The moves have also paid off: profit margins have widened by 20 percent, and the price of Coke's stock, down sharply in the pre-Goizueta decade, has doubled since he took over in 1981.

Goizueta has been a bold agent of change in a once-stodgy corporation. Highly organized

and meticulous, he has done nothing less than remake Coke's culture. "Roberto sets high standards for himself and expects everyone else to reach that level," says Sam Ayoub, the company's former chief financial officer. Goizueta has orchestrated several brilliant decisions. Perhaps equally important, he has ended almost three years of corporate infighting that had drained Coke of its energy. He replaced almost a dozen executives who were not pulling their weight to "let people know it was not business as usual." And he instituted an open-door management policy that encouraged innovation and the free exchange of new ideas.

Despite his successes, Goizueta was haunted by a problem: the steady decline of Coke's market share against Pepsi-Cola. The rival cola has been outselling Coke in U.S. food stores since 1977. And Coke had been unable to refute the "Pepsi Challenge," which convinced Americans that Pepsi tasted better than "The Real Thing." Says Goizueta: "We tried everything—more marketing, more spending. The only thing we had not tried was claiming product superiority."

Goizueta was flabbergasted by the outcry over the elimination of the original Coke. But the company's surprise may have been due to its cast of characters—several international executives who have a firm hand on Coke's global operations, but were out of touch with the symbolic meaning of their own product. "If we still had some of these Southern good ol' boys running this company instead of this international crew, maybe this never would have happened," says one Southern bottler. "They missed the mystique of Coca-Cola, if they ever knew it at all."

Erratic Memory

In retrospect, Goizueta's decision to alter the formula seems almost inevitable. He emerged as CEO following one of the worst periods in the company's history. Although Coke's former autocratic boss, J. Paul Austin, had overseen more than a decade of robust growth, the last 2½ years of his tenure as chief executive were marked by corporate infighting and confusion. Austin was suffering the early effects of Alzheimer's disease. His memory became erratic. "He would tell managers to do something one day, then ask them why they were doing such a stupid thing the next," says a former Coke executive. Austin would even wander into the wrong office and order the person sitting behind the desk to leave.

Austin may have been aware that he was becoming ill. In 1980 he made Goizueta and six other executives vice chairmen. The seven men, known inside Coke as "The Vice Squad" or "The Seven Dwarfs," battled it out for the top spot. Austin favored an operations man, Ian Wilson, to become the next CEO. He even held a dinner for Wilson and his wife at a posh Atlanta restaurant to celebrate his coming appointment.

But Austin was overruled by Robert W. Woodruff, Coke's legendary chairman, whose name in Atlanta is almost as ubiquitous as the company trademark. Woodruff ran Coke from 1923 to 1955, and even after his retirement from day-to-day operations, he exerted a patriarchal influence on company affairs. It was Woodruff who not only made the soft drink a part of Americana but also introduced Coke throughout the world. And it was Woodruff who took a liking to an intense young executive named Roberto Goizueta.

Woodruff asked Goizueta to lunch nearly every day in one of Coke's private dining rooms and often invited Goizueta to the Woodruff "plantation" in south Georgia, where the old man liked to hunt quail. "Woodruff believed in Roberto's efficiency and his demand for quality," says Ayoub. "Unlike Paul, who was very guarded, Roberto would share every detail of the business with Woodruff." Until Woodruff died on March 7 at age 95, Goizueta visited his mentor about twice a week.

Proudest Moment

Goizueta hardly fit the profile of the traditional Coke executive—a Southerner, preferably from Georgia. The son of a wealthy Havana sugar plantation owner, Goizueta came to the United States at 16 to enter Cheshire Academy, an exclusive Connecticut preparatory school. Goizueta spoke virtually no English when he arrived, but by using a dictionary and "watching the same movies over and over," he quickly learned the language. That same year he was the class valedictorian. "It was the proudest moment of my life," he says.

He graduated from Yale University in 1955 with a degree in chemical engineering and returned to Cuba. He decided not to help manage his father's plantation—an unconventional step at the time. "It's very Latin to want to own your own business," says Goizueta. "But I've always felt more comfortable as part of a bigger scene." Instead, he answered an ad in a Spanish-language newspaper to work in Coke's Cuban research labs.

He might have remained there had it not been for an old classmate in Cuba: Fidel Castro. In 1959, Goizueta, his wife, and their three children fled just a month after Castro seized power and expropriated Coke's Cuban business. Goizueta arrived in the United States with $20. "Everyone expected to go back to Cuba," he recalls. "In the Miami airport, I kept records of where all our equipment was for the time when we returned. But eventually we realized there was no place to go back to."

Corporate Politician

He resettled in Miami and commuted to the Bahamas, where he oversaw Coke's chemical research facilities. Although he acquired a reputation as an unimaginative and cautious researcher, he became known as a brilliant administrator. "He was not innovative in the labs at all," says one former top executive. "But he was an astute corporate politician, a clean-desk guy, a stickler for minute detail. He knew where every grain of sand was in the office."

Goizueta came to company headquarters in 1965, among the first of a new breed of Coke executive. Instead of choosing managers from old-line Georgia families, Woodruff and Austin were increasingly looking to Coke's rapidly expanding foreign operations for the company's future leaders. During the 1960s and 1970s, Austin brought several young managers to Atlanta who later formed Coke's executive core: the Egyptian-born Ayoub; German Claus M. Halle, now in charge of international operations in 155 countries; and Argentinian Brian G. Dyson, now the head of Coca-Cola USA. President Donald R. Keough, who hails from Iowa, jokes that he is the company's "token American."

Goizueta has continued that international spirit, but he has transformed Woodruff's empire into his own. As recently as 1981 there was only one Coke, and in Woodruff's day there was only one container—the 6½-ounce glass bottle. (Today only one-tenth of 1 percent of all Coke is sold in that bottle.) In what was considered heresy at the time, Goizueta used the sacrosanct company trademark on diet Coke. In less than three years, it became the third largest-selling soft drink in the United States. Encouraged by that success, Goizueta has attached the Coca-Cola name to five other soft drinks and has even let it grace a line of clothing.

Fire Him

He has changed Coke in more subtle ways. Woodruff, a conservative financial man, abhorred debt. He paid off all his company's loans just in time for the Great Depression, a cautious fiscal strategy that probably saved Coke from going under. And Woodruff retained his aversion to debt. When he learned that one former chief financial officer wanted to borrow $100 million at 9.75 percent to finance a new building, Woodruff replied: "Fire him! Coke doesn't borrow money!" When Goizueta took over, less than 2 percent of Coke's capital was in long-term debt. Since then, Goizueta has increased that to 18 percent and used it to restructure Coke's bottling operations and invest in Columbia's new movies. He has said he is unafraid to increase the company's debt burden should the right acquisition come along.

Perhaps Goizueta's most significant changes have come in management style: he has created an atmosphere that allows new ideas to flourish. Having come to power after the Austin era, Goizueta is particularly sensitive to the destructive potential of dissension among his top executives. While Goizueta is clearly in charge, he insists that he and his three top officers—Keough, Chief Financial Officer M. Douglas Ivester, and Ira C. Herbert, marketing director—agree before any key corporate decision is made. In fact, Goizueta once vetoed a major acquisition because one member of the team disapproved.

Yet Goizueta is a demanding boss with little tolerance for mistakes. He does not hesitate to sack an executive who is performing poorly. "Personal relations have nothing to do with business for him," says one insider. "He'll love you today and hate you tomorrow." Says Goizueta: "It irks me when somebody hasn't done his homework."

Goizueta always seems to have done his own. He is up every morning at 5:30, using the time to read the morning papers and write letters or speeches. When he arrives at headquarters in a chauffeur-driven Lincoln a few hours later, he sometimes questions his top officers about the day's news. He forbids high-level managers to take vacations in the summer, the prime soft-drink season. In fact, he sees little need for vacations at all. Some 20-year executives, who are entitled to five weeks, often take only a few days. Goizueta has taken one week a year throughout his career, although his wife persuaded him to take two weeks this year.

Quoting Grandpa

Whoever deals with him comes away impressed with Goizueta's intensity and intellect. "His mind is like a piece of crystal," says former Coke Marketing Vice President J. Wayne Jones, now executive vice president for marketing at Stroh Brewery Co. in Detroit. "He sees through issues and gets right to the heart of the matter." He also has a philosophical bent. "He uses a lot of Cuban aphorisms; you'll find him quoting his grandfather a lot," says Francis T. Vincent, Jr., chairman

of Columbia. And Goizueta says he simply enjoys mental gymnastics—"[when] you can think through a problem so hard you can develop a sweat."

True to his engineering roots, Goizueta is obsessed with detail. He checks the box-office results daily to determine how well Columbia's movies are doing, monitors Coke's stock price several times a day, and out of sheer curiosity gets involved with virtually every aspect of the business. "He wants perfection," says Ayoub. "On weekends, he would take home drafts of the speeches of his top executives and make corrections." As chief financial officer, Ayoub managed Coke's huge basket of foreign currencies. "We used to make little bets on foreign exchange," he recalls. "He used to walk into my office and bet me a dollar on what's going to happen to the sterling."

Weight Loss

Goizueta's attention to detail is most striking in his impeccable appearance. He is trim, having not gained any weight in the past eight years. Friends describe him as a man of passion and discipline. "He'll search all around his office for a piece of chocolate," says one acquaintance. "But when he finds one, he'll only take a nibble." Goizueta also is conscious of the appearances of others. He often speaks to managers about sloppily dressed or overweight employees—and even wants to send one obese vice president to a weight-loss clinic.

Coke's chairman is a different man outside the office. He enjoys playing golf with his wife, reading, lying in the sun at Sea Island off the Georgia coast, and attending Atlanta Symphony Orchestra concerts. And in a social setting, such as a cocktail party, Goizueta is an engaging conversationalist who wants to know what makes his counterpart tick. "He's the kind of fellow you enjoy talking to," says

Georgia Senator Sam Nunn, who talks with Goizueta periodically. "There's no stiffness, no big ego."

While he may seem distant on first meeting, he quickly warms up and can in a short time become fast friends with those he likes and respects, such as Herbert A. Allen, the former Columbia chairman who now sits on Coke's board. "Everybody used to say there was no way Herbert would go to Atlanta for a meeting. Herbert himself said he wouldn't do it for more than a year," says Vincent. "But well before the year was up, he said: 'I really like this guy.' Now he goes down there all the time."

Even though Goizueta is wealthy—he earned roughly $1.5 million in salary and bonuses last year—he has always tended to live modestly. He occupies the same house he bought when he came to Atlanta 20 years ago, one with a market value of roughly $150,000. But Goizueta is not averse to living well. "Your priorities change as you get older," he says. "Who knows—someday I may want a big house." But friends say his experience in Cuba, where the revolution swept away his family's wealth, taught him there were more important things than material possessions.

He returns to that experience often in his life. "It gives you a kind of inner fortitude," he says. And it has helped him put the recent series of events in perspective. "A friend of mine called the other day and said: 'You've gone through situations 10 times worse than new Coke,'" says Goizueta.

In the weeks after his decision to eliminate old Coke, even Goizueta's friends assumed he was feeling the sharp sting of public embarrassment. "He must be in tremendous pain," says one former Coke executive. "This is eating him up."

Goizueta would no more admit to failure than he would to drinking Pepsi. But he and other top Coke executives were staggered by the public response over their decision to scrap the original Coke. "We knew some people were going to be unhappy, but we could never have predicted the depth of their unhappiness," says Goizueta. "Just as I could not have predicted the emotional disruption that resulted from my leaving Cuba—you cannot quantify emotion."

In the past, Goizueta has ditched other strategies that haven't panned out. Coke bought Ronco Enterprises, Inc. in 1982 in an attempt to launch a national pasta business. But two years later, Goizueta sold the business after he decided Ronco was not meeting his financial goals. In 1983 he sold Wine Spectrum and its Taylor brand name.

Time Will Tell

To many, the decision to bring back the old Coke demonstrates Goizueta's pragmatism. Two sugar colas—three, including new Cherry Coke—are better than one, he says. While Coke has 18 percent of the take-home market, the company believes its three sugar brands can account for 26 percent within a short period. "Time will tell, but I'm willing to take bets on this one," he says.

There may still be trouble in Coke's executive offices if the new strategy fizzles. Someone, insiders say, will pay the price—no matter how well he has performed until now. "If this doesn't work, the people responsible for the new [Coke] decision will be fired," says one former executive. "Whoever is to blame, Roberto will cut his throat slowly."

Tension in the executive suite was high during this first big crisis. And some feel the free-spending marketers may be getting Goizueta's ear more often since the feisty Ayoub retired last December. Keough has historically supported Brian Dyson at almost every turn in the past—and it was Dyson's group that recommended new Coke. While Ivester, 38, is considered a top-notch finance man, his recent promotion and youth make it difficult for him to fight in the trenches with well-established executives. Some insiders worry that Goizueta is surrounded by yes-men who are too timid to challenge what appear to be prevailing attitudes.

Whether the multicola strategy succeeds, however, may be largely out of Coke's control. Several retailers say they will not give the company's cola brands any more shelf space. With roughly one third of Coca-Cola's U.S. sales coming from fast-food outlets such as McDonald's, restaurant owners will also play a significant role in determining which Coke sells best. If McDonald's, which serves roughly 500 million people every month, decides to put Coca-Cola Classic in its spigots rather than new Coke, the company faces serious problems convincing consumers new Coke is for them.

Just as Glad

The biggest decision of all may be whether to market new Coke overseas. Because the company gets more than half its earnings from international sales, some officials say the new product was conceived with the idea of increasing consumption outside the United States. Bringing out new Coke was "a global decision from the beginning," says Claus Halle.

Goizueta says the international rollout will begin soon, but some foreign bottlers fear a repeat of the U.S. experience and simply don't want new Coke. Some European bottlers say they would rather stay with the original formula. Others are just as glad as American bottlers that the old Coke has been retained. "People keep asking our delivery personnel: 'Why a new formula?'" says Peter Burfent, a bottler in Bonn. "They say the old Coke is good as is, and I'm happy the old Coke is going to remain."

If Goizueta has to deal with an international backlash, his worries have only just begun. But he remains confident of his company's strategy. "Having known in April what I know today, I definitely would have introduced the new Coke," he says. "Then I could have said I planned the whole thing." And his experience with new Coke has not curbed his desire to take risks. "An old boss once told me I was too much a man of action," says Goizueta. "But I like to quote the poet Antonio Machado, who said: 'Paths are made by walking.'" He will know soon enough whether he has taken the right path.

Send in the Clones
David Alan Evans

San Diego: When Sol Price and his son Robert decided in 1976 to open a cash-and-carry, general merchandise warehouse outlet featuring wholesale prices and no frills, Sol paid about 45 cents a share for his two-million-share stake in the Price Co. The bare-bones concept caught on like wildfire with both its members–only customers and Wall Street. Sol Price, now 67 years old and the company's chairman, has seen his initial $900,000 invest-

ment mushroom to about $140 million. Straight-talking Sol Price says that's too much.

"I think Wall Street tends to get crazy," he complains. "They fall in love . . . pretty soon they run your stock up. I hate to see the stock get hysterical and have people come in at 70 or 80." In the past year the stock has soared from a low of $26 to a high of $82.75. Currently, it's selling around $70, or at nearly 60 times trailing 12-month earnings, indicating that investors believe—or at least hope—Price Co.'s torrid growth will continue through generations upon generations of bargain-conscious shoppers.

What has folks so excited is the huge success of Price Co.'s special brand of discount retailing. Its chain of Price Club warehouses (currently there are 10) in California and Arizona sells national brands of food, liquor, and general merchandise at the lowest prices in town. By living with paper-thin gross profit margins (about 11 percent of sales versus 30 percent for traditional discounters and 40 percent for department stores), Price Co. has been able to generate enormous sales volume and rapidly escalating profits.

After a small loss in its first year (fiscal 1977, when one warehouse was in operation) on revenues of $13.2 million, both sales and earnings have shot up dramatically. In fiscal 1982, profits surged 53.8 percent to $7.9 million, or 79 cents a share on a 60.9 percent jump in revenues, to $370 million. In just the first nine months of fiscal 1983 (the year ended last Wednesday), Price dazzled Wall Street by ringing up earnings of $10.5 million, or 96 cents a share on sales of $445.1 million.

What's more, while Sol Price believes that 35 percent growth for the next two or three years "is not out of line." He thinks some of the company's fans are getting carried away with themselves. Told that some analysts figure his outfit's earnings, which perhaps soared 65 percent to $1.30 a share in fiscal 1983, will climb by over 50 percent, to $2 for fiscal 1984, and to $3 for fiscal 1985, he shrugs, "It's impossible for a company to turn out those numbers indefinitely."

No newcomer to discount merchandising (he founded the Fed-Mart chain and ran that company until 1975), Sol Price is candid about the pressure being exerted by Wall Street for his company to live up to its hefty price-earnings ratio.

I've got people coming in here, not only the analysts, but people from the institutions (which own about 25 percent of Price's stock). Pretty soon, they're telling me how much we're going to make next year. Often their expectations run counter to the long-term health of the company.

Indeed, despite its storybook success thus far, the future holds a number of question marks for Price. The company has embarked on a period of faster-than-normal expansion, finds itself a mite light in middle-management talent, and plans a major move to the East Coast, far from its cozy California-Arizona homeland. And lastly—but most assuredly not least—Price is drawing competitors like Rod Stewart draws groupies at a rock concert.

The essential ingredient in the Price Co. formula is that its Price Club warehouses are *for members only.* When the first one opened in 1976, it was limited to "wholesale" members—businesses that paid a $25 annual fee for the right to shop at the warehouse. The idea was for them to buy goods both for their own use and for resale. After a few months of disappointingly slow sales, however, the company began to extend Price Club memberships to the individuals who belong to various designated groups—and sales went through the roof. The "group" members include government employees, certain utility and transportation workers, credit-union members and high-balance depositors at some savings and loans. Group members pay no annual fee, but are charged prices 5 percent above those wholesale members pay.

"It was no stroke of brilliance," insists Sol Price.

The fact that the retail customer found it attractive is nothing new. Levitz Furniture tried to give people the impression they were walking into a wholesale warehouse. Everybody's always advertising "wholesale."

But not Price Co. In fact, the company does no advertising whatsoever. With the number of groups whose members may join the Price Club carefully restricted, those allowed in are more than willing to alert their members to this special privilege—at no expense to Price. The concern thus saves millions by not advertising. Excluding the general public also eases the worry of wholesale members that their customers will abandon them and buy directly from Price Club. And wholesale members remain very important. Although, at last count, they constituted just 12 percent of Price Club's 766,500 members, wholesalers generate 60 percent of overall sales.

Price Club warehouses appear to be designed with two things in mind: minimizing overhead and maximizing the customer's impression that he is getting a great deal. The warehouses typically are 100,000 square feet (larger than a football field) with concrete floor, high ceilings, and no air conditioning. Usually located in low-rent districts, they contain row after row of unembellished four-level steel shelves, piled high with $3 million of inventory per warehouse. "Anything that focuses people's eyes on fixtures instead of merchandise is missing the point," explains Robert Price, the company's president.

A minifleet of forklift trucks whizzes up and down the oversized aisles all day restocking the shelves with fresh merchandise, at the same time reminding shoppers that they are in a bona fide wholesale warehouse.

But in fact, the apparent abundance of inventory tends to mask a key ingredient of Price Club's success. Traditional chain discount stores carry a selection of 50,000 different items. But Price Club stocks only about 3,500. Although it carries a vast array of product categories (from tires to television sets to tuna fish), the selection of brands, sizes, and models in each category is extremely narrow. Price Club tries to stock only the best-selling items in each category.

And things sell fast. The typical customer spends between $50 and $80 in cash per shopping trip (no credit cards or charge accounts). Inventory turns over at the astonishing rate of 17 times a year, compared with 3 or 4 times for traditional retailers. Most everything sit-

ting in a Price Club warehouse today will be sold within three weeks. The company actually manages to sell most goods before having to pay its suppliers for them, avoiding the considerable expense of financing inventories.

Example of the savings that can be had: a carton of king-size cigarettes sells to Price Club wholesale members for $6.62 ($6.95 to group members); by contrast, Von's, a large southern California supermarket chain, charges $8.49. Even Glaser Brothers, an established area grocery wholesaler, admits to being underpriced by Price Club. "We can feel their effect," acknowledges Richard Stempson of Glaser Brothers. "They've created a very competitive market in San Diego."

Traditional wholesalers have certain advantages over Price Club, however. They offer credit terms, a much wider selection—and they deliver. According to Stempson, "Most retailers don't have the time to spend two hours in there pulling stock, rolling 50 cases out to their truck, and then driving back to the store. They'll accept service over price."

Because the general public is barred from Price Club warehouses, traditional retail chains haven't felt seriously threatened. "We can't see the impact," insists Peter Harris, president of Lucky Stores' department store division, which operates Gemco membership discount stores in California and Arizona. Harris nonetheless calls Price Club "a magnificent retail concept." Gemco, which also carries food, liquor, and general merchandise, extends a lifetime membership to anyone for one dollar. "We carry over 70,000 items," says Harris. "Price Club's appeal is clearly not in selection."

Price Club expanded slowly in its first six years of existence, adding a second warehouse in 1978, two more in 1979, and two more in 1981—and all but one of those in the San Diego metropolitan area. In the past 15 months, however, it has spread northward, opening two warehouses in suburban Los Angeles, and one each in San Francisco and Sacramento. A unit also has been added in Tucson. Later this year, another is slated to debut in Los Angeles and one more near San Francisco.

"With a little luck," predicts Sol Price, "we should open four or five a year (in California and Arizona)." For the next two to four years, that is, since the company's home turf, he feels, can only absorb only 10–15 more Price Club warehouses.

To help finance this hurried-up growth, Price Co. raised nearly $30 million last fall via an offering of 1 million common shares (up from the 800,000 shares initially planned). It also can draw on a $15 million line of bank credit.

In May, Price Co. announced its most venturesome move to date—including the East Coast. While the company said that no specific sites had yet been picked, it allowed as Washington, D.C., seemed to hold a lot of potential (namely, the biggest work group of them all, federal employees). The East Coast units will be operated by a new 60 percent-owned subsidiary, Price Club East, headed by Al Werner, formerly executive vice president of Best Products.

Explains Sol Price:

> We've always been thinking about how we can transpose (our concept), without having our fine team of people being diverted on airplanes all the time. We recognize there are very substantial problems in running a business where you don't have substantial local control and investment.

So the East Coast management team has been granted that control and 40 percent ownership of Price Club East. Still, even Price fan Joe Ellis, retailing analyst for Goldman, Sachs, warns that the move East is "fraught with risk in its early stages."

In Washington, Price Club for the first time will encounter serious competition in the form of a privately held Dutch company called Makro. In February 1981, Makro established an American beachhead, opening a 185,000 square-foot cash-and-carry warehouse in the nation's capital. (It has since opened warehouses in Philadelphia, Cincinnati, and Atlanta, with more units on the way.) Unlike Price Club, Makro's wholesale customers pay nothing to walk through the door. And Makro carries 35,000 items, about 10 times the assortment of merchandise offered by Price Club, as well as fresh meat and produce, both absent at Sol Price's outlets.

So far Makro has restricted its business to "true" wholesaling, ignoring the "group" member constituency courted by Price Club. However, in Chicago, a similar cash-and-carry chain, called Metro, decided in January to begin admitting group members to its three warehouses there. A privately owned German firm, Metro operates the world's largest chain of wholesale cash-and-carry warehouses and is bent on expanding its U.S. operation beyond the Windy City. "We've got 60,000 group members already and we plan to triple that by Christmas," avers David Walter, a former Price Club executive who is running Metro's U.S. operations.

And in early July a Price Club imitator, the Warehouse Club, also opened its doors in Chicago. "We look just like a Price Club," beams its president, Walter Teninga. He should know. A former vice chairman of K mart, he spent six months last year learning about Price Co. from the inside. He was hired in January to run its northern California division but left abruptly in June.

But the most significant thrust so far into what was once Price Co.'s exclusive domain has been by Wal-Mart Stores, a big, highly successful discount store operator. In April, it opened its first Sam's Wholesale Warehouse in Oklahoma City, and other units are scheduled to open later this year in Dallas and Kansas City. "They're experimental," explains Wal-Mart Vice Chairman David Glass. "We've got a lot to learn in this business." He doesn't deny emulating the Price Club operation.

"Sam's is a combination of Wal-Mart thinking and different things we observed at the Price Club."

Goldman, Sachs's Ellis predicts that if it chooses to expand Sam's Wholesale Warehouse effectively, "Wal-Mart would quickly become the national leader in the field." Acknowledges Sol Price, "Some people may go faster than we're going."

Another imitator, Club Mart of America, claims it will open its first wholesale warehouse outlet in New York City later this year. But so far, the only product it has wholesaled has been its stock. Last December, the company sold 3 million shares to insiders for 8.5 cents a share. Then, at a public offering this past May, eager investors paid retail—$5.25 each—for 1.4 million shares. Club Mart's chief operating officer is Eugene Ferkauf, who founded the ill-fated Korvettes discount chain in 1947. According to Club Mart's prospectus, Ferkauf has been an officer of two other retailers since then; one, the prospectus says, was forced into bankruptcy in 1975, while the other was "liquidated in 1981–82 pursuant to an agreement with its creditors." However, some savvy Street folk think that Ferkauf has a real shot at making a go of Club Mart.

Other Price Club look-alikes are springing up in such diverse locations as Seattle, Denver, Boise, and Indianapolis. The Indianapolis operation is run by John Geiss, a retailing consultant who advised Wal-Mart on Sam's Wholesale Club. Although Geiss obviously likes the business, he warns: "People think it's a magic formula, but you've got to know what you're doing. A lot of people starting these things are going to get killed."

Price Co.'s management is quite aware of the implications of this proliferation of clones. "I worry about it," admits Robert Price. "If they succeed it's only a matter of time before we'll be bumping heads in the same market."

A more immediate headache for Price is that over the years demand for seasoned employees to manage new Price Club warehouses has created a serious shortage of seasoned middle management. "That's a legitimate criticism," concedes Sol Price. "Unfortunately, we are always much more comfortable with people that have grown with us than people who have come to us from the outside."

Seeking to spread its risk, Price Co. recently plunked down $3 million for a one third interest in "Price Bazaar." This warehouse-like 118,000 square-foot building adjoining the Price Club in Chula Vista, California, is subdivided into dozens of selling spaces which are leased to local merchants. It has proved less successful than Sol Price had hoped. "We're just fiddling with it . . . We're sure as hell not going to go charging off and do anymore until we've figured out what it really does to us."

Besides, the company is facing a bigger hurdle at the moment: the potential backlash from its recently announced decision to begin

The Past Four Years at Price Co.

	1982	1981	1980	1979
Revenues (millions)	$370	$230	$148	$ 63
Net income (millions)	7.9	5.1	2.6	1.1
Earnings per share	.79	.52	.26	.11
Book value	2.03	1.20	.67	N/A
Stock prices				
High	48¾	22½	5¼	N/A
Low	12	5¼	2¼	N/A

N/A = Not applicable.

charging a $15 annual fee for group members of Price Club. The action has been widely interpreted as an effort to buffer the potential earnings drain from the firm's East Coast expansion. Sol Price is reluctant to discuss the thinking behind the charge although he acknowledges its risks. If just half of Price Club's 675,000 members agree to pay the $15, an additional $5 million a year will be generated. But those revenues would be more than offset by a loss of potential sales to group members who drop out.

Quite obviously, Price Co. has a lot riding on its bet that people will ante up for a bargain. And lots too on its move East.

On the evidence of the company's lofty P/E, investors are confident that the company will expand its reach and turn back the growing competition without breaking stride. Sol Price though hedges: "It's really going to come down to a question of how easy or tough this business is—and you're going to know that within a year."

Case Studies

Baird-Atomic, Inc.
Laurie Tyman and Dharmendra T. Verma

The Baird-Atomic System Seventy-Seven multicrystal scanning gamma camera was introduced into the market in 1975. At that time, the projected sales volume was 150 units within two years. However, by the end of 1977, the camera had reached only two thirds of its target sales. As a result, in January of 1978, a meeting of the key executives involved in the System Seventy-Seven was called to determine just what had gone wrong and to decide on any changes in the marketing of the camera.

Company Background

Baird-Atomic, Inc., was founded in 1936 as Baird Associates by a group of young physicists (including Walter S. Baird, the present chairman of the board) to design and sell scientific instruments. From its early days as a manufacturer of X-ray diffraction tubes, Baird Associates grew to develop scientifically complex, high-technology, analytical instrumentation. During World War II, Baird was a major supplier of scientific instruments to the U.S. government. In addition to sophisticated scientific instruments, the company supplied aircraft periscope bombsights and attack simulators for the U.S. Navy. After the war, the company emerged as a major force in the commercial and scientific instrument industry.

In the 1950s, with military contracts on the wane, Baird Associates merged with Atomic

This case was prepared by Laurie Tyman, research associate, and Dharmendra T. Verma, professor of marketing at Bentley College. Copyright © 1979 by Laurie Tyman and Dharmendra T. Verma. Reproduced by permission.

Instrument Company and eventually became Baird-Atomic, Inc. This merger provided Baird with the earliest concepts for the nuclear medicine instrument market, from which they were to build their prototype nuclear scintillation gamma camera.

In the 1960s, Baird continued to perfect the scientific instruments by computerizing them, and continued its long association with the American military by developing a biocular eyepiece for the Army Night Vision Laboratory. By the mid-1970s, Baird-Atomic was firmly entrenched as an international leader in scientific instruments and components, all working on some scientific principle involving optics—reaction to light, ultraviolet rays, or gamma radiation. In 1977, company sales amounted to $24 million.

Product Development

The entire field of nuclear medicine began in 1923 with the application of radioactive tracers to the study of the thyroid gland and its metabolism. Nuclear medicine for diagnostic work began in the early 1950s, when the medical application of radioisotopes was recognized. This required special educational courses and created the nuclear physician. The first nuclear scintillation gamma camera (the Anger camera) was built in 1956. By 1957, Baird-Atomic was designing and experimenting with its own version of a nuclear scintillation camera and became recognized as a pioneering leader in scientific achievement in nuclear medicine.

The camera evolved out of Baird-Atomic's first attempts with an Autofluoroscope multicrystal nuclear diagnostic medical instrument. This was marketed in the early 1960s and was considered a failure both in terms of technical capability and sales. The company then developed a multicrystal scanning gamma camera in 1972. This 1972 version (the System Seventy) became the System Seventy-Seven of 1975—the major difference being the added capability of doing cardiac studies.

A scintillation scanning gamma camera is a noninvasive diagnostic device, which, for ease of a commonly understood reference point, can be remotely compared to a conventional X-ray. An X-ray is termed an "active" device, whereas the S77 is a "passive" one. The difference between active and passive is that the X-ray creates an image from the radiation *generated by the X-ray machine in its X-ray tube:* the S77 measures the radiation *generated from the patient's body* due to a small amount of radioisotopes ingested prior to the System's use. The X-ray is limited to recording bone and some tissue, while the S77 can see organs, soft tissues, and cavities. Exhibit 1 compares the radiation generated by an X-ray with the gamma camera.

It is also possible to use a nuclear scanning camera instead of exploratory surgery to detect irregularities since the camera can show the extensiveness as well as location of a disorder. This results in saving a patient the pain, expense, risks, and time delays of surgery. Using a camera for diagnoses may protect a physician from possible malpractice suits since it is a noninvasive procedure, and the doctor can point to having afforded the patient the latest in diagnostic techniques before performing any surgery. Finally, the camera can prevent a patient from undergoing unnecessary surgery.

Present Marketing Approach

In the United States and Canada, the S77 has been sold by a network of four company salespeople who specialized in the gamma camera. These salespeople call on doctors within clinics and hospitals. The doctors' names are obtained from responses to S77 advertisements placed in trade journals (such as the *Journal of Nuclear Medicine*) and from informal interview cards on each person visiting the Baird-Atomic booth at trade shows and exhibitions. Baird exhibits in five national shows or "congresses" a year.

EXHIBIT 1 Comparison of X-Ray and Gamma Camera

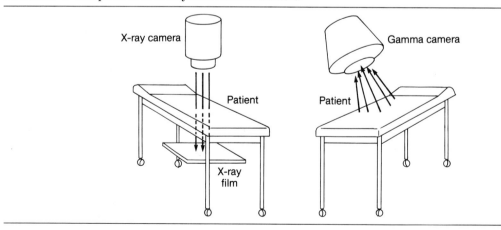

Also, when invited to do so, Baird hosts seminars at current system users' hospitals. At these seminars, system users and medical sales prospects get a chance to exchange ideas, theories, and tips on applications in using the S77. A direct-mail campaign is also employed to distribute newsletters containing news of updated options and newly discovered applications and to distribute technical papers and abstracts of presentations given at medical conferences by System Seventy-Seven users.

Often Baird-Atomic will install a demonstration instrument in a prospect's hospital for them to evaluate over a period of six months to a year. The company trains hospital personnel to operate the S77 and the hospital pays only for the overhead costs in the day-to-day operation of the unit (such as electricity and air conditioning) and for consumable items (such as radioisotopes—not sold by Baird). During the evaluation period, visits are made by the salesperson, as well as by a clinical applications expert who advises the hospital personnel in the most effective manner of using their system. At this point, the salesperson also meets with the people (usually a committee) authorized to make capital equipment expenditures.

Internationally, Baird-Atomic relies on a network of independent manufacturer's agents to make sales calls on leads generated in the same manner as domestically. Baird-Atomic exhibits in about five trade shows annually in Europe and participates cooperatively with local representatives in smaller, more local shows. Seminars and symposiums are also held in Europe, and the "loan and demo" sales tool is employed extensively. There are wholly owned company subsidiaries in the Netherlands (with jurisdiction over all of Continental Europe) and England (with responsibility for the United Kingdom). The International Operations Division of the company has the responsibility for marketing the S77 throughout the rest of the world.

Competition

In addition to having direct competitors in the form of manufacturers of other scintillation-scanning gamma cameras, other methods of noninvasive diagnoses compete with Baird-Atomic's System. These are conventional X-rays, surgery, and filmless X-rays. These three methods are only remotely competitive or apply in only one area. However, there are two other types of devices that are more in direct competition with the functions and abilities of nuclear medical scanning cameras. These are computerized axial tomography scanners (CT or CAT scanners), and ultrasound units.

CAT scanners were introduced in 1973 and were thought by some to be a great improvement over existing types of cameras. Others thought that CAT and ultrasound would outdate the scintillation camera and that by 1980 only 20 percent of all noninvasive diagnostic work in this country would be done with scintillation cameras. Exhibit 2 depicts the projected mix of diagnostic procedures in 1980.

The major differences between CAT scanners and scintillation cameras are in *cost* ($600,000 for a CAT scanner versus $160,000 for the S77), in *procedures* necessary for using the scanners (the S77 requires radioisotopes to be ingested by the patient prior to its use; CAT scanners require no such preparation), and in *applications* (the S77 specializes in cardiac studies but is poor for brain imaging whereas the CAT scanner is considered superb for brain studies but poor for doing cardiac studies). The CAT scanner, like an X-ray, is also an "active" device—it generates its own radiation from within. It avoids the shadowing effect of conventional X-rays by beaming X-rays through the patient in several directions, not just one.

The noninvasive diagnostic product market, therefore, comprises the potential users of all types of devices—CAT scanners, ultrasound, and scintillation cameras. The leader

EXHIBIT 2 Comparative Cost Analysis: Computed Tomography versus Alternative Diagnostic
Procedures: 1977 and 1980

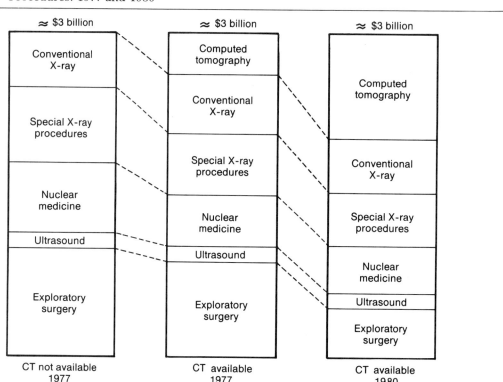

in this field, Electro-Medical, Inc. (EMI), has over a 50 percent share of the total market. The market is dominated by four big-name manufacturers: EMI, Ohio Nuclear, Pfizer, and General Electric. There were 15 main firms in the world scanner market in 1978, down from 20 in April of 1977. A chart of the remaining 15 with a description of their product and its major achievement/feature is included in Exhibit 3. This chart, from the December 21, 1977, issue of *Bio-Medical Insight,* also predicts which firms should be next to drop out of the worldwide scanner market.[1] Despite its status as an innovator in nuclear medical technology, Baird-Atomic,

with 2 percent of the U.S. market share, is not included as one of the rapidly diminishing field of 15 manufacturers of diagnostic instruments.

Since 1975 there have been no new developments among noninvasive diagnostic products—just improvements in software packages and imaging perfections. It seems all scanner and camera manufacturers are concentrating on marketing their existing products and not on engineering. Despite this trend, Baird-Atomic increased its research and development budget for nuclear medicine by 44 percent in 1976.

EXHIBIT 3 Sales and Market Shares of Manufacturers of CAT, Ultrasound, and Gamma Scanners

Company (Parent), U.S. Operating Headquarters	Total Orders Booked*	Percentage World Market Share in Units†	Most Recent Developments
American Science & Engineering, Inc., Cambridge, Massachusetts	15	<1.0	Manufacturing 2 a month. Claims to have delivered 12. Has lawsuit pending with Technicare.
Artronix, Inc., St. Louis, Missouri	65	3.1	Claims 47 head and 18 body units on order. First body unit goes into Parkland Hospital in Dallas next month.
CGR Medical Corporation (CGR/Thomson-Brandt S.A.), Baltimore, Maryland	30	1.4	One known placement at France's Hospital Lariboisiere. Introducing 20-second "ND-8000" at $500,000. Selling Varian overseas.
Elscint, Inc. (Elscint, Ltd.), Hackensack, New Jersey	10	<1.0	Placed 2 units each in United States, Israel, and in West Germany, for a total of 6 installations.
EMI Medical, Inc. (EMI, Ltd.), Northbrook, Illinois	850	40.6	U.S. sales rate down by 40%. Installed 460 units in United States, of 850 units ordered worldwide. About 300 "5005" systems installed, 175 in United States, in 1977.
General Electric Medical Systems (General Electric Company), Milwaukee, Wisconsin	150	7.2	Producing 20 a month, half for overseas. Reports 85 "CT/T" units installed and 2 "CT/M" mammography scanners in clinical trial.
Ohio-Nuclear, Inc. (Technicare Corporation), Solon, Ohio	450	21.5	Over 300 units installed. Reports 150 orders for new "2000" 2-second units. Going direct overseas.
Omnimedical, Inc., Paramount, California	10	<1.0	Latest entrant. Features low-performance, $119,500 unit. First system into clinicals by January in Los Angeles hospital.
Pfizer Medical Systems (Pfizer, Inc.), Columbia, Maryland	230	11.0	Newest is "0400" sub-5-second system with 2.6 second option. Will produce 14 a month.
Philips Medical Systems (North American Philips/ N.V. Philips' Gloielampenfabriken), Shelton, Connecticut	25	1.2	Down to 20-second scans. Has placed 5 units in United States. Coming is 2.6-second speed at $715,000. Also selling Syntex overseas.

EXHIBIT 3 *(concluded)*

Company (Parent), U.S. Operating Headquarters	Total Orders Booked*	Percentage World Market Share in Units†	Most Recent Developments
Picker Corporation (C.I.T. Financial Corporation), Cleveland, Ohio	30	1.4	Has shipped 25 "Synerview-1" systems. One-second systems expected to sell at $750,000, scheduled for mid-1978.
Searle Diagnostics (G.D. Searle & Co.), Des Plaines, Illinois	10	< 1.0	Admits to 5 units installed and monthly production rate of 2. Most likely candidate to drop out of scanner race.
Siemens Corporation (Siemens AG), Iselin, New Jersey	60	2.9	Claims 60 head units sold world-wide, 10 in United States and 33 in Europe. First 2 body units going into St. Louis and Munich. No longer repping ONI.
Syntex Medical Systems (Syntex Corporation), Palo Alto, California	40	1.9	Claims 30 units in operation. Philips will represent overseas. Reports halt on further development.
Varian Associates, Inc., Palo Alto, California	30	1.4	Claims 11 units shipped, 7 on the air. CGR has ordered 140 CT and ultrasound units for oversea sales.
Hitachi Medical Corporation (Hitachi, Ltd.), Tokyo, Japan (not sold in the U.S.)	90	4.3	Principal Japanese producer in competition with imports. Has booked about 90 systems in Japan. Domestic sales only thus far.
Total	2095	100.0	

*Includes o.c.m. arrangements, as well as upgrades and remanufactured units expressed as orders booked.
†On a unit-for-unit basis, with no dollar volume assumptions.
Source: *Bio-Medical Insight* (December 21, 1977), pp. 200–201. Reproduced with permission.

Participants at Strategy Meeting[2]

Dave Collins: Vice President of Nuclear Medicine. Chaired meeting and occasionally played "devil's advocate."

Jack Dixon: Vice President of Marketing. A newly created position filled by a newcomer to Baird. All other participants in the meeting had been with the company since the introduction of the S77.

Jim Hopkins: Research scientist
Steve McNamara: Controller
Larry Miller: Salesperson, Western Division
Andy Robbins: National Sales Manager
Bob Sanders: Salesperson, Eastern Division

Strategy Meeting: January 1978

Dave Collins: I see this meeting as a diagnostic and prescriptive session. I hope we can look at some of our past problems and come to terms with the issues that face us in marketing the System Seventy-Seven and develop a plan to respond to these in the near future.

Jack Dixon: From what I can see, little or no market research was ever done before proceeding with building the prototype and starting up production runs. Basing a whole marketing strategy for a new product on a small amount of information obtained from users of precursor systems can create problems. This may be the reason that Baird-Atomic overestimated its sales potential and thus overproduced. A full-scale market research project should be undertaken immediately, if not by my department, then by an outside consultant. This is the only way to really determine if a market exists and, if so, how large it is.

Extremely high losses in the early stages of a product's life cycle are very damaging and are not easily overcome. The recovery period takes several years if everything else goes right and sales do improve.

Andy Robbins: Well, the *U.S. Industrial Outlook* for 1978 shows that the X-ray and related electromedical equipment industry (within which the S77 falls) is ranked second in annual real rate of growth among all U.S. industries, and has grown by 23.8 percent from 1972 to 1977. The only cautionary note is in the specific area of diagnostic scanners. The *Bio-Medical Insight* at the end of 1977 was saying that "the financial forecasters are likening 1978's scanner market to a round-robin contest for survival among some fifteen firms now active in the U.S. marketplace, with 1978 telling who the survivors will be." Early this year they had quantified the year's potential unit sales in the United States to under 200 units. Only the prospect of export sales was cited as a possible saving grace for the industry. Japan was mentioned as the specific country to target. This negative view of the future is of particular interest to small firms such as ourselves, since the Big Four in the scanner market will probably survive the depressed 1978 market. However, no guarantees are being made for anyone else.

Dave Collins: OK, but there are also figures and sources that predict just the opposite of what you're saying—that the future for diagnostic devices is not pessimistic at all, but shows potential for a good rate of growth. In 1976, the world demand for X-ray and electromedical devices was estimated at $800 million (with 75 percent of the sales occurring in North America) and the predicted annual rate of growth for the industry was 8 percent. In 1977, the world market was estimated to be between $2.6 billion and $3 billion annually, and the predicted annual rate of growth for the industry was 20 percent. The prediction for rate of growth for computer-assisted diagnostic equipment (the System Seventy-Seven) specifically was 11 percent in 1977. Therefore, of the optimistic predictions, the ones made most recently tend to be the best. From this small survey, I would think that our future still looks bright, but I might agree that an intensive market study should be launched to be sure.

Bob Sanders: I think the poor reputation of the S77's predecessors in the diagnostic medicine field, particularly the Autofluoroscope, and to a lesser degree, the System Seventy, are impossible to overcome in marketing the System Seventy-Seven. We are all in agreement that the Autofluoroscope was a dismal failure, and the service problems experienced in the final stages of the System Seventy certainly did not enhance our credibility in our attempts to market our gamma camera. I haven't run into any prospects who've actually said to me—"Based on past experience with Baird-Atomic we do not feel confident that you are capable of manufacturing a quality instrument and providing reliable servicing"—yet I don't feel we can discount this type of attitude.

Dave Collins: I disagree. It's not impossible to overcome a bad reputation. Very difficult, yes, but not totally insurmountable. Besides, we've made great strides in improving our name in the past two to three years. Look, the best salesperson we have for our System is a satisfied user. Technical papers written by satisfied users in the past few years have increased and are now running at the rate of about two every quarter. What you and our other salespeople have to do is to introduce all of the work done by our System users to prospects, taking care to show cardiologists' work to other cardiologists, radiologists' comments to other radiologists, and so on, to prove to them that our equipment has widespread support. As we build up our network of satisfied users whom we can call upon for references and testimonials, our tarnished reputation will fade away completely.

Jim Hopkins: Along these same lines, there seems to be an inherent difficulty in selling to doctors to begin with. Because of the nature of medical science, physicians as a group tend to be extremely cautious in their embracing of new instruments, procedures, and techniques. Most are understandably reluctant to be the first to buy and use a new instrument, waiting instead until the instrument is perfected, "the bugs are worked out," and it becomes standard operating procedure. For example, in 1975, when both CAT scanners and scintillation cameras were available, doctors' reactions in the United States were divided between "proper medical caution" and "enthusiasm." At the same time American doctors' counterparts in England were behaving quite differently—the United Kingdom Department of Health had announced its intent to have a scanner in every hospital with a major neurological service, starting with one to a geographical area in order to get them dispersed widely and in operation as soon as possible.

Andy Robbins: It's good to see that you in Research are aware of the difficulties encountered in selling medical equipment, but I still feel we seem to be more concerned with scientific achievements and being the first to discover a new principle than with manufacturing a proven marketable product. For example, the 1975 *Annual Report* stated, "We are participating in the earliest stages of an important revolution in diagnostic medicine" and rationalized the lower than planned net income because the time and money was expended in a "continued investment in software development for application of . . . System Seventy-Seven Gamma Camera in cardiac diagnostics. . . ." Also, the budgets for research and development keep rising dramatically despite poor sales volume. I realize, of course, that the ultimate goal is to someday see the financial rewards of these scientific breakthroughs; but I feel we're sacrificing too much in sales volume and profits for the sake of "progress."

Jim Hopkins: Product improvements through research are very important. For instance, research and development for nuclear medicine increased over 44 percent in 1976, and one result was that the S77 can now perform a cardiac study in 10 minutes versus competition's 90 minutes a year earlier and our own time of 45 minutes a year earlier. As a result of our corporate objective of furthering the progress of science, the system is in the forefront of technical superiority today. It is comforting to note that we enjoy a unique position in the field of diagnosing heart disease.

Dave Collins: Saying that Baird-Atomic is not concerned with profits is a bit naive and farfetched, don't you think? We at Baird are not a nonprofit organization; it is true that there are other divisions within the organization that make a considerable profit and can thus support the efforts (although not happily) of a less successful but more scientifically and humanitarian and rewarding pursuit of developing a superior diagnostic scanning camera, and your observation that Baird-Atomic puts a great deal of importance in scientific achievement is undeniable. The recent increase in the money paid to patent issuances and the bonuses paid for the publication and presentation of technical abstracts supports this. But, as you pointed out, the ideal is to combine continuous scientific discoveries with profits, and I think we have a good shot at achieving this goal very soon.

Jack Dixon: Look, I've been doing some reading on the new developments in the diagnostic instrument market and I think what's hurting us are the new instruments that are vastly superior to nuclear scintillation gamma cameras. CAT scanners, for example, do a far better job in detecting tumors and in brain studies than our S77. Should we continue with a product that may become technologically obsolete? Its design has no possibility of ever being upgraded to perform the same studies as CAT scanners or even ultrasound.

Admitting that hindsight is a marvelous but unfair tool of analysis, I would question the wisdom of the decision to continue with the gamma camera project in 1975, two years after the invention, announcement, and promotion of the CAT scanner had begun. In fact, *Bio-Medical Insight* predicted in 1976, just a year *after* the introduction of the System Seventy-Seven, that soon we would see the rapid disappearance of the scintillation camera market. Knowing of the superiority of the CAT scanner at that time, why then didn't we put a stop to this project before spending all this money?

Dave Collins: I believe you are tending to see things only in terms of black and white, which is not fair in this situation. As you know, tumor detection and brain studies are only a few of the uses for diagnostic devices. A major application, one that is growing and where the Baird-Atomic S77 excels, is the area of cardiac studies. The scintillation gamma camera, and in particular, the Baird multi-crystal gamma camera, is far superior in diagnosing heart disease to both CAT scanners and ultrasound, and it looks as though we will retain this superiority for some time to come. In addition, the S77 can diagnose artery blockages and obstructed valves in the heart as well as the invasive procedure of catheterization can, and can thus be used to replace the painful and occasionally dangerous (especially in high-risk patients) surgical procedure of locating cardiac dysfunctions.

Because of this major area of technical superiority, and the important growing field of cardiology, I do not see the market for scintillation cameras dwindling away. In fact, I can envision it growing, due to the recognition of the importance of early detection of cardiac irregularities and the realization that an alternative must be found to the sometimes fatal diagnostic catheterization surgery.

Larry Miller: The problem is that the purchase of a highly sophisticated scanning device is viewed as an unnecessary medical expenditure. As we all know, hospitals, being nonprofit organizations, are funded through several types of public sources: community funding, trust foundations, charity drives, insurance companies, and federal and state monies. Historically, hospitals could always purchase the most expensive piece of equipment available as long as it was the best, and they could convince the appropriate committee of their need—a once relatively simple task. This is why hospital costs rose over 20 percent in 1976 whereas patient traffic remained constant. However, there is increasing concern with keeping medical expenses down. Protective regulations developed to curb rapidly made large expenditure decisions are hurting us. The Certificate of Need

(CON) was developed to ensure that instrument purchases were thought about long enough and seriously enough before money was wantonly spent.

The most important of these obstacles to closing a sale of a System is the CON. Getting this piece of paper approved by the proper authorities is the final step—and the most difficult—in acquiring the purchase order for a capital expenditure by a publicly funded hospital or clinic. Most of the time our System is an instrument classified as a capital expenditure.

The CON is now required in all 50 states and the District of Columbia for a purchase of over $150,000. Private physicians and private institutions are exempted from this legislation, but completely private practices account for only 15 percent of the total market. Not only does this regulation make it harder for a hospital to buy a piece of equipment due to justifications of the purchase, but it also causes long delays from the time the first sales call is made until the time an order is actually placed. This considerably slows the recovery period that we so desperately need after our poor start in 1975–1976.

Dave Collins: You're missing an important fact here. The S77 Basic Package is priced just under $100,000 for domestic customers. Most CONs are written for purchases of $150,000 or over. As a result, unless a customer is considering a deluxe version with several costly options, Baird-Atomic would be exempt from this CON obligation. Yes, I know the goal is to sell as fancy an instrument as possible for larger profits, and with our forte in the nuclear medicine business being cardiac studies, that requires the higher priced options. Consequently, most of our instruments will sell for over $150,000. But there are ways of getting around this numerical stopping point. Also, Baird-Atomic has never lost an order due to the veto of a CON made out for the express purpose of purchasing a S77.

Larry Miller: But Dave, that's because Baird has had such a limited market share. One of the considerations in issuing a CON is how many other systems just like it are in existence locally. Maybe Baird has never lost an order due to the CON regulation, but industry leader Ohio Nuclear estimated that the CON requirement reduced their scanner sales in 1977 by between 33 and 50 percent. In December 1977, 190 CONs for scanner and camera applications were vetoed in 30 states. We are not likely to continue our perfect record very much longer, especially if our sales and market share increase as we hope they will.

Dave Collins: Right now there are only two geographical areas that might conceivably be considered to have reached the saturation point with S77s: Philadelphia and Washington, D.C. That leaves quite a bit of room with which to work in the United States alone.

Bob Sanders: Remember, the CON and the test for saturation within a geographical area are only harbingers of things to come. The possibility of additional government regulations will serve to curb sales in the future. As the health care industry becomes a larger and larger portion of our Gross National Product, there exists the possibility that an increasing amount of government regulations, similar to the Certificate of Need legislation, will be enacted, thereby limiting the quantity of scanners and cameras sold. Not all of these regulations are designed to restrict spending; others, under the guise of product safety, for example, will serve the purpose of being so expensive to small manufacturers, such as Baird-Atomic, as to have the effect of driving them out of the market.

Overseas, government regulations for the sale of the S77 are the same as for any product of the same value being imported. The same problems are encountered with preference of native equipment over imported goods, customs procedures, tariffs, duties, international financing, local servicing, and the availability of spare parts.

Dave Collins: As I commented earlier on the subject of CON, these governmental regulations only retard sales; they do not eliminate them. Therefore, regulations such as these will not affect the volume sold; instead, they may affect the rate of growth. These regulations make life more difficult but not impossible. On the plus side, these also limit new entries to the market in the form of potential competitors.

Larry Miller: OK, but that leaves a whole other area of contention. Despite feelings that noninvasive scanning devices may represent the best breakthrough yet in avoiding surgery, their high cost, especially the costs of CAT scanners, cause a great deal of concern. Now computerized X-ray scanners are a distinct improvement for discovering heretofore undetected medical problems, but their purchase requires outlays on the order of $500,000. In fact, CAT scanners are being used as the prime examples of soaring medical costs for questionable purposes in lobbies in Washington. The National Academy of Science Institute of Medicine discourages the use of scanners, warning that strict regulation of placement and utilization must be made to control rising costs.

Steve McNamara: To refute the argument that the initial cost and routine operation and maintenance of the S77 is unjustifiably high, why not compare the cost of a scan with catheterization? The scan costs $100 to $200 and can be done on an outpatient basis; the catheterization procedure alone is $750, plus there's the cost of a few days' stay in a hospital bed and the fees for all the other medical personnel involved. This should be stressed to those who oppose it as being too expensive.

Jim Hopkins: Also, there are still doctors and hospital administrators who agree that cost cutting is important in the medical profes-

sions as it is anywhere else, but who haven't lost sight of the ultimate goal in medical science. These people are afraid that the current reaction against technology because of its high price will have the effect of stalling progress in medical science just as it is getting somewhere in its fight against disease. Medical science should never lose sight of its goal to eradicate disease, and since now it is assisted by the development of modern diagnostic equipment, it shouldn't try to destroy the biggest weapon it has to save lives in the interest of saving pennies.

Steve McNamara: This is somewhat related to financing. I don't think that lack of available financing arrangements is the cause of this lack of sales success with the system. In fact, our generosity in offering lenient credit terms may be hurting our recovery period. For example, we have extended payment terms in which 50 percent is paid now, 30 percent in 6 months, and the remaining 20 percent in another six months with zero interest. Many times the hospital reneges on the final payments, which necessitates the camera's removal (or at least threat of removal) before the balance is paid. Often the final payment is made, but at a much later date than was originally scheduled. This poor payment procedure really hurts small manufacturers like Baird-Atomic. We sorely need the cash and do not have the capital our large competitors do to absorb interest lost due to slow conversion of accounts receivable.

The sales tool of the "Loan and Demo" (L&D) unit does not help our P&L statement much either, mainly because it's not successful enough to pay for itself. Although it provides us goodwill with the hospital, it does not provide us with tangible results. Only 1 out of every 10 of these result in a sale in the United States; the percentage is higher in Europe. Also, a hospital can drag out the L&D period by claiming to be applying for approval of the purchase requisition, thereby preventing us from removing the system for several more months, until it becomes apparent that no sale will ever materialize. I would suggest that we cut back on the use of Loans and Demos as a sales tool since it is so costly and provides such a low return on our investment.

Dave Collins: Although we can all agree with you that this is a major sales expense of questionable value, before we can discard the policy we must consider what our competitors are doing. Since none of them have discounted this admittedly costly practice, we really cannot, either. Eliminating the L&D would definitely put us at a disadvantage vis-à-vis our competitors, and further illustrate to a potential customer why they should buy from the large industry leaders over the small manufacturer. Gentlemen, it is getting late. Let us continue this discussion at our next meeting, at which time we can summarize the main problems with the S77 and decide on a future plan of action.

Notes

1. The forecasting in this chart proved accurate; during the second week of April 1978, Searle Diagnostics announced discontinuation of its scanner.

2. Fictitious names.

O & E Farm Supply
T. F. Funk, E. Gimpel, and O. Guindo

It was a cool, rainy day in November of 1981 when Len Dow, manager of O & E Farm Supply was sitting in his office looking over the past season's records. He felt he had brought the fertilizer outlet a long way since he purchased it in February of 1980. Volume, which had declined to 7,000 tonnes in 1979 due to poor management, increased to 8,400 tonnes in 1980, and to 10,000 tonnes in 1981 (see Exhibit 1). Profit margins, which were also lower in 1979, had returned to the normal 6 percent level in 1981 due to Len's good managing abilities. But Len was not completely satisfied. He wanted to increase the volume and profitability of the outlet, but was not sure what direction he should take.

The Company

O & E Farm Supply is located in Goodland, a town centrally located in a major corn and potato-producing area of Ontario. (See Exhibit 2 for a map of the area.) O & E does most of its business within a five-mile radius of Goodland (60 percent); however, it does have some sales and distribution extending 20 miles from its plant (35 percent) and a very small wholesale market over 100 miles away in northern Ontario (5 percent). At the present time, O & E is involved only in the sale of fertilizers and related services. Dry-bulk blends and bagged blends make up the majority of O & E's fertilizer volume (9,000 tonnes), with 28 percent liquid nitrogen making up a much smaller portion (1,000 tonnes). Potato and vegetable farmers purchase almost 60 percent of O & E's production; corn and cereal farmers account for 33 percent; and sod farmers purchase the remaining 7 percent (see Exhibit 3).

This case was prepared by To Fo Funk, E. Gimpel, and O. Guindo of the University of Guelph. It is intended as a basis for classroom discussion and is not designed to present either correct or incorrect handling of administrative problems.

Copyright © 1982 by the University of Guelph.

EXHIBIT 1 O & E Fertilizer Sales

Year	Tonnes Liquid and Dry Fertilizers	Tonnes Micronutrients
1977	11,000	—
1978	11,000	—
1979	7,000	—
1980	8,400	10
1981	10,000	100

EXHIBIT 2 O & E's Trading Area

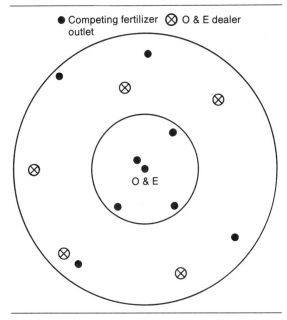

● Competing fertilizer ⊗ O & E dealer
outlet

O & E

EXHIBIT 3 O & E Fertilizer Sales by Farm Type, 1981

Farm Type	Percent of Dry Fertilizer Sales	Percent of Acres Served
Potato and vegetable	60%	35%
Corn and cereals	33	60
Sod	7	5

O & E sells a custom application service for bulk fertilizers and rents application equipment to farmers who wish to apply their own fertilizer. Current equipment consists of two dry-fertilizer spreader trucks, two feeder-delivery trucks to refill spreader trucks on the farms, and three four-tonne tractor-pulled spreaders which are rented out to customers who spread fertilizer themselves. Since Len purchased the organization, he cut the full-time staff from seven to five including himself. One of his newest employees is a young agricultural university graduate who spends most of his time in a sales capacity calling on present and potential customers in the area. Len also spends some of his time making farm calls.

Of O & E's 85 local customers in 1981, 5 were merchant dealers who resell to farmers. These 5 dealers accounted for 2,000 tonnes of O & E's business and ranged in volume from 100 to 1,000 tonnes each. For the most part these dealers are located on the fringes of O & E's 20-mile trading area. In general, of the remaining 80 local customers, Len's records showed that 70 were within 5 miles of the Goodland plant and 10 were at a greater distance. Almost all of these customers purchased more than 50 tonnes of fertilizer a year from O & E.

O & E sold 10 tonnes of micronutrients in 1980 and over 100 tonnes in 1981. Micronutrients are basic elements that a plant requires in relatively small amounts compared to the larger amounts of nitrogen, phosphorus, and potassium found in most regular, blended fertilizers. Micronutrients have been proven by university and industry research in the United States to improve the quality and yield of crops. Commercial trials carried out in Ontario have indicated similar positive results.

The Market and Competition

The total market for fertilizers in O & E's trading area has been remarkably stable at approximately 50,000 tonnes for the past several years. This is not expected to change significantly in the future, although some shifts in types used are possible. Within 5 miles of Goodland there are four major fertilizer outlets competing with O & E for approximately 25,000 tonnes of fertilizer business, and within 20 miles there are an additional three fertilizer outlets competing for the remaining 25,000 tonnes. Len estimates that there are approximately 550 farmers within a five-mile radius of Goodland.

Although the market for fertilizer is very competitive, Len feels that he has been able to better his competition by offering excellent service, by remaining open extended hours, by offering advice and timely delivery to his customers, and by knowing how to deal with the large farmer. Len quickly came to realize that farmers placed service ahead of price when deciding where to buy fertilizer as long as the price was close to that of the competition. Len felt that by offering a superior service, he had nurtured a high level of dealer loyalty in his customers, which resulted in a lower turnover relative to his competition.

Growth Opportunities

Although the business had been doing well, Len realized that growth was essential to future success. He therefore had been giving this matter considerable thought the past couple of months. So far he was able to identify several avenues of growth; now his problem was to evaluate each and arrive at some plan for 1982 and beyond.

Liquid Nitrogen

Len had been toying with the idea of getting into 28 percent liquid nitrogen in a bigger way. He estimated that the total current market in his 20-mile trading area was 4,000 tonnes of which he sold 1,000 tonnes to three corn farmers. This type of fertilizer is of interest mainly to the larger corn farmer because it can be mixed with herbicides for combined application and because of its ease of handling. Although its price per tonne is less than

the price per tonne for dry fertilizers, it is comparable in terms of price per unit of actual nitrogen. This is because it usually is less concentrated than other forms of nitrogen, such as dry urea which contains 45 percent nitrogen compared to the 28 percent concentration in the liquid form. The product is very corrosive, which means that the farmer must also purchase a stainless-steel sprayer costing about $2,000 if he is to use 28 percent liquid nitrogen. This relatively high initial capital outlay restricts use to fairly large farmers. Of the 400 corn farmers in his trading area, approximately 200 have sufficient acreage to be possible 28 percent liquid nitrogen users, and Len estimated that about 20 farmers were using 28 percent liquid nitrogen in 1981. Price is the major purchase criteria since the product is a commodity and little service is involved. Most of the volume of 28 percent liquid nitrogen is sold in December for delivery in the spring (see Exhibit 4 for costs and margins). O & E's current holding capacity is 10,000 gallons or 50 tonnes. If output is increased, additional storage and nurse tanks would have to be purchased as well as another pumping system. A pumping system costs $4,000, storage tanks costs 15 cents per gallon, and a 1,400 gallon nurse tank costs $1,000. Len feels one additional pumping system, one more 10,000-gallon storage tank, and two more nurse tanks should allow a large increase in sales. No matter what Len decided to do, he wanted to stay ahead of his competition by at least two years. Because he felt 28 percent liquid nitrogen could be a big thing in the future, he

EXHIBIT 4 Fertilizer Prices and Margins

| | Dry Fertilizers | | 28% Liquid Nitrogen | | | | Micronutrients | |
| | | | Winter | | Spring | | | |
	$/Tonne	Percent	$/Tonne	Percent	$/Tonne	Percent	$/Tonne	Percent
Average selling price	248	100	138	100	170	100	700	100
Cost of sales	203	82	131	95	136	80	595	85
Gross margin	45	18	7	5	34	20	105	15
Estimated fixed costs	$260,000		$20,000				$5,000	

was excited about this possibility. He had seen a new type of potato planter which required only liquid fertilizer. If this type of planter became popular, the potential for liquid fertilizer would increase dramatically. Despite these positive feelings about this market Len was concerned about a number of things, including the relatively low liquid nitrogen margins and the slow growth of this market in the past. He also wondered whether or not he should consider offering a weed-and-feed service where O & E would apply liquid fertilizer and herbicides for the farmer all in one operation. Len was not really sure of the demand for this service or what was involved in operating a weed-and-feed program. He did know that there was no one currently offering such a service in his area.

Micronutrients

Another opportunity confronting Len was to try to expand micronutrient sales in a major way. At the present time, O & E was a dealer for the Taylor Chemical Company, which produces and sells a complete line of micronutrients. Included in their line are manganese, zinc, iron, copper, molybdenum, boron, calcium, and sulfur. These materials are sold separately or in various combinations designed to treat specific crops. An example of the latter is the company's vegetable mix, which contains magnesium, sulfur, copper, iron, manganese, and zinc in fixed proportions. The individual materials and mixes are sold in two ways: in a dry form for mixing by the dealer with other fertilizer products, and in liquid form for spray application by the farmer on the foliage of the growing crop. Although foliar application is more bother for the farmer, and may result in some leaf burning, some farmers prefer it because they can postpone micronutrient application until visible signs of deficiencies occur. Also, there is some research which indicates that micronutrients can be most effective if absorbed through the

leaves at the peak growth period of the plant. Despite the apparent advantages of foliar application, Len had not sold any micronutrients in this form during his first two years in this business. If properly applied, he felt liquid micronutrients offered the most value to his customers, yet he noticed a great deal of reluctance and skepticism on the part of even the most progressive farmers in his area to try this product form.

Sales of the dry, mixed micronutrients had grown considerably over the past year and it appeared that the products offered real value to customers. One of Len's customers applied micronutrients to half of a large potato field and treated the other half as he normally did. The treated field yielded 327 hundredweight whereas the untreated portion only yielded 304 hundredweight. This 23 hundredweight gain resulted in a $111.55 higher revenue per acre when computed at the $4.85-per-hundredweight price to the farmer. Unfortunately, the University of Guelph, which farmers look to for technical information, is not promoting or even recommending the use of micronutrients (see Appendix B). Their soil-testing service, which analyzes soil samples for most Ontario farmers and makes fertilizer use recommendations, doesn't even include an analysis for micronutrients. The competition does not want to get involved in this business unless there is a very high demand and they start to lose their other fertilizer business. Of the 100 tonnes sold in 1981, 75 went to six large potato farmers representing 3,500 acres, 10 tonnes went to vegetable farmers, and 15 tonnes went to corn farmers (see Exhibit 5 for rates and cost per acre). Len has receiving excellent service and advice from the company distributing the micronutrients. He felt that the use of micronutrients was becoming accepted by the farmers using them, and that sales should rise in the future. Len chuckled to himself as he recalled the day two very large potato farmers who were brothers were sitting in his office and the sub-

EXHIBIT 5 Micronutrient Sales by Crop, 1981

Crop	Tonnes Sold	Acres	Application Rate	Cost/Acre
Potatoes	75	3,500	50 pounds per acre	$15.90
Corn	15	1,300	25 pounds per acre	8.00
Vegetables	10	400	50 pounds per acre	15.90

ject of micronutrients came up. One of the brothers, Jack, asked the Taylor sales rep if he thought they should be using micronutrients. The sales rep related all of the advantages of using micronutrients to them whereupon Jack turned to his brother and asked, "Well, what do you think?" Peter replied "Yes, I think we should be using them." With that Len landed a micronutrients' order worth several thousand dollars.

Len was convinced that micronutrients had potential in his area. His major concern was how he could convince farmers to spend an additional $10 to $15 per acre on a product for which there was no objective basis for determining need.

Northern Ontario

Len was also considering expanding sales in northern Ontario. Currently, he has three dealers selling bagged fertilizer for him in Sault Ste. Marie, New Liskeard, and Kenora. O & E's current volume is approximately 500 tonnes of bagged fertilizer only. Several co-op outlets have most of the market in this area. Prices are very competitive and there appears to be strong dealer loyalty to the co-ops. There are many small farms in the region with 75–100 acres of workable land per farm. The crop types in the area are mixed grain, barley, hay, and a few hundred acres of potatoes near Sudbury. On the average, farmers in northern Ontario who use fertilizer purchase 2–3 tonnes of bagged fertilizer per year and do their purchasing in the winter months. Because the retail price of fertilizer in Northern Ontario is similar to that around Goodland,

the margin to O & E is reduced by about $17 a tonne, the sum of the $12 dealer commission and the $5 freight cost. The lower margin is offset to some extent by lower personal selling costs since dealers are used. Although the growing season is only 2–3 weeks behind that of Goodland, because most sales in the area occur in the winter months, O & E's ability to service the Goodland area in the spring is not affected. One reservation about dealing with the distant northern Ontario market is that credit could be a problem, particularly because the cost of collection could run very high due to the distance involved. On the more positive side, Len is quite optimistic about the long-run potential growth of this market. He feels that there is an ultimate total industry potential in this market of 50,000 to 60,000 tonnes of dry fertilizer of which perhaps 10 to 20 percent has been developed at the present time.

Agricultural Chemicals

So far O & E's product line consisted only of fertilizers. Len observed, however, that all of his competitors carried insecticides, herbicides, and fungicides as well, and he wondered if he should be getting into this business too. Len had always believed that concentrating on one line was the way to go. Agricultural chemicals were very competitively priced leaving small margins in the neighborhood of 5–10 percent for the dealer. Len felt that farmers in his trading area bought fertilizer and chemicals each on their own merits. For example, if a dealer had a hot price on fertilizer, this would not mean that farmers also would buy their chemicals from the same dealer unless of course they were also the lowest price. At any rate, Len sized up his customers as not wanting to buy everything from one dealer, so he was satisfied to receive all of their fertilizer business and to leave the other lines to the other dealers. The set-up costs for carrying chemicals would be approximately $20,000 for an additional warehouse. No other direct costs would be attributable to the chemical line, but Len knew that servicing the line would take valuable time away from servicing and selling the fertilizer line which could possibly result in lower sales and profits. Len estimated that the average farmer in his trading area spent $3,000 to $5,000 per year on agricultural chemicals.

Dry Fertilizers

An alternative Len thought particularly attractive was to expand dry fertilizer sales in his local trading area. Although he had a substantial share of this market already, he felt he could pick up more through aggressive pricing and continued good service. He was especially interested in this alternative because no matter what he did, he knew his present plant, which was over 20 years old, would have to be upgraded. As part of his plant improvement program he planned to set up a new mixing system that would be adaptable to adding micronutrients without any downtime. This mixer could be purchased in two sizes: the smallest size was similar to his present system with a maximum capacity of 15,000 tonnes and cost $100,000, while the larger size had an annual capacity of 20,000 tonnes and cost $160,000. Because of this opportunity to increase his capacity, Len wondered if he shouldn't just try to sell more dry fertilizer to both his current customers and possibly some new ones in his local trading area. As part of his strategy to do this he was thinking about adding another person to his staff who would act as a second salesman and

develop and offer a comprehensive crop-management service to interested farmers. He was also considering the possibility of developing a local advertising program aimed at developing more awareness and interest among farmers outside his immediate five-mile concentrated area. The total cost of the new sales specialist would be about $35,000 per year, and the local advertising would cost about $10,000 per year.

The Decision

Len knew he would have to make a decision soon if he were to make some changes for 1982. Although he had identified what he thought were several good opportunities for future growth, he knew he could not pursue all of them right away, and therefore he would have to establish some priorities. To help him in this assessment, he recently wrote away to the University of Guelph and received a publication entitled "Farmer Purchasing and Use of Fertilizers in Ontario." (See Appendix A for a summary of this 1979 study.) With this new information, plus his own size-up of the situation, Len began the process of planning for 1982 and beyond. He knew that economic conditions in 1982 were not expected to be good. This made the necessity of coming up with a successful plan all the more important to Len.

Appendix A: Results of Fertilizer Marketing Research Study

1. Only 7 percent of total crop acreage in southern Ontario is not fertilized at the present time. This acreage is almost entirely in soybeans, pasture, and forages.

2. The average fertilizer application rate for southern Ontario farmers is 384 pounds per acre. Most farmers use soil-test recommendations from the University of Guelph to deter-

mine the application rate. There is some tendency for farmers to apply more fertilizer than recommended by their soil tests.

3. The major types of fertilizer used by southern Ontario farmers are dry-bulk blends and liquid nitrogen. Of lesser importance are dry-bagged fertilizers, anhydrous ammonia, and liquid mixes (N-P-K). Liquid nitrogen fertilizers are almost exclusively used by very large farmers.

4. Most farmers find the quality and availability of fertilizers to be very good.

5. In southern Ontario as a whole, a relatively small percentage of farmers purchase a large percentage of the fertilizer products sold. The breakdown is as follows:

	Percent of Farmers	Percent of Purchases
Under 25 tonnes	30%	10%
26–50 tonnes	35	25
51–100 tonnes	20	20
Over 100 tonnes	15	45

6. Over 70 percent of all dry fertilizers are sold to farmers in April and May. This figure is somewhat lower (50 percent) for liquid nitrogen.

7. Thirty percent of Ontario farmers use dealer custom application services, while 75 percent apply the fertilizer themselves, using rented dealer application equipment. There is some tendency for larger farmers to be more inclined to want custom-application services.

8. In the course of a year, farmers discuss their fertilizer program with a number of parties to get information and advice on various aspects of fertilizer use and dealer selection. The influence groups most widely consulted are the local fertilizer dealer, other farmers, and family members. In addition to these influence groups, fertilizer-company representatives, agricultural extension officials, and university scientists are consulted by some farmers. In the case of company represent-

atives and university scientists, proportionately more larger farmers visit these people than smaller farmers.

9. Farmers also obtain fertilizer information from soil-test results, various government publications, company-sponsored farmer meetings, dealer-demonstration plots, and company and dealer displays at farm shows and fairs.

10. Over 60 percent of all farmers contact more than one fertilizer dealer before making a purchase. Larger farmers have a tendency to contact more dealers than smaller farmers.

11. Over 50 percent of all farmers reported receiving an on-farm call by a fertilizer dealer in the last year. Larger farmers reported receiving more dealer call than smaller farmers.

12. In addition to fertilizers, southern Ontario farmers purchase on the average more than three other products from their fertilizer supplier. Of these, the most common are herbicides, insecticides, general farm supplies, and seeds. Large farmers are more likely to purchase herbicides and insecticides from their fertilizer supplier than are small farmers.

13. Six dealer services were identified as being essential to all but a very small proportion of farmers: (1) application equipment, which is available when needed and in good repair; (2) custom application services; (3) custom fertilizer blending; (4) fertilizer information through a well-informed staff, brochures, newsletters, and farmer meetings; (5) soil testing; and (6) demonstrations.

14. Other dealer services which were reported as being important to smaller groups of farmers were crop management assistance, help in securing expert assistance with problems, and custom herbicide application.

15. Dealer location, price, and availability of product when needed are the major factors farmers consider when selecting a fertilizer dealer. In general, dealer location and avail-

ability of product when needed are more important to smaller farmers while price is more important to larger farmers.

16. Over 45 percent of all farmers purchase fertilizer from their nearest dealer. On the average, farmers purchase from dealers located less than five miles from their farms.

17. Thirty percent of all farmers purchase from more than one dealer. Larger farmers have a greater tendency to spread their purchases over more dealers than do small farmers.

18. Analysis of dealer switching showed that one third of the farmers made no dealer changes in the past five years, one third made only one change, and the remaining one third made two or more changes. Those farmers making several dealer changes are the larger, younger farmers.

Appendix B: No Substitutes for Rotation

This past year there has been a lot of interest in Perth and Huron counties about micronutrients. There are numerous plots out this year with different formulations and mixes and ways of application, both on corn and beans. We are sure there will be a lot of discussion this winter about the subject.

Some things are becoming evident about micronutrients—at least we think they are.

The first is that you cannot expect dramatic yield increases with individual nutrients on small areas.

Secondly, none of the micronutrient sales staff has been able to explain to us the problem of overapplying micronutrients. They suggest if you put on too much potash you may tie up magnesium. If you put on too much phosphorus, you may need to put on more zinc and manganese. We believe, with our variable soils, in some fields you can put on too much zinc and manganese.

Finally these micronutrients seem to be most attractive to growers with poor crop rotations. Some of your neighbors have gone to poor crop rotations and their yields have dropped. (You know they are the ones that think Pioneer corn followed by Cargill corn is crop rotation.) Now they are searching for something to pull their yield back to former highs. Micronutrients appear to them to be an answer.

What puzzles us is why some of you are willing to spend large sums of money on products you are not sure will work: shotgun micronutrients. We both know what the problem is. You have to get more crops into the rotation, especially perennial forages. I suppose the bottom line is when you hear your neighbor talking about all the micronutrients he is using. That's just a polite way for him to tell you he has a terrible crop rotation.

This article was written by Pat Lynch and John Heard.

Acme Office Products, Inc.
James R. Stock

Herb Townsend had just returned to his office following the quarterly sales meeting of all airfreight salespeople in the midwest region, Peerless Airlines. Herb had been told by his

This case was prepared by James R. Stock of the University of Oklahoma for the purpose of classroom discussion.

Douglas M. Lambert and James R. Stock, *Strategic Physical Distribution Management.* © 1982 Richard D. Irwin, Homewood, Ill.

sales manager that Peerless, a national carrier, was embarking on an ambitious five-year plan that would expand the firm's lift capacity by 150 percent (with the addition of 28 wide-bodied jet aircraft). The increased capacity meant that Herb, as well as the rest of the Peerless airfreight sales team, would have to generate more revenues from their present customers or from new business. For some time Herb had been exploring the idea of trying to entice nonairline shippers into using the services of air freight. More specifically, Herb felt that many of the LTL shippers using motor carriers, who had been adversely affected by rising carrier rates in recent months, might be willing to consider Peerless's airfreight container rates. When container rates were first introduced to the sales force several months previously, one of the selling points was that they would directly compare with motor carrier LTL (less-than-truckload) rates on some product shipments and over some routes.

In the weeks that followed the sales meeting Herb investigated a number of industries that shipped primarily by LTL and he was able to identify several likely prospects for Peerless. One industry which seemed to offer substantial potential in terms of volume and growth was office products. Further analysis revealed that airfreight had been used in the past by companies in this industry only for emergency shipment of products. LTL shipments were the dominant method of transport in the industry, especially for small- and medium-sized companies.

Through a local library and chamber of commerce, Herb was able to develop a listing of office products firms in his sales territory. He decided that he would schedule a visit with one of the firms on the list early in the following week. As he examined the companies on the list, he saw that one firm, Acme Office Products, Inc., was located in the same general area as his regular sales calls. Herb obtained as much information as he could on the company and set up an appointment with the firm's traffic manager for early in the week.

Company Background

Acme Office Products Company is one of five prominent U.S. manufacturers of electric pencil sharpeners/letter openers. The company has shown continued growth over the past 10 years of approximately 5 percent per year. Return on investment has averaged approximately 10 percent per year over this same period. Acme has had the reputation of producing a quality product at a modest price. This has been the major objective of corporate management since the company's inception. All aggregate planning decisions are made with this philosophy in mind.

The company has one manufacturing facility which is located in Chicago, Illinois. Inventories of Acme's products are distributed through independent wholesalers in New York City, Dallas, and Los Angeles. The company uses public warehousing space in Denver, Minneapolis, and Atlanta. Additionally, the company owns a warehouse located adjacent to the plant. Essentially, the company produces only two models of pencil sharpeners—the basic model, retailing for $6.95, which is an electric pencil sharpener with no attachments; and the deluxe model, retailing for $19.95, which is both an electric pencil sharpener and a letter opener. The basic model is quite popular because of its low cost and also because of its superior quality in relation to competing electric pencil sharpeners at comparable prices.

The company services seven major markets: Chicago, Atlanta, Dallas, Denver, Los Angeles, Minneapolis, and New York City. In cities where Acme deals through wholesalers, the wholesalers are responsible for distribution of the product to retail stores. In those locations where the company uses public warehouses, and in Chicago where the company-owned warehouse is located, Acme must assume the costs for delivering its product to the retail outlets.

Acme is beginning to face severe competition from foreign manufacturers, especially in the Los Angeles market. These competitors have increased their combined market share from 5 percent to 28 percent in the Los Ange-

les market. While competition from these foreign manufacturers is not as critical in other
markets, Acme management believes that
these competitors will pose a serious threat to
these markets within the next 1–3 years.

Situation Analysis

In August 1981, Herb Townsend called on Ron
Simmons, traffic manager for Acme Office
Products. Simmons was a bit surprised to see
an airfreight salesman since in his 20 years on
the job he had really not considered airfreight
as a possible means of moving his goods. On
several occasions Simmons had arranged to
move an emergency shipment by air through
his local freight forwarder. These emergencies usually occurred around the Christmas
season and he was well satisfied with this
emergency service. However, the idea of using airfreight to move all of his products to
market did not really seem feasible from an
economic point of view.

In their initial meeting, Townsend explained
that new capacity, new rate structures, and
new services provided by the airlines were increasingly attractive to LTL surface shippers.
At this point, Townsend asked Simmons a series of screening questions about the product.
These included questions about:

1. Size of shipment.
2. Origin and destination of shipments.
3. Weight/value of shipment.
4. Seasonal patterns of shipment.
5. Present shipping costs.
6. Public warehouse costs.
7. Company warehouse costs.
8. Production patterns.
9. Customer requirements.
10. Inventory policy.

Simmons did not have all of this information readily available but promised to send

the information to Townsend as soon as it
could be collected. On his part, Townsend
promised to respond with a specific proposal
for Simmons as soon as he received the information. The information supplied by Simmons is presented in Appendix A.

Herb Townsend also requested some information from his staff support group. This information is presented in Appendix B.

Production, Inventory, and Delivery Requirements

The company presently operates a single shift
of eight hours. There are five work days per
week and a total of 250 available work days
per year (the company is shut down for two
weeks each year for remodeling, repair and
maintenance of machines, employee vacations, etc.) The production of the basic and
deluxe models of sharpeners/letter openers is
performed using workstations. Both models
share the same facilities. At each workstation, a different portion of the product is assembled and/or tested. Parts are moved
through the facility on a conveyor-belt system. The casings for each model are manufactured on premises using an automatic molding
machine. The packaging of each model is also
completely automated. The manufacturing
cycle is fairly long and completed models go
into inventory continuously as production
progresses.

Demand for the basic and deluxe models is
seasonal with peak demand being November–
December. Exhibit 1 shows orders received
by month for the past four years. Sales volume of basic models is approximately 2 to 1
over the deluxe model.

Production lots are determined by the production superintendent. No systems of annual
production budgets or monthly production
goals exist, and therefore, production is scheduled on an intuitive basis (based only on the
superintendent's past experience). Produc-

EXHIBIT 1 Orders Received (*000 Units*)

	1977		1978		1979		1980	
	Basic	Deluxe	Basic	Deluxe	Basic	Deluxe	Basic	Deluxe
January	4.8	2.4	4.7	2.4	4.9	2.4	5.4	2.8
February	5.0	2.7	4.5	2.6	5.2	2.8	5.3	3.0
March	4.7	2.6	5.0	2.6	4.8	2.7	5.2	3.1
April	4.7	3.0	5.0	2.8	5.5	3.1	5.5	2.9
May	4.6	2.7	5.2	3.2	4.9	2.8	5.3	3.4
June	4.8	3.0	4.9	3.3	5.3	3.2	5.5	3.3
July	4.9	2.8	4.9	3.2	5.1	3.4	5.3	3.2
August	4.7	2.7	5.2	3.0	4.8	3.2	5.4	3.4
September	5.0	2.8	5.3	2.7	5.0	3.2	5.2	3.0
October	4.8	3.2	5.0	2.8	5.2	3.1	5.9	3.4
November	5.8	4.0	6.0	4.0	6.4	3.8	6.8	4.2
December	6.2	4.2	6.3	4.6	6.8	4.8	7.2	4.8
Total	60.0	36.1	62.0	37.2	63.9	38.5	68.0	40.5

tion figures for each model are provided in Exhibit 2.

Delivery is a very important concern of the company. Acme's competitors have been providing almost immediate delivery and some Acme salespeople have reported that some customers (wholesalers and retailers) cited delivery problems as the reason for selection of a competitor's product. This was especially true when the wholesalers or retailers were experiencing storage and/or demand problems. In such instances, they would select against those companies with longer and/or less consistent delivery times. The whole-salers with which Acme dealt were in very strong positions and management felt that the policies of the wholesalers had to be followed. These wholesalers were considered by the industry to be the best available, even with some of their restrictive policies. The retailers were also valued highly because of their past success in selling Acme's products. Most of the difficulties with retailers had been with the newer firms (department and variety stores) rather than with the older more traditional firms (stationary and office-supply stores). The older stores tended to be more lenient with respect to inconsistency in delivery.

EXHIBIT 2 Electric Pencil Sharpener Production (*000 Units*)

	1977		1978		1979		1980	
	Basic	Deluxe	Basic	Deluxe	Basic	Deluxe	Basic	Deluxe
January	5.2	2.9	5.7	2.8	5.4	3.0	5.3	3.2
February	5.4	2.9	5.7	3.0	5.3	3.1	5.1	3.4
March	4.8	2.8	5.6	3.1	5.7	3.0	5.1	3.5
April	4.7	3.1	5.9	2.9	6.0	2.7	4.8	3.6
May	5.8	3.2	5.2	3.1	6.0	2.7	5.2	3.7
June	6.0	3.1	6.1	3.2	5.7	3.0	5.1	3.6
July	5.7	3.0	5.3	2.6	5.9	3.1	5.4	3.2
August	5.9	3.2	5.2	3.1	5.1	2.9	6.0	3.2
September	5.2	2.9	5.7	3.0	5.0	3.6	5.6	3.5
October	5.0	3.0	5.0	3.2	5.1	3.4	5.3	3.3
November	5.2	2.9	5.1	3.1	5.4	3.2	5.1	3.4
December	5.7	2.8	5.8	3.2	5.4	2.9	5.6	3.2
Total	64.6	35.8	66.3	36.3	66.0	36.6	63.6	40.8

Acme has been using a major motor carrier for the past 15 years in its shipment of goods to its major markets. Service had generally been satisfactory although on a few occasions shipments had arrived somewhat later than promised at various points. One example occurred about six months ago when a shipment was about six days late. The order was returned to Acme by the wholesaler because it had obtained a competitor's shipment the previous day. The wholesaler in Los Angeles, as well as the one in New York City, has a habit of refusing shipments that are several days late. Otherwise, service had been satisfac-

tory. Shipment times did, however, vary somewhat, depending on the point serviced. For example, shipment time between Chicago and Los Angeles varied between 3 days and 10 days, with most shipments requiring 4 to 6 days. See Exhibit 3 for shipment times between points and their respective probabilities. The probabilities had been obtained by examining shipping records over a one-year period. Shipment times were recorded and then arrayed on a graph to obtain a distribution of transit times. Probabilities were then obtained from these graphs. Loss due to theft and damage was normal for the carrier used

EXHIBIT 3 LTL Motor Transit Time

	Days in Transit	Probabilities	Average
Chicago–New York City	2–6	P(2) = .05	
		P(3) = .20	
		P(4) = .50	
		P(5) = .20	
		P(6) = .05	4 days
Chicago–Atlanta	2–6	P(2) = .30	
		P(3) = .55	
		P(4) = .05	
		P(5) = .05	
		P(6) = .05	3 days
Chicago–Dallas	2–6	P(2) = .05	
		P(3) = .20	
		P(4) = .50	
		P(5) = .20	
		P(6) = .05	4 days
Chicago–Denver	2–8	P(2) = .05	
		P(3) = .10	
		P(4) = .20	
		P(5) = .30	
		P(6) = .15	
		P(7) = .15	
		P(8) = .05	5 days
Chicago–Minneapolis	1–4	P(1) = .40	
		P(2) = .30	
		P(3) = .20	
		P(4) = .10	2 days
Chicago–Los Angeles	3–10	P(3) = .05	
		P(4) = .15	
		P(5) = .20	
		P(6) = .25	
		P(7) = .15	
		P(8) = .10	
		P(9) = .05	
		P(10) = .05	6 days

Rates apply to electric pencil sharpeners, Item No. 1265/ONMSCA13.

and the commodity carried, although reimbursement for lost, stolen, or damaged items generally took six months or longer. The company had compared rates between rail and motor carriage for its LTL shipments several years before and had found that the LTL motor-carriage rate was lower. The company had not compared rates between various modes in recent years.

As mentioned previously, there are seven major distribution points. Of these seven points the company owns or rents public warehousing space at four of them. Inventories are carried at each of these locations in amounts sufficient to handle two-months' average demand before stock-outs occur. The largest part of the inventory is comprised of the basic model of pencil sharpeners. The values of inventory at the company owned and public warehouses are shown in Exhibit 4.

EXHIBIT 4 Value of Inventory on Hand
as of 12/31/80

	Basic Model	Deluxe Model
Denver	$15,679	$ 23,940
Minneapolis	11,509	3,885
Chicago	84,095	143,640
Atlanta	16,680	26,613

Inventory is valued at retail selling price for insurance purposes. Additionally, the company ships approximately 1,260 units per month to each wholesaler in New York City, Dallas, and Los Angeles. The other distribution points are shipped units as needed when the inventory on hand at any location falls below the level representing the total of two-months' average demand. Inventory in all warehouses is comprised of the two models of pencil sharpeners.

Few raw materials are carried in inventory at the manufacturing facility inasmuch as all parts not manufactured by Acme are available from sources within the Chicago area

and delivery times for these items always average less than two days from time of order to receipt of shipment. At the Chicago warehouse a computerized inventory system is employed and management is provided with a computer printout of stock on hand at the end of each week. A clerk then determines whether the inventories have fallen below the specified levels. If so, the clerk sends an operation job ticket to the production superintendent. The superintendent usually holds these order tickets until there are enough to constitute a lot. At such time, production of the needed models is begun. With this batching of orders, lead time is reduced to one week.

An important consideration, as mentioned previously, is consistency in shipment time. Simmons has estimated that whenever a shipment exceeds its normal time in transit by a significant amount (i.e., when shipments that average two days or less take four or more days; when shipments that average more than two days but less than five days take six or more days; when shipments that average five days but less than six days take eight days or more; and when shipments that average six days to eight days take more than nine days) or whenever a stock-out occurs at either a public warehouse or wholesaler, the result is a lost sale—either because of unfilled demand in the case of a stock-out or returned orders in the case of the wholesaler.

The Air Freight Proposal

Herb Townsend told Mr. Simmons that shipping by air would reduce inventories and improve customer service. He stated that he could improve consistency of service and make this improvement at competitive transportation charges.

Simmons has provided information about current shipping methods, cost, service levels, and other aspects of company policy.

EXHIBIT 5 LTL Motor Carriage Rates (*Includes Pick-Up and Delivery*)

	Minimum Charge	Up to 500	500–1,000	1,000–2,000	2,000–5,000	5,000 or Over
		Rates per CWT Minimum Weight (in Pounds)				
Chicago–New York	11.92	8.67	8.33	7.37	6.84	5.79
Chicago–Minneapolis	10.15	7.15	6.33	5.48	5.18	4.38
Chicago–Atlanta	10.40	7.70	7.62	6.51	5.93	5.12
Chicago–Los Angeles	14.80	14.80	9.21	8.27	7.82	7.37

	Minimum Charge	Up to 1,500	1,500–5,000	5,000 or Over		
Chicago–Dallas	13.40	8.54	27.82	6.98		

	0–100 lbs.	100–150	150–200	200–250	250–300	Over 300
		Minimum Charges				
Chicago–Denver	10.42	10.69	11.88	13.09	14.23	15.83

	Less than 1,000 lbs.	1,000–2,000	2,000–5,000	Over 5,000		
		Rates per CWT				
Chicago–Denver	8.32	7.72	7.15	6.75		

Rates apply to electric pencil sharpeners, Item No. 126510NMSCA13.

Appendix A: Information Provided by Mr. Simmons, Traffic Manager, Acme Office Products Company

Cost Information

Mr. Simmons has contacted the production superintendent, Mr. Boyd, in order to obtain an accurate and up-to-date listing of cost estimates. The total costs as provided by Mr. Boyd for the basic model averaged $4, and for the deluxe model, $14. These costs did not, however, include transportation charges from point of manufacture to point of distribution. Transportation charges are presented in Exhibit 5. Wholesalers are charged $5.50 per unit for the basic model and $16 per unit for the deluxe model. This includes delivery. With this mark-up, the company realizes a modest profit on each unit sold to wholesalers. Costs of warehousing are indicated below:

EXHIBIT 6

Chicago	
Initial construction costs*	$75,000
Operating costs per year:	
Taxes	1,100
Insurance	800
Heat	2,000
Electricity	700
Labor	10,000

*Does not include depreciation of building and fixtures on a straight-line basis over a 20-year period.

At Denver, Atlanta, and Minneapolis, where public warehousing is utilized, costs are as follows:

Storage: 8 cents per carton per month.
Handling: 22.5 cents per carton per month.

Delivery costs from the warehouse to the retail outlet are comparable to the rates as shown in Exhibit 7. The delivery rate per carton is the same as the minimum charge (i.e., in Atlanta, $3.30 per carton). Mr. Boyd has estimated that inventory carrying costs average 25 percent at each location where inventory is stored.

Other data which has been collected by Mr. Boyd includes the following:

Merchandise value per pound
Basic model	$1.75
Deluxe model	$4.00

Weight per item (per pound, including package)
Basic model	4.0
Deluxe model	5.0

Turnover rate at all warehouses (per year)
Basic model	4.0
Deluxe model	2.5

Electric pencil sharpeners are packaged individually and then in cartons of 12 each. Dimensions of cartons containing either basic or deluxe models are 24" × 18" × 12".

Ending inventories as of 12/31/80 at each owned or public warehouse are:

	Units	
Location	Basic Model	Deluxe Model
Chicago	12,100	7,200
Atlanta	2,400	1,344
Denver	2,256	1,200
Minneapolis	1,656	696

Appendix B: Rate Information Provided by Peerless Airlines Staff Support Group

EXHIBIT 7 Pickup Delivery Rates (*Airfreight Shipments Only: Not Applicable to Containerized Shipments*)

	Minimum Charge	Rates per CWT Minimum Weight (in Pounds)					
		100	1,000	2,000	3,000	5,000	10,000
Pickup							
Chicago	$5.00	$2.05	$1.70	$1.30	$1.15	$1.00	$0.75
Delivery							
Atlanta	3.30	1.25	1.20	1.15	1.10	1.10	0.85
Dallas	2.80	1.30	1.20	1.05	1.00	0.75	0.65
Los Angeles	4.30	2.10	1.75	1.50	1.10	0.90	0.65
New York	6.95	3.45	3.15	3.00	2.70	2.05	1.50
Minneapolis	3.40	1.35	1.25	1.00	0.90	0.75	0.65
Denver	3.35	1.60	1.50	1.30	1.00	0.65	0.55

All pickups and deliveries within Zone A.

EXHIBIT 8 General Commodity Rates (*Airport to Airport*)

	Minimum Charge	Rates (per Pounds)				
		1	100*	1,000†	2,000	3,000
Chicago–Atlanta	$10.00	$0.16	$12.45	$11.40	$10.75	$ 9.70
Chicago–Dallas	10.00	0.18	13.15	11.40	11.40	10.80
Chicago–Los Angeles	12.00	0.32	23.50	21.15	20.45	19.70
Chicago–New York	10.00	0.17	12.45	11.40	10.75	9.35
Chicago–Minneapolis	10.00	0.12	7.90	7.15	6.80	6.30
Chicago–Denver	10.00	0.19	14.40	13.00	12.00	10.25

*Rate per 100 pounds for shipments weighing up to 999 pounds.
†Rate per 100 pounds for shipments weighing 1,000 pounds to 1,999 pounds.

EXHIBIT 9 Pickup and Delivery Rates (*Airfreight Shipments Only: Applicable Only to Containerized Shipments*)

	Type A-1*	LD-3†	LD-N‡
Pickup			
Chicago	$34.00	$19.00	$17.00
Delivery			
Atlanta	27.00	11.00	9.00
Dallas	30.00	13.00	11.50
Los Angeles	44.00	30.00	30.00
New York	81.00	34.00	29.00
Minneapolis	22.00	11.00	10.00
Denver	27.00	15.00	13.50
Breakbulk costs per container	18.00	6.00	5.00

Note: Containers are carrier owned.

*Type A-1 container (up to 425 cubic feet)—maximum gross weight, 10,000 lbs.; empty weight, 200 lbs.

†Type LD-3 container (166 cubic feet)-maximum gross weight, 3,500 lbs.; empty weight, 100 lbs.

‡Type LD-N container (110 cubic feet)—maximum gross weight, 3,100 lbs.; empty weight, 100 lbs.

EXHIBIT 10 Container Rates

	Chicago–Atlanta	Chicago–Minneapolis	Chicago–Dallas	Chicago–Los Angeles	Chicago–New York	Chicago–Denver
Type A-1 containers with net weight of 3,200 lbs. or over						
Charge per container for net weight up to 3,200 lbs.	$219.00	$153.00	$297.00	$555.00	$257.00	$321.00
Rate per 100 lbs. for net weight over 3,200 lbs.	4.80	2.75	7.25	12.55	5.95	7.85
LD-3 containers						
Charge per container	76.00	57.00	105.00	201.00	89.00	122.00
LD-N containers	41.00	n.a.	87.00	144.00	75.00	86.00

n.a. = Not available.

Alaska Native Arts and Crafts Cooperative, Inc.
G. Hayden Green and Walter Greene

The artistry of Alaska natives grew out of a spontaneous urge which embraced many motives, none of which were monetary. The pre-European Alaskan native indulged his creative prowess in embellishments of his person, in recording the details of his unique and colorful culture, and in the symbolic expression of his religion. It didn't occur to these people to create such beauty to be sold. The marketing of native crafts before the advent of the white man simply did not exist, as the native had no conception of payment for his art.

Because of the obvious and unavoidable impact of modern society upon the traditional native culture, the need of at least a minimal cash flow has become vital to the basic survival of these people. A man must have money for his snow machine or outboard motor in or-

This case was prepared by Professor G. Hayden Green of the University of Alaska and Professor Walter Greene, University of North Dakota.

Dennis H. Tootelian and Ralph M. Gaedeke *Cases and Classics in Marketing Management.* Copyright © 1986 by Harcourt Brace Jovanovich, Inc. Reprinted by permission of the publisher.

der to engage in subsistence hunting and fishing and money for oil to heat his home. Many rural natives who move to Alaska's urban communities lack the education and skills to adapt to a new lifestyle. There is infrequent employment for those who seek to live in the isolated areas of their heritage; consequently, they have discovered an important source of income is the sale of artistic creations and handcrafted items.

The survival of the Alaska Native Arts and Crafts Cooperative, the organization established over 40 years ago to market the creative expression of the aboriginal population of Alaska, has been threatened by an operating deficit. Such important issues as the preservation of a magnificent but imperiled art form versus the uplifting of a destitute and forgotten race are at stake in the formulation of the future of the Alaska firm.

Background of Alaskan Natives

Throughout northwest Alaska and parts of Canada reside a large aboriginal population which includes numerous tribes of Indians, Eskimos, and Aleuts, referred to vernacularly as natives. These people have for generations endured some of the world's harshest climatic conditions. Many native inhabitants of the north still retain a relatively traditional subsistence lifestyle, with hunting and fishing being the mainstay of their livelihood. The Bureau of Indian Affairs (BIA), federal and state agencies, and native leaders have since the turn of the century tried to reduce their dependence upon seasonality and volatility of caribou migrations, salmon runs, mammal harvesting, and the public welfare system. This has proven to be no easy task.

Many of the northern villages are hundreds of miles from each other and as much as eight hundred miles from Anchorage, the state's major population center. The harbors are often frozen eight to nine months out of the year; and only the larger communities receive commercial air transportation, which is sporadic at best. The general level of education in many villages does not exceed that of grammar school, and housing conditions are some of the worst in the United States. Most of the smaller communities and even some of the larger communities do not have public sewers or water systems. These living conditions are compounded by winter temperatures of 50° to 60° below zero, and the sun only shines three to six months out of the year. Yet the Alaskan native holds fast to a lifestyle which has been traditional since man first crossed the land bridge from Asia (see Exhibit 1).

Background of Native Arts and Crafts

One of the areas upon which concerned groups have placed much hope for shifting total dependence on subsistence living to a partial cash economy has been the development of the arts and crafts trade. These arts and crafts include ivory carving, basketry, skin sewing, dolls, and other traditional items. These products are not to be confused with curios and mass-produced knickknacks from Japan and Korea which are marketed as cheap imitations, but are works of art, with an individuality of creativity and time-consuming detail which is reflected in their costliness as well as their quality.

History of Arts and Crafts Marketing

In the past, the purchasing of native crafts was done in a very casual manner. The common means of selling work was through the local store manager who would give, if not cash, food and trade goods in return or through the local BIA teacher, bush pilot, local missionaries, and finally, the seasonal tourist and professional trader-buyer. Consequently, this marketing pattern was unsatis-

EXHIBIT 1 Location of Principal Alaskan Native Groups

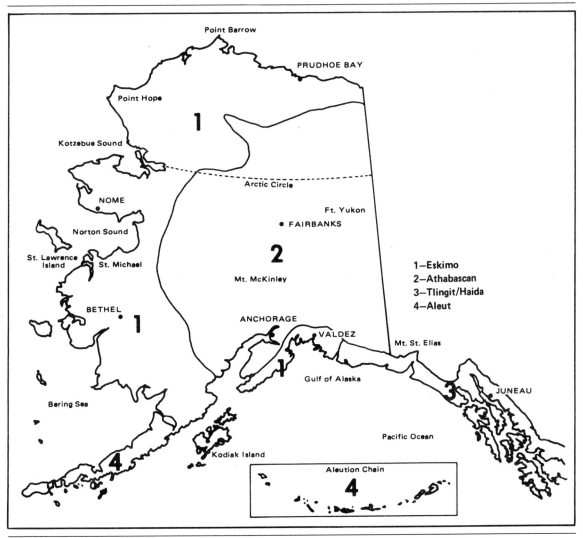

1—Eskimo
2—Athabascan
3—Tlingit/Haida
4—Aleut

factory for the craft people. Even today, professional traders seldom visit a particular village more frequently than once a month.

In 1936 a clearinghouse for native arts and crafts was formed under the sponsorship of the Bureau of Indian Affairs. The intent of the clearinghouse was to establish a marketing mechanism and maintain a central inventory of native arts and crafts. Juneau, the state capital, located in the southwestern part of Alaska and approximately 800 to 1,000 miles south of some of these villages, was selected as the headquarters. It was chosen mainly for its port which was on the regular run of the North Star, a ship that was the major source of transport in Alaska in those years. Articles were sent to Juneau on consignment, warehoused, and later marketed in retail and military stores throughout Alaska. This was an earnest attempt to resolve the natives' plight, but as a whole the program proved ineffective.

In 1956, the BIA reorganized the original clearinghouse and established a private, nonprofit cooperative, the Alaska Native Arts and Crafts Cooperative. The payment and marketing policy of the new organization remained the same as the original establishment. ANAC was not truly serving in a marketing capacity although this was to be one of its more vital functions when the organization was initiated. Instead, it continued to serve as a sort of clearinghouse for the crafts.

The managers of ANAC were not well grounded in exactly what marketing is, as funds were not used for advertising or promotional activities. Indeed, when business became poor and funds short, the books show that expenditures for advertising and travel were cut. Although the ANAC was another step forward in straightening out the crafts cash system, it was far from being a successful organization.

Operating History

In the first year of operation in 1936, ANAC's sales were $29,000. In 1938, the financial figure showed sales at $30,000. For the fiscal year 1939, a value of native arts and crafts rose to $98,000 and thereafter enjoyed a phenomenal rise until the mid-1940s. In part this

was due to contracts with the U.S. Antarctic Expedition made in 1939 and 1940 and a number of contracts with the U.S. Army for the sewing of fur garments.

Annual reports give the peak value of native arts and crafts as $485,641 during the fiscal year 1945. Immediately thereafter there was a dramatic drop in the reported value of sales to a low of $101,133.43 in fiscal year 1946. This was attributed to the decline of military personnel in Alaska from a high of 152,000 to a low of only 19,000 in 1946.

During the mid-1950s and 1960s ANAC sales declined, inventories increased, and profits declined accordingly, a trend which continued through the 1970s (see Exhibit 2).

The Controversy

During this more than 40-year period, Alaska was rampant with different groups who advocated multiple approaches to marketing the arts and crafts of the native population. Their divergent views compounded an already complex situation. Most of them were quite vociferous about their viewpoints. This field of battle had an inhibiting effect upon any spirit of conciliation and rapport. Understandably, little real communication has been established among these groups as their primary concerns were their respective "causes."

There was one faction whose overriding aim was the preservation of native arts at all costs. These people felt that the real value of

EXHIBIT 2 Alaska Native Arts and Crafts Cooperative, Inc. (*Wholesale*)

	Total Net Sales	Cost of Sales	Gross Profit	Operating and Selling Expenses	Net Operating Profit (Loss)	Total Other Income Expense	Net Profit and Losses
Representative year 1970s	$133,800.59	$ 89,346.07	$44,454.52	$58,943.63	($14,489.11)	($7,029.71)	($21,518.82)
Representative year 1960s	130,395.23	84,015.70	46,379.53	52,268.95	(5,889.42)	(7,960.71)	(13,850.13)
Representative year 1950s	181,799.49	129,669.73	52,129.76	46,696.66	5,433.10	272.87	5,705.97

native art lay in the creation of superior objects by a few talented individuals. They esteemed these objects of art as potential museum pieces and deplored the intemperate production of pieces of lesser quality as a corruptive force within the creative community. The proponents of this viewpoint turned a deaf ear to the social injustice group who propounded that the ultimate issue here was the economic betterment of the native groups and that the preservation of the art as an issue was "low man on the totem pole." This group supported the community instituting a regular production-line facility for turning out commercialized versions of native crafts for the tourist trade.

There existed another element composed of a large percentage of politically active natives whose only concern seemed to be that, whatever the program instituted, it should be completely administered by natives. It is no mystery that these people frequently came into direct conflict with that group which advocated the hiring of qualified outside administrative leadership as the most efficient way of getting things done.

The question whether or not the native people even wanted an organization for marketing their goods looms ominously in the background. The answer to this question has not always been in the obvious positive vein that is expected. Some of the leading craftsmen themselves have expressed doubt in this regard.

The New General Manager

This then was the situation when Henry Tiffany III was drafted by the board of directors of ANAC to serve as general manager of the firm and to implement some organizational changes in order to make it more responsive to the needs of Alaskan natives. Henry Tiffany came to Alaska from New York when he was in his early 20s and experienced success

in construction and real estate investments. Through repeated association, due to the mobility demanded of him by his enterprises, he became sensitive to the social and environmental difficulties unique to the Alaskan natives. This concern, as well as a natural appreciation of fine crafts and a desire to see the art form preserved, led him to accept the position as general manager of ANAC. In accepting this post he stipulated that ANAC would sever its connection with the Bureau of Indian Affairs, a condition with which the federal agency concurred.

Expansion of ANAC

After three months of research in the development of a long-range organizational plan, the directors met with the new general manager who presented to them the following proposal: ANAC would open and operate a retail outlet in Anchorage across the street from Alaska's largest hotel. The new retail outlet would include a showroom for direct sales to the public, and approximately half of the 2,000-square-foot store was set aside for craft demonstrations by the artists for the public.

At that time it was also decided that the policy of ANAC would be to encourage the creation of arts and crafts which aspired to the quality sought after by museums and exclusive art stores, and it would discourage the poorer quality of work or mass production of existing designs. Tiffany also proposed that ANAC would become involved in the training of its members and sponsoring of conferences plus promotion to the public in order to advance Alaskan crafts to acceptance as an art form.

With the approval of the board of directors, Henry Tiffany embarked on the program of expansion; and, in the ensuing months, he developed a cooperative relationship with over 120 villages statewide; and the buyer network was established in 12 of these villages.

He moved the Juneau retail operation from the back of an old building to the Juneau retail center near the ferry system and the tourist trade. To accommodate the wholesale business, a loan was obtained for a 4,000-square-foot warehouse erected near the Anchorage Municipal Airport, at which time the wholesale operation was moved from Juneau to the new facilities.

The new general manager introduced the mechanics for a rebate system to reward craftsmen for superior work whereby the buyers used a quadruplicate invoice upon which the buyer's and craftsman's names were recorded plus the item purchased. Where products sold for a higher price due to superior craftsmanship, the craftsman received a quality rebate. A system for providing craft supplies through the native stores was also introduced by Mr. Tiffany. In essence, ANAC was to provide a supply of craft materials to each village store on consignment in each village which contained an ANAC buyer. This required $300 to $500 to

EXHIBIT 3 Alaska Native Arts and Crafts, Cooperative Current Financial Statement Retail Operation

Assets:		
Current assets		
Cash	$ 3,341.89	
Credit cards and layaways	525.68	
Accounts receivable $3,816.21		
less RS. B/D (1,166.58)	3,002.74	
Total	$ 6,870.31	
Inventories (see Schedule A)		
Arts and Crafts, Juneau	$ 27,449.80	
Crafts supplies, Juneau	1,332.75	
Arts and Crafts, Anchorage	32,310.55	
General supplies	2,146.89	
Collection	26,195.80	
Total inventories	$ 89,435.79	
Total current assets		$ 96,306.10
Other assets		
Prepaid expense	$ 2,319.85	
Clearing account*	4,994.68	
Fixed assets	18,531.57	
Deposits	50.00	
Investments	30,000.00	
Total other assets		$ 55,896.10
Total assets		$152,202.20
Liabilities and capital		
Current liabilities	$114,539.49	
Long-term liabilities	195,346.75	
Total liabilities		$309,886.24
Membership fees	926.00	
Retained earnings	(93,591.73)	
Loss from operation		
(See Schedule C)	(65,018.31)	
Fees and retained earnings (Deficit)		($157,684.04)
Total liabilities and capital		$152,202.20

*Includes credit-card discounts.

supply the minimum requirements of each village.

The final and most critical element of the new program was the establishment of cash buyers in each of the craft-producing villages. The success of the rebate system and the craft supplies all hinged on having a good buyers' network. To establish such a network, it was proposed that an ANAC representative would visit each village to study the needs of the craftsman, establish a working relationship with the local governing council, study the community's social and economic base, and interview candidates who were interested in serving as ANAC buyers. The selection and existence of a buyer was completely voluntary and was determined by the local community leaders. It was agreed that most buyers would receive somewhere between 10 and 20 percent of the value of the items purchased. The buyer was left with cash ranging from between $200 and $1,500.

In addition to the expansion program, Tiffany undertook a personal campaign to educate the public in native arts and crafts—his goal ultimately being the preservation of the arts and the halting of imports and poor quality craftsmanship.

Deficits Increase at Accelerated Rate

After several months of operation, deficits amassing, and considerable creditor pressure ensuing, Henry Tiffany wrote the following memo to the ANAC board of directors.

During our expansionary period, operating deficits have continued to mount at an accelerated rate (see Exhibits 3 and 4). A major contributing force in this state of affairs is the buyer system. The system is operating at minimal efficiency due to multiple reasons. Many native buyers entered the program handicapped by both educational and cultural inadequacies. Many did not understand the record-keeping system; consequently they are often unable to account for funds either by their presence or absence. Quality is often overlooked in the subjective viewpoint of the buyers who are not capable of discerning the very best work from those pieces of less worth. Also, as a result of their cultural heritage, nepotism often sets in which further adds to the problem of second-best material being occasionally purchased for top dollars.

Another contributing factor to the monetary deficits is that retail sales in the Anchorage store are not meeting sales objectives and projections. Although the Anchorage retail outlet is in a high foot-traffic district of Anchorage and located

EXHIBIT 4 Alaska Native Arts and Crafts, Cooperative Current Financial Statement Schedule C, Income versus Expense (*Income Statement*)

	Juneau to Date	Anchorage to Date
Sales, Arts and Crafts	$57,105.32	$91,840.56
Sales, craft supplies	2,319.22	
Repair income	20.60	
Misc. income	75.60	1,502.86
Returns and allowance	(193.58)	(450.00)
Sales discounts*	(2,428.60)	(1,621.00)
Sales commission	(344.66)	(20.00)
Postage	—	68.00
Net sales	$56,553.90	$91,320.42
Inventory cost	(40,108.88)	(64,676.45)
Gross profit	$16,445.02)	$26,643.97
Expenses	48,264.60	59,842.10
Net loss	($31,889.58)	($33,198.13)

*Includes credit-card discounts.

across from the state's largest hotel, its sales are disappointing. The problem is caused in part by the fact that the store has poor window visibility and gives the impression of being more of a museum than a retail business. Consequently, I recommend we move the store to a different section of Anchorage's downtown area—one more closely associated with the native community.

Figuring largely in the failure of the expansion program coming to fruition is the evolution of a conflict arising from the very system which it doomed. The structure of ANAC is such that a larger volume of trade is essential to support the overhead incurred by the new warehouse and the two retail outlets. It has become apparent that quality artwork is not available to meet the sales volume needed to support such a system. Consequently, and contrary to the ANAC marketing philosophy, inferior work would have to be purchased to infuse the operation with the cash flow necessary to its survival. I recommend we begin to nullify the policy of expansion and initiate the mechanics of contracting ANAC's exploratory tentacles of growth into a more compact and refined body of endeavor, the aims of which are more consistent with our original goals.

In an attempt to reverse the increasing deficit position, we should sell the Juneau retail store and move the merchandise in the wholesale warehouse to the Anchorage retail establishment and sell the warehouse. The warehouse should bring a price of $185,000, which will pay off the mortgage on it. A new buyer system must also be instituted.

The financial losses incurred by the firm are of a critical nature and immediate steps must be instituted to reverse the trend. However, we should not be discouraged as ANAC is a very successful enterprise. In the early years of the formation of ANAC, our artists made, at best, a nominal wage. Today, a few artists earn a wage comparable to high-paying white-collar jobs in Anchorage, Alaska. A couple of artists have gained such national prominence that they have almost outgrown ANAC and are being courted by patrons of museums and establishments which exhibit the finest examples of American art.

Big Sky of Montana, Inc.
Anne Senausky and James E. Nelson

Introduction

Karen Tracy could feel the pressure on her as she sat at her desk late that April afternoon. Two weeks from today she would be called on to present her recommendations concerning next year's winter season pricing policies for Big Sky of Montana, Inc.—room rates for the resort's accommodation facilities as well as decisions in the skiing and food services areas. The presentation would be made to a top-management team from the parent company, Boyne USA, which operated out of Michigan.

"As sales and public relations manager, Karen, your accuracy in decision making is extremely important," her boss had said in his usual tone. "Because we spend most of our time in Michigan, we'll need a well-based and involved opinion."

"It'll be the shortest two weeks of my life," she thought.

Background: Big Sky and Boyne USA

Big Sky of Montana, Inc., was a medium-sized destination resort located in southwestern Montana, 45 miles south of Bozeman and 43 miles north of the west entrance to Yellowstone National Park.[1] Big Sky was conceived

This case was prepared by Anne Senausky and James E. Nelson. Copyright © 1978 by the Endowment and Research Foundation at Montana State University.

in the early 1970s and had begun operation in November 1974.

The 11,000-acre, 2,000-bed resort was separated into two main areas: Meadow and Mountain villages. Meadow Village (elevation 6,300 feet) was located two miles east of the resort's main entrance on U.S. 191 and seven miles from the ski area. Meadow Village had an 800-bed capacity in the form of four condominium complexes (ranging from studios to three-bedroom units) and a 40-room hostel for economy lodging. Additional facilities included an 18-hole golf course, six tennis courts, a restaurant, a post office, a convention center with meeting space for up to 200 people, and a small lodge serving as a pro shop for the golf course in the summer and cross-country skiing in the winter.

Mountain Village (elevation 7,500 feet) was the center of winter activity, located at the base of the ski area. In this complex was the 204-room Huntley Lodge, offering hotel accommodations, three condominium complexes (unit-size ranged from studio to three bedroom), and an 88-room hostel, for a total of 1,200 beds. The Mountain Mall was also located here, next to the Huntley Lodge and within a five-minute walk of two of the three condominium complexes in Mountain Village. It housed ticket sales, an equipment-rental shop, a skier's cafeteria, two large meeting rooms with a maximum occupancy of 700 persons (regularly used as sack lunch areas for skiers), two offices, a ski-school desk, and a ski-patrol room, all of which were operated by Boyne. Also in this building were a delicatessen, a drugstore/gift shop, a sporting goods store/rental shop, a restaurant, an outdoor clothing store, a jewelry shop, a T-shirt shop, two bars, and a child day-care center. Each of these independent operations held a lease that was due to expire in one to three years.

The closest airport to Big Sky was located just outside Bozeman. It was served by Northwest Orient and Frontier Airlines with con-

nections to other major airlines out of Denver and Salt Lake City. Greyhound and Amtrak also operated bus and train service into Bozeman. Yellowstone Park Lines provided Big Sky with three buses daily to and from the airport and Bozeman bus station (the cost was $4.40 one way, $8.40 round trip) as well as an hourly shuttle around the two Big Sky villages. Avis, Hertz, National, and Budget offered rent-a-car service in Bozeman with a drop-off service available at Big Sky.

In July 1976, Boyne USA, a privately owned, Michigan-based operation, purchased the Huntley Lodge, Mountain Mall, ski lifts and terrain, golf course, and tennis courts for approximately $8 million. The company subsequently invested an additional $3 million in Big Sky. Boyne also owned and operated four Michigan resort ski areas.

Big Sky's top management consisted of a lodge manager (in charge of operations within the Huntley Lodge), a sales and public relations manager (Karen), a food and beverage manager, and an area manager (overseeing operations external to the Lodge, including the Mall and all recreational facilities). These four positions were occupied by persons trained with the parent company; a fifth manager, the comptroller, had worked for pre-Boyne ownership.

Business figures were reported to the company's home office on a daily basis, and major decisions concerning Big Sky operations were discussed and approved by "Michigan." Boyne's top management visited Big Sky an average of five times annually, and all major decisions, such as pricing and advertising, were approved by the parent for all operations.

The Skiing

Big Sky's winter season usually began in late November and continued until the middle of

April, with a yearly snowfall of approximately 450 inches. The area had 18 slopes between elevations of 7,500 and 9,900 feet. The terrain breakdown was as follows: 25 percent novice, 55 percent intermediate, and 20 percent advanced. (Although opinions varied, industry guidelines recommended a terrain breakdown of 20 percent, 60 percent, and 20 percent for novice, intermediate, and advanced skiers, respectively.) The longest run was approximately three miles in length; the temperatures (highs) ranged from 15 to 30 degrees Fahrenheit throughout the season.

Lift facilities at Big Sky included two double chair lifts, a triple chair, and a four-passenger gondola. Lift capacity was estimated at 4,000 skiers per day. This figure was considered adequate by the area manager, at least until the 1980–81 season.

Karen felt that the facilities, snow conditions, and grooming compared favorably with those of other destination resorts of the Rockies. "In fact, our only real drawback right now," she thought, "is our position in the national market. We need more skiers who are sold on Big Sky. And that is in the making."

The Consumers

Karen knew from previous dealings that Big Sky, like most destination areas, attracted three distinct skier segments: local day skiers (living within driving distance and not utilizing lodging in the area); individual destination skiers (living out of state and using accommodations in the Big Sky area); and groups of destination skiers (clubs, professional organizations, etc.).

The first category typically comprised Montana residents, with a relatively small number from Wyoming and Idaho. (Distances from selected population centers to Big Sky are presented in Exhibit 1.) A 1973 study of four Montana ski areas, performed by the Adver-

EXHIBIT 1

Proximity of Population Centers to Big Sky

City	Distance from Big Sky (Miles)	Population (U.S. 1970 Census)
Bozeman, Montana	45	18,670
Butte, Montana	126	23,368
Helena, Montana	144	22,730
Billings, Montana	174	61,581
Great Falls, Montana	225	60,091
Missoula, Montana	243	29,497
Pocatello, Idaho	186	40,036
Idaho Falls, Idaho	148	35,776

Approximate Distance of Selected Major U.S. Population Centers to Big Sky

City	Distance to Big Sky* (in Air Miles)
Chicago	1,275
Minneapolis	975
Fargo	750
Salt Lake City	375
Dallas	1,500
Houston	1,725
Los Angeles	975
San Francisco	925
New York	2,025
Atlanta	1,950
New Orleans	1,750
Denver	750

*Per passenger air fare could be approximated at 20 cents per mile (round trip, coach rates).

tising Unit of the Montana Department of Highways, characterized Montana skiers as:

1. In their early 20s and males (60 percent).

2. Living within 75 miles of a ski area.

3. From a household with two skiers in it.

4. Averaging $13,000 in household income.

5. Intermediate to advanced in ability.

6. Skiing five hours per ski day, 20 days per season locally.

7. Skiing four days away from local areas.

8. Taking no lessons in the past five years.

Karen was also aware that a significant number of day skiers, particularly on the weekends, were college students.

Destination, or nonresident, skiers were labeled in the same study as typically:

1. At least in their mid-20s and males (55 percent).
2. Living in a household of three or more skiers.
3. Averaging near $19,000 in household income.
4. More intermediate in ability.
5. Spending about six hours per day skiing.
6. Skiing 11–14 days per season, with 3–8 days away from home.
7. Taking ski school lessons.

Through data taken from reservation records, Karen learned that individual destination skiers accounted for half of last year's usage based on skier days.[2] Geographic segments were approximately as follows:

Upper Midwest (Minnesota, Michigan, North Dakota)	30%
Florida	20
California	17
Washington, Oregon, Montana	15
Texas, Oklahoma	8
Other	10

Reservation records indicated that the average length of stay for individual destination skiers was about six or seven days.

It was the individual destination skier who was most likely to buy a lodging/lift package; 30 percent made commitments for these advertised packages when making reservations for 1977–78. Even though there was no discount involved in this manner of buying lift tickets, Karen knew that it was fairly popular because it saved the purchaser a trip to the ticket window every morning. Approximately half of the individual business came through travel agents, who received a 10 percent commission.

The third skier segment, the destination group, accounted for a substantial 20 percent of Big Sky's skier day usage. The larger portion of the group business came through medical and other professional organizations holding meetings at the resort, as this was a way to "combine business with pleasure." These groups were typically comprised of couples and individuals between the ages of 30 and 50. Ski clubs made up the remainder, with a number coming from the southern states of Florida, Texas, and Georgia. During the 1977–78 season, Big Sky drew 30 ski clubs with memberships averaging 55 skiers. The average length of stay for all group destination skiers was about four or five days.

A portion of these group bookings was made through travel agents, but the majority dealt directly with Karen. The coordinator of the professional meetings or the president of the ski club typically contacted the Big Sky sales office to make initial reservation dates, negotiate prices, and work out the details of the stay.

The Competition

In Karen's mind, Big Sky faced two types of competition: that for local day skiers, and that for out-of-state (i.e., destination) skiers.

Bridger Bowl was virtually the only area competing for local day skiers. Bridger was a "nonfrills," nonprofit, and smaller ski area located some 16 miles northeast of Bozeman. It received the majority of local skiers, including students at Montana State University, which was located in Bozeman. The area was labeled as having terrain more difficult than that of Big Sky and was thus more appealing to the local expert skiers. However, it also had much longer lift lines than Big Sky and had recently lost some of its weekend business to Big Sky.

Karen had found through experience that most Bridger skiers usually "tried" Big Sky once or twice a season. Season passes for the

EXHIBIT 2 Competitors' 1977–1978 Package Plan Rates,* Number of Lifts, and Lift Rates

	Lodge Double (2)†	Two-Bedroom Condo (4)	Three-Bedroom Condo (6)	Number of Lifts	Daily Lift Rates
Aspen, Colorado	$242	$242	$220	19	$13
Steamboat, Colorado	230	230	198	15	12
Jackson, Wyoming	230	242	210	5	14
Vail, Colorado	230	242	220	15	14
Snowbird, Utah	208	none	none	6	11
Bridger Bowl, Montana	No lodging available at Bridger Bowl			3	8

*Package plan rates are per person and include seven nights' lodging, six lift tickets (high-season rates).
†Number in parentheses denotes occupancy of unit on which price is based.

two areas were mutually honored at the half-day rate for an all-day ticket, and Big Sky occasionally ran newspaper ads offering discounts on lifts to obtain more Bozeman business.

For out-of-state skiers, Big Sky considered its competition to be mainly the destination resorts of Colorado, Utah, and Wyoming. (Selected data on competing resorts are presented in Exhibit 2.) Because Big Sky was smaller and newer than the majority of these areas, Karen reasoned, it was necessary to follow an aggressive strategy aimed at increasing its national market share.

Present Policies

Lift Rates

It was common knowledge that there existed some local resentment concerning Big Sky's lift-rate policy. Although comparable to rates at Vail or Aspen, an all-day lift ticket was four dollars higher than the ticket offered at nearby Bridger Bowl. In an attempt to alleviate this situation, management at Big Sky instituted a nine dollar "chair pass" for the 1977–78 season, entitling the holder to unlimited use of the three chairs plus two rides per day on the gondola, to be taken between specified time periods. Because the gondola served primar-

ily intermediate terrain, it was reasoned that the chair pass would appeal to the local, more expert skiers. A triple chair serving the bowl area was located at the top of the gondola, and two rides on the gondola would allow those skiers to take ample advantage of the advanced terrain up there. Otherwise, all advanced terrain was served by another chair.

However, if Big Sky was to establish itself as a successful, nationally prominent destination area, Karen felt that the attitudes and opinions of all skiers must be carefully weighed. Throughout the season she had made a special effort to grasp the general feeling toward rates. A $12 ticket, she discovered, was thought to be very reasonable by destination skiers, primarily because Big Sky was predominantly an intermediate area and the average destination skier was of intermediate ability, but also because Big Sky was noted for its relative lack of lift lines, giving the skier more actual skiing time for the money. "Perhaps we should keep the price the same," she thought. "We do need more business. Other destination areas are likely to raise their prices, and we should look good in comparison."

Also discussed was the possible abolition of the $9 chair pass. The question in Karen's mind was whether its elimination would severely hurt local business or would sell an all-lift $12 ticket to the skier who had previously bought only a chair pass. The issue was compounded by an unknown number of destination skiers who opted for the cheaper chair pass too.

Season pass pricing was also an issue. Prices for the 1977–78 all-lift season pass had remained the same as last year, but a season chair pass had been introduced which was the counterpart of the daily chair-lift pass. Karen did not like the number of season chair passes purchased in relation to the number of all-lift passes and considered recommending the abolition of the season pass as well as an increase in the price of the all-lift pass. "I'm going to have to think this one out carefully," she thought, "because skiing accounted for about 40 percent of our total revenue this past season. I'll have to be able to justify my decision not only to Michigan but also to the Forest Service."

Price changes were not solely at the discretion of Big Sky management. As the case with most larger western ski areas, the U.S. government owned part of the land on which Big Sky operated. Control of this land was the responsibility of the U.S. Forest Service, which annually approved all lift pricing policies. For the 1976–77 ski season, Forest Service action kept most lift rate increases to the national inflation rate. For the 1977–78 season, larger price increases were allowed for ski areas which had competing areas nearby: Big Sky was considered to be such an area. No one knew what the Forest Service position would be for the upcoming 1978–79 season.

To help Karen in her decision, an assistant had prepared a summary of lift rates and usage for the past two seasons (Exhibit 3).

EXHIBIT 3 Lift Rates and Usage Summary

Ticket	Consumer Cost	Skier Days*	Number Season Passes Sold
1977–78 (136 days' operation)			
Adult all-day all-lift	$ 12	53,400	
Adult all-day chair	9	20,200	
Adult half day	8	9,400	
Child all-day all-lift	8	8,500	
Child all-day chair	5	3,700	
Child half day	6	1,200	
Hotel passes†	12/day	23,400	
Complimentary	0	1,100	
Adult all-lift season pass	220	4,300	140
Adult chair season pass	135	4,200	165
Child all-lift season pass	130	590	30
Child chair season pass	75	340	15
Employee all-lift season pass	100	3,000	91
Employee chair season pass	35	1,100	37
1976–77 (122 days' operation)			
Adult all-day	$ 10	52,500	
Adult half day	6.50	9,000	
Child all-day	6	10,400	
Child half day	4	1,400	
Hotel passes†	10/day	30,500	
Complimentary	0	480	
Adult season pass	220	4,200	84
Child season pass	130	300	15
Employee season pass	100	2,300	70

*A skier day is defined as one skier using the facility for one day of operation.
†Hotel passes refers to passes included in the lodging/lift packages.

Room Rates

This area of pricing was particularly important because lodging accounted for about one third of the past season's total revenue. It was also difficult because of the variety of accommodations (Exhibit 4) and the difficulty in accurately forecasting next season's demand. For example, the season of 1976–77 had been unique in that a good portion of the Rockies was without snow for the initial months of the winter, including Christmas. Big Sky was fortunate in receiving as much snow as it had, and consequently many groups and individuals who were originally headed for Vail or Aspen booked in with Big Sky.

Pricing for the 1977–78 season had been made on the premise that there would be a good amount of repeat business. This came true in part but not to the extent that had been hoped. Occupancy experience had also been summarized for the past two seasons to help Karen make her final decision (Exhibit 5).

As was customary in the hospitality industry, January was a slow period and it was necessary to price accordingly. Low-season pricing was extremely important because many groups took advantage of these rates. On top of that, groups were often offered discounts in the neighborhood of 10 percent. Considering this, Karen could not price too high, with

EXHIBIT 4 Nightly Room Rates*

	Low-Season Range	High-Season Range	Maximum Occupancy
1977–78			
Huntley Lodge			
Standard	$ 42–62	$ 50–70	4
Loft	52–92	60–100	6
Stillwater Condo			
Studio	40–60	45–65	4
One bedroom	55–75	60–80	4
Bedroom with loft	80–100	90–110	6
Deer Lodge Condo			
One bedroom	74–84	80–90	4
Two bedroom	93–103	100–110	6
Three bedroom	112–122	120–130	8
Hill Condo			
Studio	30–40	35–45	4
Studio with loft	50–70	55–75	6
1976–77			
Huntley Lodge			
Standard	$ 32–47	$ 35–50	4
Loft	47–67	50–70	6
Stillwater Condo			
Studio	39–54	37–52	4
One bedroom	52–62	50–60	4
Bedroom with loft	60–80	65–85	6
Deer Lodge Condo			
One bedroom	51–66	55–70	4
Two bedroom	74–94	80–100	6
Three bedroom	93–123	100–130	8
Hill Condo			
Studio	28–43	30–45	4
Studio with loft	42–62	45–65	6

*Rates determined by number of persons in room or condominium unit and do not include lift tickets. Maximum for each rate range apply at maximum occupancy.

EXHIBIT 5 Lodge-Condominium Occupancy

In Room-Nights (1977–78)*

	December (26 Days' Operation)	January	February	March	April (8 Days' Operation)
Huntley Lodge	1,830	2,250	3,650	4,650	438
Condominiums†	775	930	1,350	100	90

In Room-Nights (1976–77)

	December (16 Days' Operation)	January	February	March	April (16 Days' Operation)
Huntley Lodge	1,700	3,080	4,525	4,300	1,525
Condominiums‡	600	1,000	1,600	1,650	480

In Person-Nights§

December 1977 (1976)	January 1978 (1977)	February 1978 (1977)	March 1978 (1977)	April 1978 (1977)
7,850 (6,775)	9,200 (13,000)	13,150 (17,225)	17,900 (17,500)	1,450 (4,725)

*A room-night is defined as one room (or condominium) rented for one night. Lodging experience is based on 124 days of operation for 1977–78, while Exhibit 3 shows the skiing facilities operating 136 days. Both numbers are correct.
†Big Sky had 92 condominiums available during the 1977–78 season.
‡Big Sky had 85 condominiums available during the 1976–77 season.
§A person-night refers to one person using the facility for one night.

the risk of losing individual destination skiers, or too low, such that an unacceptable profit would be made from group business in this period.

Food Service

Under some discussion was the feasibility of converting all destination skiers to the American plan, under which policy each guest in the Huntley Lodge would be placed on a package to include three meals daily in a Big Sky-controlled facility. There was a feeling both for and against this idea. The parent company had been successfully utilizing this plan for years at its destination areas in northern Michigan. Extending the policy to Big Sky should find similar success.

Karen was not so sure. For one thing, the Michigan resorts were primarily self-contained and alternative eateries were few. For another, the whole idea of extending standardized policies from Michigan to Montana was suspect. As an example, Karen painfully recalled a day in January when Big Sky "tried

on" another successful Michigan policy of accepting only cash or check payments for lift tickets. The reactions of credit card-carrying skiers could be described as ranging from annoyed to irate.

If an American plan were proposed for next year, it would probably include both the Huntley Lodge Dining Room and Lookout Cafeteria. Less clear, however, were the prices to be charged. There certainly would have to be consideration for both adults and children and for the two independently operated eating places in the Mountain Mall (see Exhibit 6 for an identification of eating places in the Big Sky area). Beyond these considerations, there was little else other than an expectation of a profit to guide Karen in her analysis.

The Telephone Call

"Profits in the food area might be hard to come by," Karen thought. "Last year it appears we lost money on everything we sold"

EXHIBIT 6 Eating Places in the Big Sky Area

Establishment	Type of Service	Meals Served	Current Prices	Seating	Location
Lodge Dining Room*	A la carte	Breakfast	$2–5	250	Huntley Lodge
		Lunch	2–5		
		Dinner	7–15		
Steak House*	Steak/lobster	Dinner only	6–12	150	Huntley Lodge
Fondue Stube*	Fondue	Dinner only	6–10	25	Huntley Lodge
Ore House†	A la carte	Lunch	0.80–4	150	Mountain Mall
		Dinner	5–12		
Ernie's Deli†	Deli/restaurant	Breakfast	1–3	25	Mountain Mall
		Lunch	2–5		
Lookout Cafeteria*	Cafeteria	Breakfast	1.50–3	175	Mountain Mall
		Lunch	2–4		
		Dinner	3–6		
Yellow Mule†	A la carte	Breakfast	2–4	75	Meadow Village
		Lunch	2–5		
		Dinner	4–8		
Buck's T–4†	Road house restaurant/bar	Dinner only	2–9	60	Gallatin Canyon (two miles south of Big Sky entrance)
Karst Ranch†	Road house restaurant/bar	Breakfast	2–4	50	Gallatin Canyon (seven miles north of Big Sky entrance)
		Lunch	2–5		
		Dinner	3–8		
Corral†	Road house restaurant/bar	Breakfast	2–4	30	Gallatin Canyon (five miles south of Big Sky entrance)
		Lunch	2–4		
		Dinner	3–5		

*Owned and operated by Big Sky of Montana, Inc.
†Independently operated.

EXHIBIT 7 Ski Season Income Data (*percent*)

	Skiing	Lodging	Food and Beverage
Revenue	100.0%	100.0%	100.0%
Cost of sales:			
Merchandise	0.0	0.0	30.0
Labor	15.0	15.9	19.7
Maintenance	3.1	5.2	2.4
Supplies	1.5	4.8	5.9
Miscellaneous	2.3	0.6	0.6
Total cost of sales	21.9	26.5	58.6
Operating expenses	66.2	66.4	66.7
Net profit (loss) before taxes	11.9%	7.0%	(25.2)%

(see Exhibit 7). Just then the telephone rang. It was Rick Thompson, her counterpart at Boyne Mountain Lodge in Michigan. "How are your pricing recommendations coming?" he asked. "I'm about done with mine and thought we should compare notes."

"Good idea, Rick—only I'm just getting started out here. Do you have any hot ideas?"

"Only one," he responded. "I just got off the phone with a guy in Denver. He told me all of the major Colorado areas are upping their lift prices one or two dollars next year."

"Is that right, Rick? Are you sure?"

"Well, you know nobody knows for sure what's going to happen, but I think it's pretty good information. He heard it from his sister-in-law who works in Vail. I think he said she read it in the local paper or something."

"That doesn't seem like very solid information," said Karen. "Let me know if you hear anything more, will you?"

"Certainly. You know, we really should compare our recommendations before we stick our necks out too far on this pricing thing. Can you call me later in the week?" he asked.

"Sure, I'll talk to you the day after tomorrow; I should be about done by then. Anything else?"

"Nope—gotta run. Talk to you then. Bye"—and he was gone.

"At least I've got some information," Karen thought, "and a new deadline!"

Notes

1. Destination resorts were characterized by on-the-hill lodging and eating facilities, a national market, and national advertising.

2. A skier day is defined as one skier using the facility for one day of operation.

Crowe Chemical Division
M. Edgar Barrett and Charles T. Sharpless

Michael Demming, executive vice president of the Crowe Chemical Division of Majestic Tool Company, Inc., was sitting in his Beaumont, Texas, office. It was late in the evening on a midweek day in July 1976. Demming had stayed late at the office in order to be able to spend some time assessing the ramifications of a recently announced price cut by a major competitor. The competitor, Cajun Chemical Corporation, was the industry leader in the region of the country and the market segment served by Crowe Chemical. The Louisiana-based firm was both larger and more profitable than Crowe.

The Company

Crowe Chemical was a wholly owned subsidiary of Majestic Tool. It was a small concern, with manufacturing and administrative facilities located in or near Beaumont, Texas. The firm was engaged in the production of industrial chemicals which were used primarily in the oil-refining process. Although it was far

smaller than most firms in the chemical industry, Crowe had managed to survive, and, in fact, stay quite competitive.

Crowe's divisional strategy was built on the premise that the firm would concentrate its efforts in the marketing, manufacturing, and distribution of specialty chemicals. The manufacturing process for each of the firm's products was nearly identical. With a few minor exceptions, the productive plant and equipment could be used for the manufacture and packaging of all three products.

The firm's three products were also closely related in that they required similar raw materials. One of the raw materials used to produce one of the three products (Sa 11) was itself a by-product resulting from the manufacture of another of the firm's products (Sa 10). The amount of this by-product which resulted from the manufacture of Sa 10 at the current level of production was well in excess of the firm's current and projected needs as an input to the Sa 11 production process. The excess amount of by-product was sold on the open market and treated as a reduction in Sa 10's overall raw material costs.

The sales and marketing efforts of the Crowe Chemical Division were concentrated in three Gulf Coast states. Salaried salespeople were assigned to specific geographic regions in Texas, Louisiana, or Mississippi. Price was a major consideration for the smaller refineries with which the Crowe Chemical Division often dealt. However, some degree of brand loyalty had been created as a result of long-standing customer relationships developed by the regional salespeople. The management of Crowe Chemical estimated that they held an average market share of 16 percent for Sa 10, 14 percent for Sa 11, and 8 percent for Sa 12 within the three-state region served by the firm.

Some History

Crowe Chemical Company was founded in 1939 by John Lewis Crowe. The firm benefited handsomely from the wartime economic boom. By 1946, annual sales had reached the level of $5 million. The firm continued its pattern of gradual but steady growth over the next three decades. Record sales of nearly $42 million were recorded in 1974.

J. L. Crowe resigned from his management position in mid-1973. The resignation had been planned for some time as a result of Crowe's explicit desire to free most of his time for use in family related interests and personal real estate ventures. The presidency of the firm was handed to Crowe's son-in-law, George Thompson. Crowe, however, did not totally withdraw from the ongoing activities of the firm. He had, for example, played an important role in the merger negotiations that took place during 1975.

Acquisition by Majestic Tool

Due in large part to spiraling production costs, 1975 was not a very profitable year for either Crowe Chemical or the industry as a whole. In fact, 1975 was an exceptionally poor year for the entire chemical industry. Raw material prices rose considerably. Rising labor costs and sharply higher utility rates took their toll in terms of reduced levels of profit. Finally, it was widely acknowledged that production capacity had recently grown in a manner disproportionate to increases in demand.

Crowe's common stock, traded over the counter, fell considerably in price during the year. After being the target of two unannounced takeover bids, Crowe's management sought out a friendly partner. Majestic Tool, a Louisiana-based supplier of high-technology products and services to the energy sector, ultimately entered into merger discussions with the firm.

The acquisition talks centered, at one point, on what role George Thompson would play in the emerging subsidiary. It was finally agreed that he would remain in his present capacity as chief executive officer, with responsibility for planning and personnel. The agreement stipulated, however, that one of Majestic's own people was to be brought in as executive vice president. This person, Michael Demming, had had extensive experience in industrial products and was to be in charge of day-to-day operations.

Analysis of Operating Results

Demming assumed his new position in early 1976. Several days after his arrival, he and Thompson met to review the firm's 1975 operations. The two men inspected the income statement for the year just ended (Exhibit 1), as well as several other documents recently computed by the controller's department. One of these other documents was a product-line profitability analysis for the calendar year 1975 (Exhibit 2). Another document provided information about the particular char-

EXHIBIT 1 Income Statement (*for the Year Ended December 31, 1975*)

Gross sales	$37,985,788
less: discounts	690,343
Net sales	37,295,445
Cost of goods sold	19,655,641
Gross margin	17,639,804
Operating expenses	16,980,765
Operating income	659,039
less: interest	357,143
Divisional profit (before tax)	301,896

acteristics of individual product costs, including some written comments regarding their projected behavior (Exhibit 3).

While no action was taken as a result of the discussion that took place between the two men, Thompson did express his concern about the loss shown on Sa 11. Excerpts from the conversation are included below.

George Thompson: It looks to me like we're losing our shirt on Sa 11. The results have never been great on this product, but now

EXHIBIT 2 Product Line Profitability Analysis (*for the Year Ended December 31, 1975*)

	Sa 10		Sa 11		Sa 12	
	Thousands of Dollars	**Per Unit**	**Thousands of Dollars**	**Per Unit**	**Thousands of Dollars**	**Per Unit**
Gross sales	$115,514	$7.7500	$13,517	$9.0000	$8,954	$9.5000
Discounts	194	.0969	304	.2024	192	.2037
Net sales	15,320	7.6531	13,213	8.7976	8,762	9.2963
Cost of goods sold:						
Direct labor	2,035	1.0165	3,352	2.2319	1,579	1.6753
Direct material[a,b]	1,919	.9586	1,701	1.1326	1,439	1.5268
Indirect labor	1,087	.5430	1,189	.7917	907	.9623
Fringe benefits	81	.0405	134	.0892	64	.0679
Insurance	104	.0519	79	.0526	49	.0519
Repair service	336	.1678	254	.1691	157	.1666
Power	124	.0619	94	.0626	58	.0615
Property taxes	204	.1019	154	.1025	94	.0997
Supplies	507	.2533	1,109	.7384	845	.8955
Total	6,397	3.1954	8,066	5.3706	5,192	5.5085
Gross margin	8,923	4.4577	5,147	3.4270	3,570	3.7878
Operating expenses:						
Administrative	970	.4846	628	.4181	534	.5666
Advertising	1,706	.8522	1,213	.8076	797	.8456
Depreciation	2,396	1.1969	1,906	1.2690	1,089	1.1554
Interest	164	.0819	116	.0772	77	.0817
Research and development	1,745	.8717	1,241	.8263	814	.8636
Allocated overhead	892	.4456	634	.4221	416	.4413
Total	7,873	3.9329	5,738	3.8203	3,727	3.9542
Divisional profit (before tax)	1,050	.5248	(591)	(.3933)	(157)	(.1664)
Unit sales (in barrels)	2,001,842		1,501,885		942,512	

[a]The sale of the excess by-product resulting from the production of product Sa 10, as well as the internal transfer of by-product to product Sa 11, resulted in a reduction in the recorded direct materials cost for product Sa 10.
[b]The Sa 10 by-product used in the production of Sa 11 was charged to Sa 11. It was valued at the market price of the by-product in the outside (of Crowe Chemical Division) market.

EXHIBIT 3 Controller's Analysis of Manufacturing Costs

Variable Costs

Direct labor:
: Direct labor costs have been historically treated as varying with volume of production. An identifiable number of workers, however, are paid their full weekly wages regardless of units produced.

Direct materials:
: Purchased at market price. The market is highly susceptible to the relative forces of supply and demand, but prices tend to change on a quarterly basis. See also the notes to Exhibit 2.

Fringe benefits:
: Included are compensation insurance, group health plan, and group life insurance. These programs are mandatory and the amount paid is most directly related to the amount of direct labor costs.

Supplies:
: Supplies are purchased from company offering most favorable terms. Cost is net of discounts.

Repair service:
: Has historically varied with level of production. Repair people are available on short notice in case of unforeseen downtime.

Power:
: Charged industrial rates. The total bill tends to be directly related to production volume.

Fixed Costs

Indirect labor:
: This consists largely of supervisory labor. A few laborers available to relieve workers or substitute for those on holiday and sick leave are also included.

Depreciation:
: This represents a fixed amount assigned to each product.

Interest:
: Total interest charges are divided among the products on the basis of a formula largely derived from expected unit sales.

Administrative:
: These costs represent salaries paid to executive and office personnel.

Advertising and research and development:
: The total amount of expenditures is fixed at yearly budget meetings. They may be augmented during the year at management's discretion. The total is allocated to specific products based on the same formula used for interest.

Insurance and property taxes:
: Fire, property, and vehicle insurance charges are assigned to each product line. Property taxes are based on assessed values and are considered to be fixed. They do, however, tend to rise slightly each year.

Allocated overhead:
: Other overhead costs. This category includes such things as heat, water, and janitorial services.

they've really turned bad. I wonder if we shouldn't cut back on our production and sales efforts on this one.

Michael Demming: According to the records, we've never shown a very substantial profit on this product. With the disaster of a year we've had, the loss may have been unavoidable.

George Thompson: You may be right, Mike. But, I just don't see any feasible way to lower manufacturing costs by 39 cents a barrel. We also ought to look at Sa 12. We're off-budget on that one as well.

Michael Demming: Let's hang on for another quarter, George. Making drastic changes may well do us more harm than good. If things don't improve with time, we'll have to address the issue head-on later during this year.

First-Quarter Results

Around the middle of April, Demming received an income statement for the first three months of 1976 (Exhibit 4). Much to his satisfaction, the division had managed to earn a modest profit. A week or so later, Demming

EXHIBIT 4 Income Statement (*for the Quarter Ended March 31, 1976*)

Gross sales	$9,913,923
less: discounts	180,309
Net sales	9,733,614
Cost of goods sold	4,985,357
Gross margin	4,748,257
Operating expenses	4,343,212
Operating income	405,045
less: interest	89,124
Divisional profit (before tax)	315,921

received the first quarter's version of a new product line profitability analysis form that he had specifically requested from the divisional controller (Exhibit 5). Demming inspected the report and compared the results to the previous year's operations.

Cajun Chemical's Price Announcement

During the second quarter of 1976, the Gulf Coast chemical industry suffered from the results of circumstances quite similar to those that had existed in 1975. The Crowe Chemical Division managed to keep a tight grip on their market share. Nonetheless, profits for the three-month period declined.

Even before the release of the second-quarter operating data, events took what Demming perceived to be an even more somber tone as Cajun Chemical announced a price decrease. This decrease, to be effective immediately, meant that Cajun's version of product Sa 10 would carry a net list price of $7.15 a barrel. It was this price cut that Demming had now focused upon for analysis.

Demming recalled that he and George Thompson had speculated several weeks ago that a price cut by Cajun was a possibility that they should consider. At that time, Thompson had stressed that he did not wish to sell Sa 10 below cost. He had based his view on the fact that the product was currently the division's major source of profit.

Demming also recalled a conversation of earlier in the same day with the divisional sales director. The director, Bill Sharpless, predicted that the sales volume for Sa 10 during the second half of 1976 would approximate 1 million barrels. When pressed, however, he admitted that this estimate was based on an assumption of price parity with the Cajun Chemical product. He said that sales would probably fall to around 875,000 barrels if the Cajun price cut was not met. Thompson believed it was time to make a decision about Sa 11 and to decide whether to meet the Cajun price cut.

EXHIBIT 5 Product Line Profitability Analysis (*for the Quarter Ending March 31, 1976*)

[handwritten: cont. margin = $5.09 /per unit]

Majestic Tool, Inc.: Form 640

Copies to: _____

Product Sa 10

	Standard per Unit	Total at Standard Cost and Actual Units (000s)	Total at Actual (000s)	Variance (000s)
Revenue (net sales)	$7.6533	$3,973	$3,973	—
Variable costs:				
Direct labor	1.0775	559	545	14
Direct materials	.9585	498	509	(11)
Fringe benefits	.0405	21	19	2
Repair service	.1680	87	88	(1)
Power	.0620	32	33	(1)
Supplies	.2535	132	131	1
Total variable costs	2.5600	1,329	1,325 *(2.5523)*	4
Fixed costs:				
Indirect labor	.5430	282	272	10
Depreciation	1.1969	621	599	22
Interest	.0819	43	41	2
Insurance	.0519	27	26	1
Administrative	.4846	252	243	9
Research & development	.8717	453	436	17
Advertising	.8522	442	437	5
Property taxes	.1019	53	51	2
Allocated overhead	.4456	231	224	7
Corporate overhead	.0720	37	36	1
Total fixed costs	4.7017	2,441	2,365 *(4.5556)*	76
Divisional profit (before tax)	.3916	203	283	80
Unit sales (in barrels)		519,140		
Expected sales (in barrels)	*(7.2617)*	500,000	*(7.1079)*	

[handwritten notes left margin: 114379 ; 7.65 875,000 ; 1.9860 ; 7.15 1,000,000]

[handwritten: Price elasticity = % Δ in quantity demanded / % Δ in price]

[handwritten scribbles]

Massachusetts State Lottery
Dharmendra T. Verma and Frederick Wiseman

Product (Pending)

In early February 1972, the lottery's director, assistant director, and deputy directors met to consider further steps to implement the recently enacted state lottery. They were under considerable time pressure because the bill passed by the legislature on September 27, 1971, had been designated an "emergency law" to indicate that the lottery should be made operational as soon as possible. Accordingly, a tentative decision was made to instigate the lottery in April of 1972. By the end of

January, the main staff positions had been filled and a meeting was then called to decide what kind of marketing program should be followed. The commission had already set up headquarters in a new building, purchased computer equipment, selected an advertising agency, and visited other states that had lotteries in order to gain background information. Three other states—New Hampshire,

This case was prepared by Dharmendra T. Verma of Bentley College and Frederick Wiseman, Northeastern University.

Dennis H. Tootelian and Ralph M. Gaedeke, *Cases and Classics in Marketing Management.* Copyright © 1986 by Harcourt Brace Jovanovich, Inc. Reprinted by permission of the publisher.

CM = $5.1375   *CM = 4.9013*

	Product Sa 11				Product Sa 12		
Standard per Unit	Total at Standard Cost and Actual Units (000s)	Total at Actual (000s)	Variance (000s)	Standard per Unit	Total at Standard Cost and Actual Units (000s)	Total at Actual (000s)	Variance (000s)
$8.7975	$3,265	$3,265	—	$9.2957	$2,495	$2,495	—
1.6754	622	764	($142)	1.6752	450	453	($3)
.9486	352	366	(14)	1.5268	409	409	—
.0670	25	29	(4)	.0678	18	18	—
.1680	62	60	2	.1666	45	51	(6)
.0626	23	23	—	.0615	17	17	—
.7384	274	273	1	.8965	241	231	10
3.6600	1,358	1,515 *(4.08/5)* (157)		4.3944	1,180	1,179 *(4.3925)* 1	
.7919	294	297	(3)	.9045	243	227	16
1.2690	471	476	(5)	1.0888	292	272	20
.0772	29	29	—	.0771	21	19	2
.0526	19	20	(1)	.0495	13	12	1
.4180	155	157	(2)	.5430	146	137	9
.8260	307	310	(3)	.8139	218	203	15
.8165	303	308	(5)	.7986	214	201	13
.1025	38	38	—	.0940	25	23	2
.4221	157	158	(1)	.4135	111	103	8
.0693	26	26	—	.0681	18	17	1
4.8451	1,799	1,819	(20)	4.8510	1,301	1,214	87
.2924	108	(69)	(177)	.0503	14	102	88
(8.5091)	371,185	*(8,982)*			268,413		
	375,000				250,000		

(profit per unit)

New York, and New Jersey—had already been operating lotteries.

During the strategy formulation meeting various issues were raised, including whether the lottery administrators were ready to make specific marketing plans or whether they should try to generate some primary marketing data. Some of the administrators believed that they should go ahead and specify a marketing program. They pointed to the urgency of the situation as well as to the available data from the other state lotteries. Vern Fredericks, one of the deputy directors, strongly asserted:

> We should copy the features of the other state lotteries, especially New Jersey which has been so successful. What worked well in New Jersey will work in Massachusetts. We don't have time to go around doing marketing studies here. Besides, why should a ticket buyer in Boston be any different from someone buying a ticket in New York City or Newark?

But others believed it was necessary to find out something about people's attitudes toward various aspects of a lottery. Donald Phillips, another deputy director, argued:

> It is difficult to decide on specific aspects of a lottery, such as what price to charge and what kind of prize distribution to offer, unless we know how Massachusetts residents feel. The other states have made many changes or are considering changes in their initial programs. Also, how do we decide which features to copy when we're

not sure what factors are responsible for a successful lottery? We should undertake a study to give us the kind of information we need to help design our marketing program.

Formulation and Organization of the State Lottery

The Massachusetts State Lottery was established by the "State Lottery Law" enacted by the Senate and the House of Representatives of the Commonwealth of Massachusetts on September 27, 1971.[1] The two major purposes of the lottery as stated by the majority whip of the Massachusetts House of Representatives, William Q. MacLean, Jr., were "to raise revenue for the cities and towns in Massachusetts and to decrease organized (illegal) gambling within the state."

The Massachusetts Lottery Law specified, among other things, that prizes should amount to no less than 45 percent of total revenues; that costs for operation and administration should not exceed 15 percent; and that a minimum of 40 percent should go to the state treasury for subsequent disbursement to the cities and towns. In addition, the legislative act designated the bill an "emergency law" which was to be implemented as soon as possible. The salient features of the legislation are reproduced in Exhibit 1.

The lottery commission consisted of five members, with the state treasurer serving as chairman. The other members were the secretary of public safety, the state comptroller, and two persons appointed by the governor for terms coterminous with that of the governor. The specific responsibilities of the commission are also outlined in Exhibit 1.

In November 1971, Dr. William E. Perrault, chairman of the mathematics department at Boston State College, was appointed director of the state lottery by the state treasurer with the approval of the governor. The director was responsible for the supervision and administration of the lottery.

The next few weeks were spent in setting up the organization structure and filling the administrative positions necessary to start the lottery operation. Computer equipment was purchased and a Boston advertising firm was appointed. The first-year advertising and promotional budget was approximately $1 million. By the end of January, most of the staff had been appointed and operating plans were being formulated. A partial organization chart is presented in Exhibit 2. Initial funding for the staffing requirements was provided by the state legislature with the stipulation that this money be returned to the state out of revenues from ticket sales.

The marketing staff consisted of Mr. Louis J. Totino, deputy director marketing, 3 district managers, and 18 field representatives. Each of the representatives was to service the various Massachusetts retail outlets which would be licensed to sell the lottery tickets. In addition, the commission entered into a $300,000 contract with a Cambridge-based major consulting firm, Arthur D. Little, Inc. The objective of the contract was to advise in the planning, design, and implementation of the lottery.

Other Forms of Gambling in Massachusetts

In addition to the lottery there were several other types of legal gambling in Massachusetts. These were pari-mutuel horse and dog racing and beano. Total receipts to the Commonwealth from horse and dog racing had increased from $19.4 million in 1968 to almost $29 million in 1971.[2] Beano was expected to return at least $1 million (10 percent of gross receipts) to the state in 1972.

Recent changes had been made in the Massachusetts laws to allow Sunday horse racing

EXHIBIT 1 The Massachusetts State Lottery Act—Selected Sections

Section 23. There shall be, in the office of the state treasurer, a state lottery commission, hereinafter called the commission, consisting of the state treasurer, the secretary of public safety or his designee, the state comptroller or his designee, and two persons to be appointed by the governor for terms coterminous with that of the governor. No more than four members of the commission shall be of the same political party. The state treasurer shall be the chairman of the commission.

Section 24. The commission is hereby authorized to conduct a state lottery and shall determine the type of lottery to be conducted, the price, or prices, of tickets or shares in the lottery, the numbers and sizes of the prizes on the winning tickets or shares, the manner of selecting the winning tickets or shares, the manner of payment of prizes to the holders of winning tickets or shares, the frequency of the drawings or selections of winning tickets or shares and the type or types of locations at which tickets or shares may be sold, the method to be used in selling tickets or shares, the licensing of agents to sell tickets or shares, provided that no person under the age of twenty-one shall be licensed as an agent, the manner and amount of compensation, if any, to be paid licensed sales agents, and such other matters necessary or desirable for the efficient and economical operation and administration of the lottery and for the convenience of the purchasers of tickets or shares and the holders of winning tickets or shares. . . .

The commission shall make a continuous study and investigation of the operation and administration of similar laws in other states or countries, of any literature on the subject which from time to time may be published or available, of any federal laws which may affect the operation of the lottery, and of the reaction of citizens of the commonwealth to existing and potential features of the lottery with a view to recommending or effecting changes that will tend to better serve and implement the purposes of the state lottery law.

Section 25. The apportionment of the total revenues accruing from the sale of lottery tickets or shares and from all other sources shall be as follows: *(a)* the payment of prizes to the holders of winning tickets or shares which in any case shall be no less than forty-five percent of the total revenues accruing from the sale of lottery tickets; *(b)* the payment of costs incurred in the operation and administration of the lottery, including the expenses of the commission and the costs resulting from any contract or contracts entered into for promotional, advertising or operational services or for the purchase or lease of lottery equipment and materials which in no case shall exceed fifteen percent of the total revenues accruing from the sale of lottery tickets, subject to appropriation; and *(c)* the balance to be used for the purposes set forth in clause *(c)* of section thirty-five [...shall be credited to the Local Aid Fund . . . and shall be distributed to the several cities and towns in accordance with preestablished provisions.].

Section 27. No person shall be licensed as an agent to sell lottery tickets or shares if such person engaged in business exclusively as a lottery sales agent. Before issuing such license the director shall consider the financial responsibility and security of each applicant for licenses, his business or activity, the accessibility of his place of business or activity to the public, the sufficiency of existing licenses to serve the public convenience, and the volume of expected sales.

Section 29. No person shall sell a ticket or share at a price greater than that fixed by the commission. No person other than a licensed lottery sales agent shall sell lottery tickets or shares, except that nothing in this section shall be construed to prevent any person from giving lottery tickets or shares to another as a gift.

No ticket or share shall be sold to any person under age eighteen, provided that a person eighteen years of age or older may purchase a ticket or share for the purpose of making a gift to a person under age eighteen.

Source: The Commonwealth of Massachusetts, Chapter 813, Act H 5925, 1971.

and to increase the length of the racing season. Also, additional bingo legislation was being considered which would increase the maximum allowable daily prize from $50 to $200, allow games on Sunday, and allow each licensee to hold more than one game per week.

Illegal gambling also thrived within the state, with the most well-known varieties being off-track betting and the "numbers" game. Officials of the state legislature believed that sales of the lottery tickets and the fact that no more local newspapers published the "number" would cut down revenues in the "numbers" by about 20 to 25 percent.

Background on Other State Lotteries

New Hampshire Sweepstakes

In 1963, the state legislature of New Hampshire passed the "New Hampshire Sweep-

EXHIBIT 2 Partial Organization Chart

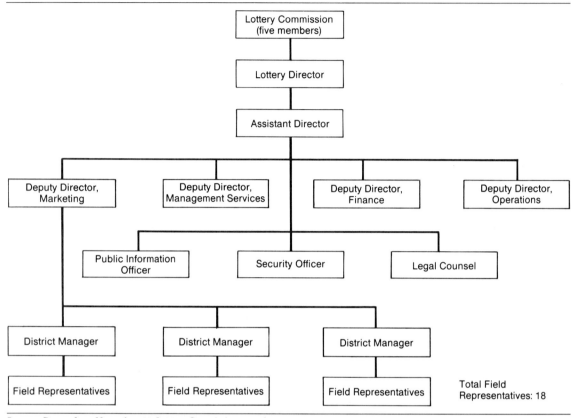

stakes Law." This law set up a sweepstakes commission with responsibility to "conduct public drawings at such intervals and in such places within the state as it may determine."[3] The stated purpose of the sweepstakes, the first of modern times in the United States, was to provide New Hampshire's cities and towns with additional revenue to aid in defraying educational costs.

The state law limited participation in the sweepstakes to individuals over 21 years of age. The law also specified that tickets, priced at $3 by the sweepstakes commission, could be sold only at state-owned liquor stores and at state-regulated horse race-

tracks. Further, as part of the act creating the sweepstakes, the legislature included a provision which made it possible for any city or town, by referendum, to elect not to have tickets sold within its boundaries.

Only one sweepstakes drawing was held during each of the first two years of operation, 1964 and 1965. The exact prize distribution, which totaled approximately 35–40 percent of gross revenue, was a direct function of tickets sold. Top prize was $50,000 and additional major prizes were set at $25,000, $12,500, and $10,000. In all, there were approximately 400 prizes awarded for each $500,000 worth of tickets sold, over 95 percent of these being consolation prizes between $100 and $500.

In 1964, gross revenue from the first sweepstakes drawing totaled $5.7 million. After accounting for operating expenses, the commission was able to return a total of $2.8 million to the cities and towns in which tickets were sold. Ticket sales for the following year declined almost 20 percent and there was approximately a $300,000 reduction in revenue returned by the state.

A consumer study, conducted by a University of New Hampshire professor in 1965, revealed a number of insights into the characteristics of the typical purchaser. Among these were that (1) 88 percent of all buyers came from out of state, and (2) among neither residents nor nonresidents was the number of tickets purchased significantly related to family income. A more complete discussion of the findings of the New Hampshire consumer study is given in Exhibit 3.

In an attempt to increase yearly gross revenue, the commission decided to have two drawings in 1966. The result of this change was unexpected as gross revenue again fell significantly. The following year brought about the first major change in the running of the sweepstakes. The state legislature granted permission for tickets to be sold at sweepstakes commission offices, at toll booths along the state highway and, most importantly, at retail business establishments. It was expected that with the increased number of ticket outlets, sales and interest in the sweepstakes would also increase. In anticipation of this, the commission decided to conduct three drawings in 1967. This marketing program remained in force through 1970. The result of this strategy was a substantial decline in sales during the first two years, followed by a leveling off at approximately $2 million during the next two years. The gross revenues, operating expenses, prizes paid, and educational aid contribution figures for the years 1964–1970 are given in Exhibit 4.

New York State Lottery

New York had considered having its own lottery for many years, but it was not until the initial success of the New Hampshire sweepstakes that the New York state legislature passed "The New York State Lottery Law" in 1965 and 1966.[4]

The New York law required that 45 percent of the gross receipts of lottery ticket sales be applied exclusively for the purpose of providing aid to primary, secondary, and higher education and for providing scholarships. It also provided that no more than 40 percent of the proceeds be awarded as prizes and no more than 15 percent be used for all administrative expenses including promotion and commissions to vendors.

New York's marketing program differed significantly from that of New Hampshire. Tickets were priced at one dollar and drawings were scheduled monthly. The advertising campaign centered around the purpose of the lottery and used the theme: "Give a dollar to education." It was believed that people would not mind contributing to educational costs if they also had a chance of winning a large amount of money at the same time. This approach was also expected to minimize social criticism of the lottery.

Distribution, as in the New Hampshire plan, was very limited and tickets could be purchased only at about 4,000 banks and at government buildings. These outlets were chosen by the New York Lottery Commission in order to gain respectability for the lottery and to minimize the risk of underworld influence and other forms of corruption. The prize structure for the monthly lottery was established on the basis of each million tickets sold. A total of $400,000 was to be allocated among approximately 1,100 winners. The major prizes were $100,000, $50,000, $5,000, and $2,000. There were also 10 $1,000 winners. The remainder of the prizes were for $500 and $100.

EXHIBIT 3 New Hampshire Consumer Study

The characteristics of purchasers of New Hampshire tickets can be summarized as follows:

1. 88% come from out of state.
2. 67% are male.
3. 80% of the men and 60% of the women are married.
4. 82% support four persons or less.
5. 50% are between 40 and 60 years of age.
6. 75% purchased three tickets or less.
7. 50% obtained the ticket themselves.
8. 10% made a special trip to get the tickets.
9. 52% of the nonresidents are in New Hampshire for recreational purposes.
10. 65% completed high school and 11% have more than college training—levels of educational achievement which are significantly above the national average.
11. 31% have incomes of $10,000 or more, 75% have incomes over $5,000 and 10% have incomes below $3,000—the income pattern being significantly higher than the national average.
12. In terms of income and education levels, resident winners are not as different from the state population as nonresident winners are from the national population.
13. Residents tend to buy more tickets per purchaser than nonresidents.
14. Resident and nonresident winners are comparable in the relationship which exists between family incomes and the number of persons supported.
15. Among neither residents or nonresidents is the number of tickets purchased related significantly to family income.

These findings provide a picture of sweepstakes participants which is quite different from that which might have been anticipated on the basis of historical precedent. If, as the analysis shows, the number of tickets purchased is unrelated to income, why are the poor not participating much more heavily in the sweepstakes?

At least three intuitive explanations for these results can be offered. It is clear that the majority of the purchasers come from outside of New Hampshire. Federal statutes limiting the use of the mails for lottery purposes were enacted before the turn of this century and remain in full force. As a result, the buyer, or someone acting for him, must personally come to New Hampshire to obtain a ticket. For nonresidents to get a ticket, therefore, some travel will be required. However, travel is not something the poor or their friends can readily afford, particularly for recreational purposes.

A second factor, the price of the tickets, may also have an impact. At three dollars each, tickets are not easily obtained by those who prefer to do their gambling on the basis of a nickel, dime or quarter a day.

Finally, the sweepstakes is essentially an "investment" form of gambling in that the results are not known until well after the ticket has been picked out. This lag has probably contributed to the noticeable lack of interest inveterate and professional gamblers have demonstrated in the sweepstakes. Perhaps the poor who gamble do not like the deferred outcome this form of wager entails as much as they like gambling where results are known within 24 hours.

The "typical" sweepstakes ticket purchaser appears from this study to be a middle-aged married man who has a good education and is earning a relatively high income with which he supports a small family. He has come to New Hampshire for the purpose of having a good time, which apparently includes buying a few sweepstakes tickets.

As a means of raising public revenue, the New Hampshire Sweepstakes does not appear to be extracting a disproportionate amount of money from those in society who are least able to pay for government services.

Source: New Hampshire Sweepstakes Commission. Survey conducted by Professor S. Kenneth Howard, University of New Hampshire, 1965.

EXHIBIT 4 New Hampshire Sweepstakes, Operating Results, 1964–1970

Year	Gross Revenue	Operating Expenses	Prizes Paid	Net to Education
1964	$ 5,740,093	$1,172,010*	$1,799,995	$ 2,768,088
1965	4,566,044†	678,679	1,400,000	2,487,365
1966	3,889,056	633,447	1,414,993	1,840,616
1967	2,577,341	578,578	943,565	1,055,198
1968	2,054,434	364,162	800,150	890,122
1969	2,017,667	358,710	790,599	868,358
1970	2,019,367	391,208	791,596	836,563
Total	$22,864,002	$4,176,794**	$7,940,898	$10,746,310

*Includes $587,710 paid to Internal Revenue Service for 10 percent wagering tax.

†Includes $664,448 refund from Internal Revenue Service, including interest.

**Includes $580,876 paid to State Liquor Commission for sale of tickets; therefore, total revenue paid to state—$11,327,186.

Source: New Hampshire Sweepstakes Commission.

Ticket sales for the first 10 drawings (June 1967 through March 1968) averaged 5.3 million tickets per month. This level was below expectations based on the performance of the New Hampshire Sweepstakes.[5]

On April 1, 1968, a law passed by the United States Congress took effect which restricted banks from being used as outlets for selling lottery or sweepstakes tickets in any state. This required the New York Commission to adopt a new distribution policy. Foremost consideration was given to those outlets which were reputable and willing to provide the necessary push in the selling of tickets. Hotels, motels, drug and variety stores were the types of stores that were sought. Licenses were granted to 13,000 business establishments and a 5 percent commission on ticket sales was to be paid to all vendors. (In New Hampshire, the sales commission was 4 percent for state stores and 8 percent for private vendors.) The immediate consequence of the required change in distribution policy was a reduction in ticket sales as is shown in Exhibit 5.

New York, as well as New Hampshire, also came under the provisions of a second federal law. This one prohibited information regarding any aspect of a lottery or sweepstakes from being communicated in a media vehicle which crossed over state lines. Hence, no radio or television advertising of any sort was allowed. Even winners could not be identified or interviewed over radio or television networks. Further, only those newspapers that were distributed within the state could be used for transmission of lottery information. With such restriction, point-of-purchase displays, billboards, and in-state newspapers became heavily used as the means by which the lottery or sweepstakes commission communicated with their potential purchasers.

During the fiscal years April 1968 through March 1969 and April 1969 through March 1970, New York ticket sales totaled nearly $49 million and $47 million, respectively. Both years' sales were considerably below the average $5.3 million in ticket sales of the first 10 months. During 1970–1971, bonus $2 and $3 lotteries were scheduled to be held on an alternating quarterly basis in an attempt to stimulate sales. Further details of these special lotteries are given in Exhibit 6 which is the promotional piece displayed at outlets selling lottery tickets. Ticket sales increased during the fiscal year 1970–1971 to $70 million, with the $3 summer special lottery contributing a record $17 million to gross revenues. Also, the New York commission held three special 50 cent weekly lotteries on a test basis in November, December, and January. Gross sales averaged approximately $900,000.

EXHIBIT 5 Gross Receipts of New York State Lottery, by Month *(Millions of Dollars)*

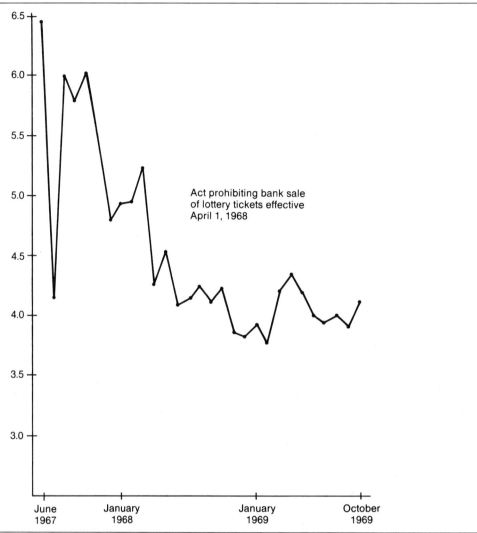

Source: New York State Lottery Commission records.

The $2 lottery had not been started. Exhibit 7 shows the sales record, by month, for all drawings held between April 1970 and March 1971.

New Jersey State Lottery

In January 1971, New Jersey became the third state to commence lottery operations.[6]

The New Jersey lottery differed from the New Hampshire and New York lotteries in a number of ways: tickets were priced at 50 cents; drawings were held weekly; vending machines as well as sales personnel were used to sell tickets; supermarkets were emphasized heavily in the distribution network; and tickets could be purchased from vending machines up until the day of the drawing.

EXHIBIT 6 New York State Lottery Promotion

Somebody's always winning the New York State Lottery...

it might as well be you!

MORE THAN $80 MILLION IN PRIZES
PAID TO OVER 200,000 WINNERS

(front)

Tickets are on sale at more than 13,000 business establishments licensed by the Division of the Lottery throughout the State.

Results of all drawings are published in newspapers throughout the State and posted by sales agents. Winners are notified by phone or wire.

BUY YOUR TICKETS IN COMBINATIONS

DL - 601 (7/71)

(back)

Can win you $100,000!	Top Prize $25,000 a year for life	Can make you a Millionaire!
or one of these other		(payable $50,000 a year for 20 years)
Grand Tier Prizes	$500,000 GUARANTEED	Other Grand Tier Prizes
(for every million tickets sold)	Other Grand Tier Prizes	• $100,000 • $50,000
• $50,000 • $5,000	• $75,000 • $40,000	• $25,000 • 10 at $10,000
• $2,000 • 10 at $1,000	• $15,000 • 10 at $5,000	Consolation Prizes
Consolation Prizes	Consolation Prizes	• 10 at $5,000 • 10 at $4,000
• 300 at $500	• 500 at $1,000	• 10 at $3,000 • 10 at $2,000
(per million tickets sold)		• 100 at $1,000
plus thousands of $100 prizes	plus thousands of $300 prizes	plus thousands of $500 prizes
Tickets on Sale Every Month	**Tickets on Sale Aug. - Sept. 1971**	**Tickets on Sale Oct. - Nov. 1971**

EXHIBIT 7 New York State Lottery Operating Results, 1970–1971

Sales Month*	Gross Sales	Commissions Retained	Net Revenues
April 1970	$ 3,948,275.00	$ 225,076.05	$ 3,723,198.95
May	3,785,567.00	215,748.37	3,569,818.63
June	3,688,096.00	208,424.99	3,479,671.01
July	3,309,573.00	188,538.28	3,121,034.72
August	3,220,801.00	182,954.10	3,037,846.90
September	3,169,871.00	179,665.78	2,990,205.22
Summer Special ($3)	16,747,581.00	940,210.68	15,807,370.32
October	3,606,144.00	205,326.78	3,400,817.22
November 50-cent Special	765,752.00	55,861.20	709,890.80
November	3,384,900.00	193,798.70	3,191,101.30
December 50-cent Special	1,001,995.50	74,312.91	927,682.59
December	3,276,925.00	188,588.16	3,088,336.84
Holiday Special ($3)	8,667,298.00	489,182.02	8,178,115.98
January 50-cent Special 1971	938,887.00	69,265.66	869,621.34
January	3,303,844.00	189,728.95	3,114,115.05
February	3,806,400.00	218,178.34	3,588,221.66
March	3,461,860.00	197,549.83	3,264,310.17
Total	$70,083,769.50	$4,022,410.80	$66,061,358.70

*Net revenues are collected in the month following the sales month.

Source: New York State Lottery Commission.

As in New York, New Jersey's prize distribution was based on the sale of one million tickets. For each million tickets there were 1,000 prizes with the total prize money amounting to $158,000 to be distributed as follows:

Number of Winners	Prize
1	$50,000
9	4,000
90	400
900	40

Since, by state law, a minimum of 45 percent of gross revenue had to be returned in the form of prize money, $67,000 was left undistributed. This money was used to finance a special "millionaire's" drawing in which the prize distribution was as follows:

Number of Winners	Prize
1	$1,000,000
1	200,000
1	100,000
7	10,000
215	500
2,025	100

New Jersey promoted its lottery heavily with the use of newspaper, billboard, and point-of-purchase advertisements and promotional materials, such as placemats which were given to restaurant owners to be used on their tables (see Exhibit 8).

Tickets were sold at approximately 6,000 retail establishments with the heaviest concentration being at large supermarkets. Vending machines were also placed at high-traffic locations such as bus, train, and airport terminals. A 5 percent commission was paid to vendors for each ticket sold. In addition, bonus money totaling 1 percent of gross revenue was paid to outlets that sold prize-winning tickets. For example, the outlet selling the "millionaire" winning ticket was given a $10,000 bonus.

In its initial year of operation, the New Jersey lottery sales totaled 282 million tickets (see Exhibit 9 for weekly sales data). The New Jersey State Lottery Planning Commission in 1970 had said, "Our estimate of gross revenues for the first full year of operation will be about $30 million, although there is a sub-

EXHIBIT 8 New Jersey State Lottery Promotion

HOW TO WIN IN THE NEW JERSEY LOTTERY

BUY A TICKET!

You can't win if you don't have a ticket. Buy as many as you want, each week. Tickets are 50¢ each. You have a chance to win $50,000, or other cash prizes ... EVERY WEEK! Tickets can be purchased from any of the thousands of Licensed Agents throughout New Jersey. Look for the Official Lottery Sign in the window. There's an agent near you.

SIGN YOUR TICKET!

Very important! Write your name on the back of your ticket. Now, only you can collect if your ticket wins.

LOOK AT THE DRAWING DATE

Could be your lucky day. On that date, the WINNING NUMBER will be announced for the Lottery in which your ticket is entered. Winning number is published in New Jersey newspapers each week, and posted by all Licensed Agents.

CHECK YOUR LOTTERY TICKET NUMBER

See if all or part of your Lottery Ticket Number wins! For example—On Jan. 7, 1971, the Winning Number was 394584. Here were the winners:

Lottery Ticket No. 394584 ... $50,000
Lottery Ticket No. *94584 ... $4,000
Lottery Ticket No. **4584 ... $400
Lottery Ticket No. ***584 ... $40
Lottery Ticket No. ***84 ... $4 ... Entry into a 50¢ Millionaire Semi-Final Drawing.

IF YOU'RE A CASH WINNER...

take your ticket in person to any N.J. State Motor Vehicle Agency. DO NOT MAIL. After your ticket is validated, you will receive your check.

Our Stakes are the greatest!

MAY WE RECOMMEND

Food for thought ... bound to make your mouth water. We cooked it up to whet your appetite while you're waiting for your order. Eat hearty! Then treat yourself to lottery tickets on your way out.

Good luck!

New Jersey State Lottery

Benefits State Education and Institutions

Important Information. All determinations of winners are subject to Lottery Commission rules and regulations. Winners must claim their prizes within one year following date of drawing. Ticket void if torn or altered. Valid only for drawing date shown on ticket. New Jersey State Lottery is not responsible or accountable for lost or stolen tickets.

HOW THE 50¢ MILLIONAIRE DRAWING WORKS...

If you're a winner with the last 2 correct digits in any Weekly Drawing, you have a chance to become a millionaire! KEEP YOUR TICKET and watch for the announcement of the 50¢ Millionaire Semi-Final Drawing in which your ticket is entered. There will be several during the year—whenever the revenue from the sale of Weekly Tickets warrants the awarding of 50¢ Millionaire prizes!

There are two parts to the 50¢ Millionaire Drawing—the Semi-Final Drawing and the Final Drawing. At the Semi-Final Drawing the SERIAL NUMBER on your winning Weekly Ticket is all important. A 3-digit number will be drawn as the Semi-Final Winning Number. Check to see if the last 3 digits of the Serial Number on your eligible ticket exactly matches the Semi-Final Number.

For example—On Feb 25, 1971, the Semi-Final Number was 460 Serial Number—***460 (Last 3 digits matched) ... became a Finalist, guaranteed at least $500.
Serial Number—****60 (Last 2 digits matched) ... became a $100 winner.

NEW JERSEY STATE LOTTERY COMMISSION

50¢ Lottery 50¢

LOTTERY | B | SERIAL NO. 157460 | DRAWING DATE 1-7-71

THIS IS YOUR LOTTERY TICKET NUMBER 643184

Sample Winning Ticket

- Correct last 3 digits of Serial Number
- Correct Drawing Date
- Correct last 2 digits of Ticket Number

IF YOU'RE A SEMI-FINAL WINNER...

take your ticket to any N.J. State Motor Vehicle Agency. After your ticket has been validated, if you're a FINALIST, you will be invited to a Final Drawing. If you're a $100 winner, a check will be forwarded to you.

NOW, THE FINAL DRAWING!

In this drawing, your name is used, so you must identify yourself within the published time limit before the drawing. You, or your representative, will take part in the Final Drawing process. As a Finalist you can win prizes from $500 up to $1,000,000! First Prize is $1,000,000 ($50,000 a year for 20 years), Second Prize, $200,000 ($20,000 a year for 10 years), Third Prize, $100,000 ($10,000 a year for 10 years), and seven Fourth Prizes of $10,000 each. All other Finalists receive $500 each.

PLAY NOW! PLAY OFTEN...

This is America's Most Rewarding Lottery. Every ticket you buy goes a long way toward the improvement of State Education and Institutions. Help yourself and others.

EXHIBIT 9 New Jersey State Lottery Operating Results, 1971

1971 Drawing Date		Total Number of Tickets Sold (in Millions)	1971 Drawing Date		Total Number of Tickets Sold (in Millions)	1971 Drawing Date		Total Number of Tickets Sold (in Millions)
January	7	4.7	May	6	5.9	September	2	5.3
	14	2.5		13	6.0		9	5.3
	21	3.7		20	5.9		16	5.2
	28	3.9		27	5.9		23	5.4
							30	5.5
February	4	4.9	June	3	5.9	October	7	5.5
	11	5.8		10	5.8		14	5.5
	18	5.8		17	5.9		21	5.4
	25	5.7		24	5.9		28	5.5
March	4	5.9	July	1	5.8	November	4	5.4
	11	6.1		8	5.6		11	5.5
	18	6.1		15	5.4		18	5.4
	25	6.0		22	5.4		24	5.3
				29	5.4			
April	1	6.0	August	5	5.3	December	2	5.4
	8	5.9		12	5.2		9	5.1
	15	5.9		19	5.2		16	5.3
	22	5.6		26	5.3		23	5.2
	29	5.8					30	5.0
Total for 1971								282.3

Source: New Jersey State Lottery Commission.

stantial amount of possible error in this figure. The potential revenues, of course, may be somewhat higher, but some margin must be allowed for errors and experimentation in the initial stages." Thus, the first-year sales totaling $141 million far exceeded the planning commission's estimate.

Recent Developments

Both New Hampshire and New York reacted to the New Jersey success by changing many of the basic characteristics of their own lotteries.

New Hampshire. New Hampshire, which had expanded its number of retail outlets to 850 in 1971, decided to institute a weekly 50-cent drawing in addition to its now quarterly $3 sweepstakes drawing. Drawings were held each Friday and tickets could be purchased as late as Tuesday. On Wednesday, tickets for the following week's drawing were put on sale. Also, a bonus drawing was scheduled in October of each year with the top prize being $100,000. A June 25, 1971, news release by the sweepstakes commission concerning this new lottery is shown in Exhibit 10. During the first week of the 50-cent ticket, 207,957 tickets were sold and for 1971, gross lottery revenue (which included the $3 sweepstakes and the 50-cent drawings beginning July 23) amounted to $4.3 million.

New Hampshire also added a new dimension to the purchase of lottery tickets which was called the "uniticket." This permitted any resident or visitor to the state to buy a 50-cent lottery ticket for a 12-, 24-, or 52-week period at a cost of $6, $12, or $25, respectively. Further, subscribers could select their own number and were also guaranteed renewal rights on this number. Advertisements suggested that residents and tourists purchase unitickets for themselves, or as gifts for friends, relatives, or associates.

EXHIBIT 10 New Hampshire State Lottery News Release

NEW HAMPSHIRE
SWEEPSTAKES COMMISSION
State House Annex, Concord, N.H.

50/50 N. H. SWEEPS POISED FOR TAKEOFF

NEWS RELEASE

FOR RELEASE

June 25, 1971

The Sweepstakes Commission announced today that tickets for the new 50/50 N. H. Sweeps will go on sale at all outlets on July 14. The ticket price has been set at 50¢ and provides a chance at a top prize of $50,000, as well as hundreds of other prizes.

Public drawings will be held every Friday morning beginning July 23. The first drawing will take place on the State House Plaza in Concord. Prizes will be determined by a randomly selected 5-digit number. Each ticket has a 5-digit Sweeps number. If a ticket matches the winning 5-digit Sweeps number for that drawing date, the holder of that ticket wins at least $5,000 and qualifies for a super drawing with a chance to win $50,000 or $10,000. It is estimated that super drawings will be held every 2 or 3 weeks, depending on ticket sales. A variety of additional prizes of varying amounts will be awarded. The prize schedule is best explained by example.

Selected Winning Sweeps Number	Your Sweeps Number	Prize
12345 12345	12345	— $5,000 Minimum. Chance at $10,000 or $50,000
12345 12345	X2345	— $500
12345 12345	XX345	— $50
12345 12345	XXX45	— Weekly Bonus Chance at $500 next week
12345 12345	XXXX5	— Hold for special BONANZA drawing to be held at least quarterly with minimum prize pool of $50,000.

Flyers will be distributed within the next several days explaining the prizes and drawings in greater detail. All existing sales outlets will be selling the 50/50 Sweeps tickets along with the regular $3.00 Sweeps tickets. It is anticipated about 200 additional private outlets will be authorized by the Commission.

The Commission explained that the new 50/50 N. H. Sweeps is patterned after the successful New Jersey Lottery; however, the Commission believes that the N. H. program provides a more exciting prize structure. In the New Jersey program there is an 8-day delay between the end of sales and the weekly drawing. This has been eliminated in the N. H. program since the drawing will take place during the same week. This improves the action. This is in harmony with one of the slogans for the new 50/50 N. H. Sweeps program, "Where the Action Is!"

Source: New Hampshire Sweepstakes Commission.

Three further changes in this marketing program were made in 1971 to increase the number of winners. The first was that buyers of the 50-cent ticket were given 10 $3 sweepstakes tickets if their weekly ticket number was one more or one less than the winning number. The second change established a "scramble bonus" in which a ticket holder won $25 if his ticket contained the five digits of the winning ticket number in any order. The third change was to increase the number of prize winners for the $3 sweepstakes ticket. The new prize distribution for each 100,000 tickets sold was as follows:

Number of Winners	Prize
1	$50,000
1	10,000
1	5,000
5	2,000
20	500
100	100
300	50

New York. New York, like New Hampshire, also changed its lottery substantially. The $1 monthly ticket was discontinued and replaced by a weekly 50-cent ticket; the prize structure was changed; and the distribution network was streamlined by dropping a number of outlets. A news release issued by the New York State Lottery Commission in January 1972 described the new 50-cent lottery.

New York State's 50-cent lottery offers the advantages of fast action and fast payoff. Drawings are held weekly on Thursday at various locations within New York state. Tickets may be purchased from any of approximately 7,200 licensed vendors. A new lottery begins each Wednesday . . . For each series of one million 50-cent tickets sold, 10,000 prizes are offered weekly.

The prizes, for each million tickets sold, are:

1 first prize	$50,000	All six digits of winning number (in exact order)
9 second prizes	$5,000	Last five digits
90 third prizes	$500	Last four digits
900 fourth prizes	$50	Last three digits

Those holding the last two digits (9,000 per million tickets sold) will participate in the next bonus drawing and should retain their tickets to await the results of that drawing. . . . Of the more than 7,200 vendors licensed to sell lottery tickets, virtually every line of business is represented, including supermarkets, department stores, hotels and motels, restaurants, drugstores, variety stores, specialty shops, bars, liquor stores, and others.

The New York Commission decided against the policy of awarding large major prizes in its bonus drawing. Instead, they selected a prize distribution which featured a relatively large number of smaller prizes. For example, if $150,000 was available in the bonus pool,[7] the prize distribution would be:

Number of Winners	Prize
1	$22,500
1	7,500
6	1,500
79	379
945	85

The first 50-cent drawing took place on January 20, 1972, and sales of 3.2 million tickets were recorded. During the subsequent four weeks, sales of 3.6 million, 4.0 million, 4.2 million, and 4.8 million tickets, respectively, were achieved.

New Jersey. As New Jersey entered into its second year of operation, two changes were announced by the New Jersey Lottery Commission. The first was to offer a subscription ticket which was identical to New Hampshire's "uniticket" except for the fact that an individual was assigned a number, rather than being able to select his own. The second was to double the total number of ways that buyers could qualify into the "millionaire" drawing. This was done by making all those with tickets whose first two numbers matched the winning number eligible for the drawing. A new prize distribution was also established creating 2,000 more cash prizes in the "millionaire" drawing, which was held once every five or six weeks.

Number of Winners	Prize
1	$1,000,000
1	200,000
1	100,000
27	10,000
443	500
4,252	100

Present Situation. In preparation for the February meeting, staff members of the Massachusetts Lottery Commission had prepared two summary tables showing comparative data on the other three states and their lottery operations. These are presented in Exhibits 11 and 12. At this same time, two other states—Connecticut and Pennsylvania—had decided to start lotteries and were in the process of preparing plans for their newly created state lotteries. Also, New Hampshire, fearing lost sales from the soon-to-start Massachusetts lottery, had under consideration further changes in its sweepstakes. One such plan involved daily drawings with a 25-cent ticket price. It was in this general context of

EXHIBIT 11 Summary: Structure of State Lotteries, January 1972

State	Price	Frequency of Drawing	Prize Distribution*		Number of Outlets
			Number	**Amount**	
New Hampshire	50 cents	Weekly	1	$5,000 minimum— chance at $50,000 or $10,000	850
			9	500	
			90	50	
			900	Bonus chance of $500 in the next drawing	
			119†	25 (Scramble Bonus)	
	$3	Quarterly	1	$50,000	
			1	10,000	
			1	5,000	
			5	2,000	
			20	500	
			100	100	
			300	50	
New York	50 cents	Weekly	1	$50,000	7,200
			9	5,000	
			90	500	
			900	50	
	$3	Infrequent intervals	1	50,000 a year for twenty years	
			1	100,000	
			1	50,000	
			1	25,000	
			10	10,000	
			10	5,000	
			10	4,000	
			10	3,000	
			10	2,000	
			100	1,000	
				plus an unspecified amount of $500 prizes depending on the number of tickets sold	
New Jersey	50 cents	Weekly	1	$50,000	6,000
			9	4,000	
			90	400	
			900	40	

*Prize distribution is based on sales of 100,000 tickets for New Hampshire and 1,000,000 tickets for New York and New Jersey.
†Maximum number. The actual number of $25 prizes depends upon the number of different digits in the week's winning number.
Source: Various state lottery commissions.

EXHIBIT 12 Comparative Data—State Lotteries

	First Year Lottery Revenues*		1971 Lottery Revenues		1971 Estimates		
State	Total (in Millions)	Per Capita	Total (in Millions)	Per Capita	Population (in Thousands)	Number of Households (in Thousands)	Per Capita Income
New Hampshire	$ 5.7	$ 7.70	$ 4.3	$ 5.81	738	225	$3,608
New York	61.7	3.39	70.1	3.85	18,237	5,893	4,797
New Jersey	141.1	19.60	141.1	19.60	7,168	2,218	4,539
Massachusetts	—	—	—	—	5,689	1,760	4,294

*The first year of operation for the various state lotteries was as follows: New Hampshire, 1964; New York, 1967–1968; and New Jersey, 1971.
Source: Various state lottery commissions and the *Statistical Abstract of the United States: 1971.*

uncertainty and time pressure that the director of the Massachusetts lottery had called the February staff meeting.

Notes

1. The bill was passed by a two thirds majority overriding the veto of the governor: by a 171 to 33 vote in the state house of representatives and a 26 to 13 vote in the state senate. No public referendum was required in Massachusetts.

2. Total pari-mutuel handle from horse and dog racing was $308.9 million; total attendance was $4.4 million during the 439 racing days.

3. New Hampshire Sweepstakes Law, chapt. 284, Sect. 21, p. h.

4. State law required passage by two successive sessions of the legislature in addition to a public referendum. The referendum, held at the general election in November 1966, passed by a 2 to 1 margin.

5. See Exhibit 11 for comparative data on the three states with lotteries.

6. The act creating the lottery was approved by residents at the general election on November 11, 1969, by a 4.5 to 1 margin.

7. The $150,000 would come from prize money that was undistributed in the 50-cent weekly prize distribution.

Plas-Tech Corporation (B)[1]
Charles H. Patti

In late 1957 George Atkin left an important position with a major oil firm to start his own business. Although Atkin was fully aware of the high failure rate of new business ventures, he possessed a combination of talents and experience which he believed would contribute heavily to the success of his new business.

After graduating from MIT as a chemical engineer, Atkin went to work for one of the country's largest oil companies. Within three years he was put in charge of an industrial products development project that was to explore new ways of adapting polyethylene for industrial use. As part of this project, Atkin supervised and then directed the commercial development of polyethylene film.

Polyethylene film became so popular with industrial customers that within six months after its development Atkin was made general manager of a new operating division. The objective of this new division was to manufacture and market polyethylene (plastic) film to a variety of industrial markets.

Under Atkin's direction, this new division developed into a highly profitable operation. Sales grew rapidly and demand soon began to exceed supply of the raw material.

Although the production and manufacturing of plastic film is not technically complicated, Atkin was among the few in the industry with firsthand experience in both production and marketing the product. He had the unique combination of engineering-manufacturing know-how and proven administrative abilities. At age 30, George Atkin felt the time was right for him to try his own business. In October of 1957 he moved to Des Moines, Iowa, and started the Plas-Tech Corporation to manufacture and market a line of disposable polyethylene film for industrial and consumer use.

Polyethylene Market

Polyethylene represents both the fastest-growing and the largest segment of the plastics packaging industry. In 1960 the dollar volume of polyethylene sold was $660 million. In 1971 the same figure was $3.3 billion. Of the

This case was prepared by Charles H. Patti. The original Plas-Tech case was prepared by Charles H. Patti and appeared in *Advertising Management: Cases & Concepts*, by Charles H. Patti and John H. Murphy, Grid Publishing, Inc., 1978.

©1978 Charles H. Patti, professor of marketing, College of Business Administration. University of Denver, Colorado.

TABLE 1 Production of Plastic Packaging Materials *(in Millions of Pounds)*

Type	1967	1968	1969	1970	1975	1980	1985*
Plastic containers							
Bottles	357	380	443	491	791	1,273	2,051
Tubes	20	24	25	23	32	42	57
Molded polystyrene containers	350	360	375	400	607	864	1,229
Transparent films							
Cellophane	385	360	350	340	350	375	392
Polyethylene	735	795	895	975	1,670	2,514	4,199
Other plastic film	198	240	277	300	918	1,832	2,493
Totals	2,045	2,159	2,365	2,529	4,368	6,900	10,421

*Projected.

2.5 billion pounds of plastic packaging materials produced in 1970, polyethylene accounted for nearly 1 billion pounds, or 35 percent of the total. In 1980 the figures were 6.9, 2.5, and 36 percent respectively (see Table 1).

Among the factors influencing the rapid growth of polyethylene are its relatively low price (polyethylene is the lowest-priced transparent material in the world), its strength and versatility, and the development of high-speed and dependable equipment that prints, bags, and wraps.

Industrial Market

Nearly 65 percent of the polyethylene film is consumed by the industrial market (shipping bags, liner film, and construction film). The balance of film production is accounted for by the consumer market (household wrap and bags). Although now growing very rapidly, consumer applications of plastic film were developed several years after the introduction of the product to the industrial market.

The industrial market is made up of government, industrial, commercial, and institutional users. Major users of the product are building material suppliers, mobile-home manufacturers, hospitals, food processors, contractors, and apparel manufacturers.

Consumer Market

Disposable plastic bags are sold in a variety of sizes and used for several household purposes—lawn and garden care, garbage and waste containers, food storage, and the packaging of miscellaneous household items. The total market for disposable plastic bags at the consumer level was approximately $520 million in 1975, $810 million in 1980, and projected to over $1 billion by 1985 (see Table 2).

Although brands are not very important in marketing plastic film to the industrial market, almost all of the film produced for consumer use is sold under a brand name—the brand name of either the manufacturer or the distributor. The rapid growth and high profit potential of consumer plastic bags and wrap have attracted many competitors. While to-

TABLE 2 Industry Sales of All Disposable Plastic Bags

Year	Retail Dollar Volume ($000)	Percent Increase
1967	$ 10,000	0
1968	25,000	150
1969	100,000	300
1970	275,000	175
1975	520,000	125
1980	810,000	31
1985[a]	1,231,000	52

[a]Projected.

day there are literally dozens of brands on the market, three brands dominated the field during the early stages of the product's life cycle (see Table 3).

Growth of Plas-Tech Corporation

Because Atkin had extensive experience in manufacturing and marketing film to the industrial market, he directed Plas-Tech's initial efforts along these same lines.

During the late 1950s and early 1960s, Plas-Tech manufactured a variety of sizes and gauges of plastic bags and film for industrial users. The product was manufactured in the company's 150,000-square-foot manufacturing and warehouse facility in Des Moines and marketed by a staff of 6 full-time, "inside" salespeople and 15 sales agents located throughout the United States.

Although competition was keen, a favorable economic climate, a rapidly increasing demand for the product, and a continuing supply of raw materials needed to manufacture the film combined to make Plas-Tech a

successful operation. In addition to factors beyond his control, Atkin felt his company was enjoying success because of manufacturing efficiencies and low marketing costs. Selling to industrial markets required almost no advertising. Also, sales personnel were being paid on a commission system; therefore, there were few fixed costs in the promotion program.

Development and Marketing of "Big Boys"

1970–1975

During the late 1960s Atkin began planning for entry into the consumer goods market. Several firms were already marketing plastic film for consumer household use, and the products of these firms were eagerly accepted by consumers. Consumer sales were increasing rapidly and the profit margins on plastic film were considerably higher at the consumer level than at the industrial level. In 1970, after 18 months of product development and

TABLE 3 Retail Sales of Plastic Bags: 1971

Type of Bag	Estimated Sales (in $ Millions)	Brand	Sales (in $ Millions)	Share of Market (Percent)
Household/lawn	200.0	Brand "A"	74.0	37.0
		Brand "B"	46.0	23.0
		Brand "C"	34.0	17.0
		All others	46.0	23.0
Food storage	45.0	Brand "C"	22.5	50.0
		Brand "A"	9.9	22.0
		Brand "B"	4.5	10.0
		All others	8.1	18.0
Waste disposal	155.0	Brand "A"	55.8	36.0
		Brand "B"	51.2	33.0
		Brand "D"	23.3	15.0
		All others	24.8	16.0
Total market	400.0	Brand "A"	139.7	34.9
		Brand "B"	101.7	25.4
		Brand "C"	56.5	14.1
		Brand "D"	23.3	5.8
		All others	78.9	19.7

testing, Plas-Tech entered the consumer market with Big Boys, a line of plastic bags for household use.

Creative Strategy

Plas-Tech's advertising agency suggested that Big Boys be positioned as the bag offering the consumer the best value. Although most plastic bags are identical in construction, Big Boys' reinforced bottom seam provided more strength than any other bag on the market. Furthermore, all of the leading brands were priced approximately 10 to 15 percent higher than Big Boys. Therefore, a creative strategy built around "Big Boys—the extra-strength bag with the lowest price"—appeared to offer a strong selling idea with high saliency for the consumer.

Distribution and Promotion

The normal chain of distribution for this product is from manufacturer to wholesaler to retail outlet to the ultimate consumer. The leading national brands were all heavily advertised via television, magazines, newspapers, and radio. There was also a need for promotion and advertising to the trade; therefore, co-op advertising, trade deals, cents-off coupons, and point-of-purchase materials were used extensively. However, it was generally felt that mass consumer advertising was the most important promotional tool in stimulating and controlling brand demand (see Table 4).

In 1971 Plas-Tech decided to introduce Big Boys on a market-by-market basis. Big Boys were first introduced in Des Moines and supported by little consumer advertising. Distribution was secured primarily through personal selling and price discounting. During the brand's first year in the market, Plas-Tech spent $50,000 for Big Boys advertising and most of this was spent on material to support the selling effort of wholesalers. While advertising costs were kept at a minimum, distribution was slow. Fourteen months after the product had been introduced, Big Boys had limited distribution in Des Moines, Iowa; Lincoln, Nebraska; Rockford, Illinois; and several other medium-sized Midwest markets.

1975–1981

During the late 1970s the plastic-bag market continued to expand at a rapid pace. The product category became a household staple as consumers learned to appreciate the convenience, flexibility, and low cost of polyethylene.

By 1980 nearly 75 percent of all households used plastic garbage bags and trash-can liners and 70 percent of all households used plastic sandwich bags or food bags.

Attracted by the continued growth of this market and its profitability, private brands began appearing in the early 1970s. The private or store brands were eventually joined by generics, and by 1980 the consumer had a wide choice of brands. As the national brands continued to fight to hold their market share, national advertising intensified (see Table 4).

Although the Big Boy brand was able to survive the 1970s, George Atkin was less than completely satisfied. Although he had developed a good product and was able to survive a 10-year market struggle against companies much larger than his, he knew he really had not seriously penetrated the market positions of the industry leaders. He frequently wondered if his original marketing plan of minimal consumer promotion and market-by-market introduction had been the best strategy. With 10 years of data to examine, he was often bothered by the correlation between industry share of advertising and market share. Tables 5, 6, and 7 present a summary of past Big Boy advertising, Plas-Tech sales, and Big Boys distribution.

TABLE 4 Advertising Expenditures and Market Shares of Leading Brands of Plastic Bags and Wrap for Consumer Household Use: 1971, 1976, 1981

Brand	1971			1976			1981		
	Advertising Expenditure ($000)	Share of Advertising (Percent)	Market Share (Percent)	Advertising Expenditure ($000)	Share of Advertising (Percent)	Market Share (Percent)	Advertising Expenditure ($000)	Share of Advertising (Percent)	Market Share (Percent)
A	$ 3,500	34.3	34.9	$ 7,307	33.0	32.4	$12,740	35.0	34.3
B	2,750	26.9	25.4	6,665	30.1	28.9	9,246	25.4	24.4
C	2,500	24.5	14.1	4,473	20.2	16.7	6,188	17.0	12.1
D	812	8.0	5.8	2,318	10.7	7.1	4,041	11.1	5.1
E	600	5.8	3.0	1,271	5.6	4.1	3,895	10.7	3.9
Big Boys	50	0.5	0.4	105	0.4	2.3	291	0.8	3.0
All others	N/A	N/A	16.4	N/A	N/A	8.5	N/A	N/A	17.2
Totals	$10,212	100.0	100.0	$22,139	100.0	100.0	$36,401	100.0	100.0

TABLE 5 Big Boys Advertising Media Analysis: 1971, 1976, 1981

Year	Advertising Budget	Advertising Media Used
1971	$ 50,000	Direct mail to wholesalers and retailers
		Newspapers (co-op)
		Outdoor
1976	$105,000	Newspapers
		Outdoor
		Radio
1981	$291,000	Newspapers
		Sunday supplements
		Outdoor
		Radio
		Television

TABLE 6 Plas-Tech Corporation Sales: 1957–1985

Year	Total Sales	Sales of Big Boys	Percent of Total Sales
1957*	$ 5,000	$ 0	0
1960	240,000	0	0
1965	2,870,000	0	0
1970†	8,565,000	428,250	5.3
1971‡	14,000,000	1,680,000	13.6
1975	38,044,000	14,260,000	59.9
1980	61,868,000	24,300,000	64.7
1985§	103,341,000	45,547,000	78.8

*Company was formed in October 1957.
†Big Boys brand introduced.
‡First full year of Big Boys sales.
§Projected.

Current Situation

Next week George Atkin would present a new long-range plan for Big Boys to his board of directors. Industry projections were quite encouraging and he didn't want to let another opportunity escape him.

Note

1. The data presented in this case were taken from a number of sources including *Industry Surveys,* Simmons Market Research Bureau, Inc., the National Flexible Packaging Association, and *Advertising Age.* Also, much of the information has been disguised and does not describe the actual situation in the plastic bag and wrap industry.

TABLE 7 Geographic Distribution of Big Boys: 1971, 1976, 1981

Big Boys Markets	Time Period Distribution Achieved		
	1970–1971	1972–1976	1977–1981
Illinois			
Alton		√	
Aurora		√	
Belleville		√	
Bloomington			√
Champaign-Urbana			√
Decatur			√
DeKalb	√		
East St. Louis		√	
Elgin		√	
Freeport	√		
Galesburg		√	
Moline	√		
Normal			√
Pekin		√	
Peoria		√	
Rockford	√		
Rock Island	√		
Springfield			√
Iowa			
Ames	√		
Burlington		√	
Cedar Rapids		√	
Council Bluffs		√	
Des Moines	√		
Ft. Dodge	√		
Ft. Madison		√	
Iowa City		√	
Marshalltown	√		
Mason City		√	
Ottumwa	√		
Waterloo		√	
Kansas			
Lawrence		√	
Topeka		√	
Wichita			√
Missouri			
Columbia		√	
Independence			√
Jefferson City		√	
Joplin			√
Kansas City			√
Springfield			√
St. Joseph		√	
St. Louis			√
Nebraska			
Grand Island		√	
Hastings		√	
Lincoln	√		
North Platte			√
Omaha	√		

SECTION 5

Implementing Marketing Programs

*T*he single-most important tangible result of strategic marketing planning is a document known as the marketing plan. Although there are innumerable variations of marketing plans, all good plans share five common elements. First, the plan stipulates the marketing objectives to be achieved; proper objectives statements relate quantified targets to be attained to certain time frames. Next, broad strategies or guiding statements are given about marketing decision variables. These strategies are broken down into action steps, or tactics, that specify in great detail the activities that must be implemented to execute the strategies. Third, coordination of marketing activities is achieved through the assignment of responsibilities; that is, someone is identified as the person responsible for the implementation of each action step. Finally, target dates for the completion of action steps are established.

It is best to envision the marketing plan as a road map rather than a sacred document. With a road map, as you drive toward your destination, landmarks along the way coincide with those on the map. More important, if you wander off the correct road, signals alert you to this fact. The marketing plan has its own signposts, for if action steps are not implemented by target dates, signals are given that the objectives may not be achieved. Similarly, intermediate achievements act as landmarks; these can be compared to intermediate objectives to see how well the plan is fulfilling its expectations. If actual performance levels are below expectations, alternative or contingency plans can be elicited to bring the company back on track. Some companies, because of their competitive environments, must be constantly vigilant about progress, and must have contingency plans waiting in the wings at all times.

The comparison of actual to expected performance is called effectiveness. Another gauge of a marketing department's progress is efficiency, which relates to the resources used to achieve objectives. For most marketers, the relevant efficiency measurement is determined by comparing monthly marketing department expenditures to a preset budget. Beyond this barometer, many financial ratios, such as return on investment or marketing performance measures like stock turnover, indicate how efficiently the marketing resources have been utilized to achieve objectives.

Together, effectiveness and efficiency indicants comprise the early warning system for the company, alerting it to the time when the control function of the marketing plan should swing into action.

The widespread proliferation and declining costs of computer technology have opened the door for most companies to build and maintain accurate marketing information systems that track progress toward objectives, generate indicants of efficiency, and maintain a host of other types of information useful in assessing the company's marketing health. To develop such a system, a company identifies the monitors useful to marketing managers in observing the performance of units for which they are responsible and designs a system that collects, tabulates, and reports the information to the managers frequently and in timely fashion. The adoption of workstation personal computers permits a marketing manager to peruse reports, delve into data files, and perform additional analyses to gain insights into how well marketing activities are accomplishing the marketing plan's objectives.

About the Readings

We begin the readings for this section with an article on the "new priority" in marketing mandated by natural-market fragmentation. Lifestyle changes, demographics, sophisticated marketing research techniques, and aggressive competitors are causing companies that historically have been successful mass marketers to rethink their strategies and adopt target marketing. This change forces them to constantly monitor the results of marketing strategies and to fine-tune their marketing mixes. Although this reading contains many business examples, we have placed it in the conceptual category because its theme is pervasive and vital in managing marketing programs. The next reading examines companies that are wholly opposite to mass marketers—those who are highly successful despite their low market shares. The article is both informative about the circumstances of effective versus ineffective low-share companies, and points out some striking marketing management differences between the two. The third conceptual article is written by a well-respected professor who is a marketing management observer and commentator. It discusses the vital role played by marketing research in marketing management decision making and monitoring of results. The author makes a strong case that failure to include marketing research in marketing planning and management is associated with small and/or competitively disadvantaged companies who would do well to rethink their budgets.

The first company related article tells of Wall Street investors who look to how well companies manage their marketing relative to demographics as a means of assessing stock values; obviously, companies with good marketing management systems are smiled upon. The next reading's central topic is the Burger King franchise system. It describes how Burger King has attempted to hold franchise owners to its marketing programs and policies. The article is especially instructive about the daily control difficulties encountered by companies who must dominate their channels of distribution to achieve maximum effectiveness. The last article describes the ever-changing network television battlegrounds where ABC, NBC, and CBS juggle and counterbalance television shows against one another to gain audience statistics and lure advertising dollars; in the television industry, success is redefined weekly ∎

Conceptual Readings

Marketing: The New Priority
Business Week *Cover Story*

Question: What do John Sculley and James J. Morgan have in common? Answer: Each is an experienced, highly regarded consumer goods marketer who has recently moved to a top job at a large corporation. Sculley, an alumnus of PepsiCo Inc., is now president of Apple Computer, Inc. Morgan, who came from Philip Morris, Inc., is chairman of Atari, Inc. In the past, Apple and Atari had concentrated more on developing new technologies than on understanding the dynamics of the marketplace—and suffered because of it. The recruitment of Sculley and Morgan is one of the more visible signs that marketing has become the new corporate priority.

Vast economic and social changes have made better marketing an imperative. Realization of that fact has set off a near free-for-all in recruiting circles for successful marketers, now hotter prospects for high-level jobs than executives with financial experience. Companies of every stripe are looking for managers, presidents, or chief executive officers who can not only develop long-term product strategies but also instill an entrepreneurial spirit into corporations that, more often than not, practice risk avoidance.

No Bean Counters

Says Gerard R. Roche, chairman of Heidrick & Struggles, a top recruiting firm: "Nobody wants bean counters now. Everybody wants a president with marketing experience—someone who knows about product life cycles and developing product strategies." James R. McManus, chairman of Marketing Corp. of America, a consulting firm, agrees: "Today,

companies realize that their raw material, labor, and physical-resource costs are all screwed down and that the only option for dramatic improvement will come from doing a better marketing job."

As companies define marketing more clearly, they no longer confuse it with advertising, which uses media to let consumers know that a certain product or service is available. In essence, marketing means moving goods from the producer to the consumer. It starts with finding out what consumers want or need, and then assessing whether the product can be made and sold at a profit. Such decisions require conducting preliminary research, market identification, and product development; testing consumer reaction to both product and price; working out production capacities and costs; determining distribution; and then deciding on advertising and promotion strategies.

Simple as those steps may sound, many of them were all but forgotten in the 1970s, when inflation kept sales pacing upward and marketing was of secondary importance. Corporate strategies emphasized acquisitions, cash management, or the pursuit of overseas markets. Then came the recession, with its stranglehold on consumer spending, and companies were forced into trying to understand what made the domestic marketplace tick. They soon discovered that demographic and lifestyle changes had delivered a death blow to mass marketing and brand loyalty. A nation that once shared homogeneous buying tastes had splintered into many different consumer groups—each with special needs and interests.

The emergence of this fragmented consumer population, together with an array of economic factors—intense international competition, the impact of rapid technological change, the maturing or stagnation of certain markets, and deregulation—has altered the shape of competition. "If you have to change how to compete, then all of a sudden marketing is a very important function," says Robert D. Buzzell, a Harvard University School of Business Administration professor who specializes in strategic market planning.

Rallying Cry

Robert L. Barney, chairman and CEO of Wendy's International, Inc., understands this all too well. "The main thrust today is taking business away from the competition, and that fact, more than any other is modifying our business," he explains. To pick up market share, the fast-food and hamburger chain is trying to build up its breakfast and dinner business, to achieve greater store efficiencies, and to introduce a slew of new products that will attract a broader spectrum of consumers. Wendy's has not only raised its ad budget by 45 percent but also increased its marketing staff to 70, from 10 five years ago. "You have to outexecute the competition, and that's why marketing is more important than ever before," asserts Barney.

The realization that marketing will provide the cutting edge in the 1980s not only has hit well-known packaged goods marketers—such as Procter & Gamble, Coca-Cola, and General Foods—but is affecting industries that used to be protected from the vagaries of consumer selling by regulatory statutes. Airlines, banks, and financial-services groups are looking for ways to grow and prosper in an environment of product proliferation, advertising clutter, escalating marketing costs, and—despite advances in research and testing—a dauntingly high rate of new-product failures.

With marketing the new priority, market research is the rallying cry. Companies are trying frantically to get their hands on information that identifies and explains the needs of the powerful new consumer segments now being formed. Kroger Co., for example, holds more than 250,000 consumer interviews a year to define consumer wants more precisely. Some companies are pinning their futures to product innovations, others are rejuvenating timeworn but proven brands, and still others are doing both.

Unquestionably, the companies that emerge successfully from this marketing morass will be those that understand the new consumer environment. In years past, the typical American family consisted of a working dad, a homemaker mom, and two kids. But the 1980 census revealed that only 7 percent of the 82 million households then surveyed fit that description. Of those families that reported children under the age of 17, 54 percent of the mothers worked full- or part-time outside their homes. Smaller households now predominate: more than 50 percent of all households comprise only one or two persons.

Men Alone

Even more startling, and most overlooked, is the fact that 24 percent of all households are now headed by singles. This fastest-growing segment of all—up some 80 percent over the previous decade—expanded mainly because the number of men living alone increased. Some 20 percent of households include persons 65 or older, a group that will grow rapidly. Already, almost one out of six Americans is over age 55.

These statistics are significant to marketers. "It means that the mass market has splintered and that companies can't sell their products the way they used to," says Laurel

Cutler, executive vice president for market planning at Leber Katz Partners, an advertising agency that specializes in new products. "The largest number of households may fall into the two-wage-earner grouping, but that includes everyone from a manicurist to a Wall Street-type—and that's really too diverse in lifestyle and income to qualify as a mass market." Cutler foresees "every market breaking into smaller and smaller units, with unique products aimed at defined segments."

Even the automakers agree. "We've treated the car market as a mass one, but now I'm convinced that concept is dead," says Lloyd E. Reuss, general manager of General Motors Corp.'s Buick Motor Division. Reuss now believes in target marketing: specific products and ads aimed at selected groups.

Canned Health

Despite this segmentation, there is enormous common interest in convenience, service, health, cost, and quality. Some companies have already translated these desires into successful products. Makers of soft drinks sell caffeine- and sugar-free products to health- and calorie-conscious consumers. Diet and low-salt foods have found a small but growing number of takers, and so too have high-quality frozen entrées. Robert A. Fox, the first marketing oriented CEO in Del Monte Corp.'s 65-year history, has wasted little time getting the company into fancy frozen-food products. And he has repositioned its existing line of canned vegetables and fruits as low-salt and low-sugar items.

Philadelphia's ARA Services, Inc. offers the patrons of its workplace cafeterias the option of picking up full dinners for consumption at home. It has also acquired a day-care operation and expanded the number of centers from 40, in 1980, to more than 150. "Changing demographics have a tremendous influ-

ence on the services we provide," affirms Joseph Neubauer, ARA's CEO. He says the changes have given marketing "one of the key roles—if not the key one—in corporate strategy."

As families and dwellings grow smaller, the need for more compact products and packages grows more pressing. General Electric Co. downsized its microwave oven and then modeled it to hang beneath kitchen cabinets, thereby freeing valuable counter space. The result: GE went from an also-ran in this category to a strong number two.

How-To Data

Yet many new consumer segments are not being mined. Men, for instance, are probably the most ignored of all buying groups—especially for household items. A recent study by Langer Associates, Inc. found that men living alone were indeed interested in furniture, cooking, and cleaning and resented their "domestic dummy" stereotype. What they wanted, and what they were not getting, was straightforward how-to information from peer figures.

Teenagers too have become a much larger shopping force. A Yankelovich, Skelly & White, Inc. poll, undertaken with Seventeen magazine, found that nearly 75 percent of teenage girls with working mothers now regularly shop for groceries. Yet few companies try to reach this group to sell anything but games, records, and clothes.

Many companies still gear their products and ads to 18 to 34 year olds, who dominated the marketplace of the 1970s but have been supplanted in power and size by the 25 to 45 year olds. "Youth reflected everything we did as a culture for a long time, but that's not where the bulge is today," says Paula Drillman, executive vice president and director of research at McCann-Erickson, Inc.

The Changing Market

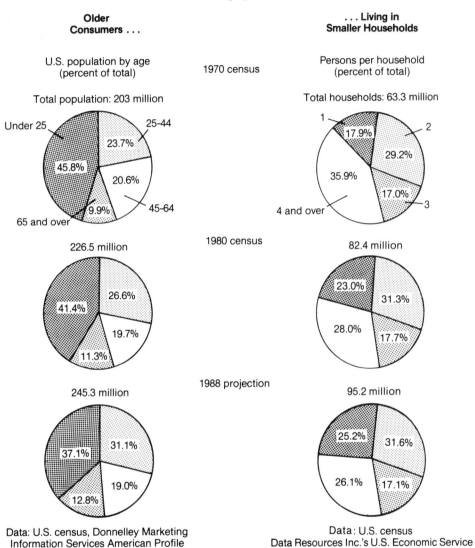

Older Consumers . . .

U.S. population by age
(percent of total)

. . . Living in Smaller Households

Persons per household
(percent of total)

1970 census

Total population: 203 million

Under 25 — 45.8%
25–44 — 23.7%
45–64 — 20.6%
65 and over — 9.9%

Total households: 63.3 million

1 — 17.9%
2 — 29.2%
3 — 17.0%
4 and over — 35.9%

1980 census

226.5 million

26.6%
41.4%
19.7%
11.3%

82.4 million

23.0%
31.3%
28.0%
17.7%

1988 projection

245.3 million

31.1%
37.1%
19.0%
12.8%

95.2 million

25.2%
31.6%
26.1%
17.1%

Data: U.S. census, Donnelley Marketing
Information Services American Profile

Data: U.S. census
Data Resources Inc.'s U.S. Economic Service

This means that companies must sell to an older, better educated consumer who regards the marketplace with a jaundiced eye. Drillman, for one, believes that this skepticism accounts for the slow growth of brands in such industries as liquor. "The shopper is saying, 'Why should I pay so much more for Smirnoff when all I do is put it in a glass and mix it with something? Vodka is vodka is vodka.'"

This indifference to brands is partly the result of the massive proliferation of consumer goods. In an attempt to fire up sales, companies have been swamping the market with new products and line extensions backed by ads, coupons, giveaways, and sweepstakes. For instance, of the 261 varieties of cigarettes for sale today, about half are 10 years old or less.

Me, Too

This huge influx of products has shifted the balance of power from manufacturers to retailers. Lawrence C. Burns, a partner with the Cambridge Group, a Chicago firm of marketing consultants, finds that

> Stores are eliminating slow movers and won't take on any new products unless they are assured of good inventory turns and margins. They want proof that a product really is a success, and the only way companies can provide that is through more regional roll-outs and more test marketing.

But achieving those affirmative results is more difficult because so many of the offerings are basically parity items. Says Robert E. Jacoby, chairman and CEO of Ted Bates Worldwide, Inc.: "We seem to be experiencing a never-ending flow of me-too products or line extensions, which makes it difficult to make a unique claim about the product." Roy Grace, chairman and executive creative director of Doyle Dane Bernbach, Inc., seconds that view. He comments, "If a new technology appears, most companies can quickly copy it or acquire it. So it's really hard to gain a competitive advantage."

Examples of this difficulty abound. Aseptic packaging, a technology for putting food and drinks in specially prepared foil or cardboard pouches that require no refrigeration, has been embraced by nearly all juice makers during the past 18 months. And after the Food & Drug Administration ruled last summer that aspartame, a natural sweetener, could be used in soft drinks, all the major manufacturers raced to reformulate their diet brands to include it. Even Procter & Gamble Co. is eas-

ing up on its age-old philosophy of testing a product for years and bringing it to market only when convinced that some claim of superiority can be made. P&G has rushed its Citrus Hill brand into the spurting orange juice category, even though it admits it cannot make any unique claims for the juice.

The result is a vicious cycle. With the plethora of new choices, products have much shorter life spans, so a steady flow of new items is needed to keep sales curving upward. "The number of entrants in a given category has increased, and the implication is that there is greater market segmentation and shorter product life cycles," points out Derwyn F. Phillips, executive vice president at Gillette North America. "And we find ourselves really working hard at projecting a given brand's life cycle—when the bell curve is likely to peak and the point at which it is no longer intelligent to support a given brand."

Phillips says that Gillette is now trying to speed up new-product development to prevent its combined market share in a category from shrinking. Half of the company's $2.2 billion revenues last year came from products that did not exist five years ago.

Despite advances in the technology of testing, the level of new-product casualties remains astonishingly high. Two out of three new entries still fail—the same proportion as in the 1960s—while the cost of introducing a new item has skyrocketed. An outlay of some $50 million is needed to launch a national brand in a major category. P&G is said to be spending almost $100 million to roll out Citrus Hill orange juice.

Analysis Paralysis

At those odds and prices, companies are understandably wary about committing themselves to high-risk endeavors. They are demanding more research, more strategic planning, and more "review" committees to weed out problems. More often than not, however, the result of all these checks is total confusion and inactivity. Ellen I. Metcalf, a senior consultant with Arthur D. Little, Inc., reports:

> In some companies, you can spend six weeks going through psychographics, trend-line analysis, quarterly consumer reports, scanner data from grocery products—rooms just full of data. Then you ask, "How do you use this information?" And they say they don't know what to do with it.

Ad agencies, in particular, resent the analysis-paralysis climate. "There are more and more people [at a company] who can say no and very few who can say yes," laments Barry Loughrane, president and CEO of Doyle Dane. This risk-avoidance atmosphere worries Allen G. Rosenshine, chairman and CEO of ad agency Batten Barton Durstine & Osborn, Inc. "Everyone has developed a corporate timidity." That, along with the B-school mentality—quantify everything, take few chances—is threatening the entrepreneurialism that companies need if they are to grow, he feels.

But the outlook may not be altogether bleak. Enlightened companies have recognized the challenge and are radically overhauling their operations to put more emphasis on marketing, seeking top marketing executives, and changing the nature and scope of their jobs. Lester B. Korn, chairman of Korn/Ferry International, says he recently filled the top marketing slot at a major consumer goods company—a $350,000-a-year post that typifies the trend to give marketing more clout. "Companies want marketing executives to be responsible for total business results—they're putting the profit-and-loss in with the job—and that's a big step forward from the past, when they had only been responsible for volume and share growth," he says. Companies hope to create a culture that

encourages more risk taking, accepts some failures, and rewards success.

The hottest companies to recruit from are P&G, Johnson & Johnson, Philip Morris, General Foods, and Thomas J. Lipton—large, disciplined consumer-product marketers with broad product lines. "These companies teach their people how to create profitable product lines in brutally competitive industries, and their consistency is what makes them so attractive," says J. Gerald Simmons, president of Handy Associates, Inc.

Support Systems

Some executive-search specialists express reservations, however, about placing a P&Ger. "Their support system is just so strong that they end up working for the system rather than being creative," says David S. Joys, executive vice president of Russell Reynolds Associates, Inc. "Many clients prefer that a P&G executive go to another company first, and then they'll go after him."

Today, most companies believe that their brightest chances for success in coming years will hinge on the development of innovative products aimed at specific consumer niches. But because of the risks, they are trying to direct development efforts toward producing related items in order to achieve economies of scale and a greater overall market share. "You have to go into areas where you have some right to be in that category," says McManus of Marketing Corp. "Companies that go with a product in search of a market or one that has no fit with their existing businesses are doomed to a bloody nose."

Hershey Foods Corp. learned that very lesson when it tried to get into the canned frosting business. Hershey's problem: it did not have a cake mix to support its frosting, unlike its chief competitors, General Mills, P&G, and Pillsbury. These rivals discounted the frosting and made up the difference on the cake batter. Hershey, with no companion product to fall back on, had to discount its product to stay in the market. "The competition was suicidal, and while we could have stayed in the market, it wouldn't have been prudent," says Jack Dowd, Hershey Chocolate Co.'s vice president for new-product development. "But you've got to have the right to fail."

The company has recouped with its new Hershey's chocolate milk, packaged in a rich brown container that makes chocoholics drool in anticipation. Hershey had planned to have the chocolate milk in four markets by the end of the year, but strong demand has already put it in 12 cities, and the figure is growing.

Hang with It

To minimize the risk of failure with new products, experts make several recommendations. "Companies need to have a high-level executive who will champion the new creation—hang with it—and move fast," says Cutler of Leber Katz, which since 1969 has helped clients develop 10 major brands, including Vantage brand cigarettes, with no failures. "It's vital to get a pilot product up quickly, test consumers' reactions to it, refine it, and get it going."

Speed, however, is not the hallmark of many companies. Up to seven years can elapse between the time a new product is proposed and its nationwide distribution. A product developed in 1976 may meet with wholly different market conditions when it finally makes its debut in 1983. "Developing a new product is like shooting a duck," observes Gary W. McQuaid, marketing vice president at Hershey's. "You can't shoot it where it is; you've got to shoot it where it's going to be."

Aiming too far ahead of the market is just as risky, of course. But for some companies, such as automakers, the lengthy time it takes to develop a new product leaves no choice. "When we commit to a car, we're four years away from production," says F. James McDonald, GM's president. "How many people today know what they want four years from now? We really have to roll some dice."

The task of understanding and predicting consumer behavior has led to a nearly insatiable hunger for market research. But experts in the field caution companies about switching from one new technique to another, and they suggest that keeping a steady information base will allow for more accurate projections and comparisons with previous years. Cutler believes that new products often misfire because they "are assigned to junior people at either the company or agency level, since the most experienced people do not want to take their eyes off the main brands. But it is imperative that the team have broad knowledge and have clout—in order to see the new product through review committees and then to get it on the shelf."

Given the slim odds for scoring a new-product hit, many executives are trying to breathe new life into dying brands. "There are dozens of older brands lying around that have been neglected over the years," says Chester Kane, president of Kane, Bortree & Associates, a new-product consulting group. "Companies must discover ways to make them viable for today's consumer."

Right Guard Reborn

Gillette is trying for just such a comeback with its Right Guard deodorant, which dropped from a huge 25 percent share of the deodorant market in the mid-1960s to 8 percent today. The company was loath to let the bronze-canned brand die, since it had produced $500 million in profits during its 23-year life span. For the past two years, all departments—research, marketing, research and development, manufacturing, sales, and finance—as well as the product's ad agency, Young & Rubicam, Inc., have been getting together monthly to coordinate plans for rejuvenating Right Guard. Last June, Gillette put the deodorant into new, bold-stripe containers and began a $28.2 million ad campaign—the most expensive in the company's 82 years. Gillette says the deodorant's sales are running 14 percent higher than planned.

Whether a product is new, old, or rejuvenated, the task facing all marketers is to differentiate it from competitors' offerings. The consumer must be made aware of its usefulness and given a reason to choose it over all other brands. "The financial-services companies are having trouble with this," remarks Russell Reynolds' Joys. "They all want a product portfolio that matches the competitors' offerings, but they also must come up with unique products—carrying higher gross margins—for the salesmen to really focus on."

Federated Department Stores, Inc. is grappling with these issues. Fearful that its core department stores were losing their identity with consumers because of the rapid growth of designer labels and discounters, it has set up a buying office for the purpose of creating private-label goods that would be sold only in its better stores. As a first step, the company has brought out a line of sheets and towels under the "Home Concept" name. The idea is to develop unique, high-quality merchandise that carries a higher profit margin and is different from anything a consumer could buy at a rival department store or discounter—even a Federated-owned one, such as Gold Circle Stores.

Advertising plays a major role in carving out distinct identities for consumer products. The push is on for harder hitting, product-selling ads and the increased use of sales-promotion devices, such as direct mail and rebates. Broadcast television is still the preferred medium, because cable is not yet in enough homes, and viewership data are still too sketchy to make it efficient as an audience-targeting device. However, specialty publications are getting more play from companies that wish to reach a particular market group—usually a working population that may not have the time to read more general media or watch TV.

Nukes and Bagels

Furthermore, companies are consolidating their accounts at a few full-service agencies, rather than letting a number of agencies handle various brands. They are doing this on the theory that the more important an account is to an agency, the higher the quality of attention the client is likely to receive. Then too, that policy promotes efficiency and more unified marketing, especially for companies that sell overseas. To capitalize on the consolidation trend, Bates has centralized in New York its operations for key multinational clients, including Colgate-Palmolive Co. and Mars, Inc. The strategy is to develop "benchmark ads" that can be launched in the United States and then adapted for use all over the world.

The need to reorganize corporate priorities to meet the changing marketplace has caused several companies—quietly and almost surreptitiously—to start their own in-house venture-capital operations. Companies such as Seagrams, R. J. Reynolds, and Gillette have begun either funding or acquiring small, diverse businesses in market segments that hold promise. By experimenting in areas as disparate as nuclear medicine (Seagrams) and bagel chains (Reynolds), these companies can explore the intricacies of the medical or fast-food businesses—categories that are likely to become increasingly important—with little risk.

Gillette North America's just-begun ventures council—composed of its domestic divisional presidents and three corporate executives—has been charged with ferreting out opportunities, not necessarily in the consumer packaged-goods area. "The level of maturity of some of our businesses says to us that it is very important that we invest dollars today to grow higher-yield businesses for tomorrow,"

says Gillette's Phillips. "We are trying to motivate people inside and outside the company to help us develop new opportunities for the future."

The Surprising Case for Low Market Share
Carolyn Y. Woo and Arnold C. Cooper

Can businesses with small market shares be successful? If so, what strategies characterize such businesses? This article seeks to answer these questions by using research on 126 businesses, 40 of which have demonstrated superior performance despite low market shares.

Strategists tend to place much importance on having high market-share positions. Bruce Henderson of the Boston Consulting Group observed: "In a competitive business, it [market share] determines relative profitability. When it does not seem to do so, it is nearly always because the relevant product market sector is misdefined or the leader is mismanaged."[1] One study, based on analysis of data at the Strategic Planning Institute in Cambridge, Massachusetts, concluded that "a difference of 10 percentage points in market share is accompanied by a difference of about five points in pretax ROI."[2]

High market share is frequently seen as offering businesses a number of attendant advantages, including economies of scale, brand-name dominance, and greater bargaining power with suppliers, distributors, and customers.

These correlations have often been interpreted to mean that businesses with low market shares inevitably have poor long-term prospects. Accordingly, analysts usually advise such businesses to build market share or reposition themselves so that they dominate some market segment. And, they contend, if neither action is feasible, the small-share business should be harvested or divested. Since only a few businesses are market-share

leaders, presumably such dismal prognoses apply to most companies.

Each of these alternatives can cause serious problems. Building market share is a risky, costly activity that can ignite retaliatory actions by competitors. For low-share businesses in particular, share building may not even be possible because of limitations of resources or market influence. To reposition in an effort to dominate a market segment, a company must have product- and market-development capabilities. Harvesting or divestiture may be especially difficult in the multibusiness corporation because facilities, distribution channels, or customers are shared with other units in the company. Legal or social pressures may make it difficult to leave a business, and finally, those companies that lack attractive investment alternatives may realize little benefit from harvesting funds.

All of these concerns suggest that simple prescriptions do not apply to low-share businesses. Moreover, recent research suggests that pessimism about the prospects of low-share businesses is not always warranted. In 1978, Richard G. Hamermesh and associates reported on three companies they had studied—Burroughs, Union Camp, and Crown Cork & Seal—which had all been highly successful despite low-share positions.[3] They concluded that the strategies of these companies were characterized by the following: creative market segmentation, efficient research and development expenditures, controlled growth, and strong leadership. A subsequent study by William K. Hall identified companies in eight mature industries that had exhibited outstanding performance despite nonleadership positions.[4] The experiences of these companies demonstrate that market leadership is not always necessary to attain the lowest cost position. They also show that the lowest cost position is not required to achieve high margins.

Both studies show that long-run competitive success is feasible despite low market-share position.

A New Approach

This article reports findings from a research project that examines a much larger number of businesses than the studies just mentioned and that looks at a number of factors associated with strategy. We have focused on two sets of broad questions, both relating to high-performing, low-share companies: (1) What kinds of industry settings do these businesses enter? What types of products do they offer? (2) How do these businesses compete? Do they allocate resources in distinctive ways to achieve a competitive advantage?

For a given business, performance might be expected to depend both on the product, market, and industry characteristics that determine its competitive environment and on its business strategy, i.e., the way it competes within that environment.

The businesses in this sample were chosen from the PIMS data base.[5] Each business is defined as "a division, product line or other profit center within its parent company, selling a distinct set of products or services to an identifiable group or groups of customers, in competition with a well-defined set of competitors." We studied a total of 649 domestic manufacturing companies for the period 1972 through 1975. From this group, we sought to identify low-share businesses that achieved superior returns without diminishing their market shares. To qualify, businesses had to show a pretax return on investment of at least 20 percent. Their market shares could not exceed 20 percent of the combined share of their three largest competitors. Of the 649 businesses, 40 met these requirements.

It should be noted that the managements of these businesses estimated their own market shares, defining the market in terms of the customers they sought to serve. It is clear that the market definitions used directly affect a company's market share; however, these are the market definitions used by managements in their own planning. It should also be noted that, because of the nature of the PIMS data base, most of these were divisions of large corporations, not free-standing small businesses.

For contrast, we compared these high-performing businesses with two control groups: effective high-share businesses and ineffective low-share businesses. The definitions of those groups and the number of businesses in each category are shown in Exhibit 1.

EXHIBIT 1 The 126 Companies We Studied

Type of Business	Pretax Return on Investment	Relative Market Share	Number of Businesses
Effective low share	20% or higher	20% or lower	40
Effective high share	20% or higher	125% or higher	39
Ineffective low share	5% or lower	20% or lower	47

The Best Circumstances

For proprietary reasons, the names of the companies or the industry segments they serve are not given in the data base. However, we do know the characteristics of their industries, as reflected by 13 different factors. These factors are the nature of the product, the degree of product standardization, the importance of auxiliary services, the stage of product life cycle, purchase frequency by both immediate and end users, geographic scope, industry value added, industry concentration, number of competitors, industry growth, market growth, and frequency of product changes (see Exhibit 2). In examining these environmental characteristics, we can determine whether high-performing, low market-share businesses sell in markets with distinctive characteristics.

Using a statistical technique called "cluster analysis," we could classify the environments of the 126 businesses into six groups.[6] These six groups, shown in Exhibit 3, differ in a number of dimensions but particularly in the nature of the products and their market growth rates. These six groups do not describe all possible environments, but do include the settings of the 126 businesses we studied. Bear in mind that businesses within a group do not necessarily compete with each other; rather, they compete in environments with common characteristics.

The distribution of effective low-share businesses and the two control samples in these six groups is displayed in Exhibit 4. Most of the effective low-share businesses are found in three environments: those designated as groups three, four, and six. Group four contains almost 50 percent of these high performers; this is an environment characterized by businesses offering standardized industrial components and supplies in low-growth markets. Another 25 percent are included in group six, an environment also characterized

EXHIBIT 2 Dimensions of Market Environment and Competitive Strategy

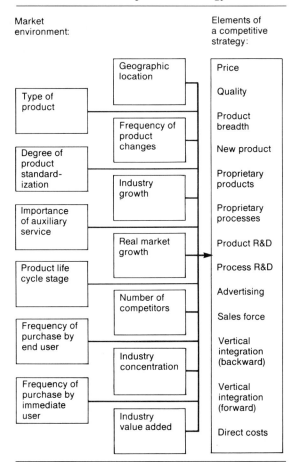

by slow market growth, but which has industrial components that are less standardized and that are experiencing some product changes. Group three, which contains 15 percent of these high-performing businesses, includes mature consumer durables and capital goods in slow-growth markets.

The environments where we found most of the high-performing, low-share businesses share certain characteristics, some of which are very different from the environmental characteristics often thought to be most promising for smaller businesses.

EXHIBIT 3 Characteristics and Composition of Market Groups

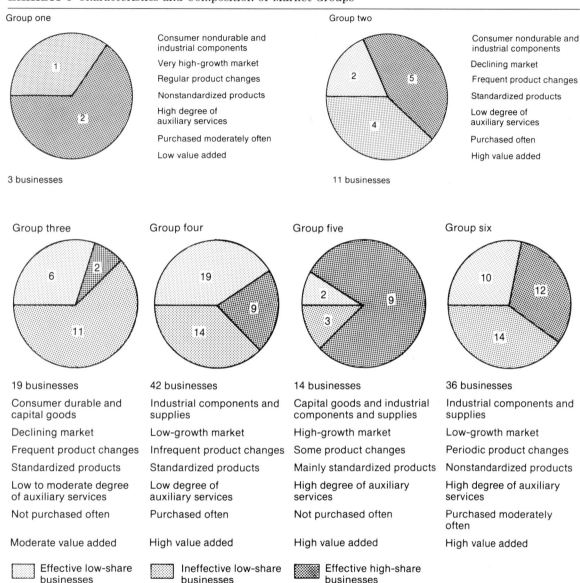

Group one

1
2

3 businesses

- Consumer nondurable and industrial components
- Very high-growth market
- Regular product changes
- Nonstandardized products
- High degree of auxiliary services
- Purchased moderately often
- Low value added

Group two

2
5
4

11 businesses

- Consumer nondurable and industrial components
- Declining market
- Frequent product changes
- Standardized products
- Low degree of auxiliary services
- Purchased often
- High value added

Group three

6
2
11

19 businesses

Consumer durable and capital goods

Declining market

Frequent product changes

Standardized products

Low to moderate degree of auxiliary services

Not purchased often

Moderate value added

Group four

19
9
14

42 businesses

Industrial components and supplies

Low-growth market

Infrequent product changes

Standardized products

Low degree of auxiliary services

Purchased often

High value added

Group five

2
3
9

14 businesses

Capital goods and industrial components and supplies

High-growth market

Some product changes

Mainly standardized products

High degree of auxiliary services

Not purchased often

High value added

Group six

10
12
14

36 businesses

Industrial components and supplies

Low-growth market

Periodic product changes

Nonstandardized products

High degree of auxiliary services

Purchased moderately often

High value added

☐ Effective low-share businesses

▦ Ineffective low-share businesses

▨ Effective high-share businesses

1. **Profitable low-market-share businesses exist in low-growth markets.** Groups four and six, which account for 72.5 percent of profitable low-share businesses, are characterized by real (inflation-adjusted) growth rates of zero to 1 percent. This may seem surprising because limited opportunities and low profits are often thought to be associated with low-growth markets. High-growth markets, however, are turbulent arenas where competitors

EXHIBIT 4 Distribution of Effective Low-Share Businesses and Two Control Groups across
Six Market Groups

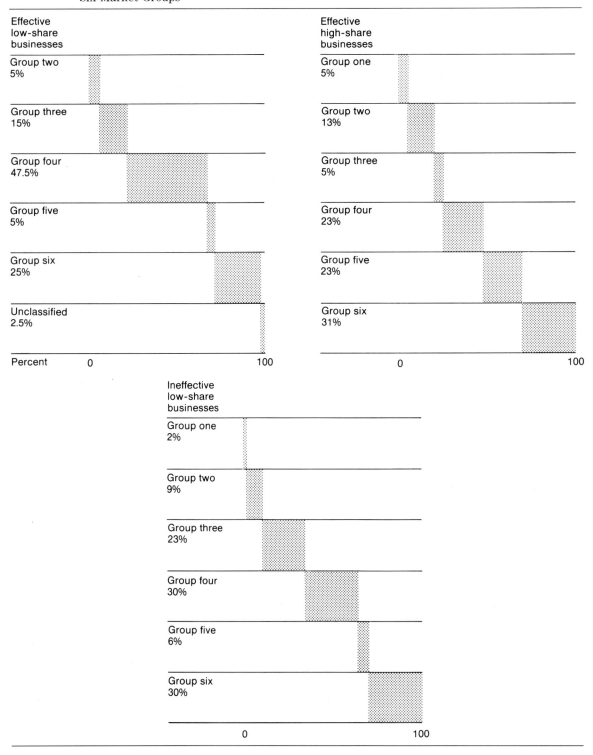

try to grab share leadership before the market stabilizes. During this period, competition can be intense. Rapid product and process changes add to the uncertainty. Often a shakeout period follows, when weak competitors are forced to exit. This turbulence is repeated when the market reaches a stage of negative growth.

Profitable low-share businesses thrive between these two stages. Most of them seek mature though nondeclining markets with low real growth. Such markets seem to provide a more stable environment, in which there is less elbowing to gain market share. Hence this structure makes it easy for all players to define and protect their positions.

2. **Their products don't change often.** The mature markets mentioned previously also have low levels of product and process change. The concentration of profitable low-share businesses in this environment is surprising. High rates of change benefit companies that can move quickly, as well as those seeking product differentiation opportunities. Low-market-share companies are often expected to benefit from such environmental changes.

Frequent changes may, however, force all members of an industry to spend heavily on product introduction as well as on research and development, which is difficult for smaller businesses that have less revenue to support these activities. High rates of change may also force smaller producers to scrap production tools and dies before their useful lives run out. By contrast, the greater production volumes of businesses with large market shares may mean that tools and dies are depreciated and ready for replacement sooner. Moreover frequent changes also reduce the stability of markets and may be a reflection of greater competitive intensity.

3. **Most of their products are standardized and they provide few extra services.** Smaller businesses are often viewed as having the flexi-bility that permits them to cater to customers' special needs. They might be expected to avoid direct competition with large corporations' standardized products. They are often advised to choose fields in which competition is based on custom products or auxiliary services such as engineering consultation, frequent on-site visits, or maintenance and repair.

Contrary to expectations, 72.5 percent of successful low-share performers competed in markets characterized by standard products (groups two, three, four, and five). Moreover, the markets were not heavily supported by auxiliary services.

Competing in such markets permits focused strategies, in which companies need not incur the costs of providing custom products or special services. These market characteristics may stem from the nature of industrial components and supplies, which (as we discuss next) are the main products of successful low-share businesses. These products often require little subsequent servicing or technical support.

4. **Most of them make industrial components or supplies.** All businesses in groups four and six and some in two and five manufacture industrial components and supplies. These represent 70 percent to 80 percent of successful low-share performers in our sample. Purchase decisions for industrial products are based largely on performance, service, and cost. In industrial markets, it may be possible for small-share businesses to develop strong relationships with selected customers through emphasis on performance variables important to them. Advertising, normally thought to have high economies of scale, is usually less important for industrial products; therefore, small-share businesses are at only a minor competitive disadvantage.

In addition, purchases of industrial products are frequently governed by contracts. This guarantee of a market puts the sellers in a better position to project sales volume, capital spending, and costs.

5. **These products and supplies are purchased frequently.** Market share appears to be less important for products that need to be bought often. More than half the low-share businesses studied produced such items (groups two and four). For such products, customers tend to rely more on experience and less on the brand name of market leaders for indications of reliability and performance. Thus, the share advantage of market leaders is less pronounced in these markets.

In addition, the rate of product purchases is likely to affect the requirement for working capital. High purchase frequency usually leads to faster turnover of inventory and receivables, allowing for quicker recovery of capital. Indeed, in our study, businesses making frequently purchased products had lower working-capital ratios than others.[7]

6. **Profitable low-share businesses are in industries with high value added.** Companies in these industries often enjoy margins wide enough to absorb cost increases from suppliers or price declines in the markets they serve. High value-added industries are less likely to invite forward integration by suppliers or backward integration by customers. When the value-added factor is high, many opportunities exist for differentiation according to product characteristics and cost structures. In this study, 82.5 percent of successful low-share businesses are in such industries (groups two, four, five, and six).

Which Strategies Work Best

How do high-performing, low-share businesses compete in particular environments? Competitive strategy is reflected by the emphasis organizations place on such variables as relative prices, quality, product-line breadth, emphasis on new products, and advertising and selling efforts. (A more complete listing of factors comprising competitive strategy is contained in Exhibit 2.)

Examining market groups three, four, and six, where nearly 90 percent of these successful low-share businesses are clustered, we find distinctive patterns of competitive strategy in each environment.

1. **A strong focus tailored to environmental differences.** These successful businesses are distinguished by highly focused strategies. They do not try to do everything. They compete in carefully selected ways with the competitive emphasis differing according to the market environment.

Effective low-share businesses had similar strategies in groups four and six, both of which involve the sale of components and supplies. In group four, where products are standardized and undergo little change, successful low-share businesses are distinguished from the two control groups by their orientation toward low costs, low prices, and high quality. Though these characteristics are also present in group six, the high-performing, low-share businesses in this group are notable for their lower product R&D allocations and lower levels of backward integration. Products in group six undergo frequent changes. Hence, careful monitoring of product R&D is important to achieve a balance between long-term competitive position and short-term profitability.

In this market environment, we found that successful low-share businesses adopted a very conservative posture toward R&D, spending yet achieved ROIs exceeding 20 percent over four years. Though the long-term success of this approach has not been proved, a lower R&D emphasis did not reduce the competitiveness of these businesses in the four-year period we observed. The lower vertical integration policy also contributed to success by providing these low-share businesses with greater flexibility to respond to changes, which minimized the disadvantage of their lower volumes.

In the mature consumer durables and capital goods area (group three), which contains 15 percent of our sample, effective low-share businesses adopt an aggressive marketing strategy and place less emphasis on quality, competitive prices, or research and development. The heavy emphasis given to marketing, particularly in the use of their sales forces, compensates for the other shortcomings of these businesses. Their reputations for quality were lower than competitors', and their product lines were not as broad. Yet these businesses command high prices. They sustain higher direct costs and have less forward and backward integration than do competitors. Despite weaker positions in cost, quality, and product value, a targeted marketing focus enables these businesses to derive rather strong margins from a low-share position in a declining market environment.

2. **A reputation for high quality.** Except for those businesses in group three, effective low-share performers consistently turned out high-quality products. Superior performance and reliability may be particularly important competitive weapons in the sale of industrial components and supplies. Knowledgeable buyers and frequent use lead to constant evaluation of tangible product characteristics.

3. **Medium to low relative prices complementing high quality.** The majority of successful low-share performers had lower prices than competitors (72.5 percent in groups four and six). Like product quality, competitive prices are particularly important in the environments in which these businesses compete. Buyers of industrial products are well informed and often enjoy strong bargaining positions in dealing with suppliers. When switching costs are low, buyers can solicit bids from eager suppliers. Within these mature, technologically stable markets, price might be expected to be an important consideration in purchase decisions. Note that the combination of high product quality and lower price means that these businesses offer their customers exceptionally good value.

4. **Low total cost.** Relatively low costs presumably permit low-share businesses to offer high-quality products at low prices and still show high profits. It follows that effective low-share businesses have lower unit costs than do ineffective low-share businesses. How do they achieve low costs? (After all, they do have higher unit costs than the market-share leaders because of smaller production volumes and less vertical integration.) In part, by concentrating on a narrow line of standardized products. These high-performing, low-share businesses also spend less on product R&D, advertising, promotion, sales force support, and new product introduction.

Strategies of Poor Performers

Interestingly, there are no substantial differences in the environments chosen by effective and ineffective low-share businesses. Both have more than 80 percent of their businesses in groups three, four, and six. The differences between these two groups of companies relate more to how they compete in each environment.

By contrast, low-performing, low-share businesses compete aggressively along many fronts; they might emphasize broad product lines, advertising, selling expenses, product R&D, and process R&D. They also have considerable vertical integration, which requires still more resources. Their price-quality performance is below that of their competitors. We observed the absence of a clear focus in all three market groups (three, four, and six) where we compared these low-performing, low-share businesses with high-performing, low-share businesses.

In general, the resource allocation patterns of ineffective low-share performers are similar to those of effective large-share businesses. The latter offer a broad line of products complemented by aggressive marketing, selling, R&D, and new-product introduction. They are also highly integrated vertically. While both groups emphasize a large number of competitive weapons, small-share businesses lack the sales volume to support such broad-scale aggressive strategies.

Implications for Success

First, low market share does not inevitably lead to low profitability. Despite the well-accepted correlation between market share and profitability, market share is not a necessary condition for profitability. The dismal prospects often foreseen for low-share businesses do not always come to pass—certainly not to this sample of 40 businesses, all very profitable despite low-share positions.

Since these businesses have low market shares and are positioned in low-growth markets, they would usually be classified as candidates for harvesting or divestiture. The performance of these 40 businesses demonstrates that such blanket recommendations should be considered with care.

Second, a stable market environment contributes to low-share success. The performance of effective low-share businesses depends on both the characteristics of their industry settings and their business strategies. The successful businesses tend to concentrate in competitive environments somewhat different from those of effective large-share businesses, but similar to those of ineffective low-share performers. These environments are not characterized by an absence of large market-share businesses, as might be expected if "niche" strategies were followed. Rather, the overriding feature is stability. Low market growth, infrequent product and process changes, high value added, and high purchase frequency all contribute to more predictable and less turbulent environments. These markets are unlikely to attract new competitors, but they may be viewed as unexciting by existing competitors. As such, competitors' divisions may receive less top-management attention and staff support, and they may be staffed by less able and creative managers.

Third, selectivity is a key to low market-share success. Effective low-share businesses compete in distinctive ways. They normally offer superior products at prices lower than competitors. This supports the traditional wisdom that success in any business ultimately depends on the benefits provided customers.

The most distinctive feature of these strategies is selective focus. They do not copy the strategies of market leaders (unlike ineffective low-share businesses). These high-performing, low-share businesses choose particular bases of competition, such as product quality and price. They then limit their expenditures in other areas of competition, such as product R&D, product-line breadth, or marketing expenditures, so that they can achieve high performance despite relatively limited sales volume.

The specific strategy of any business must be tailored to its capabilities and the requirements of its competitive environment. Small-share businesses clearly vary widely in their possibilities. But the experience of these 40 companies demonstrates that success is possible for well-positioned and well-managed small-share businesses.

Notes

1. Bruce D. Henderson, *Henderson on Corporate Strategy* (Cambridge, Mass.: Abt Books, 1979), p. 94.

2. Robert D. Buzzell, Bradley T. Gale, and Ralph G. M. Sultan, "Market Share—A Key to Profitability," *Harvard Business Review*, January–February 1975, p. 97.

3. Richard G. Hamermesh, M. Jack Anderson, Jr., and J. Elizabeth Harris, "Strategies for Low Market Share Businesses," *Harvard Business Review*, May–June 1978, p. 95.

4. William K. Hall, "Survival Strategies in a Hostile Environment," *Harvard Business Review* September–October 1980, p. 75.

5. PIMS (Profit Impact of Market Strategy) is a research program sponsored by the Strategic Planning Institute in Cambridge, Massachusetts, and includes more than 1,000 member businesses.

6. For a detailed discussion of the methodology, refer to Carolyn Y. Woo and Arnold C. Cooper, "Strategies of Effective Low Share Businesses," *Strategic Management Journal*, July–September 1981, p. 301.

7. A correlation coefficient of + .26 was obtained between purchase frequency and working-capital-to-revenue. Based on the definition of the purchase frequency variable, the coefficient indicated that longer time periods between purchases (infrequently purchased products) were correlated with higher working-capital-to-revenues ratios.

Research's Place in the Marketing Budget
A. Parasuraman

Most managers will agree that the timely availability of relevant information from the marketplace is of major importance for achieving commercial success in today's business world. Yet, it is unclear whether, and to what extent, firms do more than merely acknowledge the importance of marketing research, which is the key to relevant market information.

Some past studies have concluded that United States firms do not spend enough on marketing research.[1] Other studies have criticized U.S. firms for being too "consumer" or "marketing" oriented.[2] These critics have argued that such an orientation is at least partly responsible for the economic woes of U.S. firms, and the erosion of their competitive strength vis-à-vis that of foreign firms. In other words, they have indirectly accused U.S. firms of placing an overemphasis on marketing research, perhaps at the expense of basic R&D and truly innovative products.

Given these apparently conflicting schools of thought, it will be instructive to ascertain the actual extent of emphasis being placed on marketing research by U.S. firms. Specifically, what share of their marketing budgets gets allocated to marketing research? Do company characteristics such as the type of firm, its size, its profit orientation, and competitive strength have a bearing on the relative emphasis placed on marketing research? I sought answers to such questions through a study that I recently completed. The answers which I obtained were insightful and thought provoking.

The sample for the study consisted of 1,000 firms in the United States, chosen randomly from the 1980 edition of *Dun and Bradstreet's Million Dollar Directory*. Questionnaires were mailed to the marketing departments of these firms. A total of 261 firms responded to the survey. Of the individuals filling out the questionnaires, 27 percent were presidents, 33 percent vice presidents or VPs-marketing, 29 percent were marketing managers, sales managers, advertising managers, or marketing research directors, and the remaining 11 percent had a variety of titles such as owner, assistant to the president, and management trainee. Thus almost all the respondents held middle- or upper-management positions. Statistical tests showed no significant differences between the firms that responded and the initial sample, with respect to annual sales revenue and number of employees.

The respondents provided the following information about their firms:

■ The percentage of total marketing expenditures (that is, the market budget) used for marketing research expenditures (including the purchase of commercial marketing research services, if any) during the past year.

■ Size as indicated by annual sales revenue and number of full-time employees.

■ Number of different product and/or service categories marketed.

■ Type of firm: "manufacturing" (that is, consumer and/or industrial goods manufacturer) or "nonmanufacturing" (that is, retailer, wholesaler/industrial distributor, financial institution, or firm offering other than financial services).

■ Extent of overall competition within the firm's industry.

■ The firm's own competitive position relative to other firms in its industry.

■ Whether the firm's top management placed higher emphasis on long-term or short-term profits, or about equal emphasis on both.

Not Much for Research

Of the 261 respondents, 143 indicated that their firms spent *no* money on marketing research during the past year. Among the 237 firms that responded to the question about the share of the marketing budget allocated to marketing research, the average allocation per firm was a mere 2.2 percent. Even among the 94 firms that spent some of their marketing budgets on research, the average allocation was only 5.5 percent (see Table 1). Apparently, U.S. firms are still placing relatively little emphasis on marketing research. This casts a shadow of doubt on the validity of criticisms that an overemphasis on marketing

research may be responsible for the waning of U.S. competitive strength in the marketplace.

There were some interesting variations in the patterns of monetary allocations made to marketing research across firms with different characteristics. Table 2 provides a summary of these variations.

Size of Firm

There is a significant association between the size of a firm and the likelihood of its allocating at least some money to marketing research. The larger a firm—based either on its annual sales revenue or the number of full-time employees it has—the more likely it is to allocate some of its marketing budget to marketing research. The last column of Table 2 shows the average percent allocation to marketing research by firms within each size category. This raises a couple of intriguing questions: Could it be that firms that are larger got that way, at least in part, due to their greater emphasis on marketing research? Or, could it be that larger firms are more likely to feel that they can "afford" to spend money on marketing research due to their size? Obviously, any conclusive answers to such questions, based solely on the descriptive data collected in this study, will be speculative. Nevertheless, if smaller firms tend to shy away from marketing research due to a belief that they cannot "afford" it, they need to realize that such a belief may be no more than a myth. Small firms can afford to spend money on market-

TABLE 1 Share of Marketing Budgets Allocated to Research

Percentage of Budget Allocated to Marketing Research	Number of Firms	Percentage of Firms
None	143	54.8%
1% or less	32	12.3
From 1% to 5%	40	15.3
From 5% to 10%	12	4.6
From 10% to 20%	6	2.3
From 20% to 40%	4	1.5
No response	24	9.2
Total	261	100.0

ing research, and can profit from doing so, if they take a little time to become familiar with the potential applications and benefits, as well as pitfalls, of marketing research.[3]

Number of Product/Service Categories

There is no significant direct association between the product "assortment" of a firm (that is, the number of product/service cate-

gories marketed) and the likelihood of its spending some money on marketing research. However, as can be seen from Table 2, it is interesting that firms marketing a medium-sized assortment of categories (10 to 49) are somewhat more likely to have spent money on marketing research than firms marketing a narrower, or wider, assortment. Also, on the average, such firms allocated a larger share of their budgets to marketing research.

TABLE 2 Relationships between Characteristics of Firms and Their Expenditures on Marketing Research

Characteristics of Firms	Number (%) of Firms Allocating		Total Number (%) of Firms	Average % of Marketing Budget Spent on Marketing Research
	Nothing to Marketing Research	Some Funds to Marketing Research		
Sales revenue				
Less than $5 million	53 (77%)	16 (23%)	69 (100%)	1.65%
$5 million to less than $25 million	63 (67)	31 (33)	94 (100)	1.51
$25 million and over	27 (36)	47 (64)	74 (100)	3.50
Number of full-time employees				
Less than 100	92 (77)	27 (23)	119 (100)	1.34
100 to 499	41 (57)	31 (43)	72 (100)	2.60
500 and over	10 (22)	36 (78)	46 (100)	3.63
Number of product/service categories				
Less than 10	83 (65)	45 (35)	128 (100)	1.81
10 to 49	28 (50)	28 (50)	56 (100)	3.21
50 and over	32 (63)	19 (37)	51 (100)	1.99
Type of firm				
Manufacturing	71 (51)	67 (49)	138 (100)	3.15
Nonmanufacturing	72 (73)	27 (27)	99 (100)	0.81
Competition in firm's industry				
Weak to moderate*	25 (54)	21 (46)	46 (100)	2.42
Intense	66 (59)	46 (41)	112 (100)	2.16
Very intense	52 (66)	27 (34)	79 (100)	2.04
Firm's competitive position				
Average or below average†	64 (66)	33 (34)	97 (100)	1.58
Above average	79 (56)	61 (44)	140 (100)	2.58
Firm's profit orientation‡				
High emphasis on long-term profits	55 (62)	33 (38)	88 (100)	2.07
Equal emphasis on long- and short-term profits	59 (64)	33 (36)	92 (100)	2.59
High emphasis on short-term profits	29 (51)	28 (49)	57 (100)	1.65

*Only 2 of the 46 firms in this category indicated that competition in their industries was "weak"; all of the rest said competition was "moderate."

†Only 10 of the 97 firms in this category indicated that their competitive position was "below average"; the rest indicated "average."

‡On a 7-point scale, in which 7 = very high emphasis on long-term profits and 1 = very high emphasis on short-term profits, firms scoring above 4 were placed in the first category and those scoring below 4 were placed in the third category; the rest (those scoring exactly 4) were placed in the middle.

Type of Firm

Table 2 shows a significant relationship between the "manufacturing" or "nonmanufacturing" nature of a firm and the likelihood of its spending money on marketing research. The average allocation to marketing research made by manufacturing firms was 3.51 percent vis-à-vis the average allocation of only 0.81 percent made by nonmanufacturing firms. This finding is consistent with a traditional belief that nonmanufacturing firms lag behind manufacturing firms in terms of researching their markets and customers.

Competition

Let us first look at the overall level of competition in a firm's industry and its relationship, if any, to the firm's expenditures on marketing research. In this regard, the pattern revealed by Table 2 was not statistically significant. However, it is interesting that firms in industries characterized by "intense" or "very intense" competition appear to be more likely to do little or no marketing research compared to firms in less competitive industries. Firms in highly competitive industries, perhaps due to their preoccupation with maintaining their market shares through lower prices, heavy advertising, and the like, may not be giving adequate consideration to marketing research. If so, such firms would do well to rethink their marketing priorities. For, when we look at the relative competitive position of firms within their respective industries, Table 2 shows that the "above average" firms are more likely to have spent some money on marketing research. Furthermore, such firms allocated a larger share of their budgets to marketing research than competitively weaker firms (2.58 percent versus 1.58 percent). These findings offer some food for thought, although inferring a causal connection between emphasis on marketing research and competitive strength within an industry is somewhat speculative.

Profit Orientation

The overall association between the three types of profit orientation (shown in Table 2) and the likelihood of spending any money on marketing research was not statistically significant. However, the results in Table 2 still offer some interesting insights. Firms with a high emphasis on short-term profits were most likely to have allocated some funds for marketing research; but, surprisingly, the average budget share allocated by such firms to marketing research was only 1.65 percent—the lowest share among the three sets of firms classified according to their profit orientation. One possible explanation for this is that many firms with short-term profit emphasis may be engaging in so-called quick and dirty research for evaluating marketing tactics (for example, price cuts, sales promotions, and so on) aimed at boosting sales and profits in the short run. They may be doing little, if any, strategy oriented research (such as market potential studies, customer segmentation studies, and so on) which may be expensive, but is essential for sound long-term strategy formulation. The results suggest that firms placing medium or high emphasis on long-term profits are less likely than others to do any marketing research; however, if such firms do spend any money on marketing research, they are perhaps likely to engage in relatively more expensive, "strategic" (rather than "tactical") research, as evidenced by their higher average percent allocations to marketing research.

Missed Opportunities

In addition to shedding light on the share claimed by marketing research from the marketing budgets of a variety of firms, the results of this study have some important implications for marketers. In pondering these implications, however, it should be noted that this study investigated only the share of marketing budgets allocated to marketing research rather than the actual dollar expenditures on it. Thus the budget share allocated can only be viewed as a surrogate measure of the relative emphasis placed on marketing research. Another caveat to bear in mind is that the firms in this study reported their budget allocations only for the past year. Hence, a firm indicating that no part of its marketing budget was spent on marketing research may have done some marketing research in years preceding the past year. Nevertheless, the aggregate patterns of responses across different cross-sections of firms at least raise some intriguing issues that marketers ought to mull over.

The relatively low emphasis that U.S. firms are apparently placing on marketing research is not supportive of recent criticisms that they may be overemphasizing marketing research to the detriment of their competitive strength. Indeed, the results of this study suggest that U.S. firms—especially those that are relatively small in size, those that are in the nonmanufacturing sector, and those that are competitively weak and/or operate in intensely competitive industries—would do well to consider allocating a larger share of their marketing budgets for research purposes.

Pinpointing the causes for the rather low budget allocations for marketing research may border on being conjecture. However, I would like to proffer the following as plausible reasons for the low average budget allocations:

Lack of management support for, or trust in, marketing research.

Misunderstanding, or maybe even lack of knowledge, about the potential benefits of marketing research.

An erroneous belief that a firm simply cannot "afford" marketing research due to the nature of the circumstances under which it operates.

A deliberate management decision not to engage in marketing research, based on careful and objective evaluation of the potential benefits and costs of marketing research.

Firms that are shying away from marketing research for reasons other than the last one may be unintentionally passing up potential marketing strengths that can accrue through marketing research. In such firms both managers and researchers must shoulder the responsibility for ensuring that marketing research gets the kind of objective consideration that it deserves. Managers must put aside their subjective beliefs about marketing research and view it with an open mind. Researchers must provide managers with an objective picture of the pros and cons of marketing research. They must be prepared to defend specific research projects on the basis of their net monetary benefit, which is obviously of primary concern to managers. Establishing the productivity of marketing research in monetary terms may indeed pose a challenge that researchers must diligently confront in order to increase managers' faith in marketing research.

Notes

1. See, for example, C. E. Eldridge, "Role of Marketing Research," *Printers Ink,* August 11, 1967, pp. 36ff; see also, Blair Little and Robert G. Cooper, "The Role of Marketing Research in New Technology Ventures," *Research Management,* May 1977, pp. 20–25.

2. See, for example, Peter C. Riesz, "Revenge of the Marketing Concept," *Business Horizons,* June 1980, pp. 49–53; and, Roger C. Bennett and Robert G. Cooper, "The Misuse of Marketing: An American Tragedy," *Business Horizons,* November-December 1981, pp. 51–61.

3. For a discussion related to this issue, see S. W. Brown, "Gaining Valuable Market Research Information Through Arrangements with Universities," *Journal of Small Business Management,* April 1977, pp. 34–40; see also, A. Parasuraman, "Marketing Research by a Small Industrial Firm: A Case Study," *Industrial Marketing Management,* August 1978, pp. 238–42.

Company Readings

Counting on Wall Street
Olivia Schieffelin Nordberg

"You can't use demographic data to buy stocks," says Harold L. Vogel, vice president in the Securities Research Division of Merrill Lynch. But knowing something about demographics can improve investment performance, according to analysts.

Wall Street uses demographics to pinpoint opportunity. Population trends are particularly important for telephone companies, utilities, and regional banks. Atlantic City Electric, an unattractive stock for years, began to do well when the casinos came to town because they brought with them the increased population that allowed the utility to grow.

And it was partly the "huge size" of the market area that made Harold M. Levine, vice president at E. F. Hutton, recommend First Interstate, a bank holding company in Los Angeles with operations in 11 western states with burgeoning population and personal income. "The growth in Nevada was so strong," comments Levine, "that it encouraged me to look at other companies there as well."

Health industry stocks have been good performers of late. Providers of nursing homes and health care services, like Comprehensive Care and Beverly Enterprises, have done well and should continue to grow partly because of the aging of the American population. For investors in the lens business too, things look bright. According to James T. Morton, vice president, Chase Special Equities, "everyone of us will ultimately need to wear glasses after age 65." And the number of Americans over age 75 will grow more than 72 percent by the year 2000.

The baby-boom's passage through life so far has helped account for the rise and fall of the stock value of companies that make blue jeans,

soft drinks, and fast food. Now the baby boomers are reaching the family formation stage of the life cycle, with healthy implications for companies in the housing and forest-product industries, and for consumer durables, such as washing machines. These underlying growth trends were short circuited in the 1980–82 period by soaring interest rates and high unemployment, but demand for housing is waiting to be unleashed.

Companies like Mohasco, which manufactures carpet and furniture, are also expected to do well in this market, according to Edward E. Johnson, director of the Johnson Redbook Service, a division of Prescott, Ball & Turban, Inc. So are those textile companies with a large commitment to carpets and domestic textiles (sheets and towels), like Burlington, West Point Pepperell, and Springs Industries. Johnson, who issues a weekly comment on the effects of consumer trends on the retail, apparel, textile, and chemical industries, says that even the companies that make the fiber for carpets, like Allied Corp., should benefit.

The changing population mix should also help the apparel industry. "People buy more apparel as they get older and as they earn higher incomes," Johnson notes. The increase in the number of working women, as well as a shift in the 1980s back to the "dress-up era of the 1960s versus the dress-down era of the 1970s," in Johnson's judgment, will benefit stocks like Warnaco, which owns Warner's Foundation Garments; White Stag and Hathaway Shirts; Russ Togs, which makes Crazy Horse apparel; and Palm Beach,

© August 1983 *American Demographic.*

which owns Evan Picone, manufacturers of women's business clothes.

Other analysts also stress that age and income are the most interesting demographic variables. Morton, who follows such restaurant companies as Charthouse, explains that the dining-out preferences of 18 to 25 year olds differ considerably from those of 25 to 34 year olds. The younger group eat fried foods, drink no alcohol, do not care about the service, and are price conscious. The older group have tastes that encompass more than hamburgers, drink alcohol, and are interested in decent service.

Investment hopes for the future are personified in the cute faces of the baby boomers' own babies. Wall Street is looking with new enthusiasm at the rise in the annual number of births and the obvious beneficiaries, Gerber and its competitors, Johnson & Johnson, and Beechnut—manufacturers of baby foods.

But you can't buy stock in Beechnut (it is privately owned), so which do you invest in, Gerber or Johnson & Johnson? Which company has the stronger management? Which puts less sugar in the beans? And what happens if baby-boom parents decide it is healthier or cheaper or more chic to make and mash their own baby food instead of buying the little jars? Knowledge of the numbers needs to be tempered with attention to changing tastes and attitudes.

Consumer behavior, not demographics, accounts for the recent lackluster performances in the stock market of record distributors and bicycle manufacturers, says Merrill Lynch's Vogel, because consumers spent an unprecedented—and unpredictable—$6 billion in video arcades, rather than in record or bike stores over the last few years. "When a static demographic group is offered a strongly competitive alternative to leisure spending," Vogel declares, "the pie has to be cut up. In the absence of the video-game boom, records and bikes might have held on."

Avoiding Risk

The second major use of demographic data on Wall Street is analyzing and defining risk—the flip side of identifying opportunity. "Winning will take care of itself; it's avoidance of loss that is crucial," says Clifford Rand of Cowen Asset Management Company. "If you don't know the demographics, and they're not in your favor, you're in trouble," comments Morton of Chase.

Prescott's Johnson points to several companies in the junior apparel business that have already been hurt by the disappearance of the teenager, among them Petrie, Brooks Fashions, and Miller Wohl. These companies are all switching into clothes for older ages, and analysts are waiting for them to turn around.

Good Management

Investment analysts strongly believe that even in a static market good management makes the difference. Once a promising demographic area has been identified, "finding the lock" is essential, according to Rand of Cowen Asset Management.

When money managers evaluate the management of a company—for example, if a communications company claims its programs are reaching particular audiences—an analyst will double-check the demographics with Simmons or Nielson or other of the syndicated readership and audience measurement services to validate the company's claim. If a product has a "most likely" demographic market, and the manufacturer is not making any special effort to reach that market, an analyst will be skeptical of statements by marketing management.

Levine at E. F. Hutton points out the implications of this sort of analysis for the banking industry. "In the 1960s people banked where they lived; in the 1970s they banked where they worked; now they bank where they shop. And in the late 1980s and the 1990s people will bank where they have their telephone, television, or computer." In such a nationwide banking system, telephone numbers and zip codes will be the key to locating clients for potential financial services. Levine is watching to see which banks will be strong in that marketing effort.

Poor Economy

In making an investment decision, Levine gives a 20 percent weight to demographics but 50 percent to the individual company. The remaining 30 percent is economics. Analysts agree that the state of the general economy overrides demographics (of course, changing demographics affect the economy too, and vice versa). Boating equipment is faring poorly in the market, Merrill Lynch's Vogel says, because high proportions of the demographic group most likely to buy outboard engines—blue-collar workers in their 30s and 40s in the Midwest—have been laid off.

The poor performance of Disneyland in the mid-1970s came about both because of a decline in the number of young children, and because of OPEC. "We didn't have the demographics and we did have a gas shortage," Vogel says. Such information as production indexes, the money-supply figures, help-wanted ads, and box-car loadings, often affect the economy much more than the shifting population.

Time and Money

The short lifetime of information in the securities market and the short-term pressure to perform ("You're as good as your last transaction," says one analyst) force advisors to concentrate on the short run, rather than the longer trends of most demographic changes.

Demographic trends are valuable background information, but stock market trends rise and fall from week to week.

Some investment researchers do find a longer term use for demographic data. For example, Rosanne Cahn, vice president and economist in the Research Department of Goldman-Sachs, is studying projections of the slowed growth of the labor force during the 1980s as one ingredient in a forecast of productivity. If productivity grows, she reasons, the inflation outlook may be improved, which in turn would reduce upward pressure on interest rates. The end result might be to make investment a better idea.

In the same vein, Cahn is looking at the shift into the higher savings age groups projected for the 1990s, when the baby boomers will begin to reach their mid-40s. Then more savings dollars will be chasing the same number of savings vehicles. This trend should help to raise the price of assets.

But decisions are increasingly made in Washington, not in the marketplace, which makes forecasting risky. According to Chase's Morton, the success of the hospital supply and health care companies may be due less to the aging of the population than to government incentives to figure out cheaper ways to care for convalescent patients than in hospital beds. Federal policies—such as a statement about interest rates by the head of the Federal Reserve—have an immediate effect on the market.

Finding Data and Clients

Wall Streeters use demographic data from a variety of sources: the Census Bureau, consultants, market research companies, and private data companies. Often data from private companies are paid for with "soft dollars." An analyst gets research reports from a data company. The data company then bills the brokerage house that handles the analyst's buying and selling. So it is the client, in the end, through his commissions on stock transactions, who pays for Wall Street's data.

Finding clients is the one area where everyone in the securities business uses demographic data. In "selling on the front lines," investment analysts have lots of help, not from the Census Bureau, but from the people who provide lists of yacht club members, recent Cadillac purchasers, and zip codes where there is extensive building of additions to private homes. "Brokers have to prospect in areas where there are high returns," notes one—just like other salespeople.

Yet there is no standard approach to locating clients, according to a knowledgeable Wall Street source. "Some people rely on social contacts and spend their lives in bars and restaurants. Others earn their living by calling people up out of the blue." But basically, he observes, new clients come through one of two routes. "The first is a snow job, whereby silver-tongued thieves sell people a bill of goods. The other is simply doing good work and making money for the client."

Indeed, the success of brokers in doing a good job and finding customers partially ac-

counts for the recent acquisition of several brokerage firms by larger companies, as in the cases of Prudential-Bache, Shearson-American Express, and Sears' purchase of Dean Witter Reynolds, Inc. They are all after the same client, whether to execute his order on the stock exchange or sell him a credit card or a dishwasher.

If Wall Street were objective, more attention might go to demographic data. But few analysts start with a demographic trend and then explore its investment implications. Rather, they check to see if the trend confirms a prior hunch. Confides a stock researcher laughingly, "Research is more of a rationalization or a sales tool in the report that's written up by the average brokerage firm than it is analysis. Usually the guy has a company he loves."

"Sure I see the P25 series," says Vogel, referring to the regular Census Bureau report. "It's fine and interesting to know the details and major trends, but our job is to make money in the stocks. The long-term view is okay—but so much intervenes."

Burger King Puts Down Its Dukes
Lee Smith

Hold the pickles,
Hold the lettuce.
Special orders
Don't upset us.
All we ask is that you
Let us serve it your way.

Hold the jingle. The Burger King hamburger chain has abandoned that bouncy promise to build its sandwiches to suit the customer. Tailoring Whoppers was manageable when relatively few fast-food fanciers were coming through the doors. But now so many are lining up, at least at peak hours, that special orders are, well, upsetting. Burger King will still

make it your way if you insist, but isn't going to invite you to and rather hopes you won't.

Unlike the customers, some other people are not going to have things their way at Burger King any longer—even if they ask the Burger King franchisees. Burger King's 2,726 or so restaurants—"stores," as the fast-food industry calls them—fall into three main categories. In the smallest group are the 466 owned and operated by Burger King itself, a subsidiary of Pillsbury Co. Another 771 are operated by independent franchisees on land or in buildings belonging to Pillsbury. The great majority —a total of 1,489—are operated by franchisees who own the land and buildings themselves, or rent them from someone other than Pillsbury.

That third group—the "DTLs," which stands for Direct to Licensee, meaning that title to the real estate was transferred directly from the seller to the franchisee—has troubled Burger King for years. The DTLs cost the company a lot of money, and some of them have grown so big they threaten the burger sovereign. Now, however, Burger King has subdued one of those dukes, Horn & Hardart Co., which owns 20 franchises in the New York City area. It has boxed in another, and sent a message to the rest of its ambitious franchisees: Burger King is having things its way.

In the beginning, the franchisees could pretty much write their own ticket. James W. McLamore and David R. Edgerton, a pair of young Miami restaurateurs, had little but a concept to offer when they set out in 1959 to clone a nationwide chain of Burger Kings from their five stores in Florida. To attract entrepreneurs and investors they gave away exclusive rights to large territories and allowed franchisees to buy land and build as many stores as they liked. A franchisee was free to sell sections of his territory to others if he wanted; he could even diversify into other fast-food businesses.

Burger King exacted a modest price in return. A franchisee made a one-time payment of $25,000 for his franchise and equipment. Thereafter, he paid the chain as little as 1 percent of sales—less than a third of what franchisees who sign up today are sending back to Miami.

A Voracious Clone

The arrangement worked brilliantly for McLamore and Edgerton. By 1967 the chain had grown to 274 stores, and the two founders sold out to Pillsbury for $18 million. But it wasn't just Burger King that had expanded. Some of its franchisees did at least as well, and one of them grew at such a phenomenal rate that it threatened to devour the parent.

The voracious clone belonged to Billy and Jimmy Trotter, sons of a wealthy Louisiana rice broker, who bought a Burger King outlet in 1963. Over the next seven years they multiplied it almost two dozen times. In 1969 they took the company public as Self-Service Restaurants, Inc. (since changed to Chart House, Inc.).

The following year Self-Service helped itself to a property that catapulted it into fast-food's big league. Self-Service discovered that five franchisees who held 99-year rights to a territory that included Chicago, potentially one of the richest markets in the country, wanted to sell out. The Trotters were eager to buy, even though the Chicago group had already built 66 stores, which made it three times as large as Self-Service. As if that weren't brazen enough, Self-Service was competing for those stores with Pillsbury, which wanted to reclaim the Chicago territory for itself.

One night during a snowstorm, Billy Trotter flew into Chicago and bought the five out for $8 million in cash, notes, and stock. The next day, when the weather cleared, the Pillsbury party arrived in town to discover that a faster food company had been there first.

That began a war that raged for years. Self-Service thrived. From owning 100 Burger King outlets with sales of $32 million in 1971, it mushroomed to 351 stores and revenues of $186 million last year. Along the way, it bought out two chains of steak houses as well—Cork 'N Cleaver and the Chart House group in California, whose name it adopted.

Chart House got so big that the company set up its own training and inspection programs and even its own commissaries to supply far-flung stores with meat, onions, and other grist.

So strong and independent did Chart House become that it decided it could run Burger King better than Pillsbury—and made a grab for it. "The problem with Pillsbury was that there were people in the organization who didn't really want to be in the fast-food business," says Braxton I. Moody III, who guided Chart House through most of the 1970s and retired recently as chief executive.

Burger King Bites Back

As Moody tells the story, Chart House offered Pillsbury $100 million for Burger King in 1972. Pillsbury declined. Then Chart House suggested that both companies spin off their Burger King properties to form a separate Burger King entity. "I understand that was defeated by the Pillsbury board by only one vote," says Moody. People at Pillsbury say they can't recall either proposal.

Having failed to swallow Burger King at a single sitting, Chart House continued to nibble off pieces. It bought up nine stores from franchisees in Boston and 13 stores in Houston. This time, Burger King bit back and sued Chart House and the Boston franchisees for disregarding Pillsbury's right of first refusal. Ultimately Chart House and Pillsbury compromised, with Chart House reluctantly agreeing to release its hold on Boston in exchange for keeping its new Burger Kings in Houston. "In the six months in which we had those Boston stores, earnings went up," says Moody. "When Pillsbury took over, they went down again."

While McDonald's prospered through the early 1970s, Burger King floundered. Although Pillsbury did not break out earnings figures for Burger King during those years, analysts were estimating that the profits of company-owned stores were lower than those of the franchisees. Pillsbury tried to make its stores and the system more profitable, but some of its efforts succeeded only in worsening the normal strains between franchisor and franchisee.

The franchisee, of course, is interested in the bottom line—in his store's profit and loss. The franchisor is more interested in the top line. Apart from a one-time franchise fee of $40,000, Pillsbury gets most of its revenue from the franchisee's sales—3.5 percent of sales as a royalty; 4 percent for the marketing fund, most of which buys TV advertising; and, if Pillsbury owns the land and building, an additional 8.5 percent as rent. (McDonald's levies a franchise fee of $12,500, a royalty of 3 percent, a marketing fee of 3 percent, and rent of 8.5 percent.) So the franchisor, understandably, always wants to increase sales. The franchisee does too—except when boosting sales pushes costs so high that his profit goes down. The slight but crucial difference led to what Burger King veterans recall as the hospitality feud.

In 1974, in an effort to increase sales during the peak lunchtime period, Pillsbury required all new Burger King stores to be equipped for the "hospitality system"—multiple lines such as McDonald's was using. (A rule of thumb in the industry is that customers grow impatient if they have to wait more than five minutes.) Pillsbury also urged franchisees to shift to multiple lines in existing stores. Chart House refused to make the change, complaining that the additional cash registers and extra help would cost more than the increased sales would justify. Following Chart House's lead, many smaller franchisees put off adopting the hospitality system as long as they could. Gradually, they have begun to use multiple lines, but only because sales have increased by enough to make them economical.

Ads Aimed at Kids

Eventually, Pillsbury Chairman William H. Spoor rescued the deteriorating situation. In 1977 he hired Donald N. Smith, then 36 and the third-ranking executive at McDonald's, as

Burger King's chief executive. Smith brought McDonald's techniques with him, right down to its approach to making french fries, which aficionados had long preferred to Burger King's. Smith also redirected the advertising campaign, pointing it squarely at children; although it is parents who decide that the family will go out to dinner, the children often dictate where. Adroitly, he persuaded franchisees to remodel their stores along more elegant lines (softer lighting, real shrubbery rather than plastic) by redecorating Pillsbury's own stores first.

Such innovations made Burger King prosperous. McDonald's is still far and away the leader in fast food, with gross sales of $5.4 billion last year. (Most of that stayed in the hands of the franchisees; $1.9 billion flowed through to the company's income statement.) Kentucky Fried Chicken was second with over $2 billion in sales, and Burger King a respectable third with $1.5 billion. Pillsbury earned $21.3 million from Burger King in 1979, or about a quarter of its entire profit.

Smith also began to remake Burger King's franchise system on the McDonald's model. Burger King had hardly been alone in giving away vast territories to franchisees. McDonald's passed through a similar stage, but soon tightened its policy to make empire-building impossible. Today McDonald's owns or leases nearly all of the land and buildings used by its 5,747 stores.

The advantages of ownership are compelling. The land is an appreciating asset and the building a source of depreciation write-offs. Moreover, as the franchisee's landlord, the franchisor has power. McDonald's franchisees, for example, are not allowed to own any other fast-food restaurants, and they have no territorial rights or protection. "The only thing they guarantee is that they won't let someone else open a McDonald's at the same street address you have," says Irwin S. Kruger, who has two McDonald's franchises in New York City. At the other extreme is

Wendy's, which still encourages the growth of large franchisees. That policy has enabled it to balloon from 100 to 1,881 stores in the past five years.

For new Burger King franchisees, Smith established a far more demanding contract. Today they must agree not to own any other fast-food business and to live within an hour's drive of their Burger King store, which makes it difficult for a franchisee to own more than a dozen restaurants. The official reason for such strictures is to make certain that the proprietor, and not simply a manager, is always nearby to give the store his personal attention. But this explanation is less than convincing. Pillsbury-owned stores, after all, are run by professional managers, not proprietors. The real reason for the new rules is to stop franchisees from getting too big.

Smith reached an accommodation with Chart House. As in the past, Chart House may build as many Burger Kings as it likes in the Illinois territory. But it has agreed not to expand elsewhere without Pillsbury's prior approval. On another crucial matter, the two burgermakers do not see eye to eye. Moody believes that Chart House may operate other food businesses as long as they are not hamburger stores—a freedom that would allow it to buy some Texas barbeque restaurants it has an option on. Smith, however, says that Pillsbury isn't prepared to give Chart House any such freedom in the future.

Still, the most divisive issue does seem to have been resolved: Smith won Chart House's respect. "The previous management was very arrogant," says Moody. "Smith is an operating guy, and he understands the operating guy's problems."

A Snake and a Mongoose

With Chart House domesticated, Smith turned to a final challenge—the pointed thrust of Horn & Hardart. The creator of New

York City's Automats, Horn & Hardart had fallen on hard times by the early 1970s and decided to turn most of its famous but empty restaurants into Burger Kings. "We were considered quite a coup for Pillsbury back in those days," Barry W. Florescue, Horn & Hardart's 36-year-old chairman observes wistfully. "They featured us in their annual report. It was a great relationship."

But the relationship turned as sour as a week-old milk shake when the hard-driving Smith and the ambitious Florescue got to know each other. "Those two get along like a snake and a mongoose," says an executive of another fast-food chain. From Smith's point of view, Florescue was a threat and possible usurper. An accountant by training, Florescue had taken over Horn & Hardart by ousting the previous management. "Barry doesn't really accept the idea of partnership," says Smith. "I'm not sure he really has the personality of a franchisee."

Smith rejected Horn & Hardart's proposal to build eight new stores a year in New York. He limited the company to half that number and barred it from building elsewhere. Today Florescue reflects on Smith's diktat with bemused derision: "Burger King is taking the attitude that it is blessing you by giving you a franchise. McDonald's can get away with that argument; it really *is* blessing you by giving you a franchise. But Burger King isn't there yet. McDonald's has more capital in its balance sheet than Burger King and the rest of Pillsbury combined."

Horn & Hardart defied Smith by purchasing a group of eight Burger Kings in Orange County, California. Burger King sued the sellers, arguing that they had ignored Burger King's right of first refusal. A federal court in Miami has upheld Burger King, effectively canceling the sale.

Whatever goodwill remained was extinguished in a series of legal counterpunches. Smith told Florescue that unless he signed an agreement to make no acquisitions anywhere without Burger King's approval, Horn & Hardart would not be allowed to open the four new stores it was building in New York.

Not only did Florescue refuse, he signed an agreement with Arby's, a purveyor of roast-beef sandwiches, to build a series of Arby's stores in New York, the more the better. Smith notified Florescue that such a deal with another fast-food chain violated Horn & Hardart's franchise agreements with Burger King. Florescue retaliated by suing Burger King for violating antitrust laws. After six months of bargaining, the litigants are settling their argument out of court.

More Dough for Pizza Hut

However this particular battle may end, Smith will have won the larger war: Horn & Hardart will not become an independent force within Burger King, determining for itself its size and territory—and neither will any other franchisee. Smith, his mission accomplished, is leaving Burger King in mid-June to join PepsiCo as president of its food-service division, whose troubled Pizza Hut chain presents some familiar challenges—declining sales and profits, and the presence of large, independent franchisees.

As for Horn & Hardart, it will turn to other interests, including a vestigial chain of Automats now being restored, a hotel and casino in Las Vegas, a flourishing mail-order business, and, of course, its Arby's stores—at least until Arby's too begins to wonder whether it is a dog being wagged by a tail.

Squeeze on the Networks
Steven Flax

In three manic weeks of July the TV networks sold a record $2 billion of commercials for the 1983–84 season, late September to late April. On one memorable day ABC did over $170 million of business. Salespeople stumbled out of ABC's New York offices at 4 A.M., eyes glazed and fingers cramped from writing orders. But all this glorious selling obscured the real news: the networks were unable to raise prices as they once had, and a continuing rise in programming costs threatens to pinch the free-spending industry.

The advance marketing of commercial time is broadcasting's equivalent of the running of the bulls at Pamplona. Advertisers hang back as long as they dare, hoping to force the networks to lower their asking prices. But when one buys, the whole crowd stampedes toward Broadcast Row along New York's Avenue of the Americas, waving dollars. One advertiser can hold out against network demands only while they all hold out. Once selling starts, fear of being squeezed out of a big series like "Dynasty," the ABC show that has bumped "Dallas" as the audience favorite, sets the Madison Avenue bulls rampaging, despite prices that call for deep pockets. "Dynasty" costs $179,000 for a 30-second commercial. Thirty seconds on a run-of-the-mill prime-time program can cost $75,000.

This year, as has been the case for the last 15 years, the buyer who set off the stampede was William Claggett, vice president and advertising director of St. Louis-based Ralston Purina. Claggett, whose company spends an estimated $70 million annually advertising pet foods and cereals on network TV, says buying early lets him get exactly the shows and dates Ralston Purina wants.

Claggett adds that he can buy faster partly because he has more autonomy and collects more information earlier than most advertising managers. He also negotiates directly with the networks rather than through an agency. Though some people in the ad business would dispute him, Claggett believes that there is sometimes a cost advantage in buying first because "nobody has bought, so nobody knows what the price is. We seldom get burned by being first."

The networks offer only part of their inventory of time before the season starts, the amount depending on how each sees the season unfolding. In industry jargon, the early sales are called up-front sales, as opposed to scatter sales made later. In deciding how many commercials to leave unsold, the networks take into account not only the economy and attractions like the Olympic Games, but also what they expect from their shows. Being an unknown quantity, a new show might not command a top price up front, but if it proves popular, the price for scatter sales would rise.

Because the Olympics eat up so much prime time, the price of the remaining stock of prime-time commercials on all three networks would be expected to rise. Earlier this year rumors swept through the trade that prime-time prices would go up almost 30 percent for 1983–84. The speculation did not seem farfetched. Next year the broadcasters get a triple dip of good tidings. The Olympics will coincide with an economic recovery and a presidential election—and broadcasters setting ad rates count on incumbent presidents seeking reelection to stimulate economic growth.

During the last such confluence of good portents, the networks were able to increase prime-time prices some 25 percent over the previous year, even in inflation-adjusted dollars. But this time around the networks were able to achieve rate increases on up-front sales of no more than 11 percent over last year

© September 5, 1983, *Fortune* magazine.

after adjustment for inflation—little more of an increase than in recession-ridden 1982.

According to McCann-Erickson, the fifth-largest advertising agency in the world, major advertisers like Procter & Gamble and General Foods have reduced the proportion of their ad budgets that goes to network TV. (Top-spending P&G will shell out $335 million this year for all advertising.) The diverted money is finding its way to local stations and cable. Within the broadcast industry, McCann-Erickson's report is discounted as a bargaining ploy in the incessant ad-agency quest for lower rates. But one TV executive acknowledges that the time may be coming when network price increases will no more than match increases in inflation.

Cable TV and such fledgling threats as subscription TV and direct broadcast by satellite continue to make inroads in the prime-time market. Independent TV stations—those unaffiliated with the networks—also continue to siphon off viewers. In the last two years 37 new independent stations have started up in markets served by network stations. In the offing is Metromedia's scheme of linking up independent stations in what would amount to a fourth network, showing made-for-cable movies and other programs. Last season the three networks' combined average share of viewers watching TV in prime time fell to a new low of 81 percent. Ten years ago it was 90 percent.

One potential bright spot for the networks is the Federal Communications Commission's (FCC) tentative decision in August to allow them to own program syndication rights and share in the profits of producers, which they've been barred from doing since 1970. The FCC ruling could give access to $800 million in added annual revenues—but it is unlikely much of that will be chalked up soon on the networks' income statements.

Squeezed by competition and their inability to raise prices with the old abandon, the networks must also contend with the rise in programming costs. Though they've been barred from producing much of their own programming, they pick up most of the tab for it—the major expense for all networks. According to FCC reports, from 1971 to 1980 the annual three-network cost of producing and buying programming more than tripled, to $3.1 billion, growing at a compound annual rate of 14.4 percent. Meanwhile gross advertising revenues, the major source of income for the three networks, grew only 13 percent a year, to $4.7 billion in 1980.

In later years of the period the disparity between the growth of revenues and programming costs became dramatically worse. From 1977 to 1980 gross advertising revenues grew at an 11.6 percent annual compound rate while program costs grew at 18.4 percent. The FCC no longer collects these data, but there is no convincing evidence that the trend had been reversed. At ABC, prime-time programming costs in the 1981–82 season were a dangerously high 73 percent of the network's prime-time revenues, compared with less than 58 percent in 1977.

What the narrowing gap between revenues and programming costs does to profit margins can be clearly seen at CBS. For the last four years CBS has been champ in the audience ratings for both prime-time programs and news. Theoretically the network's high ratings mean it can command the highest prices for commercials. Yet even at CBS costs from 1978 to 1983 went up at a 14 percent compound annual rate while revenues were growing at only 12 percent. During those five years the CBS Broadcast Group added about $800 million in new revenues, for a total of $2.2 billion, but operating earnings increased only a little over $30 million, to $274 million. And even that addition to profits would have been missed had it not been for a strike by the Screen Actors Guild in 1980, which let CBS save money by using reruns.

Recently all the networks claim to have cleaned up their cost-cutting acts. They are authorizing fewer pilots for possible new series, encouraging producers to shoot with videotape, which is cheaper than film, paying less for feature movies, putting freezes on hiring, and rejecting stars' demands for raises—even at the risk of hurting the popularity of big-drawing programs. Such decisions take guts on the part of a TV executive.

But other instances make one wonder how deep the cost-cutting really goes. CBS News recently generated headlines by laying people off. The total involved: 14 out of 1,500 employees in the news division. ABC sent the entire crew of "The Love Boat," a comedy about a cruise ship, to film in China. Just how much pictorial value the authentic location will have when the episodes are viewed on a small TV screen remains to be seen.

Over at NBC, Robert C. Butler, the chief financial officer, recently deplored the horrendous costs of earlier NBC shows like "Supertrain," a series about an atomic-powered cross-country train, which exploded to nearly $1 million an episode in 1979—an extraordinary cost then. Said Butler: "I guarantee that could not happen now." Yet NBC has authorized Steve Bochco, who produces NBC's hit "Hill Street Blues," to build a 1,300-seat baseball stadium in California to use in the filming of a new blue-collar serial "Bay City Blues." The series, woven around a minor-league baseball team, will routinely use hundreds of extras for crowd scenes at the ball park. Each episode of the new series will cost nearly $1 million—not much more than usual these days. Still, NBC Chairman Grant Tinker says about the expense of the show, "Don't think that wasn't hernia producing. We bought trusses for all concerned when we signed off on that one. But we felt the series was worth the cost."

Tinker's painful decision illustrates the networks' dilemma. They must risk huge sums to get the size—and kind—of audience that will draw advertising dollars. Nowadays advertisers buy TV time based largely on the demographic makeup of the audience. This is much more important than brute ratings, which measure households watching a program. (One point in the ratings indicates that 833,000 households were tuned in.) The best buy for the advertiser is the network that is most cost-effective at providing the kind of audience desired. In most cases buyers of TV commercials are looking for an audience of high-spending adults aged 18 to 49 living in urban and suburban counties.

More advertising dollars are thrown at the 18 to 49 group than at any other. Even though ABC has been second in the prime-time ratings for the last few seasons, it has been particularly successful at delivering these viewers, and its sales and profits reflect that. Last year ABC's broadcast operations brought in revenues of $1.83 billion—more than either CBS ($1.7 billion) or NBC ($1.6 billion). According to John Reidy, a security analyst at the brokerage firm of Drexel Burnham Lambert, ABC's operating profits of $262 million were more than those of the other two networks combined; Reidy estimates that CBS's operating profits were $180 million and NBC's a mere $30 million.

CBS's relatively unimpressive profitability is not just the result of the long-term cost-price squeeze. The network has also been penalized recently by two policy changes that worked out poorly. The first involved the number of commercials CBS chose to sell up front. In mid-1982, in setting up-front sales strategy, CBS's economists told the sales planning and marketing staff that the recession would soon be over. Expecting commercials sold later in the season—scatter sales—to command much higher prices than those sold up front, CBS purposely offered fewer prime-time commercials than usual. (When asked why ABC didn't do the same, the ABC vice president in charge of sales, H. Weller "Jake" Keever, said, "We don't run this department based on theories of economics. Remember what Casey Stengel said: 'If you're going to predict, then you better do it often.' ")

The bulk of CBS's unsold time was in the second and third quarters of this year, but scatter sales went soft, leaving CBS with lots of high-priced time on its hands. Early in the second quarter, says James Rosenfield, executive vice president of the CBS Broadcast Group, "we sat here and saw the locomotive come and run over us and there was nothing we could do about it." The misjudgment cost CBS around $50 million in revenues.

This year, with the economy exploding at up-front time, a strong case might be made for holding inventory off the market and waiting for high-priced scatter sales. But this time CBS shunned the risks: it went into the up-front market in a big way, selling an estimated $690 million of prime-time commercials, perhaps $140 million more than it sold last year. "Nobody around here had the stomach to take the gamble," says Rosenfield.

The other big change in strategy at CBS has to do with demographic guarantees for up-front buyers. These guarantees assure advertisers that if their commercials don't get the desired audience in a certain demographic category—say, women from 18 to 49 years old—then the network will supply free commercials called "make-goods" to produce the desired population of viewers.

CBS had given such guarantees for several years, but dropped them last year because according to the corporate brass the network was finding itself in a strange new position. It was still garnering the highest ratings, but the network's heretofore stable demographics turned unpredictable. "We began to see wild swings," says one executive. "Even though we were up last year in total homes, we were down 16 percent in women aged 18 to 49, and were also down in women 25 to 54."

Such erratic demographics handed CBS a financial problem. To continue giving guarantees could cost the network dearly in make-goods. So it stopped offering guarantees. But advertisers were hooked on paying only for the target audiences they wanted. Viewers outside that category were superfluous. Now CBS is once again giving what in effect are demographic guarantees, though the network insists that it is not *contractually obligating* itself to give freebie commercials to up-front buyers if they don't reach the desired audiences.

For all the networks, ratings and demographic reach have never been more important—which means that programming has never been more important. Naturally, all are going into the new season with high hopes for their lineups of shows—though to outsiders the hopes in some cases may look overblown.

CBS has 16 successful prime-time series returning, nine of which were among last season's top 15. One or more of these shows—"60 Minutes," "Magnum, P.I.," "Dallas," or one of the others—will be shown each night. CBS is also counting on new shows like "Whiz Kids," a look-alike of the hit movie *War-Games*. It'll also offer "Scarecrow and Mrs. King," in which a suburban housewife gets involved in the doings of a secret agent (a kind of Erma Bombeck meets James Bond).

CBS has a possible weakness this season: the network is leaning heavily on movies or miniseries in prime time. It is running them three evenings a week, preceding two of them with new series. The untried lead-ins, as they're known in the industry, could be a liability if they don't succeed in attracting large audiences that might stay tuned for the movies.

At NBC, fortunes have improved in the two years since Grant Tinker became chairman and chief executive. Seeking to bring the network out of the ratings basement, Tinker has based his turnaround strategy on the nurturing of quality programs until they develop a sufficient audience. "Hill Street Blues," a well-written story about some inner-city cops, didn't do well for a couple of seasons, then caught on with audiences while winning several Emmies and a Peabody award. This year Tinker renewed "Cheers," a literate situation comedy set in a Boston bar, even though last season it got only a 21 percent share of the audience. By comparison, CBS killed "Gloria," an "All in the Family" spin-off that attained a fairly respectable 28 percent share.

For those who prefer mindless fare, Tinker has served up such shoot-and-smash-'em-up shows as "The A-Team," in which a posse of mayhem-minded borderline sociopaths go around and beat up on even bigger meanies, all for the sake of justice. It's a violent, Sam Peckinpah version of the "Lone Ranger" with a cadre of vigilantes; and its ratings have been going through the roof. Even "The A-Team's" reruns got a 30 percent share in the ratings this summer. "The A-Team" may not be quality programming, but speaking as corporate chairman, Tinker says: "I'm glad the show's on NBC. We have to have something for everybody." The networks, he adds, "have bored the asses off audiences for quite some time."

NBC's demographics have improved with Tinker's new mix of programming, which is bringing in larger numbers of the young, urban, and well-off viewers that advertisers want. This, more than ratings—where NBC still stands last—has put money in the till. Last year NBC's prime-time 30-second spots ranged from $50,000 to $135,000. For next season they are ranging from $75,000 to $185,000—putting it right up with the other networks again. During this year's up-front selling, NBC sold $700 million of prime-time commercials, 12 percent more than last year.

For the new season, besides "Bay City Blues," NBC is bringing to the tube two highly touted new shows, both with unlikely premises. One is called "The Manimal," in which a psychology professor transforms himself into a variety of animals to fight crime in New York. The other, called "Mr. Smith," is the story of a talking orangutan with an IQ of 256.

ABC's 1983–84 season shapes up best. During the last season, it whittled CBS's lead in prime time to half a rating point and retained its leadership in the demographic categories advertisers want. This year, besides its stable of successful offerings like "Dynasty" and "The Love Boat," ABC will be introducing shows that some in the advertising community view as potential blockbusters. "Hotel," a series about the doings at the exclusive St. Gregory Hotel, is produced by Aaron Spelling and Douglas Cramer, who are also behind "The Love Boat," a show "Hotel" closely resembles. Another promising series is "Oh, Madeline," a wacky comedy along the lines of "I Love Lucy"; it features comedienne Madeline Kahn.

ABC also boasts a lucrative sports menu: the World Series, a full schedule of "NFL Monday Night Football," and both the winter and summer Olympic Games. The Olympics are such a special attraction that ABC has been able to raise prices several times (most recently in June) during the two years the network has been selling commercials for the games. So far ABC has sold over $600 million of Olympics ads. It paid $316.5 million for rights to the Olympics.

The problem for ABC in the coming season is in the daytime. That's a surprise because the network's daytime schedule, featuring soap operas like "General Hospital," has been first in the ratings for 5½ years. But recently CBS, usually a poor second in the soapstakes, has suddenly begun catching up in the ratings. For ABC the daytime downdraft meant that it was able to raise the prices of daytime commercials only 10 percent to 14 percent up front—far less than the increases of 17 percent to 20 percent it got for them last year during the recession. For CBS the audience shift brought price increases of 25 percent for daytime commercials. These changes have a big impact on profits. Daytime commercials bring less money than those in prime time because audiences are smaller, but daytime shows are much cheaper than prime-time shows to produce.

These are not exactly hard times on Broadcast Row, but except for CBS's creditable showing in up-front daytime sales, the boosts networks were able to impose this year for commercials were less than might have been expected. With costs still rising and fat price increases hard to achieve, the coming network slugfest looks even fiercer than customary. As usual, the knob turners will decide the victor.

Broadcasting has always had a creative side that is resistant to cost controls, but the networks have to live within their ad revenues. In an era of shrinking audience shares, profitability will depend on an unceasing businesslike managing of costs.

Case Studies

The Milwaukee Blood Center
Patrick E. Murphy and Ron Franzmeier

The Milwaukee Blood Center (MBC) was established in 1946 by the Junior League to meet the emerging needs for blood in the Milwaukee area. The MBC has experienced substantial growth and is now a major regional blood center. The Milwaukee Blood Center is a member of two blood-banking trade associations—American Association of Blood Banks and Council of Community Blood Centers. MBC is affiliated with the Medical College of Wisconsin. For a discussion of the current state of blood donation in the United States, see the Appendix.

In 1976, the Milwaukee Blood Center moved to a new location at the western edge of the downtown area and adjacent to Marquette University. Within several blocks of their location there are five hospitals which MBC serves. The first floor of the building was renovated for use in blood collection. Free parking is provided behind the building for donors. The MBC also makes extensive use of the five mobile units for drawing blood at business and organization sites. Furthermore, three satellite stations are utilized in suburban and neighboring city locations.

Current Situation

In fiscal 1979, volunteer donors in southeastern Wisconsin gave 91,500 units of blood to support patients' needs in the 33 hospitals that the Milwaukee Blood Center served. As Exhibit 1 shows, donations have increased steadily during the decade of the 1970s and the 1979 total was 5,500 over the previous year.

However, local demand for blood *exceeded* local donations by 3,100 units which had to be obtained from other blood centers. The major objective of donor-recruitment programs is to make this region self-sufficient.

Eighty percent of the blood collected in the region was given by members of 900 donor clubs sponsored by business, schools, churches, and other civic, labor, and community groups in southeastern Wisconsin. The other 20 percent was drawn from individuals at MBC's central location in Milwaukee and part-time satellite stations located within the six-county area that the center serves.

These donors made it possible for the Milwaukee Blood Center to keep pace with the increasing demand for blood products in the region. Patients in the 33 hospitals served by the center required 5,400 more units of whole blood and packed red blood cells than were needed in 1978. The MBC also experienced a dramatic increase in the need for blood components.

The increased need for blood and blood components is related in part to the growing number of open heart, hip replacement, and kidney transplant operations being performed. Regular transfusions of blood platelets are demanded by a growing number of patients undergoing chemotherapy for cancer.

A Marketing Approach

Administrators at MBC felt that the amount of blood collected from donor clubs was

This case was prepared by Patrick E. Murphy and Ron Franzmeier as a basis for classroom discussion rather than to illustrate either effective or ineffective handling of an administrative situation. Copyright © 1980 by Marquette University.

EXHIBIT 1 Number of Volunteer Blood Donations, Milwaukee Blood Center, 1970–1979*

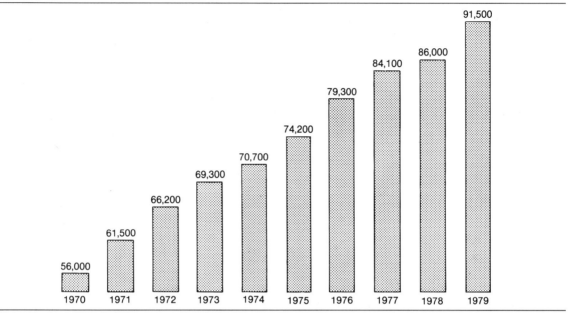

*During fiscal year 1979, 60,000 donors provided the 91,500 units of blood collected in the region. As demand continues to increase, the Blood Center must recruit more donors to avoid having to ask for more donations each year from the same people.

reaching a steady-state position. In fact, a few mobile drives had to be canceled because of layoffs or slowdowns at local industries. Also, the demographic projections for the southeastern Wisconsin area indicate that the area will not grow in population. Therefore, the administration felt that a program aimed at the individual donor was needed. To facilitate this process the Milwaukee Blood Center sought the services of a local marketing consulting firm.

With the assistance of the consultant, the administrators were able to relate the marketing mix elements to the process of blood donation. The product/service that they are offering is the unique satisfaction which the donor receives from the act of contributing a pint of his/her blood. This satisfaction cannot be derived from writing a check or volunteering time. The price not only represents real cost of physical discomfort of the donor, inconvenience, and time lost that could be spent in other ways, but also the psychological cost of fear of the total experience. The place or distribution element is directly related to the center's location or availability of mobile units or satellite stations. Finally, promotion entails the personal selling effort engaged in by the donor recruiters and the mass-media efforts. The Milwaukee Blood Center employs four full-time donor recruiters who call on industry and other donor clubs.

The mass-media promotion used by the Milwaukee Blood Center took the form of public service announcements. These announcements are free, but often aired late at night or at times when few people are watching or listening. Also, publicity is utilized by the Blood Center when they are experiencing a large shortage of donations. The problem with this type of promotion is that the Blood Center has no real control over the frequency with which their message reaches the target audience. Therefore, the Blood Center has relied heavily on other means of reaching prospective donors such as printed brochures, direct-mail materials, and telephone solicitation.

Marketing Research

The consultant and administration agreed that before a marketing program could be developed for the MBC, marketing research was necessary. Specifically, they needed to know more about their market area's donation patterns and certain attitudes of thought leaders and donors toward the Blood Center.

One part of the marketing research encompassed a study of the present geographic market area. It includes six counties which comprise the southeastern region of Wisconsin. These counties are: Milwaukee, Waukesha, Ozaukee, Washington, Racine, and Kenosha. Exhibit 2 shows the population and donation profile of this area for fiscal 1979. One important figure in this table is the percentage of population which actually donates. It is only 3 percent for the Blood Center area while the national figure is between 5 and 6 percent. In the county-by-county breakdown, Racine and Kenosha residents are not donating at a percentage equal to their population proportion.

A second phase of the initial marketing research effort entailed a "thought leader" study. Approximately 10 governmental and mass-media leaders in Racine, Kenosha, and Waukesha were interviewed regarding their perception of attitudes that people in their area had toward the Blood Center. Thought leaders in Milwaukee were not surveyed because the Blood Center administrators had frequent contact with them. One consistent finding was that they felt there was some reluctance of people in these cities to donate to the "Milwaukee" Blood Center. Most citizens did not realize that the Blood Center served the entire southeastern Wisconsin region.

Research was also conducted with first-time donors. One hundred first-time donors were surveyed via telephone. They were prompted to donate by the 1979 Winter Blood Telethon which was carried by a local television station. These donors were asked why they had never donated before. Their responses are shown in Exhibit 3. The most frequently mentioned reason was, "No one ever asked me to donate." Some of the more obvious reasons like "too busy" and "afraid to

EXHIBIT 2 Market—Donor Statistics

Region's population	1,710,000			
Donors	55,000 (3.2%)			
Donations needed	102,000 (6%)			
		Counties Served by Milwaukee Blood Center: Population and Donation Profile		
	Population	% of MBC Region Population	Units Drawn in County	% of Total Units Drawn in MBC Region
Milwaukee	982,000	57.4%	56,000	61%
Waukesha	276,000	16.1	15,800	17
Ozaukee	68,000	4.0	4,200	5
Washington	80,000	4.7	4,000	4
Racine	178,000	10.4	6,600	7
Kenosha	126,000	7.4	4,000	4
Other	—	—	1,400	2
Approximate Region totals	1,710,000	100	92,000	100

EXHIBIT 3 Reasons Why People Have Not Donated Blood Before

		Was a Reason	Was Not a Reason	No Answer/ Don't Know
a.	You thought you had a medical condition which kept you from giving.	16%	83%	1%
b.	You thought giving blood was painful.	29	70	1
c.	You never knew your blood was needed.	30	70	0
d.	You were afraid of giving blood.	30	70	0
e.	You didn't know where to go to give blood.	31	69	0
f.	The location of the MBC was inconvenient.	22	77	1
g.	No one ever asked you to donate before.	62	37	1
h.	You were too busy to give blood.	37	61	2

give" were designated by a much smaller percentage of donors.

Another survey was conducted at the downtown Milwaukee drawing station. Donors were asked to fill out a short questionnaire while they were being served refreshments after donating. Four hundred and sixty-two donors responded over a two-week time period. One of the major findings of this survey was that nearly one third of the respondents (32.4 percent) indicated that they would be likely to donate more often if there was a drawing station located more conveniently to their home.

Conclusion

When the consultant presented these research findings to the administration of MBC, they indicated that the consultant should develop a comprehensive marketing strategy (plan) based on these results. The administrators urged the consultants to be innovative and not to be concerned about organizational resistance to change. The only limiting factors that the administration placed on the marketing plan was that they could not afford paid television advertising. Major mass-media resources for the Milwaukee area are shown in Exhibit 4. The Milwaukee Blood Center's Board of Directors is scheduled to meet in three weeks and the administrator wants to present the comprehensive marketing program to them at that time.

Appendix: Current Status of Blood Donation in the United States

The blood collection system in America is going through some major changes, which may not be fully understood by the public.

Credits for Donating

There used to be a national system of credits for blood donors (hence, the concept of blood "banking"). If you gave a pint of blood, a credit was given to you, your family, or whomever you designated to be the recipient of that credit. If you or your family needed a blood transfusion, you could draw on those credits and did not have to worry about re-

EXHIBIT 4 Major Mass-Media Resources in Milwaukee-Area

		Newspaper		
	Name	**Circulation**	**Frequency**	**Cost ($ per Column Inch)**
Milwaukee	Journal	329,000	Daily	$13.58
	Sentinel	165,205	Daily	7.84
	Post	262,000	Weekly (suburban)	3.92
Kenosha	Kenosha News	31,620	Daily	4.84
	Kenosha Labor Press	21,500	Weekly	3.92
Racine	Labor News	16,000	Weekly	3.05
	Journal Times	40,000	Daily	4.75
Waukesha	Freeman	26,000	Daily	3.86

		Radio	
	Name	**Format**	**Average Cost ($ per 30-Second Spot)**
Milwaukee	WTMJ	Mid Road	$67.50
	WOKY	AM Rock	35.00
	WZUU	FM Rock	27.00
	WBCS	Country/West	22.00
Kenosha	WLIP	Mid Road	7.75
	WJZQ	FM Rock	6.35
Racine	WRJN	Mid Road	7.50 per spot
	WRKR	AM Rock	11.00 per spot
	WWEG	Country/West	10.00 per spot

placing the blood. Those who had no credits for previous donations were assessed a penalty charge, called a nonreplacement fee, unless they were able to find someone who would donate to replace the blood used.

This system of credits proved very costly to maintain and involved the transfer of paper credits rather than blood. It also seemed to place an unfair burden on the elderly and others who did not have friends or family members able to replace the blood used. For these reasons, nearly 80 percent of the blood centers in the country have dropped the system of credits and no longer charge a nonreplacement fee. Blood is simply made available to all who need it and the only charge made is for the costs of collecting and processing it (and this is covered by most insurance programs).

Paid Donors

It was very common practice at one time for donors to be paid for the blood they gave. Re-

search has determined that the incidence of Infectious Hepatitis in blood from donors who have been paid is far greater than that in blood which comes from volunteer donors. As a result, most communities no longer pay donors or offer them any reward of monetary value.

Regional Blood Centers

At one time, many small communities had their own blood program—usually organized by the local hospital and industry leaders. Physicians have conducted research into how to use blood efficiently, and about how to separate it into various components. Today, a patient is rarely given whole blood. They receive only those components which are required.

Testing, processing, and separating blood into its components required specialized staff and equipment which would be very costly to duplicate in every community. As a result, the country's blood collection system is being regionalized. Blood is being collected in small communities, but it is transported to regional blood centers where it is processed. The blood is stored at these centers, with the quantities and types of blood needed being returned to the small towns so that their supply is always adequate.

As a result of this regulation, many of the small-town blood programs are now a part of larger regional programs. They are subject to new regulations and have suffered a loss of local identity.

Fewer Restrictions on Donors

Research has greatly improved our understanding of how disease is and is not transmitted through blood transfusions. As a result, many people who once were rejected as blood donors because of some childhood disease can now donate. At one time, the average rejection rate was 12 percent (i.e., 12 percent of the people who came in to donate were rejected as donors on the basis of their medical history). Today, only 5 percent of those who come in are turned away because of past illnesses.

Donors between the ages of 17 and 65 who are in good health are eligible to donate. In special circumstances individuals older or younger than those ages may be donors. A person may donate once every 10 weeks (5 times per year). However, individuals who do donate in the United States usually do so less than once a year.

Home Tractor, Inc.
Charles M. Futrell

Home Tractor, Inc. manufactures six major product lines: push lawn mowers, power lawn mowers, riding mowers, garden tillers, lawn tractors, and garden tractors. The company is divided into five geographical regions. As shown in Exhibit 1, annual sales have steadily increased to $362.6 million as of 1980. In fact, sales have increased at a more rapid rate than industry demand, and the company's market share has been increasing.

Jim Tanner, national sales manager, takes great pride in these figures and has always felt his group was working at their maximum potential.

Market Information System

At the beginning of 1980 a market information system (MIS) was installed to provide a

EXHIBIT 1 Home Tractor, Inc. Sales

Year	Company Sales Volume (Millions)	Industry Demand (Millions)	Share of Market (Percent)
1972	$265.1	$16,150.1	1.64%
1973	280.0	17,200.0	1.63
1974	287.0	17,289.2	1.66
1975	294.4	17,420.2	1.69
1976	303.4	18,059.6	1.68
1977	315.2	18,541.2	1.70
1978	337.4	19,736.2	1.71
1979	340.8	19,929.8	1.71
1980	362.8	20,839.0	1.74

continuous audit of the firm's marketing operation. It was hoped that the MIS would aid in the allocation of time and dollars in such a way as to generate higher sales volume and net profits by concentrating market effort in the most profitable areas. The company wanted to examine market segments and determine which were producing the majority of sales and profits so management could divide the total marketing resources in the most efficient manner. Because different net profits and sales are often contributed by different product lines, price lines, and geographical areas, management wanted to direct the majority of marketing expenditures at those areas in which the profit, sales, or a profit-sales ratio's return per marketing dollar spent was the highest. As one manager said: "We must allocate our funds where we get the most bang for the buck." It was felt that MIS could aid in such things as sales forecasting, evaluating market position, production planning, inventory control, sales-force planning, and appraising pricing, advertising, sales promotion, and distribution strategies.

An important part of MIS is the computer-generated data used to assist the sales analyst. Corporate management wanted to examine the extent to which the so-called 80-20 principle was operating. They realized that a major part of the company's sales and profits may directly result from a small number of customers, products, or geographical areas. It

was felt that some marginal or unprofitable products, geographical areas, or customers should be carried in order to complement the existing product line and encourage sales volume in the more profitable areas. Furthermore, MIS could be used to examine the effect that averaging, summarizing, and aggregating data has on the true sales or profit picture. Management did not want to assume that, just because sales were increasing, this meant that the company's operations could not be improved.

Financial Analyses

One of the first reports generated by MIS was the income statement shown in Exhibit 2. The contribution margin approach, rather than the full cost approach, was used to prepare the income statement. As shown, variable costs (those that fluctuate with net sales volume), including marketing and manufactur-

EXHIBIT 2 Home Tractor, Inc., Income Statement, Contribution Margin Approach

	Entire Company (000)	Southwest (000)	Southern (000)	Eastern (000)	Western (000)	Midwest (000)
Net sales	$362,600	$68,898	$68,756	$78,522	$74,274	$72,150
Less variable costs						
Manufacturing costs	238,606	44,094	45,244	52,610	50,506	46,152
Marketing costs						
Sales commissions	11,536	2,342	2,062	2,506	2,674	1,952
Transportation and shipping	2,418	602	472	334	426	584
Warehousing	806	152	148	172	134	200
Credit and collection	1,184	374	352	386	280	422
Assignable costs						
Salaries: salespeople	36,920	7,398	6,608	7,272	7,446	8,196
Salaries: marketing manager	2,308	400	446	474	462	526
Advertising	6,804	1,396	1,362	1,486	1,272	1,288
Sales promotion	2,872	576	580	636	554	546
Total variable and assignable costs	304,084	57,334	57,254	65,876	63,754	59,866
Contribution margin	58,516	11,564	11,502	12,646	10,520	12,284
Nonassignable costs						
Institutional advertising	810					
Fixed costs						
General administration	4,054					
Manufacturing	46,092					
Net income (before taxes)	7,560					

ing costs, are first subtracted from net sales for each segment. This contribution margin is the amount that each respective segment contributes to company overhead and to net profits. Nonassignable costs and fixed costs are not allocated to the segments. The contribution margins serve as measures of relative profitability. Tanner noted that the Western region was the lowest in terms of profitability. He also observed that if regions were ranked in terms of profitability the Eastern region would be the most profitable.

Management was pleased to see that every region was making a positive contribution to net profits and overhead. Several managers suggested that there was no need to continue the analysis. However, Tanner asked that this contribution margin approach be extended to product line (see Exhibit 3). He was somewhat surprised to see that the lawn tractor line was unprofitable. It appears from certain territorial analyses that the very profitable garden tractor line may be compensating for the lawn tractor line's losses. He could not tell from this analysis alone the reason for the poor performance of the lawn tractor line. Industry demand for lawn tractors may have declined and the firm may not have anticipated this economic fact; or the new model of lawn tractor may have mechanical defects or poor aesthetic features. "We don't know, but what

I am sure of is that management should take appropriate measures to find out what the problem may be. Maybe MIS is better than I first felt it was because, without this analysis, the success of our other product lines may have hidden this from us," stated Tanner.

Regional Sales Analysis

Tanner requested a regional breakdown of company sales volume. Last year he had developed a retail sales index to serve as a relative measure of the dollar volume of retail sales that normally occur in each region. Based on that index he had established quotas for the sales regions, districts, and individual territories. As shown in Exhibit 4, all except the Western region were meeting quotas. Tanner did not know why sales were down. He called John Anderson, the Western regional sales manager, and asked him to look into the matter and report back to him in two weeks. Anderson knew sales were slow; however, he had not been that concerned until now.

Western Sales Region

To examine the $478,000 loss Tanner used the district sales breakdown shown in Exhibit 5.

EXHIBIT 3 Home Tractor, Inc., Income Statement, Contribution Margin Approach *(By Product Line)*

	Company (000)	Push Mowers (000)	Power Mowers (000)	Riding Mowers (000)	Garden Tillers (000)	Lawn Tractors (000)	Garden Tractors (000)
Net sales	$362,620	$66,900	$44,734	$70,342	$17,352	$33,114	$119,168
Less variable costs							
Manufacturing	238,606	47,662	29,792	45,454	11,260	39,668	64,770
Marketing	16,564	2,916	2,652	3,162	532	2,848	4,464
Assignable costs	48,904	8,150	7,654	8,776	2,000	6,446	15,860
Total variable and assignable costs	304,084	58,728	40,098	57,932	13,792	48,980	85,904
Contribution margin	58,516	8,172	4,636	12,960	3,560	(4,886)	34,074
Nonassignable costs	810						
Fixed costs	50,146						
Net income (before taxes)	7,560						

EXHIBIT 4 Home Tractor, Inc., Regional Breakdown of Sales

Region	Retail Sales Index	Expected Sales (000)	Actual Sales (000)	Dollar Deviation
Midwest	99	$71,848	$72,100	+ 252
Southwest	95	68,946	68,948	+ 2
Southern	9	64,592	68,756	+4,164
Eastern	105	76,204	78,522	+2,318
Western	103	74,752	74,274	− 478

EXHIBIT 5 Home Tractor, Inc., Western Region Sales

District	Expected Sales (000)	Actual Sales (000)	Dollar Deviation
Washington	$ 8,970	$ 8,994	+ 24
Idaho-Oregon	7,850	7,842	− 8
Northern California	21,602	21,014	−588
Southern California	36,330	36,424	+ 94

EXHIBIT 6 Home Tractor, Inc., Western Region, N. California District Sales

Salesperson	Expected Sales (000)	Actual Sales (000)	Difference	Performance Index*
J. Boles	$5,696	$5,792	+ 96	101
L. Stark	5,584	4,842	− 742	86
J. Dozzier	6,012	6,046	+ 34	100
A. Penny	4,310	4,334	+ 24	100

*(Actual Sales/Quota) × 100.

It was very apparent that the northern California sales district was experiencing problems. He called Kurt McNeal, the district manager, and asked him why sales were down. Kurt said "John, I was just about to call you. I'm getting ready to fire Leslie Stark. His sales are down. You know he is in the process of getting a divorce and his personal life must be getting in the way of business." "Have you talked to him?" asked Tanner. "Yes, he claims competition is using that area as a test market for a new line of garden tractors. However, I suspect he is not working very hard and the competition is stealing our business. You know we have some large retail chain accounts there and we cannot afford to lose that business. So let's replace him." "Before you do Kurt, look over some of the data I'm mailing you, then talk to Leslie. After this, if you still feel you should let him go, you have my permission. I'm not sure he's doing so badly compared to the rest of you."

Up until this time McNeal had been working with total sales figures and figures that salespeople developed on their own, so it was difficult for him to break out sales data. In fact,

EXHIBIT 7 Salespeople's Dollar Gain or Loss over Expected Sales

| | J. Boles | | L. Stark | | J. Dozzier | | A. Penny | |
| | Expected Sales (000) | Actual Sales (000) | Expected Sales (000) | Actual Sales (000) | Expected Sales (000) | Actual Sales (000) | Expected Sales (000) | Actual Sales (000) |
Products								
Push mowers	$ 939	$1,009	$1,032	$1,044	$ 999	$1,008	$ 588	$ 605
Power mowers	630	609	544	540	971	980	686	702
Riding mowers	207	160	208	234	896	900	848	851
Garden tillers	1,072	1,112	1,098	1,096	1,291	1,295	873	858
Lawn tractors	1,670	1,702	1,526	1,616	733	735	635	652
Garden tractors	1,178	1,200	1,176	312	1,122	1,128	680	666
Totals	5,696	5,792	5,584	4,842	6,012	6,046	4,310	4,334

EXHIBIT 8 Salespeople's Percentage Gain or Loss

| | Percentage Gain or Loss Over Last Year | | | | Percentage Gain or Loss Over Last Year | | |
	Territory	District	Region		Territory	District	Region
J. Boles				J. Dozzier			
Push mowers	7.0	8.9	7.6	Push mowers	9.0	8.9	7.6
Power mowers	− 3.4	− 1.5	3.7	Power mowers	1.0	− 1.5	3.7
Riding mowers	− 1.7	41.4	3.8	Riding mowers	1.7	−41.4	3.8
Garden tillers	3.6	−14.8	− 4.2	Garden tillers	5.2	−14.8	− 4.2
Lawn tractors	1.9	8.2	11.5	Lawn tractors	1.6	8.2	11.5
Garden tractors	10.1	−18.6	− 9.1	Garden tractors	21.6	−18.6	− 9.1
L. Stark				A. Penny			
Push mowers	11.0	8.9	7.6	Push mowers	8.6	8.9	7.6
Power mowers	− 2.2	− 1.5	3.7	Power mowers	3.1	− 1.5	3.7
Riding mowers	.4	41.4	3.8	Riding mowers	.8	41.4	3.8
Garden tillers	− 8.2	−14.8	4.2	Garden tillers	− 15.4	−14.8	4.2
Garden tillers	8.2	−14.8	− 4.2	Garden tillers	15.4	−14.8	− 4.2
Lawn tractors	15.2	8.2	11.5	Lawn tractors	− 10.5	8.2	11.5
Garden tractors	−46.3	−18.6	9.1	Garden tractors	− 4.0	−18.6	9.1
Garden tractors	46.3	−18.6	− 9.1	Garden tractors	4.0	−18.6	− 9.1

he really did not want to do it. He felt it was the company's job and not his responsibility. If sales were down they would let him know. Up until recently he had always met his overall sales quota. Several days after the conversation with Tanner, McNeal received the data shown in Exhibits 6, 7, and 8. It was amazing to him to see this much detail in the data. When he saw that Stark was the only person selling below quota and in fact making the district's performance look bad, he made up his mind to fire Stark.

Volunteers in Health Care, Inc.
Joanne G. Greer

Volunteers in Health Care, Inc. (VHC) was a nonprofit corporation that was organized in 1968 to provide medical, psychological, and dental care for the medically indigent and other selected low-income populations in the northern suburbs of an Eastern city. The founders, a group of medical doctors who were predominantly psychiatrists, were still active in the group, although younger colleagues had assumed some of the management.

The original group of physicians augmented their ranks with their own former students, younger colleagues, and professional friends. There had never been a problem with recruitment of volunteer medical professionals, and the medical director had to decline additional volunteers in certain speciality areas. For example, there was consistently an excess of volunteers in pediatrics. A CPA, a former member of the board of directors, performed the annual financial audit free of charge. There had never been a volunteer lawyer,

however, in spite of efforts to recruit one. In addition, no one with formal training in business management had ever been involved in VHC. The value of services donated in the most recent year, based on the county health department wage schedule, is displayed in Exhibit 1.

The founders had multiple interests in the organization, including the following:

1. Indignation about the plight of elderly persons and children who "fell through the cracks" of the health care system. Such persons either had too much income to qualify for welfare or did not apply for it. But because they or their parents were unemployed or marginally employed, they lacked private health insurance or were insured only intermittently. Preventive health care, such as

This case was prepared by Joanne G. Greer, Ph.D.

Reprinted with permission of Macmillan Publishing Company. From Thomas V. Greer, *Cases in Marketing*, 3rd ed. Copyright © 1983.

EXHIBIT 1 Estimated Value of Donated Services

Number of Volunteers	Staff	Hours	Rate	County Pay Rate
14	Physicians	1,306	$23.02	$30,064.12
22	Board members*	781	23.02	17,978.62
12	Psychologists	1,145	15.99	18,308.55
20	Nurses	779	9.69	7,548.51
5	Lab technicians	159	8.84	1,405.56
4	Medical students	24	8.84	212.16
2	Dietitians	61	10.63	648.43
12	Clinic assistants	411	6.05	2,486.55
2	Registrars	51	6.05	308.55
7	Office	209	7.72	1,613.48
1	Auditor	80	23.02	1,841.60
101		5,006		$82,416.13
		FICA		5,266.39
		State unemployment		1,648.32
		Workmen's Compensation		346.14
		Total		$89,676.98

*Board member compensation is the same for all board members, physician, nonphysician, professional, or client, according to county policy.

checkups, shots, and monitoring of chronic illnesses such as high blood pressure, was particularly lacking. Hospital care was less of a problem because hospitals built with federal or state funds could not turn indigents away. A major regional children's hospital, although a private foundation, also accepted all indigent patients.

2. A research interest in psychosomatic disorders and a related need to stay active in general medical work, although they earned their living as psychiatrists.

3. A desire to demonstrate to their psychiatric colleagues the effectiveness of "talk" therapy with lower-class persons, who in the United States usually were given tranquilizers when stressed or depressed. The founders were particularly influenced in this research interest by the writings of psychiatrists who had worked in the British national health service.

VHC provided services at six sites, visiting a different site each evening from 7:30 to 10:30 P.M. The sites were located in county-subsidized housing units which were reserved for the elderly and a few totally disabled persons. Paid county employees furnished other services to these buildings, such as security guards, maintenance, and minimal recreational programs. Most residents lived on social security incomes from retirement or from total disability ratings, and had too much income to qualify for the state's medicaid program but too little income to afford private doctors' fees. Transportation to physicians was a severe problem even to residents who had funds to pay the doctors' charges, because public transportation was poor and they were fearful of being injured while entering and leaving buses and crossing busy streets.

The space for the medical clinics at each site was donated by the county, although it was not exclusively dedicated to VHC. Examining rooms were often utilized by other personnel, such as county social workers, outside of clinic hours, and the only space reserved for VHC was a large closet at each site to hold basic equipment such as centrifuges and equipment for specimen collection. Patients made appointments by telephoning VHC's one-room office, located in a converted former county school building, which had been subdivided for use by various volunteer groups. Each evening a volunteer registrar picked up the files of patients expected at the clinic, set up the examining rooms, and arranged folding chairs at the waiting area. He or she greeted the patients, supervised their flow through the clinic, and recorded the services rendered. Payments were accepted on a voluntary system, and the usual total receipts for an evening were less than $10, with individual payments as low as 50 cents. Many paid nothing, although recently a sign had been posted stating, "VHC is staffed entirely by volunteers. Contributions gratefully accepted."

In reality, VHC had four paid staff: a nurse, a social worker, a secretary, and a lower-level manager who was promoted from secretarial work. The nurse took calls from patients, made appointments, and made decisions during the day about patient emergencies. For example, she might consult by telephone with a patient's doctor at his regular employment, or direct a patient to go to the hospital emergency room for a medical crisis. The social worker assisted new patients in contacting various sources of volunteer or tax-subsidized services in the county. Patients requiring medical services not available through VHC were assisted by the social worker to find local sources of help. For example, a patient requiring oral surgery for receding gums was put in touch with the clinic of a local dental school, and a nutritionist was found to assist several diabetic patients with menu planning on a fixed income.

Wives of the male physicians and their women friends sometimes volunteered for typing and filing for a few hours a day, and the supply of clerical help was more than adequate. It was particularly easy to get office volunteers ever since the county had recently moved VHC to an attractive suite in a new senior citizens day-care center. VHC had had only one daytime professional volunteer, a retired social worker, who made home visits and school visits to coordinate care for children receiving psychotherapy from VHC evening volunteers. She also took initial case histories of psychotherapy patients, which were presented to volunteer therapists at their weekly group meeting so they could each choose the type of patient they preferred working with. She had recently resigned, and psychotherapists now received only a name and telephone number for each referral.

Psychotherapists also had to "hustle" office space in the county buildings to see their patients, because there wasn't sufficient auditory privacy to conduct psychotherapy in the physician's examining rooms during evening clinics, even when the rooms were free.

Nevertheless, there was no lack of psychotherapists because of an important career benefit they received by volunteering. Several distinguished senior professors of psychiatry provided the volunteers with free case supervision, a form of tutorial teaching, for each of their clinic cases. Ordinarily, such supervision cost $60 to $80 an hour, and therapists regarded supervision by a well-known educator as a prestige form of continuing education.

VHC's sources of income and types of expenditures for the past year are displayed in Exhibits 2 and 3. The main sources of income were grants from United Way, the county health department, and an "adolescent parent" grant program. The services to adolescent mothers and their infants had been eliminated from the state and federal plans for the coming fiscal year, so no further funds would be available from that source. The previous week United Way had notified the chairman of the VHC board of directors that no further United Way funds would be available until VHC performed an evaluation and

EXHIBIT 2 Volunteers in Health Care, Inc. Statement of Revenues and Expenditures and Changes in Fund Balance

Most Recent Fiscal Year Ended June 30	
Revenues	
United Way	$50,962.00
County Health Dept.	17,385.00
CETA	1,041.01
Medical fees	15,409.00
Donations	550.00
Interest	211.49
Miscellaneous	144.34
Total revenues	$82,148.26
Expenditures	
Program	
Clinic	62,558.51
CETA	5,914.77
Adolescent Parent Education	6,282.93
Total Program	$74,756.21
General and administrative	14,932.28
Total expenditures	$89,688.49
Excess of revenues (deficiency) over expenditures	(7,540.23)

EXHIBIT 3 Volunteers in Health Care, Inc. Analysis of Functional Expenditures Most Recent Fiscal Year Ended June 30

| | Program | | | General and | |
	Clinic	CETA	Total	Administrative	Total
Salaries and registrar fees	$51,062.97	$775.25	$51,838.22	$13,653.00	$65,491.22
Payroll taxes	4,257.86	51.55	4,309.41	1,169.92	5,479.33
Employee benefits	1,102.03	—	1,102.03	310.84	1,412.87
Total personnel costs	56,422.86	826.80	57,249.66	15,133.76	72,383.42
Interest	—	—	—	5.59	5.59
Transportation	4,171.82	—	4,171.82	77.95	4,249.77
Contributions	—	—	—	—	400.00
Depreciation	424.50	—	424.50	92.32	516.82
Insurance	2,567.00	—	2,567.00	87.00	2,654.00
Laboratory fees	3,288.20	—	3,288.20	—	3,288.20
Office supplies and expenses	1,302.60	—	1,302.60	367.40	1,670.00
Repairs and maintenance	650.26	—	650.26	159.50	809.76
Medical supplies	1,471.40	—	1,471.40	—	1,471.40
Telephone	427.65	—	427.65	646.41	1,074.26
Miscellaneous	296.13	—	296.13	1,036.58	1,332.71
	$71,022.42	$826.80	$71,849.22	$17,606.71	$89,455.93

hired a professional manager. United Way also objected to the research interest the physicians had in the patients, in spite of the fact that any patient included in a research study signed an informed consent form. The fees received from medicare, medicaid, and the county health department grant would not be sufficient to even maintain current operations, much less recruit a manager. Some of the patients had private health insurance, but the largest company refused to consider VHC for direct payment because VHC did not have a fixed fee schedule for services, but simply accepted whatever the patient was willing to pay. Consequently, the patients collected the insurance reimbursements and usually pocketed them, making a token donation to VHC. One patient was known to have collected $500 from an insurance company in reimbursement for psychotherapy visits, had donated $50 to VHC, and then used the remainder to take a vacation.

Two letters to the insurance company to negotiate a contract for direct payment to VHC had received short, stereotyped responses of refusal, signed by a correspondence clerk.

In a special meeting to discuss strategy, board members were offended by United Way's demand for an evaluation. Claire Washburn, the board president and wife of a former volunteer, commented, "Our program is sterling, and it breaks my heart to think they would question our integrity." Dr. Vincent Jones, one of the original founders, questioned whether the United Way's funds were worth the effort and wanted to pursue more vigorously obtaining direct reimbursement status with private insurors. VHC was currently receiving a grant from the county health department because VHC could care for the medically indigent more cheaply than county clinics, and Dr. Jones thought the county would give more business if pressed. He also thought there was a possibility of taking over the county operation completely, under a "capitation rate" payment arrangement. The county clinics had high costs, were poorly run, and had just received a large amount of negative coverage in the news media.

Because the county clinics primarily delivered care to medically indigent children, assuming responsibility for these patients would enable VHC to use the volunteer pediatricians it was currently turning away for lack of work.

Under the capitation rate mode of payment, the responsible payor, in this case the county, negotiates a per-head annual payment with a health care provider, usually a clinic. The health care provider is responsible for service even if the provider incurs a loss. On the other hand, the provider receives the payment for all covered persons, even those who use no services that year. Medicaid experiments with capitation rate had been quite successful in that equal-quality care for patients with lower annual costs had resulted. Under capitation rate reimbursement, there is no financial incentive for the provider to

provide unnecessary services, or to "ping-pong" the patient from doctor to doctor.

Washburn, the board president, was hesitant at the risks involved in giving up the United Way money, but Barry Water, a community activist board member, noted that if VHC dropped out of United Way, it would be completely free to hold its own annual fund-raising drive, an activity that United Way strongly discouraged in recipient agencies. He also noted that the children's hospital had successfully gone this route. Washburn pointed out that some response had to be made to United Way's request for an evaluation of the VHC program, but she, for one, had no idea how to go about it, particularly in light of United Way's expressed dislike for research in the clinics.

Modern Plastics (A)
Tom Ingram and Danny N. Bellenger

[handwritten: Develop several forecasts]

Institutional sales manager Jim Clayton had spent most of Monday morning planning for the rest of the month. It was early July and Jim knew that an extremely busy time was coming with the preparation of the following year's sales plan.

Since starting his current job less than a month ago, Jim had been involved in learning the requirements of the job and making his initial territory visits. Now that he was getting settled, Jim was trying to plan his activities according to priorities. The need for planning had been instilled in him during his college days. As a result of his three years' field sales experience and development of time-management skills, he felt prepared for the challenge of the sales manager's job.

While sitting at his desk, Jim recalled a conversation that he had a week ago with Bill Hanson, the former manager, who had been promoted to another division. Bill told him that the sales forecast (annual and monthly) for plastic trash bags in the Southeast region

would be due soon as an initial step toward developing the sales plan for the next year. Bill had laughed as he told Jim, "Boy, you ought to have a ball doing the forecast being a rookie sales manager!"

When Jim had asked what Bill meant, he explained by saying that the forecast was often "winged" because the headquarters in New York already knew what they wanted and would change the forecast to meet their figures, particularly if the forecast was for an increase of less than 10 percent. The experienced sales manager could throw numbers together in a short time that would pass as a serious forecast and ultimately be adjusted to fit the plans of headquarters. However, an inexperienced manager would have a difficult time "winging" a credible forecast.

This case was coauthored by Tom Ingram, University of Kentucky, and Danny N. Bellenger, Georgia State University.

Cases in Marketing Management, rev. ed. Kenneth L. Bernhardt and Thomas C. Kinnear, © 1981 Business Publications, Incorporated.

[handwritten: assume done for volume in cases]

[handwritten: minimum acceptable]

Bill had also told Jim that the other alternative meant gathering mountains of data and putting together a forecast that could be sold to the various levels of Modern Plastics management. This alternative would prove to be time consuming and could still be changed anywhere along the chain of command before final approval.

Clayton started reviewing pricing and sales volume history (see Exhibit 1). He also looked at the key account performance for the past two and a half years (see Exhibit 2). During

files: mktg (s forcasts) MP(c)

EXHIBIT 1 Plastic Trash Bags—Sales and Pricing History, 1975–1977

	Pricing Dollars per Case			Sales Volume in Cases			Sales Volume in Dollars		
	1975	1976	1977	1975	1976	1977	1975	1976	1977
January	$6.88	$ 7.70	$15.40	33,000	46,500	36,500	$ 227,000	$ 358,000	$ 562,000
February	6.82	7.70	14.30	32,500	52,500	23,000	221,500	404,000	329,000
March	6.90	8.39	13.48	32,000	42,000	22,000	221,000	353,000	296,500
April	6.88	10.18	12.24	45,500	42,500	46,500	313,000	432,500	569,000
May	6.85	12.38	11.58	49,000	41,500	45,500	335,500	514,000	527,000
June	6.85	12.65	10.31	47,500	47,000	42,000	325,500	594,500	433,000
July	7.42	13.48	9.90*	40,000	43,500	47,500*	297,000	586,500	470,000*
August	6.90	13.48	10.18	48,500	63,500	43,500	334,500	856,000	443,000
September	7.70	14.30	10.31	43,000	49,000	47,500	331,000	700,500	489,500
October	7.56	15.12	10.31	52,500	50,000	51,000	397,000	756,000	526,000
November	7.15	15.68	10.72	62,000	61,500	47,500	443,500	964,500	509,000
December	7.42	15.43	10.59	49,000	29,000	51,000	363,500	447,500	540,000
Total	7.13	12.25	11.30	534,500	568,500	503,500	3,810,000	6,967,000	5,694,000

*July–December 1977 figures are forecast of sales manager J. A. Clayton and other data comes from historical sales information.

EXHIBIT 2 1977 Key Account Sales History *(in Cases)* (72% of total sales)

p.545 Portfolio

60%

Customer	1975	1976	First Six Months 1977	1975 Monthly Average	1976 Monthly Average	First Half 1977 Monthly Average	First Quarter 1977 Monthly Average
Transco Paper Company	125,774	134,217	44,970	10,481	11,185	7,495	5,823
Callaway Paper	44,509	46,049	12,114	3,709	3,837	2,019	472
Florida Janitorial Supply	34,746	36,609	20,076	2,896	3,051	3,346	2,359
Jefferson	30,698	34,692	25,044	2,558	2,891	4,174	1,919
Cobb Paper	13,259	23,343	6,414	1,105	1,945	1,069	611
Miami Paper	10,779	22,287	10,938	900	1,857	1,823	745
Milne Surgical Company	23,399	21,930	—	1,950	1,828	—	—
Graham	8,792	15,331	1,691	733	1,278	281	267
Crawford Paper	7,776	14,132	6,102	648	1,178	1,017	1,322
John Steele	8,634	13,277	6,663	720	1,106	1,110	1,517
Henderson Paper	9,185	8,850	2,574	765	738	429	275
Durant Surgical	—	7,766	4,356	—	647	726	953
Master Paper	4,221	5,634	600	352	470	100	—
D.T.A.	—	—	2,895	—	—	482	—
Crane Paper	4,520	5,524	3,400	377	460	566	565
Janitorial Service	3,292	5,361	2,722	274	447	453	117
Georgia Paper	5,466	5,053	2,917	456	421	486	297
Paper Supplies, Inc.	5,117	5,119	1,509	426	427	251	97
Southern Supply	1,649	3,932	531	137	328	88	78
Horizon Hospital Supply	4,181	4,101	618	348	342	103	206
Total cases	346,007	413,217	156,134	28,835	34,436	26,018	17,623

41958.33

the past month Clayton had visited many of the key accounts, and on the average they had indicated that their purchases from Modern would probably increase about 15–20 percent in the coming year.

Schedule for Preparing the Forecast

Jim had received a memo recently from Robert Baxter, the regional marketing manager, detailing the plans for completing the 1978 forecast. The key dates in the memo began in only three weeks.

August 1	Presentation of forecast to regional marketing manager.
August 10	Joint presentation with marketing manager to regional general manager.
September 1	Regional general manager presents forecast to division vice president.
September 1– September 30	Review of forecast by staff of division vice president.
October 1	Review forecast with corporate staff.
October 1– October 15	Revision as necessary.
October 15	Final forecast forwarded to division vice president from regional general manager.

Company Background

The plastics division of Modern Chemical Company was founded in 1965 when Modern Chemical purchased Cordco, a small plastics manufacturer with national sales of $15,000,000. At that time the key products of the plastics division were sandwich bags, plastic tablecloths, trash cans, and plastic-coated clothesline.

Since 1965 the plastics division has grown to a sales level exceeding $200 million with five regional profit centers covering the United States. Each regional center has manufacturing facilities and a regional sales force. There are four product groups in each region:

1. Food packaging: Styrofoam meat and produce trays; plastic bags for various food products.

2. Egg cartons: Styrofoam egg cartons sold to egg packers and supermarket chains.

3. Institutional: Plastic trash bags and disposable tableware (plates, bowls, and so on).

4. Industrial: Plastic packaging for the laundry and dry-cleaning market, plastic film for use in pallet overwrap systems.

Each product group is supervised jointly by a product manager and a district sales manager, both of whom report to the regional marketing manager. The sales representatives report directly to the district sales manager but also work closely with the product manager on matters concerning pricing and product specifications.

The five regional general managers report to J. R. Hughes, vice president of the plastics division. Hughes is located in New York. Although Modern Chemical is owned by a multinational oil company, the plastics division has been able to operate in a virtually independent manner since its establishment in 1965. The reasons for this include:

1. Limited knowledge of the plastic industry on the part of the oil company management.

2. Excellent growth by the plastics division has been possible without management supervision from the oil company.
3. Profitability of the plastics division has consistently been higher than that of other divisions of the chemical company.

The Institutional Trash Bag Market

The institutional trash bag is a polyethylene bag used to collect and transfer refuse to its final disposition point. There are different sizes and colors available to fit the various uses of the bag. For example, a small bag for desk wastebaskets is available as well as a heavier bag for large containers such as a 55-gallon drum. There are 25 sizes in the Modern line with 13 of those sizes being available in 3 colors—white, buff, and clear. Customers typically buy several different items on an order to cover all their needs.

The institutional trash bag is a separate product from the consumer-grade trash bag which is typically sold to homeowners through retail outlets. The institutional trash bag is sold primarily through paper wholesalers, hospital supply companies, and janitorial supply companies to a variety of end users. Since trash bags are used on such a wide scale, the list of end users could include almost any business or institution. The segments include hospitals, hotels, schools, office buildings, transportation facilities, and restaurants.

Based on historical data and a current survey of key wholesalers and end users in the Southeast, the annual market of institutional trash bags in the region was estimated to be 55 million pounds. Translated into cases, the market potential was close to 2 million cases. During the past five years, the market for trash bags has grown at an average rate of 89 percent per year. Now a mature product, future market growth is expected to parallel overall growth in the economy. The 1978 real growth in GNP is forecast to be 4.5 percent.

General Market Conditions

The current market is characterized by a distressing trend. The market is in a position of oversupply with approximately 20 manufacturers competing for the business in the Southeast. Prices have been on the decline for several months but are expected to level out during the last six months of the year.

This problem arose after a record year in 1976 for Modern Plastics. During 1976, supply was very tight due to raw material shortages. Unlike many of its competitors, Modern had only minor problems securing adequate raw-material supplies. As a result the competitors were few in 1976, and all who remained in business were prosperous. By early 1977 raw materials were plentiful, and prices began to drop as new competitors tried to buy their way into the market. During the first quarter of 1977 Modern Plastics learned the hard way that a competitive price was a necessity in the current market. Volume fell off drastically in February and March as customers shifted orders to new suppliers when Modern chose to maintain a slightly higher than market price on trash bags.

With the market becoming extremely price competitive and profits declining, the overall quality has dropped to a point of minimum standard. Most suppliers now make a bag "barely good enough to get the job done." This quality level is acceptable to most buyers who do not demand high quality for this type of product.

Modern Plastics versus Competition

A recent study of Modern versus competition had been conducted by an outside consultant to see how well Modern measured up in several key areas. Each area was weighted according to its importance in the purchase decision, and Modern compared to its key competitors in each area and on an overall basis. The key factors and their weights are shown below.

		Weight
1.	Pricing	.50
2.	Quality	.15
3.	Breadth of line	.10
4.	Sales coverage	.10
5.	Packaging	.05
6.	Service	.10
	Total	1.00

As shown in Exhibit 3, Modern compared favorably with its key competitors on an overall basis. None of the other suppliers were as strong as Modern in breadth of line nor did any competitor offer as good sales coverage as that provided by Modern. Clayton knew that sales coverage would be even better next year since the Florida and North Carolina territories had grown enough to add two sales-

EXHIBIT 3 Competitive Factors Ratings *(by Competitor*)*

Weight	Factor	Modern	National Film	Bonanza	South-eastern	PBI	BAGCO	South-west Bag	Sun Plastics	East Coast Bag Co.
.50	Price	2	3	2	2	2	2	2	2	3
.15	Quality	3	2	3	4	3	2	3	3	4
.10	Breadth	1	2	2	3	3	3	3	3	3
.10	Sales coverage	1	3	3	3	4	3	3	4	3
.05	Packaging	3	3	2	3	3	1	3	3	3
.10	Service	4	3	3	2	2	2	3	4	3

Overall Weighted Ranking†

1. BAGCO	2.15	6. Southeastern	2.55
2. Modern	2.20	7. Florida Plastics	2.60
3. Bonanza	2.25	8. National Film	2.65
4. Southwest Bag (Tie)	2.50	9. East Coast Bag Co.	3.15
5. PBI (Tie)	2.50		

*Ratings on a one to five scale with one being the best rating and five the worst.

†The weighted ranking is the sum of each rank times its weight. The lower the number, the better the overall rating.

EXHIBIT 4 Market Share by Supplier, 1975 and 1977

Supplier	Percent of Market 1975	Percent of Market 1977
National Film	11	12
Bertram	16	0*
Bonanza	11	12
Southeastern	5	6
Bay	9	0*
Johnson Graham	8	0*
PBI	2	5
Lewis	2	0*
BAGCO	—	6
Southwest Bag	—	2
Florida Plastics	—	4
East Coast Bag Co.	—	4
Miscellaneous and unknown	8	22
Modern	28	27
	100	100

*Out of business in 1977.

Source: This information was developed from a field survey conducted by Modern Plastics.

EXHIBIT 5 Characteristics of Competitors

National Film	Broadest product line in the industry. Quality a definite advantage. Good service. Sales coverage adequate, but not an advantage. Not as aggressive as most suppliers on price. Strong competitor.
Bonanza	Well-established tough competitor. Very aggressive on pricing. Good packaging, quality okay.
Southeastern	Extremely price competitive in southern Florida. Dominates Miami market. Limited product line. Not a threat outside of Florida.
PBI	Extremely aggressive on price. Have made inroads into Transco Paper Company during 1977. Good service but poor sales coverage.
BAGCO	New competitor in 1977. Very impressive with a high-quality product, excellent service, and strong sales coverage. A real threat, particularly in Florida.
Southwest Bag	A factor in Louisiana and Mississippi. Their strategy is simple—an acceptable product at a rock bottom price.
Sun Plastics	Active when market is at a profitable level with price cutting. When market declines to a low profit range, Sun manufactures other types of plastic packaging and stays out of the trash bag market. Poor reputation as a reliable supplier, but can still "spot-sell" at low prices.
East Coast Bag Co.	Most of their business is from a state bid which began in January 1976 for a two-year period. Not much of a threat to Modern's business in the Southeast as most of their volume is north of Washington, D.C.

people to the institutional group by January 1, 1978.

Pricing, quality, and packaging seemed to be neither an advantage nor a disadvantage. However, service was a problem area. The main cause for this, Clayton was told, was temporary out-of-stock situations which occurred occasionally primarily due to the wide variety of trash bags offered by Modern.

During the past two years, Modern Plastics had maintained its market share at approximately 27 percent of the market. Some new competitors had entered the market since 1975 while others had left the market (see Exhibit 4). The previous district sales manager, Bill Hanson, had left Clayton some comments regarding the major competitors. These are reproduced in Exhibit 5.

Developing the Sales Forecast

After a careful study of trade journals, government statistics, and surveys conducted by Modern marketing research personnel, projections for growth potential were formulated

by segment and are shown in Exhibit 6. This data was compiled by Bill Hanson just before he had been promoted.

Jim looked back at Baxter's memo giving the time schedule for the forecast and knew he had to get started. As he left the office at 7:15, he wrote himself a large note and pinned it on his wall—"Get Started on the Sales Forecast!"

EXHIBIT 6 1978 Real Growth Projections by Segment

Total industry	+5.0%
Commercial	+5.4
Restaurant	+6.8
Hotel/motel	+2.0
Transportation	+1.9
Office users	+5.0
Other	+4.2
Noncommercial	+4.1
Hospitals	+3.9
Nursing homes	+4.8
Colleges/universities	+2.4
Schools	+7.8
Employee feeding	+4.3
Other	+3.9

Source: Developed from several trade journals.

SECTION 6

Marketing's Broadening Roles

*B*usiness has been variously blessed and chastised for its effects on society. In fact, this society has long had a love-hate relationship with the business sector. Americans' history of materialism and conspicuous consumption parallels labor-management clashes, environmental abuse, and consumerism movements. The average customer, for example, must own an automobile but is appalled at the depletion of our fossil fuels; he buys and consumes fast foods in large quantities but is highly critical of the chemicals used by these companies to preserve freshness or enhance taste; he calls himself law abiding yet uses a small radar detector to avoid being caught when speeding; he disdains pollution of all types but persists in buying goods and services from companies that are known polluters. To say the least, the typical consumer is inconsistent when it comes to consumption and societal welfare.

To understand marketing's role in the larger society, it is important to note that marketing is the *only* business function that interfaces directly with society. Each company assigns marketing the task of sensing consumer needs, wants, and problems, which are articulated so that the company can respond through product innovation or modification, price adjustment, changes in channels of distribution, or promotional program refocus. To accept this view means seeing marketing as communicating what society wants to the business, which in turn can respond with appropriate products and services. However, not everyone holds this view; many prefer to see a sense of corporate responsibility applied to marketing decisions. Clearly, for example, companies in certain industries—such as liquor, cigarettes, drugs, or movie making—have attempted to establish industrywide standards. It is obvious, however, that marketing in general has the power to set tastes, determine fashion, define materialism, create standards of living, and even accentuate the norms of bizarre elements of society. Although there are regulatory agencies and many laws that constrain business practices, it is impossible to legislate controls for *all* marketing practices. Thus, it is worthwhile instead to mention what are considered some of the major areas of marketing's responsibilities to society.

The following list of items is representative of some of these responsibilities. Since the list is not exhaustive, it should be treated as thought provoking and indicative of the types of concerns companies should have for society.

1. The responsibility to market safe products.
2. The responsibility to advertise in good taste.
3. The responsibility to protect the environment.
4. The responsibility to discourage abnormal and antisocial behavior.
5. The responsibility to price products equitably.
6. The responsibility to sponsor charitable and patriotic events.
7. The responsibility to help customers decide intelligently.
8. The responsibility to give full disclosure.
9. The responsibility to provide reasonable service.
10. The responsibility to compete in the spirit of free enterprise.

About the Readings

The first conceptual reading reveals how changing marital patterns have created a new type of man and new attitudes about masculinity. Household and other domestic chores are increasingly being shared by married couples or performed by single men. Working wives, single-parent households, and extended bachelorhood are all being used by marketers as segmentation factors, and advertising is accelerating the social acceptance of these living preferences. In other words, marketing is helping society redefine the traditional family unit. The second article in this section raises a philosophical question about the ownership of creativity; it is especially salient for marketing executives who brainstorm and design strategies daily. When an employee leaves a company or is let go, what are the rights and obligations of each party with respect to proprietary knowledge? The article points out that the answers to these questions are difficult and that we will see increasingly more instances of court cases in the next decade.

The first company article describes the Charlie Chaplin advertising campaign adopted by IBM for its Personal Computer. The well-known silent-movie comic figure was intentionally selected to soften IBM's industrial product image in the consumer goods market. But, more important, the article illustrates how a company's choice of an advertising theme may accelerate the process of adopting an innovation, and may steer customers toward more efficient methods of doing things. The next article—on Kodak—describes what is happening to this company, despite its position as a market leader, as it experiences the public rush toward electronic gadgets, especially foreign-made electronic products. Kodak is portrayed as a hibernating American bear about to waken to a new world of Japanese high-technology and cosmopolitan consumer tastes. Although the company personifies traditional American values, it must change if it is not to become a dinosaur. The last article is about the restoration of free enterprise in the telephone industry. For years AT&T and the U.S. government fenced with each other, but divestiture was ultimately mandated. Now AT&T must completely reconceive its corporate values while serving the public and fighting competition. Given the vital role played by telecommunications for every U.S. citizen, business, and nonprofit organization, there are difficult questions to be answered concerning rate adjustments, quality of service, long-standing contracts, and regional identity ■

Conceptual Readings

New Men
Eileen Prescott

When Dagwood wore an apron in the old television series, "Dagwood and Blondie," he became the butt of some classic one-liners with surefire results. A man in an apron was always good for a few laughs. But the laughing has stopped.

Today, men are wearing aprons, cooking dinner, washing dishes, going shopping, and taking care of the children—with major consequences for American business.

"A profoundly important change is happening," says Alice Goldberg, vice president and director of research at Benton & Bowles. Just as marketers have settled down after a wrenching upheaval in the women's market in the 1970s, they now have to rewrite the book on men.

The change is already evident in advertising and marketing. Taster's Choice, for example, recently replaced the image of a woman on their instant-coffee label with that of a man. Swanson has repackaged its frozen dinners as "Hungry Man" meals. Reggie Jackson is now the face behind the Panasonic microwave oven.

Though in the past commercials portrayed men either as Marlboro Men or as kitchen klutzes (with little in between), today's television viewers have been treated to advertising showing a man baking a cake, a father feeding his baby, and even a male shopper in rapt conversation with Mr. Whipple about the merits of Charmin bathroom tissue. A man in a toilet-paper commercial was once unthinkable.

In a complete reversal of content and format three years ago, *Esquire* magazine became the closest publication to a men's "service book" on the market and a first among men's magazines. Once heavy on politics and Burt Reynolds, today *Esquire* is full of helpful ideas on looking good, dressing well, the latest makeovers, hair, travel, home, and food—subjects men's magazines didn't often mention a decade ago. In a different kind of switch, traditional women's magazines like *House Beautiful* and *Food and Wine* have introduced "fast, easy food" sections which insiders say are designed to attract male readers.

Men's New Demographics

These innovative marketers are responding to the remarkable new demographics of men. A record-breaking divorce rate and a new acceptance of being single are responsible for a staggering increase in the number of men living without a woman. Since 1960 men's median age at first marriage has risen two full years to 24.8 years (see Exhibit 1). The proportion of men waiting to marry until their early thirties has doubled during the last decade, while the number of men living alone has nearly doubled, to 7.5 million—39 percent of all people living alone (see Exhibits 2, 3, 4, and 5). Of special interest to marketers is the fact that of the men who live alone, about half are young and never married, unlike women living alone, half of whom are 65 or older and widowed. Nearly one third of men living by themselves are between the ages of 25 and 34; more than half are under 45 years old.

EXHIBIT 1 Men by Age: 1982*

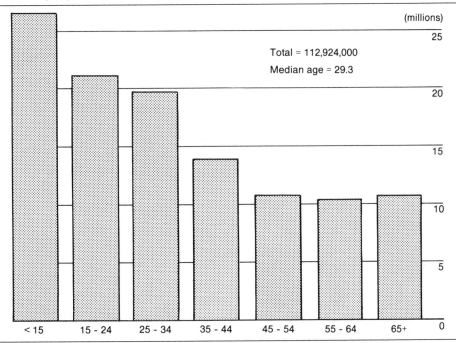

Total = 112,924,000
Median age = 29.3

(millions)

*The median age of men is still below 30, while that of women is above 30 because more boys are born than girls and women live longer than men.

EXHIBIT 2 Never-Married Men by Age: 1970–81*

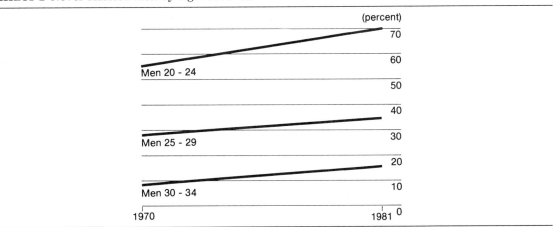

(percent)

*A larger proportion of men are remaining single until their 30s today, resulting in a rising age at first marriage for men and women.

EXHIBIT 3 Householder Status of Men*

Numbers in Thousands	1982		1970		% Change
	Number	Percent	Number	Percent	1970–82
Husbands in married-couple families	49,630	81.3%	44,728	86.9%	11.0%
with children less than 18	24,465	40.1	25,532	49.6	− 4.2
with no children less than 18	25,165	41.2	19,196	37.3	31.1
Male family householders	1,986	3.2	1,228	2.4	61.7
with children less than 18	679	1.1	341	0.7	99.1
with no children less than 18	1,307	2.1	887	1.7	47.4
Male nonfamily householders	9,457	15.5	4,063	7.9	132.8
living alone	7,482	12.3	3,532	6.9	111.8
other	1,975	3.2	531	1.0	271.9

*In 1970, half of male householders lived with a wife and children. Today, only 40 percent do, and the proportion of men who live alone or with unrelated people has nearly doubled.

EXHIBIT 4 Male Family Householders*

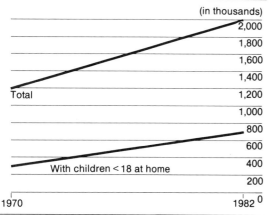

(in thousands)

Total

With children < 18 at home

1970   1982

*Though an increasing number of men are heading families with no wife present, a minority of them are single-parent families (with children under 18 in the home).

Another two million men are family heads without a wife, 62 percent more than in 1970. And over 16 million men are single but live with friends, parents, or lovers. The trend toward single living will continue through the 1980s. By 1990, fully 45 percent of all households are expected to be headed by a man or woman without a spouse. Twenty-nine percent will be headed by a woman and 16 percent by a man.

Today's men are facing questions Dad never told them about—like: Who's going to do the laundry and clean the bathtub? In this post-feminist era, a fellow certainly dares not ask his girlfriend for help. After all, real women don't do bathtubs.

"By mandate," explains Adam Stagliano, vice president of Yankelovich, Skelley & White, "men have had to get involved with traditional women's roles." The territorial lines are less clearly drawn, he says, and in general there is "an attitudinal acceptance" of men's role in the home. "If women can go to work and buy insurance," he says, "men should buy groceries and raise children. We see this blurring of roles as a given. And we don't see any turnaround."

Judith Langer, whose New York-based market research firm (Judith Langer Associates) has been studying single men for more than three years, is no longer surprised when she hears men comparing brands of cleanser and floor polish. Langer, whose clients include AT&T, Bristol-Myers, Gillette, PepsiCo and other major corporations, claims: "Male householders accept their new domestic role as a fact of life. It is acceptably masculine to care about one's house."

Langer dubs the men who have most willingly adopted the new roles the "Settlers." "These men," she has observed, "seriously think about and talk about the best way to clean walls, remove spots, make dinner, and find a detergent." One 31-year-old man in

EXHIBIT 5 Persons Living Alone by Age and Sex: 1981*

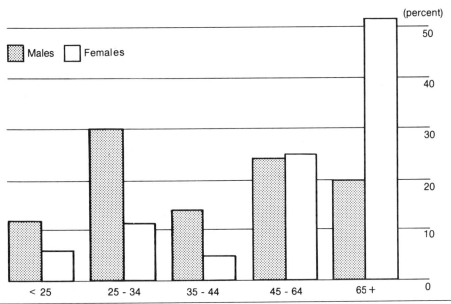

*The age profile of men who live alone is strikingly different from that of women who live alone. Over half of women who head single-person households are elderly, while half of men who head such households are younger than 45.

Langer's group admitted, "I don't want people to think I'm a slob. I want to make a good impression. I don't want to have to apologize for dirty dishes or dirty floors."

Although many household chores are as great a bore for men as for women—like the bathroom and the laundry—men are taking an interest in some duties, especially cooking. What began as necessity has become an accepted responsibility and even a pleasure, and one they won't easily give up, argues Langer. One New York interviewee said that if he married again, he would insist on preparing at least 60 percent of all meals.

"Single men," remarks Langer, "are determined to play a household role even if they marry or live with a woman." A Nashville man summed up his reasons this way: "I think most people benefit from taking care of themselves. You should take care of your own house, in a figurative as well as literal way."

Changing Marriages

The phenomenon is by no means limited to single men. Marrieds too are participating more in the home. Goldberg at Benton & Bowles is convincing on the subject. "Men are really actively involved in the home in doing the things which were traditionally women's work. It's more than just a 'helping out.' It's a real, participatory, ongoing assuming of a lot of tasks." The figures support her. The agency's 1980 study, *Men's Changing Roles in the Family of the 1980s,* found that men cooked meals, did laundry, shopped, and helped with the children in what Goldberg considers significant numbers. Some 33 percent cooked an entire meal at least once in a two-week period, 80 percent did the main grocery shopping for the family, and 29 percent did laundry.

A Cunningham & Walsh study in 1980 reported similar findings. A survey of 1,000 households showed that one third of men cooked a full meal at least once a week, and that some 80 percent did grocery shopping. Two out of five did dishes, and half said they vacuumed most of, if not all of, the time. Though husbands this active were a minority of the sample, Cunningham & Walsh concluded: "They will grow into a significant segment demanding the attention of marketers."

Joseph H. Pleck, program director of the Wellesley College Center for Research on Women, and author of *The Myth of Masculinity,* considers these findings consistent with his own observations. "Husbands are definitely spending more time in housework and child care," he says unequivocally. Exactly how much time they are spending, however, is elusive.

John Robinson of the University of Michigan, in his study *Changes in Americans' Use of Time,* charted the change in men's household participation over a 10-year period—1965 to 1975. He measured a 7 percent increase in men's activity in the home, a figure which Pleck considers high. "When you're working with large-scale national samples," he explains, "7 percent is a tremendous change." During those years, the number of women in the work force increased 21 percent.

Kathryn Walker, a Cornell University researcher, examined two-parent households with children in a study measuring change in time use in the home between 1968 and 1976. Husbands' time spent in housework increased a surprising 30 percent.

Although it is still impossible to quantify what men are doing in the home, the gap between the amount of time spent by women and by men in home duties is closing. Robinson's study also spotted a marked decline in women's time at household tasks. He noticed a drop of 15 to 20 percent between 1965 and 1975, "the largest change ever in the history of time-use studies," says Pleck. The decrease, which occurred equally among women in the labor force and stay-at-home housewives, indicates to Pleck that there may be a movement toward a balancing out of household time.

Especially meaningful, claims Lydia O'Donnell, research associate at Wellesley's Center for Research on Women, is that men have developed an "ethic of involvement," a belief that sharing jobs at home is the "right" thing to do, a phenomenon Cunningham & Walsh noticed too. Although the Benton & Bowles study still showed a high degree of conflict and ambivalence among men when it comes to sharing housework, some 88 percent of their sample believed a man should help with housework if his wife works outside the home. Although O'Donnell still finds men choosing to do the more pleasurable tasks—leaving diapers and ovens to their wives—she feels their contributions come from "the right intentions."

Good for Men

When men share housework, there may be reason to believe that it is good for them. William R. Beer, professor of sociology at Brooklyn College and author of *Househusbands: Men and Housework in American Families,* studied 56 married men from a broad range of age, income, educational, and ethnic groups who perform between 30 and 70 percent of all the housework. He reported that his subjects by and large felt positive results from participation in the home, not the least of which was an improved marital relationship.

Moreover, by participating in housework, "work outside the home often tends to become less central to a man's self-definition," Beer explains. "A man comes to define himself more in terms of home relationships and nonoccupational work than exclusively in terms of his occupation." Goldberg has also observed this side effect. Often when a man is very involved at home, she has noticed, "the work ethic isn't the be-all and end-all."

Many sociologists view men's sharing of household chores as a shedding of old values, not the least of which is the "controlled, macho" image. Peter Stein, associate professor of sociology at William Paterson College and author of *Single Life,* believes that a growing number of men—most of them in the under-40 age group—are indeed less constricted by tradition. "Men are freer to express what they feel and want," he says. "It's less an 'oddball' position." He points to an ever-increasing number of male support organizations, men's newsletters, "talk" sessions, books, and parenting groups like New York's The Fatherhood Project, created to help men experience fathering more fully.

Although the shift seems clear, some people (including wives of men who don't lift a finger) still do not accept that a change has occurred. Judith Langer has found that most companies are slow to respond to this and other demographic changes. Often clients decline to include men in their samples, even when Langer strongly recommends it. Although 40 percent of supermarket shoppers today are male (of whom 28 percent are shopping alone), marketers often claim that the male market is too small to be significant or that women still make the buying decisions. What is worse, advertisers tend to talk down to men, Langer says, presenting them as "know-nothings" or "tag-alongs." "The image of the 'boob' hits a sore spot and makes it harder for men to adjust to their new roles," she warns. Men are resentful of the topsy-turvey "bachelor pad" image and irritated when guests joke about their "domestic talents."

Procter & Gamble, the nation's heaviest advertiser, maker of Zest, Ivory, Scope, Pampers, Bounce, Crest, and Attend, believes that few of its brands really "have application to the men's market," according to Ed Plowden, an executive in their media department. "Most of the purchasing decisions," he emphasizes, "are made by women." However,

Procter & Gamble put a toe in the water recently with its male oriented Charmin commercial, designed to appeal to a "dual audience" of prime-time female and male viewers. But the water is still too cold for the company to jump into male-only media.

At *Sports Illustrated,* it has taken four years —and blood, sweat, and tears—to convince advertisers that men not only buy cars, beer, and stereo equipment, but coffee, cereal, and soup.

Jackie Fowler, recently named apparel advertising manager at *Sports Illustrated,* was one of the staunchest advocates of selling packaged goods in a men's magazine. "At first," she recalls, "people didn't care to listen. The woman was still the primary market and men were only secondary." But Fowler points to "startling, compelling reasons" why she kept up the fight. "You look at the research and you see that men are doing much more in a domestic way."

The persistence paid off. Some advertisers have started to believe and these days you will find Maxwell House coffee, Sure deodorant, Nutri-grain cereal, Campbell's soup, and Planter's peanuts on the pages of the magazine. "In the past," Fowler explains, "Planter's may have advertised once at football season, once at baseball season. Now they're in all year."

Why did it take so long? "Addressing the male market just didn't set right with people," she believes. "These companies had been successful and you don't knock success." But times are tougher. Today, in a battle for market share, they are being forced to look in new directions. "But it kind of hurts," she quips. "Traditions die hard."

Competition for market share and a need to segment markets may indeed be prompting skeptics to take a second look at men. "Segmenting is the key to marketing right now," says Adrienne Darling of Young and Rubicam. "We need to be able to target groups individually." The firm's recent study of American singles was designed to help clients zero in on singles as a group, and Darling expects that Young and Rubicam will focus on men alone in the near future, since they consider the single male "a totally new consumer."

Meet the New Man

What are the characteristics of these "new" men? Can they be segmented easily by age, income, education, and lifestyle? What products are they likely to buy? Alice Goldberg calls men who strongly believe in and actively do housework the "Progressives." These men are the most active and committed to equality between the sexes and tend to be younger (50 percent are under 35), well educated (40 percent are college graduates), and moderately affluent (40 percent make more than $20,000).

But it may not be that easy to segment this growing market. "Class certainly isn't a factor," argues O'Donnell at Wellesley, who has found that blue-collar men take over many household tasks traditionally assigned to women when their wives are working, especially when there are children present. She considers job pressures more relevant. "Where husbands have very high-powered jobs, the men do less. They're out all the time."

Although Langer has found that younger, educated men are most inclined to embrace egalitarian values, she too has noticed blue-collar husbands participating.

Adam Stagliano thinks that household involvement is prominent among younger, upscale groups, but emphasizes that his firm has observed roles changing across the board in many age, income, educational, and ethnic groups.

Both Stein and Langer correlate a husband's domestic role with the duration of the marriage. "In the 20-year relationships," notes Langer, "there is more stress and strain

with men who have not adjusted to new values about household sharing." And even among people in their 30s, Peter Stein observes, there are often serious problems with a man's household role if the couple has been married a long time. Often second marriages—even between older individuals—begin with more contemporary thinking.

Few industry people talk about this movement without mentioning the baby boomers, those born in the 1950s and 1960s. Women of this generation are determined to participate fully in the work force, and today two out of three baby-boom women work. Their values—incubated in the liberal 1960s—are inescapably present at many levels of American life, and the home is no exception. Some say the "ethic of involvement" started with this generation.

Whether a working wife is a factor in men's activity in the home is debatable, however. Though it is a logical correlation, Pleck for one says his research shows no data confirming the connection. A 1979 study conducted by the Newspaper Advertising Bureau indicates that nonworking and working wives alike report that their husbands do virtually the same amount of work around the home.

On the other hand, both Benton & Bowles and Cunningham & Walsh research contradict this position. Both say that men with working wives are far more likely to contribute to household chores. The discrepancy baffles industry experts, though one possibility is that the change in values brought about by working women has seeped into society and affected the families of working and nonworking wives alike.

If working wives are a factor, more sweeping changes may be in store by the end of the decade. In 1980, 56 percent of working women worked only part time or for less than 50 weeks a year. But as more women choose year-round, full-time, and continuous employment, men may play an even greater role at home. Moreover, many people, including

Alice Goldberg, believe that the men now doing more in the home constitute "thought leaders" and that their new values will permeate society more widely in the future.

Men as Consumers

Some studies have been done to date on what kind of consumers men themselves are and may become. For marketers, segmenting men is difficult because the new male is still "selecting" the household jobs he does. As the Cunningham & Walsh study showed, "A man may act differently in different areas. The involved cook may be a lazy housekeeper; the fastidious duster might survive on fast food."

One thing seems clear, however. Men who do housework value convenience and speed in their selection of products and services, even if this means additional cost. They are likely to use outside services (laundromats, dry cleaners) because, as Langer points out, they have no guilt about not doing it all themselves, as women sometimes do. Like women, they prefer what's fast and easy, but they are willing to pay more for it than women are.

In the kitchen, these men like machinery and gadgetry as much as in the workshop, delighting in clever juicers, microwaves, food processors, and innovative items, like one man's favorite, the "quick release ice-cube tray." They are as efficiency oriented at home as in the office. One New York man in Langer's study selected his supermarket because it had a computerized checkout.

Clearly single men are having an impact on the marketplace in new ways, but the Benton & Bowles study also showed conclusively that married men are having a powerful impact too. Benton & Bowles's survey revealed that 63 percent of married men were involved in the purchase of cereal, for example, 40 percent helped choose toothpaste, and 44 percent the household soap—every one a traditional female purchase.

"The high level of influence on brands," Goldberg concludes, "undoubtedly comes about through the growing involvement of men in tasks like meal preparation, child care, laundry, and other home activities. Men's role as consumers has major ramifications for product development, advertising, media selection, and research."

She expects to see a steady increase in the attention marketers pay to men, with more advertising directed to them, and more awareness of their new image. "We are already seeing men in nontraditional roles, and we are likely to see more of it—more men showing emotion, caring, concern, tenderness, softness—traditionally female attitudes. The wave of the future," she predicts, "will be toward a wide-ranging adoption of these emerging values and greater acceptance of the flexibility of men's and women's family roles."

In the future, single men will continue to seek a stable and comfortable home environment. Working wives and a new acceptance of men's role at home will spur more husbands to experimentation, with one ironic twist. Many men may have to face the dilemma which now confronts women: that of how to balance home interests with career demands. As William Beer at Brooklyn College suggests, household responsibility will change the way they view themselves as men.

For advertisers, the shift will demand new thinking. Langer insists advertisers should not portray men as klutzes but as capable homemakers. Fowler at *Sports Illustrated* adds that men will need direction, and that advertisers who take a service oriented approach will prosper.

Goldberg believes the revolution is imminent. "It's not such an oddity to see men in nonconventional roles," she feels. "In five years or so we'll hardly be paying any attention it will be so commonplace. You won't even think twice about a man baking a cake."

Who Owns Your Brains?
Kevin McManus

Top executives from archrivals Hertz and Avis usually don't have cozy chats. But on February 4, 1982, Joseph Vittoria, president of Hertz Europe, huddled with Avis CEO J. Patrick Barrett in the TWA Ambassador Lounge at JFK Airport. Subject: the presidency of Avis. Vittoria was en route to his Hertz post in London, and Barrett wanted to sound him out before the plane took off.

Within weeks of the clandestine meeting, Vittoria agreed to leave the driver's seat of Hertz Europe and try harder at Avis, where he is now president. He is also a defendant in a notable—and increasingly common—kind of lawsuit. His ex-employer claims he had no right to change hats and head up the competition. This, despite the facts that Vittoria had been removed from the presidency of Hertz and that the company's parent, RCA, was known to be ready to sell it.

The question raised in the Vittoria case is rock-bottom fundamental: What right does an executive have to use what he or she learned in one job at a new job at another company? It's not an easy question, and there are no simple answers. This is not a question of secret formulas or of patents or of working prototypes, but of matters that are far more subtle. As the rising number of lawsuits testifies, employers feel increasingly forced to throw legal obstacles in the path of employees aiming to work for the opposition or set up their own competing shops. After all, competitors do lure away key people just for what they know of a given process or marketing plan. Venture capitalists are always waiting in the wings, ready to back a good idea. And executives are increasingly immune to sentiments like loyalty. Peter Rabinowitz, president of the Boston recruiting firm P.A.R. Associates, puts it very well: "Job candidates are saying to me, 'I wasn't too crazy about going to IBM or TI and all the bureaucracy that went with

it, but I knew it would be a good ticket.' " Is that stealing? Or just being smart? Increasingly, the courts are having to decide.

At high-tech companies especially, you can easily run afoul of these questions when you jump ship. Computer industry leader IBM, for example, is breaking new legal ground as it stalks ex-employees it thinks are walking away with the company jewels. "IBM is sort of the trend setter in litigation," notes Steven Brill, publisher of *American Lawyer.* "And computer technology is just one area. We see law firms developing specialties in different kinds of trade-secret litigation that just didn't exist before."

One law firm, Brown & Bain of Palo Alto, which does indeed specialize in trade-secret litigation and numbers IBM among its clients, is swamped. "Business is very good," says Philip Berelson, a partner in the firm. "We have more requests for our services than we can really handle out of this office at this time."

It's hard to predict under what circumstances an employer will actually sue a defector, let alone who will win in court. But the particulars of some recent cases offer guidelines. One is obvious: the better your chances of doing real damage, the heavier the lawyers come down. The Hertz complaint against Avis, for example, contains a number of charges, including breach of contract and pirating of employees. But the most serious one alleges that Vittoria conspired with Avis to steal key information from Hertz before he resigned.

Here are some recent suits involving giant companies.

■ In California, IBM is suing a group of former employees who recently started a company called Cybernex Corp. to make thin-film, read/write recording heads. These tiny, intricate devices go into disk drives for the kind of computer that supports the work of, say, airline reservation clerks. IBM alleges that the employees, who helped develop such devices at IBM, misappropriated its technology when they set up Cybernex.

■ In Houston, Texas Instruments has charged a group of former employees with using TI trade secrets in setting up a personal computer company. The upstart, Compaq Computer Corp., has filed a countersuit claiming that TI is trying to drive it out of business.

■ In Boston last year, Merrill Lynch sued Jeffrey Wilgus, a broker who had resigned to join Bache in the same city. There the issue was Wilgus' solicitation of his Merrill Lynch clients after he departed—an act forbidden by his contract.

In the IBM case, Cybernex is accused of misappropriating virtually the entire IBM process for making recording heads. According to the complaint:

> It is inconceivable that an organization could have duplicated IBM's thin-film head production process without access to IBM trade secrets and confidential information, especially in the short period the founder defendants and Cybernex devoted to this effort.

Cybernex set up its San Jose, California, production facility in less than eight months and began shipping prototypes of its product less than a year after that. IBM claims to have spent 14 years—"an arduous process of trial and error"—perfecting its process.

Responds Cybernex cofounder and President William Klein:

> About 10 companies make this product. We have independently developed what we think is a much better process than most of them have, and many of the people involved never worked for IBM.

Figuring out who is right has led the judge into such a technical maze that he has enlisted the aid of a patent attorney. Significantly, he has not issued an injunction to put Cybernex out of business—as IBM requested—while he studies the charges.

Whatever the outcome, IBM's action by itself sends all its employees a message: hands off company ideas. It frequently does so, even in its annual report:

> Our investments in research and development and the innovative ideas of our employees are IBM's stake in the future. We will do everything appropriate to safeguard those assets.

A 1982 case left no doubt that that warning has teeth. IBM sued three executives for starting a company while still employed by IBM. The sole purpose of the firm, Bridge Technology, apparently was to sell design information about unannounced IBM products in the personal computer field. Within weeks of filing a 23-page amended complaint, IBM won an injunction that prevented the employees from designing or making any computer products at issue in the case for three years. The court also ordered the employees—two senior engineers and a marketing executive—to give back to IBM portions of the salaries they were paid before being fired in September 1982.

The Texas Instruments dispute with Compaq Computer, while similar to IBM's case against Cybernex, illustrates the use of a countersuit as part of a defense. A group of TI employees, led by Joseph Canion, broke away from the company in late 1981 and early 1982. They formed Compaq to produce and market a personal computer. Entrepreneurial daring be damned, TI alleges that Compaq employees stole trade secrets and infringed a number of TI patents in making its computer. Compaq calls all of those patents invalid, unenforceable, or not infringed upon. Furthermore, reads its countersuit, "None of the former TI employees were requested to divulge or use any confidential information of TI in their work for Compaq."

Trade secrets are also at issue in the Hertz-Avis case, but the court documents are rich with accusations of the sort of wrongdoing, mainly on the part of Joseph Vittoria, that any discontented, sought-after, top-level executive could blunder into.

The dispute seems to center on Vittoria's actions between early February and mid-April of last year. In January 1982 Vittoria had been sent to London as president of Hertz Europe. He says he was unhappy about the assignment because it was a demotion (his previous title was vice chairman) and because he did not want to move his family to London. He began to commute, returning to New York every other weekend. He also put out feelers for another job.

On Thursday, February 4, as he was at home packing for a flight back to London, he got a call from an executive recruiter doing a search for Avis. "Did you know Avis was looking for a president?" he was asked. No, Vittoria said, but he was interested. The recruiter arranged for him to meet later that day with Avis CEO J. Patrick Barrett. The spot they agreed on was the TWA Ambassador Lounge at Kennedy Airport, not far from Avis' Long Island headquarters.

At that meeting Barrett confirmed that Avis was looking for a president, but nothing was settled. Two weeks later they met again, at the Sky Club in Manhattan, but again no commitment was made. In mid-March Vittoria learned from another recruiter in London that the Avis presidency had been given to Howard Miller, and Vittoria was asked if he was interested in the job of executive vice president. He said he was.

On his next visit home, on March 25, Barrett asked Vittoria to dinner on Long Island and there offered him the executive vice presidency of Avis. Vittoria accepted. "It was a verbal agreement," he explains. "I knew it was good, but I didn't want to resign from Hertz until I had the offer in writing. I went back to London and conducted business as usual."

On his next visit home, at Easter, Vittoria received Avis' offer in writing. The following Monday, April 12, he tendered his resignation to Hertz President Bennett Bidwell. "Ben asked me to give him a couple of days," he recalls. "Two days later, on April 14, I went back to him and he offered me full pay to go home and not work for a year and a half, until my contract ran out." (In an affidavit, Bidwell said he offered Vittoria full pay to act as a consultant to Hertz, and that Vittoria told Bidwell that he "probably would not" end up working for a competitor.) Vittoria went to Avis instead, and was later followed by about 15 Hertz executives. He was eventually named president.

Hertz is arguing that the Kennedy Airport meeting and others were not for the purpose Vittoria has described. In a court memorandum Hertz claims that, for a period early in 1982, Vittoria was essentially "serving two masters." Specifically, he is alleged to have taken an "eight-day tour through Europe gathering Hertz' documents and trade secrets."

The accusation is "nonsensical," says Vittoria, who believes the suit is simply a tactic to impede Avis. "Hertz is a very aggressive company," he says. "They've owned 'No. 1' for years and they guard that jealously. When someone comes along with any kind of a real threat, they unleash all the weapons in their arsenal."

State Supreme Court Judge Leonard Cohen, who is hearing the case, conceded in an interview that he is not sure whether there *are* trade secrets in the car rental business. In any event, last January he ordered Avis to return to Hertz a number of documents that were supposedly taken to Avis by departing Hertz employees. However, and more important, he refused to grant Hertz' request that Vittoria and other former Hertz employees be forbidden to keep working for Avis. The case could still come to trial.

An interesting facet of the dispute is Vittoria's contract with Hertz, which specifically forbade him to compete with his employer for two years after he left the company—a "restrictive covenant." Vittoria contends that Hertz itself broke that contract first, by demoting him. Judge Cohen appears to agree since he has not stopped Vittoria from working for Avis.

By and large, noncompete contracts such as Vittoria's are being looked at skeptically by judges. "In effect, they attempt to deprive people of making a living after leaving jobs," says Joseph Auerbach, a practicing attorney and a professor at the Harvard Business School, "and the courts are not going to do that—with a signed contract or without one."

Jeffrey Wilgus, the broker sued by Merrill Lynch, signed a noncompete agreement when he joined Merrill in 1975. In January 1981 he quit the firm's Boston office and went to work for Bache in the same city. Upon arriving at his new job, Wilgus wrote letters to about 70 of his biggest customers at Merrill, asking them to stay with him at Bache. Merrill sued, citing the noncompete agreement he had signed, and asked $900,000 in damages (thrice Wilgus' gross production in 1981). Wilgus ended up paying Merrill Lynch $12,500, but he was allowed to keep all his clients.

But the Vittoria and Wilgus cases should not be taken as evidence that courts will shoot down all noncompete agreements. Rather, says Stanley Lieberstein (author of *Who Owns What Is in Your Head?*), the courts regard unfavorably those agreements that are too sweeping with respect to either time or geographic area. More enforceable, he says, are noncompete clauses that call for the employee not to work for competitors for, say, only six months after leaving. And the more effective contracts, Lieberstein says, are likely to limit the geographic area in which the employee may not compete.

Disclosure agreements designed to protect company secrets are taken much more seriously by the courts. An employee need not even sign a contract containing a disclosure agreement for it to be enforceable. That is, each employee is said to have a "fiduciary duty" to his employer not to disclose trade secrets.

Aware of the difficulties in enforcing overly comprehensive contracts, companies are increasingly resorting to agreements that specify what areas of a person's job are confidential. Lieberstein, who writes such contracts for client companies, advises that disclosure clauses should simply warn employees that some or all of the information they're working on may be proprietary. And he suggests that employees be obligated to check with the company before disclosing any such proprietary information while employed or afterward.

An especially fuzzy area in most contracts has to do with notes, memos, reports, and other documents that an employee may take with him to augment what's in his head. Harvard's Auerbach offers the hypothetical example of a physicist employed by a firm that designs nuclear power plants. The physicist has been doing research in the firm's laboratory for 10 years. He has signed an agreement that the firm owns all of the inventions he produces while employed there. Furthermore, he has agreed to leave behind his notebooks if he should quit the job.

"His notebooks are the critical thing," says Auerbach.

In them he has 10 years of experiments listed—and the ones that failed are just as important as the ones that succeeded, so he doesn't repeat the failures. Now he accepts an offer from another firm . . . and . . . off he goes with his notebooks. Does the company have a right to get them back? Can it prevent someone else from seeing his notebooks? The answer is yes.

In the real world, of course, employees often take with them documents they have amassed on the job—from Rolodexes to rejected proposals—and companies have had only limited success in getting them back.

When Jeffrey Wilgus left Merrill Lynch, for example, he was later able to contact his customers because he had taken with him copies of records listing their previous transactions, current holdings, addresses, and phone numbers. The photocopying, he said, was done at Bache before Wilgus quit Merrill Lynch.

"It wasn't a matter of giving the pages to Bache," Wilgus explains.

They were *my* pages. What I did was basically what all brokers did and still do when they quit. When you leave a brokerage house, the house you're going to has everything set up so that the day you walk in the door you're in business.

"That may be standard practice, but it's certainly not accepted by all firms—especially ours," says a Merrill Lynch lawyer.

What we object to is when a broker copies his records well in advance and notifies his customers beforehand that he is leaving. He solicits them to join him at the new brokerage house and puts all the information on transfer forms—before he quits. And then he piously pretends that it was not done that way and that he never really solicited the customers but that the customers loved him and wanted to join him.

Wilgus likely was spared a harsher penalty than his $12,500 fine because he sent out his letters of solicitation only after giving notice to Merrill.

The issue of missing documents came into play in George Ball's celebrated defection last July from E. F. Hutton to Prudential-Bache. Shortly after Ball left, E. F. Hutton Chairman Robert Fomon sent a letter to Prudential Chairman Robert Beck. In the letter Fomon pointed out that Ball's copy of the June production run of account executives had not been seen since Ball left. Also, Fomon wrote, one of the employees who had followed Ball to Pru-Bache had apparently taken with him a copy of Hutton's institutional mailing list.

According to Fomon, Ball himself answered the letter, saying simply that neither item had been taken. "George said he did not have any proprietary information," Fomon recalls, and adds, "I don't believe that." In spite of this, Fomon contends he never considered suing Ball—who, strange to tell, had not signed a contract—or any other Hutton employee who went to Bache. "What do you get by suing someone?" Fomon asks. "I've got better things to do with my time than be involved in lawsuits."

Such forbearance should not be counted on, however. And if you should be sued after leaving an outfit, your defense in court could cost a fortune even if you win. Consider the case of Philippe Villers, founder of Automatix Inc., a robotics company based in Billerica, Massachusetts.

In April 1979, while a senior vice president at Computervision, a computer-aided design company he helped found, Villers approached the executive committee with an idea for a robotics venture. His 80-page proposal was accompanied by a two-hour verbal presentation. His idea was rejected.

"The consensus was that the company was stretched too thin to undertake such a venture at that time," Villers recalls. "It was growing at the rate of about 100 percent per year, and in my view that's the very time you should plant seeds." Villers decided to plant the seed himself. He left Computervision in September and founded Automatix shortly thereafter.

Nine months later Computervision sued him for, among other things, theft of robotics secrets and loss of a corporate opportunity. The case dragged on for two years before a jury found Villers innocent. His defense hung on his presentation of the plan to the executive committee and Computervision's rejection of the idea. The jury ruled that once turned down, the idea did, indeed, belong to Villers.

Yet the victory was costly. "I recovered my court costs," he says, "but that's a joke because they amounted to about $4,000. I spent close to $150,000 on attorneys' fees."

If you do leave your company to join the opposition or start your own firm, here are some tips to keep in mind that improve your chances of escaping a lawsuit.

■ Beware of disclosing "trade secrets." In your new job you will inevitably draw on your career experience, of course. But, at least in the eyes of your ex-employer, you will inevitably exploit what may be considered "proprietary information." According to Lieberstein, there is a difference between using such information and formally disclosing it—a difference the courts weigh heavily. What, precisely, constitutes a trade secret? "A trade secret," says Lieberstein, "is something that is not generally known in the trade or industry to which it applies, and which provides its owner with a competitive advantage." However, he cautions: "In a given case a trade secret is what a judge says it is."

■ Make it clear, before you leave, that you have no intention of using trade secrets to the company's disadvantage. It's a good idea to have your new employer write your old one, formally stating that you will not be asked to divulge trade secrets.

■ To be safe, take no printed material with you when you leave, other than purely personal papers. (That includes photocopies.) If you are ever sued, the fact that you did take documents could tip the scales in the plaintiff's favor in a close case. Even your Rolodex remains company property if it contains names and addresses of customers, says Joseph Auerbach.

■ If you are establishing your own company, try to remain friendly with your ex-employer. If sensitive customer lists are involved, you may be able to agree to leave certain accounts alone for a specific period—and thereby forestall a suit.

Where's the right and where's the wrong in all this? Some of the suits may be sheer harassment to discourage employees from going over to competitors. But before throwing your sympathy to the little individual over the big, soulless corporation, keep in mind that there are two sides to the issue. A highly successful entrepreneur talks about what he calls "the dark side of venture capital"—where employees working on a product leave the company, get financial backing, and beat their old employer to the marketplace with its own idea. Such incidents are not rare. And the line between aggressive entrepreneurship and outright stealing is becoming increasingly blurred.

—————————— *Company Readings* ——————————

Using Yesterday to Sell Tomorrow
Daniel Burstein

The offices of Lord, Geller, Federico, Einstein on Madison Ave. outwardly look like any agency that handles classy clients in the ranks of *The New Yorker,* Steinway pianos, and Hennessy cognac. But step inside VP-creative Bob Tore's office, and you feel you have stumbled accidentally into Charlie Chaplin's dressing room. Derbies, canes, and mustaches seem to be flying frenetically about the room; photographs, storyboards, and sketches featuring Chaplin's *Little Tramp* character dot the walls and floor.

Lord, Geller *is* in fact Charlie Chaplin's dressing room. It is the shop where the idea was first conceived two years ago to use a Chaplin character to introduce the new International Business Machines Corp.'s Personal Computer and where new Chaplinesque ideas have continued to flourish through three TV commercials (a fourth will be aired shortly) and some two dozen print ads for the IBM PC.

The IBM PC appeared on the market in late 1981, amid skepticism as to whether IBM could effectively compete in the domain of the wizards and wunderkinds whose maverick entrepreneurialism had built Apple, Radio Shack, and the rest of what was then the personal computer industry. Since that time, however, IBM has gobbled up market share so voraciously that its engineering specifications are now on the verge of providing the microcomputing world with its first-ever standardization. With close to 10 percent of all personal computers now bearing IBM's name and an estimated 20,000 being shipped monthly, IBM is expected to overtake the six-year-old Apple II in the near future as the most popular of personal computers. At last December's Comdex, the biggest annual computer trade show, the new products that received the most enthusiasm were hardware and software specifically designed to be compatible with IBM.

Computer trade analysts generally judge the IBM PC to be an excellent product. They give high marks as well to the extended capability model known as the XT, which was unveiled in March, and to the growing library of software produced under IBM's name. But what IBM did that was unprecedented was to bring its vast prestige to a field that had previously asked consumers to spend several thousand dollars on machines manufactured by companies with brief or nonexistent track records.

Although priced initially at almost $4,000—considerably higher than the orchard of Apples and Tandy Corp.'s (Radio Shack) TRS-80s—the IBM offered something special. In the words of *Fortune:* "Big Blue's logo on the front inspires customer confidence that no other company can match." William F. Ablondi, an industry analyst with Future Computing of Richardson, Texas, goes a step further: "What IBM has done is add credibility to the whole personal computing industry."

The IBM PC arrived just at the point when such machines were beginning to win wide acceptance. In 1980, less than half a million units of all types of personal computers were shipped: 1982 saw that figure climb to 3.5 million. Mr. Ablondi predicts that 1983 will see last year's figure double to 7 million. It appears that IBM entered the market at just the point when experienced number crunchers, tinkerers, and electronics enthusiasts had given way to the ordinary mortal as the chief personality in computer buying's demography.

In developing an advertising strategy, IBM knew it wanted to break down widespread public fear of the computer, demonstrate the essential simplicity of its operation, and popularize its many applications. IBM strategies wanted to reach out to the millions still unaware of what computers could do for them or how cost efficient they might be. But IBM also wanted to create a unique identity for its PC that would distinguish it both from other IBM products and from the plethora of other personal computers. And that's where Charlie Chaplin fit in.

"Charlie Chaplin's Little Tramp character is lovable to all kinds of people at all ages," says Tom Mabley, senior VP-creative director of Lord, Geller. "He's vulnerable, but he's clever. He has incredible problems, but he always finds a solution. He's an individual. . . . He's Everyman."

Mr. Mabley, 49, arrived at Lord, Geller from J. Walter Thompson Co. in January, 1981. (Lord, Geller is a JWT Group subsidiary.) IBM's personal computer was then top secret, but Lord, Geller—already responsible for IBM's corporate-image advertising—had been asked to design a campaign for it.

"I couldn't talk to anyone about it, and I couldn't find much to read about it," says Mr. Mabley. "I closed my door for a month and read every computer magazine I could find. I was trying to figure out how to tell the history of the computer in a 30- or 60-second spot." Soon Bob Tore arrived from Foote, Cone & Belding and was teamed with Mr. Mabley on "IBM's big secret."

Neither Mr. Tore nor Mr. Mabley remembers exactly how the Chaplin idea first came up, but both are certain that when it did, they knew it was perfect. Mr. Tore's recollection is visual:

We were talking about the problems of big computers and their unfriendliness. We had the idea of showing the history of the computer shrinking—a big white box in a white, sterile room that would get smaller and smaller. We wanted to have a person reacting to it, and with all that white background, we obviously needed a character in a black suit to stand out. That became Charlie.

Mr. Mabley recalls it this way:

We wanted a figure to represent us, but with Dick Cavett doing Apple and Bill Cosby doing Texas Instruments, the field was getting a little cluttered. We knew we wanted a single, friendly person who would represent Everyman. But we didn't really see a need for on-camera dialog. That pointed to mime.

We talked about Marcel Marceau for about 10 minutes, and considered a few other ideas. We quickly developed criteria for who this mime should be and ended up with the conclusion that it could only be Charlie Chaplin. After that, Bob Tore and I were on a roll, and everything began to work.

For the next few months, Mr. Mabley, Mr. Tore, and others at Lord, Geller honed the Chaplin concept into a storyboard for a 60-second TV spot they called "House."

Eventually, it would be this ad—remarkably unchanged when it aired in September 1981, from its first storyboard—that would kick off the campaign and establish Charlie Chaplin as IBM's silent spokesman.

The ad opens with a big white block designed to abstract the concept of a mysterious, foreboding machine. A voice-over describes the way early computers were like closed doors for most people. Then the block sprouts a door that the Chaplin character tries to penetrate, only to have it slam in his face. Suddenly, the block begins to shrink, ultimately becoming box size.

Chaplin breaks open the box, takes out the personal computer, scans a "how-to" book, and within seconds is sitting in his white designer chair at a white table ready to work at his white computer, which will make him more productive and more creative.

At the narrator's mention of creativity, Chaplin sniffs a red rose in a white vase on the table; the rose, intended, according to Mabley, to symbolize "creativity and individuality," became a second constant along with Chaplin himself. It was to be used as an ending point in future commercials and in print ads, as well. On TV, the voiceover concludes with a message about IBM personal computers that strikes a happy ending right out of a Chaplin film.

Convinced they had a winning concept, Messrs. Tore and Mabley nevertheless proceeded to develop other options for IBM, as did other teams at Lord, Geller. All the concepts stressed the notion of friendliness in the face of high technology. One team, for example, suggested using the Muppets. But in their hearts, the Lord, Geller people wanted to go with Charlie Chaplin for the TV campaign, while pursuing other themes for the projected print campaign.

The day came for unveiling the "House" spot to IBM, along with the other ideas. Mr. Mabley recalls IBM's executives as being "intrigued, pleased with the originality and the clarity of the message." The green light was given to proceed with filming House for broadcast spots that would follow the first announcement of the PC.

Two problems immediately presented themselves: finding an actor who did a good Charlie Chaplin routine and securing the rights from the Chaplin family to use the likeness of the *Little Tramp* character.

"The law is fuzzy about what becomes of the rights to an individual's likeness after his death, but IBM, being who they are, wanted to be absolutely sure," says Mr. Mabley. An agreement was reached with Bubbles, the Chaplin family organization that licenses use of characters he portrayed, for exclusive rights to use the *Little Tramp* image in the advertising of office and data processing equipment.

Scouting for an actor required auditioning more than 30 Chaplin imitators in both New York and Los Angeles. Videotapes were requested from agents and talent casters; exciting prospects were auditioned in person. Lord, Geller knew they had their man when they saw Billy Scudder, a 43-year-old Chaplin actor who has been doing the Little Tramp at parties, restaurants, and amusement parks—including southern California's famous Knott's Berry Farm—since 1971. "He doesn't look anything like Chaplin without makeup—he looks more like James Dean," says Mr. Mabley of the actor. "But when he puts on his costume and begins moving and gesturing, he is absolutely Charlie Chaplin. He's an excellent actor, dancer, and mime."

Mr. Scudder's numerous faces and tricks are crucial to the element of delight in the ads—the visual subtleties that make the viewer want to see it again as soon as it ends. "I just react the way Charlie would to things," says Mr. Scudder. "The essence of the character is in the vulnerability. IBM is such a big, powerful company. By using Charlie, the element of fear disappears."

As Lord, Geller swung into action, the creative team expanded to include writer Arlene Jaffe and producer Bob Dein. Jeff Lovinger was called in to direct "House," owing to his reputation for sensitivity to the nuances of lighting and design—key factors in a commercial done entirely on a white background. David Horowitz wrote the music after immersing himself in original scores written by Chaplin and other music of the Chaplin era. The camera itself was cranked down to 15 frames per second instead of 24 to suggest the stilted motion of Chaplin's early "flicks."

As soon as the commercial appeared, it was a success. "I think its secret was that the whole gestalt of the campaign was so friendly, human, and communicative," says Ms. Jaffe, whose contributions on the IBM campaign have just earned her the title of vice president at Lord, Geller, according to Mr. Mabley.

Individual ads from the campaign won a slew of 1981 awards, including an Andy and International Broadcasting Award and awards from the Art Directors Club and International Film and TV Festival of New York. And "Bakery" was selected as one of *Advertising Age's* best commercials of 1982.

T. David McGovern, advertising manager for the personal computer at IBM's system products division in Boca Raton, Florida, is unabashedly enthusiastic about the Chaplin campaign. "Over the years IBM developed an image that was very professional but sometimes cold," he says.

> This is part of the efforts to soften the image and make it more human. We are sensitive to not doing anything to hurt the overall image of the company. We couldn't do anything as wild as Federal Express, for example. But we wanted something bold and memorable. That's why Chaplin works so well for us—there's a classic flavor to it.

The "House" commercial got rave notices in the trade and generated extremely positive audience responses. But by December 1981, Lord, Geller and IBM reached a critical juncture. They had to decide whether future IBM PC commercials would continue to be based on the Chaplin character and whether to replace the non-Chaplin print ads with print versions of the character created for broadcast.

"We heard Lord, Geller's presentation of an all-Chaplin campaign versus a diversified campaign," Mr. McGovern recalls.

> When I saw what they planned to do, I knew the all-Chaplin campaign was the way to go. It was so bold and distinct. Among all the key people in the decision process, there was no doubt about it.

Throughout 1982, a series of print ads featuring the Chaplin character unfolded in newspapers, newsweeklies, business magazines, science publications, and the computer trade press. They retained the originality and cleverness of the TV campaign, but were able to provide more detailed information about the computer and its applications.

Headlines and key images were funny and reinforced the Chaplin theme: "Keeping Up with Modern Times," said one, borrowing its title from Chaplin's most famous movie while depicting him roller skating through a trail of paperwork. Those two-page spreads explained the essential uses of a personal computer in layman's terms while incorporating a technical specifications box for the more computer literate.

Two-third-page ads also were designed to explain specific software applications in the same vein: "How to Balance the Books," with Chaplin balancing 12 books behind his back supported by his left foot along with an explanation of accounting software; "How to Move a Paragraph," with Chaplin leaning against a wall of copy and pushing it aside for word processing.

As 1982 went on, the TV spots continued. "House" gave way to "Bakery" and then "Hats," featuring clever routines in which Charlie solved the production problems of his bakery and the accounting problems of his home business with the help of an IBM PC. The effort to preserve the Chaplinesque theatrical magic continued: The camera was still undercranked, and the colors were muted to suggest the past. In "Hats"—where the personal computer saves the day for Charlie's Hat of the Month Club business in his home—IBM used a Los Angeles house that Chaplin himself had employed as a set decades earlier. The fourth commercial, featuring an office setting, also is filled with Chaplin references and may prove to be the funniest yet.

The cost of all this creativity, talent, and attention to detail is high. Neither Lord, Geller nor IBM will discuss specific figures for production costs of the TV spots, but IBM's Mr. McGovern emphasizes that in representing not just the PC but all of IBM, "We can't afford to do anything less than first class. The production values must be very high, we can't skimp on sets or extras, we can't shoot on videotape."

Mr. McGovern is still more closemouthed when it comes to the subject of just how much the whole campaign is costing IBM, but analysts say it is certainly the most expensive computer advertising campaign ever undertaken on TV. *Business Week* recently estimated that IBM will spend $13 million on TV ads for the PC in 1983, a figure Mr. McGovern neither confirms nor denies.

Despite the high costs of TV advertising, most manufacturers of personal computers believe it is the preferred medium for establishing product awareness in a field jammed with competing products. By some estimates, as much as 75 percent of personal computer advertising dollars are spent on TV, for an industrywide total that reaches upward of $200 million for all companies now using TV time.

Although TV has been used heavily for the Chaplin campaign, it has been part of a strategy that balances broadcast and print. "There is nothing that can match the drama and excitement of television," says John Steinle, the IBM account supervisor at Lord, Geller. "But our print campaign adds the educating, the detail, the how-to that we can't provide in a broadcast medium." Concurs IBM's Mr. McGovern:

> Television can't be used in isolation. It is the most powerful awareness-building tool there is, but we need print to explain the uses and applications of the product that can't be condensed into 30 or 60 seconds.

The Chaplin theme has even been extended beyond both print and broadcast to an innovative collateral campaign designed by the agency Muir Cornelius Moore, which includes among other things a Charlie Chaplin theatri-

cal trunk replete with hats, canes, and life-size Chaplin cutouts for use in dealerships where the PC is sold.

One question logically posed by all the emphasis on the Chaplin theme, when compared with the futurism and stress on high technology in the campaigns of some other manufacturers, is whether IBM might be going too far away from its image as the technology leader, especially considering that the movie *Modern Times* (1935) was something of a slam against impersonal technology. Future Computing's Mr. Alblondi doesn't think so. "They may have succeeded just as well in certain corporate circles with a straight-laced motif," he says.

> But personal computers should not be sold purely as technical tools. They are personal tools, and the Chaplin motif has given IBM a very effective personality for the general population.

Even for reaching the sophisticated computer literate, Lord, Geller believes the Chaplin campaign is still the right stuff. Print ads recently have been designed for computer trade publications to recruit software writers, and they too share the Chaplin imprint. Moreover, manufacturers of software and peripherals have begun to pick up on the Chaplin motif and make allusions to it in their ads. A program designed for use on the IBM PC called IRMA, for example, shows a young woman being handed the Chaplin rose and proceeds to explain what happens when Charlie and Irma get together.

While Lord, Geller is flattered by ads by other agencies that build on the Chaplin concept, there have been problems. The manufacturer of a portable computer published ads showing its customer blithely bounding downstairs, computer in hand, as Charlie Chaplin, uncomfortably lugging his nonportable IBM, trailed far behind. The message was obvious, but the ad didn't last long after the Chaplin family pointed out that exclusive use of the character for computer ads was in the hands of IBM.

The simple beauty of the Chaplin campaign notwithstanding, IBM's marketing strategy for the personal computer is considerably more complex. Observes Robert Ozankan of Manhattan's ComputerLand store, part of the chain that is the PC's biggest distributor: "People don't walk in and say I saw Charlie Chaplin and now I want to buy an IBM, no matter how good the ads are."

For IBM, the selling of the PC represented its first major venture outside the confines of its own selling organization. Recognizing that one of the biggest problems with other personal computers was a lack of support (dealer advice and assistance to the customer in learning to use the machine and servicing it after purchase), IBM knew it had to have a support system worthy of its reputation. It chose distributors carefully (ComputerLand, Sears, Macy's Compushop, etc.), and it has put some emphasis on a co-op advertising program that includes dealer listings and toll-free phone numbers.

New products are expected soon from IBM in both hardware and software relating to the personal computer. The price of the PC—

slashed by 15 percent in March—also is expected to continue falling as demand increases. For the growing number of customers who find themselves bewildered by the complex process of matching the right computer with the right software and peripherals, the idea of an integrated family of IBM personal computer products is an appealing one.

You can expect Charlie Chaplin to be around for the foreseeable future, then, as IBM seeks to bring the frontier of technology to our fingertips. "Chaplin says a lot about our product at a glance now," says Mr. McGovern. "We save words and time by maintaining that image. There's a lot of value in that as the product family grows."

At Lord, Geller itself, the Chaplin campaign is a source of intense pride. "So often in this business the greatest ideas are never produced," says Bob Tore.

They end up on the floor or in your personal book. But this is a case where a great idea was produced.

You can't imagine how good it feels when I'm sitting around at home with my wife and kids and Charlie comes on TV.

Embattled Kodak Enters the Electronic Age
Thomas Moore

Inside the neat, period-piece brick buildings of Eastman Kodak's headquarters and manufacturing plants, spread over 3,000 acres in Rochester, New York, the slow, deliberate master of the photographic industry is whipping itself into a war frenzy. Kodak is arming to take on the combined might of the Japanese, Silicon Valley, IBM, Xerox, Du Pont, and a host of other forces that are threatening its profitability. The $10.8-billion-a-year company has finally decided, after 10 years of watching and waiting, to enter the burgeoning electronics and video businesses in a big way. By its annual meeting next spring, if not sooner, Kodak will announce the formation of an electronics division that it has been quietly and carefully nurturing for the past seven years.

The company is counting on products from the new division to lift its sagging fortunes. Competition from upstart film companies has sent its profit margins into an extended decline and it faces an even greater long-run challenge from new technologies. Kodak's plan is to hang onto its markets (and profits) by combining electronics with its optics and film know-how. Down the road, the company plans to use electronics to enter new markets as well, as it already has so successfully with its high-speed copier machines. Kodak's Ektaprint machines have made serious inroads on Xerox's dominance in the top end of the copier business. Three out of every four dollars spent on new research projects next year will go into electronics, and the company is adding 10 electrical engineers for each new chemical engineer it hires. The operative word among its executives, after a token protestation about not abandoning photography, is *imaging.* Says research director Leo J. Thomas, 46, "We have a mandate to integrate electronics into the fiber of this company over the next five years."

Talk like that signals a veritable reformation at Kodak. The company viewed its cofounder, George Eastman, as deserving a place in the pantheon of the gods and elevated the chemical film technology he pioneered into a religion. Long after Eastman's suicide in 1932, Kodak clung to his cautious ways. If George didn't do it, his successors didn't either. The company passed up an invention called xerography, leaving the new technology to a then-tiny Rochester company called Haloid. Kodak let Polaroid have the instant-camera business to itself for nearly 30 years. Wags joked that Eastman's ghost presided at board meetings.

The conservative strategy paid off despite the missed opportunities, at least through the 1960s. Kodak continually extended the frontier of film chemistry. Its technological edge, coupled with economies of scale from huge production runs, gave Kodak a virtual monopoly in photographic film and paper and made it one of the most profitable blue chip companies in the world.

That approach plainly isn't working anymore. Over the last decade Kodak's profit margins have declined from 15.7 percent of sales in 1972 to 10.7 percent last year. But it wasn't until the first quarter of this year, when the company announced a shuddering 73 percent decline in earnings, that outsiders realized how seriously Kodak's situation had deteriorated. Most of the decline was due to the onetime costs of a special, early retirement program, much of which will be made up in payroll savings during the remainder of the year. But operating earnings alone fell 24 percent, a decline that continued in the second quarter and may persist for the entire year. The company's stock, once a superstar, has been the worst performer among the Dow Jones industrials lately. In a raging bull market, Kodak has fallen 27 percent from a high of $98 last October. The stock is at less than half its price of a decade ago.

Kodak's inner peace was rudely disrupted in the 1970s when Japanese film manufacturers broke its lock on the lucrative color film and paper markets, which historically accounted for 75 percent of the company's profits. The Japanese, led by Fuji Photo Film, improved their production efficiencies and quality to the point where most consumers couldn't see much difference. At the same time, Kodak did little to improve its own productivity in the face of rising costs. When the Japanese began to compete aggressively in price, they not only cut into Kodak's market share but also squeezed its margins. Some analysts estimate that its share of the U.S. photographic paper business plummeted from 92 percent to 50 percent during the 1970s. The Japanese gains in the film market came mostly at the expense of secondary companies like GAF, but Kodak is now feeling the pressure as well.

The advent of video cameras and recorders unsettled Kodak's markets even more. Despite being priced much higher than Kodak's latter-day Brownies, video products have been selling faster and faster ever since Sony introduced its Betamax machine in 1975. Home video is now a $3 billion business in the United States—already a fifth the size of the photographic industry. For the first five months of this year, according to Mark Obenzinger, a security analyst with Lehman Brothers Kuhn Loeb, shipments of video recorders are up 104 percent and video cameras 22 percent. The recorders and cameras don't use any film, of course, and Kodak doesn't make videotape. Photo specialty stores are adding video equipment to their wares to make up for lost sales in conventional photography.

Former Kodak Chairman Walter Fallon, the tough technocrat who was heralded at his retirement party this June as the man who made the elephant dance, attributes the company's poor performance to adverse economic conditions rather than false steps. In particular, he bemoans the markets outside the United States, where Kodak makes 40 percent of its sales and has achieved much of its growth in recent decades.

Kodak's new chairman, Colby Chandler, 58, an amiable "down easter" who drives a pickup truck to work, says profits will recover with the world economy. Wall Street is less sanguine. The first-quarter earnings decline, following a 6 percent drop in 1982, sent previously upbeat analysts scurrying to their calculators to revise their estimates for the year. Kodak earned $1.16 billion, or $7.12 per share, in 1982. Some analysts now figure it will be lucky to make $5 per share this year—little more than half what they were predicting 12 months ago.

Kodak's record over the last decade suggests that recovery alone won't be enough to restore prosperity. Of four major product lines launched under Fallon, only the high-speed copiers are paying off. The Ektaprint copiers, which receive top marks in quality and reliability, have become the company's fastest-growing product line. Kodak executives say the seven-year-old Ektaprint business, if spun off as a separate company, would make the *Fortune* 500.

The company wasn't so lucky with the Kodamatic instant camera, basically a Polaroid clone that came out just as instant cameras were losing popularity. Analysts doubt that the Kodamatic has made any money for the company. Kodak's president, Kay Whitmore, 51, says the camera's future will depend on whether a new feature that allows users to peel the photo from its bulky chemical backing boosts sales.

The Ektachem 400, a two-year-old blood analysis machine that uses dry chemical slides rather than liquid solutions, got off to a poor start because it performed only a limited number of tests and proved unreliable. The machine was supposed to preserve Kodak's faltering presence in the health care market. Sales of X-ray film, under pressure from competitors like Du Pont and from filmless scanners, have gone nowhere for three years. The company is hoping for better results with a new blood analyzer, the Ektachem 700. The machine performs 25 series of tests, half again as many as its predecessor can do. An operator can order up a test simply by touching a word on a video screen. The machine can be tied into computerized patient records and clinical data sources. Kodak foresees smaller versions of the machine for use in doctors' offices.

Kodak's disc camera, launched with much hoopla last year as a replacement for the phenomenally successful pocket Instamatic, has also proved disappointing. The company shipped eight million disc cameras last year, a first-year record for a new camera format. But more than a million of those cameras were sitting on dealer shelves after Christmas. Hot-selling 35-mm point-and-shoot cameras are now priced as low as most disc models, and pictures from the tiny disc negatives are grainier than buyers expected. The graininess has cut down picture taking by photo enthusiasts who bought the disc as a secondary snapshot camera. Says Sean Callahan, editor of *American Photographer,* "The disc has charming cosmetics, but after four or five rolls the quality of the pictures outweighs the convenience."

The disc has sold poorly in Europe and Japan, the two largest markets outside the United

States and ones that are more accustomed to 35-mm quality. "To say the disc has not met company projections abroad," says one industry source, "would be inaccurate. It's getting murdered."

Kodak denies that sales in those two markets, where its regular cartridge-loaded cameras have never sold well, are worse than anticipated. "The novelty factor has worn off in Europe," says J. Phillip Samper, 49, the new head of the photographic division. "Now we just have to get out there and move the cameras." The company's research shows 90 percent of disc users in the United States are satisfied with the camera, and that its high "yield rate"—93 percent of the pictures are printable as opposed to 75 percent for the pocket Instamatic—more than makes up for the graininess.

The disc's future is being decided this summer. Picture taking is heaviest in summer and dealers gauge the activity to determine their camera orders for the Christmas selling season. But the camera already seems unlikely to enjoy the 8- to 10-year life cycle of its popular predecessors—and may last only half as long. A shorter life would give Kodak less time to recover its development costs, which security analysts estimate at over $300 million.

The uneven performance of its new products and the most serious competition in its history have stirred the Kodak elephant into action—even into uncharacteristic flashes of anger. Walter Fallon is said to have pounded the table when he learned that Fuji had snatched the sponsorship of the 1984 Olympic games while his negotiators dithered. If somewhat belatedly, the company has launched a major program to coordinate planning around the world, increase productivity, and reduce costs. Two years ago the company reshuffled some of its foreign production. Many of Kodak's international divisions were manufacturing identical products for their regions, often at higher costs than at the main factory in Rochester. Kodak brought the high-cost for-

eign manufacturing home—just in time for part of the $55 million in productivity gains to be offset by the strong dollar, which boosted the cost of the products when exported.

This year Kodak instituted a special early retirement program, announced it was postponing next year's pay raises for six months, and made its largest layoffs in a decade. Says Whitmore, "We are looking less at reducing a given percentage of people than whole functions."

Chandler, who made his mark by leading Kodak's assaults on Polaroid and Xerox, criticizes what he says was an ad hoc approach to product development and has ordered up the company's first corporatewide strategic plan. "We can no longer be all things to all people," he says. "Kodak is a little like the government in that it takes things on much easier than it can get rid of them."

Traditionally dominated by its technical side, Kodak has given its marketing departments a louder voice, if not the final say, in the company's direction. Kodak's two marketing stars, Samper and Wilbur Prezzano, 42, manager of worldwide marketing, have moved up to the second and third spots in the unofficial line of succession after Whitmore. Kodak has never allowed a marketer to run the company. Gerald Zornow, chairman from 1972 to 1976, got closer than any other, but still was number two to Fallon.

Kodak also has abandoned some of its fusty ways and finally adopted tactics that have long been standard procedure at other multinationals. It has created a marketing intelligence group, issued its first significant debt ($275 million of convertible debentures), purchased more than $1 billion in tax-benefit leases, and started hedging its foreign-currency risks in the futures market.

Most important, Kodak has finally decided it would rather switch than fight, and has joined the electronics revolution. Over the last decade the company made sure its research labs kept up to speed with fast-changing video technology. In fact, it developed a video system of its own in the early 1970s. "We had a hell of a good product," recalls Zornow. "We had both a video-movie and a still camera, and the quality of the image was excellent on a TV screen. We killed it off, though, when we found out what the costs were."

To get a window on the video business, Kodak also bought a small California company called Spin Physics in 1972 that specialized in magnetic recording heads for high-density data storage. But Kodak sat on its video know-how in the 1970s and decided to commit its resources to instant cameras and copiers instead.

The company has now changed its mind. Among other reasons, Kodak was mightily annoyed when Sony upstaged its announcement of the disc camera last year by unveiling a "revolutionary" video still camera called the Mavica and promising to have it on the market in the United States right about now. Kodak knew that current solid-state sensors could not capture anywhere near as much picture "information" as silver-emulsion film. Sony's best sensors last year contained about 280,000 picture elements, compared with the four million-plus needed to match the comparatively poor quality of the ordinary 110-size negative that is used in pocket Instamatics.

The video picture looked all right on a TV screen, but was fuzzy when printed. Given the high cost of the sensors, the camera itself would have to be priced over $1,000, making it too expensive, in Kodak's opinion, for a mass market. But the idea of taking pictures, showing them on a TV set, printing out hard copies, and then erasing the tape to take more, all without having to buy film and send it to a developer, caused quite a stir in the photographic world. The technical problems were lost on a public accustomed to the wonders of electronics.

Instead of ignoring Sony as in the past, Kodak decided to reveal its own electronic imaging capability—and zap Sony's Mavica. Last October at the Photokina trade fair in Cologne, West Germany, Kodak demonstrated a video display unit that allows disc film negatives to be shown in color on a television set. Thomas, the research director, made it a point to give a personal demonstration of the new device to his counterparts at Sony. The video display unit was conceptually inferior to what Sony had in mind: the disc film still had to be sent to a developer and could not be erased. But the demonstration revealed that Kodak had a solid-state sensor with 50 percent more pictorial capability than Sony's "state of the art" Mavica. "They were very impressed," says Thomas. Today Sony doesn't like to talk about the Mavica, except to say that Japanese newspapers are now experimenting with a black and white version. It has nothing to say about the color version anymore.

That Kodak exhibited its video display unit, which is still under development, was unprecedented for the company. Kodak usually doesn't hint at what it has in the laboratory until the product is ready to sell. Not only did the gesture demonstrate Kodak's strength in electronics, it also showed a new competitive zeal that the company will sorely need in the frenetic electronics business.

Kodak's experiences with electronics haven't all been so positive. It has run into a host of problems with Atex, a manufacturer of electronic publishing systems for newspapers and magazines that it bought in 1981—only its second major acquisition in over 50 years. A typical high-tech success story, Atex was started in 1972 by three entrepreneurs, literally working in a garage, and grew to become the leader in its field, doing $50 million of business a year when Kodak bought it. Since then, the three founding partners and eight vice presidents have departed. Kodak found itself stuck with a system of "dumb" terminals dependent on central computers when the industry was moving to "smart" terminals with computer capabilities built in. Atex is quickly losing its technological lead in the industry.

"The people at Kodak are hardworking but bureaucratic," says Al Edwards, a former Atex vice president who defected to Systems Integrators, Inc., Atex's top competitor, because he couldn't abide Kodak's poky pace. "They do not understand the competitive nature of computer technology. You sometimes have to react to the marketplace on a weekly basis. At Kodak, if you came up with an idea, it would be five years before you saw the product."

Edwards estimates Atex shipments will be down about $20 million this year and the company will lose money. Kodak maintains it is still the market leader and that sales will be about the same as the $85 million last year. "Sure, some people have left here and we've had some bad times," says Joseph Quickel, 62, Atex's third chief executive under Kodak. "But that's one of the hazards of the electronics business, and now we've successfully made the transition."

Spin Physics has fared better under Kodak's stewardship. It continues to be a leader in its field, and two of its products will be seminal to Kodak's electronics effort: a new high-density magnetic surface for both tape and computer discs, and a high-speed video system that can play back the action of fast-moving equipment in slow motion so engineers can analyze problems visually.

Spin Physics has been so successful in the magnetic recording business that Kodak, after holding the subsidiary at arm's length for a decade, has decided to embrace it as one of three building blocks of the new electronics program. The other two blocks: a solid-state research laboratory and a facility to design and produce integrated circuits.

One important question about Kodak's electronics effort is whether a big, stodgy company in gray, nonswinging Rochester can attract and hold the notoriously disloyal elec-

tronics cowboys who thrive best in Silicon Valley. Kodak has had no trouble recruiting electrical engineers. But finding managers with an electronics background has been tougher. James Lemke, a cofounder of Spin Physics who stayed with the company, was offered a top job at the new electronics division but turned it down because he didn't want to move from California to Rochester. Still on Kodak's payroll, Lemke is helping to set up the Center for Magnetic Recording Research at the University of California at San Diego. The center, supported by Kodak, IBM, and more than a score of other companies, is the country's first pooled research effort in magnetics.

Kodak has yet to name a director for the new division, and hasn't filled other important slots. "We clearly have to attract people into the company who don't exist here now," says President Whitmore. That in itself will be a major departure for Kodak; few if any of its senior executives ever worked for another corporation. Gerald Zornow, for one, doubts that outsiders can successfully adapt to the Kodak culture. "They tried some people from the outside before and it never worked out," he says. "Kodak is like an old family that grows up together, and it is tough for outsiders to fit in."

Venturing into the volatile electronics business obviously is a gamble for Kodak, but the company doesn't have much choice. A competitive electronic still camera is at least a decade away, and electronic imaging technology will probably never fully match the quality of silver-based film. Amateur and professional photography will always be a large business, though possibly a much diminished one. Video has already begun to undercut many of Kodak's consumer and commercial applications. TV news film, for instance, has been eliminated by the immediacy of videotape. To the extent people use the latest generation of small video cameras to shoot movies of the kiddies, still photography suffers.

The biggest question about Kodak is how well it can play in a different and tougher game. Increasingly, Kodak will be competing in a business where it is not the worldwide leader, where it does not have a technological edge, and where it does not have a significant cost advantage. And it will not have a unique strategy. The same competitors that have bedeviled Kodak in the photographic business are also going electronic. Fuji, the fastest comer in film, makes videotape. Canon, Minolta, Olympus, and Pentax—companies that

bested Kodak in still camera technology—already sell TV cameras.

All corporations must be alert to changes in their technologies and their markets. Its move into electronics, however tardy, indicates that Kodak has the flexibility to adapt to a new world. Considering the company's roots, that's not terribly surprising. The lesser known of its cofounders was a man named Henry A. Strong who decided to gamble that young George Eastman's dry photographic plates might lead to something. Strong made buggy whips.

Ma Bell's Kids Fight for Position
Brian O'Reilly

Imagine you're in the class of a business-school professor gone mad. "Ladies and gentlemen," he announces, a wicked gleam in his eyes. "For our next assignment, we're going to take apart what is, measured by assets, the world's largest corporation. Until now, this company has been a monopoly selling telephone service in the United States. We will divide it into eight huge parts and you"—he thrusts a finger toward the class—"you will be chief executive of one of these parts. You must convert your company from a full-fledged monopolist to part-monopolist, part-entrepreneur. You must fight off competitors. You must keep the phones ringing and keep almost three million shareholders happy. You will be playing by entirely new rules but"—he smiles slyly—"you won't know what all the rules are."

He pauses to let the assignment sink in, then adds: "Well, ladies and gentlemen, as the management consultants say, what are you going to do first thing Monday morning?"

As anyone who has been awake for the last year knows, the assignment is hardly academic. The breakup of American Telephone & Telegraph Co., barely six months away, has

set off a frantic scramble by AT&T executives who must, many for the first time in their lives, grapple with strategic planning, devise new ventures, restructure their organizations, reconstitute their corporate personalities, and come up with new names to match. Moans the chairman of a local Bell company: "It's like taking apart a 747 in midair and making sure it keeps flying."

Anyone who has been around Bell System executives recently hears a mysterious phrase repeated like an incantation: "One-one-eighty-four." It's not the number of some arcane Federal Communications Commission decision or the combination to the lock on somebody's footlocker, but the date when the world as Bell managers know it will come to an end. Next New Year's Day, AT&T is due to spin off its 22 wholly owned telephone companies, from New Jersey Bell to Pacific Telephone, which will get about three quarters of AT&T's $155 billion of year-end assets. The telcos, as they're called, will remain largely intact and retain their present names, but will be reorganized into seven regional holding companies. The regional companies' principal business will be providing local phone service—"selling dial tones," as telephone people say—but they may also extend their wings into entirely different, unregulated ventures. Their wingspread could be wide. On average each regional will start with roughly $17 billion in assets. Their territories will range from 2 to 14 states.

A smaller but still enormous AT&T will remain, made up of five parts with some $43 billion in assets. The reconfigured AT&T's largest part will be the long-distance phone service division, an expanded version of the current Long Lines. Other parts are Western Electric, a mammoth manufacturer that makes equipment for the telephone companies; Bell Labs, which serves the Bell System's research and development needs; American Bell, which markets equipment and communications services to business and residential users; and AT&T International, an overseas marketer of equipment and services. A stockholder who owns 10 shares of AT&T today will get 10 shares of the new AT&T and one share in each of the seven regionals.

The old AT&T existed in a state possibly best described in terms of Zen: it was its own supplier and its own market to a degree almost unique. That closed-loop existence having been plucked apart, the eight new entities are struggling to define their aspirations and relationships. The new AT&T does not simply serve the interests of its former children but also competes with them—and sometimes with itself. Having lost its sense of oneness, it's groping for an unambiguous mission of its own.

The upheaval began 17 months ago, when Charles L. Brown, AT&T's chairman, announced that the company had agreed to divest itself of the local telcos to end a seven-year-long antitrust suit brought by the Justice Department. Rulings by federal Judge Harold Greene during the trial had prompted concern at AT&T that the case was going badly. So as Brown says, "We seized the initiative. We now have our fate in our own hands."

As originally negotiated with the Justice Department, the plan would have given the local monopoly phone business to the seven regionals and reserved for AT&T the right to enter competitive businesses. The theory was that this would eliminate the danger of AT&T's using its monopoly position to gain advantages in competitive markets. But Judge Greene has been reviewing the terms under which the case was settled, and has ordered changes in the plan that have blurred the boundaries between businesses and created confusion. For example, he ordered that one competitive business, publishing and selling advertising for the Yellow Pages, would stay with the regionals rather than move to AT&T. A $3-billion-a-year business, the Yellow Pages can earn a rate of return considerably higher than that of the monopoly phone service; many state regulators now tap those profits to help defray the cost of local phone service, and Greene may have wanted them to retain that option. In hopes of stimulating competition, Greene also allowed the regionals to sell telephone equipment to homes and businesses, something reserved exclusively for AT&T in the original draft of the consent decree. These rulings have made the judge a powerful if unpredictable force in restructuring the industry.

To outsiders the Bell System often appears a monolith whose executives are stamped from identical molds (Bell-shaped heads, goes the cliché). But any notion that the breakup is producing a bunch of cloned companies that will respond to the competitive challenges they face with Rockette-like similarity is wildly wide of the mark. Although the seven regionals' assets, revenues, and customer bases will be roughly the same, their history, geography, leadership, growth rates, and political and regulatory environments have already begun to stamp them with unique personalities.

The clash of personalities comes through immediately as the regionals take their first tentative steps to define themselves. Jack A. MacAllister heads a 14-state Western region that spreads over 43 percent of the continental United States but holds a bare 4 percent of AT&T's shares. Come the breakup, MacAllister figures, his regional had better have an exciting image to attract investors. So his was the first company to come up with a name—US West. The omission of "Bell" from the name is no accident. "US West is not a telephone company," MacAllister declares. It might compete anywhere in any business, he says, and he has been crisscrossing the country trying to leave a good impression with investment analysts—to whom he hands out cowboy spurs.

By contrast, the only other regional to have adopted a name—NYNEX—is in the Northeast, which has 51 percent of AT&T's shares. NYNEX's boss, Delbert C. Staley, thinks his company needs no new image. "You can do a lot of advertising and hooplaish stuff, but it doesn't change the business," he shrugs. "You build on an image of steady performance and I don't have much to gain by trying to convey a big change in direction. I'm not sure I know what US West has in mind." Zane E. Barnes, who will head the Southwest region, jokes that US West sounds like an airline. Barnes plans to keep the Bell name because "it plays well in Peoria."

Though a divestiture is underway, mergers are taking place too. Most regions are being formed by the joining of two to five previously separate Bell companies, so the issue of who calls what shots at what level in the organization immediately arises.

Thomas E. Bolger, who will step down as executive vice president of AT&T to head the Mid-Atlantic region, plans to run his company with a firm hand at the top. "A problem at AT&T," he says, "was that all the parts didn't always pull together." The head of the Midwest regional, William L. Weiss, perceives Ma Bell's management failings quite differently. He thinks AT&T's marketing was too centralized, with the result that managers became "less creative and more dependent on the sig-

nal caller." So while Mid-Atlantic's business plan calls for a highly regimented marketing approach throughout the region, the Midwest will operate as a decentralized confederation of five companies. One of these companies, Michigan Bell, hired the Boston Consulting Group to help produce its marketing plan, while Booz Allen & Hamilton came up with one for the region as a whole.

Motivating former monopolists requires vast changes in the way executives are assessed and rewarded. At the typical telephone company, managers are judged more by the service they provide than by their contribution to the earnings. The Pacific region is reorganizing along lines of business whose performance can be judged by profits—one company to sell phone service, another to sell unregulated equipment, and so on. Salaries way down into lower management ranks will be tied to profitability.

The efforts to create a new culture will be put to the test when the companies start selling equipment. In the past, the telcos handled Western Electric equipment almost exclusively. They didn't sell it, but leased it to customers. Under the divestiture agreement, the regionals may not manufacture telephones, switchboards, and other "customer premises" equipment, but they can begin buying this equipment from suppliers and reselling it beginning next year. So far, only two regionals, Pacific and NYNEX, have officially declared they will sell equipment, but they all have indicated that they probably will. One reason for caution: Greene hasn't ruled on whether the regionals will be allowed to stamp the Bell logo on what they sell. AT&T wants to restrict their use of the famous bell-within-a-circle to the Yellow Pages and the local monopoly phone business (say, on repair trucks and in ads). The regionals want to use the logo as broadly as possible.

When they do come to market with equipment, the regionals will confront a new offspring of their former parent. AT&T's

American Bell subsidiary, with thousands of employees and stores coast to coast, has a jump on the regionals, having sold equipment to homes and businesses since last January. American Bell's appearance has created a profound change in the regionals' relationship with Western Electric. As things stand today, Western must sell its customer premises equipment through American Bell. So if the regionals want to buy Western equipment for resale, they must buy it from their competitor. H. Trevor Jones, who is expected to head the Pacific region's equipment-sales subsidiary, doesn't seem enamored of that idea. "I have no concern about Western's quality, but there are other good manufacturers out there," says Jones. "If I buy Western I get no price break and no product differentiation from American Bell. That doesn't suggest much of an advantage for me."

The regionals are now thinking about what kinds of equipment make sense to sell. The basic residential telephone is surprisingly unpopular with the people who have for so long operated under the name of the man who invented it. "It's a commodity business now," says Richard J. Santagati, head of marketing at NYNEX. "You can buy a telephone everywhere and we're not equipped to compete with that." NYNEX would consider retail outlets only to sell high-margin items like Speakerphones and burglary warning devices. Pacific wants to get into residential phone sales but doesn't want to invest in retail stores right away or send telephone men out to people's houses. Still operating under the ideal of universal service, regulators may force some companies to act as the source of last resort where telephones aren't available in stores. If that happens, the companies are inclined to send the phones by parcel post with instructions on how to hook them up.

Business equipment is another matter: the regionals seem confident they can make money on it, though their rationales differ. The Mid-Atlantic region will closely coordinate the

groups selling equipment and such business services as WATS. "You don't make a great deal selling someone else's equipment," says A. C. Tedesco, a marketing official there. "Equipment is an opener—a way to build a relationship with a customer and sell other services." At Pacific, by contrast, Trevor Jones, the man who is setting up the equipment-marketing subsidiary, has been told his future is tied directly to the profitability of equipment sales. "I'm well aware of the importance of a healthy phone network to the company," Jones says, "but it's not my job to push its use. I'm focused on meeting a customer's equipment needs."

Another important marketing issue remains in doubt: Should a regional selling equipment or other unregulated items be allowed to derive special benefit from its relationship to the monopoly phone operation? The companies know they risk successful antitrust prosecution if they use the regulated monopoly phone business to subsidize equipment sales and undercut competing vendors. But what about market information that the monopoly business has privileged access to? Should the regulated side of the business tell the unregulated side's sales department when a corporate customer's call volume goes up and he looks like a good prospect for an electronic switchboard? The companies are frank to say they would love to make that connection. Competitors are equally frank in their opposition.

The decree that giveth to the telcos also taketh away. To open phone service to greater competition, the divestiture agreement provided that the regions be carved into geographical sections now called LATAs (for local access and transport areas). Maine has 1 LATA, California 10. A regional will be forbidden to carry traffic between the LATAs in its territory; that business will be reserved for long-distance carriers, including AT&T, MCI, Sprint, and others. Today, Pacific Telephone handles the traffic between areas that will be designated LATAs in California; on January 1 it will carry none of that traffic.

The regionals worry about potential competition even within their LATAs. This could happen if, as seems likely, state regulators continue to adhere to the principle, enshrined in the Communications Act of 1934, that telephone service should be universally available regardless of how profitable a customer is to serve. Under this principle, regulators often require companies to subsidize service to high-cost areas with profits made elsewhere. For example, Pacific says, the California Public Utilities Commission set rates three times higher than costs in the heavily trafficked corridor between San Francisco and San Jose to help compensate for below-cost rates on service to out-of-the-way places. Rival carriers could siphon off business from Pacific by cutting prices in the corridor.

Among the regionals, the strategies being adopted to deal with this kind of threat are remarkably varied. The possibility of competition practically dominates Pacific's thinking these days. "The most important thing we can do for the next 10 years is protect the local network," says Donald E. Guinn, the region's boss. Alone among regionals, Pacific has asked the state regulators for an outright ban on competition inside the LATAs. NYNEX is worried about cable-TV operators trying to steal data traffic. So it's thinking about building and owning cable systems to close off that possibility.

Another threat to the regionals is called bypass. It may occur when a big telephone user decides the local company charges too much to ferry calls from his offices to a long-distance carrier and makes arrangements to bypass the local phone company entirely. A venture including Western Union and Merrill Lynch plans to bypass New York Telephone. It will run high-capacity fiber-optic cables connecting various Manhattan offices to satellite dishes on Staten Island, whence phone calls

and data will be beamed heavenward for long-distance transmission.

Long-distance carriers, eager to grab business, might build their own connections direct to big customers' offices. These carriers may most notably include the regionals' erstwhile colleagues at AT&T. Morris Tanenbaum, an executive vice president of AT&T who is due to head the long-distance operation next year, says his decision on whether to bypass the local phone companies will depend on how state regulators set local rates. "If the local companies are efficiently and appropriately priced," Tanenbaum says, "we would have little incentive to bypass." But he expects to be making direct connections with big long-distance customers if local rates are "substantially higher" than the price at which he can supply the service.

Because the regionals will handle calls only within their limited zones, AT&T's long-distance operation will acquire most telco employees and switching facilities now associated with long-haul traffic. This means the AT&T long-distance operation will more than double its assets to over $20 billion and triple employees to 120,000. The carrier's biggest challenge will be building an image among phone users who have many more choices about long-distance service than they used to. The task, as an AT&T magazine put it recently, is establishing an "invisible product in the minds of 66 million prospective customers." Though AT&T still carries 96 percent of all long-distance calls, its market share is being eroded by low-priced companies like MCI, which perpetuates a feisty image by offering, among other ploys, free phone calls on Mother's Day "in honor of Ma Bell."

Tanenbaum says he expects AT&T to be viewed as the nation's high-quality provider of long-distance service. "We have operator-handled calls," he says, distinguishing AT&T from other services in which the live voice is never heard. "You can get a human being to help you." Analysts believe AT&T will be able to maintain a price premium above its long-distance competitors. But Tanenbaum knows AT&T will have to drop prices on profitable, high-density routes where it is vulnerable to competition.

Not even the regionals have given up hope of stealing some long-distance business from AT&T. Though the divestiture plan prohibits them from owning long-distance equipment, they have asked Judge Greene to let them rig up existing facilities so that their own employees can call each other anywhere in their regions on an in-house network. Bolger of Mid-Atlantic breaks into a grin when asked if his network couldn't someday be converted to a commercial long-distance carrier stretching from New York City to Washington, D.C. He says, "I expect we'll have those restrictions lifted someday."

AT&T's long-distance operation has already begun experiments on repricing services to better match packages designed by the competition. For an additional monthly fee, for instance, callers can get half off on night calls or—for the garrulous—a low hourly rate. Additional innovation may lead to increasingly varied prices and services. "If there's a place where we haven't been nearly as effective in the past as we must be in the future," Tanenbaum told a meeting of top managers recently, "it is coming expeditiously to the determination of what the customer wants. This ball game will go to those who are there first with the right services."

What the customer wants is a question that for the regionals takes on meaning far beyond the boundaries of their monopoly phone business. They will be free, as a telephone man says, to pursue ventures as varied as "grazing sheep and making potato chips." By using the holding-company form, the regions hope to make it difficult for the regulators to grab the profits from the new businesses to subsidize local phone rates, as they did with the Yellow Pages. The limits of diversification are left to Judge Greene. The companies must convince

him that they will not be able to take advantage of their regulated business to squash competitors.

So far, they are being cautious. "New ventures are not the answer to a maiden's prayer," says Guinn of Pacific. Several regional executives doubt that new ventures will contribute as much as 20 percent to their earnings in 10 years. But all have set up systems to review new possibilities and some have looked at as many as 20.

Several ideas haven't gotten far. US West proposed using the phone lines to monitor oil production from remote wells but raised little interest from potential customers. One outstanding, if unappreciated, talent the companies have may get broader application: NYNEX considers itself so good a bill collector—less than 1 percent of its bills are unpaid—that it is thinking about performing similar services for others. But bill collecting may not be a transferable talent; phone companies are good at it partly because they can rip out your phone.

The new ventures that are starting to move are closely related to the regionals' existing businesses. US West is streamlining the Yellow Pages operations it will get with its local companies and has visions of expanding the business outside the region. The company is thinking about going after Illinois Bell, for instance, which lets an outside company, Reuben H. Donnelley Corp., publish and solicit ads for its Yellow Pages. The Midwest region, of which Illinois Bell will be a part, is considering the creation of highly specialized Yellow Pages that will appeal to narrow audiences. Illinois Bell already has an edition for tourists that goes into Chicago hotel rooms. NYNEX is thinking about using its Yellow Pages sales staff to solicit ads for cable-TV operators in the region. Taking a different approach, Southeast is looking at ways to wring more money out of its switching system. Modern electronic switches can perform many exotic services, such as forwarding a person's calls to his office after he has left home. The Southeast company notes that many small independent phone companies in its region don't have comparable facilities, and it may arrange to perform these functions for them.

One of the regionals' most dramatic new offerings will be cellular radio—a technology that will vastly increase the number of car telephones. The service is due to start in Chicago this fall and should prove popular. But no one knows how profitable it will be. The FCC has been giving the local telephone companies a franchise in each city in which they have applied. It is also giving a franchise to a competitor, usually a consortium of companies. Forming consortiums and getting regulatory approval takes time, so the telephone companies will usually be first into the market. Once the rivals come on board, however, the phone companies will face the threat of a price war.

Bell planners expect they will have to compete on cost, since most agree that neither side will have a technological advantage. "I tell my people they're going to be in the gasoline business," says Robert G. Pope, strategic planner for Southwestern Bell. "I don't want to hear anything but how they're going to bring down costs." Joseph H. Johnson, the marketing chief at Midwest, utters what sounds like a prayer for industrial statesmanship: "You have to hope that both players understand the game. If one hauls off and cuts the price he can do great damage to both parties."

Perhaps the most intriguing prospect of all is what might be called the home of the future. The Southeast regional has been experimenting with videotex, which among many other things, allows a person to use a home terminal to do his banking, order airline tick-

ets, and call up remote data bases for news or financial information. Southern Bell provided the transmission facilities for a trial in Coral Gables, Florida, last year; the Knight-Ridder newspaper chain supplied programming, and AT&T furnished the terminals. Southern Bell is now installing switching systems that make possible the transmission of phone calls and videotex data into the home simultaneously on a single line. Knight-Ridder and Southern Bell will begin a commercial videotex operation in Coral Gables in September and plan to expand into major Florida cities. Southeast won't say how many customers it needs to break even but predicts that it will have 5,000 in Florida by next year and $60 million in revenues there by 1987.

Is the Southeast's pursuit of videotex a better route to success than the Southwest's plan to stick to its knitting? Is US West's attempt to radically change its telephone company image wiser than NYNEX's emphasis on being a reliable purveyor of dial tones? Only time will tell. The upheaval underway won't end on New Year's Day but is the beginning of an evolution that will never go away.

AT&T's long war with the government was partly of its own making: its leaders thought they knew what was best for the customer and resisted, to the point of anticompetitiveness, rival efforts to develop new approaches. The antitrust settlement deliberately alters the nation's telephone system in a way that will force the phone companies to respond quickly to customers' needs or lose their business. The current strivings of AT&T and the regionals suggest that, contrary to fears that divestiture would destroy the world's greatest telecommunications system, a new, more competitive one may be emerging.

Case Studies

GMC Truck and Coach Division
Frederick D. Sturdivant

In late 1969, a two-part series of articles appeared in the *Washington Post* concerning one owner's mechanical problems with three new GMC-chassied school buses. Written by Colman McCarthy, a member of the editorial page staff, the articles opened the larger question of school bus safety.

The owner involved was John Donovan, an independent operator in the Washington area, whose drivers transported about 260 children every day to several Washington private schools for an annual fee of about $200 per student. Mr. Donovan claimed to have spent 225 hours trying to resolve what he called unsafe conditions with the buses, and the buses were not yet four months old. Mr. Donovan's problems had started on September 2, 1969, when he and two other drivers picked up the buses in High Point, North Carolina, and were forced to make at least 12 stops for repairs on the way back. Three days later, two of the three buses failed state safety inspections. It was then that Mr. Donovan began keeping a diary of the time spent repairing the buses or taking them to the dealer to be repaired. According to Mr. Donovan, the subsequent three months were the most "frustrating, nightmarish period in my life. Caring for the buses—to keep them safe for the kids who ride them—so dictates my life that nearly everything else is blocked out."[1]

A partial list of the malfunctioning or broken equipment included excessive oil consumption and leakage, gasoline leakage, tires which would not hold proper air pressure, loose exhaust hangers, broken motor mounts, burned clutches, and rattling transmissions. Mr. Donovan claimed to have talked with at least five other owners who had similar problems with the same GMC V-6 model bus.

In a summary portion of the first *Washington Post* article, Mr. Donovan was described as being "convinced that General Motors has not been adequately concerned about him or his buses. Nor does the U.S. government appear to be much concerned about the safety of schoolchildren."[2] The second article explained how Mr. Donovan had begun to get action. Assuming that "no major corporation like GMC would knowingly sell unsafe goods to the public," Mr. Donovan was "overwhelmed by not knowing which of the many GMC buttons he should press for relief."[3]

Mr. Donovan finally talked to a newsman who then made several inquiries. Within a day or so, Mr. Donovan received a telephone call from a high GMC official in Pontiac, Michigan, who said that two engineers were being flown in to make things right. That same evening, three local GMC representatives were in Mr. Donovan's apartment discussing his problems with him. Two days later, Kimball Firestone, grandson of the founder of the rubber company, offered to replace all 18 tires on Mr. Donovan's buses.

Virginia Knauer, a presidential assistant for consumer affairs, referred to Mr. Donovan's problems in a Philadelphia speech two weeks later. "If these problems exist on a national basis," she stated, "then there is no question that action should be taken on this matter immediately."[4] The second *Washington Post* article questioned whether other owners of GM

Frederick N. Sturdivant, *Corporate Social Challenge*, rev. ed., © 1981 Richard D. Irwin, Homewood, Ill.

products "have to talk to a newsman before action is taken" and concluded with a plea for action regarding school bus safety to "avoid a tragedy before it happens."[5]

The effect of these articles on General Motors and the effectiveness of the corporation's response can best be determined with further background regarding school bus production and safety records.

Background on Production

The production of school bus chassis was a miniscule part of General Motors' total domestic business. GM would produce about 4.4 million cars in 1969, and the Truck and Coach Division would produce an additional 834,000 trucks of all types.[6] School bus chassis were only a slightly modified truck chassis, and the 4,000 or so that would become school buses were included in this total.[7]

The entire market for school buses was not large. About 25,000 to 30,000 new buses were purchased every year, usually by school boards who almost always purchased from the lowest bidder. This buying procedure tended to restrict engineering and safety research, as models carrying additional research and development costs would inevitably be higher priced relative to competition. The purchase of school buses was complicated by the fact that the bus bodies were built by independent manufacturers, and the buyer actually bought the bus from distributors for the body maker. Mechanical maintenance was performed by designated dealers for the chassis maker.

There were six major body makers in the United States: Superior (the largest, selling about 8,000 units per year), Wayne, Ward, Carpenter, Bluebird, and Thomas.[8] Most of these manufacturers had plants located in the Southern states. Mr. Donovan's buses, for example, were picked up at the Thomas factory

in North Carolina. These constructors would place their bodies on whatever chassis the customer specified. The most popular chassis was International Harvester, because it was the cheapest. General Motors' share of the chassis market fluctuated between 12 and 20 percent annually.

Background on Safety

The singling out of school buses as unsafe vehicles was puzzling to many industry observers, who knew that about 25 schoolchildren had been killed while passengers in school buses in 1969. Compared with an automobile deathrate of 2.4 per 100 million miles in 1968, the school bus rate was only 0.06 per 100 million miles, or 40 times safer.[9] If passenger miles were compared, the difference would be even more dramatic.

There were good reasons why school buses had compiled such an impressive safety record. They were large and very visible to other drivers. They generally operated at much slower speeds than other vehicles at other than peak accident times. They were rarely operated at night. What accidents there were usually were attributed to driver error. School bus drivers worked inconvenient hours at low pay. Occasional outbursts by unruly students made working conditions very unpleasant at times. As a result, it was hard to find experienced drivers, and housewives and juveniles were pressed into service. Some states were so desperate for drivers that a "special license" to operate a school bus was granted to persons who had not qualified for a regular driver's license![10]

The high incidence of driver error meant that no more than about a half dozen deaths per year could be attributed to mechanical malfunctions. Even minimal safety modifications would raise the cost of new school buses at least 5 percent.[11] Given an average year's production, the total cost of these improvements would be somewhere around $12 million, and these improvements would protect only those students riding *new* buses. If children's lives could be quantified in dollars and cents, then an average of one life could be saved by the total $12 million annual expenditure.[12]

Safety and Mr. Donovan's Specific Problems

It was apparent to GM officials that some of the problems reported by Mr. Donovan, such as the alleged 12 stops for repairs he made getting his buses home, were the result of inadequate dealer preparation. Other problems were annoyances that were probably manufacturing shortcomings. None were, in GM's view, safety related. More correctly stated, almost *any* vehicular deficiency could be seen in some context to be safety related. Wind noise, or thinly padded seats, for example, could be seen to contribute to driver fatigue and could therefore be a safety hazard. The safety-relatedness of problems outlined in the initial articles could be placed in perspective as follows.

1. The brake hose which was rubbing the wheel drag line may have been worn through by repeated rubbing, but would not have caused the brakes to fail, as alleged. The buses involved had dual brake systems and automatic warning lights to prevent the complete loss of stopping ability.

2. The oil and gas leaks (which were fixed by the dealer a month before the article appeared) were wasteful but not hazardous.

3. The tires which allegedly did not hold their full air pressure were warranted by Firestone, not GM.

4. Exhaust-pipe hangers and exhaust fittings in general had been a continuing problem for fleet operators of all types of equipment for decades, because of the extreme vibration to which very long exhaust pipes were subjected.[13] Customer maintenance personnel often rigged their own solutions to this problem. The danger of carbon monoxide poisoning through any exhaust failure was extremely remote.

5. Clutch wear had historically been extremely sensitive to driver technique. Repeated failure was almost always due to riding or slipping the clutch on a constant basis. Even a severely burned-out clutch would not be a safety problem, as it would only preclude the use of full power.

6. Transmission "rattle" was unpleasant, but bus chassis were built to be simple and rugged, not necessarily smooth and quiet.

Perhaps the most convincing argument regarding the safety-relatedness of these problems was that not one of them was known to have caused an accident or near accident.

Alternative Responses

One possible corporate response to the school bus safety issue would be to make no statement and take no special action whatsoever. This would be likely to reinforce the impression of cold uncaring management at GM that was the theme of the original articles. A second approach would be to take no special action but reply with the type of cost-benefit analysis developed earlier. This plan would open GM to the charge of placing a dollar value on innocent lives. Either of these approaches was especially troublesome, as the children of congressmen and diplomats were among those who rode in Mr. Donovan's buses.

The most aggressive approach would be to recall[14] a number of the 1969 buses in order to inspect and, if necessary, fix the kinds of problems alleged to be occurring. GM had recalled about 10,450 (1967 and 1968) school buses in mid-March in order to replace a rubber seal that would allow brake fluid to leak under unusual braking conditions. Although there had been no deaths or injuries from failure of this part, GM airmailed the parts to all their distributors with instructions that the parts be hand delivered to dealers.[15] About a month later, the same buses were recalled when more than one seal was found to be involved.[16] One drawback of recent recall campaigns was that they were expensive and had been treated in the press not as responsible actions of concerned manufacturers, but as admissions of wrongdoing by the manufacturers.

Action Taken

On December 22, the second and final article appeared in the *Washington Post.* That same day, Martin Caserio, General Motors vice president and general manager of the Truck and Coach Division, attended a joint press conference in Washington with Joseph Clark, head of the Defects Review Division of the Transportation Department's National Highway Safety Bureau. Mr. Clark said that the bureau had been investigating the complaints for 11 days and would continue the investigations until safety questions were resolved. Mr. Caserio announced that the company was sampling owners of 1969 model buses to determine how widespread the complaints were. He reiterated that GM did not feel that any of the existing defects were safety related, but would recall them for repair if necessary.

Mr. Caserio further disclosed that GM had been inspecting all school buses off its production line for a little more than a year and that dealers also inspected for defects. He then added that "We think they [the inspections] did work," but if there was correctional work to be done, "we'll step up to our responsibility." Virginia Knauer, President Nixon's Special Assistant for Consumer Affairs, told newsmen that she had been assured by GM

President Edward Cole of the company's intention to recall the buses if GM's investigation showed it to be advisable.[17]

In mid-February, the results of the GM survey of 850 of the 4,000 owners of 1969 GM-built chassis were available. Mr. Caserio disclosed in a letter to Virginia Knauer that some of the same problems reported earlier had become apparent, especially those regarding tail-pipe hangers, clutch durability, and front-brake hoses. He also announced that GM had placed a resident inspector at each plant where bus bodies were mounted on GM chassis.[18] Four days later, GM announced the recall of 4,269 (1968 and 1969) buses for installation of new brake-hose retaining springs in order to prevent the possibility of brake-line chafing which could result in the loss of hydraulic brake fluid. GM added that it had received no reports of accidents attributable to the problem and that the buses involved had dual-brake systems and automatic warning signals to prevent the complete loss of stopping ability if the brake line were worn through.[19]

On July 11, new GM board chairman James Roche talked about corporate communications with consumers.

> We've had warranty policies and believe we've had a pretty responsible record, but like so many other things a better job can always be done. Had we not been able to satisfy our customers reasonably well over the years, in a business such as ours where we depend for a large percentage of our business on repeat customers, we wouldn't be in the position that we're in today. But there are new standards by which people are evaluating products, and it is incumbent on us, if we're going to compete in this business, to meet those expectations.[20]

One month later, GM's third recall of school buses for brake repair since March 1969 was undertaken. More than 10,000 school buses built during 1969 and 1970 were involved. The problem involved the possible distortion of a brake master-cylinder reservoir cover by excessive tightening. The defect had been picked up in a manufacturing check, and no accidents or consumer complaints had been involved.[21]

That same month, the National Transportation Safety Board concluded that the construction of school bus bodies encouraged "shearing" in an accident. "Shearing" left knifelike "cookie-cutter" edges of sheet metal that contributed to death and injury. The board recommended that manufacturers set rivets closer together, through guidelines specified by the National Education Association.[22]

General Motors agreed to a further recall urged by the Department of Transportation in January 1971. About 9,600 (1967 through 1969) school buses were recalled to modify clutch parts. While disagreeing with a government conclusion that "all parts of the clutch control linkage" were subject to failure, GM said that "We feel it is better to call back the vehicles to modify them to eliminate even the most remote chance of having schoolchildren injured in an accident."[23]

In May, about 1,700 (1970 and 1971) V–6 engined school buses were recalled for inspection or replacement of throttle parts. No accidents had been reported due to failure of the part.[24] About 900 rear-engined school buses and 19,000 trucks built in 1960 through 1965 were recalled the following month for installation of a clutch and flywheel replacement kit. According to the National Highway Traffic Safety Administration, the recall was voluntary on the part of GM. Observers estimated the cost of the campaign at up to $4 million.[25]

On March 11, 1972, the *Saturday Review* published an expanded version of the John Donovan story written by the original *Washington Post* reporter.[26] The tone of the article, which was subsequently published as part of a book on corporate irresponsibility,[27] was captured in the following paragraph.

> Down the line of corporate responsibility, someone had those thoughts about cheapening the exhausts and mounts, someone seconded those thoughts, and someone else carried them out. Death and injury resulted, and surely GM regrets it. Yet millions of dollars of the $22 billion profit resulted also, and it is not likely that GM has regrets about that.[28]

The article also revealed how some information was gathered from GM officials in interview situations. The three GMC officials who met in Mr. Donovan's apartment, for example, were evidently not aware until the meeting was nearly concluded that Colman McCarthy, who was sitting in on the conversation, was a *Washington Post* reporter.[29] Mr. McCarthy, however, claimed to have clearly stated that he was a *Washington Post* writer immediately upon being introduced. Mrs. Donovan sat in another room during the conversation, making notes in shorthand.[30]

Two weeks after the *Saturday Review* article was published, a train hit a school bus near Nyack, New York, killing five children. Although neither mechanical failure nor a GM chassis was involved, the accident focused attention on school bus safety.

The eighth GM bus recall since early 1969 was announced the following month. The power-steering units of 2,500 (1963 through 1965) buses were to be checked for metal cracks.[31]

In the summer of 1972, emphasis on governmental regulation of bus safety standards intensified. The Department of Transportation required each state to form an agency for pupil transportation,[32] and issued new safety standards regarding windows and emergency exits to go into effect in September 1973.[33] Senator Jacob Javits (R., N.Y.)[34] and Representative Les Aspin (D., Wis.)[35] introduced bills authorizing the establishment of extended safety requirements.

In September, the National Transportation Safety Board urged that the structural strength of school bus bodies be increased. One analysis indicated that the specifications would require joints five times as strong as those currently used.[36] Earlier that month, General Motors had unveiled a "safety bus" in *Life* magazine. The bus featured a top emergency exit, special padded seats, and a dramatically downsloping hood to aid driver visibility at school bus stops.[37] The Wayne Corporation unveiled the "Lifeguard" bus in April 1973, claiming that it had spent four years and millions of dollars in its development. Special features included five rather than 33 separate outside panels, special seats, larger emergency windows, guardrails, and a larger windshield.[38]

By September 1974, the Wayne bus had been joined on the market by Ward's "Safety Bus," which featured three times the usual number of fastening rivets. Each sold for about 5 percent more than ordinary buses.[39] In addition, instrumented crash-test results involving multiple impacts on a Superior bus of standard construction were reported. The $300,000 program undertaken at Superior's expense by an independent testing agency revealed that, after multiple impacts, no penetration into the passenger area, no significant panel separation, and no "cookie-cutter" edges were apparent. Seats remained anchored, and no other specific dangers were identified.[40]

Note

In June 1976, the base price for a 60-passenger, Superior-bodied, GMC-chassied school bus meeting Ohio state safety standards was about $12,500. That price did not include heater and defroster, electric signs, or other options. On October 26, 1976, new federal safety standards regarding rupture-proof gasoline tanks, offset seating, emergency side-door provisions, and special padded seats were to go into effect. These standards would decrease the capacity of the same basic unit from 60 to 48 passengers and increase the price to about $15,500 per unit.

Notes

1. Colman McCarthy, "Three GMC School Buses and One Man's Ordeal," *The Washington Post*, December 15, 1969, p. A20.

2. Ibid.

3. Colman McCarthy, "Troubled School Bus Operator Begins to 'Get Action.' " *Washington Post*, December 22, 1969, p. A16.

4. Ibid.

5. Ibid.

6. *Ward's 1971 Automotive Yearbook* (Detroit: Ward's Communications, 1971), pp. 80–81, 84.

7. *The Wall Street Journal*, December 23, 1969, p. 8.

8. Estimate based on personal communication with knowledgeable industry sources.

9. *Iron Age*, 207, no. 18 (May 6, 1971), p. 23.

10. Floyd Miller, "Bus Crash," *Reader's Digest*, June 1973, p. 248.

11. *McCalls Magazine*, September 1974, pp. 50–51.

12. A 5 percent increase in cost would be about $400 per bus. For 30,000 buses per year, the total is $12 million. The average bus life is about six years so that only about one sixth of the children to be saved would be riding in and protected by new buses.

13. *Fleet Owner*, 65, no. 4 (April 1970), p. 187.

14. A recall involves the identification of a suspected problem common to a specific run of vehicles, and the contacting of the owners of those vehicles to offer inspection and/or repair of the suspected problem at company expense. Most recalls in 1969 were initiated by the manufacturers involved.

15. *The Wall Street Journal*, March 19, 1969, p. 5.

16. *The Wall Street Journal*, April 18, 1969, p. 14.

17. *The Wall Street Journal*, December 23, 1969, p. 8.

18. *The Wall Street Journal*, February 16, 1970, p. 8.

19. *The Wall Street Journal*, February 20, 1970, p. 5.

20. *Business Week*, July 11, 1970, pp. 72–73.

21. *The Wall Street Journal*, August 11, 1970, p. 7.

22. *The Wall Street Journal*, August 27, 1970, p. 2.

23. *The Wall Street Journal*, January 25, 1971, p. 6.

24. *The Wall Street Journal*, May 17, 1971, p. 4.

25. *The Wall Street Journal*, June 11, 1971, p. 10.

26. Colman McCarthy, "The Faulty School Buses," *Saturday Review*, March 11, 1972, pp. 50–56.

27. Robert L. Heilbroner, *In the Name of Profit: Profiles in Corporate Greed* (Garden City, N.Y.: Doubleday Publishing, 1972).

28. McCarthy, "Faulty School Buses," p. 51. The $22 billion profit figure cited is cumulative profit from 1947 to 1969. According to the 1969 General Motors *Annual Report,* total sales for the year were $24.3 billion and net income was $1.7 billion.

29. Ibid., p. 55.

30. Ibid., p. 54.

31. *The Wall Street Journal,* April 14, 1972, p. 16.

32. *The Wall Street Journal,* May 10, 1972, p. 12.

33. *Automotive Industries,* 146, no. 12 (June 15, 1972), p. 86.

34. *1972 Congressional Quarterly Almanac,* p. 928.

35. *Automotive Industries,* 147, no. 4 (August 15, 1972), p. 66.

36. *The Wall Street Journal,* September 25, 1972, p. 28.

37. *Life,* September 8, 1972, p. 63.

38. *Fleet Owner,* 68, no. 4 (April 1972), p. 50.

39. *McCalls Magazine,* September 1974, pp. 50–51.

40. *Automotive Industries,* 151, no. 6 (September 15, 1974), pp. 62–63.

Demarketing by Ontario Hydro
J. A. Barnhill

Ontario Hydro Corporation was established in 1903 for the purpose of providing "power at the lowest possible cost" to people of Ontario. In 1906, distribution of electric power commenced. Seventy years later, the corporation was producing and distributing power to 8.5 million people, directly and indirectly, through a network of 353 municipal utilities located throughout the 412,500-square-mile Province of Ontario.

Ontario Hydro is the second largest utility in North America, surpassed only by the Tennessee Valley Authority (TVA). In 1977, the corporation had a peak generating capacity of 21 million kilowatts, approximately one quarter of Canada's electrical capacity. This power supplies the nation's leading industrial province, which accounts for more than half of Canada's manufactured goods, 30 percent of its agricultural and paper products, and 80 percent of its steel and automobile production.

Ontario Hydro has three main roles:

1. Producer of power. In the decade 1966–1976, Ontario Hydro's peak capacity increased from 8.5 million kilowatts to 19.7 million kilowatts. The number of "ultimate customers" served by the corporation and its municipal utilities rose from 2,188,000 to 2,710,000.

2. Wholesaler of power. Ontario Hydro delivers power to 353 municipal utilities throughout the province. These utilities own and operate their distribution systems and are responsible for the retail distribution of power to most of the cities, towns, and villages of Ontario.

3. Retailer of power. Just over 100 large industrial customers and some 770,000 rural customers, in areas outside the jurisdictions of the municipal utilities, are supplied directly by Ontario Hydro. The primary retail distribution line exceeds 56,000 circuit miles.

The purposes, business operations, and regulation of the corporation are outlined in the Power Corporation Act of Ontario and various other statutes and pieces of legislation. While Ontario Hydro's board reports to the Minister of Energy, the corporation has been subjected to recent inquiries by the Ontario Legislature's Select Committee on Energy and a Royal Commission on Electric Power Plan-

This case was prepared by J. A. Barnhill of Carlton University, Ottawa, Canada. Reproduced by permission.

ning. Power rates (prices) are regulated by the Ontario Energy Board.

The Environment of Ontario Hydro

Politicogovernmental Influences

No single factor in the corporation's recent situation has impacted as much as politico-governmental actions, most notably the decision by the Ontario government to cut $6.5 billion from Ontario Hydro's $36 billion, 10-year capital expansion program, cut $50 million from its 1976 operating budget, and reduce the corporation's borrowings by $1.5 billion during the period 1976–1979. In the view of the corporation's president, the net effect will be:

> Ontario consumers between now [mid-1977] and 1985 must lower their expectations by 4 million kilowatts of generating capacity that simply won't be there. That's twice the power provided to Ontario by Niagara Falls.

Governmental constraints on Ontario Hydro have precipitated a major change in the direction and marketing orientation for the corporation. In the past, corporate planning and strategies started with demand forecasts. But, as the chairman of Ontario Hydro has stated,

> No longer can Hydro forecast demand 10 years out, plan the most economic system to supply it, go out and borrow whatever amount of money is necessary, and build it. Now, money, the availability of capital, is where we must begin.

What prompted the Ontario provincial government to constrain the spending for a basic public utility? The answer lies in the same reason the government curtailed expenses in other sensitive public services; for example, health care and education—fiscal restraint. The progressive conservative government declared it was going to have a balanced budget by 1981.

Socioeconomic Conditions

While the economy of Canada in general and Ontario more specifically, has manifested substandard performance, for example, an average inflation rate of more than 10 percent for 1974–1977 and unemployment increasing to the worst absolute levels since the Great Depression, the public's energy use and expectations continued to grow. In the decade 1966–1976, demand (and supply) for electric power grew at a rate of 7 percent compounded annually. The cutbacks of capital expansion necessitated a diminution of demand to 6 percent compounded annual growth through to 1985 if reliable service was to be probable, if not certain. But the evidence of societal support for diminished use of energy was not encouraging to Ontario Hydro management. A 1976 national opinion poll revealed that, as an issue of importance, Canadians ranked energy sixth after inflation, unemployment, environment/pollution, taxation, and United States investment in Canada.

Not only do Canadians not perceive energy conditions to be of high-level importance, but their expectations appear to be insensitive to the realities of energy supply. For example, in December 1976, abnormally cold weather pushed demand for electricity to unusually high levels across Canada. In Ontario, a public dispute over transmission line routing had locked in almost 1,000,000 kilowatts of power at the Lennox Generating Station. On December 1, 1976, cracked boiler-hanger rods were discovered in another generating station. Despite public appeals through the various media to shift the usage of electrical power to "off-peak times," on December 3, Ontario Hydro cut service to both interruptible "A" and "B" customers and implemented voltage reductions. On December 6, similar circumstances resulted in the corporation cutting service to interruptible customers, terminating a 100,000 kilowatt power sale to the Province of Manitoba and bringing in 620,000 kilowatts from the United States. The "stickiness" of demand and other public expressions during the difficult conditions of December 1976, led the chairman of Ontario Hydro to state, in March 1977, that

> It is frightening to hear of the high expectations that some people have of us—that regardless of what happens, Hydro will be ready to fill any energy gaps. These expectations seem to have little regard for the limitations we have to contend with in putting new facilities in place including the extraordinarily long lead times for generating facilities that run out as far as 12 years and more—if we can get the necessary approvals to build them at all.

Supply and Demand Factors

As the executive officers of Ontario Hydro have emphasized and the December 1976 situation outlined above illustrates, supply and demand for electric power need adjustment in Ontario (and across Canada). Exhibit 1 illustrates the corporation's supply (generation) and demand (load) situation through to 1988. Assuming the historic 7 percent compounded annual growth rate, the load forecast (demand) will exceed generating (supply) capability. Predictions are that by the winter of 1979–1980 a service reliability problem will start. By 1985, a shortfall of 2,400 megawatts, or twice the maximum demand to

EXHIBIT 1 Ontario Hydro Generation and Load Situation *(1976–88)*

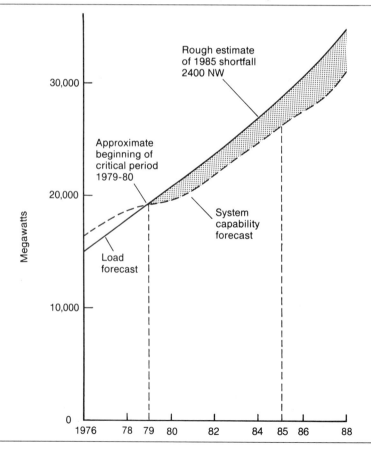

date of Toronto Hydro (the electric utility of Canada's largest city), will occur. As the projections extend into the late 1980s the excess of demand in relation to supply increases.

Ontario Hydro and Energy Conservation

The corporation has changed its market philosophy from consumer to conserver. The former director of sales is now the director of energy conservation. Forecasting has been reoriented to the supply of capital and electric power and away from customer demand. The load planning process was reversed in 1976. According to the general manager of marketing:

> Until this year, our process has been to start with a load forecast, make plans for whatever new generation was going to be required to meet the forecast, then borrow whatever funds were needed to carry out the plan. This year, for the first time, the process has been reversed. The starting point is the assessment of how many capital dollars will be available to us; this determines how much plant we're going to have; and our load forecast merely determines what kind of action we're going to have to take, to make sure the load doesn't exceed our generating capability.

While consideration and some speeches have been given on government regulation of electric energy, the corporation has ostensibly opted for conservation as its strategy in the foreseeable future. Ontario Hydro Chairman Robert Taylor has stated, "We must commit ourselves wholeheartedly to the objective of limiting the growth of electric power consumption in this province." The prime goal of the corporation is to reduce annual growth in consumption from a long-term average of 7 percent to 6 percent starting in 1976. The new, conservation oriented aims and strategies are not without some conflicting pressures, among them being the following:

1. Electricity, being more versatile and adaptable for most users than any other form of energy, will have increased demand while fossil fuels will decline and other energy sources become feasible.

2. Our whole socioeconomic structure is increasingly dependent on continuous and dependable supply. In every facet of life, substitution of energy for human effort continues.

3. Electricity cannot be stored. It must be available in the highly variable quantities required, at the locations required, continuously.

What makes these pressures more difficult, even threatening, are the prospects of demand conditions that will overwhelm the voluntary nature of conservation and lead to government controls. Several risk scenarios have been developed by various members of Ontario Hydro's management. For example:

> There is a risk that we have underestimated the problem, and it relates to two possible conditions: (1) That the province comes . . . out of the present economic trough with higher-than-normal growth rates. It has done this more often than not in the past. . . . (2) That customers will substitute electric power for other fuels in substantial amounts. We are already getting inquiries from industrial customers whose discussions with gas companies have led them to approach us about future supplies . . . this is a very real concern.

Another risk envisaged by Ontario Hydro relates to the questionable effectiveness of the conservation strategy. Its president has said:

> The evidence is conflicting, but in total it suggests that Canadians haven't yet got the message about conserving resources despite some attention-getting kicks in the pocketbook.

Other market related factors also threaten the conservation strategy. Changing Canadian lifestyles have increased the demand for more household electrical appliances and their use, particularly at peak hours, that is, 6 to 8 A.M. and 5 to 7 P.M., has taxed the electrical power supply system. Related to the expanding uses of electrical energy is the prodigal use of it. For a long time, Canada has been, next to the United States, the highest per capita user of energy in the world. "We probably enjoy the same position on the list of per capita wasters of energy." Fundamental to the wasteful behavior of energy users is their disposition toward conservation. For, as the chairman of Ontario Hydro states in reference to rate increases and conservation:

> Customers who conscientiously begin reducing their consumption of electricity will still find their bills continuing to go up, which doesn't make our job of getting the conservation message across any easier.

Moreover, while a temporary emergency makes headlines, there is little evidence that consumers are concerned about a probable energy crisis in the future.

Against these pragmatic considerations are the consequences perceived by Ontario Hydro if voluntary measures fail to bring demand into line with supply. If conservation efforts fail, one corporation executive envisions the following: (1) a faltering and uncertain power supply with an unacceptable number of interruptions; (2) a less attractive place for investment; (3) a decline in new production and the creation of jobs; (4) a lower rate of growth in all sectors; (5) controls such as those imposed on inflation by the Canadian federal and provincial governments.

The Evolution of Demarketing by Ontario Hydro

While Ontario Hydro's management and marketing activities are ostensibly discouraging the overall as well as selective time segments of demand, the concept of demarketing per se does not exist in the corporation. Nevertheless, its administrative actions clearly mani-

fest demarketing and its several facets merit closer examination.

Demarketing Aims

As a general objective, Ontario Hydro is to provide electric energy to its customers on a reliable (i.e., at all times), constant (i.e., without voltage reductions), and universal (i.e., to all applying or approved customers) basis. While this aim provides an ideal general direction for the corporation, the forecasted shortfall between future supply and demand has led to a clear demarketing goal. In Ontario, the goal is to reduce the growth of demand for electric energy by 1 percent annually to 1985; that is, from 7 percent compounded annual growth to 6 percent compounded annual growth. In addition to this goal, Ontario Hydro wants to shift demand from peak periods; that is, 6 to 8 A.M. and 5 to 7 P.M. These aims are dramatically different from the corporation's marketing orientation of 1968, at which time the assistant general manager of marketing stated:

> From a marketing viewpoint we are in business to make known to all existing and potential consumers the many advantages available to them from the use of electricity; to see that our customers are given every opportunity to use our product; to encourage them to use our product for any purpose which appeals to them—provided they are prepared to pay the lowest price at which we can make it available.

Hydro Markets

Ontario Hydro segments its markets into residential, industrial, and commercial. Exhibit 2 depicts the use of electricity by these three major market segments. Residential and commercial use have grown considerably; that is, combined use has increased from 21.5 million megawatt hours in 1966 to 44.4 million megawatt hours in 1974, a jump of 107 percent in 8 years. Commercial use increased 131.4 percent between 1966 and 1974. Indus-

EXHIBIT 2 Estimated Primary Electricity Use by Major Market Segments

	1966		1971		1974	
	Million Megawatt Hours	**Percentage**	**Million Megawatt Hours**	**Percentage**	**Million Megawatt Hours**	**Percentage**
Residential[a]	12.6	28.8	19.3	31.0	23.8	31.4
Industrial[b]	22.2	50.9	29.0	46.3	31.4	41.5
Commercial[c]	8.9	20.3	13.9	22.3	20.6	27.1
Total	43.7	100.0	62.2	99.6	75.8	100.0

[a]Residential load includes bulk-metered apartments and seasonal and farm residences.
[b]Industrial load contains all secondary (manufacturing) and primary industries, including nonresidential portion of farm load.
[c]Commercial load represents all loads associated with construction, retailing, institutional, and utility services, including street lighting.

EXHIBIT 3 Saturation of Residential Appliances, Ontario

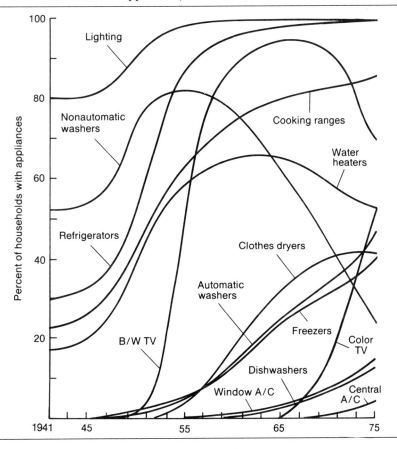

trial use, by comparison, increased at a decreasing rate during the 8-year period.

Ontario Hydro's residential segment has been disaggregated further. Exhibit 3 indicates the trends for appliances in Ontario households between 1941 and 1975. High levels of saturation have been reached for television (121 percent), lighting, refrigerators, electric ranges, and clothes washers (i.e., combining nonautomatic and automatic types).

There have been some significant declines in levels of appliance saturation; notably, non-automatic washers, electric water heaters, and clothes dryers. The dilemma posed to Ontario Hydro's conservation strategy is the prospect of rapid growth for some appliances such as color television, air conditioning, water heaters, and residential space heating.

In 1975, electricity accounted for nearly 10 percent of the total residential space-heating market in Ontario, a tenfold increase in 12 years. Of greater future impact on the conservation strategy is the growth in electrical space heating in new residential construction. Exhibit 4 shows the number of new dwellings with electrical heating being installed as well as the percentage share of new dwellings with electrical heating installations.

The growth in aggregate consumption and specific uses of electrical energy is evidence that Ontario Hydro customers have not had a conservation ethos in the past. While there is evidence that energy consumers will cut back

EXHIBIT 4 Electric Space Heating Share in New Residential Construction *(Ontario)*

Year	New Dwelling Starts	Electrical Heating Installations in New Dwellings	Percentage Share
1959	54,158	380	0.7
1960	42,282	524	1.2
1961	48,144	999	2.1
1962	44,306	2,679	6.0
1963	55,957	4,169	7.5
1964	65,617	8,284	12.6
1965	66,767	9,861	14.8
1966	52,355	11,662	22.3
1967	68,121	11,446	16.8
1968	80,375	10,600	13.2
1969	81,446	13,700	16.8
1970	76,675	13,770	18.0
1971	89,980	21,742	24.2
1972	102,933	25,870	25.1
1973	110,536	27,120	24.5
1974	85,503	20,520	24.0
1975	—	—	25.7 (prel.)

Sources: Stats. Can.: New Residential Construction (#64-002). Power Market Analysis Department, Ontario Hydro.

their use in emergencies—for example, in December 1976, Ontario users of electricity cut their use by 350,000 kilowatts—in general the growth of electrical (and other forms of) energy consumption increases steadily. To change this propensity, Ontario Hydro has embarked on a "demarketing" campaign that includes the major marketing mix components: pricing, promotion, products, and distribution.

Pricing

Since 1976, Ontario Hydro has initiated a series of substantial rate increases, that is, from 10 percent to more than 22 percent annually. As the corporation's chairman has stated:

> The price of electricity must reflect the financial realities of the exploding cost of producing and distributing electric power in today's world.

In addition to the financial realities, prices are being set to encourage the "prudent use of electricity." In early 1976, Ontario Hydro restudied and reformulated its pricing policies and practices. It shifted away from historical average costs to marginal cost pricing, that is, the cost of the last unit of energy produced. The rationale given for this pricing change is to set more realistic rates and to induce more efficient use of electrical energy.

Promotion

Since the early 1960s, there has been a major transition in the themes of Ontario Hydro's promotion. "Live Better Electrically—Hydro Is Yours" was the corporation's main advertising theme until 1964. Many of the more than 350 municipal utilities as well as appliance dealers and other members of the private sector continued to use this theme until the early 1970s. The Live Better Electrically oriented advertising was aimed at increasing demand for electricity. It emphasized the promotion of a wide variety of appliances, especially the major applications such as water heating, cooking, and clothes drying which were also being competitively advertised by the gas companies.

In the mid-1960s, the general promotional theme was reoriented to electrical modernization, clearly oriented to the use of electricity. A prevalent slogan in 1965 was "Electric Heating Is the Superior Heating System." One special promotion offered a free electric blanket ($29.95 value) with the purchase of a new electric clothes dryer at any store featuring the Hydro Special.

The transition of Ontario Hydro's advertising to the theme of wise use started in 1971. In May of that year, the corporation made a "major revision" in its marketing policy objectives. Of particular relevance to Ontario Hydro's promotional strategy were the first two objectives: "To make known to the people of Ontario the advantages of electricity"; and "To see that consumers are provided with the opportunity to share in these advantages." Further, by way of explanation, the corporate marketing plan stated:

> There is a distinction between the people of Ontario sharing in the advantages and a few people exploiting them. These words are therefore intended to convey two shades of meaning—one of equitable distribution from which follows the idea of a limited total advantage—once again reflecting scarcity. What has been abandoned is the notion of abundant power.

By early 1973, the promotion of wise use and energy conservation messages were launched. The "Waking up to the wise use of electricity" advertisement placed in May 1973 included reference to the limitations of fuel resources.

In the agricultural sector, promotion was oriented to consumption until the early 1970s. In the mid-1960s, Ontario Hydro's advertising slogan was "Farm Better Electrically." During the period 1969–74, the advertising emphasis was on controlled environment and economic efficiency of operating the farm. In 1974,

there was reference to well-insulated farm buildings. By 1975, the conservation message was quite explicit in the farm advertising.

Industrial and commercial promotion evolved from an emphasis on electricity use in the mid-1960s to its present emphasis on conservation. Common to this period's advertising is the economic rationality of efficient use of electricity.

In 1975, Ontario Hydro introduced an energy management program. The program was directed at industry. Manufacturers, especially American subsidiaries, were found to be the most responsive companies. To convey substantive information in a reasonably concise format, Ontario Hydro provides a monthly bulletin entitled *Energy Management.* Since June 1976, the phrase "for the conservation of electricity," has been added to the publication's masthead. Contents of the bulletin are predominantly reports of the ways companies and public institutions have been able to save energy and operating costs.

Related to the energy management publication program is an Ontario Hydro "walkthrough" program. One or more electrical use experts tour a company or public institution, at their request, and point out ways electricity can be saved. Response by industrial, commercial, and public organizations has been very strong. While their primary motive for conserving energy is to cut operating costs, a secondary motive is the recognition of social and public responsibilities.

While Ontario Hydro has made increasing efforts to promote conservation in the energy market, it has been an example of conservation itself. The corporation's head office, occupied since 1975, was designed, in part, to save energy. The total energy consumption, including hot water and cooking use for Hydro Place is estimated by the designer to be under 54,000 BTUs per square foot per year. This is significantly less than the 120,000 BTUs per square foot per year consumption of the average building of similar size.

Products/Services

The walk-through program and energy management publication are two services launched under Ontario Hydro's conservation program. In addition, a consulting service is offered to commercial operators. Major energy and cost savings have been achieved by supermarkets, industrial plants, educational institutions, and building owners/operators working in collaboration with Ontario Hydro personnel.

During the past two years, the highest product research and development priority has been to develop a heat pump optimally suited for Ontario climatic conditions. In climates more temperate than that of Ontario, the heat pump can produce two or more units of heat for one of electricity. Any significant advance in heat-pump efficiency, especially under colder climate conditions, is expected to greatly expand the market for them.

Water heaters present another opportunity for energy conservation development. In Ontario, water heaters represent about 30 percent of residential electricity use. Given the actual and potential increased periodic use of water heaters, Ontario Hydro is involved in the development of timers and other means of decreasing the amount of energy they require.

Distribution

Distribution of electrical energy is one of the main operating functions of Ontario Hydro. In April 1977, a load management department was set up to ensure that the distribution of electricity was optimized. Given the forecasted shortfall between supply and demand in the 1980s, electricity loads will require increasing improvements in forecasts, planning, utilization, and controls. At present, load forecasts are based on econometric models. These "probability-based" models, while sensitive to error factors, such as variability and reliability of inputs, rely heavily on environmental elements such as political and economic conditions and energy prices. They also rely on inputs from Ontario Hydro regional offices and the municipal utilities. Load forecasts have repeatedly shown a need for load planning that will increase efficiency and shift loads for optimal utilization. As the Load Management Department manager observed: "Less energy use does not necessarily improve load management. The main objective is to change the time of use." More specifically, the peak loads of 6 to 8 A.M. and 5 to 7 P.M. must be decreased or shifted to earlier or later times of the day and night, or both. Several load-shifting alternatives have been considered, including energy and heat storage, heat pumps, and heating and freezer timers.

Notes

1. Philip Kotler, *Marketing for Nonprofit Organizations* (Englewood Cliffs, N.J.: Prentice-Hall, 1975).

2. Philip Kotler and Sidney J. Levy, "Demarketing, Yes, Demarketing." *Harvard Business Review,* November–December 1971, pp. 74–80.

National Container Corporation
Alan R. Beckenstein and H. Landis Gabel

In the spring of 1977, James S. Schultz, vice president in charge of the container division, was perplexed by a credit report given him by Robert Crane, his vice president of sales. It was not at all customary for Schultz to review an application for credit from a prospective customer of the sister paper division. After receipt of an application from a new customer

This case was prepared by Alan R. Beckenstein and H. Landis Gabel of the University of Virginia. Copyright 1977 by the Colgate Darden Graduate Business School Sponsors, University of Virginia, Charlottesville, Virginia. Reproduced by permission.

account, the credit department generally made preliminary evaluations, then circulated the report among sales personnel of all divisions for any additional information. If a salesperson had any pertinent knowledge of the applicant's financial standing or reputation, they would write them on this report. Crane would then initial and route the report back to the credit department, usually without comment.

On this application for the Foldex Corporation, however, Crane had written:

> In spite of the preliminary rejection by Credit, I believe that it is in the best interest of this company to approve the new credit account. Foldex, one of our competitors in the container business, is a new company which has shown a remarkable facility for gaining new orders in this depressed market. Its financial condition should improve markedly with sales generated this quarter and projected for the remainder of the year, particularly if general market conditions improve. In view of the paper division's operating rate of less than 90 percent and need for additional output, this credit application should be approved.

On a separate sheet Crane had written, "Your concurrence on my evaluation, if noted on this report, should assure positive action by Credit."

This commentary struck Schultz as unusual in two respects. First, it was very much unlike Crane to have any great concern for the welfare of the company's other two divisions, Paper and Forest. In fact, to a large degree his compensation was made up of bonuses based on three factors: total container division sales, container division operating profits, and a subjective evaluation of container division performance in relation to the other divisions. Second, and even less characteristic, was Crane's unseemly concern for a competitor. The paper and paperboard supplied to Foldex would be converted into folding paper cartons that would compete with National's container sales efforts. This unusual intervention by Crane demanded further explanation.

Schultz sat idly for several minutes after meeting with Crane. As he had suspected, other factors had motivated Crane on the Foldex application. St. Paul Converting and the Covington Paper Companies had previously supplied Foldex with its paper and board needs. St. Paul, a leader in the container industry, and Covington were both integrated companies. Foldex, solely a converted products manufacturer, was thus a customer for paper and paperboard but a competitor for containers and other converted products. The way Crane explained it, Foldex had consistently undercut St. Paul and Covington in competitive bidding. First St. Paul, then Covington refused to supply Foldex with paper and paperboard, claiming delinquent accounts as the motivating factor. Foldex had been refused by still another supplier before approaching National. Crane then received a phone call from his counterpart at Foldex, who charged that there was a conspiracy to drive his company out of business. He warned that if National did not supply them, they would have to conclude that National was part of the conspiracy and that appropriate legal action would be taken.

Schultz considered three alternatives: (1) concur with Crane's recommendation and strongly approve the application; (2) concur with the preliminary rejection of the Foldex account; or (3) make no comment and simply route the application back to the credit department. Schultz wondered about the probable consequences of each action. Still more, he worried that any decision he would make could be misconstrued. He reflected on the events that had preceded the decision he must make.

National Container Corporation is engaged in the manufacture and distribution of all forest products. An integrated processor, its three major product lines are logs, paper and paperboard, and converted products. Corresponding to the product lines, the company has three divisions: forest, paper, and con-

EXHIBIT 1 Sales and Income for the Years Ending December 31, 1972–1976 *(in Millions of Dollars)*

	1976	1975	1974	1973	1972
Container division					
Sales	66.9	58.4	63.6	55.1	50.4
Net income after tax	1.4	3.0	4.9	3.9	3.7
Paper division					
Sales	49.8	40.8	28.9	27.7	25.4
Net income after tax	2.9	2.5	1.7	1.9	1.7
Forest division					
Sales	14.2	11.4	12.6	12.2	11.2
Net income after tax	0.9	0.5	0.8	0.7	0.7

tainer. The converted products, principally paper-folding cartons, had long been the primary contributor to total sales and earnings. Recently, however, the paper and paperboard line had become increasingly profitable and surpassed the converted products line in earnings. Exhibit 1 shows the sales and income data by operating divisions for the period 1972–1976.

Folding cartons and other containers had been extremely profitable items for National in the early 1970s, prompting expansion from four plants to five, plus additions to the other plants. Investment in plant and equipment steadily increased from 1971 to 1976, until expansion plans were substantially completed in early 1976. Exhibit 2 shows these expenditures, as well as shipments and capacity utilization for the five-year period, 1972–1976.

The paper container industry is loosely concentrated in terms of the national market, with the four largest companies typically accounting for 20 to 25 percent of total sales. By year-end 1976, there were 612 plants in the United States producing folding boxes and other paperboard containers. An abundance

of raw materials and a rather simple production process make entry into the industry easy. An equity investment of $125,000 to $200,000 is sufficient to start up a competitive container plant.

While containers do vary as to dimensions, weight, and color, they are substantially identical, no matter who produces them, when made to particular specifications. To the purchaser the product is homogeneous; the dominant competitive dimension is price. There is substantial geographical differentiation. High transportation costs, because of the low value of the product in relation to its bulk, coupled with numerous producing mills, create regional markets. Recently, there has been some substitution from paper to plastic packaging, although no long-term trend appears clear. The substitution appears directly related to changes in the price of paper packaging.

Almost 35 percent of total tonnage sales is made on the basis of negotiated contracts, usually for periods of a year or longer. Spot transactions comprise the other 65 percent of total tonnage sales; a spot transaction is a sale resulting from an order of a stated kind and

EXHIBIT 2 Plant Expansion, Shipments, and Operating Rates for the Years Ending December 31, 1972–1976

Container Division	1976	1975	1974	1973	1972
Additions to plant and equipment (millions of dollars)	6.7	10.2	8.9	6.3	1.5
Shipments (thousands of tons)	161.2	149.8	165.1	154.0	142.5
Operating rate (%)	82.7	78.2	96.8	95.3	92.4

quantity of containers to be delivered on a specified date. The price is generally determined by competitive bidding. It is common for purchasers to buy from two or more suppliers concurrently.

Because packaging is such a small percentage of the cost of the final product, industry demand is inelastic. Industrywide price changes will not, up to a certain point, visibly affect the total quantity purchased. In periods of generally rising container prices, purchasers are able to absorb costs as well as pass on the increased costs to the ultimate consumer. This results partly because of the low cost percentage of the final product but also because the final product; for example, a box of cereal, is generally a consumer staple which is relatively price insensitive. On the other hand, in a period of level demand, the primary effect of price changes among competitors is a reallocation of market share among the producers.

Schultz was promoted to head the container division in March of 1975, when his predecessor left to become president of St. Paul Converting Company, a major competitor. Schultz had been vice president of production in the division, an office which now reported directly to him. Also working closely with and subordinate to Schultz was the divisional vice president of sales, Robert Crane. Crane supervised six district sales managers and a marketing manager.

Market demand for all paper and allied products turned soft in early 1975, just as Schultz assumed his new office. While tonnage and sales dollars remained relatively constant, rising costs cut deeply into earnings. Only the paper division among National divisions was able to better the industrywide trend because of improvements in its coated book and kraft papers. By 1976, market conditions had improved for most of the industry, but folding paper carton prices remained stagnant and profit margins were further eroded. Demand was slack in part because of

increased substitution of plastic containers. On the cost side, in a few short years, energy costs had increased by 400 percent and both raw material prices and labor rates grew at a faster pace than container prices. In addition, similarly to the increased investment in plant and equipment at National, capacity had been greatly extended throughout the carton industry. This led to intense price competition, which reduced container division's profits to a 10-year low.

In large measure the difficulties were beyond Schultz's control. The overcapacity condition at National resulted from the decisions of his predecessor. Further, the high fixed costs in the container plants require a high operating rate for profitability, yet with slack demand and rigorous competition in an undifferentiated product line, the only way to load the plant is to lower price. Even this response is self-defeating, as a cut by one producer is soon matched and bettered by competitors.

It was against this backdrop that the September 1975 Western States Paper Trade Association's annual meeting was conducted. Early on in the proceedings, the president of St. Paul, his former boss, and a small group of executives representing the other industry leaders, had approached Schultz and suggested, without much subtlety, that the only way to save themselves from ruinous price competition was to work together to increase prices. The plan suggested was a simple bid-rigging enterprise. In the paper container industry, short-term contracts in spot transactions are entered into on an almost daily basis, usually for 50,000 to 500,000 units per contract. The manufacturers detail their needs for bids among the container producers. By the use of "cover bids," producers could act among themselves to accommodate one another. For instance, National could tell other competing carton companies that it had made a bid at a certain price on a new carton container for a certain facial tissue. The other carton manufacturers would agree to bid higher so that National would be awarded the contract. St. Paul would agree to bid at the higher price because in return St. Paul would expect to receive similar assistance from National.

Though not thoroughly versed in the antitrust laws, Schultz suspected that a price-fixing attempt such as this was a direct violation of the Sherman Antitrust law. He knew of two instances in the past five years in which some of his competitors had been indicted for price fixing, with some of the officers eventually going to jail. In fact, because of this awareness of the increasing enforcement activity by the Department of Justice, he had previously sought a company policy statement to be distributed among all sales personnel, the marketing personnel, and the purchasing agents. This statement was subsequently authorized and distributed. The text of this statement is reproduced in Exhibit 3.

Schultz recalled quickly extricating himself from the gathering, grabbing Crane by the arm, and retreating to the safe confines of the bar. The penalties for violations of the antitrust laws could be severe and were further strengthened by recent legislation. Formerly a misdemeanor, the violation was now a felony offense with a maximum jail sentence of three years. Schultz had met neither Haldeman nor Mitchell from the Nixon administration and had no intention of making their acquaintances in the near future in jail.

In the year following that meeting, however, market conditions worsened for the container division. Schultz feared that an actual loss was possible for the calendar year 1976. Prices for the carton products had to improve, and Schultz felt the only way this could occur would be to control production and raise prices. Prices could not be fixed, but at the least the story had to be told.

One of the section panels at the trade association annual meeting provided for industry projections and analyses by various operating officers. At the very least, Schultz felt compelled to comment on the overcapacity situation and remark on the deleterious effects of recent price warfare. As long as he steered an independent course—let the others take any tack they wanted—he could avoid any price-fixing problems. He consulted with Crane several times on the content of the speech. Crane agreed the speech was a good idea and also made a few suggestions.

EXHIBIT 3 National Container Corporation Corporate Policy

Subject: Compliance with Antitrust Laws

National Container Corporation considers strict compliance with all provisions of the antitrust laws as an integral part of company policy. It is the responsibility of the manager of each division or unit to see that this policy is known and observed by all those under his supervision, particularly in the area of sales, marketing, and purchasing.

Violations of the Company policy and the underlying antitrust laws can have a serious, adverse, and lasting effect on the Company, its operations and its growth. Therefore, a deliberate and willful violation of this policy, in the absence of mitigating circumstances, will be sufficient grounds for dismissal. In addition, violation of the antitrust laws could result in criminal or civil proceedings against the responsible employee and the Company.

Your attention is particularly directed to the prohibitions of the antitrust laws against concerted action with competitors on such subjects as prices, customers, terms of sale, and other competitive matters. It is especially important that you avoid both any actual violation and any conduct which might be misconstrued as such a violation.

When an employee who has acted in good faith upon the advice of counsel for the Company nevertheless becomes involved in an antitrust proceeding, the Company will be prepared to assist and defend the employee. However, if an employee is convicted of violating the law, the Company cannot, as a matter of law, save the employee from whatever criminal penalty the court may impose upon the employee as a consequence of such conviction.

This policy applies to the Company, which, as used in this policy statement, includes all of its affiliated companies and subsidiaries.

At the September 1976 annual meeting of the trade association, Schultz carefully avoided contacts with the group that had approached him the prior year. Indeed, those members seemed to avoid him. The main issue at the meeting was a proposed modification of trade association activities, consisting primarily of the addition of a statistical reporting service, called the "open competition plan." This plan is reproduced in Exhibit 4. The major argument of the proponents was that implementation of the plan would reduce market uncertainties and allow management to plan more efficiently. The cost of errors in market judgments based on sketchy information would hence be minimized. After cursory discussion of the proposed changes, and with little opposition, the modification was approved. National Container voted in favor of the modification.

Schultz felt that his presentation, reproduced in Exhibit 5, was very well received, and he returned from the meeting gratified with having vented some frustration and expressed his concerns. Crane stayed at the meeting site several days longer, having stated a desire to follow-up some contacts made with customers at the meetings.

In early October 1976, Schultz received a phone call from Crane. The call concerned a problem that affected not only National but the industry as a whole, particularly in the past two years of soft demand. The problem was the age-old game of playing two ends against the middle. Purchasing agents would detail their order requirements and phone a number of salespeople for bids. The purchasing agent might then call all the salespeople who had delivered higher bids, informing them of the low bid. The salespeople would then have the option of beating that price or losing out on the order. This practice might continue through three or four iterations until a final bid was reached. The problem was further heightened for the producers when the purchasing agent threw out a "phantom" bid, a low bid which did not actually exist. If in the first round of bidding, purchasing agents could not get other salespeople to beat the low bid, they might approach the low bidder and tell of a lower bid they might have to meet to get the order. Because of the antitrust laws, any exchange of price information between competitors on specific bids could be a violation; hence, competitors were hesitant to contact one another on information delivered by the purchasing agents. Only later, on an informal basis, would a salesperson sometimes learn that a bid was fraudulent by checking with a competitor. The result was that even a low bidder would occasionally beat its own bid in order to win the bid, and there was little the salespersons could do to defend themselves against the practice.

As well as Schultz could recall, the conversation lasted only several minutes.

Crane: Those blasted P.A.s have been at their games again this past week. In two regions where we had good competitive bids we were

---

EXHIBIT 4 Open Competition Plan

Statement of Purpose

The purpose of this plan is to disseminate among members accurate knowledge of production and market conditions so that each member may gauge the market intelligently instead of guessing at it; to make competition open and aboveboard instead of secret and concealed; to substitute, in estimated market conditions, frank and full statements of our competitors for the frequently misleading and colored statements of the buyer.

The Open Competition plan is a central clearinghouse for information on prices, trade statistics, and practices. By keeping all members fully and quickly informed of what the others have done, the work of the plan results in a certain uniformity of trade practice. There is no agreement to follow the practice of others, although members do naturally follow their most intelligent competitors, if they know what these competitors have been actually doing.

EXHIBIT 4 *(concluded)*

Membership Requirements

Each member shall send to the Secretary:

1. A daily report of all sales actually made, with the name and address of the purchaser, the kind, grade and quality of cartons sold, and all special agreements of every kind, oral or written with respect thereto.
2. A daily shipping report, with exact copies of the invoices, all special agreements as to terms, grade, etc. The classification shall be the same as with sales.
3. A monthly production report, showing the production of the member reporting during the previous month, with the grades and thickness classified as prescribed elsewhere in this plan.
4. A monthly stock report by each member, showing the stock on hand on the first day of the month, sold and unsold, with the total of each kind, grade and thickness.
5. Price lists. Members must file at the beginning of each month price lists showing f.o.b. shipping point, which shall be stated. New prices must be filed with the association as soon as made.
6. Inspection reports. These reports are to be made to the association by a service of its own, established for the purpose of checking up grades of the various members. The association will provide for a chief inspector and sufficient assistants to inspect the stocks of all members from time to time.
7. All of these reports by members are subject to complete audit by representatives of the association. Any member who fails to report shall not receive the reports of the Secretary, and failure to report for twelve days in six months shall cause the failing member to be dropped from membership.

Association Duties

The Secretary is required to send to each member:

1. A monthly summary showing the production of each member for the previous month, subdivided as to use, grade, kind, thickness, etc.
2. A weekly report, not later than Saturday, of all sales, to and including the preceding Tuesday, giving each sale and the price, and the name of the purchaser.
3. On Tuesday of each week the Secretary must send to each member a report of each shipment by each member, complete up to the evening of the preceding Thursday.
4. He must send a monthly report, showing the individual stock on hand of each member and a summary of all stocks, sold and unsold. This report will be referred to by the managing statistician as the monthly inventory of the stock of each member.
5. Not later than the 10th of each month the Secretary shall send a summary of the price lists furnished by members, showing the prices asked by each, and any changes made therein must be immediately transmitted to all the members.
6. A market report letter shall be sent to each member of the association pointing out changes in conditions both in the producing and consuming sections, giving a comparison of production and sales and in general an analysis of the market conditions.
7. Meetings shall be held once a month in St. Louis or at points agreed upon by members. It is intended that the regular meetings shall afford opportunity for the discussion of all subjects of interest to the members.

Later Amendments to the Plan

1. In order that members may more conveniently attend, there shall be four districts, in each of which a monthly meeting will be held.
2. A questionnaire will be sent to all members prior to the meeting. From the replies received, supplementing the other reports, the statistician will compile his estimate of the condition of the market, actual and prospective, which will be distributed to the members attending each meeting and mailed to those not present.

    Among the questions are the following:

    What was your total production during the last month?

    What do you estimate your production will probably be the next two months?

    Do you expect to shut down due to any shortage or for any reasons?

    If so, state how long you expect your mills to be idle.

    What is your view of market conditions for the next few months?

    What is the general outlook for business?

    State all reasons for your conclusions.

EXHIBIT 5 Speech Delivered to Western States Paper Association Annual Meeting, September 15, 1976. "Outlook for 1977," by James S. Schultz

I think I would have to start by saying what I am sure a substantial portion of other industry executives will be saying: that on balance we have been disappointed that the general level of activity in the North American paper and container industry has not picked up in 1976 as much as one would have hoped from the vantage point of a year ago. Looking at 1977, specifically in the paper-folding container area which is the mainstay of National's business, we have to view the approaching year with some caution as it certainly looks now as if a major pickup in general demand is not likely to occur before 1978.

The experiences of the past few years—rapidly escalating raw material costs, fourfold increases in power costs, shortages and violent changes in market demand—have forced us to reassess some treasured assumptions and have helped us to conclude that some very basic changes in our future planning are essential. Cost problems in the areas of energy, labor, materials, and pollution regulations will continue to be acute. While paper and board companies, and paper divisions, have been able to increase their prices in the past year, gains in carton prices have been nominal at best. This stems from overcapacity which has prompted cutthroat bidding practices in futile efforts to load plants. It can't be done with current demand—it just cuts container margins. Improvement in margins is of paramount concern to National. Price increases across broad product lines are essential in order to recover some of these sharp cost increases. This also reflects upon our ability to attract capital to increase capacity which provides, in turn, increased employment. But capacity additions are in the long term. As far as my company is concerned, we will be extremely cautious in making any substantial additions to current plant. The ROI is just too low for new mill construction. Attacking cost problems can be extremely profitable, and that's our current game plan. If there is no increase in production, generally, then there is going to be good business. No company is safe in increasing their production. If they do, they will be in bad shape, because demand will not support the additional production. Certainly, National Container Corporation is adjusting its production scheduling appropriate to current demand.

Historically, change has always been resisted mightily. This will never be truer than in 1977. The greatest thing managers in the paper industry can do in 1977 is to know the facts and make the best possible decisions out of the information that they have gathered. This is the stuff of success, and there is no other.

informed of a low bid that we had to beat to get the business. In the Pacific Region in particular, I have good reason to believe we had the lowest bid, though I'm not so sure about the Mid-East bid.

Schultz: They just don't let up, do they? Say, in that Mid-East bid, was that for the new market penetration in Indiana?

Crane: Yeah, the Clarksville area where they have a lot of those small independent suppliers. That's what I mean. Even if we felt there was another low bid and we still wanted to fill the order at a lower price, we still can't indiscriminately undercut the independents because of a possible charge of price discrimination. The only defense the Robinson-Patman Act gives us here is a good faith attempt to meet competition. And we can't really rely on that unless we verify prices of our competition. We've batted this around long enough, don't you think? We've got to get some con-

trol over this phantom bidding. Look, all it takes is a simple phone call to the supposed low bidder. If the P.A.s learn we're verifying the information they give us, they'll play it straight. Cutthroat competition is bad enough without having to beat imaginary competitors.

Schultz: O.K., look, you know the pressure we're under to meet our profit targets, and if we don't meet them our year-end bonus is shot. I would say to put an end to it where you can use verification for an excuse in checking with competitors, but it's sticky. Maybe you should check with our general counsel. Still, we should stop their cheating. Look, you've got a job to do—as far as I go, I know nothing. All right?

Crane: O.K. I can take it from there.

Schultz heard nothing more from Crane on the subject. Several months later, he asked

EXHIBIT 6 Western States Paper Trade Association—Monthly Report on Bidding and Prices *(Cumulative)*

Bid Date	Quantity Ordered	National	St. Paul	Covington	Mar-Vel	Foldex	Harrington
Sept. 27	180,000	$.0156	$.0160	$.0148	$.0156	$	$.0170
Sept. 30	100,000	.0156	.0148	.0150			.0170
Oct. 4	50,000	.0160	.0156	.0150	.0148		.0170
Oct. 8	160,000	.0148	.0160	.0150	.0150		.0156
Oct. 15	275,000	.0156	.0146	.0148	.0148		.0148
Oct. 16	300,000	.0148	.0146	.0148			.0144
Oct. 18	150,000	.0142	.0144	.0148	.0150		.0144
Oct. 22	250,000	.0160	.0160	.0150	.0150		.0148
Oct. 26	320,000	.0160	.0160	.0160	.0158		.0160
Oct. 29	80,000	.0160	.0162	.0160	.0160		.0158
Nov. 2	400,000	.0160	.0162	.0162	.0162		.0164
Nov. 12	380,000	.0162	.0160	.0164	.0162		.0162
Nov. 14	45,000	.0162	.0162	.0162	.0160		.0164
Nov. 16	85,000	.0162	.0164	.0162	.0162		.0160
Nov. 19	240,000	.0164	.0164	.0162	.0164		.0164
Nov. 19	160,000	.0166	.0162	.0166	.0164		.0164
Nov. 26	110,000	.0162	.0166	.0164	.0164		.0164
Nov. 28	425,000	.0160	.0166	.0166	.0162		.0166
Dec. 3	280,000	.0166	.0166	.0166	.0162		.0158
Dec. 4	315,000	.0166	.0166	.0156	.0158		.0166
Dec. 8	140,000	.0166	.0168	.0166	.0154		.0166
Dec. 15	380,000	.0168	.0164	.0168	.0154		.0168
Dec. 17	250,000	.0168	.0144	.0168	.0154		.0168
Dec. 27	150,000	.0166	.0170	.0170	.0170		.0170
Jan. 3	260,000	.0170	.0168	.0170	.0170		.0170
Jan. 7	120,000	.0170	.0172	.0170	.0170		.0168
Jan. 10	65,000	.0172	.0172	.0172	.0170		.0172
Jan. 13	375,000	.0172	.0172	.0170	.0172		.0172
Jan. 15	140,000	.0170	.0174	.0172	.0172		.0172
Jan. 20	80,000	.0174	.0172	.0174	.0174	.0166	.0174
Jan. 24	170,000	.0174	.0172	.0174	.0174	.0166	.0174
Jan. 27	140,000	.0174	.0164	.0174	.0174	.0166	.0174
Jan. 31	180,000	.0164	.0164	.0164	.0164	.0166	.0162
Feb. 3	260,000	.0164	.0164	.0164	.0162	.0166	.0164
Feb. 6	70,000	.0164	.0164	.0162	.0164	.0160	.0164
Feb. 11	390,000	.0164	.0172	.0162	.0164	.0172	.0164
Feb. 14	280,000	.0170	.0172	.0172	.0172	.0172	.0172
Feb. 21	350,000	.0172	.0170	.0172	.0172	.0172	.0172
Feb. 24	175,000	.0172	.0172	.0172	.0172	.0172	.0170
Feb. 25	130,000	.0172	.0172	.0172	.0170	.0172	.0172
Feb. 28	125,000	.0172	.0174	.0172	.0172	.0170	.0172
Mar. 3	260,000	.0174	.0174	.0172	.0174	.0168	.0174
Mar. 6	180,000	.0174	.0174	.0164	.0174	.0168	.0174
Mar. 10	90,000	.0162	.0174	.0174	.0174	.0164	.0164
Mar. 14	360,000	.0158	.0174	.0174	.0160	.0160	.0162
Mar. 17	95,000	.0160	.0156	.0160	.0160	.0154	.0156
Mar. 19	285,000	.0160	.0148	.0160	.0158	.0152	.0156
Mar. 24	470,000	.0150	.0144	.0154	.0150		.0152
Mar. 26	380,000	.0144	.0150	.0152	.0152		.0160
Mar. 28	240,000	.0160	.0166	.0154	.0150	.0174	.0160

Crane how the new program was working out. Crane reported that it was the best thing they could have done. They detected three fraudulent bids, in several regions, in the first month of the verification program. Thereafter, according to Crane, they had had no such problems, and it was this that accounted for very recent price improvements.

Prices continued to improve marginally for most container orders, and despite some softness in March, prices beginning in April 1977 were substantially improved over the previous year's levels. Operating rates were up and Schultz felt that increased demand for containers was finally mitigating the overcapacity problem of the past two years.

Schultz had been reviewing the trade association's monthly summary of prices and production by members, when the credit evaluation on Foldex was delivered to his desk. After conferring with Crane, he was clearly worried about the antitrust threat posed by Foldex. Before deciding on the disposition of the credit report, Schultz pored over the trade association statistics once more. Among other things that worried him was the data on bids for facial tissue containers. The cumulative summary of the last six monthly reports is shown in Exhibit 6.

Author Index

Reading Index

Case Index

*This book has been set Compugraphic
8600, in 10 and 9 point Century
Book, leaded 2 points. Section
numbers are 16 point Century Bold
and section titles are 24 point
Century Bold. The size of the type
page is 37 picas by 46 picas.*